The Economic Development of the United Kingdom
since 1870
Volume I

The Economic Development of Modern Europe since 1870

Series Editor: Charles Feinstein
  Chichele Professor of Economic History
  All Souls College, Oxford

The Economic Development of the United Kingdom since 1870
Volume I

Edited by

Charles Feinstein

Chichele Professor of Economic History
All Souls College, University of Oxford

THE ECONOMIC DEVELOPMENT OF MODERN EUROPE SINCE 1870

An Elgar Reference Collection
Cheltenham, UK • Lyme, US

Published by
Edward Elgar Publishing Ltd
8 Lansdown Place
Cheltenham
Glos GL50 2HU
UK

Edward Elgar Publishing, Inc.
1 Pinnacle Hill Road
Lyme
New Hampshire 03768
US

A catalogue record for this book is available from the British Library.

Library of Congress Cataloguing in Publication Data
The economic development of the United Kingdom since 1870 / edited by
    Charles Feinstein.
        (The economic development of modern Europe since
    1870; 9) (An Elgar reference collection)
        Includes bibliographical references and index.
        1. Great Britain—Economic conditions—19th century. 2. Great
    Britain—Economic conditions—20th century. I. Feinstein, C. H.
     II. Series. III. Series: An Elgar reference collection.
    HC255.E34 1997
    330.941'08—DC21   97–22601
     JK   CIP

ISBN 1 85278 670 1 (2 volume set)

Printed and bound in Great Britain by
Hartnolls Limited, Bodmin, Cornwall

Contents

Acknowledgements

The editor and publishers wish to thank the authors and the following publishers who have kindly given permission for the use of copyright material.

Academic Press Ltd for article: Andrew Kilpatrick and Tony Lawson (1980), 'On the Nature of Industrial Decline in the UK', *Cambridge Journal of Economics*, **4** (1), March, 85–102.

Allen & Unwin for excerpt: W. Arthur Lewis (1978), 'The British Climacteric', in *Growth and Fluctuations, 1870–1913*, Chapter V, 112–34 and 309–11 (notes).

Banca di Roma for article: D.E.H. Edgerton (1994), 'British Industrial R & D, 1900–1970', *Journal of European Economic History*, **23** (1), Spring, 49–67.

Blackwell Publishers Ltd for articles: E. Rothbarth (1946), 'Causes of the Superior Efficiency of USA Industry as Compared with British Industry', *Economic Journal*, **LVI** (223), September, 383–90; John Saville (1961), 'Some Retarding Factors in the British Economy before 1914', *Yorkshire Bulletin of Economic and Social Research*, **13**, 51–60; S.N. Broadberry and N.F.R. Crafts (1990), 'Explaining Anglo-American Productivity Differences in the Mid-Twentieth Century', *Oxford Bulletin of Economics and Statistics*, **52** (4), 375–402.

Cambridge University Press for excerpts and article: H.J. Habakkuk (1962), 'Technology and Growth in Britain in the Later Nineteenth Century', in *American and British Technology in the Nineteenth Century: The Search for Labour-Saving Inventions*, Chapter VI, 189–220; David S. Landes (1965), 'Some Reasons Why', in H.J. Habakkuk and M. Postan (eds), *Cambridge Economic History of Europe*, Chapter V, Volume VI, 553–84; Bernard Elbaum and William Lazonick (1984), 'The Decline of the British Economy: An Institutional Perspective', *Journal of Economic History*, **XLIV** (2), June, 567–83; R.E. Rowthorn and J.R. Wells (1987), 'De-Industrialization in the UK: Three Theses' and 'Towards a Better Past', in *De-Industrialization and Foreign Trade*, Chapters 10 and 11, 207–48, notes and references.

Frank Cass & Co. Ltd for article: T.R. Gourvish (1987), 'British Business and the Transition to a Corporate Economy: Entrepreneurship and Management Structures', *Business History*, **XXIX** (4), October, 18–45.

Harvard University Press for excerpts: Charles P. Kindleberger (1964), 'Technology', in *Economic Growth in France and Britain 1851–1950*, Chapter 7, 135–56 and references; Leslie Hannah (1980), 'Visible and Invisible Hands in Great Britain', in Alfred D. Chandler, Jr and Herman Daems (eds), *Managerial Hierarchies. Comparative Perspectives on the Rise of the Modern Industrial Enterprise*, Chapter 2, 41–76.

Institute for Fiscal Studies for article: P.J. Forsyth and J.A. Kay (1980), 'The Economic Implications of North Sea Oil Revenues', *Fiscal Studies*, **1**, 1–28.

Macmillan Press Ltd for excerpt: G.N. von Tunzelmann (1982), 'Structural Change and Leading Sectors in British Manufacturing, 1907–68', in Charles P. Kindleberger and Guido di Tella (eds), *Economics in the Long View. Essays in Honour of W.W. Rostow*, Chapter 1, Volume 3, 1–49 and bibliography.

Oxford University Press for articles and excerpt: E.H. Phelps Brown with S.J. Handfield-Jones (1952), 'The Climacteric of the 1890's: A Study in the Expanding Economy', *Oxford Economic Papers*, **4**, 266–90; H.W. Richardson (1961), 'The New Industries between the Wars', *Oxford Economic Papers*, **13**, 360–84; R.C.O. Matthews, C.H. Feinstein and J.C. Odling-Smee (1982), 'The Rate of Growth and the Proximate Sources of Growth' and 'Causes and Consequences of the Growth of Total Factor Input and Total Factor Productivity', in *British Economic Growth 1856–1973*, Chapters 16 and 17, 497–550, notes and references.

Past & Present Society for articles: Patrick K. O'Brien (1987), 'Britain's Economy Between the Wars: A Survey of a Counter-Revolution in Economic History', *Past and Present*, **115**, May, 107–30; M.J. Daunton (1989), '"Gentlemanly Capitalism" and British Industry 1820–1914', *Past and Present*, **122**, February, 119–58.

Weidenfeld & Nicolson and St Martin's Press for excerpt: Peter L. Payne (1990), 'Entrepreneurship and British Economic Decline', in Bruce Collins and Keith Robbins (eds), *British Culture and Economic Decline*, 25–58.

In addition the publishers wish to thank the Library of the London School of Economics and Political Science and the Marshall Library of Economics, Cambridge University for their assistance in obtaining these articles.

Introduction: Themes in the Economic Development of the United Kingdom since 1870[1]

Charles Feinstein

More than a hundred years of scholarship devoted to description, analysis and appraisal of the economic development of the United Kingdom since 1870 has generated an enormous literature. By far the most difficult problem posed by any attempt to assemble a collection of readings on this subject is thus the exceptional wealth of material from which to choose. With so much available, an individual selection will probably seem arbitrary or capricious, and it may be helpful to make explicit the few general guidelines underlying the present choice.

The one issue which has dominated research into the modern economic history of the United Kingdom is the fall from pre-eminence since the late 19th century, the loss of its position as the world's leading industrial nation. Numerous writers – economists and historians, politicians and government officials, businessmen and trade unionists – have contributed their views to a prolific and long-running debate over this painful and persistent process of relative decline. From this rich source I have selected as the subject for this collection a range of macro-economic issues relating to the pace and pattern of Britain's long-run economic growth. Was the pace of Britain's growth diminishing? If so, why was Britain slowing down and falling behind? Was productivity lower than it should have been? Why were American, German and other exporters gaining ground in Britain's traditional overseas markets, even outselling Britain at home? Were the fatal weaknesses and short-comings in performance, economic or social or political? Was it the fault of management or workers, capitalists or bankers, trade unions or family firms, teachers or policy-makers?

Given this decision as to the primary subject, I have selected material relating to a small number of closely related themes so as to give a greater degree of cohesion and continuity to the collection. The papers are grouped in eight separate parts, although there is inevitably some degree of overlap and several of the papers deal with topics relevant to more than one of these headings. The first of the eight parts provides a broad overview of Britain's growth, and the second and third cover the general issues of growth and retardation from late Victorian and Edwardian times to the present. The next four are devoted to the principal factors which have been advanced as explanations for Britain's apparent inability to sustain

1. I am grateful to my colleagues, James Foreman-Peck and Avner Offer for their forthright comments on my preliminary choice of articles for this volume, and to Anne Digby for suggesting valuable improvements to this Introduction.

its competitive position; and the final part consists of case studies of key industries chosen to illustrate many of these general themes.

The choice of this particular subject means, of course, that many equally important and interesting topics could not be covered but, even within this restricted field, it has been necessary to omit some outstanding contributions and some relevant topics. The omission of which I was most conscious concerned the frequent debates over economic policy and the role of the state, but this is only one of several significant issues for which there was no space.

My second criterion was the accessibility of the original publication, and on this ground I excluded all articles which first appeared in the *Economic History Review*. The *Review* is undoubtedly the premier journal for the publication of research on the economic history of the United Kingdom, but it is very widely available in both institutional and personal libraries, and I decided that it was more appropriate to use the limited space for papers which were less readily available.

Subject to these two constraints, the choice of individual papers was designed to include a representative selection of the seminal contributions which have stimulated further debate and research, to convey a sense of the variety of views held by writers on these topics, and to indicate the richness and quality of the research by British and American scholars on the economic development of the United Kingdom since 1870. I have included both detailed accounts of original research and broader surveys of the literature on specific topics. Some of the selections are representative of traditional forms of historical scholarship and literary style, others embody the 'new economic history' approach, with its emphasis on quantitative methods and the explicit use of economic theory. Some authors take the principles of orthodox neo-classical economics as the starting point for their analysis, others give greater weight to institutional determinants of economic change. In total there are 46 items by 55 writers, most written as self-contained articles but some extracted from larger studies. Many of the selected items will be familiar to most readers, but I have tried to include a few which may be less well known.

Overview

The collection begins with two contributions designed to provide an overall picture of Britain's economic growth and structural change. The first is from the book by Matthews, Feinstein and Odling-Smee (1982*).[2] In this extract they report the major findings of their elaborate quantitative investigation of Britain's long-run economic growth from 1856 to 1973. They used the new quantitative evidence on the growth of aggregate GDP and its components constructed by Feinstein (1972), and applied a growth accounting approach to determine the proximate sources of growth over this period. They then analysed the underlying factors responsible for the observed trends in factor supplies and in demand.

The second, by von Tunzelmann (1982*) applies input–output methods to analyse the process of structural change in the manufacturing sector from 1907 to 1968. He shows that

---

2. Full references are given at the end of this Introduction for works not reproduced in this collection. If all or part of the work is reproduced, this is indicated by a * after the date.

productivity increases within sectors were a much more important source of growth than the reallocation of factors between sectors, and thus plays down the significance of the concept of leading sectors. His research also casts doubt on the idea that a group of new industries constituted a special 'development block' with significant internal linkages which isolated them from the old staple industries, and gave them a special prominence in inter-war economic growth.

Retardation and the Victorian Climacteric

Part II of Volume I covers the long-standing controversy about the timing, extent and causes of the process of retardation in the late 19th or early 20th century. Modern discussion of this old theme was initiated in the early 1950s by Phelps Brown (1952*), and still continues. He argued that there was a check to growth in the United Kingdom caused by a slowdown in productivity. Such a slackening was evident in two independent measures of growth, one based on a deflated series of money incomes, the other on an index of industrial production, but these two series diverged between 1870 and 1900. Over these decades real income per head continued to rise strongly, whereas the growth of industrial productivity had already come to an end. After further investigation Phelps Brown (1952*, para. 8) concluded that there was, 'enough agreement of independent evidence to make it clear that some checks to the rise of productivity in industry and agriculture underlay the set-backs to real income a head and real wages in the United Kingdom *about the turn of the century*'.

Phelps Brown's conclusions were soon challenged by Coppock (1956), who elaborated certain key themes previously outlined by Arthur Lewis (1949). In Coppock's view the only 'genuine climacteric' in productivity was the one shown by the index of industrial production, and in this series the check to growth had occurred in the 1870s. He dismissed the apparent break in the trend in the 1890s shown by the real income series as the result of deficiencies in the price index used as a deflator.

These early studies stimulated numerous distinguished contributions to the debate from both sides of the Atlantic.[3] Their approach was generally qualitative and analytical and, although some appeal was made to statistical evidence, they were not primarily concerned with measurement and quantification. The great majority accepted retardation as an established fact, and their principal concern was to explain why this had occurred. Only a few voices, notably those of Musson (1963) and Wilson (1965), were raised to suggest that perhaps the picture of retardation was being over-stated.

McCloskey (1970) then threw down a provocative challenge to the received views which had emerged from the earlier literature. Victorian Britain, he declared, did *not* fail. Limitations on the demand side – more particularly the slow growth of exports – which Lewis (1949), Meyer (1955), Coppock (1956) and others had suggested as the proximate cause of Britain's deceleration, were of no consequence. He could also find no significant weakness on the

---

3. A selection of influential work in chronological order from 1955 onwards would include: Meyer (1955), Saul (1960), Saville (1961*), Habakkuk (1962*), Musson (1963), Kindleberger (1964*), Landes (1965*), Richardson (1965), Wilson (1965), Levine (1967), McCloskey (1970), Lewis (1978*), Elbaum and Lazonick (1985), Kennedy (1987) and Kirby (1992).

supply side. On the contrary, he observed an economy, 'not stagnating, but growing as rapidly as permitted by the growth of its resources and the effective exploitation of the available technology'. To support this analytical argument he presented new estimates of the rate of growth of real GDP and of total factor productivity, and claimed that both showed sustained growth until the end of the century: 'There was a dip of productivity in the 1900s, but it was too short, too late, and too uncertain to justify the dramatic description "climacteric"' (McCloskey, 1970, p. 459).

This was an extremely stimulating paper, but not everyone found the arguments persuasive and the debate continued. Kennedy (1974) immediately took issue with McCloskey's analysis, arguing that there were aspects of the British performance which warranted criticism, notably those caused by imperfections in the capital market (see further the discussion of this topic in Part II of Volume II). Arthur Lewis (1978*) then made a further constructive intervention. Where others had overlooked or merely noted the awkward discrepancy between the income and output data identified by Phelps Brown, he attempted to grapple directly with this problem. He compiled new estimates from the output side and used these as the basis for an illuminating analysis of the issues.

The new quantitative evidence on the growth of aggregate GDP and its components constructed by Feinstein (1972) helped to provide a sounder basis for the study of these trends in this and subsequent periods.

More recently, the work of Maddison (1982) has greatly facilitated comparison with growth performance in other countries. Lee (1984*) has sought to move attention away from the industrial sector by charting the rise of the services. Feinstein (1990) has reviewed the literature from the standpoint of the income date, emphasizing the strong evidence of a period of stagnation in the growth of real wages in the Edwardian period; while Crafts *et al.* (1989) and Mills and Crafts (1996) have used the latest econometric techniques to question the whole notion of a late 19th century climacteric in the growth of industrial production.

Relative Decline: The Inter-war and Post-war Periods

In the next set of readings (Part III of Volume I) the focus is enlarged to take in discussions of Britain's performance and relative decline after 1914. The economic history of the period between the two world wars is dominated by cyclical fluctuations and by the mass unemployment which emerged early in the 1920s, rose still further in the great depression of 1929–32, and remained high even during the recovery of the 1930s. The varied analyses which have been made of the possible causes of this inability to achieve a better balance in the labour market are not directly represented in this collection, but are reviewed by O'Brien (1987*). His paper also provides an excellent account of recent assessments of the great debates between Keynes and his opponents about the role of fiscal, monetary and exchange rate policies as a cause of the difficulties experienced in the 1920s, and as a possible cure for the problems of unemployment.

Issues of longer-term growth and relative performance were not crowded-out by these cyclical problems, and remained a major source of concern for students of these years. Re-assessment and analysis of the performance of the inter-war economy was initiated by

Richardson (1961*), Aldcroft (1966, 1967) and Dowie (1968) in the 1960s, and continued by Buxton (1975) and Alford (1981). One of the central issues which they addressed was the role of the new industries (such as electricity, motor vehicles and chemicals), and their ability to compensate for the decline of the old staple industries, such as coal, cotton, shipbuilding and engineering. The paper in Part I by von Tunzelmann (1982*) is also a major contribution to this discussion. The case studies in Part IV of Volume II illustrate inter-war developments in two of these new industries: motor vehicles (Church and Miller, 1977*) and chemicals (Reader, 1979*), while Lorenz (1991*) provides an evolutionary explanation for the long-run decline of one of the old industries, shipbuilding.

Investigation of trends in British economic growth over time was supplemented by comparisons of levels of efficiency in Britain and the United States, and this became a notable feature in the evaluation of Britain's economic performance. Whenever close comparisons could be made, the American firms were found to produce appreciably more per hour than their British counterparts; the differential could be as much as 100 per cent of the British output. Such contrasts were particularly significant in those industries where the two countries produced essentially the same product using the same machinery. Striking disparities in productivity had been the subject of numerous comments by individual visitors and official delegations from the United Kingdom to the United States ever since the mid-19th century, and were confirmed by Rostas (1948) in a systematic statistical comparison across a range of industries. Both Anglo-American and Anglo-German productivity have been studied in recent work by Broadberry (1993), Broadberry and Crafts (1990*) and Broadberry and Fremdling (1990).

The first attempt to provide a rigorous explanation for the superior efficiency of American industry was made by Erwin Rothbarth (1946*). One of his suggestions was that a crucial source of the difference in performance was the stimulus to labour-saving equipment provided by the high cost of labour in the United States, and this, in turn, he attributed to the greater abundance of land. The effects of labour scarcity on mechanization and technical progress were investigated in great depth in an illuminating study by Habakkuk (1962*), and the fascination of the topic stimulated further important contributions, notably those of Temin (1966), Ames and Rosenberg (1968) and David (1975). The influence of relative factor supplies is examined by Harley (1973–74*) in the context of its impact on production techniques (see Part I of Volume II) and by Crafts and Thomas (1986*) in relation to the overseas trade of the United Kingdom (see Part III of Volume II).

Many of the themes already noted re-appeared in the discussions of British economic growth in the years after the Second World War. Even though performance in the 1950s and 1960s was relatively good by Britain's own historical standards, a number of other countries were achieving much higher rates of growth. There was mounting dissatisfaction within Britain, and a renewed search for causes and culprits. The recent collection of studies edited by Crafts and Toniolo (1996) is an outstanding comparative survey of post-war growth.

One of the more striking new developments which attracted considerable attention during the 1970s, both in popular discussion and academic research, was the declining proportion of the labour force employed in manufacturing, a phenomenon which came to be known as de-industrialization. In the United Kingdom, a process of absolute decline began in the mid-1960s and accelerated dramatically after 1979. Absolute or relative decline was also evident in many other advanced economies. The crucial question is whether this was the result of the success or the failure of the manufacturing sector. It could be interpreted as a success if the process were driven by rapid growth of manufacturing productivity so that the necessary labour force fell even though output was increasing. It would be an indication of failure if output and employment were falling because industry was unable to compete with its international rivals in home and foreign markets.

Bacon and Eltis (1976), Singh (1977), Blackaby (1979) and Kilpatrick and Lawson (1980*) made notable contributions to an initial exploration of the causes and consequences of this phenomenon. Many of the crucial analytical and empirical issues were then examined and clarified in an extremely thorough and wide-ranging investigation by Rowthorn and Wells (1987*). The main conclusions of their study are reproduced in the extract reprinted in Part III of Volume I.

A further possible explanation for the decline of manufacturing was the discovery and exploitation of North Sea oil and gas. Once Britain became a major oil producer there was a marked improvement in the balance of payments and a rise in the real exchange rate. This in turn made exports of manufactures less competitive, and resulted in a substantial transfer of labour from manufacturing to other sectors. This represented a major change in Britain's economic circumstances and provoked a number of writers to examine its impact. Forsyth and Kay (1980*) were among the first to raise the issue; the main subsequent empirical studies were Bond and Knobl (1982) and Rowthorn and Wells (1987*). The topic also stimulated a number of innovative theoretical papers.

The next four parts of this collection are devoted to broad themes which have figured prominently in all discussions of the reasons for Britain's failure to grow as rapidly, or to be as efficient, as some of its rivals. On the supply side there has been an energetic and continuous hunt for deficiencies in the quality of managerial and entrepreneurial performance, in the attitudes and education of the labour force, and in the operation of capital markets. On the demand side there has been discussion about the possible adverse effects of the size of the market and of either the level, or the rate of growth, of demand.

Entrepreneurship, Management and Technical Change

Part IV of Volume I covers eight contributions to the discussion of the criticism most frequently raised: the shortcomings of British entrepreneurs and, in particular, their slowness in adopting new technology. Payne (1990*) reviews very clearly the successive contributions to a long debate, and there is a valuable survey in Coleman and Macleod (1986).

Habakkuk (1962*, p. 212) was one of the first of the post-war scholars to consider this issue, and the upshot of his lucid and balanced assessment of the period before 1914 was that the entrepreneurs were effectively exonerated: 'The entrepreneurial deficiencies to which the performance of the British economy is attributed can plausibly be explained as a consequence of that performance'.

Others took a different view. For a time there seemed no end to the list of failings of which those in charge of British industry were accused. They were conservative, complacent, unreceptive to new ideas; they set too much store by practical experience and neglected – or, indeed, despised – education and science; they clung to outdated equipment because they failed to distinguish technical from physical obsolescence; they invested too much in the old staples and neglected the new industries; they were guilty of nepotism and irrational attachment to the family firm; and, above all, they were sadly lacking in the cultural and sociological values which could have promoted a more dynamic and prosperous economy.

Aldcroft (1964), Landes (1965*) and Levine (1967) were in the vanguard of this attack; Landes's caustic description conveys the stark and unrelenting tone of some of the comments (1965, p. 563):

> Thus the Britain of the late nineteenth century basked complacently in the sunset of economic hegemony. In many firms, the grandfather who started the business and built it by unremitting application and by thrift bordering on miserliness had long died; the father who took over a solid enterprise and, starting with larger ambitions, raised it to undreamt-of heights, had passed on the reins; now it was the turn of the third generation, the children of affluence, tired of the tedium of trade and flushed with the bucolic aspirations of the country gentleman... Many of them retired and forced the conversion of their firms into joint-stock companies. Others stayed on and went through the motions of entrepreneurship between the long weekends; they worked at play and played at work.

For a time these harsh critics carried all before them, even though careful studies by Kindleberger (1964*), Saul (1962, 1967, 1968), Wilson (1965) and Coleman (1973) posed new issues and significantly modified the portrayal of unrelieved weakness in British industrial leadership. Then a formidable new group of scholars came rushing forward in defence of British entrepreneurship. They published a series of innovative studies in which the principles of orthodox neo-classical economic analysis were applied to specific British decisions which had frequently been taken to sustain the case made by the critics, for example, the failure of the cotton industry to introduce the ring spindle and of the steel industry to exploit the rich ore deposits of the Midlands.

The central argument of this new group was that in almost all the cases examined it was possible to demonstrate that the businessmen had made rational, profit-maximizing decisions. They should thus be found 'not guilty' and acquitted. The leading exponents of this view were McCloskey (1971, 1973) and Sandberg (1969, 1974*), and McCloskey and Sandberg (1971) is a triumphal summary of their views. The approach is illustrated in Lindert and Trace (1971*), although this was one of the exceptions to the general thrust of these contributions, since their research showed that there had been some delay in the introduction of the new Solvay process by the chemical industry.

This vindication of British industry was in turn subject to criticism by a new generation of scholars, led by Elbaum and Lazonick (1984*, 1986). They highlighted a distinction between *management*, which consisted of routine decision-making within given constraints; and *entrepreneurship*, which required innovative action to change these constraints, a point Allen (1981) had also made. On this view the McCloskey–Sandberg defence may have exonerated managers making customary decisions in a routine situation, but British entrepreneurs were still guilty as charged. They had failed to make the innovations – for example, in production, marketing, corporate structure or industrial relations – which would have removed existing constraints and so created a new context in which managers could operate.

This conceptual distinction is pertinent and useful, and should not have been overlooked. However, Saxonhouse and Wright (1984, 1987) have shown that the attempt to identify the relevant constraint does not work well in the case of the cotton industry; and Dintenfass (1988*) has exposed weaknesses in the application of this approach to the coal industry. Kirby (1992) is also critical of the approach.

These varied criticisms of the early studies which relied on strong cultural and socio-logical characteristics for their explanations of retardation and relative decline have not deterred modern writers from taking a similar position. Wiener (1981) and Barnett (1986, 1995) have been especially influential in the expression of such views, and their work has aroused considerable popular interest. However, many economic historians, including James and other contributors to Collins and Robbins (1990*), Harris (1990), and Edgerton (1991) have argued vigorously that they find little evidence to support this approach in their reading of the historical record. Pollard (1990, p. 173) summed up his wide-ranging comparative evaluation as follows: 'There is more doubt, amounting almost to certainty of the contrary, whether the British entrepreneur of the age was inferior to any other in Europe, and whether British culture was more harmful to industrial entrepreneurship than that of contemporary Europe'.

While the studies so far noted have tended to see the issues in terms of the performance of the individual entrepreneur, the next group of papers in this part of Volume I have a different focus, looking in one case at the effects of a broad socio-economic system and in the other at corporate and managerial structures. The first is associated with the work of Cain and Hopkins (1993), and their concept of 'gentlemanly capitalism'. This approach was developed in the context of their innovative and comprehensive treatment of the phenomenon of British imperialism, but in their presentation it is also of considerable relevance in understanding the performance of the domestic economy. They delineate an economy and society in which the landed interest was originally the controlling group, but which changed after 1850 as representatives of the fast-growing service and financial sectors moved to occupy the dominant positions. London re-asserted its pre-eminence as the centre of power, and the interests of industry and the provinces were subordinated to those of the City and the services. The most significant expression of the new elite's powerful influence on policy-making is seen in Britain's support for free trade, financial orthodoxy and the gold standard, all policies of uncertain benefit to the industrial sector.

It is thus the consequences of this loss of influence – rather than the performance of individual industrialists – which Cain and Hopkins see as the central determinant of Britain's loss of industrial dynamism. As is usually the case, such grand and sweeping generalizations are at once stimulating and vulnerable to detailed criticism. Daunton (1989*) uses the abundant historical records of a leading London firm as the basis for a careful criticial appraisal of these concepts and hypotheses.

The other major new avenue for the investigation of British business performance was opened by the pioneering work of Chandler (1962, 1977). Among his central themes was the importance of the growth and diversification of the large-scale corporation and the crucial role of managerial hierarchies and of multi-divisional corporate stuctures. He showed how vital strategic decisions were taken by the 'visible hand' of management, not left to the market. Chandler originally developed these ideas to explain the growth and success of large corporations in the United States, but the contrast with the survival of the family firm in the United Kingdom provided an obvious subject for investigation. Hannah (1974, 1976, 1980*) and Gourvish (1987*) were the leading figures in initiating this research, and subsequently Chandler (1990) also dealt at length with the British business scene. The merits and weaknesses of this approach are subtly probed in a review article by Supple (1991).

The extent and quality of the research and development undertaken by British industry has recently been raised as a further element in the debate about Britain's economic performance. The topic was first addressed by Sanderson (1972) and Saul (1979), and achieved greater prominence when Mowery (1986) argued that weaknesses in this area were a significant cause of Britain's relative decline. However, this view is strongly challenged in the paper by Edgerton (1994*) and in further research reported in Edgerton and Horrocks (1994).

Labour, Trade Unions, Skill and Education

Volume II opens with a set of articles devoted to another favourite candidate for writers searching for a culprit for Britain's inadequate performance: the attitudes of workers (or trade unions) to machinery, the inadequacies of their training and education, and the effort they exerted. As the Webbs (1897*) note, at the beginning of the 19th century the attitude of handicraftsmen to the introduction of machinery was frequently outright opposition, with riots and machine-burning as the most extreme expression of this hostility. By the end of the century the introduction of new equipment was no longer resisted directly, but there were fierce disputes over the terms on which it should be used. In their discussion, the Webbs give particular attention to the conflicts over the level of wages appropriate under the changed conditions created by new equipment. They also discuss disagreements over the way in which the equipment was to be used, and illustrate their account with instructive examples from the cotton, printing, boot and shoe, and shipbuilding industries.

It was these explicit or tacit understandings between employers and workers with respect to the number and qualifications of the labour to be employed, and the speed or intensity with which the new equipment would be operated, which were of vital importance in determining what effect the innovation would have on productivity. In industries where little or no equipment was used, such as the building trades, it was still possible for workers to restrict output in various ways. The popular name for these practices was 'ca canny'. The results of an informal inter-war investigation of the extent to which this was customary, undertaken by a group sympathetic to the concerns of labour, are reported in the extract from Hilton *et al.* (1935*).

In recent years the attitudes and practices of labour and management have been examined in both historical and contemporary studies. A variety of points of view on this question are expressed in works such as Price (1980), Gospel and Littler (1983), Harrison and Zeitlin (1985), Fox (1985), Zeitlin (1987) and Gospel (1992). Pencavel (1977*) draws on the experience of the coal mining industry to provide a more analytical discussion of the effects of trade unions from the perspective of an industrial relations economist. In the context of the post-war period, Kilpatrick and Lawson (1982*) emphasize workplace conflict over the organization of production as one of the principal reasons for the poor competitive performance of the United Kingdom economy.

A very different distinguishing characteristic of the British workforce was its high level of skill, and it is the consequences of this feature which Harley (1973–74*) explores. His starting point is the apparent paradox that although the 19th-century British economy had an abundance of capital compared with other countries, it persisted in using relatively labour-intensive processes. The aspect of this pattern which probably attracted the most adverse comment was the slowness to adopt the capital-intensive 'American system of manufacture', based on standardization, interchangeable parts, special purpose machine tools and assembly-line production. The explanation Harley advances for this turns on the hypothesis that Britain had an abundant supply of *skilled* labour relative to the rest of the world. He argues that this had a fundamental influence on the choice of production technique and the nature of international specialization, and supports his analysis by reference to the experience of the shipbuilding, textile, iron and steel, and engineering industries.

The question of whether Britain failed to provide an adequate education for its workers has been a controversial topic since the late 19th century. The many issues in this debate were concisely reviewed by Sanderson (1988*) in a paper which he has brought up to date for this collection. The historical issues were considered at length by Pollard (1989), together with the related questions of the content and suitability of the training provided by the public schools and universities for those who might become the leaders of British industry. Unlike many other commentators, his overall verdict was reasonably favourable to that of the education system and, in particular, he was critical of the widely expressed view that Germany was much more successful in this sphere. Prais (1993) provides an excellent assessment of similar issues in a contemporary context.

Capital Markets and Imperialism

The papers in Part II of Volume II cover a number of themes relating to the working of the capital market. Cottrell (1979) is an informative introduction to the historical background, and Michie (1988*) surveys the large literature devoted to the question of whether the progress of home industry and the economic infrastructure were impeded by a lack of capital. The reason most commonly given for suggesting this is the extraordinarily high level of overseas investment in the late Victorian and Edwardian periods.

Kennedy (1976, 1984*, 1987) has been the most vigorous exponent of the view that this was the crucial factor which deprived the domestic economy of the capital needed for modernization and expansion. In particular, he argued that potential purchasers of industrial securities had access to significantly less information than would-be sellers. This fundamental asymmetry distorted, and perhaps even destroyed, the functioning of the markets for these risky assets, and so helps to explain why such a large share of British savings was channelled abroad. The argument against this or other forms of market failure has been put most strongly by McCloskey (1981).

Edelstein (1982*) also examined the question of capital market imperfections as part of his wider assessment of British overseas investment in the age of high imperialism. However, his careful quantitative study found no support for the view that there was a bias in the market which predisposed it to support foreign issues at the expense of home investment. The larger question of whether or not Britain gained from imperialism has recently been the subject of renewed research and debate, with impressive contributions from Davis and Huttenback (1986), Hopkins (1988), Pollard (1989), Cain and Hopkins (1993), Offer (1993) and Edelstein (1994). O'Brien (1988*) surveys many of the key questions.

An alternative version of the argument claims that the country failed to maintain the desired levels of investment in domestic industry because the British banking system was not willing to provide the necessary finance. Banks were too cautious in their acquisition of assets and too concerned to maintain their own liquidity and profitability. In this form the criticism has been made with remarkable persistence from the 19th century to the present day. The attitudes and policies of the British commercial banks are frequently contrasted with those of Germany's investment banks, and it is claimed that the latter institutions and practices were much more suitable for the promotion of rapid economic growth. However, recent research by Ross (1990*) casts considerable doubt on the traditional story of the banks' reluctance to provide finance for industry, as does the work of Watson (1996) on the specific experience of the brewing industry. This long-running debate over the role of the banks is reviewed in Capie and Collins (1992) and in Collins (1995).

International Trade and Demand

Since at least the time of the industrial revolution the relatively small British economy has exported a very large share of its output, and so trade has been a potentially important influence on growth. Developments in the international economy are also in large measure exogenous and so represent possible independent explanatory factors for cyclical fluctuations and long-run trends in British output. As noted above, a number of authors, including Lewis (1949) and Coppock (1956), argued that it was the slowdown in exports in the late 19th century, following the rise of foreign competition from the USA, Germany and other late-starters, which was primarily responsible for the corresponding slowdown in British growth. The export-led economy of the late 18th century had become 'export-retarded'.

The exact nature and importance of the possible links between exports and the perform-ance of the domestic economy is carefully explored in a number of the papers. Saul (1965*) surveys the changing pattern of British overseas trade in the pre-1914 period, and the influence of foreign trade is the critical factor in the explanation for the relative decline of the pre-1914 British steel industry suggested by Temin (1966*). Beckerman (1965*) con-structs a model of export-led growth as the basis for his projection of Britain's economic growth in the late 20th century.

The lecture by Sayers (1965*) includes a helpful exploration of the effects of foreign industrialization. This can be beneficial ('complementary') if it leads to an increase in incomes within these countries and thus provides larger markets for British exports; it will be adverse ('competitive') if the late-starters become more efficient in producing goods for sale in competition with United Kingdom production.

Matthews (1973*) incorporates these ideas in his analysis of these relationships over the whole period from the mid-19th century to the 'golden age' of the 1950s and 1960s. His framework covers not only the direct link between foreign growth and British trade and payments, and the impact of the exchange rate and other institutional features of the pre-vailing international monetary system, but also the possible feedback from slower growth in Britain to the balance of payments. He identifies several channels through which domestic production and productivity might have been significantly affected, including the direct demand effects of rapid or sluggish export growth, the adverse impact on domestic investment created both by diminished profits and by a greater inducement to invest overseas, and deflationary policies imposed by the authorities in order to protect the reserves.

The repeal of the corn laws and the adoption of a free trade policy is often presented as a fundamental institutional change which not only boosted employment and income in the manufacturing sector at the expense of agricultural interests, but also made a substantial contribution to Britain's economic growth. The first serious attempts to overturn this commitment and to introduce tariff protection were made at the turn of the century, and it remained a major subject of debate and political controversy until the general election of 1931 finally gave popular backing to the supporters of the tariff. Major recent studies of the policy changes include Capie (1983), Rooth (1993) and Marrison (1996).

In a characteristically pugnacious paper, McCloskey (1980*) takes a different view of the impact of free trade in the mid-19th century. He argues that its importance has been greatly exaggerated, and that its contribution to Britain's expansion during the mid-Victorian boom was relatively small; indeed, it may even have retarded growth through its adverse effects on the terms of trade. The paper by Foreman-Peck (1979*) describes a static partial equilibrium model and shows how this can be used to analyse the effect of tariff protection on the motor industry. His findings are that protective duties were a major influence on the growth of the industry in the inter-war period, and that it would probably have been beneficial if they had been introduced before 1914.

On a different theme Crafts and Thomas (1986*) attempt to analyse the pattern of Britain's international trade in manufactures in relation to the factor inputs used for different categories of product. They distinguish three factors of production: capital, human capital and unskilled labour, and then examine the relationship between these inputs and the level of net or gross exports. Their main finding is that over the years 1910–1935 the United Kingdom had a comparative advantage in goods which were intensive in the use of unskilled labour, and a comparative disadvantage in those which were intensive in the use of human capital.

There has been a notable persistence in the attention given to all of the themes covered in these two volumes. The process of relative decline has continued remorselessly, attempts to explain why this has occurred have a disturbing longevity. The present collection has highlighted four broad categories of explanation, three on the supply side covering management, labour and capital; one on the demand side. Within each of these fields the criticisms of the British economy which were first made in the 19th century were restated in commentaries on the inter-war period, and emerged yet again, freshly discovered, in post-mortems on performance after the Second World War. The implication might be that neither those who manage the economy nor those who narrate and appraise its performance have learnt as much as they should from the historical record.

Bibliography

Aldcroft, D.H. (1964), 'The entrepreneur and the British economy, 1870–1914', *Economic History Review*, **17**, 113–34.
Aldcroft, D.H. (1966), 'Economic progress in Britain in the 1920s', *Scottish Journal of Political Economy*, **13**, 297–316.

Aldcroft, D.H. (1967), 'Economic growth in Britain in the inter-war years, a re-assessment', *Economic History Review*, **20**, 311–26.

Alford, B.W. (1981), 'New industries for old? British industry between the wars', in R. Floud and D.N. McCloskey (eds), *The Economic History of Britain since 1700, I*, 2 vols, 1st edn, Cambridge: Cambridge University Press, **2**, 208–31.

Allen, R.C. (1981), 'Entrepreneurship and technical progress in the Northeast Coast pig iron industry: 1850–1913', *Research in Economic History*, **6**, 35–71.

Ames, E. and Rosenberg, N. (1968), 'The Enfield Arsenal in theory and history', *Economic Journal*, **78**, 827–42.

Bacon, R. and Eltis, W. (1976), *Britain's Economic Problem: Too Few Producers*, London: Macmillan.

Barnett, C. (1986), *The Audit of War*, London: Macmillan.

Barnett, C. (1995), *The Lost Victory: British Dreams, British Realities, 1945–50*, London: Macmillan.

Blackaby, F. (ed.) (1979), *De industrialization*, London: Heinamann.

Bond, M.E. and Knobl, A. (1982), 'Some implications of North Sea Oil for the UK economy', *IMF Staff Papers*, **29**, 363–97.

Broadberry, S.N. (1993), 'Manufacturing and the convergence hypothesis: what the long-run data show', *Journal of Economic History*, **53**, 772–95.

Broadberry, S.N. and Fremdling, R. (1990), 'Comparative productivity in British and German industry, 1907–37', *Oxford Bulletin of Economics and Statistics*, **52**, 403–21.

Buxton, N. (1975), 'The role of the new industries in Britain during the 1930s: a reinterpretation', *Business History Review*, **94**, 205–22.

Cain, P.J. and Hopkins, A.G. (1993), *British Imperialism, Crisis and Deconstruction, 1914–1990*, London: Longman.

Capie, F. (1983), *Depression and Protectionism: Britain between the Wars*, London: Allen and Unwin.

Capie, F. and Collins, M. (1992), *Have the British Banks Failed British Industry? An Historical Survey of Bank/Industry Relations in Britain, 1870–1990*, London: Institute of Economic Affairs.

Chandler, A.D. (1962), *Strategy and Structure: Chapters in the History of American Business*, Cambridge, Mass.: Harvard University Press.

Chandler, A.D. (1977), *The Visible Hand – the Managerial Revolution in American Business*, Cambridge, Mass.: Harvard University Press.

Chandler, A.D. (1990), *Scale and Scope: Dynamics of Industrial Capitalism*, Cambridge, Mass.: Harvard University Press.

Coleman, D.C. (1973), 'Gentlemen and players', *Economic History Review*, **26**, 92–116.

Coleman, D.C. and Macleod, C. (1986), 'Attitudes to new techniques: British businessmen, 1800–1950', *Economic History Review*, **39**, 588–611.

Collins, M. (1995), *Banks and Industrial Finance in Britain, 1800–1939*, Cambridge: Cambridge University Press.

Coppock, D.J. (1956), 'The climacteric of the 1890s: a critical note', *Manchester School*, **24**, 1–31.

Cottrell, P.L. (1979), *Industrial Finance, 1830–1914, The Finance and Organization of English Manufacturing Industry*, London: Methuen.

Crafts, N.F.R. and Toniolo, G. (1996), *Economic Growth in Europe since 1945*, Cambridge: Cambridge University Press.

Crafts, N.F.R., Leybourne, S.J. and Mills, T.C. (1989), 'The climacteric in late Victorian Britain and France: a reappraisal of the evidence', *Journal of Applied Econometrics*, **4**, 103–17.

David, P.A. (1975), *Technical Choice, Innovation and Economic Growth: Essays in American and British Experience in the Nineteenth Century*, Cambridge: Cambridge University Press.

Davis, L.E. and Huttenback, R.A. (1986), *Mammon and the Pursuit of Empire: The Political Economy of British Imperialism, 1860–1912*, Cambridge: Cambridge University Press.

Dowie, J.A. (1968), 'Growth in the inter-war period: some more arithmetic', *Economic History Review*, **21**, 93–112.

Edelstein, M. (1994), 'Imperialism: cost and benefit', in R.C. Floud and D.N. McCloskey (eds), *An Economic History of Britain since 1700, II*, 3 vols, 2nd edn, Cambridge: Cambridge University Press, **2**, 173–96.

Edgerton, D.E.H. (1991), 'The prophet militant and industrial: the peculiarities of Corelli Barnett', *Twentieth Century British History*, **2**, 360–79.

Edgerton, D.E.H. and Horrocks, S.M. (1994), 'British industrial research and development before 1945', *Economic History Review*, **47**, 213–38.

Elbaum, B. and Lazonick, W. (eds) (1986), *The Decline of the British Economy*, Oxford: Oxford University Press.

Feinstein, C.H. (1972), *National Income, Expenditure and Output of the United Kingdom, 1855–1965*, Cambridge: Cambridge University Press.

Feinstein, C.H. (1990), 'What really happened to real wages?: trends in wages, prices, and productivity in the United Kingdom, 1880–1913', *Economic History Review*, **43**, 329–55.

Fox, A. (1985), *History and Heritage: The Social Origins of the British Industrial Relations System*, Oxford: Oxford University Press.

Gospel, H.F. (1992), *Markets, Firms and the Management of Labour in Modern Britain*, Cambridge: Cambridge University Press.

Gospel, H.F. and Littler, C.R. (1983), *Management Strategies and Industrial Relations, an Historical and Comparative Study*, London: Gower.

Hannah, L. (1974), 'Managerial innovation and the rise of the large-scale company in interwar Britain', *Economic History Review*, **27**, 252–70.

Hannah, L. (1976), 'Strategy and structure in the manufacturing sector', in L. Hannah (ed.), *Management Strategy and Business Development*, London: Macmillan.

Harris, J. (1990), 'Enterprise and welfare states: a comparative perspective', *Transactions of the Royal Historical Society*, Fifth Series, **40**, 175–95.

Harrison, R. and Zeitlin, J. (1985), *Division of Labour: Skilled Workers and Technological Change in Nineteenth Century Britain*, Brighton: Harvester Press.

Hopkins, A. (1988), 'Accounting for the British Empire', *Journal of Imperial and Commonwealth History*, **16**, 234–47.

Kennedy, W.P. (1974), 'Foreign investment, trade and growth in the United Kingdom, 1870–1913', *Explorations in Economic History*, **11**, 415–44.

Kennedy, W.P. (1976), 'Institutional response to economic growth: capital markets in Britain to 1914', in L. Hannah (ed.), *Management Strategy and Business Development*, London: Macmillan.

Kennedy, W.P. (1987), *Industrial Structure, Capital Markets and the Origins of British Economic Decline*, Cambridge: Cambridge University Press.

Kirby, M.W. (1992), 'Institutional rigidities and economic decline: reflections on the British experience', *Economic History Review*, **45**, 637–60.

Levine, A.L. (1967), *Industrial Retardation in Britain, 1880–1914*, London: Weidenfeld and Nicolson.

Lewis, A.L. (1949), *Economic Survey, 1919–1939*, London: Allen and Unwin.

Maddison, A. (1982), *Phases of Capitalistic Development*, Oxford: Oxford University Press.

Marrison, A. (1996), *British Business and Protection, 1903–1932*, Oxford: Oxford University Press.

McCloskey, D.N. (1970), 'Did Victorian Britain fail?', *Economic History Review*, **23**, 446–59.

McCloskey, D.N. (ed.) (1971), *Essays on a Mature Economy: Britain after 1840*, London: Methuen.

McCloskey, D.N. (1973), *Economic Maturity and Entrepreneurial Decline: British Iron and Steel, 1870–1913*, Cambridge, Mass.: Harvard University Press.

McCloskey, D.N. (1981), *Enterprise and Trade in Victorian Britain*, London: Allen and Unwin.

McCloskey, D.N. and Sandberg, L. (1971), 'From damnation to redemption: judgements on the late Victorian entrepreneur', *Explorations in Economic History*, **9**, 89–108.

Meyer, J.R. (1955), 'An input–output approach to evaluating British industrial production in the late nineteenth century', *Explorations in Entrepreneurial History*, **8**, 12–34.

Mills, T.C. and Crafts, N.F.R. (1996), 'Trend growth in British industrial output, 1700–1913: a reappraisal', *Explorations in Economic History*, **33**, 277–95.

Mowery, D.C. (1986), 'Industrial research 1900–1950', in B. Elbaum and W. Lazonick (1986), *The Decline of the British Economy*, Oxford: Oxford University Press, 189–222.

Musson, A.E. (1963), 'British industrial growth during the 'great depression' (1873–96): some comments', *Economic History Review*, **15**, 529–33.

Offer, A. (1993), 'The British Empire, 1870–1914: a waste of money?', *Economic History Review*, **46**, 215–38.

Pollard, S. (1989), *Britain's Prime and Britain's Decline: The British Economy 1870–1914*, London: Edward Arnold.

Pollard, S. (1990), 'Reflections on entrepreneurship and culture in European societies', *Transactions of the Royal Historical Society*, Fifth Series, **40**, 153–73.

Prais, S.J. (1993), 'Economic Performance and Education: The Nature of Britain's Deficiencies', *Proceedings of the British Academy*, **84**, 151–208.

Price, R. (1980), *Masters, Unions and Men: Work Control in Building and the Rise of Labour, 1830–1914*, Cambridge: Cambridge University Press.

Richardson, H.W. (1965), 'Retardation in Britain's industrial growth, 1870–1913', *Scottish Journal of Political Economy*, **12**, 125–49.

Rooth, T. (1993), *British Protectionism and the International Economy, Overseas Commercial Policy in the 1930s*, Cambridge: Cambridge University Press.

Rostas, L. (1948), *Comparative Productivity in British and American Industry*, Cambridge: Cambridge University Press.

Rowthorn, R.E. and Solomou, S. (1991), 'The macroeconomic effects of overseas investment on the UK balance of trade, 1870–1913', *Economic History Review*, **44**, 654–64.

Sandberg, L. (1969), 'American rings and English mules', *Quarterly Journal of Economics*, **83**, 25–43.

Sanderson, M. (1972), 'Research and the firm in British industry', *Science Studies*, **2**, 107–51.

Saul, S.B. (1960), *Studies in British Overseas Trade*, Liverpool: Liverpool University Press.

Saul, S.B. (1962), 'The motor industry in Britain to 1914', *Business History*, **5**, 22–44.

Saul, S.B. (1967), 'The market and the development of the mechanical engineering industries in Britain, 1860–1914', *Economic History Review*, **20**, 111–30.

Saul, S.B. (1968), 'The machine tool industry in Britain to 1914', *Business History*, **9**, 22–43.

Saul, S.B. (1979), 'Research and development in British industry from the end of the nineteenth century to the 1960s', in T.C. Smout (ed.), *The Search for Wealth and Stability*, London: Macmillan, 114–38.

Saxonhouse, G.R. and Wright, G. (1984), 'New evidence on the stubborn English mule and the cotton industry', *Economic History Review*, **37**, 507–19.

Saxonhouse, G.R. and Wright, G. (1987), 'Stubborn mules and vertical integration: the disappearing constraint', *Economic History Review*, **40**, 87–94.

Singh, A. (1977), 'UK industry and the world economy: a case of de-industrialization', *Cambridge Journal of Economics*, **1**, 113–36.

Supple, B. (1991), 'Scale and scope: Alfred Chandler and the dynamics of industrial capitalism', *Economic History Review*, **44**, 500–514.

Temin, P. (1996), 'Labor scarcity and the problem of American industrial efficiency in the 1850s', *Journal of Economic History*, **26**, 277–98.

Watson, K. (1996), 'Banks and industrial finance: the experience of brewers, 1880–1913', *Economic History Review*, **49**, 58–81.

Wiener, M.J. (1981), *English Culture and the Decline of the Industrial Spirit, 1850–1980*, Cambridge: Cambridge University Press.

Wilson, C. (1965), 'Economy and society in late Victorian Britain', *Economic History Review*, **18**, 183–98.

Zeitlin, J. (1987), 'From labour history to the history of industrial relations', *Economic History Review*, **40**, 159–84.

Part I
Long-Run Growth: An Overview

[1]

CHAPTER SIXTEEN

The Rate of Growth and the Proximate Sources of Growth

This chapter and the next summarize some principal conclusions, review their relation to one another, and consider unanswered questions. For the benefit of readers in a hurry, we have tried to make them self-contained in substance, though not in methodology or documentation.

A summary of trends in the rate of growth and its proximate sources between 1856 and 1973 is given in Tables 16.1–16.4. These tables bring together some of the principal findings discussed more fully in Chapters 2, 3, 4, 5, and 7. Growth rates over the standard phases used in this book are shown in the top half of these tables, with wartime phases italicized. These are followed by a view over longer periods: here 1856–1913 is treated as a single period, and war and postwar phases are amalgamated (this irons out a tendency to opposite movements in certain variables between periods of war and peace). Our main story starts in 1856, but rather less reliable data relating to 1800–1860 (for Great Britain only) are given for comparison in Table 16.1; statements made in the text do not embrace that period except where indicated.

A pictorial representation is given in Figure 16.1. The growth rates here shown relate to the standard periods, except that 1873–1913 is divided into subperiods at 1899, and the postwar period is divided at 1964.*

OUTPUT AND INCOME

The rates of growth of GDP and GDP per head followed a roughly U-shaped pattern over the period 1856–1973 (Table 16.1): a long intermediate period of slow growth separated initial and terminal periods of

---

*Growth rates for the subperiods 1873–99 and 1899–1913 are unreliable, because large discrepancies exist between the growth rates yielded by the income, output, and expenditure measures of GDP (see Appendix L).

[The appendices have not been reproduced here.]

498   AN OVERALL VIEW

TABLE 16.1

Growth of Gross Domestic Product and Growth of Gross Domestic Product and Real Disposable Income per Head of Population, 1800–1973

(Annual percentage growth rates)

| | | | Contribution of: | | |
Period	GDP (1)	GDP per head (2)	Income from abroad (3)	Terms of trade (4)	Real disposable income per head[a] (2) + (3) + (4) (5)
Standard phases:					
1856–1873	2.2%	1.4%	0.1%	0.2%	1.7%
1873–1913	1.8	0.9	0.1	0.0	1.0
1913–1924	*–0.1*	*–0.6*	*–0.1*	*0.3*	*–0.4*
1924–1937	2.2	1.8	0.0	0.3	2.0
1937–1951	*1.8*	*1.3*	*–0.3*	*–0.3*	*0.7*
1951–1973	2.8	2.3	0.0	0.1	2.5
Combined periods:					
1800–1860[b]	2.6	1.3	0.0	–0.2	1.1
1856–1913	2.0	1.1	0.1	0.0	1.2
1913–1937	1.1	0.7	0.0	0.3	0.9
1937–1973	2.4	1.9	–0.1	0.0	1.8
1856–1973	1.9%	1.2%	0.0%	0.1%	1.3%

Source: Tables 2.4, 3.17; Feinstein 1978.

   Note: Transwar periods are shown in italics in the tables in this chapter.

   [a]Readjusted to market prices. The readjustment affects the following periods: 1924–37 (–0.1); 1913–37 (–0.1); 1951–73 (0.1).

   [b]Data for Great Britain.

faster growth. The differences in rates of growth between periods were not enormous, but neither were they trivial. In no period did the rate of growth approach that achieved in the postwar period by France and West Germany, let alone Japan. However, the range between periods was of the same order of magnitude as the *average* difference over the long run between the British growth rate and U.S. or continental growth rates. By all criteria, growth in the postwar period was higher than in any earlier period. When the postwar period is amalgamated with the transwar period, 1937–51, the extent of its superiority over earlier periods is reduced but remains substantial by comparison with all other periods after 1873.

The bottom point of the U was reached in the first quarter of the twentieth century. Growth in the period 1899–1913 was significantly slower than in 1873–99 (Fig. 16.1), and across World War I real GDP did not rise at all.

The rate of growth per head in the United Kingdom was persistently lower than in most other industrial countries from the 1870's onward, by an average margin of about 1 percent a year (Table 2.5). It is difficult to generalize about which were the periods of greatest short-fall, since the timing of periods of more or less rapid growth differed considerably between other industrial countries, especially between the United States and continental Europe. The British U-shaped pattern is not prominent in most other countries, though all enjoyed faster growth in the postwar period than earlier.

The persistent shortfall in the British growth rate meant, of course, that the level of income in the United Kingdom declined steadily relative to that in other countries. This, together with the associated decline in Britain's share in world trade, is the basis of the popular notion of continuous deterioration in British economic performance. That notion is not warranted by comparison of the domestic growth rate in successive periods. Are other symptoms discernible of continuous deterioration in the United Kingdom's performance? One might so consider the trend decline in the balance of payments on current account as a percentage of GNP (Table 14.7). This decline was not a steady one; it took place mainly across World War I and in the interwar period. It is not self-evident in what sense it is a measure of economic performance, but it could be regarded, at the least, as posing a threat. Another feature that might be regarded as ominous was the trend decline in the rate of profit per unit of capital (Tables 6.12, 6.13). The timing of that

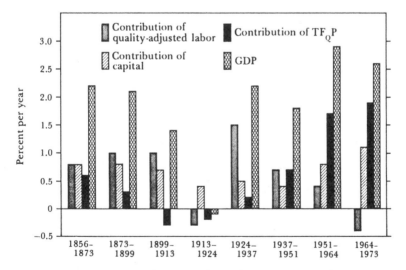

Fig. 16.1. Growth of gross domestic product and its sources by period, 1856–1973

decline was complicated by the wars and the interwar depression, but the underlying trend appears to have been fairly steadily downward for over a hundred years. The effect on the profit rate of the decline in profits' share was augmented by a rise in the capital-output ratio (measured gross, at current prices). Contrary to what might have been expected, however, the large decline in the profit rate was not accompanied by any trend decline in the rate of capital accumulation.

The broad pattern of differences between periods in the rate of growth of real disposable income was due to corresponding differences in the rate of growth of GDP. However, changes in the other two elements affecting real disposable income — property income from abroad and the terms of trade — were also important in some phases (Table 16.1, columns 3 and 4). The most striking instance was the change between 1924-37 and 1937-51, when a reduction in the annual percentage rate of growth of GDP per head of 0.5 was transformed into a reduction of 1.3 in the rate of growth of real disposable income per head. Also noteworthy was the effect of changes in income from abroad and the terms of trade in raising the rate of growth of disposable income per head in 1856-73 over what it had been in 1800-1860.

THE PROXIMATE SOURCES OF GROWTH

The growth-accounting method (discussed in Chapter 1) divides the proximate sources of growth of GDP additively into growth of total factor input (TFI) and growth of total factor productivity (TFP). This division is a convenient way of classifying information; it does not prejudge issues about ultimate causes. TFI in turn contains two elements, labor input and capital input, which are weighted in accordance with their distributive shares in GDP. The figures are shown in Table 16.2. These figures relate to the variants of the TFI and TFP concepts that we have denoted by TF_QI and TF_QP, that is to say, quality improvements in labor (defined below) are included in TFI, not in TFP. At various points later in this chapter we shall have occasion to use alternative concepts, TF_YI and TF_HI, and correspondingly TF_YP and TF_HP, in which the labor component in TFI is measured respectively in man-years and man-hours, without adjustment for quality.

A corresponding division of the sources of growth on a per-head-of-population basis is shown in Table 16.3. Abstracting in this way from the effects of population growth serves, of course, to reduce the rates of growth of TFI and its components, while leaving unaffected the rate of growth of TFP.

We now consider in turn the rates of growth of labor input, capital input, TFI, and TFP.

TABLE 16.2

Growth of Labor, Capital, Total Factor Input, and Total Factor Productivity, 1856–1973

(Annual percentage growth rates)

			Contributions to TF_oI of:			
Period	Quality-adjusted labor (1)	Capital (2)	Quality-adjusted labor (3)	Capital (4)	TF_oI (5)	TF_oP (6)
Standard phases:						
1856–1873	1.4%	1.9%	0.8%	0.8%	1.6%	0.6%
1873–1913	1.7	1.9	1.0	0.8	1.8	0.0
1913–1924	*−0.4*	*0.9*	*−0.3*	*0.4*	*0.1*	*−0.2*
1924–1937	2.1	1.8	1.5	0.5	2.0	0.2
1937–1951	*1.1*	*1.1*	*0.7*	*0.4*	*1.1*	*0.7*
1951–1973	0.1	3.2	0.1	0.9	1.0	1.8
Combined periods:						
1856–1913	1.6	1.9	1.0	0.8	1.8	0.2
1913–1937	0.9	1.4	0.5	0.5	1.0	0.1
1937–1973	0.5	2.4	0.3	0.8	1.1	1.3
1856–1973	1.2%	2.0%	0.7%	0.7%	1.4%	0.5%

Source: Tables 4.7, 7.1, 7.4.

TABLE 16.3

Growth of Labor, Capital, and Total Factor Input per Head of Population and Growth of Total Factor Productivity, 1856–1973

(Annual percentage growth rates)

			Contributions to TF_oI per head of:			
Period	Quality-adjusted labor per head (1)	Capital per head (2)	Quality-adjusted labor (3)	Capital (4)	TF_oI per head (5)	TF_oP (6)
Standard phases:						
1856–1873	0.6%	1.1%	0.3%	0.5%	0.8%	0.6%
1873–1913	0.8	1.0	0.5	0.4	0.9	0.0
1913–1924	*−0.9*	*0.4*	*−0.6*	*0.2*	*−0.4*	*−0.2*
1924–1937	1.7	1.4	1.2	0.4	1.6	0.2
1937–1951	*0.6*	*0.6*	*0.4*	*0.2*	*0.6*	*0.7*
1951–1973	−0.4	2.7	−0.3	0.8	0.5	1.8
Combined periods:						
1856–1913	0.7	1.0	0.5	0.4	0.9	0.2
1913–1937	0.5	1.0	0.3	0.3	0.6	0.1
1937–1973	0.0	1.9	0.0	0.6	0.6	1.3
1856–1973	0.5%	1.3%	0.3%	0.4%	0.7%	0.5%

Source: Tables 3.17, 7.1, 16.2.

Inputs: Labor

The rate of growth of quality-adjusted labor input is equal to the sum of the rates of growth of man-hours and labor quality (Table 16.4). The rate of growth of man-hours was on balance negative after 1913. It can in turn be divided into contributions from population growth, participation rates and unemployment, and hours of work (Table 16.4, columns 1–3). The rate of growth of labor quality, which was always positive, is here defined to consist of changes due to the following: education; age-sex composition; diminution in the weight of Ireland (before 1914); and increases in the intensity of work associated with reductions in hours per man (Table 4.7). Other sources of change in labor quality are included, not in TFI, but in TFP.

The measures of man-hours are reasonably firm statistically. The same cannot be said of the measures of labor quality. This applies particularly to the items relating to education and the intensity of work. The inclusion of the item relating to the intensity of work serves to mitigate the effects of changes in hours of work on the measure of labor input; the extent of changes in hours of work differed greatly between periods, and some mitigation is certainly appropriate, but the amount is largely a matter of guesswork. The unreliability of the item relating to education probably matters less for comparison of periods than it does for the relative rates of growth attributed to TFI and TFP over the period as a whole. The quantity of schooling embodied in the labor force grew at a fairly even rate after 1880; unevennesses in the rate of growth between successive age-cohorts were largely damped out in the labor force as a whole. Any substantial differences between periods in the contribution of education would therefore have to have arisen from unmeasured changes in the quality of education. However, the estimate of the absolute magnitude of the contribution made by education to improvement over time in the quality of the labor force is subject to a very wide margin or error. Using conventional methods, we have estimated it at 0.5 percent a year on average, an estimate that may err on the high side. If a lower estimate were adopted, the rate of growth of TFP in 1873–1913 would no longer be zero, though it would still be lower than in other peacetime periods.

Given these definitions and measures, with all their imperfections, what picture emerges? The rate of population growth underwent a once-for-all fall from around 0.9 percent a year before 1914 to around 0.5 percent a year after that. This was not the only source of decline in the rate of growth of labor input. The rate of growth of labor input per

TABLE 16.4

Sources of Growth of the Labor Input, 1856–1973

(Annual percentage growth rates)

Period	Population (1)	Man-years in employment per head of population (2)	Man-hours per man-year in employment (3)	Total man-hours (1) + (2) + (3) (4)	Quality adjustment per man-hour (5)	Quality adjusted labor input (4) + (5) (6)
Standard phases:						
1856–1873	0.8%	0.1%	−0.9%	0.0%	1.4%	1.4%
1873–1913	0.9	0.0	0.0	0.9	0.8	1.7
1913–1924	0.5	−0.9	−1.9	−2.3	1.9	−0.4
1924–1937	0.4	0.8	0.3	1.5	0.6	2.1
1937–1951	0.5	0.3	−0.7	0.1	1.0	1.1
1951–1973	0.5	−0.1	−0.9	−0.5	0.6	0.1
Combined periods:						
1856–1913	0.9	0.0	−0.3	0.6	1.0	1.6
1913–1937	0.4	0.0	−0.7	−0.3	1.2	0.9
1937–1973	0.5	0.0	−0.8	−0.3	0.8	0.5
1856–1973	0.7%	0.0%	−0.5%	0.2%	1.0%	1.2%

Source: Tables 3.10, 3.17, 4.7.

head of population actually declined more than the rate of population growth: from 0.7 percent a year in 1856–1913 to 0.0 in 1937–73 (Table 16.3, column 1). The main single source of this was a speeding-up in the rate of decline of hours of work. In none of the three combined periods — 1856–1913, 1913–37, and 1937–73 — was there any net change in participation rates: the trend rise in the female participation rate was offset by the trend increase in the duration of education, earlier retirement, and a less favorable age-distribution.

Over a very long period the trend was thus a decline in both the rate of growth of labor input and the rate of growth of labor input per head of population. Over the shorter time spans of our standard periods, these movements were not smooth. There were violently discrepant movements in 1913–24 and 1924–37. Labor input per head of population fell steeply between 1913 and 1924, mainly on account of abnormally large reductions in hours and the rise in unemployment; the effects of these reductions were of about the same size, after allowance for an intensity offset to the reductions in hours. Between 1924 and 1937, on the other hand, labor input per head of population rose greatly, chiefly on account of an increase in the proportion of those of working age. This was the deferred and temporary result of the once-for-all reduction in the rate of population growth: there were fewer children, but the elderly still belonged to cohorts substantially smaller than those of working age. The weighted contribution to the growth of real disposable income per head in the interwar period made by increase in labor input per head, as here estimated, was 1.2 percent a year, exceeding the average over the period 1856–1973 as a whole by 0.9 of a percentage point (Table 16.3, col. 3). It is interesting to note that this abnormal contribution of 0.9 was three times as great as the contribution made by the improvement in the terms of trade, the item most commonly cited as a special factor making for rising real income in that period.

Within the period 1937–73 the rate of growth of quality-adjusted labor input per head fell substantially, as well as being lower on average than in earlier periods. In 1937–51, 1951–64, and 1964–73, respectively, the annual percentage rates were 0.6, 0.1, and −0.9. Between 1951 and 1973 total quality-adjusted labor input scarcely rose at all, and total man-hours worked (without quality-adjustment) fell significantly — a point of contrast both with earlier peacetime experience in Britain and with the postwar experience of most other advanced industrial countries. The historically high rate of growth of GDP was thus achieved despite the trend in labor input, not because of it.

Inputs: Capital

The movements over time in the rates of growth of the capital stock and the capital stock per head of population conformed after a fashion to those in GDP (Tables 16.2, 16.3). They were notably higher in the postwar period than in earlier periods. However, differences between the combined periods 1856–1913, 1913–37, and 1937–73 were not enormous, and they are further scaled down in the calculation of the contribution to the rate of growth of TFI, where they are multiplied by a coefficient of less than a half (capital's distributive share). The increase in capital's contribution to the rate of growth of TFI in the postwar period partly offset the decline in the contribution from the labor side. The rate of growth of the capital stock was lower in transwar periods than in peacetime periods, as would be expected. Rather more surprisingly, variations between peacetime periods were smaller than in the case of labor input.

Within the postwar period the rate of growth of the capital stock, and its estimated contribution to growth, followed a pronounced long swing, rising up to about 1968 and then falling (Fig. 11.1). This long swing is reminiscent of the long swings in domestic capital formation before 1914, but the order of magnitude of the upward phase of the postwar long swing was altogether greater. It would require a future downward phase of unprecedented severity and duration to reduce the postwar rate of capital accumulation to the long-term historical average. Thus, in order for the long-term rate of capital accumulation, even starting from 1937, to be reduced to its historical average, it would be necessary for the annual percentage rate of increase of the capital stock to be at its war-period rate (1.0) for over 20 years from 1973.

The Weights of Labor and Capital in Total Factor Input

The growth-accounting measure weights the contribution of labor and capital in TFI according to their distributive shares in GDP.

Over the period 1856–1973 as a whole there was a downward trend in property's share in national income and in the profit rate. The downward trend was not equally rapid in all periods, but from the 1870's onward it was persistent and large. Property's share in GNP fell from nearly half in the early 1870's to barely more than a quarter in 1973. This fall was not due to rent, whose share fell steeply across the wars but rose enough to compensate in peacetime; nor was it due to income from abroad, whose share in 1973 was almost the same as it had been in 1856, after a huge intermediate rise and fall. The fall was due predominantly to profit's share in trading income. The consequence of the fall in property's share in GDP is that a considerably lower weight in the measure of TFI is given to capital in the postwar period than in the nineteenth century.

The postwar period is the only one in which the weighting makes a significant difference in the measurement of TFI. In earlier peacaetime periods the rates of growth of quality-adjusted labor and capital were quite close to each other, so any weighting would give much the same result. In 1951–73 the rate of growth of TF_qI, as measured, was 1.0 percent a year; had pre-1914 weights been used, it would have been 1.4 percent. This is not a negligible difference, but it does not alter the general picture.

Whether it is appropriate to give capital input a diminishing weight over time in this way depends on what caused the decline in profits' share — itself of course a question of much interest. There are two possible types of explanation: (1) a neoclassical type of explanation, in terms of a less-than-unit-elasticity of substitution between labor and capital (or else a capital-saving bias in technical progress, the two being difficult to distinguish, as is well known), combined with a willingness of investors to continue capital accumulation in face of a falling profit rate; (2) an explanation in terms of an increase over time in labor's bargaining power, possibly due to a trend increase in labor shortage, constituting a change favorable to labor in the degree of monopoly in labor and product markets, taken together. Both types of causes appear to have played a part, and they interacted with each other. *

Insofar as the explanation lay in changes in the degree of monopoly, it did not necessarily betoken a corresponding change in the relative marginal products of labor and capital. It is possible, therefore, that the rate of growth of TFI in the postwar period is somewhat under-estimated relative to earlier periods.

Total Factor Input and Total Factor Productivity

Over the period 1856–1913 as a whole growth of TFI contributed 1.4 percent a year to the growth of GDP and growth of TFP contributed 0.5 percent a year. Their contributions to the growth of GDP per head were more nearly equal: 0.7 percent from TFI per head and 0.5 percent from TFP. However, there was virtually no increase at all in TFP between 1873 and 1937, a period of nearly two-thirds of a century. This does not mean, of course, that there was no technological advance during that period. Certainly there was. What it *does* mean is that the whole of the net increase in labor productivity over that period is capable, according to the present measures, of being attributed to increases in the capital stock and improvements in the quality of labor (both of which had, as one effect, the promotion of technical advance). Other sources of improvements were in net offset by tendencies inimical to productivity. Some of these operated in particular sectors, such as commerce and mining, other perhaps more generally.

Some of the changes between periods in the rate of growth of TFI were quite large, but they did not follow any regular pattern, nor were they related in any regular way to changes in the rate of growth of GDP. Only in the trans–World War I recession, and to a lesser extent in the interwar period (as compared with 1873–1913), did change in the rate of growth of TFI make a major contribution to the change in the rate of growth of GDP. The decline in the rate of growth of GDP in the period before 1914 was due to TFP, not TFI. So was the historically high rate of growth of GDP in the postwar period. Variations in the rate of growth of GDP, and in particular the U-shaped pattern, thus arose more from TFP than from TFI.

The U-shaped pattern in the rate of growth of TFP was a smooth one, *including* war periods (Fig. 16.1). Moreover, estimates for years

---

*The possible effects of a third cause, foreign trade, are discussed below, p. 529.

before 1860 indicate that the downward phases of the U had already begun early in the nineteenth century; and, at the other end of the story, the rate of TFP growth continued to increase within the postwar period up to 1973 (though not beyond). The complications caused by wars, depressions, and statistical deficiencies make it impossible to say whether the U-shaped movement was really a continuous one or whether the underlying phenomenon consisted rather of a limited number of steps — downward at some point in the second quarter of the nineteenth century and again in the first quarter of the twentieth century, upward in the interwar period and after World War II. The low point in Table 16.2 is located in the period 1913–24, when TFP growth (measured, it must be remembered, excluding the effects of improvements of labor quality) was actually negative. When 1899–1913 is taken as a separate period, as in Figure 16.1, instead of being incorporated in 1873–1913, as in Table 16.2, it comes out fractionally worse than 1913–24. On any reckoning, the low point in the rate of growth of TFP came in the first quarter of the twentieth century.

In the foregoing we have reviewed trends in the rates of growth that actually occurred and their proximate sources in the sense used in growth-accounting. It remains to consider causes and consequences in a more fundamental sense.

CHAPTER SEVENTEEN

Causes and Consequences of the Growth of Total Factor Input and Total Factor Productivity

THE QUESTIONS TO BE ASKED

Why is it necessary to go beyond the enumeration of the proximate sources of growth, as described in the preceding chapter?

There is no presumption that the rates of growth of labor, capital, and TFP are ultimate independent variables. The need to consider their *causes* is therefore plain enough. Those causes may be endogenous to the growth process, or they may be of a kind that can reasonably be treated as exogenous. The latter, by definition, mark the end of the road for this investigation. Insofar as the growth of TFI or TFP was endogenous, it was part of the mechanism of the growth process. That mechanism determined the ultimate impact on growth of the exogenous forces, whether those impinged directly on the variable concerned or on one of the other variables.

It is perhaps a little less obvious why it is necessary to consider further the *consequences*, for the growth of output, of growth in labor, capital, or TFP; for the growth-accounting identity may appear to have already answered that question. However, this is not really so. There are quite a number of complications. Any consideration of the consequences means consideration of counterfactual alternatives — of which interperiod comparisons are one case. Growth-accounting is concerned with the counterfactual consequences of alternative overall rates of growth of labor, capital, and TFP, irrespective of their causes. But one may instead wish for some purposes to consider the counterfactual consequences of some particular exogenous influence on TFI or TFP. In an extreme case, a change in one of these could produce no change at all in actual TFI or TFP; for example, a demographically induced rise in the labor supply could lead merely to an equal increase in unemployment. Whatever counterfactual question is asked, the working of the whole system has to be taken into account. It cannot be assumed, for example, that variations in the rate of growth of the labor input will leave unaffected the rates of growth of capital and TFP. Moreover — a more technical point — the coefficients in the growth-accounting identity, even supposing they correctly identify marginal products at the points observed, cannot be assumed to remain valid if one is contemplating the effects of a different rate of growth of an input over a substantial period.

These considerations can be made more concrete by relating them to theoretical models of economic growth.

Take the elementary neoclassical model. In this model supply creates its own demand (business cycles being allowed as a possible exception). The underlying supply-side variables are population growth and technical progress. These are exogenous. They determine the long-run equilibrium rate of growth of output — the "natural" rate in the sense of Harrod. Investment is a function of income, and the rate of capital accumulation is therefore primarily an endogenous variable, though the ratio of investment (savings) to income is exogenous.

This model contains important elements of truth. The rate of growth of supply does have at least *some* tendency to communicate itself to the rate of growth of demand. There are at least *some* exogenous elements in the rates of growth of the labor supply and technical knowledge and in the savings ratio. It is part of the task of the economic historian to identify them.

But there are important qualifications, particularly in regard to demand. It cannot be taken for granted that demand wholly accommodates itself to supply, even in the long run. Equally, it cannot be taken for granted that the rates of growth of labor and TFP are wholly exogenous; they may be influenced by endogenous forces, including the pressure of demand. These questions require investigation, as do the forces determining demand itself. Because of the role of demand, the treatment of the effects of increase in labor input and the effects of increase in capital input cannot be fully symmetrical: both contribute to the growth of supply, but expenditure on capital accumulation direcly generates demand in a way that an increase in the size of the labor force does not.

Further complications result from relaxing the assumption of a closed economy made in the neoclassical model in its elementary form. It is not just that the exogenous elements affecting the rate of growth of TFP must now be defined to include innovations originating abroad. In addition, foreign trade may affect the rate of growth of TFP by affecting the relative size of sectors, since sectors may differ in their susceptibility to productivity improvements. Moreover, if capital is internationally mobile, domestic savings are no longer identically equal to domestic investment, and insofar as savings are a function of income the link between domestic investment and income is weakened. Finally, the self-balancing forces in the balance of payments do not work perfectly or instantaneously. Hence foreign trade and payments provide a further reason why the rate of growth of output may from time to time diverge from the natural rate.

These considerations are important. They indicate that the rate of growth is not necessarily to be explained exclusively, or even primarily, by exogenous supply-side forces. Attention has to be given to the interaction of those with demand—its growth, level, and structure. Investment and foreign trade and payments are the principal elements of demand in this connection.

We may nonetheless organize the discussion by continuing to focus on the growth-accounting categories. We shall accordingly consider in turn the causes and consequences of the rates of growth of labor, capital, and TFP, taking due account of the various interactions mentioned. An alternative, equally valid, way of structuring the discussion would be in terms of categories of exogenous influences, irrespective of whether their impact was on labor, capital, or TFP, or on all of these. It is convenient to do this in the case of international trade and payments. This is dealt with in a separate section, which therefore complements the sections on the growth-accounting categories.

In the light of the foregoing, the following are among the principal questions to which we must address ourselves in considering the British experience:

(1) How exogenous was the rate of growth of the labor input? Did it communicate itself to the rate of growth of demand and output?

(2) How endogenous was investment? How did variations in investment, whether endogenous or exogenous, affect the rate of growth of output through their effects on (a) the supply of capital capacity, and (b) demand?

(3) Did foreign trade cause demand to grow at other than the "natural" rate? Did it affect supply by its effects on the rate of growth of TFP or on the rate of capital accumulation?

(4) What were the domestic or foreign exogenous forces affecting the rate of growth of TFP? How much was the rate affected by demand? How far was the growth of TFP itself communicated to demand?

The foregoing enumeration of questions matches the arrangement of the next four sections, which deal in turn with labor, capital, foreign trade and payments, and TFP. We then conclude the main part of this chapter by looking at matters chronologically and reviewing the principal forces that affected the rate of growth of output in each period.

THE GROWTH OF LABOR INPUT

Causes

The proximate sources of growth of labor input were summarized in the preceding chapter (Table 16.4; see Tables 3.17 and 4.7 for a fuller breakdown). The main sources of differences in the growth rate between periods were demographic change and changes in hours of work. War losses were important in World War I, as were the rise in unemployment across World War I and its fall across World War II. Changes in age- and sex-specific participation rates largely canceled out.

In the light of this, how far is the rate of growth of the labor input to be deemed to have been determined by exogenous forces and how far was it a function of the demand for labor?

Changes in the rate of natural increase, together with their effects on age distribution, both of which were important, plainly rank as exogenous (save in the broadest and most long-run sense). At the other extreme, changes in unemployment were plainly endogenous. One might expect the rate of net migration to be an endogenous variable, but it was in fact mainly determined by conditions abroad and, latterly, by social policy. It would probably have been affected, but only to a minor extent, had the domestic demand for labor been other than it was. Changes in participation rates — more married women working, earlier retirement, and longer schooling — were in part sensitive to the demand for labor. However, to a large extent they reflected social change and the *existence* of economic growth, rather than its precise rate in any particular period. Much the same may be said of the progressive improvement in the quality of labor brought about by education.

Changes in hours of work were of major importance, both for the long-run trend in labor input and for its variation between periods. Their status regarding exogeneity is peculiar. Reduction in hours of work did not take place at a steady rate but were concentrated, with ratchet effects, in phases when the bargaining power of labor was strong: in the early 1870's, in 1919, in 1948–49, and in the postwar period. Their timing resembled that of the rise in *money* wages rather than that of the rise in real wages. There was some very long-run trend for the rate of reduction of hours to speed up, and this too is consistent with labor's bargaining power having been an important influence. The bargaining power of labor was in turn a function largely (though not wholly) of the demand for labor. Long-run changes in hours were thus endogenous, but in a perverse direction (in contrast to the normal rise and fall in hours over the business cycle). This, it should be understood, is a description of what actually occurred, not a statement of a general law. The bargaining power of organized labor is not solely a function of the pressure of demand, and if it had been — or were to be in the future — strong for other reasons, it could be used to push down hours of work during a period of low demand.

The major observed rises and falls between periods in the rate of growth of labor input thus did not occur in response to changes in the same direction in the demand for labor. Counterfactually, higher demand for labor would have elicited higher supply through some channels, but the net outcome would have been uncertain on account of the tendency to a perverse response in hours of work.

Consequences

No one would maintain that variations in the rate of growth of labor input were the principal causes of the variations in the rate of growth of GDP. The single most important change in the rate of growth of labor — its fall, chiefly due to demographic causes, from about 1 percent a year in 1856–1913 to about half of 1 percent a year in 1913–73 — was in fact accompanied by scarcely any change in the rate of growth of GDP between those very broad periods. But one pair of observations is no basis for generalization, and the question remains what effects growth in labor supply had or might counterfactually have had in various periods, both on GDP and on GDP per head of population.

This raises extremely general and controversial theoretical questions about whether there is an inherent long-run tendency to full employment, and if so what the mechanism is.

One hypothesis regarding the mechanism is that cyclical upswings have (or sometimes have) an anti-damped or unstable tendency that brings them up against a full-employment ceiling. Hence the faster that ceiling rises, the faster the long-run rate of growth. This is easily understandable. Insofar as growth presses against a labor shortage, labor is a constraint, and the rate of growth of the labor supply directly affects the rate of growth of output.

Was the labor supply a constraint on growth or would it have been if its growth rate had been lower than it was? Assuming that the rate of growth of labor productivity is taken as given, labor supply was obviously a constraint in the period 1937–73, when there was full employment at cycle peaks. This is not refuted by the occurrence at postwar cycle peaks of another constraint, in the form of the balance of payments, since balance-of-payments difficulties may well have reflected underlying supply constraints. It is consistent with the slight decline in the rate of growth of GDP between 1951–64 and 1964–73, accompanying a less rapid growth of labor input (itself due mainly to demographic causes and to trends in hours of work). In this connection, it is interesting to speculate on how the trend in output might have been affected if government had not chosen, for social reasons, to impose restrictions on immigration in the early 1960's, thus preventing the domestic labor force from being augmented by immigrants to the extent that it was in West Germany and France.

A full-employment ceiling can scarcely be said to have been reached, even at cycle peaks, before World War II, except in a few sectors and possibly more generally on one or two occasions (1872–73, 1920). Labor supply was not in general a constraint on output in the interwar period, apart from certain sectors affected by rearmament in the late 1930's; but the question can still be asked whether it would have been a constraint if the rate of growth of the labor supply had not been so exceptionally high. The increase in employment (3 million between 1924 and 1937) much exceeded the number of unemployed at the end of the period (1.8 million in 1937). So if there had been *no* increase in the labor supply, GDP could not have risen as much as it did. Likewise, output could scarcely have risen as much as it did if the labor force had risen only at the same rate as population (even leaving aside hours of work); it would then have been some 1.8 million less in 1937 than it actually was, a difference equal to the entire number of the unemployed. However, it was not a necessary condition of the observed GDP growth, on this reckoning, that the labor force should have risen *faster* in 1924–37 than in 1873–1913. If the number of workers had instead risen at the same rate as in 1873–1913, there would have been only some 0.7 million fewer than they actually were, and the difference could surely have been made up by drawing on the pool of unemployed. A similar conclusion probably holds in relation to the period before 1914. Given the existence of concealed unemployment and the extent of emigration at that time, it is difficult to believe that labor would have become a constraint on growth if the rate of growth of the labor force had been less by a moderate amount than it actually was. But labor would have become a constraint if its supply had not increased at all.

In view of what was said earlier about exogeneity, these conclusions do not need to be much qualified on account of the possibility of induced changes in the labor supply. However, there is more ground for objecting to the *ceteris paribus* assumption about labor productivity. There is certainly reason to suppose that shortage of labor in the postwar period was partly responsible for the high rate of capital accumulation, and possibly of TFP as well. We revert to this below.

In periods when the labor supply was not directly a constraint on output, did the rate of growth of the labor supply nonetheless influence the rate of growth of output in other ways? In order for it to have done so, it would have needed to influence the rate of growth of demand for output; otherwise its effect would merely have been on unemployment (or underemployment), and the change in the labor *supply* would not have resulted in any actual change in labor *input*. Possible channels are through effects on the real wage, or on the efficiency wage (in the case of improvements in labor quality), or on the money wage and hence on international competitiveness and/or real balances. These effects cannot easily be traced. But they cannot be precluded. There is reason to suppose that changes in the supply of labor due to changes in hours of work had a more direct effect on the demand for labor and hence on output than did changes in the supply of labor due to changes in numbers, because reductions in hours of work tended more directly to affect costs. Indeed, they may have reduced the demand for labor by more than they reduced the supply; the large reductions in hours in the 1870's, and in 1919 were followed by unusually severe unemployment. Since these reductions were themselves largely the lagged consequence of high demand, there was here a factor making for oscillations. It is possible that a similar cyclical effect has, since 1973, attended the large reduction in hours of the postwar period.

Our general conclusions about the role of the labor supply in the several periods are these. In the postwar period and in 1937–51 the slow growth of the labor force was a constraint on growth, subject, however, to offsets in the shape of induced increases in capital accumulation and TFP, to be discussed below. It is doubtful whether the abnormally high rate of growth of the labor supply in the interwar period, by previous standards, was either a necessary condition for the growth of GDP that occurred or a direct influence in promoting it. But if the labor supply had grown only at the same rate as population in the interwar period, a labor bottleneck could have been encountered. Moreover, given that the interaction of forces on the supply side and on the demand side caused GDP in the interwar period to grow at the rate it did, the increase in labor input per head of population did permit a correspondingly rapid increase in income *per head*, and in that sense our conclusions in Chapter 16 about the importance of this source of growth in the interwar period stand. In regard to the period 1913–24, the great reduction in hours of work, which was one of the principal sources of the fall in labor input, did contribute to the reduction in the demand for labor and the setback to output. Finally, before 1914, a complete absence of growth in the labor supply would certainly have affected the growth of GDP. Moreover, improvements in education probably increased the employability of labor. But the rate of growth of GDP would probably not have been affected much if the labor supply had grown at a moderately faster or slower rate than it did.

Where does this leave "labor's contribution to GDP growth," as measured by the growth-accounting conventions of Table 16.2? It is perhaps not too bad as an indicator of the effects of labor-force growth in the very long run and in certain periods, including the postwar period. But exogenous changes in the labor supply cannot be assumed to be translated automatically into changes in the demand for labor. Nor can they be assumed to leave unaffected the rates of growth of the capital stock or of TFP. Hence "labor's contribution to GDP growth" is not a good measure of the extent to which differences between periods in exogenous sources of labor-supply growth were the causes of differences between periods in the rate of growth of GDP. Nor is it a good counterfactual measure of the likely effects of alternative rates of growth of the labor supply in particular periods. However, nothing that has just been said invalidates it as an indicator of labor's contribution to growth *on the production function side*, and hence as an indicator of the contributions to growth, *given* the demand for final output, that must have come from the other elements on the supply side, namely growth of the capital stock and growth of TFP.

THE GROWTH OF CAPITAL INPUT

Causes

The constancy in the rate of growth of the domestic capital stock in broad peacetime periods before World War II is remarkable. The annual percentage rates were 1.9 in 1856–73, 1.9 in 1873–1913, and 1.8 in 1924–37 (along with an estimated 2.0 in 1830–60; Feinstein 1978: 86).

This constancy up to the postwar period did not reflect immutability in the components of the Harrod identity (growth rate of the capital stock equals the savings-income ratio divided by the capital-output ratio). Overseas investment made for important divergences between savings and domestic investment. In the interwar period the depression caused the savings-income ratio to be lower and the capital-output ratio higher than before 1914, but the adverse effects of those movements on the rate of domestic capital accumulation were almost completely compensated for by the reduction in the proportion of savings devoted to overseas investment. In the postwar period the savings-income ratio was somewhat higher than it had been before 1914 (and *a fortiori* higher than in the interwar period); but compared with the pre-1914 period it was the lower rate of overseas investment that was, in the arithmetic of the Harrod identity, the most important source of the higher rate of domestic capital accumulation. This higher rate occurred notwithstanding a significantly higher current-price capital-output ratio, brought about by a once-for-all rise in the relative price of capital goods across World War II.

One would expect the rate of capital accumulation to be more endogenous to the growth process than the rate of growth of labor input and less influenced by outside forces (apart from wars). However, the distinction between induced and exogenous movements in the labor supply has some counterpart in the distinction between influences on capital formation arising from the side of the schedule of the marginal efficiency of investment (MEI) and influences arising from the side of the schedule of the supply price of finance (SPOF). Changes in investment due to changes in MEI are likely to reflect and reinforce other influences making for growth. Changes arising from the side of SPOF have more claim to rank as independent influences on the rate of growth.

The effects of these two classes of changes are best considered separately for the three broad sectors distinguished in Table 17.1. The trend in each was different, and only in the case of industrial and commercial investment was the rate of growth of the fixed capital stock, averaged over the trans–World War II and postwar periods, higher than the average for earlier periods.

The conclusion reached in Chapter 13 was that differences between broad periods in the rate of growth of *industrial and commercial* fixed capital chiefly reflected movements in MEI. There were some important trends in the SPOF schedule (see below); but it is doubtful whether the MEI schedule in industry and commerce was sufficiently elastic in the long run for movements in SPOF by themselves to have been capable of causing large changes in investment (as opposed to changes in the profit rate).

TABLE 17.1

Growth of the Gross Domestic Fixed Capital Stock in Three
Broad Sectors, 1856–1973

(Annual percentage growth rates)

Sector	1856–1873	1873–1913	1913–1937	1937–1973
Industry and commerce[a]	2.5%	2.2%	1.2%	3.1%
Infrastructure[b]	3.0	2.4	1.2	2.1
Dwellings	1.5	1.9	2.3	2.0

Source: Table 11.1; basic statistics (Appendix N).
[a]Manufacturing, mining, construction, distributive trades, finance, and miscellaneous services.
[b]Gas, electricity, water, transport, communications, and public and professional services.

There was some downward trend in the rate of growth of the industrial and commercial capital stock running through the long swings of the pre-1914 period. It was attributable to a decline in the rate of TFP growth and a decline in international competitiveness. There was a more substantial reduction in the interwar period: apart from the obvious effects of the depression, including its important psychological effect in preventing investment in many sectors of industry from responding much to the recovery of GDP in the 1930's, there was apparently in this period some capital-saving bias in technical progress. The rate of growth of the capital stock in the postwar period exceeded that in earlier times by a greater margin in industry and commerce than in infrastructure or dwellings. The causes responsible for this historically high rate of industrial and commercial investment included improved confidence, faster output growth, and labor shortage, particularly in commerce. The response of investment to faster output growth was a reinforcer of other sources of growth; its response to labor shortage (itself caused partly by full employment and partly by slow growth of the labor force) was not a reinforcer of another source of high growth, but an offset to a potential source of low growth.

Shifts in the SPOF schedule appear to have had less effect on differences between periods in the rate of growth of industrial and commercial fixed capital than they had on differences within periods, that is to say, between phases of the long swing before 1914 and between parts of the postwar period. In the early 1950's some classes of investment were still held up by shortages and controls, themselves the result of government's perception of pressures on the economy, and thus a manifestation of a high SPOF, interpreting that concept broadly. From then until the late 1960's SPOF in manufacturing was reduced by increasingly generous tax treatment. These changes in SPOF within the

postwar period strengthened a long-swing tendency that would probably have existed anyway on account of trends in MEI.

Investment in *infrastructure and dwellings* likewise largely reflected
and reinforced the general trends in the economy, while also being
influenced by certain Schumpeterian elements (the falloff in investment in transport after the main railway-building period of the mid-
nineteenth century; the growth of the electricity supply industry;
suburbanization in the 1930's). The influence of SPOF was greater,
however, than in the case of industrial and commercial investment.
The demand for dwellings was responsive to its cost, and its cost was in
turn affected not only by productivity in the construction industry, but
also by the rate of interest and government policy. The increase in the
rate of growth of the stock of dwellings in 1873–1913 compared with
1856–73 and its further and larger increase in 1913–37 compared with
1873–1913 were opposite to the trends in industry and commerce and
in infrastructure, and it is possible that they reflected partly a taking-
up of slack in the supply of finance – crowding-in. In the postwar period the amount and timing of investment in transport and in social
capital such as schools and hospitals were chiefly determined by the
government's perception of pressures on the economy. The steep decline in these classes of investment in wartime was a more extreme example of the crowding-out manifested to some extent in parts of the
postwar period.

In two senses adjustments in SPOF, if not in the SPOF schedule,
were necessary conditions of the observed movements in investment. In
the first place, the savings had to be forthcoming to match the investment. How was this achieved? Before 1914 the link between savings
and domestic investment was not close, because capital export was
large and variable. In the interwar period savings were reduced by the
depression. This was reversed in the postwar period. For more obscure
reasons, there was a rise within the postwar period in the personal savings ratio, and this helped to finance the rising ratio of investment to
income. Finally, government savings were a much higher proportion of
GNP in the postwar period than previously. This must be ranked,
along with restrictions on capital export, as an autonomous factor,
serving to increase the availability of finance for domestic investment
compared with earlier periods.

In the second place, some explanation is needed of the following
paradox. The rate of profit on trading capital underwent a long-run
decline, and though the particular steps in this decline were matched
for the time being by falls in investment (in the 1870's and 1880's, the

1920's, and the 1970's), the long-run decline itself was not accompanied by a decline in the rate of capital accumulation, but rather the contrary. There must therefore have been a trend reduction in the acceptable rate of return on investment. In part this may be taken to mean simply that suppliers of finance had no choice but to put up with whatever rate of return was available. Also of substantial significance, however, was a trend reduction in the degree of imperfection in the capital market, attributable chiefly to the increase in the proportion of the economy in the hands of public joint-stock companies, to the increase in their size, and to the expansion of the equities market. This reduced the gap between the supply price (actual or imputed) of finance to the enterprise and the yield available to the rentier.

It may be noted that the maintenance of investment in face of the declining trend in profitability is not to be explained by an increase in public investment relative to private investment. Leaving aside dwellings, investment in the never-public sector was a significantly *higher* proportion of total investment in the postwar period than in the interwar period.*

Consequences

The rate of capital accumulation can influence the rate of growth of GDP in two separate ways: through its effect on demand and through its effect on productive capacity. We consider these in turn.

Effect on demand. As noted earlier, the existence of this (Keynesian) effect deriving from investment expenditure is a feature of increases in the capital input that does not have a parallel in the case of increases in the other factor, labor.

The effect was particularly apparent in the postwar period. High investment (itself largely endogenous in origin) was the major source of the high level of demand, and the high demand in turn not only en-

---

*A related question may be asked here in parentheses. Was the downward trend in the profit rate the principal reason for the trend increase in the size of the public sector (as, for example, in Italy in the 1930's, when the bankruptcy of much of industry brought it under the aegis of the state?) The answer is, on balance, no. A fall in profits was, it is true, the main reason for the nationalization of the railways (and, after the end of our period, of the firms taken over by the National Enterprise Board). It was also the cause of the decline in the private rented sector of the market for dwellings; but there the fall in profitability was of the government's own making through rent control. Declining profitability was not the main reason for the nationalization of utilities, coal-mining, steel, and aviation, or for the expansion of education and health. Moreover, certain industries that suffered severe reductions in profitability in one phase or another remained in the private sector — agriculture, building, and the bulk of manufacturing. Most of the public sector, it may be noted, enjoys natural protection from foreign competition, and is therefore sheltered from pressure on profitability from that source.

sured high employment, but also contributed to the growth of TFP (see below). Conversely, in the interwar period output would have grown faster if demand had been higher, and demand would have been higher if investment had not been depressed by other forces making for slow growth.

The Keynesian effect of high investment did not operate in all circumstances. It was certainly present in some degree in the period before 1914, but its operation then is clouded by the long-swing alternation of domestic investment and capital export. In the postwar period, at least one of the influences on SPOF favorable to investment, namely the historically high government saving propensity, was not such as in net to make for higher demand. In several periods high MEI in one sector meant high SPOF to another sector, damping the overall result, as noted above in the case of dwellings. And of course if investment had been *higher* than it was in the postwar period, there would have been at least some crowding out of other classes of expenditure, since the economy was in general near to full employment.

Effect on productive capacity. This is what is in principle measured by "capital's contribution to GDP growth," in growth-accounting. That measure provides a starting point. It indicates that if, in the postwar period, the capital stock had grown at only the same rate as it did in the interwar period, the annual rate of growth of GDP would have been lower than it was by 0.4 percentage point: quite a large part of the difference between the two periods in the rate of growth of GDP (0.6), but quite a small part of the difference between them in the rate of growth of GDP per man-hour (2.6).

That measure is subject to a good many qualifications. Apart from any more fundamental objections, it takes the capital-elasticity of output as given, an assumption that is not necessarily justifiable if one is considering what the consequences would have been had the rate of growth of the capital stock been higher or lower than it actually was over a substantial number of years. The measure does not therefore dispense with the need to look at the circumstances of individual periods.

It is a reasonable conjecture that if the rate of capital accumulation in the postwar period had really been kept down to what it was between the wars, the detriment to the rate of growth of productive capacity would have been greater than just indicated, on account of the need to embody at least parts of the historically high rate of growth of TFP in new equipment.

The opposite contingency has been the subject of much controversy. What would have happened in the postwar period if, say, firms had been generally more optimistic and their investment plans had not been discouraged by stop-go, i.e. by the peculiar pattern of the British postwar business cycle, with its relatively short upswing phases? In manufacturing, the sector of chief interest in this connection, there was a rising capital-output ratio and a falling trend in the profit rate. Prima facie these features suggest diminishing returns rather than any capital shortage; they suggest that if extra investment had been undertaken, it would as such have yielded only limited benefit. In some industries, indeed, over-investment as it was led to blatant excess capacity, though the prime example was not in manufacturing but in electricity supply.

This macro-evidence is not decisive. Inadequate expansion of capacity may ultimately lead to the under-use of even what capacity there is, if customers become discouraged by supply difficulties. Hence a rising capital-output ratio does not *necessarily* betoken diminishing returns. Moreover, greater confidence or greater availability of funds for capital investment might conceivably have caused the investment to have been of higher quality, and so conduced to faster growth in TFP. However, cross-section evidence within manufacturing does not indicate a positive correlation between the rate of capital accumulation and the rate of growth of TFP (Appendix J).

The period 1873–1913 has points in common with the postwar period. Then too the trend of the capital-output ratio was upward, and that of the profit rate downward. There is therefore a presumption that if the rate of domestic investment had been higher, say, on account of a more domestically oriented capital market, the potential gain to output would have been no more than limited.

The answer is less doubtful in the case of the interwar period. Though the profit rate was not particularly high, it did not have a downward trend, nor was the capital-output ratio rising. If industrial investment had not been depressed by the state of confidence, output could have expanded more in the late 1930's, when bottlenecks were encountered in some sectors; moreover, industry would have been better placed to take advantage of its opportunities in the early postwar years.

To conclude. Trends in the rate of capital accumulation in the British economy were mainly determined by trends in the marginal efficiency of investment and were thus endogenous to the growth process. They served, by their effects on both supply and demand, to magnify the effects on output created by variations in the rate of growth of TFP. They likewise served to amplify the effects of variations in demand arising from other sources, and they were a channel by which demand affected the rate of growth of supply. These sources of feedback were somewhat reduced, but by no means eliminated, by a certain tendency for high MEI in one sector to crowd out investment in other sectors.

Capital accumulation did not, apparently, serve to magnify the effects on output of variations in the rate of growth of the labor supply, but rather at least in the interwar and postwar periods to offset them, though less than completely. It is doubtful whether investment would have been stimulated by a faster rate of growth of labor input than actually occurred, at least if it had taken the form of greater quantity rather than improved quality. It is also doubtful whether a higher level of investment, due to exogenous causes such as greater availability of finance, would, in the absence of other changes, have made a major difference to the growth rate of GDP over most of the period.

THE ROLE OF INTERNATIONAL TRADE AND PAYMENTS

Discussion so far in this chapter has focused on the causes and consequences of the rates of growth of labor and capital, the constituents of TFI. Before we go on to treat TFP similarly, as we do in the next section, it is convenient at this point to adopt a different and complementary approach, focusing attention, not on one of the growth-accounting categories, but on a class of exogenous influences and structural relationships that affected all of those categories, namely the influences and relationships involved in Britain's international trade and payments.

The effects of international economic transactions were largely on demand: its growth, its level, and its structure. Did they cause the rate of growth of demand to diverge from the "natural" rate, i.e. the rate of growth of supply? Did they affect supply itself by their effects on the rate of capital accumulation? Or by their effects on the rate of growth of TFP?

The main questions here concern the causes and consequences of changes in Britain's relative standing among industrial countries. Also significant, however, were certain other world events exogenous to British economic growth, and we shall deal with those first.

Exogenous World Events

World demand. In the postwar period the high level of world demand helped sustain high demand in Britain. In particular the absence of major world recessions (before 1974) was the main reason why cyclical fluctuations in Britain were milder in the postwar period than previously. In the interwar period demand in Britain was depressed by the world recession of the 1930's and by the recession that affected most of Northern Europe in the early 1920's. These trends in demand affected GDP and its growth directly by affecting the utilization of resources and indirectly by their effects on capital accumulation and TFP.

Primary-product prices. Most of the major movements in Britain's terms of trade were due to movements in primary-products prices, exogenous from the British point of view. They affected real disposable income directly — favorably during the interwar period and unfavorably across World War II — and they also tended to affect it indirectly by their effects on the balance of payments, and hence on demand. The 1950's and early 1960's offered an unusually favorable conjunction of improving terms of trade and strong world demand. (The deterioration in the terms of trade from 1974 was likewise unusually unfavorable in coinciding with a world recession.)

Loss of overseas assets. The influences considered under the two previous headings affected all or many industrial countries, not just Britain. Peculiar to Britain were the effects of the two world wars on the value of overseas assets, and hence on income from abroad. The decline in the value of overseas assets, from the the high point in 1913, was almost wholly due to the wars — partly to war finance and partly to the reduction by wartime inflation in the real value of overseas assets denominated in money terms. The estimated decline amounted to some 15 percent of the total UK net capital stock (domestic and overseas together) in the case of World War I and no less than 28 percent in the case of World War II. These losses put pressure on the balance of payments and affected GNP directly, through the consequent loss of income from abroad. The direct effect on GNP was doubtless less than would have followed from the loss of a corresponding amount of domestic capital (since in that case the average product of the capital lost would have much exceeded the marginal product of a unit of capital). On the other hand, the loss of overseas assets did not have the benefit of creating a *tabula rasa* for new investment, as the destruction of domestic assets might have done.

The foregoing effects were important. They are easy to understand. Much more complex were the effects to be considered under the next heading.

Britain's Relative Standing Among Industrial Countries

The period from 1800 until 1973 may for this purpose be divided schematically into three phases.

(1) In the first half of the nineteenth century Britain was enabled, by exporting, to expand its output of manufactures, chiefly textiles, by much more than would have been justified by the structure of domestic demand. This was achieved largely by sharply increased productivity, which reduced the prices of exports and so allowed Britain to move along foreigners' demand curves. The domestic benefit of the rise in productivity and in GDP was thus subject to an offset due to the deterioration in the terms of trade.

(2) The third quarter of the century was a transitional period in which Britain remained the predominant producer of manufactures and was able to continue to increase its exports at a rapid rate (though less rapidly after 1860 than previously). This was notwithstanding that the prices of exports ceased to fall and even rose. There was in this phase an acceleration in the rate of economic growth abroad; foreigners' demand curves were shifting upward. In this period international transactions had a uniquely favorable effect on the growth of real income in the United Kingdom. Industrialization was being promoted by rapid growth in export demand; the terms of trade were improving; and capital export had already produced a substantial increase in income from abroad.

(3) In the fourth quarter of the nineteenth century and throughout the twentieth century, Britain was no longer the only industrial country; the *proportion* of world demand for manufactures met by Britain became, as it had not been before, no less important than the *level* of world demand for manufactures in determining the demand for British manufactures. Hence Marshall's dictum that after 1870 it is no longer possible to write *British* economic history. After 1870 British economic history has to be understood partly in terms of the theory of the location of industry.

Our interpretation is consistent, subject to some significant qualifications, with the following commonly held characterization of trends in the century after 1870. Industrial production and productivity were growing faster in other countries than in the United Kingdom, whether because they had more arrears of industrial development to make up or because conditions there were more conducive to TFP growth or to capital accumulation. The resulting international competition put pressure on prices and profits in British manufacturing (i.e. in the tradables sector). This discouraged investment in manufacturing, making either for a reduction in total capital formation or for a shift of capital formation into capital exports or into the domestic non-tradables sector. The growth of GDP was thereby retarded, and retarded, moreover, to a heightened extent (a) because the rate of growth of TFP in manufacturing is partly a function of the rate of growth of output of manufactures, and (b) because the needed adjustments in the structure of domestic output tended to occur with a lag, so that there was chronic trouble with the balance of payments, leading to deflationary pressures.

The qualifications to this description are, first, that the quantitative importance of the effects of the processes just described on the British rate of growth is less clear than the direction of those effects, and, second, that those processes did not take place in a uniform manner. We now consider the periods more closely.

Pre-1914. This period exhibits many of the characteristics described. There was a decline in the balance of trade in manufactures as a proportion of GNP, and also in agriculture, a tradable sector that in this period suffered even more from international competition; there was a fall in the profit rate in the 1870's and 1880's, not fully retrieved thereafter; there was a downward trend in the rate of growth of the capital stock in manufacturing, partly offset by an opposite movement in dwellings (a non-tradable sector); and, of course, there were very large capital exports.

Capital exports gave the pre-1914 period some peculiar features. The two great phases in the history of Britain's overseas assets — their rise from 1850 to 1913, their decline from 1913 to 1951 — did not have symmetrical causes. The rise was due to economic conditions; the fall was due to wars. A really high level of capital exports requires two circumstances not usually present together: a strong balance of payments on current account and an inducement to invest a large proportion of the country's savings abroad rather than at home. This unusual combination of circumstances emerged in the third quarter of the nineteenth century, because exports were not yet too much affected by foreign competition and at the same time the expected MEI abroad was high relative to the expected MEI at home because of territorial expansion in countries of recent European settlement. The necessary combination of circumstances persisted in 1873–1913, but now the source of the strength in the balance of payments on current account was to an increasing extent the earnings on the accumulated overseas investment: the earlier strength of the current-account balance was providing a source of continuing strength. The growth of income from abroad allowed overseas investment to remain at an average of 5 percent of GNP, notwithstanding a trend decline in the remainder of the balance of payments on current account as a proportion of GNP. Hence there was in this phase no balance-of-payments aggravation of the ill-effects of declining competitiveness on industrial investment. Indeed it is arguable that the strengthening of the overall balance by the increase in income from abroad was itself a part-cause of the declining competitiveness, through its effects on relative prices ("Dutch disease").

The pattern described contributed to the retardation of growth of real disposable income in the period 1873–1914 compared with 1856–73 through its effects on (1) the terms of trade, which now ceased to improve—not a fortuitous event, but an inherent part of the underlying change, reflecting the increased competition in export markets; (2) the rate of growth of TFP (see below); and (3) to a small extent, the rate of capital accumulation. Because the overall balance of payments was not under pressure, ill-effects through the level of activity were not prominent and had nothing like the importance they had in the interwar period, but they do seem to have been present to some degree.

The ill-effects of international economic relations on the rate of growth in this period should not be exaggerated. The relationship between the foreign trade position and the growth of GDP or TFP was not simple or direct. It is reasonable to suppose that the decline in the rate of growth of net exports of manufactures brought about some reduction in the scope for growth economies. But the timing of changes in the rate of growth of TFP in manufacturing and of changes in the rate of growth of net exports does not suggest a close connection between the two: there was little or no decline in the rate of growth of TFP in manufacturing until the period 1899–1913, and in that period net exports were booming.[1]

Some of the ill-effects of foreign trade were, moreover, inevitable. Britain, as the early starter, could plainly not be expected to complete the process of absorbing surplus labor by industrialization before continental countries had even started to do so. Likewise, it was inevitable that the potential obstacle to world industrialization arising from food supply should have been removed by investment in New World infrastructure rather than by investment in British agriculture. The rate of capital accumulation did decline significantly in manufacturing (and still more in agriculture), but over the economy as a whole the decline was slight, and the nonmanufacturing investment undertaken did yield a return. In Chapter 15 we offered the guess that about half of the decline between 1856–73 and 1873–1913 in the rate of growth of TFP was due to the effects of the country's changed international position, including both changes due to events abroad and the reinforcing effects

through international transactions of changes in the rate of growth of
TFP originating at home.

World War I and the interwar period. In the interwar period
adverse underlying trends in competitiveness continued to be felt, in
more acute forms—partly a deferred penalty for the long period of
slow TFP growth that had gone before, though World War I speeded
up the decline in Britain's share in world markets, in services as well as
in goods. As a result of the war income from abroad fell as a proportion
of national income, instead of rising, as it had formerly done. The combination of these circumstances led to a balance-of-payments problem
of a kind not experienced before 1914. These unfavorable developments on the international front, together with the world depression of
the 1930's, were the main cause of the low aggregate demand in the interwar period and its effects in the form of discouragement to industrial
investment and declining TFP in sectors affected by the underemployment of labor. However, the main feature of the behavior of TFP in
this period—its faster growth in most sectors compared with before
1914—is not explicable by trends in the country's international transactions, unless in the most general sense that changes on the international
front were part of a general process of shake-up following the war. The
effects of the balance of trade on the demand for manufactures were
more unfavorable in the interwar period than before 1914, but whatever ill-effects this may have had on the rate of growth of TFP in manufacturing were outweighed by forces working in the opposite direction.

World War II and the postwar period. Across World War II there
was a major break from long-run trends. Britain's share in world exports actually rose; imports declined steeply as a proportion of national
income; and the main export sector, manufacturing, experienced an increase in profitability and, for the first time for over a hundred years, a
substantial increase in its share of the labor force (the subsequent
decline in this proportion, from its high point in the early 1950's, left it
still in 1973 well above its historical average). Foreign trade was the
main source of the increase in the level of demand compared with the
1930's. All this reflected the temporary absence of competition from
war-devastated countries, helped by the devaluation of sterling against
the dollar. It produced a short-lived situation with certain resemblances to the third quarter of the nineteenth century. Its erosion
resembled what occurred after that period, but with some differences
and at a faster tempo. The resemblances were declining competitiveness, pressure on profitability, and hence pressure on capital accumula-

tion in manufacturing, which as in the earlier period reached its peak before capital accumulation in the rest of the economy. One difference was that in the postwar period pressure was felt through the balance of payments, which on this occasion was not being helped by rising income from abroad on the scale of 1870–1914. There was not (until 1973) any substantial adverse trend in the actual balance of payments on current account as a proportion of national income, but an underlying tendency to one can be held to have been present, inasmuch as the trend in the pressure of demand during the 1960's was downward in the United Kingdom and upward in most of the rest of the industrial world. (The latter fact, incidentally, tells against the hypothesis that the balance-of-payments pressures were the result of a tendency to chronic excess absorption.) Balance-of-payments pressure was largely responsible for the peculiar time pattern of the British business cycle in 1951–73, with downswings on the average longer than upswings, and the whole cycle short and not severe. Another difference from the pre-1914 period was that since the rates of capital accumulation (industrial as well as total) and TFP growth were high by historical standards, any ill-effects from the international side were ill-effects relative to what might have been, not (as they had been before 1914) relative to what had actually occurred earlier.

As in 1870–1914, some erosion of the initial position was inevitable, as other countries made good their arrears. But the erosion would not have continued as long as it did, had there not been other forces making for slower growth in TFP in Britain than abroad. It is not consistent to argue *both* that Britain was at a disadvantage by having been in the lead in the early postwar period while Germany and Japan were able to make a fresh start, *and* that once those countries had taken the lead, the cumulative advantages of that lead made their position impregnable. It is clear enough that in the postwar period foreign competition reduced profitability, MEI, and hence capital accumulation in the tradables sector. The effect on the growth of TFP is less apparent. Whereas in 1870–1914 pressure on the tradables sector from foreign competition can be held to have inhibited the transfer of underemployed labor from agriculture, that is not applicable to the postwar period. We may grant that there was *some* adverse effect, and that it reinforced shortfalls arising from other causes in the rate of growth of TFP compared with abroad. This is, however, a far cry from the view that has sometimes been held of the balance of payments as in itself the dominant or sole constraint on the growth rate.

A word may be said, finally, about two related topics, the effect of foreign trade on trends in profitability and the role of exchange-rate policy in the interwar and postwar periods.

In Chapter 16 reference was made to the long-run downward trend in profits' share and in the profit rate (more fully dealt with in Chapter 6). In most of the phases in which there were substantial movements in profitability (profits' share in trading income), trends in international competitiveness were in the right direction to explain them. This applies to the rise in profits' share in 1856–73; to its falls in the 1870's and 1880's and again after World War I; and to the temporary rise in profitability in manufacturing across World War II and its subsequent decline during the postwar period. It does not apply well to the acceleration in the decline in 1968–73, since in that phase competitiveness, following devaluation, was for a while better than before. Nor does it apply well to the sharp fall of profitability in the services sector across World War II.

It is easily understandable that there should be a relationship between profitability and international competitiveness. Profits accrue as quasi-rents, so in the short-run changes in the world prices of tradables relative to domestic costs impinge mainly on profits. Moreover, insofar as there was *chronic* pressure on competitiveness after 1870, it would account for profitability being chronically below a steady-state equilibrium *level*. It is not clear, however, that declining competitiveness can account for the trend *fall* in profits' share after the 1870's, a fall that, moreover, would have been even more pronounced had capital export not provided an outlet for savings. In the long run one would expect the supply of capital and its allocation between sectors to adjust. Whatever the effect of foreign trade on the level of output or on its structure, it is not obvious why it should as such in the long run affect the distribution of the value of output between labor and capital.* Though foreign trade accounts for much of the *timing* of the trend fall in profitability, other causes have to be sought for the trend itself.

The relationship between profitability and the exchange rate is, of course, that devaluation has as one of its immediate effects an increase in profits' share. The function of exchange-rate changes is to facilitate adjustments called for by underlying circumstances. In addition to its

---

*To the extent that influences from the side of foreign trade caused TFP and hence GDP to rise less fast than they would have otherwise done, foreign trade must indeed have *tended* to lower the profit rate. But since the rate of growth of TFP was not actually falling in the twentieth century, this cannot be invoked to explain the fall in the profitability that *did* occur.

effects on profits' share, devaluation raises the prices of tradables relative to the prices of non-tradables and usually, though not necessarily,
lowers the terms of trade.

A decision to adopt a lower exchange rate than $4.86 in the 1920's
would have had these effects. The adjustments needed were large and
difficult, on any policy. An increase in the relative price of tradables
would have encouraged the growth of newer export industries and
helped the balance of payments, but it would not have solved the problems of the old staples. Its effectiveness would, moreover, have depended on public willingness to accept the effects on real wages of a less
rapid improvement than actually occurred in labor's share and in the
terms of trade. It would also have depended on the response of other
countries to the devaluation of sterling.

The decision to devalue in 1949 contrasts with the return to the
pre-1914 parity in 1925 and was perhaps the single most important
point of difference between postwar and interwar government policy.
It facilitated the major break from past trends after World War II in
Britain's international trading position. The adjustments required in
this period were admittedly easier than the adjustments that had to be
made after World War I, because of buoyant world demand and because of the more appropriate structure of manufacturing inherited
from the war and the 1930's. No one disputes that further adjustments
had become necessary by the mid-1960's. The debate about whether
the devaluation of 1967 should have been made earlier or not at all is a
debate about whether this particular device sufficiently facilitated adjustment — a similar doubt as may be felt about the alternative policies
available in 1925, and one apparently given substance by the continuing balance-of-payments troubles experienced after 1967. These
troubles however, were partly the result, not of the intractability of the
problem as it existed in 1967, but of the subsequent change, exogenous
from Britain's point of view, in the trend in primary-product prices.

Conclusions About the Effects on the Growth Rate

Let us now summarize the answers to the questions that were put at
the beginning of this section.

Did international influences cause demand to tend to grow less
rapidly than supply and hence cause output to grow at less than the
"natural" rate? There are obvious difficulties in defining a "natural"
rate of growth for such an open economy as Britain's in abstraction
from international trade; but, briefly, the answer is yes, for much of
the period. It is plainly so for 1913–24, and also, though to a less

degree, for 1873–1913 and the interwar period. For the postwar period, there is no clear answer. On the one hand, high and rapidly growing demand in the rest of the world was a major plus by comparison with almost all earlier periods; on the other hand, the increase in foreign competition made the resultant benefit less than that derived by other countries, to say the least.

Did foreign trade and international capital movements adversely affect supply by their influence on the rate of capital accumulation? Before 1914, not much — less than might have been expected. In the interwar period, certainly. In the postwar period foreign trade affected at least the timing of the fall in profitability in manufacturing and so discouraged investment in that sector. This has to be seen, however, in conjunction with the abnormal stimulus to investment in manufacturing arising from the side of foreign trade at the beginning of the postwar period.

Did foreign trade affect the rate of growth of supply by its effects on the rate of growth of TFP? This is largely related to the first question. Adverse effects can be traced in 1873–1913. The main trends in TFP in the interwar period do not appear to have been at all directly due to foreign trade. The effects in the postwar period are ambivalent. The influence of foreign trade does not go far to explain the U-shape of the very long-run movement in the rate of growth of TFP, which is further discussed in the next section.

THE GROWTH OF TOTAL FACTOR PRODUCTIVITY

TFP is a weighted average of the productivity of labor and the productivity of capital. As noted above, the rate of growth of TFP was the principal proximate source of variations between periods in the rate of growth of GDP per head of population.

The Time Pattern to Be Explained

The rate of growth of TFP was the prime example of the U-shaped time pattern. However, this time pattern, as it was shown in Table 16.2 and Figure 16.1, requires some comment and some qualification. The rate of growth of TFP in 1924–37 and 1937–51 was much affected by its behavior in commerce and by the movements of factors between that sector and the rest of the economy. Both of these were largely reflections of changes in the amount of concealed unemployment. A better indication of the underlying pattern in those periods is given by the rate of intra-industry growth in TFP in the rest of the economy (Table 17.2 , row 2). This was significantly higher in 1924–37 than in

TABLE 17.2

Growth of Total Factor Productivity Including and Excluding Commerce and Quality-Shift, 1856–1973

(Annual percentage growth rates)

Category	1856–1873	1873–1913	1924–1937	1937–1951	1951–1973
(1) Rate of growth of TFP	0.9%	0.5%	0.7%	1.4%	2.3%
(2) Rate of growth of TFP, excluding contributions from commerce and quality-shift	(0.5)*	(0.1)*	0.7	0.4	1.6
(3) Rate of growth of TFP in manufacturing	0.9	0.6	1.9	0.9	2.4

Source: Tables 7.2, 8.3, 9.7.

Note: The figures do not relate to the same concept of TFP as that used in Table 16.2 and Fig. 16.1, namely TF_QP, because sectoral data on labor quality are not available. The concept of TFP used in this table, namely TF_rP for 1856–1913 and TF_wP for 1924–73, serves to allow for the only part of labor-quality change that has a major effect on comparisons between periods, the 100% increase in intensity of work assumed to have accompanied the reduction in hours in 1856–73. For definitions of the alternative concepts of TFP, see p. 199.

TFP in rows 1 and 2 is based on the average of the GDP estimates from the expenditure, income, and output sides. Commerce and manufacturing in rows 2 and 3 are estimated from the output side.

*Quality-shift is assumed to be 0.25.

1873–1913. It underwent a large setback in 1937–51, not surprisingly. It then improved further in the postwar period. This improvement after the two wars, following a decline up to World War I, is the pattern to be considered.

Trends in the rate of growth of TFP, excluding commerce and quality-shift, exhibit broadly the same pattern as trends in manufacturing, also shown in Table 17.2. These trends were pervasive throughout the economy (with the exception of the period 1937–51). TFP grew more rapidly in 1924–37 than in 1873–1913 in every sector except commerce, and it grew more rapidly in 1951–73 than in 1924–37 in every sector without exception. This pervasiveness of trends between broad periods — less pronounced within periods — is a characteristic to be borne in mind in seeking explanations. The rate of growth of TFP in individual sectors was the dominant influence on the rate of growth of TFP in the economy as a whole. The effects of shifts of weights between sectors with different levels or rates of growth of TFP were small by comparison, both in absolute amount and in their contribution to differences between periods.

Causes

We now turn to an analysis of the forces responsible for the U-shaped pattern in the rate of growth of TFP. Four broad categories are considered: (1) the rate of growth of demand (including one aspect of economies of scale); (2) the level of demand; (3) the introduction of new technology; (4) the sociocultural factors reflected in the attitudes of labor and the quality of management. There is some overlap between them, as well as between them and the effects of foreign trade, already discussed.

The rate of growth of demand. Fast growth of demand, at least for a single industry and maybe for the economy as a whole, conduces to rapid growth of TFP by facilitating embodied technical progress, opening the way for enterprise (great generals are not made in peacetime) and lessening labor resistance to change. A special case of this relationship is that put forward in the Kaldor-Verdoorn hypothesis, according to which the tendency operates in manufacturing only but extends to the economy as a whole because of manufacturing's importance; the effect can then result from a switch in demand to manufacturing, typically because of foreign trade, as well as from rapid growth in demand in the economy as a whole.*

The period in which this effect was most apparent was 1873–1913. Trends in foreign trade then affected adversely the rate of growth of TFP in some manufacturing industries and still more so in agriculture. Perhaps surprisingly, the effect in agriculture had considerably greater impact on TFP in the economy as a whole than did the effect in manufacturing. Output in agriculture fell absolutely between 1873 and 1913. At the same time the rate of decline of the agricultural labor force diminished somewhat, no doubt largely because there were less opportunities for employment elsewhere in the country. The result was a fall in the rate of growth of TFP in agriculture that accounted for about a third of the fall between 1856–73 and 1873–1913 in the rate of growth of TFP in the economy as a whole.

The trouble with the Kaldor-Verdoorn hypothesis as applied to later periods is not that it is necessarily wrong as a counterfactual proposition, but that it is largely irrelevant to the explanation of interperiod differences in the rate of growth of TFP in the United Kingdom. The rate of growth of output of manufactures was the same in the interwar period and in the postwar period, and therefore does not help to explain why TFP grew more rapidly in the postwar period. Similarly, since the rate of growth of output of manufactures was the same in the two parts of the postwar period, 1951–64 and 1964–73, it does not help to explain why TFP grew more rapidly in the second of these. The output of manufactures did grow faster in 1924–37 than in before 1914, so

---

*An alternative version of the hypothesis, relating productivity growth in manufacturing to the growth of inputs rather than of production, must be considered refuted by the empirical evidence both on the UK time-series and on international comparisons.

the hypothesis works in the right direction to explain the rise between those periods in the rate of growth of TFP. But in this instance it explains too much, since in manufacturing the increase in TFP growth was greater than the increase in output growth, so the hypothesis implausibly implies negative marginal costs; moreover, the increase in the rate of output growth arose from domestic absorption rather than from the balance of trade, the most likely source of an *exogenous* change of demand. Cross-section studies of manufacturing industries do give some indication of the presence of a Kaldor-Verdoorn relationship. The most reasonable conclusion is that the growth of output did make some contribution, though not the sole contribution, to the higher rate of growth of TFP in manufacturing achieved in the interwar period compared with before 1914; and that, though change in the rate of growth of manufacturing output does not explain why TFP grew faster in the postwar period than in the interwar period, the lack of such change between those periods may have been part of the reason why TFP growth increased *less* in manufacturing than in most other sectors.

As a counterfactual proposition, the Kaldor-Verdoorn hypothesis is less attractive for the postwar period than for 1873–1913. In the postwar period there was less slack in the economy, and faster growth in the demand for manufactures would have had more tendency to be halted by supply-side bottlenecks before it could begin to generate dynamic economies of scale.

The level of demand. Like rapidly growing demand, a high level of demand may conduce to a high rate of growth of TFP, and for much the same reasons. It may enable enterprising new men to come to the fore; facilitate mobility; dispel restrictive labor practices by reducing fear of technological unemployment; and induce innovations to overcome labor shortages. On the other hand, it may enable inefficient firms to survive; destroy labor discipline; weaken the inducement to cut costs; and defer needed changes in industrial structure or attitudes. Any of these effects may be important. They are not trivial matters. But the net outcome cannot be predicted *a priori*, nor is it easy to test empirically. Some of the above effects do not seem to have been significant in Britain: neither the extent of labor restrictive practices nor labor mobility bore any clear relationship to the prevailing level of demand. The relationship between the level of demand and the growth of TFP is not necessarily monotonic. The pattern Denison has conjectured as the most conducive to economic growth — predominantly strong demand, punctuated by short sharp recessions — was not the pattern of British business cycles in *any* period. If Denison is right, it could help to explain why TFP generally rose less rapidly in Britain than elsewhere.

However, the evidence suggests that the high level of demand in the postwar period had a net favorable effect, and a substantial one, on the growth of TFP (as well as being favorable to capital accumulation). Certainly this was so in the important commercial sector. In one sector, construction, full employment appears to have had an adverse effect on the level of TFP (if not on its growth rate). The sector was not large enough for the movement of TFP there to have much effect on the movement of TFP in the economy as a whole; however, the fall in TFP in construction across World War II had some significance in raising the price of capital goods and reducing the profit rate earned on them.

Though the high level of demand in the postwar period thus had a positive effect on TFP growth, Kendrick's finding (1973: 41–51) that the depression of the 1930's led to a slowdown, not subsequently made good, in the growth of TFP in the United States does not hold for the United Kingdom. On the contrary, as already noted, TFP grew more rapidly in 1924–37 than in 1873–1913 in every sector other than commerce. Was this *notwithstanding* the uniquely low level of demand, or was it, partly, *because* of it? Did the favorable effects on TFP of low demand in that phase preponderate over the unfavorable ones? Schumpeter saw the business cycle as a wave of creative destruction, upswing and downswing both playing their part, and this idea could be extended to the longer alternations represented by the interwar and postwar periods. Good effects exercised by the depression on the growth of TFP are more dubious and were certainly smaller than the good effects of the high level of demand in the postwar period; moreover, the depression had some deferred ill-effects, such as discouraging the training of skilled labor, as well as direct and immediate ill-effects on the utilization of resources and capital accumulation. However, it would not be inconsistent to suggest that, as far as the growth of TFP is concerned, both the high demand of the postwar period and the low demand of the interwar period had *some* good effects.

The introduction of new technology. It is helpful to draw a distinction here between innovations that originated in Britain and those that where wholly or largely initiated abroad and taken up in Britain after some delay.

In the first half of the nineteenth century only the domestic source of innovation was important to Britain, and the increase in TFP up to about 1860 was largely dependent on the mechanization of the textile industries and the construction of the railways. When this process was completed, the effect was sufficient to bring about an appreciable deceleration in the growth of TFP. The second half of the century brought no new domestic innovations with effects comparable to the earlier advances in textiles. Some key improvements were not widely taken up in Britain, most notably the Gilchrist-Thomas process in the production of basic steel and the use of electricity as a source of motive power.

As industrial leadership passed from Britain, so the possibilities increased for adopting innovations pioneered abroad. Both *a priori* reasoning and empirical evidence (Table 2.5, Fig. 2.2) create a presumption of international convergence in productivity levels. The further a country lags behind the leading country or countries, the greater the scope for catching up and the faster the rate of growth of TFP that can be expected, other things being equal. In principle, an increase over time in the rate of growth of TFP in the British economy would be expected on this account.

The catching-up hypothesis has to be considered in conjuction with the hypothesis of the disadvantage of an early start. That asserts that the existence of old-vintage capital, non-human and human, slows down the adoption of innovations, because the old capital is not itself adaptable to the new methods and has demolition costs, physical or social. This hypothesis has been applied in many contexts. One is the explanation of Britain's technological lag in the last quarter of the nineteenth century. Another relates to more recent times, when West Germany, it is claimed, was able to renew its status as late starter because of the destruction of old capital by bombing.* The hypothesis has a good deal of plausibility — especially in its most general applications, that is to say, the persistence of outdated attitudes among labor and management, often reinforced by common-interest groups — and it has relevance to the general problem of Britain's slow rate of growth. It is not directly antithetical to the catching-up hypothesis, and indeed to some extent concerns a different point (old age brings disadvantages, whether or not new ideas are being introduced by the younger generation). It does mean, however, that the existence of a technological gap provides less easy scope for increasing TFP in an old industrial country than in a new one, and thus helps to explain why the convergence phenomenon is less apparent in the British case than in others. Only on extreme assumptions, however, does it remove altogether (or reverse)

---

*Other cases in which the early-start hypothesis has been invoked include, for the pre-1914 period, gas delaying electricity, mules delaying ring-spindles, Bessemer converters delaying the open-hearth process, and the Leblanc process delaying the Solvay process in soda-making, as well as the logically different and simpler case of the depletion of the most accessible mineral deposits; and for the postwar period, the dispersed location of the motor industry, the over-defensive orientation of early postwar investment (above, pp. 394–95) and, at a regional level, the less rapid growth of industry in traditional locations, like Merseyside and Glasgow, than in newer ones.

the presumption that the opening up of a technological gap increases the scope for innovation. It does not apply, for example, in industries where there is freedom of entry and new firms (or new divisions of multiproduct firms) can set up free from the millstones that encumber the old ones. Let us proceed, then, on the assumption that Britain's international standing in relative productivity did at least to some extent affect the scope for growth in TFP in the manner postulated by the catching-up hypothesis, and consider how it affects the view taken of performance in each period.

Before 1873 the United Kingdom had the world's highest GDP per man-year. In some sectors, possibly in manufacturing as a whole, the United States was already leading, but the scope for catching up by the United Kingdom was still small.

At the beginning of the period *1873–1914* GDP per man-year in the United States was equal to Britain's. In the course of the period the United States progressively moved ahead of Britain. So did Germany in some sectors. There was thus increasing scope for catching up by the United Kingdom. The decline over time in the British rate of growth of TFP after 1873 therefore implies a *greater* decline in the rate of growth of TFP relative to what might have been expected. It leaves correspondingly more to be explained.

World War I widened the productivity gap between the United Kingdom and the United States. Some improvement in the rate of growth of TFP in *1924–37* was therefore to be expected, compared with earlier. The improvement that did occur, however, was larger than can easily be accounted for by the increase in the scope for catching up; the increase in the scope for catching up was part of a continuous process, whereas the improvement in the rate of growth of TFP was abrupt and already in evidence in the 1920's. On this reckoning, there must have been domestically originating sources of improvement as well.

1951–73 is the most difficult period to characterize. World War II increased the productivity gap between Britain and the United States, as World War I had done. Moreover, the postwar rate of growth of productivity in the United States was faster than before, betokening a more rapid extension of the production frontier. The improvement in the UK growth rate compared with the prewar rate more than matched the improvement in the United States: for the first time since the Civil War, the British rate of growth of productivity was not below the American. Thus the United Kingdom shared in whatever was the source of the U.S. improvement, and rather more besides. As in the interwar period, the improvement appears to have been more than can be accounted for by the increase in the size of the initial gap (though this must be a subjective judgment), and domestic sources have to be sought. However, other countries showed a much greater break from their past. In particular, the gap separating France and Germany from the U.S. level of productivity, which proportionally had changed little before World War II, now narrowed rapidly, and those countries overtook the United Kingdom. The experience of those countries does not negate the evidence for domestic sources of improvement in Britain, but it implies that those countries had much stronger sources of domestic improvement.

Some of the specific advances to which this hypothesis of technological lag and catching up might apply are the use of electricity for power, the internal combustion engine, the production of synthetic dyestuffs and other chemicals, the development of the basic process and the open-hearth furnace in steel making, the spread of mechanization, and the use of automatic machinery.[2] These are all areas in which Britain fell behind its competitors on the Continent and in the United States in the period after 1870, and even if there were often sound economic reasons for the reluctance of British management to introduce new technology, the effect was seen in the slow growth of TFP. Conversely, some part of the improvement in TFP growth in the interwar period can be attributed to a belated introduction and extension of these innovations.

In the early 1950's the scope for technological catching up by Britain was again large. In the subsequent period the pace of world technological advance was more rapid than in earlier periods. Innovation took place on a wide front throughout the industrial world (including Britain), and the increase in the number of countries at a comparable stage of technological development facilitated international learning. Outstanding innovations of the period came in electrical engineering and electronics (including computers and the use of automated machinery), in aircraft, in the development of synthetics, antibiotics, and other products by the chemical industry, and in the peaceful application of nuclear power. Mention may also be made of new managerial techniques, such as stock control, largely derived from operations research, which (like many of the above) had its origins in World War II; these techniques were akin to technological advance, rather than the consequence of changes in the personal qualities of management of the kind to be considered under the next heading.

Neither technological innovation nor catching up is, of course, an inevitable or automatic process.[3] The extent to which other factors facilitated or obstructed them must be analyzed. These factors include the level and rate of growth of demand, already considered, and the socioeconomic forces of labor and management, to which we now turn. Changes in the attitudes of labor and in the quality of management are the most truly exogenous and least quantifiable of the possible causes of TFP change. They are thus not very well suited for study from the macro-economic data on which this book is based. So in a sense our inquiry ends with a question mark. Certain observations can, however, be tentatively made.

Attitudes of labor and quality of management. British workers have been said for over a hundred years to be more adverse to change, to flexibility in working practices, and to a fast tempo of work than their foreign counterparts, this aversion being expressed both through trade unions and, informally, through the attitudes of individuals and groups. Even allowing for frequent exaggeration, the testimony to this effect is too strong to be dismissed. The origins of the phenomenon have been sought in numbers of causes: the tradition of craft unionism and the slow rate of growth in industrial employment, both related to the country's early start on the path of industrialization; the absence, by comparison with the United States, of a flow of immigrants of mixed nationalities; the absence, by comparison with Germany and Japan, of traumatic setbacks to the standard of living that forced the practice of each-man-for-himself. *Changes over time* in labor attitudes in the United Kingdom have some, but only limited, relevance to the explanation of changes over time in the rate of growth of TFP. For reasons that are not entirely clear, industrial relations markedly deteriorated in the 20 years before World War I, and the rate of growth of TFP reached its nadir at the same time. The decline in labor militancy after 1926 probably assisted TFP growth. It is unclear whether change in labor attitudes in the postwar period, compared with earlier periods, was on balance such as to contribute to faster growth of TFP or to inhibit it. With a faster underlying rate of technical change, a given degree of labor resistance to change mattered more, labor attitudes and technical progress thus having a multiplicative rather than an additive effect on the growth of TFP.

It is a well-known contention that the quality of entrepreneurship declined in late-Victorian and Edwardian Britain. If true, it would help to explain the decline in the rate of growth of TFP in that period. The argument is that any corps of industrial leadership will deteriorate over time if there is not enough infusion of new talent, and that the values of late-Victorian Britain, reflected and reinforced by the educational system, did not direct enough able people that way: the most successful in business were drawn into the lifestyle of the landed gentry, and the middle classes looked for their careers to the professions, the public service, and jobs in the Empire. The educational system reflected these goals and neglected engineering and chemistry.

Not all the arguments that have been advanced in this regard stand up to examination. However, there is enough direct evidence about motivation, recruitment, and education to justify the inference of some falling off in entrepreneurship in the late nineteenth century, quite apart from indirect evidence afforded by the performance of the economy. Much of this falling off (including that due to the expansion of Empire, a point of difference from other industrial countries) can be traced directly or indirectly to the early start of British economic growth and to the economy's consequent temporary world leadership.

The attitudes and institutions just referred to outlived the circumstances of their origin. However, they did gradually alter. The timing of that gradual and incomplete alteration is consistent with the improvements in the rate of growth in TFP after World War I and again after World War II.

The alteration came about partly because of the jolts administered by the two wars, which upset institutions, compelled a reexamination of attitudes, and led people and firms into activities they would not otherwise have contemplated. The effects of wars and other political upsets have been made the basis of a general theory of economic growth by Olson (1978).* There is no need to go all the way with him in order to recognize that the adverse effects of the wars on the capital stock and the foreign trade position were significantly offset by the shake-up of attitudes and institutions, governmental as well as private.† Jolts may also have been administered (in accordance with the Schumpeterian idea) by the depression of the 1920's *and* by the boom of the postwar period.

Consequences

So much for the causes affecting the rate of growth of TFP. Its consequences can be more briefly treated. The question is, did the rate of growth of TFP affect the rate of growth of GDP?

---

*Olson's theory has particular reference to common-interest groups (cartels and labor unions) that retard growth.

†Changes in government attitudes on aspects of policy indirectly affecting TFP — demand management, health, education, and to some extent science — were probably the most important. Governments throughout the postwar period also concerned themselves more than before with policies designed to improve productivity directly, and there were some successes, but the result of these policies generally fell below expectations, and it is doubtful whether in net they contributed substantially — if indeed at all — to overall growth in TFP.

Insofar as the rate of growth of TFP was a function of the rate of growth of demand, the answer is plainly yes: it was part of an endogenous cumulative process.

More generally, in those periods when demand was pressing against a ceiling of productive potential, anything making for fast or slow growth in TFP was bound to translate itself into the rate of growth of GDP.

The less easy question concerns the effects of changes in TFP due to exogenous causes (technological or sociocultural) or to perversely endogenous ones (low demand stimulating high TFP growth) in periods when the economy was not pressing against a ceiling. The issue resembles the issue about the effects of exogenous changes in the labor supply. However, there are good reasons for supposing that the answer is more straightforward than in that case. TFP growth not only raises the ceiling on output, but it also reduces costs, and so facilitates its own absorption, by improving international competitiveness, as shown by evidence from all periods. Moreover, insofar as it requires to be embodied in new equipment, it contributes directly to demand by stimulating gross investment.

In principle, of course, fast growth in TFP could lead to slow growth in TFI rather than to fast growth in output. To some extent that may have happened in the interwar period, when there was spare labor to draw on and when, moreover, the capital-saving element in TFP growth was prominent and kept down investment in some sectors. Even in that period, however, growth in TFP in the construction industry was an important element in stimulating the building boom. In general, we need not feel much doubt that growth in TFP, whether exogenous or endogenous, was both a necessary and a sufficient condition for growth in GDP, while recognizing that the effect was not in all cases necessarily one for one, and that its magnitude depended partly on the form of the growth of TFP and on its sectoral incidence, especially on the extent to which it generated demand by improving international competitiveness.

CHARACTERISTICS OF THE SUCCESSIVE PERIODS

So far this chapter has considered, one by one, the various factors in British economic growth. Let us now, at the risk of some repetition, review matters from the other angle, chronologically.

The Pre-1914 Period

GDP grew more slowly in 1873–1913 than in 1856–73. This slowdown was not due to any change in the rate of growth of labor input: population and employment grew at a constant rate (cycles and long swings apart), and indeed in 1873–1913 there were less reductions in hours of work and rather more improvement in the quality of the labor force (in education and age composition) than in 1856–73. Nor was there a decline in the rate of domestic capital accumulation; there was admittedly some decline in the rate of investment in industry and commerce, but this was matched by a rise in house-building, and the rising capital-output ratio in industry does not suggest a capital short-age. The decline was in the rate of growth of TFP. TF_QP did not in-crease at all over the period 1873–1913 as a whole, and it actually declined after 1899.

TF_QP had not grown all that rapidly before 1873 either, and the falloff, at least until 1899, was therefore not so enormous. But com-parison with other countries suggests that TFP ought to have increased *more* rapidly after 1873 than before. In that sense, the comparison of successive periods understates the deterioration.

Part of the explanation was the increase in foreign competition. Its most visible effect was on agriculture, which suffered both a decline in the rate of growth of its output and a slowdown in the trend rate of reduction of its labor force, the latter due, presumably, to diminished scope for absorption of labor elsewhere in the economy, itself partly related to the slower rate of growth of net exports. As was argued above (pp. 533–34), the effect of foreign competition on TFP in manufactur-ing is more doubtful, though there probably was some.

A further part of the explanation lies in certain special factors. In textiles there was already a decline in the rate of growth of TFP some time before 1873, attributable to the exhaustion of the once-for-all effects of the industrial revolution. In mining, where there was an ab-solute fall in output per man (not merely in TFP), classical diminishing returns played a part. But for the economy as a whole more general ex-planations must be sought. Deteriorating industrial relations in the lat-ter part of the period were one. Decline in entrepreneurial vitality may have been another. It is possible that both of these were affected (with different timing) by a vicious circle between performance and remu-neration, the decline in industrial profit rates in the 1870's and 1880's having harmful effects on the recruitment and motivation of entrepre-neurs, and the check to real wages after 1900 souring industrial rela-tions. No offsetting incentive effect could be expected from the con-comitant increase in income from abroad.

The surprisingly small part of the falloff in the rate of growth of overall TFP that was attributable to manufacturing appears on the face of it to militate against both the foreign-competition hypothesis, as normally stated, and the entrepreneurial-deficiency hypothesis (though not against the industrial-relations hypothesis); and there remain some puzzling features about the period. These are especially concerned with the timing of movements within it and their relation to long swings. The falloff in the rate of growth of TFP was not continuous but was temporarily arrested in the 1890's. Both in 1873–90 and in 1899–1913 there were elements of demand deficiency, though with different origins: in 1873–90 largely foreign competition, in 1899–1913 the long-swing fall in domestic construction and perhaps an adverse real-balance effect created by the rise in world prices. It is arguable that demand deficiency of one kind or another ultimately accounted for the major part of the falloff in the rate of growth of TFP in the period 1873–1913 as a whole compared with 1856–73 and also for the more severe falloff after 1899. However, demand deficiency cannot explain why the rate of growth of TFP in most sectors was so much lower than it came to be in the interwar period. This *is* indicative of entrepreneurial deficiencies or other supply-side sources, which doubtless interacted with demand.

World War I and the Interwar Period

Such a large gap opened up between supply and demand in the interwar period that it is tempting to regard demand-side forces as the only ones relevant to the explanation of the actual movement of output. However, exogenous trends in supply did contribute as well to the decline in GDP across World War I, and they were the main cause of the better trend performance in the interwar period compared with 1873–1913.

The absolute fall in GDP across the war, not made good till the late 1920's, is one of the most spectacular features of recent British economic history. Its main constituent, from the growth-accounting point of view, was the fall in labor input. Three sources had about equal effects in reducing the annual percentage rate of growth of (quality-adjusted) labor input from 1.7 in 1873–1913 to −0.4 in 1913–24: population growth, hours of work, and unemployment. The causes of the movement in the three were to a large extent independent of each other, and to that extent the magnitude of the movement had a fortuitous element. Population growth (affected by war casualties and the influenza epidemic) and hours of work (affected by immediate postwar labor militancy) were supply-side factors, both much influenced in their different ways by the war itself. Unemployment, of course, was a demand-side factor, though a subordinate part may also have been played by the rapid transwar rise in the real wage (comparable in origin, and indeed partly due to, the reduction in hours).

In regard to the movement of TFP across the war, there is not so much to explain. The performance was bad (TF_QP is estimated to have been lower in 1924 than in 1913); but the trend was not worse than 1899–1913, and the underlying trend was probably somewhat better, since TFP in 1924 was no doubt depressed by below-capacity working.

The importance of the supply constraints was apparent in 1920, when unemployment was extremely low yet GDP was 5 percent below 1913. The ensuing major decline in demand arose from the side of foreign trade. How much of it would have happened if there had not been a war can only be a matter of speculation. The balance of trade would certainly have deteriorated because of foreign competition anyway, very likely to nearly the same extent. But the disappearance of the support formerly given to the overall balance of payments by increasing income from abroad was a new feature, directly attributable to the war. So, doubtless, were the violent price movements and ensuing depression that affected most of Northern Europe in the early 1920's.

The recovery in 1924–37 was not to any large extent due to a reversal of the specific causes responsible for the previous contraction. The balance of payments on current account continued to have a downward trend; unemployment did not diminish; there was only a slight increase in hours of work.

On the supply-side the two new features were an abnormally rapid increase in the proportion of population of working age and a much improved rate of growth of TFP in most sectors—better than in 1873–1913, let alone 1899–1913. The first was purely demographic. In regard to TFP, there is no single simple answer to the question why it took a turn for the better in this period rather than a bit sooner or a bit later. The factors at work included belated adaptation to earlier sources of technical innovation, stimulated by the increase in the size of the productivity gap compared with the United States, by the jolt to the system administered by the war, and possibly also in some sectors by the depression; a decline in labor militancy in the aftermath of the General Strike of 1926, affected also by the growth of industry in new regions lacking old traditions of labor relations; and possibly improvements in entrepreneurship, particularly in recruitment.

On the demand-side the main source of growth was investment, chiefly in dwellings and in manufacturing (where investment, though still low absolutely, rose considerably under the influence of rearmament in the 1930's). Some growth in demand originated in foreign trade, but less than in any other peacetime period: the gain from the fall in the import propensity, due mainly to the fall in the prices of primary products, was largely offset by the continuing poor performance of exports.

If exogenous influences on the rates of growth of labor input or TFP had been *much* less favorable in the interwar period — if, for example, TFP had continued to decline at the same rate as in the years before World War I — the actual rate of growth of output would not have been possible. If they had been only *slightly* less favorable, it is not clear, in view of the slack in the economy, that output would have risen more slowly than it did, *provided* demand had risen at the same rate. But it is unlikely that that proviso would have been met, particularly if the difference had been in TFP. Higher real costs would have inhibited the growth of investment (notably in dwellings) and possibly made the balance of trade worse as well. This is quite apart from the importance of the interwar growth of TFI and TFP in establishing the productive potential that more directly constrained output during and after World War II.

World War II and the Postwar Period

There is an extraordinary contrast in respect of demand between the transitions across World War I and World War II. Yet in other respects the two wars had many similar features: large losses of overseas assets and consequent problems for the balance of payments; low domestic investment; jolts to established attitudes and, partly in consequence, improvement after the war in the rate of growth of TFP; increased involvement of government in economic affairs.

Among the many points of contrast between the two transwar phases, four may be singled out.

(1) The pressure of demand on the eve of the war was different. The existence of slack in the economy at the outset of World War II gave a margin from which to satisfy increased aspirations generated during the war.

(2) The scope for increasing exports was greater after World War II, on account of the greater setback to competitors, the more appropriate structure of industry developed before and during the war, and the decision not to adhere to the prewar parity.

(3) Transition from the war economy was smoothed by the much longer continuation of controls after World War II, and this helped

prevent a recurrence of the pattern of violent postwar boom and slump of 1919–21. This, along with the absence after World War II of a *world* recession like 1921, is the difference most directly relevant to the contrasting behavior of demand.

(4) In the aftermath of World War II there was a sense of national unity conspicuously lacking after World War I. Great attention had been paid to morale during the war, the fighting itself had been less traumatic, and a reformist government with a strong majority was elected in 1945. The exact effects of this different mood are difficult to pinpoint. At the least it helped avoid the industrial unrest of 1919. It probably had a more general effect too on the performance of labor and management.

In the postwar period itself growth in the British economy was more rapid than in earlier periods, by a substantial margin, though less rapid than in most other industrial countries (as it had been since 1870). Britain shared, in its fashion, in the outstanding postwar performance of the world economy.

As in earlier periods the rate of growth actually achieved was the result of forces on both the supply side and the demand side, interacting with each other. TFP in the economy as a whole increased much more rapidly than in any previous period (though in manufacturing the improvement over the interwar period was only moderate). In part this represented a catching up of accumulated arrears. In part it resulted from changes in business attitudes, facilitated by the jolt administered by World War II and manifested in increased sophistication in management and some redirection of talent and education. In part it resulted from faster and more broadly based technical progress throughout the world.

The predominantly high level of demand not only ensured that supply was taken up, but also contributed to the rate of growth of supply itself. It did this by encouraging capital accumulation and by stimulating the growth of TFP, particularly in the service sectors. Capital accumulation was a reinforcing element in growth, encouraged both by the rapid *growth* of output (permitting a correspondingly rapid growth of savings and also helping to keep up the marginal efficiency of investment) and by the high *level* of output. The process was a circular one in that the fast rate of growth of output, permitted by supply, was a contributing cause of the historically high rate of investment, which itself was a principal source of high demand (along with the growth in world trade and, probably, government commitment to the goal of full employment). The period thus had some of the characteristics of a business-cycle boom, but augmented and prolonged by an additional source of feedback not present in the textbook model of the business cycle, namely feedback through the supply side. Demand acted as a reinforcer of supply—as it had not done in the interwar period.

The generally buoyant level of world demand made an important contribution to the high average level of demand, compared with the past, and in that respect international trade acted as a benign reinforcer of fast growth. However, at the same time trends in the country's international position probably acted as a malignant reinforcer of the tendency to grow slowly *relative* to other countries: this tendency led to weakened competitiveness; hence to balance-of-payments trouble; hence to the distinctive British postwar cyclical pattern in which downswings (though not severe) lasted longer than upswings; and hence to ill-effects on confidence and on the growth of TFP compared with that enjoyed elsewhere. This ambiguous effect of foreign trade—favorable compared with the past, unfavorable compared with other countries—may be contrasted with its unambiguously adverse effect in the 40 years before 1914, when changes in Britain's competitive position tended to slow down its growth relative to its own past as well as relative to other countries.

GDP grew fast in the postwar period despite a rate of growth of labor input that was, primarily for demographic reasons, not only unprecedentedly low but declining; and the labor input per head of population was declining more rapidly than in earlier periods, with the exception of the period 1913-24. Labor shortage, due to this cause and to full employment, might in theory have either stimulated investment or discouraged it. In the event, it stimulated it. Such a response carried with it an inherent threat of diminishing returns to investment. The rate of capital accumulation did in fact begin to tail off in the course of the 1960's—in manufacturing earlier than in most other sectors—and the capital-output ratio began to show a marked tendency to rise after 1968. Thus indications of an end or at least a slowing down of the postwar boom were apparent well before the world recession that began in the course of 1973.

EPILOGUE: THE PERIOD SINCE 1973

Throughout this book we have deliberately avoided carrying the story beyond the watershed of 1973. Our approach has been based mainly on comparisons of cycle peaks, and there has been none worthy of the name since 1973. We have, moreover, been aware that nothing dates a work of history more surely than an attempt to bring its coverage up to the moment of writing. Let us, however, conclude with some brief and tentative remarks.

The recession since 1973 has been a world phenomenon. The falloff in the rates of growth of production and productivity relative to previous trend has been of the same order in most other industrial countries as in the United Kingdom, though their actual rates of growth have remained higher. Similarities between the United Kingdom and other countries in the impact of the recession on output have been more important than differences between them. Since both the causes and the consequences of the recession were worldwide, systematic discussion of them lies far beyond our scope. We can, however, usefully say something about what the magnitude of the change in the United Kingdom has been and consider how far it suggests that the historically high growth rate of 1951–73 was a flash in the pan.

Since 1973 Britain has suffered the severest setback to output *relative to previous trend* of any peacetime period since the middle of the nineteenth century. Real GDP in the late 1970's fell below the previous trend line by more than it did in the 1870's, the most severe recession before 1914; and a much longer time has passed without substantial signs of recovery than in the 1930's. Only the setback across World War I was more severe — albeit by quite a large margin.

The year 1979 saw the end of the limited upswing that began in 1975, following the absolute fall in real GDP in each of the two previous years. It therefore provides a convenient benchmark for the comparison of rates of growth of TFP, the variable that chiefly distinguished earlier periods from one another.

Between 1973 and 1979 the annual percentage rate of growth of $TF_{H}P$ in the economy as a whole was about 0.7, compared with 2.3 in 1951–73; it was close to the average figure for the century before 1951 (0.8). Even less favorable is the comparison in manufacturing, where output fell absolutely between 1973 and 1979 and the absolute level of $TF_{H}P$ remained about constant. The rate of growth of $TF_{H}P$ in manufacturing averaged over the whole period from 1951 to 1979 was little higher than it was in the interwar period.

These comparisons are too gloomy as indicators of underlying trends in TFP. TFP has always been temporarily below trend in recession years, and 1979 was still a year of recession, as measured not only by unemployment, which may be an unreliable indicator, but also by survey data on the proportion of firms restricted in their output by lack of orders. It is obvious that in all countries the decline in demand played a large part in the setback to TFP, especially in the years immediately after 1973. However, the improvement in productivity in the limited recovery after 1975 was much less than would have been expected on the precedent of earlier postwar recessions. This has been true of most sectors in most countries. Admittedly, there has been no postwar precedent for a recession of such magnitude, and the possibility cannot be ruled out that the slowdown in the rate of growth of productivity in Britain and in other European countries was entirely cyclical in nature. That it was cyclical in *origin* is indeed much the most likely hypothesis. But whether it was cyclical in the sense of being speedily reversible is much less clear; there may have been a downward ratchet. This is suggested not only by the occurrence of certain supply-side bottlenecks, but also by the experience of the United States, where a similar slowdown in productivity growth occurred even though by 1978 unemployment was not abnormally high.

This has been taken to indicate either a decline in the underlying rate of growth of productivity or else a once-for-all reduction in the level of productivity. The reasons for such a change, if it has occurred, remain fundamentally unclear. Denison (1979a, 1979b), who has made the most thorough attempt at quantification of possible causes, found that the sum of the effects of the various possible causes he could identify fell far short of explaining the slowdown in productivity growth in the United States. The same appears to hold for the United Kingdom (Sheriff 1979). The whole matter is thus obscure. Even if it were agreed that the ultimate cause was some kind of downward ratchet effect brought about by the recession, the way in which it affected productivity would remain to be determined.

The exact extent of short-run excess supply in the late 1970's is not entirely relevant to the assessment of the long-run trend in TFP. Short-run bottlenecks have not been unknown in all recessions. Still less does the occurrence of a prolonged and severe recession as such imply a permanent fall in the underlying rate of growth of TFP — though in all bad recessions there have been people who drew this inference. However, prolonged setbacks to the rate of growth of TFP *have* occurred, most notably at the beginning of the twentieth century, so a recurrence cannot be ruled out on grounds of historical precedent.

Prediction is not part of our aim, and we shall not try to evaluate the effects of certain features of the post-1973 period that are completely new, like the rise in energy prices, British membership in the EEC, the exploitation of North Sea oil, or the possibility of persistent high inflation independent of the level of activity. More appropriate in the context of a historical study is to conclude with a few words on which of the principal forces making for historically fast growth in the United Kingdom in 1951–73 appear in the light of subsequent events to have been of a permanent kind, and which of a transitory kind.

(1) There is no convincing evidence that the speedup on the strictly technological side was other than permanent. This holds both for the world as a whole and for the United Kingdom. Though some of the United Kingdom's improvement over earlier periods came from catching up with improvements already in use abroad, the scope for such catching up did not diminish in the course of the postwar period, but if anything the reverse. Nor is there any reason to suppose that the improvement in the quality of management was other than permanent.

(2) The high average level of demand between 1951 and 1973 not only ensured the take-up of supply, but also contributed to the rate of growth of supply. High demand proved compatible with non-accelerating inflation until toward the end of the 1960's. This compatibility now appears to have been transitory. Given the determination of governments to try to stop inflation, it follows that the reinforcement to rapid growth that was derived from high demand (at home and abroad) must regretfully be deemed to have been transitory too. This does not mean that advances in the *level* of TFP achieved under that stimulus were such as to be lost, only that the more rapid trend *rate of growth* due to that cause was once-for-all.

(3) During almost the whole of the postwar period up to 1973 the investment-income ratio was rising. Such a trend could clearly not be maintained indefinitely. It is the feature of the postwar period most manifestly indicative of a long swing, providing some basis for the contention that a growth boom of record proportions, like the postwar one, was likely to be followed by a setback even apart from inflation.

These considerations suggest that part of the excess of the growth rate achieved in the postwar period over that achieved in earlier periods was due to causes that were transitory. They also suggest, however, that not all of it was of that nature, either in respect of the level of productivity attained as a result of the growth or in respect of the continuing growth rate itself.

Notes

1. Annual percentage rates of growth of net exports of manufactures were as follows: 1857–73, 2.4; 1873–99, 0.6; 1899–1913, 2.9 (Schlote 1952). Rates of growth of TFP in manufacturing are given in Appendix L.

2. On Britain's record in technological innovations in these and other fields, see M. Frankel 1955; Habbakuk 1962; Saul 1962, 1967; Kindleberger 1964; Levine 1967; Aldcroft 1968; Landes 1969; McCloskey 1971, 1973; Byatt 1979.

3. On the factors influencing the diffusion of technology, see Mansfield 1968; Rosenberg 1976. See also Peck 1968.

References

Aldcroft, D. H. ed. 1968. *The Development of British Industry and Foreign Competition.* London.

Byatt, I. C. R. 1979. *The British Electrical Industry, 1875–1914: The Economic Returns to a New Technology.* Oxford, England.

Denison, E. F. 1979a. *Accounting for Slower Growth: The United States in the 1970s.* Washington, D.C.

———. 1979b. "Explanations of declining productivity growth," *Survey of Current Business,* 59.8, part 2 (Aug.): 1–25.

Feinstein, C. H. 1978. "Capital accumulation and economic growth in Great Britain, 1760–1860," in vol. 7 of *Cambridge Economic History of Europe.* Cambridge, England.

Frankel, M. 1955. "Obsolescence and technological change in a maturing economy," *American Economic Review,* 45.3 (June): 296–319.

Habakkuk, H. J. (1962), "Fluctuations in house-building in Britain and the United States in the nineteenth century," *Journal of Economic History,* 22.2: 198–230.

Kendrick, J. W. 1973. *Postwar Productivity Trends in the United States, 1948–69* (National Bureau of Economic Research). New York.

Kindleberger, C. P. 1964. *Economic Growth in France and Britain, 1851–1950.* Cambridge, Mass.

Landes, D. S. 1969. *The Unbound Prometheus.* Cambridge, England. (Originally published in 1965 as "Technological change and development in Western Europe, 1750–1914," chap. 5, part 2, vol. 6 of *The Cambridge Economic History of Europe.*)

Levine, A. L. 1967. *Industrial Retardation in Britain, 1870–1914.* London.

McCloskey, D. N. 1973. *Economic Maturity and Entrepreneurial Decline: British Iron and Steel, 1870–1913.* Cambridge, Mass.

———, ed. 1971. *Essays on a Mature Economy.* London.

Mansfield, E. 1968. *The Economics of Technical Change.* New York.

Olson, M. 1978. "The political economy of comparative growth rates," in *U.S. Economic Growth from 1976 to 1986: Prospects, Problems and Patterns.* Washington, D.C.

Peck, M. J. 1968. "Science and technology," in R. E. Caves et al., *Britain's Economic Prospects.* Washington, D.C.

Rosenberg, N. 1976. "On technological expectations," Economic Journal. 86.343 (Sept.): 523–35.

Saul, S. B. 1962. "The motor industry in Britain to 1914," *Business History,* 5 (Dec.): 22–44.

——. 1967. "The market and the development of the mechanical engineering industries in Britain, 1860–1914," *Economic History Review*, 20.1 (April): 111–30.

Schlote, W. 1952. *British Overseas Trade from 1700 to the 1930's.* Westport, Conn.

Sheriff, T. D. 1979. "The slowdown of productivity growth," unpublished National Institute of Economic and Social Research Discussion Paper 30.

[2]

1 Structural Change and Leading Sectors in British Manufacturing, 1907–68

G. N. VON TUNZELMANN

59–107
[82]

/UK/ Ō14
L60
N63
N64

I believe we shall increasingly interpret a significant element in the interwar sluggishness of Western Europe as due to the process of disengagement from the old leading sectors of the pre-1914 and wartime years and to the rather slow preparation for the age of high mass-consumption which, in the 1950s, at last fully seized Western Europe, as the lessons of income analysis were learned and the old men of steel and electricity and heavy chemicals were superseded by the bright young men of automobiles and plastics, electronics, and aeronautics. (*The Stages of Economic Growth*)[1]

Professor Rostow's concept of 'leading sectors' has attracted most favourable notice in the case of the United Kingdom in applications to the classical Industrial Revolution period, that is, Rostow's 'take-off'. Nevertheless it is obvious from repeated utterances throughout his major works on economic growth (*The Stages of Economic Growth* and *The World Economy: History and Prospect* being the two most extensively considered here) that the concept is intended to apply at each stage of modern economic growth, and that technical change within industries and structural transformations among various industries constitute the essence of the 'analytical bone-structure'. It is, however, the case that his work fits readily (and often explicitly) into a substantial corpus of work by economic historians and economists both for Western Europe as a whole (pioneered by Schumpeter and Svennilson[2]) and for Britain in particular. On the

1

2   *Applications and Cases, Part II*

latter score, the rise of the so-called 'new industries' in the interwar years (especially) has been a popular theme since the time itself. Its popularity was accentuated in the 1960s through an extensive body of writings by H. W. Richardson and D. H. Aldcroft.[3]

As makes intuitive sense, the study of twentieth-century growth both by Rostow and by Richardson and Aldcroft comprehends demand as well as supply elements – in Rostow's case, suggested by the reference to the 'lessons of income analysis' in the opening quotation here and of course by the whole terminology of an 'age of high mass-consumption'. In my view the fusing of demand and supply sides by British writers, although carried out in the best interests of depicting economic growth and history 'in the round', has had the undesirable effect of confusing the nature of the argument(s); for example, in delineating the hypotheses to be tested and more simply in defining what exactly were the 'new industries'. In this critique I shall be concentrating on the supply side, trusting that the neglect of a richer dimension will be partially offset by a sharper focus on the particular aspects studied. However, problems of simultaneity remain, so that demand-side influences on the variables measured are included.

It has already been noted that at various points Professor Rostow alludes to both intra-sectoral technical change and inter-sectoral structural shifts. For their part, Aldcroft and Richardson originally stressed both the shifts in resource allocation towards new industries and what they considered to be a high rate of technical improvement within the new industries. Subsequent 'arithmetic' by J. A. Dowie (1968) severely mauled the latter of these hypotheses. In the wake of Dowie's article they wrote:

> Thus the improvement in the residual [i.e. total factor productivity] in the interwar years was in large part due to shifts in resource allocation within the industrial sector and a fairly rapid rate of technical improvement which affected both old and new industries alike. (Aldcroft and Richardson, 1969, p. 22).

Despite Dowie's attack on the notion of innovations clustering predominantly in the new industries and the apparent acceptance of the criticism by Aldcroft and Richardson themselves, a recent and fairly critical summary of the argument by B. W. E. Alford (1972, p. 14) concluded that the Aldcroft–Richardson view 'has almost developed into a new orthodoxy'.

Structural Change in British Manufacturing, 1907–68   3

The only formal attempt that I am aware of to break down the argument further in fact preceded Aldcroft and Richardson – Salter (1966) referred to 'shifts in resource allocation within the industrial sector' as the 'shift effect' and rates of technical improvement within all industries as the 'intensity effect', and those terms will be borrowed here. Especially as Salter's book, *Productivity and Technical Change*, is much better known for its contribution to the theory of the economics of technological change than to British economic history, it is worth considering Salter's findings in a little more detail. Salter began by pointing out (see especially his Appendix A3, pp. 184–5) that the appropriate way to divide movements in output per head into shift and internal components was multiplicatively, not additively. Let O_{it} equal output in the ith industry in year t, E_{it} likewise be employment and P_{it} ($= O_{it}/E_{it}$) output per head in that industry at year t. Then overall productivity change can be decomposed as:

$$\frac{\sum_i P_{it}}{\sum_i P_{i0}} = \underbrace{\frac{\sum_i P_{it} E_{it}}{\sum_i P_{it} E_{i0}} \cdot \frac{\sum_i E_{i0}}{\sum_i E_{it}}}_{\text{(a)}\qquad\text{(b)}} \cdot \underbrace{\frac{\sum_i P_{it} E_{i0}}{\sum_i P_{i0} E_{i0}}}_{\text{(c)}}$$

In this decomposition, (a) and (b) together measure the increase in output, subject to the restrictions that output per head in each industry does not change and that the total labour force stays constant – in other words, the 'shift' effect. Component (c) is a base-weighted index of output per head, subject to the restriction that employment in each industry does not change, that is, it measures the 'intensity' effect.

Two elaborative points are given special attention by Salter. The first is that output has to be valued at some set of prices that still need to be defined (the actual set chosen can be selected independently of the decomposition above) – if instead current prices are utilised in an inflationary world virtually everything is bound to accrue to the 'intensity' effect through the consequences of $M3$ (or whatever). Secondly, the overall productivity growth can equally well be decomposed using productivity rather than employment for the base weighting:

$$\frac{\sum\limits_i P_{it}}{\sum\limits_i P_{i0}} = \frac{\sum\limits_i P_{i0} E_{it}}{\sum\limits_i P_{i0} E_{i0}} \cdot \frac{\sum\limits_i E_{i0}}{\sum\limits_i E_{it}} \cdot \frac{\sum\limits_i P_{it} E_{it}}{\sum\limits_i P_{i0} E_{it}}$$

The first two components on the right-hand side are now a base-weighted 'shift' effect and the last one a current-weighted 'internal' effect.[4]

On the basis of his sample of industries (28 selected industries), Salter showed that decisions as to these weightings substantially affected the result. The results he published set year 0 at 1924 and year t at 1948 for employment weightings of 0 (that is 1924, corresponding to the first decomposition above), of t (that is 1948, corresponding to the second decomposition), and of an inter-mediate weighting (1935) they were as shown in Table 1.1. Thus using the first formulation of the problem, the shift and internal effects were about equal in their contribution to overall growth in labour productivity; using the second, the internal effect was over $2\frac{1}{2}$ times as powerful as the shift one.

Salter argued that there was little to choose between the weighting schemes; theoretically they were of equal merit. If one is going to argue a case against (or for) a certain cohort of entrepreneurs for their failure (or success) in shifting into new lines of activity it may seem fairest to them to judge them in terms of the

TABLE 1.1   *Salter's break-down between 'internal' and 'shift' effects*

Employment weights		1924	1948
1924	Internal	100	136
	Shift	100	133
	Total	100	181
1935	Internal	100	150
	Shift	100	121
	Total	100	181
1948	Internal	100	152
	Shift	100	119
	Total	100	181

SOURCE W.E.G. Salter, *Productivity and Technical Change*, 2nd edn (Cambridge University Press, 1966) pp. 150–1.

relative productivities of alternatives they were facing at the time, that is in terms of the second formulation. On the other hand, much of the new industry debate, for the late nineteenth century as much as for the twentieth, has been conducted as if entrepreneurs were blessed with perfect foresight about *future* relative productivities – in which case the former decomposition is appropriate.

It also needs mentioning that the analysis is conducted on *labour* productivities, whereas the Aldcroft–Richardson quote above clearly relates to total factor productivities. Dowie (1968) has comparisons of the two for the industrial divisions he employs. The data are at present hopelessly inadequate to pursue this point much farther in the present paper.

Rostow has always emphasised that leading sectors derive their significance from their backward, forward, and lateral linkages to the rest of the economy. Thus he has been concerned to draw out the repercussions of their growth on a wide range of supporting (and to a large extent, dependent) industries. Appendix C of *The World Economy*, for instance, is a rough computation of the size of the United States 'motor vehicle sectoral complex' for the early 1970s (Rostow, 1978, pp. 670–5). For Britain, and especially interwar Britain, authors like Richardson and Aldcroft have accepted that the new sectors in themselves were still a fairly small portion of total output, but their significance was magnified partly by their input–output links with so many other industries (for example, because some new industries were considered to be crucial capital-goods industries) and partly by their links with one another. Richardson emphasised the deadweight of overcommitment to nineteenth-century export staples (such as textiles, steel, coal, and shipbuilding) hindering the expansion of the economy in the early years of the present century. The very inter-relationship between the staples (coal being used in steel-making, steel in shipbuilding, and so forth) made recovery all the more difficult and helped obstruct new activities. A wholly new 'development block' (to use a phrase originally devised by E. Dahmén [1955], subsequently borrowed by Richardson), less dependent on those decaying staples and their problems of over-manning and obsolete plant and equipment was ideally required. Thus he was led to emphasise the interdependence of the new industries (for example, 'New industries tend to have closer input–output connections with each other than with other industries in the economy' (Richardson, 1967, p. 95 – see also Rostow (1978, p. 209)).

6   *Applications and Cases, Part II*

The final characteristic often asserted for new industries that will be examined in this paper is their greater impact on output than on employment. Again in referring to the interwar period, Rostow (1978, pp. 208–9) states that,

> The three great new leading-sector complexes which had emerged before the First World War continued to move forward in the erratic, distorted environment of the interwar years: the internal combustion engine, electricity, and chemicals. They supplied elements of growth and development to the most advanced part of the world economy; but, except in the United States of the 1920s, they could not by themselves bring about an environment of relatively full employment in any of the major economies.

However a few pages later he qualifies the assumptions on which these statements partially rest, in noting that,

> Although electricity production itself is (like oil refining) a highly capital-intensive industry, the whole sectoral complex, including the building of power stations and lines, generators, radios, vacuum cleaners, refrigerators, irons, and other electric-powered household gadgetry of high mass-consumption, created substantial increases in employment. (ibid., p. 214)

This qualification foreshadows my own discussion of the point below. The main thrust of the argument is preserved in the view of Richardson and Aldcroft for the UK that, whilst the new industries could take much of the credit for a satisfactory growth of manufacturing output, they did less to assist by way of expanding employment opportunities, since their technology was highly labour-saving. Hence, in part, the coexistence of high unemployment and the upsurge of these new industries in the 1930s.

I

The information necessary for a more extended test of the sources of productivity change in industry has come from re-processing the major Censuses of Production from 1907 to 1968. The ultimate objective is to obtain estimates of net output, employment, and labour productivity, all broken down by standard region at as disaggregated a level of industry as possible. At the time of writing, the data are ready on an industrial base back to 1907 and on a regional plus industrial base from 1948 to 1968. Since 1970 the collection of industrial statistics has been restructured and it will not be possible to link my regional results with those published for the 1970s.

The problem all researchers have encountered in using the Censuses of Production is that the classification of regions changes frequently (on every occasion studied here up to 1948, then again between 1958 and 1963), while the industrial classification is always changing. The former problem does not greatly affect us in this paper (except for the Northern/Southern Ireland difficulty for 1907), but the latter is a considerable obstacle. The Business Statistics Office's recent *Historical Record of the Census of Production 1907 to 1970* (1978, p. x) reckons that the scope of only about twenty industries out of the 150-odd it examines remained 'virtually unchanged'.

More usually the definition of an industry changed, and the difference compared with 1968 tended to be greater the earlier the census was held. Some industries increased in importance over the years, in some cases starting as specialist sub-divisions within industries in earlier censuses and later appearing as separately distinguished industries for which a full range of industrial statistical data was published, such as Soft drinks, Printing ink, Aluminium and aluminium alloys, and Refrigeration machinery industries. Conversely, some industries important in the earlier censuses declined in importance and were relegated to sub-industry status such as Wallpaper, Matches, and Pens, pencils and artist's materials industries. Many activities, once regarded as being within the scope of the census of production, were subsequently transferred to the distribution or service sectors, and there are also instances of the reverse happening (ibid.).

On the (periodically-revised) Standard Industrial Classification (SIC) industry is classified first by order (loosely speaking, the two-digit level), and beyond that by Minimum List Heading (MLH; the three-digit level). Sub-industries frequently were moved from order to order or MLH to MLH (for example ice cream began in the bread and biscuit industry before being transferred to milk and milk

8   *Applications and Cases, Part II*

products). Not the least contribution of the *Historical Record* (ibid.,
pp. 80–102) are general footnotes covering twenty-three large and
closely-written pages describing changes that have occurred among
and within industrial classifications. The compilers (H. Gracie and
I. Duncan) have made extensive efforts to realign categories in
order to preserve some sort of continuity – and their account of their
procedures makes clear that this can only be achieved by considerable guesswork. Even so, the extensive footnoting just mentioned largely comprises classificatory changes that the compilers
were *not* able to take into account.

My own compilations began before (and were ignorant of) the
appearance of the *Historical Record*, but do not simply duplicate it, as
the classificatory connections through time are made in a quite
different way. The original census forms are not available for public
inspection and unlikely ever to be so unless the law is changed. My
procedure began with the observation that in every major census of
production there are figures, broken down by region, etc., – not only
for the year in question but for the preceding major census. Since in
nearly every case (1958–64 is the main exception) these figures in the
later census differ substantially from those in the earlier one, my
assumption is that they represent a reclassification of the earlier
year's data to the later year's system. Roughly speaking, on this
basis it was possible to extrapolate backwards from 1968 to each
preceding census in turn. As the quotation given above from the
Historical Record would imply, the probability is that the divergence
between my extrapolations and actuality would be greatest for
1907, and this must be borne in mind in what follows. However in
the overwhelming majority of cases the results produced by this
procedure look sensible. To take an extreme example, figures for
employment in the milk and milk products industry (MLH 215)
obtained by my procedure can be compared with those published in
the *Historical Record* as in Table 1.2.

TABLE 1.2   *Employment in milk and milk products, 1930–68, in thousands*

	1930	1935	1948	1951	1954	1958	1963	1968
Historical record	9.6	20.6	52.8	63.5	23.6	30.2	27.1	70.6
Present figures	26.5	40.5	52.8	63.5	64.1	82.1	73.7	70.6

SOURCES: Business Statistics Office, *Historical Record of the Census of Production 1907 to 1970*
(London: HMSO, 1978) p. 5; own calculations.

Structural Change in British Manufacturing, 1907–68 9

The major disparities in this example arise from the presence or absence of the heat treatment of milk; in most industries the differences are minor.

My data have been prepared only for manufacturing industry so far. This limitation makes the tests of the role of leading sectors, for example, particularly inadequate, with electricity supply being overlooked. The *quid pro quo* of declining sectors like coal mining is also misrepresented. Whether the results for manufacturing alone can be extended to non-manufacturing industry remains to be seen. The level of disaggregation achieved depended on the information available: I took as my guide the derivation of reasonable *regional* data for the postwar (that is 1948–68) period. The 1968 SIC system of 17 industrial 'orders' was preserved throughout, but at the more disaggregated MLH level it would not have been possible to sustain the 1968 format without wild extrapolation. Sub-aggregations therefore had to be undertaken, resulting in a classification more like the 1958 SIC pattern (furthermore, the level of breakdown required of the 1968 system, for example in electronics, was of little relevance for earlier years in many of the cases). I ended up with 103 industries for the years 1948–68; shrinking slightly to 100 for the interwar period and 96 for 1907. The least satisfactory aspect was that in the engineering industries particularly, large residual categories like 'general mechanical engineering' remained. Over shorter periods of time than 1907–68 it would, of course, be possible to do something about this shortcoming.

The final data problem turns out to be more serious, and the solutions offered so far much rougher. This concerns price deflators. As Salter pointed out, price comparisons are the very essence of productivity assessments through time. Other things being equal (that is the demand side and the general price level), technological change will lower costs and prices and hence be understated by the changes of net output relative to employment actually observed. Unlike Salter, I have made no attempt in this paper to redress the balance for individual industries. Any conclusions about relative rates of technical change, etc., therefore must be taken with a grain of salt. For the 'shift' versus 'internal' effect comparisons, I have simply deflated by a general price index. A windfall gain of relative price for one particular industry (occurring, it can be supposed, for demand-side reasons) is here treated as part of the productivity gain of that industry. Since newer industries are the most likely beneficiaries of such windfalls, their contribution is to that degree overstated.

It quickly became apparent that it was insufficient to plug in any readily-available price index for output – weird results emerged for the Korean War period, etc. Instead separate deflators had to be developed for inputs and outputs. For 'gross output', that is including intermediate payments, I used the Board of Trade index for wholesale prices for output of manufactured products for the postwar period, adjusted for prices in the food-processing industries before 1954 (the *Historical Record* 1978, Appendix II, Table (i)) advises using this index; the data are more accurately specified in Mitchell and Jones (1971, pp. 188–9). The link back from 1948 to 1935 was made using an implicit deflator derived from the work of Brown (1954) in comparing the results of the censuses of those two years. For the interwar period I have compared changes in gross output with changes in the volume of production (available for each industry and sub-industry in the 1935 Census), and aggregated. For 1907 the deflator for GDP developed by Feinstein (1972), adjusted for Northern/Southern Ireland, etc., was used. For intermediate inputs I developed separate series for food, fuel, textiles, and machinery, etc. (accorded weights of 15, 10, 20, and 55 respectively). The Board of Trade indices of industrial materials prices (Mitchell and Deane, 1971, pp. 476–7, and Mitchell and Jones, 1971, pp. 188–9) and the censuses of production themselves were again the chief sources. The price index for net output then emerged implicitly from the separate deflations for gross output and for purchased inputs.[5]

Perverse results still occurred. For the period 1924–30, gross output prices fell, but input prices fell much faster (especially of course in 1929–30; see Rostow (1978, p. 206)), with the result that the implicit price index for net output rose markedly between 1924 and 1930. The outcome is a sharp decline in aggregate productivity between 1924 and 1930 (see the second column of Table 1.3), and in general the ensuing calculations that rely on 1930 net output prices in some way are not to be taken too seriously. In similar vein, though less dramatically, the years of the early 1950s, in the aftermath of the Korean War boom, still behave chaotically.

With these reservations in mind, we may turn first to Table 1.3. The change in aggregate productivity in the second column is divided into 'shift' and 'internal' components using either base-weighted employment (that is, the first formulation above – perfect foresight of future relative productivities) in the third and fourth columns, or base-weighted productivity (that is, the second

Structural Change in British Manufacturing, 1907–68   11

TABLE 1.3   *Productivity change broken down by 'shift' and 'internal' components, between censal years, 1907/68 (MLH level of disaggregation)*

	Percentage change in aggregate employment	Percentage change in aggregate productivity	'Shift' component base-weight employment	'Internal' component base-weight employment	'Shift' component base-weight productivity	'Internal' component base-weight productivity
1907/24	9.8	18.5	3.7	14.5	2.4	15.9
1907/30	10.2	0	2.8	−2.4	2.7	−2.3
1907/35	12.8	40.0	6.6	32.0	3.6	35.8
1907/48	40.3	36.6	4.9	30.2	7.8	26.7
1907/51	50.7	84.6	7.4	72.4	7.2	72.7
1907/54	55.2	108.8	10.9	89.0	6.3	97.0
1907/58	57.3	97.3	15.0	72.3	8.3	82.9
1907/63	60.2	127.6	17.6	94.2	10.2	107.2
1907/68	57.7	182.5	16.6	143.1	9.7	158.3
1924/30	0.4	−14.5	2.7	−16.5	1.3	−15.4
1924/35	2.8	18.4	2.9	15.3	2.8	15.5
1024/48	27.8	16.2	2.8	13.1	5.5	10.2
1924/51	37.3	55.0	4.0	49.2	5.4	47.3
1924/54	41.4	75.2	6.4	65.0	5.7	66.0
1924/58	43.3	67.3	10.1	52.2	8.1	55.0
1924/63	46.0	92.9	12.0	72.4	9.7	76.0
1924/68	43.6	139.0	11.6	114.4	9.2	119.0
1930/35	2.4	30.4	1.0	29.2	0.6	29.7
1930/48	27.3	32.9	2.3	29.9	5.8	19.3
1930/51	36.8	65.2	3.6	59.2	5.5	56.3
1930/54	40.8	85.9	5.3	76.3	6.3	74.6
1930/58	42.8	86.4	8.6	71.7	9.4	70.4
1930/63	45.4	115.0	10.2	94.8	11.4	92.7
1930/68	43.1	164.0	10.0	139.7	11.1	137.3
1935/48	24.3	1.0	1.7	−0.7	5.3	−4.1
1935/51	33.6	27.7	2.5	24.3	5.0	21.4
1935/54	37.5	43.8	4.1	37.9	5.4	36.2
1935/58	39.4	42.7	7.2	32.9	8.4	31.4
1935/63	42.0	64.4	8.9	50.7	10.4	48.8
1935/68	39.7	102.4	8.6	86.0	9.8	83.9
1948/51	7.5	27.3	0	27.5	−0.3	27.8
1948/54	10.6	44.0	0.5	43.5	−1.8	46.8
1948/58	12.2	41.5	2.3	38.4	0.8	40.6
1948/63	14.2	63.0	4.2	56.6	1.9	60.2
1948/68	12.4	100.8	4.2	92.9	1.4	98.1
1951/54	3.0	14.0	0.4	13.6	−0.2	14.3
1951/58	4.4	2.8	2.5	0.4	1.1	1.7
1951/63	6.3	18.7	4.2	13.9	2.4	16.0
1951/68	4.6	48.5	4.1	42.7	2.0	45.5

Continued overleaf

TABLE 1.3 *Continued*

	Percentage change in aggregate employment	Percentage change in aggregate productivity	'Shift' component base-weight employment	'Internal' component base-weight employment	'Shift' component base-weight productivity	'Internal' component base-weight productivity
1954/58	1.4	−8.5	2.1	−10.4	1.8	−10.2
1954/63	3.2	5.6	3.9	1.6	3.4	2.1
1954/68	1.6	31.7	3.7	26.9	3.2	27.6
1958/63	1.8	15.3	1.9	13.1	0.9	14.3
1958/68	0.2	42.6	1.8	40.1	1.8	40.1
1963/68	−1.6	23.3	0.1	23.2	0.1	23.2

NOTE   For sources and methods, see text.

formulation) in the fifth and sixth columns. It will be recalled that these two pairs of columns should multiply out to give the second column, aggregate productivity change (in fact there are slight discrepancies in some cases, arising out of rounding of the original data).

The first observation to be made is that by and large it makes little difference whether employment or productivity is base-weighted, in sharp contrast to the conflicting results Salter obtained, as quoted above. It is, however, true that pairs of years involving 1948 (Salter's terminal year) do provide some of the biggest disparities in the Table – for his own pair (1924/48) the shift effect is twice as large using the 1948 weight for employment as using the 1924 weight (oddly enough this is the reverse of his conclusion). Part of the reason for the difference in our findings may be Salter's sample, which as he admits is biased towards industries with high output and employment variances. However the main reason is probably the difference in our procedures for deflation, as discussed above, although for 1935/48 both Salter and I use Brown.

There is some support in the Table for the long-swing pattern enunciated by Rostow (1978 – Rostow's terminal dates are 1920, 1936, 1951, and 1972), though it will be remembered that the figures in the second column are a guide to technical change only with severe reservations.

The more significant result is the eclipse of the shift component by the internal component in accounting for such productivity growth as here measured; particularly in the long term. Whereas Salter's results quoted earlier gave the shift component up to equal importance, here it is outgunned by five to ten and sometimes twenty to one in the longer run. It is, however, always positive, that is the changes were always beneficial to productivity in aggregate, which is more than can be said for some shorter periods of the internal effect. In other words, in those pairs of years it is preventing aggregate productivity from sagging as much as it might otherwise have done.

What can account for this finding? It may be thought that the shift component is being understated through simultaneity, for example as labour shifts (relatively) into higher-productivity industries, that every process will reduce the productivity advantage of the more productive sectors. A moment's further thought, however, will suggest that such an event is likely to expand still further the 'internal' effect, and indeed in a rough calculation partially allowing for diminishing returns below, I show that the outcomes are persistently a further diminution of the 'shift' effect.

It is supposed in the calculation that the kinds of labour released from relatively declining sectors will be as productive as their counterparts in advancing sectors when they move to join them there. There are obvious reasons for doubting this assumption. Take the case of female versus male workers – employers may be supposed, on the basis of the well-known perpetuation of wage differentials, to perceive real or imaginary differences in capabilities between female and male labour. A rough calculation using Census of Population (occupational) data for the postwar period showed a relatively larger decline in female employment in old industries than their absorption into new industries. This, however, was entirely the result of the textiles and clothing industries. If they are omitted from the calculation, the requirements for males (proportionately speaking) in new industries are more than met. Obviously it is extreme ad-hockery to omit textiles and clothing in this way; a justification could be that many of the remaining old industries (like iron and steel, coke ovens, some machinery manufacture, railway vehicles, shipbuilding, timber; but unlike textiles and clothing) could be regarded as inculcating skills and attributes of considerable use for subsequently redeployed labour. Clearly this matter needs much further consideration than it is given here.

Such understanding as can be advanced here is obtained by breaking the shift and internal components for all industries as in

TABLE 1.4   Contribution of each industry to 'shift' effect, between censal years (MLH level of disaggregation)

Industry	Order	1907/24	1907/30	1907/35	1907/48	1907/51	1907/54	1907/58	1907/63	1907/68
Food, drink, tobacco	III	−.0077	−.0060	−.0109	−.0093	−.0098	−.0128	−.0121	−.0108	−.0149
Coal and petroleum products	IV	.0062	−.0010	−.0006	.0005	.0005	.0027	.0024	.0025	.0024
Chemicals and allied	V	.0047	.0047	.0088	.0091	.0124	.0133	.0166	.0205	.0204
Metal manufacture	VI	.0011	.0016	.0011	.0021	.0033	.0013	.0017	.0015	.0022
Mechanical engineering	VII	.0005	.0026	.0019	.0001	.0014	.0051	.0052	.0005	.0028
Instrument engineering	VIII	−.0003	−.0000	−.0005	−.0011	−.0013	−.0007	−.0005	−.0018	−.0018
Electrical engineering	IX	.0004	.0025	.0008	−.0057	−.0061	−.0045	−.0042	−.0091	−.0068
Shipbuilding	X	.0027	.0010	.0046	.0016	.0048	.0045	.0050	.0089	.0067
Vehicles	XI	.0009	.0033	.0036	−.0013	.0036	.0103	.0103	.150	.0131
Other metal goods	XII	.0003	−.0005	−.0013	−.0024	−.0025	−.0025	−.0026	−.0054	−.0005
Textiles	XIII	.0092	.0275	.0305	.0220	.0182	.0456	.0685	.0750	.0593
Leather and fur	XIV	.0004	.0003	.0004	−.0002	.0006	.0008	.0014	.0013	.0014
Clothing and footwear	XV	.0134	.0118	.0176	.0244	.0320	.0356	.0419	.0478	.0510
Building materials etc.	XVI	.0011	.0012	.0006	.0002	.0006	.0005	.0026	.0032	.0045
Timber and furniture	XVII	.0004	−.0006	−.0014	−.0000	.0007	.0011	.0016	.0014	.0012
Paper and printing	XVIII	.0026	.0053	.0053	.0026	.0054	.0044	.0043	.0040	.0035
Other manufacturing	XIX	−.0001	.0022	.0013	.0013	.0027	.0018	.0009	.0020	.0021
Total		.0358	.0559	.0619	.0439	.0665	.1066	.1430	.1594	.1387

Structural Change in British Manufacturing, 1907–68 15

TABLE 1.4 *Continued*

Industry	Order	1924/30	1924/35	1924/48	1924/51	1924/54	1924/58	1924/63	1924/68	1930/35
Food, drink, tobacco	III	.0062	–.0001	–.0034	–.0063	–.0089	–.0067	–.0071	–.0098	–.0015
Coal and Petroleum products	IV	–.0002	–.0005	.0001	–.0004	.0023	.0015	.0023	.0024	–.0003
Chemicals and allied	V	.0002	.0027	.0058	.0087	.0096	.0127	.0162	.0160	.0019
Metal manufacture	VI	.0005	–.0006	.0014	.0018	.0001	.0007	.0007	.0011	.0000
Mechanical engineering	VII	.0010	.0014	.0001	.0011	.0040	.0038	.0007	.0023	.0005
Instrument engineering	VIII	–.0000	–.0002	–.0009	–.0010	–.0006	–.0005	–.0015	–.0016	–.0001
Electrical engineering	IX	.0005	.0002	–.0039	–.0043	–.0033	–.0035	–.0069	–.0054	.0002
Shipbuilding	X	.0024	–.0015	–.0000	.0020	.0019	.0023	.0053	.0064	.0021
Vehicles	XI	.0011	.0018	–.0006	.0023	.0065	.0068	.0106	.0117	.0010
Other metal goods	XII	–.0012	–.0012	–.0021	–.0017	–.0019	–.0019	–.0023	–.0041	–.0007
Textiles	XIII	.0161	.0184	.0147	.0121	.0315	.0519	.0571	.0540	.0023
Leather and fur	XIV	.0000	–.0000	–.0003	.0004	.0007	.0013	.0011	.0013	–.0001
Clothing and footwear	XV	–.0012	.0053	.0133	.0176	.0198	.0249	.0291	.0326	.0061
Building materials etc.	XVI	.0005	.0002	.0003	.0007	.0008	.0024	.0028	.0036	–.0001
Timber and furniture	XVII	–.0011	–.0019	–.0005	–.0001	.0001	.0008	.0008	.0008	–.0005
Paper and printing	XVIII	.0029	.0031	.0015	.0034	.0029	.0031	.0029	.0025	.0007
Other manufacturing	XIX	.0005	.0006	.0003	.0019	.0017	.0014	.0018	.0016	.0005
Total		.0286	.0275	.0257	.0380	.0673	.1010	.1134	.1153	.0121

Continued overleaf

TABLE 1.4 *Continued*

Industry	Order	1930/48	1930/51	1930/54	1930/58	1930/63	1930/68	1935/48	1935/51	1935/54
Food, drink, tobacco	III	−.0029	−.0050	−.0076	−.0053	−.0061	−.0086	−.0000	−.0016	−.0044
Coal and petroleum products	IV	.0002	−.0005	.0025	.0016	.0022	.0028	.0003	−.0007	.0027
Chemicals and allied	V	.0052	.0083	.0090	.0124	.0157	.0157	.0043	.0071	.0076
Metal manufacture	VI	.0018	.0032	.0022	.0028	.0014	.0014	.0017	.0033	.0028
Mechanical engineering	VII	−.0003	.0006	.0034	.0033	.0005	.0021	−.0005	.0003	.0029
Instrument engineering	VIII	−.0008	−.0009	−.0005	−.0004	−.0013	−.0015	−.0006	−.0007	−.0005
Electrical engineering	IX	−.0030	−.0037	−.0029	−.0033	−.0059	−.0048	−.0027	−.0027	−.0023
Shipbuilding	X	−.0005	.0012	.0012	.0015	.0043	.0053	−.0024	−.0020	−.0018
Vehicles	XI	−.0007	.0017	.0053	.0056	.0089	.0104	−.0012	.0006	.0036
Other metal goods	XII	−.0016	−.0012	−.0014	−.0014	−.0018	−.0033	−.0012	−.0000	−.0008
Textiles	XIII	.0090	.0065	.0180	.0339	.0377	.0372	.0075	.0059	.0158
Leather and fur	XIV	−.0003	.0003	.0006	.0012	.0010	.0011	−.0002	.0005	.0007
Clothing and footwear	XV	.0144	.0187	.0209	.0259	.0301	.0336	.0089	.0116	.0132
Buidling materials etc.	XVI	.0008	.0012	.0014	.0028	.0028	.0033	.0012	.0017	.0017
Timber and furniture	XVII	.0005	.0013	.0016	.0023	.0023	.0014	.0008	.0018	.0021
Paper and printing	XVIII	.0002	.0015	.0022	.0024	.0022	.0020	−.0007	−.0003	.0013
Other manufacturing	XIX	.0001	.0019	.0018	.0017	.0020	.0017	.0001	.0011	.0009
Total		.0219	.0353	.0575	.0868	.959	.0999	.0152	.0257	.0457

Structural Change in British Manufacturing, 1907–68   17

TABLE 1.4 Continued

Industry	Order	1935/58	1935/63	1935/68	1948/51	1948/54	1948/58	1948/63	1948/68	1951/54
Food, drink, tobacco	III	-.0021	-.0026	-.0045	-.0021	-.0035	-.0018	-.0022	-.0042	-.0014
Coal and petroleum products	IV	.0016	.0023	.0033	-.0004	.0018	.0012	.0016	.0020	.0010
Chemicals and allied	V	.0111	.0142	.0144	.0003	-.0005	.0024	.0042	.0039	-.0008
Metal manufacture	VI	.0034	.0017	.0017	-.0007	-.0007	.0002	.0001	.0005	-.0001
Mechanical engineering	VII	.0027	.0004	.0020	.001	.0007	.0014	.0004	.0012	.0004
Instrument engineering	VIII	-.0004	-.0012	-.0014	-.0001	-.0001	-.0001	-.0005	-.0007	-.0001
Electrical engineering	IX	-.0027	-.0050	-.0041	-.0007	-.0008	-.0017	-.0031	-.0027	-.0004
Shipbuilding	X	-.0015	.0005	.0010	.0019	.0018	.0021	.0050	.0060	.0001
Vehicles	XI	.0039	.0068	.0085	.0007	.0018	.0025	.0062	.0077	.0008
Other metal goods	XII	-.0009	-.0012	-.0025	.0001	.0002	.0001	.0002	-.0002	-.0002
Textiles	XIII	.0310	.0347	.0347	-.0005	.0011	.0088	.0138	.0156	.0021
Leather and fur	XIV	.0013	.0011	.0013	-.0000	.0001	.0005	.0004	.0005	.0000
Clothing and footwear	XV	.0177	.0213	.0248	-.0009	.0002	.0033	.0060	.0091	.0012
Building materials etc.	XVI	.0031	.0030	.0035	.0003	.0005	.0011	.0014	.0016	.0002
Timber and furniture	XVII	.0028	.0028	.0016	.0003	.0007	.0011	.0014	.0008	.0003
Paper and printing	XVIII	.0017	.0017	.0016	.0008	.0010	.0014	.0013	.0013	.0007
Other manufacturing	XIX	.0006	.0008	.0007	.0005	.0006	.0003	.0002	-.0000	.0001
Total		.0734	.0805	.0855	.0000	.0049	.0231	.0362	.0423	.0041

Continued overleaf

TABLE 1.4 *Continued*

Industry	Order	1951/58	1951/63	1951/68	1954/58	1954/63	1954/68	1958/63	1958/68	1963/68
Food, drink, tobacco	III	.0005	.0003	−.0012	.0025	.0020	.0008	−.0001	−.0011	−.0008
Coal and petroleum products	IV	.0010	.0011	.0010	.0005	.0003	−.0003	−.0003	−.0013	−.0010
Chemicals and allied	V	.0024	.0040	.0035	.0031	.0048	.0046	.0010	.0006	−.0010
Metal manufacture	VI	.0008	.0003	.0004	.0008	.0002	.0003	−.0001	.0000	−.0001
Mechanical engineering	VII	.0011	.0004	.0012	.0006	.0004	.0010	.0002	.0007	.0003
Instrument engineering	VIII	−.0000	−.0004	−.0007	−.0000	−.0003	−.0006	−.0002	−.0006	−.0004
Electrical engineering	IX	−.0011	−.0025	−.0022	−.0006	−.0021	−.0019	−.0012	−.0012	−.0001
Shipbuilding	X	.0004	.0028	.0035	.0003	.0027	.0034	.0023	.0030	.0004
Vehicles	XI	.0015	.0049	.0065	.0008	.0052	.0057	.0044	.0047	.0016
Other metal goods	XII	−.0003	−.0003	−.0007	.0000	−.0003	−.0006	−.0004	−.0005	−.0001
Textiles	XIII	.0103	.0150	.0164	.0070	.0124	.0144	.0055	.0084	.0038
Leather and fur	XIV	.0004	.0004	.0004	.0003	.0003	.0004	.0000	.0000	.0000
Clothing and footwear	XV	.0043	.0071	.0100	.0031	.0057	.0087	.0024	.0052	.0027
Building materials etc.	XVI	.0009	.0013	.0016	.0008	.0010	.0013	.0004	.0007	.0003
Timber and furniture	XVII	.0009	.0010	.0008	.0006	.0007	.0005	.0001	.0001	.0001
Paper and printing	XVIII	.0012	.0012	.0012	.0006	.0006	.0006	−.0000	.0001	.0001
Other manufacturing	XIX	.0000	−.0003	−.0005	−.0000	−.0004	−.0006	−.0005	−.0007	−.0004
Total		.0243	.0363	.0412	.0205	.0332	.0377	.0136	.0183	.0061

Table 1.3 down into contributions from individual industries, as in Table 1.4 and 1.5. Since there is little difference in general between the results of different weighting patterns, I have worked henceforth on the basis of base-weighting employment. Unfortunately the measures for the shift effect used for Table 1.3 do not disaggregate in a way that is both simple and meaningful. Statistically speaking, the reason is the presence of the term $\Sigma E_{it}/\Sigma E_{i0}$ in the relevant equations; all industries are having their labour force deflated by this factor, irrespective of their own performance with regard to employment. Thus if an industry's level of productivity is below average (in year t in the first formulation; year o in the second) it will tend to add a negative contribution to the overall total, whether it gained or released labour on balance. It seemed more appropriate to devise a measure of industrial contribution which resulted in a positive contribution towards 'shift' if *either* an industry with productivity above average gained labour *or* an industry with productivity below average released labour (the gains and losses being defined relative to the national change, $\Sigma E_{it}/\Sigma E_{i0}$). Conversely if an industry with productivity above average released labour or one with below-average productivity gained it, the contribution would be negative. Several possibilities for such a measure commend themselves; the one adopted here consisted of computing the expression $(P_{it}-\bar{P}_t)\ (E_{it}-E_{i0}.\ \overline{\Delta E})$, where the terms are as before and $\overline{\Delta E}$ is shorthand for the aforementioned national change in employment $(=\Sigma E_{it}/\Sigma E_{i0})$.

The trouble with this measure, and of others I tried, is that it fails to aggregate simply to the national 'shift' component. The shift factor that emerges from this expression is highly dependent on the level of disaggregation maintained. Suppose one takes an industry like vehicles which has large sub-industries (like motor vehicles and aerospace) with high productivity and growing fast, and equally large sub-industries (like railway carriages and locomotives) of low productivity growing slowly or declining. Calculated at the two-digit level, the expression just discussed will yield a small contribution, positive or negative; however at the three-digit level its contribution will be large and positive. The figures in Table 1.4 are all calculated at the three-digit level (the MLH level) then re-aggregated at the end to the two-digit level. There is no straight-forward way of undertaking still further disaggregation to see the consequences, but in the reverse direction it is possible to recalculate the Table directly at the two-digit level. As the example just given implies, the contribution of vehicles then drops sharply away, as do those, to a lesser extent, of coal and petroleum products and of textiles. Most industries, as one would expect, show a mild decline in contribution for most pairs of years. The industry that really loses from being exhibited, as here, on the basis of MLH-disaggregation is food, drink, and tobacco, which at the direct two-digit level shows mainly (small) positive contributions rather than largish negative ones. This results from declining employment in one or two of its particularly high-productivity sub-sectors (brewing and malting in the earlier years, later grain milling).

With that rather quirky exception, the picture is dominated by the positive contributions of two industries normally thought of as 'new' – chemicals and vehicles – and even more two 'old' industries –textiles and clothing. However some new industries (instrument engineering and electrical engineering) yield generally negative contributions, lowering the overall contribution of new industries and giving rise to the possibility that, say, the positive contribution of vehicles may come from its declining as well as its expanding sub-branches. A different classification is required to shed more light on the new industry debate, and this will be done after considering Table 1.5.

Industry-by-industry disaggregation of the 'internal' effect suffers from none of the statistical ambiguities of that for the shift. The contribution of industry i is given as $E_{io}(P_{it}-P_{io}.\overline{\Delta r})$, with $\overline{\Delta r}$ here the implicit price deflator for net output discussed above. This aggregates perfectly simply to the national total for the 'internal' effect as given in Table 1.3. The general pattern in Table 1.5 is not vastly dissimilar to that in Table 1.4, with powerful contributions from chemicals, textiles and clothing. Food, drink and tobacco joins them in importance, while vehicles slip back a little; but by and large the contributions are much more evenly shared around than is the case with the shift effect.

The tables give the lie to the traditional 'over-commitment' view of a deadweight of manpower in the decaying export staples. If anything, their shedding of labour accounted for more of the rise in productivity for the country as a whole than did the rising share of labour in the fast-growing industries (remember that all figures in both Tables 1.4 and 1.5 are a compound of productivity and employment factors). However to trace this in more detail a sharper set of distinctions between old and new is called for.

We come back to Rostow. As the quotation at the beginning of

Structural Change in British Manufacturing, 1907–68   21

TABLE 1.5   Contribution of each industry to 'internal' effect, between censal years

Industry	Order	1907/24	1907/30	1907/35	1907/48	1907/51	1907/54	1907/58	1907/63	1907/68
Food, drink, tobacco	III	.0410	.0168	.0875	.0166	.0534	.0882	.0832	.1110	.1761
Coal and petroleum products	IV	−.0021	−.0009	.0014	−.0040	−.0038	.0051	.0021	.0034	.0121
Chemicals and allied	V	.0052	.0010	.0227	.0049	.0275	.0470	.0445	.0601	.0878
Metal manufacture	VI	−.0033	−.0179	.0191	.0170	.0645	.0873	.0786	.0796	.1039
Mechanical engineering	VII	−.0049	−.0134	.0094	.0071	.0367	.0577	.0464	.0630	.0995
Instrument engineering	VIII	.0003	−.0001	.0011	.0006	.0024	.0045	.0039	.0048	.0069
Electrical engineering	IX	.0020	.0007	.0052	.0027	.0086	.0120	.0113	.0137	.0211
Shipbuilding	X	−.0038	−.0036	.0122	.0112	.0275	.0413	.0359	.0447	.0657
Vehicles	XI	−.0028	−.0015	.0091	.0053	.0166	.0253	.0195	.0248	.0311
Other metal goods	XII	−.0028	−.0111	.0078	.0128	.0416	.0497	.0424	.0512	.0806
Textiles	XIII	−.0344	−.0106	.0166	.0979	.2114	.1853	.1133	.1685	.2835
Leather and fur	XIV	.0028	−.0005	.0033	.0079	.0076	.0085	.0063	.0099	.0148
Clothing and footwear	XV	.0259	.0088	.0505	.0598	.0850	.1033	.0866	.0169	.1520
Building materials etc.	XVI	.0120	.0034	.0214	.0179	.0363	.0471	.0390	.0526	.0715
Timber and furniture	XVII	.0082	−.0007	.0124	.0144	.0268	.0355	.0316	.0434	.0694
Paper and printing	XVIII	.0240	.0086	.0342	.0245	.0686	.0717	.0607	.0800	.1158
Other manufacturing	XIX	.0028	−.0026	.0058	.0054	.0138	.0200	.0177	.0243	.0388
Total		.1445	−.0237	.3197	.3022	.7245	.8896	.7230	.9418	1.4309

Continued overleaf

TABLE 1.5 *Continued*

Industry	Order	1924/30	1924/35	1924/48	1924/51	1924/54	1924/58	1924/63	1924/68	1930/35
Food, drink, tobacco	III	−.0205	.0354	−.0177	.0140	.0435	.0398	.0668	.1201	.0521
Coal and petroleum products	IV	−.0003	.0025	−.0014	−.0002	.0066	.0050	.0053	.0128	.0022
Chemicals and allied	V	−.0048	.0172	−.0008	.0198	.0377	.0357	.0507	.0776	.0216
Metal manufacture	VI	−.0117	.0201	.0178	.0581	.0769	.0705	.0714	.0929	.0287
Mechanical engineering	VII	−.0085	.0142	.0118	.0392	.0598	.0510	.0649	.1005	.0189
Instrument engineering	VIII	−.0003	.0011	.0003	.0025	.0052	.0047	.0056	.0085	.0012
Electrical engineering	IX	−.0025	.0066	.0015	.0135	.0210	.0198	.0246	.0403	.0097
Shipbuilding	X	.0007	.0107	.0104	.0205	.0296	.0267	.0325	.0463	.0079
Vehicles	XI	−.0060	.0108	.0048	.0258	.0422	.0347	.0476	.0595	.0165
Other metal goods	XII	−.0069	.0089	.0131	.0361	.0430	.0376	.0457	.0688	.0155
Textiles	XIII	−.0615	−.0146	.0486	.1358	.1213	.0662	.1157	.2072	.0363
Leather and fur	XIV	−.0029	.0005	.0041	.0040	.0048	.0029	.0063	.0105	.0030
Clothing and footwear	XV	−.0108	.0161	.0243	.0397	.0522	.0420	.0564	.0867	.0255
Building materials etc.	XVI	−.0072	.0074	.0043	.0189	.0276	.0220	.0339	.0506	.0149
Timber and furniture	XVII	−.0062	.0031	.0050	.0136	.0201	.0174	.0260	.0455	.0101
Paper and printing	XVIII	−.0127	.0090	.0003	.0381	.0403	.0314	.0484	.0791	.0208
Other manufacturing	XIX	−.0032	.0042	.0045	.0126	.0178	.0147	.0224	.0371	.0064
Total		−.1653	.1531	.1308	.4917	.6497	.5221	.7243	1.1440	.2914

Structural Change in British Manufacturing, 1907–68 23

TABLE 1.5 *Continued*

Industry	Order	1930/48	1930/51	1930/54	1930/58	1930/63	1930/68	1935/48	1935/51	1935/54
Food, drink, tobacco	III	−.0024	.0213	.0519	.0590	.0907	.1492	−.0433	−.0225	.0021
Coal and petroleum products	IV	−.0016	−.0009	.0056	.0049	.0053	.0120	−.0028	−.0018	.0025
Chemicals and allied	V	.0038	.0224	.0408	.0426	.0597	.0881	−.0155	.0006	.0157
Metal manufacture	VI	.0300	.0628	.0798	.0806	.0822	.1031	.0005	.0273	.0402
Mechanical engineering	VII	.0191	.0420	.0633	.0602	.0750	.1126	−.0007	.0190	.0363
Instrument engineering	VIII	.0006	.0025	.0056	.0057	.0068	.0101	−.0006	.0012	.0040
Electrical engineering	IX	.0048	.0171	.0270	.0289	.0348	.0556	−.0052	.0071	.0164
Shipbuilding	X	.0096	.0159	.0245	.0249	.0308	.0442	.0006	.0042	.0085
Vehicles	XI	.0118	.0317	.0507	.0474	.0636	.0779	−.0046	.0134	.0296
Other metal goods	XII	.0230	.0436	.0511	.0499	.0596	.0849	.0056	.0233	.0295
Textiles	XIII	.1022	.1661	.1562	.1182	.1693	.2522	.0481	.0986	.0925
Leather and fur	XIV	.0124	.0060	.0068	.0057	.0094	.0137	.0036	.0025	.0031
Clothing and footwear	XV	.0389	.0471	.0598	.0556	.0715	.1040	.0084	.0152	.0240
Building materials etc.	XVI	.0127	.0257	.0353	.0334	.0482	.0690	−.0023	.0094	.0176
Timber and furniture	XVII	.0149	.0224	.0306	.0305	.0421	.0686	.0063	.0133	.0202
Paper and printing	XVIII	.0144	.0513	.0527	.0498	.0704	.1065	−.0059	.0262	.0269
Other manufacturing	XIX	.0085	.0145	.0201	.0189	.0280	.0445	.0007	.0060	.0100
Total		.3027	.5916	.7618	.7162	.9474	1.3962	−.0071	.2431	.3791

Continued overleaf

TABLE 1.5   *Continued*

Industry	Order	1935/58	1935/63	1935/68	1948/51	1948/54	1948/58	1948/63	1948/68	1951/54
Food, drink, tobacco	III	.0055	.0301	.0754	.0191	.0407	.0436	.0648	.1053	.0180
Coal and petroleum products	IV	.0021	.0023	.0065	.0005	.0065	.0053	.0060	.0118	.0061
Chemical and allied	V	.0159	.0300	.0529	.0243	.0436	.0438	.0642	.0970	.0161
Metal manufacture	VI	.0395	.0416	.0586	.0337	.0484	.0460	.0487	.0696	.0117
Mechanical engineering	VII	.0328	.0440	.0742	.0298	.0550	.0486	.0650	.1085	.0217
Instrument engineering	XIII	.0039	.0049	.0078	.0033	.0063	.0061	.0076	.0124	.0027
Electrical engineering	IX	.0173	.0231	.0427	.0184	.0320	.0325	.0418	.0701	.0117
Shipbuilding	X	.0083	.0113	.0180	.0064	.0137	.0130	.0180	.0293	.0049
Vehicles	XI	.0261	.0399	.0528	.0261	.0488	.0433	.0610	.0832	.0193
Other metal goods	XII	.0279	.0358	.0562	.0211	.0290	.0266	.0361	.0585	.0065
Textiles	XIII	.0614	.1002	.1628	.0362	.0325	.0104	.0376	.0808	—.0020
Leather and fur	XIV	.0022	.0028	.0084	—.0009	—.0004	—.0013	.0010	—.0038	—.0004
Clothing and footwear	XV	.0200	.0308	.0525	.0054	.0112	.0082	.0157	.0309	.0050
Building materials etc.	XVI	.0153	.0269	.0451	.0108	.0186	.0167	.0269	.0426	.0064
Timber and furniture	XVII	.0194	.0289	.0509	.0060	.0106	.0100	.0183	.0357	.0040
Paper and printing	XVIII	.0229	.0394	.0685	.0281	.0282	.0224	.0370	.0604	.0005
Other manufacturing	XIX	.0089	.0155	.0270	.0066	.0099	.0087	.0165	.0290	.0028
Total		.3293	.5074	.8602	.2749	.4348	.3841	.5661	.9287	.1358

TABLE 1.5 *Continued*

Industry	Order	1951/58	1951/63	1951/68	1954/58	1954/63	1954/68	1958/63	1958/68	1963/68
Food, drink, tobacco	III	.0094	.0250	.0563	−.0066	.0076	.0345	.0166	.0474	.0263
Coal and petroleum products	IV	.0037	.0046	.0100	−.0026	−.0014	.0044	.0017	.0087	.0058
Chemicals and allied	V	.0090	.0242	.0505	−.0052	.0082	.0306	.0162	.0419	.0221
Metal manufacture	VI	.0021	.0040	.0202	−.0072	−.0055	.0085	.0014	.0162	.0127
Mechanical engineering	VII	.0066	.0190	.0543	−.0120	−.0011	.0306	.0120	.0466	.0308
Instrument engineering	VIII	.0013	.0024	.0064	−.0011	−.0000	.0037	.0012	.0053	.0041
Electrical engineering	IX	.0057	.0124	.0348	−.0047	−.0019	.0222	.0079	.0315	.0233
Shipbuilding	X	.0017	.0046	.0118	−.0024	.0002	.0064	.0027	.0089	.0038
Vehicles	XI	.0067	.0203	.0389	−.0110	.0017	.0219	.0143	.0368	.0186
Other metal goods	XII	−.0009	.0056	.0222	−.0058	.0001	.0145	.0064	.0209	.0132
Textiles	XIII	−.0289	−.0078	.0276	−.0206	−.0037	.0249	.0163	.0420	.0190
Leather and fur	XIV	−.0009	.0006	.0026	−.0009	.0003	.0019	.0011	.0024	.0011
Clothing and footwear	XV	−.0015	.0041	.0165	−.0050	−.0002	.0103	.0047	.0146	.0078
Building materials etc.	XVI	.0011	.0084	.0205	−.0041	.0024	.0127	.0065	.0167	.0087
Timber and furniture	XVII	.0005	.0062	.0190	−.0026	.0023	.0131	.0048	.0152	.0086
Paper and printing	XVIII	−.0107	.0007	.0201	−.0089	.0011	.0180	.0118	.0307	.0171
Other manufacturing	XIX	−.0009	.0051	.0149	−.0029	.0025	.0111	.0059	.0151	.0091
Total		.0039	.1394	.4265	−.1036	.0162	.2692	.1315	.4010	.2320

this paper makes clear, it is oversimplifying things to conjecture leading sectors that operated throughout the first two-thirds of this century. Rostow's more recent thoughts, in *The World Economy*, however indicate a rather higher degree of continuity. Chapter 28 on Great Britain notes that steel, which had become a leading sector in the 1870s, had ceased to lead by the 1920s; motor vehicles are estimated to have become a leading sector in the 1920s and ceased to lead in the 1960s; and electricity to have become a leading sector in the first decade of this century and forecast to cease leading in the 1970s. Nitrogen, plastics and resins, and synthetic fibres all achieved their maximum rate of expansion in the first half of this century but were individually too small to act by themselves as leading sectors (all these observations from Rostow (1978, Table V-2, p. 379)). The earlier cross-country comparisons of trend periods and business cycles in *The World Economy* (Chapters 14–17, 22–5) reinforce the argument from an internationalist perspective. As already quoted, 'the internal combustion engine, electricity, and chemicals' lead for the interwar period (ibid., pp. 208–17, 227, 335–6). The next trend period Rostow identifies, 1936–51, is more confused because of the wars, but the same underlying pattern is present.

> Energy consumption increased modestly, on balance, between 1938 and 1948, lifted notably by the U.S. figures; but it then moved forward rapidly, with electricity, petroleum, and natural gas increasing their share of the total, as against coal . . . Like electricity, the other interwar leading sectors (e.g., motor vehicles and chemicals) quickly re-emerged and moved forward at high rates, with the age of plastics coming into its own. (ibid., pp. 231–2, also pp. 235–6)

Finally – so far as my study is concerned – for the trend period 1951–72:

> For Western Europe as a whole, for example, Table III-59 shows the disproportionate rise down to 1963 in the three leading sectors which had begun to emerge before 1914 – motor vehicles, chemicals, and electricity – sectors which cushioned the stagnation of the interwar years, and finally carried Western Europe forward at relatively full employment in the 1950s and 1960s. (ibid., p. 261)

In this period there is especially great emphasis on electric-powered consumer durables and electronics (pp. 260–3).

As already stated, my data for non-manufacturing industry such as electricity supply still remain to be prepared. Within manufacturing itself, I have therefore taken electrical goods and equipment, motor vehicles, aircraft, and chemicals as 'leading sectors' for the period studied here. Since there are other sectors – some of which have already been mentioned – which are individually too small for Rostow to classify them as leading sectors but which nevertheless clearly impart some of the sectoral growth impetus, I have further subsumed the leading sectors into a wider group of 'new industries' – the additions being petroleum refining, non-ferrous metals, constructional and mechanical handling equipment, instrument engineering, man-made fibre production (weaving cannot be separately measured in these data), rubber, and plastics products (plastics manufacture is already included in chemicals). The 'old staples' are probably less contentious to define (see the list at the foot of Table 1.6) – marginal candidates like wood products (based on ibid., p. 260) and steel tubes can be dropped and others included with very little alteration to the results (certainly per capita).

Net output, employment, and labour productivity according to these breakdowns are given in Table 1.6. It will be seen from Part B of the Table that net output in 'new industries' rose from less than 10 per cent of net output in manufacturing as a whole in 1907 to 38 per cent by 1968. Employment in these industries rose from under one-fourteenth of the total for manufacturing in 1907 to about one-third by 1968. Conversely, net output of the 'old staples' as here defined fell from over half the total for manufacturing in 1907 to little more than one-fifth in 1968. In terms of growth rates (Part C of the Table) it will be noted that the fastest rates of growth of *employment* in leading sectors and new industries were probably experienced during the First and Second World Wars (that is in 1907/24 and 1935/48). Fastest rates of growth of *net output* and *productivity* however occurred in 1948/54, consonant with Rostow's reference (1978, pp. 231–2, 235–6) to the end of the period 1936–51 (though it must be remembered that problems with price deflators severely affect this particular conclusion).

For leading sectors and new industries generally, there does seem to be some indication of inversity between rates of growth of employment and those of real net output (these latter being the

TABLE 1.6   *Net output, employment, and labour productivity in 'leading sectors', 'new industries', and 'old staples', censal years, 1907/68*

(A) Levels

	Leading sectors			New industries			Old staples		
	Net output	Employ-ment	Pro-ductivity	Net output	Employ-ment	Pro-ductivity	Net output	Employ-ment	Pro-ductivity
	£m	000s	£/man	£m	000s	£/man	£m	000s	£/man
1907	31.5	235.4	133.7	45.3	340.5	132.9	250.9	3123.9	80.3
1924	136.3	520.8	261.8	188.9	732.0	258.0	527.0	3023.9	174.3
1930	161.8	599.8	269.8	222.7	832.9	267.4	447.1	2815.1	158.8
1935	203.1	710.9	285.7	271.1	965.9	280.7	451.1	2676.9	168.5
1948	758.6	1294.6	586.0	1026.1	1736.4	590.9	1388.0	2784.3	498.5
1951	1062.4	1432.4	741.7	1436.9	1914.8	750.4	1684.2	2908.7	579.0
1954	1475.9	1580.8	933.6	1965.7	2095.0	938.3	1891.1	2856.0	662.1
1958	2021.7	1729.5	1169.0	2606.6	2271.9	1147.3	2159.7	2622.6	823.5
1963	3020.9	1924.4	1569.8	3991.1	2556.5	1561.2	2488.9	2377.7	1046.8
1968	4230.5	1900.0	2226.6	5777.2	2591.1	2229.6	3231.1	2149.8	1503.0

TABLE 1.6 *Continued*

(B) *Shares*

	Leading sectors			New industries			Old staples		
	% of all manu-facturing	% of all manu-facturing	% of national average	% of all manu-facturing	% of all manu-facturing	% of national average	% of all manu-facturing	% of all manu-facturing	% of national average
1907	6.6	4.7	138.3	9.4	6.9	137.4	52.3	62.9	83.0
1924	11.5	9.6	120.8	16.0	13.4	119.1	44.6	55.5	80.4
1930	13.8	11.0	125.9	19.0	15.2	124.8	38.1	51.5	74.1
1935	15.9	12.7	125.1	21.2	17.2	122.9	35.3	47.8	73.8
1948	19.4	18.6	104.4	26.2	24.9	105.2	35.5	40.0	88.8
1951	20.9	19.1	109.2	28.3	25.6	110.5	33.2	38.9	85.3
1954	23.6	20.5	114.9	31.4	27.2	115.5	30.2	37.1	81.5
1958	25.6	22.1	115.7	33.0	29.1	113.5	27.4	33.6	81.5
1963	27.8	24.2	114.7	36.7	32.1	114.1	22.9	29.9	76.5
1968	27.7	24.3	114.0	37.8	33.1	114.1	21.1	27.5	76.9

Continued overleaf

TABLE 1.6 *Continued*
(C) *Growth Rates*

	Leading Sectors		New industries			Old staples		
	% p.a.	% p.a.	% p.a.	% p.a.	% p.a.	% p.a.	% p.a.	% p.a.
1907/24	9.0 (5.0)	4.0 (0.2)	8.8 (4.8)	4.6	4.0 (0.2)	4.5 (0.6)	−0.2	4.7 (0.8)
1924/30	2.9 (0.5)	0.5 (−1.9)	2.8 (0.4)	2.2	0.6 (−1.8)	−2.7 (−5.0)	−1.2	−1.5 (−3.9)
1930/35	4.7 (9.0)	1.2 (5.3)	4.0 (8.3)	3.0	1.0 (5.1)	0.2 (4.3)	−1.0	1.2 (5.4)
1924/35	3.7 (4.8)	0.8 (1.9)	3.3 (4.5)	2.6	0.8 (1.9)	−1.4 (−0.3)	−1.1	−0.3 (0.8)
1935/48	10.7 (3.3)	5.7 (−1.3)	10.8 (3.4)	4.6	5.9 (−1.1)	9.0 (1.8)	0.3	8.7 (1.5)
1948/51	11.9 (13.9)	8.2 (10.1)	11.9 (13.9)	3.3	8.3 (10.2)	6.7 (8.5)	1.5	5.1 (7.0)
1951/54	11.6 (9.8)	8.0 (6.3)	11.0 (9.2)	3.0	7.7 (6.0)	3.9 (2.3)	−0.6	4.6 (2.9)
1954/58	8.2 (0.2)	5.8 (−2.0)	7.3 (−0.6)	2.0	5.2 (−2.6)	3.4 (−4.3)	−2.1	5.6 (−2.2)
1948/58	10.3 (7.7)	7.1 (4.6)	9.8 (7.2)	2.7	6.9 (4.3)	4.5 (2.0)	−0.6	5.1 (2.7)
1958/63	8.4 (4.9)	6.1 (2.7)	8.9 (5.4)	2.4	6.4 (3.0)	2.9 (−0.4)	−1.9	4.9 (1.6)
1963/68	7.0 (3.9)	7.2 (4.1)	7.7 (4.6)	0.3	7.4 (4.3)	5.4 (2.3)	−2.0	7.5 (4.4)

NOTES For sources, see text.
Parenthesised figures in Part C of the table are deflated values, using the net output deflator discussed in text. Composition of each grouping is as follows (MLH numbers in parentheses):

Leading sectors
Chemical and allied (271/9)
Electrical engineering (361/9)
Motor vehicles (380/2)
Aerospace equipment (383)

New industries
Leading sectors plus:
Mineral oil refining (262)
Lubricating oils and greases (263)
Non-ferrous metals (321/3)
Construction equipment (336)
Mechanical handling equip. (337)
Instrument engineering (351/4)
Production of man-made fibres (411)
Rubber (491)
Plastics products (496)

Old staples
Coke ovens and mfd. fuel (261)
Iron and steel (general) (311)
Steel tubes (312)
Iron castings, etc. (313)
Textile machinery etc. (335)
Shipbuilding and marine engineering (370)
Locomotives and railway track equipment (384)
Railway carriage etc. (385)
Textiles except MMF (412/29)
Leather and fur (431/3)
Clothing and footwear (441/50)
Pottery (462)
Timber and furniture (471/9)

parenthesised figures in Part C of Table 1.6) and real productivity (displayed likewise) – a kind of inverse Verdoorn effect. Consistent with the frequently-heard complaints about labour dilution during the World Wars, etc., one might posit that through diminishing returns the rate of growth of labour productivity is ultimately hampered by a fast rate of growth of the workforce. The simple correlation coefficient between real productivity growth rate and employment growth rate for new industries is –0.86; so long as 1948/ 58 is treated as one period and 1924/35 similarly. Using parameters estimated from this equation, it is possible to recalculate 'shift' and 'intensity' effects akin to those of Table 1.3. Using values for P_{it}, E_{it}, etc., taken from Part A of Table 1.6 – that is a very high level of aggregation – I find that the 'shift' effect would have been reduced by about forty per cent in most pairs of years if employment in the new industries had grown only at the rate of all other industries. Since hypothetical productivity would have risen considerably faster than the actual, the 'intensity' effect would have risen more than commensurately. There are so many improbable assumptions in this computation that it does not bear elaboration, but the direction of effect is probably correct. A final and possibly interesting inference from the Table is that no such inversity is evident for the old staples ($r = -0.11$) but productivity growth in the old staples is quite well correlated ($r = 0.69$), and positively, with productivity growth in the new industries. This may suggest a 'lateral' linkage in Rostow's sense – productivity growth in new industries spinning off to older industries, for example through their provision of cheaper and better capital goods or through demonstration effects. However this linkage does not appear to hold for the interwar period when (cf. Dowie, 1968) productivity grew fastest in old staples at times when their labour shake-out was greatest. Much more work especially on the problem of price deflators is necessary before these propositions can be affirmed more strongly (or indeed rejected).

We can now make more precise the contribution of each group of industries to the shift and internal effects spelled out in Table 1.3. In Table 1.7 it will be noted that in every pair of years but one (1954–8) the old staples account for more than three-quarters of the total shift effect. As before, my conclusion is that collectively they cannot take as much of the blame as is often levelled against them for Britain's slow rate of economic growth. Again also, the internal effect is more evenly divided – indeed the shares over the longer runs are very like the shares of the respective industries in manufacturing

TABLE 1.7   *Contribution of 'leading sectors', 'new industries' and 'old staples' to 'shift' and 'internal' effects, between censal years, 1907/68*

	Leading sectors				New industries				Old staples			
	% of Total Shift Effect	Growth Rate, Shift Contribution	% of Total Internal Effect	Growth Rate, Internal Contribution	% of Total Shift Effect	Growth Rate, Shift Contribution	% of Total Internal Effect	Growth Rate, Internal Contribution	% of Total Shift Effect	Growth Rate, Shift Contribution	% of Total, Internal Effect	Growth Rate, Internal Contribution
1907/24	18.5	.03	5.8	.05	22.8	.04	6.3	.05	106.7	.17	45.3	.37
1907/30	19.0	.04	-6.8	.01	17.8	.04	-14.2	.01	79.2	.16	146.8	-.15
1907/35	20.7	.05	9.8	.11	20.5	.05	13.1	.15	88.4	.20	36.9	.40
1907/48	3.8	.00	3.2	.02	8.2	.01	3.9	.03	112.2	.09	71.3	.48
1907/51	13.1	.01	6.0	.10	24.0	.03	7.7	.03	82.7	.09	61.0	.84
1907/54	16.7	.03	7.9	.14	23.7	.04	10.5	.19	81.9	.15	55.3	.85
1907/58	14.3	.03	9.0	.12	16.8	.04	11.2	.15	86.5	.19	52.0	.63
1907/63	13.2	.03	9.2	.15	18.0	.04	11.9	.19	85.8	.18	51.4	.71
1907/68	13.6	.03	8.7	.19	19.8	.04	11.6	.25	90.3	.16	51.5	.91
1924/30	5.4	.01	6.5	-.18	4.6	.01	8.4	-.23	76.8	.22	15.3	-.43
1924/35	14.6	.04	20.0	.27	13.6	.04	27.2	.37	76.1	.21	24.8	.34
1924/48	2.6	.00	2.6	.01	7.9	.01	5.7	.03	110.2	.09	87.8	.45
1924/51	13.8	.02	10.5	.19	14.7	.02	15.6	.27	86.4	.10	56.4	.91
1924/54	16.7	.03	13.7	.28	22.8	.04	26.3	.53	82.8	.15	49.1	.93
1924/58	13.4	.03	15.7	.23	15.1	.04	19.3	.28	85.2	.21	45.3	.63
1924/63	12.4	.03	15.6	.27	14.3	.03	21.9	.38	88.8	.18	43.8	.71
1924/68	12.2	.02	14.3	.34	15.7	.03	20.5	.48	90.9	.17	44.2	.93
1930/35	22.1	.06	14.6	.84	20.1	.06	19.4	1.11	86.1	.25	40.1	2.24
1930/48	4.7	.00	5.3	.09	8.6	.01	8.4	.14	111.8	.10	69.8	1.07
1930/51	14.9	.02	10.7	.29	17.0	.02	16.0	.43	88.7	.12	54.7	1.34

Structural Change in British Manufacturing, 1907–68   33

1930/54	17.6	.04	14.0	.42	21.5	.05	19.8	.59	81.7	.17	48.3	1.31
1930/58	14.6	.04	15.2	.37	15.4	.04	20.1	.48	82.7	.22	45.8	1.02
1930/63	14.3	.03	15.5	.42	13.8	.03	21.9	.57	88.6	.20	42.4	1.03
1930/68	14.1	.03	14.8	.50	15.8	.03	21.2	.68	91.0	.17	42.5	1.23
1935/48	4.2	.00	347.8	−.19	9.8	.01	448.9	−.25	101.5	.06	−982.8	.52
1935/51	18.7	.02	7.9	.12	19.5	.02	14.3	.21	80.2	.08	65.0	.92
1935/54	18.6	.04	15.1	.29	24.0	.05	21.9	.42	76.0	.15	50.1	.92
1935/58	15.4	.04	17.0	.24	16.2	.04	22.4	.31	79.0	.21	46.8	.63
1935/63	14.2	.04	17.5	.37	13.6	.04	25.1	.52	79.5	.20	41.5	.83
1935/68	15.3	.03	16.5	.40	17.5	.03	23.6	.56	86.8	.15	40.4	.91
1948/51	−144.0	−.10	24.0	2.15	−295.2	−.20	32.9	2.93	466.1	.31	29.4	2.62
1948/54	−4.1	−.01	27.3	1.89	29.3	.03	35.9	2.45	93.8	.10	26.6	1.84
1948/58	7.8	.02	30.1	1.10	11.7	.02	37.1	1.34	82.8	.17	22.9	.85
1948/63	9.2	.02	28.6	1.01	11.2	.02	37.4	1.29	87.5	.15	23.6	.84
1948/68	6.6	.01	26.1	1.09	11.0	.02	34.8	1.41	93.5	.13	26.5	1.11
1951/54	−16.9	−.02	33.1	1.47	−2.2	−.00	42.1	1.87	116.4	.17	20.7	.93
1951/58	8.0	.02	553.9	.31	10.0	.03	474.7	.26	80.6	.22	−564.6	−.32
1951/63	9.1	.02	40.6	.46	8.4	.02	51.1	.57	86.5	.17	8.0	.09
1951/68	6.4	.01	28.6	.68	7.3	.01	38.0	.89	92.7	.14	22.9	.55
1954/58	14.1	.05	18.4	−.48	15.4	.05	31.1	−.81	66.1	.24	36.4	−.96
1954/63	15.3	.03	81.3	.15	14.8	.03	97.3	.17	76.8	.16	−64.8	−.12
1954/68	9.7	.01	27.7	.52	9.2	.01	37.6	.69	87.1	.13	22.8	.43
1958/63	14.8	.02	39.6	1.02	10.6	.01	42.4	1.09	90.9	.10	14.3	.37
1958/68	.08	.00	27.0	1.03	−5.5	−.01	38.1	1.43	111.7	.10	21.6	.83
1963/68	−2.9	−.00	27.2	1.23	−22.9	−.01	38.4	1.72	137.1	.10	22.1	1.01

NOTES For sources and methods, see text.

The 'Percentage of Total Effect' columns are percentages of the two effects for each pair of years quoted in Table 1.3. The 'Growth Rate of Contribution' columns are annual growth rates of the effects computed for each grouping (growth rates are used here rather than the simple ratios used earlier to abstract from the effect of the passage of time). Both sets of data are quoted since, for example, 100 per cent of a very small or negative number may not be especially impressive (see 1935/48 and 1951/58 for good examples).

employment in the base year (Part B of Table 1.6). In effect, productivity growth has behaved even-handedly.

II

The extension of the 'leading sectors' to comprise a wider range of new industries, as in Tables 1.6 and 1.7, on one level gives a more adequate representation of the role of leading sectors in sectoral change. On the other hand, it risks going too far afield in search of growth nodes – it is obvious that part of the expansion of the rubber industry, to take just one example, results from that of motor vehicles and aerospace (etc.). Even among the primary leading sectors there could have been powerful interdependencies. As Rostow himself points out,

> The three complexes [internal combustion engine, electricity, and chemicals] were related in significant ways. The automobile (and truck), for example, depended on rapidly evolving chemistries of oil refining and rubber manufacture, as well as on the battery, spark plugs, and other light electrical gear. Electric power played a large role in the production of many of the new chemicals. (Rostow, 1978, p. 209)[6]

Above all, the whole range of Rostovian backward and forward linkages to other industries is overlooked. Finally, the links with non-manufacturing industry need further consideration.

If allowance is made for all the backward and forward linkages and interdependencies, then, how much did the expansion of the new industries contribute to economic growth at large? In this paper I tackle this huge question by looking at just one of the 45 spans of years for which the earlier calculations were undertaken: the years from 1930 to 1935. The 1930s have received particular emphasis from some British economic historians, including H. W. Richardson. He states

> By 1930 this burden of "over-commitment" [to the old export staples] was being cast off. Connected with this was the fact that by 1930 the new industries, after two decades of gradual growth, were just beginning to reach the mass production stage of

development, and this revealed new output potentialities. (Aldcroft and Richardson, 1969, p. 251)

Though both Richardson and Aldcroft, *inter alia*, have had occasion to grant the usefulness of input-output methods for resolving the kinds of issues they pose, neither they nor others have gone so far as, for instance, formal computation using the 'Leontief inverse'. Soon after Leontief's own pioneering work on the interwar American economy, Tibor Barna devised an input–output table for the UK for 1935.[7] Barna divided the economy into 36 sectors; by and large his divisions have been imitated in postwar input–output tables for this country (unsurprisingly, since all relate back to the census of production), and will be used in what follows hereafter. Richardson and Aldcroft both (independently) accept Barna's table and his sub-divisions in their writings; so that the degree of interdependence, which is obviously a function of the precise industrial breakdown, is based on a mutually-agreed framework. The classifications are, however, quite different in many cases from the 1958/68 SIC categories used earlier in this paper, and could scarcely be re-developed in that system without a massive amount of work.

The overall contribution of new industries will be studied here in the manner of much present-day historiography by evaluation of the counterfactual outcomes. The same point has indeed been made implicitly by Richardson himself: 'It is obvious that without the new industries – motor-cars, rayon, household appliances, radio and electrical engineering, for example – the increase in productivity and real income would only have been very small compared with what was actually achieved in the interwar period' (Aldcroft and Richardson, 1969, p. 270). The simplest procedure is to suppose that the output (and therefore the derived demands) of new industries were not to have risen at all since 1930 – how much lower would 1935 output then have been? More moderate and plausible counterfactuals such as permitting the new industries to grow at average industrial rates can be gauged in this light. Thus I retain final demands (consumption, exports, etc.) of all other industries at the levels they actually attained in 1935, and attempt to assess the effect on their aggregate gross output (final plus intermediate demands) of the reduction in inter-industry demand arising out of this hypothetical failure of new industries to improve their sales one iota over 1930 levels.

Before this calculation can be carried out, two statistical obstacles have to be overcome. The first follows from the fact that Barna's input–output table is drawn up in terms of current (1935) prices, as opposed to say physical quantities. As such, this raises complications for the counterfactual comparison with 1930. According to Stone and Rowe (1966, Table 24, p. 58) the average price of motor cars consumed in Britain fell from £279 in 1930 to £213 in 1935. Use of current prices for both years might well bias the inter-industry effects downwards. Unfortunately it is not enough to correct for the 1930 level of purchases by converting their physical amounts into an average sales value for 1935. Not only were cars getting cheaper between 1930 and 1935, they were also getting smaller (see Richardson, 1967, pp. 84, 120). The depression years marked the heyday of the introduction of popular small models, like the Morris Eight and the Ford Eight. What is wanted is to correct the 1935 average price by an allowance for changes in 'quality' (size, etc.) since 1930. This amounts to an analogue of the so-called 'hedonic' price index often used to evaluate hypotheses about consumer demand for automobiles; whereby prices are adjusted for differing power, handling, braking, styling, etc., as the consumer detects them in varying sales mixes. My analogue requires the producer's point of view rather than the consumer's. The nearest approach to this ideal readily obtainable is to take the various categories of, say, vehicle (private cars, commercial passenger vehicles, goods vehicles, motor cycles, tractors, pedal cycles, etc.), subdivide so far as is possible by size (horse-power for private cars, passenger and freight capacity for commercial vehicles), and weight each quantity by 1935 price weights. In fact, the Census of Production gives private cars in six groupings (8 HP and under; 8 to 12 HP; 12 to 16 HP; 16 to 20 HP; over 20 HP; and unclassified including taxicabs), internal-combustion passenger vehicles in four, and internal-combustion goods vehicles in five. The same could be done, at varying levels of disaggregation (greatest for chemicals), for electrical engineering, electricity supply, and chemicals and allied industries. It may be noted in passing that this procedure partially obviated the well-known difficulties about input–output coefficients changing through time.

The second data problem is that some of the new industries – rayon and silk, scientific instruments, and electricity supply are those considered here – constitute sub-sectors of the classifications adopted by Barna. Accordingly I had first to deduct the derived demands for the remainder of the relevant classification (cotton, gas and water supplies, and unspecified metal goods other than precision instruments). This had to be done by trial and error; substituting suitable levels of final demand for all other new industries and sub-industries in each case. In theory this could lead to multiple solutions because of the interdependencies, but in practice the reductions in output of cotton, gas and water, and other unspecified metal goods were so small that the trial and error procedure seems accurate enough up to the level of rounding employed.

Standard input–output procedure of course requires the computation of a matrix of input–output coefficients, $A = [a_{ij}]$ ($i = 1, 2, \ldots, 36; j = 1, 2, \ldots, 36$), where the cell components – the a_{ij} – represent the proportion of industry i's gross output coming as an intermediate input from industry j. In addition the vectors $x = (x_i)$ and $c = (c_i)$ are defined, each of 36 elements, representing gross outputs and final demands respectively, for each industry. Prediction then generally involves substituting in new values for the final demands (a new vector c), and establishing the inter-industry effects through the computation of the 'Leontief inverse', $(I-A)^{-1}$.

The basic counterfactual used here however required a slightly different technique. In general I did not have available 1930 data on final demands. I could, though, acquire 1930 material on gross outputs from the Census of Production. Thus my problem was one of setting the gross outputs of the new industries (or sub-industries) at their 1930 levels (measured in 1935 prices), whilst the final demands of all other industries were maintained at 1935 levels. In this way, the task is reduced to solving 36 equations in 36 unknowns (7 unknown c_i's for the new industries and 29 unknown x_i's for the rest). With appropriate algebraic transformations this could be effected using standard simultaneous-equations methods. The results are summarised in Table 1.8.[8] In column (ii) appears the difference between the levels of gross output actually achieved in 1935, according to Barna, and the levels that would have prevailed if the physical quantities of product of the new industries had stayed at 1930 rather than rising to 1935 levels. For the new industries themselves, these differences are obtained from the census, suitably price-and-quality-adjusted. For the remaining industries, the differences reflect the hypothesised diminution of their gross output when the derived demands of the expansion of new industries are eliminated.

TABLE 1.8   *Actual gross outputs and final demands of all sectors, 1935, compared with two hypothetical solutions (£ million)*

Industry	(i) Actual gross output	(ii) Change 1930/35 method I	(iii) Change 1930/35 method II	(iv) Actual final demand	(v) Change 1930/35 method I	(vi) Change 1930/35 method II
Agriculture, forestry, etc.	293.8	−0.2	−40.7	230.5	—	−38.43
Coal mining	146.5	−7.3	−23.1	64.5	—	−0.02
Other mining	21.9	−0.6	−5.9	3.2	—	−0.06
Building materials	62.2	−0.9	−25.1	15.2	—	−15.18
China and glass	32.4	−1.2	−17.9	13.9	—	−13.87
Coke ovens	17.3	−0.8	−9.2	4.8	—	−4.77
Chemicals, etc.	93.2	−16.4	−16.4	48.3	−13.5	−6.17
Soap, polishes	39.2	−0.1	−0.1	34.7	—	−0.01
Oils, paints	81.8	−1.8	−10.3	26.2	—	−0.06
Iron and steel manufactures	193.2	−11.0	−72.0	39.8	—	−0.07
Non-ferrous metals	57.2	−3.8	−35.8	15.8	—	−15.77
Shipbuilding	46.5	−0.1	−41.4	39.3	—	−39.24
Mechanical engineering	186.9	−3.6	−157.3	128.0	—	−127.96
Electrical engineering	109.6	−43.9	−43.9	70.5	−35.5	−28.20
Motor and cycle	171.5	−49.2	−49.2	120.5	−38.7	−34.60
Aircraft	14.4	−5.2	−5.2	13.3	−4.8	−4.80
Railway rolling stock	44.9	−0.4	−25.0	17.2	—	−17.16
Metal goods n.e.s.	173.4	−6.2	−131.0	104.9	−1.3	−104.81
Cotton and silk	211.4	−20.5	−7.9	83.3	−13.3	−0.07

	(i)	(ii)	(iii)	(iv)	(v)	(vi)
Woollen and worsted	142.2	−0.4	−3.7	55.0	—	−0.06
Hosiery and lace	48.4	−0.0	−0.1	42.7	—	−0.03
Other textiles	61.1	−0.8	−4.3	26.4	—	−0.08
Textile finishing, etc.	32.1	−2.3	−1.2	0.1	—	−0.08
Leather and fur	47.1	−0.7	−1.7	17.6	—	−0.06
Clothing	222.4	−0.0	−0.5	207.5	—	−0.04
Food processing	406.0	−0.1	−7.1	303.6	—	−0.02
Drink and tobacco	360.8	−0.3	−0.6	306.7	—	−0.07
Manufactures of wood	98.6	−1.3	−9.2	56.5	—	−0.08
Paper	74.8	−1.4	−6.1	20.6	—	−0.04
Printing and publishing	145.7	−2.7	−12.6	70.2	—	−0.07
Rubber	28.4	−2.3	−19.2	15.9	—	−15.85
Miscellaneous manufactures	24.2	−0.1	−0.4	20.4	—	−0.00
Building and civil engineering	470.6	−0.3	−74.2	321.5	—	−61.10
Gas, electricity and water	242.5	−59.5	−59.5	159.6	−48.6	−37.50
Distributive services	1700.6	−14.0	−482.1	1298.4	—	−399.80
Other services	1348.5	−1.0	−8.3	1305.5	—	−0.04
Total	7458.0	−267.8	−1408.3	5302.3	−155.7	−966.17

NOTES For sources see text.
Method I = using simultaneous equations (dashes in col. (v) are zeroes by assumption).
Method II = using linear programming.
All figures rounded to one decimal place for cols. (i)–(v) and two decimal places for col. (vi).
Industrial groupings follow Barna (1952).

The direct effect measured by the net decline in gross output as estimated by simultaneous equations is 3.6 per cent, which can be taken as big or small, depending on the point of view of the observer. It will naturally be larger for a longer period. On the other hand, it is probably greatly overstated through assuming zero substitution, that is through assuming that if (say) electricity supply does not grow, no other form of power supply will be forthcoming to fill the void.

More constructively, perhaps, the indirect effects may be seen by comparing the decline in gross outputs, set out in column (ii), with those of final demands in column (v). If attention is limited to the 33 secondary industries by omitting agriculture and the two service sectors, the decline in final demands is actually greater proportionately (6.3 per cent) than that of gross outputs (6.1 per cent), though by very little. In other words, as it turns out, one would obtain virtually the same impression about the impact of the new industries over the years 1930/5 by means of a rough-and-ready calculation based on final demands (consumption, capital formation, exports, etc.) as with the more sophisticated input–output approach incorporating inter-industry linkages.[9]

This modified input–output approach is tantamount to imposing the heaviest burden of adjustment to a world of stagnant new industries on the final demands for those new industries. For most of the new industries the proportionate fall in final demand therefore comes out greater than that in gross output. This is in keeping with the 'age of high mass-consumption' kind of stress on burgeoning consumption levels for the products of new industries – motor cars, vacuum cleaners, radios, and the like. On the other hand, the method of estimation does lead to a result that seems historically implausible. The hypothesised reduction in, say, electricity supply does little to lower the portion of outputs of all other industries going to satisfy final demands. The gross output of industries other than new industries is reduced primarily by the smaller *input* requirements of new industries, rather than the smaller output consequences. In other words, backward linkages are looked after better than forward linkages. This is clearly doing an injustice to Rostow and to Richardson.

Constraints can be introduced into the problem to help cope with this objection. For a second solution, I chose to impose the constraint that final demands for new industries should not be permitted to fall by a greater proportion than their 'actual' fall in gross outputs. This would prevent the adjustment coming wholly through sacrifices in final consumption of electricity, etc., and thereby require the electricity supply available to other industries to fall. The problem to be solved was set out as:

$$\text{Min} \sum_{i \neq n} \Delta x$$

$$\text{subject to} \quad A\Delta x + \Delta c = \Delta x \quad (\text{all } i)$$

$$\Delta x \leqslant 0$$

$$\Delta c \leqslant 0$$

$$\Delta c \geqslant -c$$

$$\frac{\Delta c_n}{c_n} \geqslant \frac{\Delta x_n}{x_n} \quad (n = 7, 14, 15, 16, 34)$$

$$\Delta x_n \text{ given}$$

From the basic theory of linear programming, it follows that an optimum will lie in a corner of the feasible solution space. In this example, as becomes apparent in comparing columns (iv) and (vi) of Table 1.8 this means that for 31 of the 36 industries, final demands will change by either the minimum or the maximum allowable (I altered the x_i in discrete jumps of £0.1 m, so that zero is only approximated in most cases). Now, this may seem as arbitrary as the first method of solution by simultaneous equations. In part it is; but it does help to indicate what would happen were a more historically plausible set of constraints to be found. The coefficients of the input–output matrix assure that the old staples like iron and steel, shipbuilding, railway vehicles, and coke ovens – together with mechanical engineering, parts of which (at least) are often regarded as nineteenth-century staples – will always figure prominently among the industries most badly affected by a retardation of structural change, no matter what other counterfactuals are attempted with new industries in the interwar economy. On the other side, some of the more dependent new industries, like rubber and non-ferrous metals, are also severely hindered. But the overriding impression is the opposite of a new block of industries with weak links back to the lumbering export staples – the most powerful linkages run backwards and forwards to the selfsame export staples. The linear programming approach does seem to have been successful (whatever its other limitations) in picking up some of the forward linkages, as was asked of it. The case of shipbuilding provides a good example. It was not an industry that acted as an important input to any new industry (or any industry, for that matter); it is completely cut back as in column (vi) of Table 1.8 because of significant forward linkages from iron and steel and especially mechanical engineering.

The other side of the 'development block' concept, of strong interdependencies among the leading sectors themselves, is less straightforward to assess from this information, since any reasonable test is eliminated by assumption. It is noteworthy that if the outputs of the remaining leading sectors are consecutively reduced to 1930 levels, the 1935 gross output of chemicals is reduced by just 2.0 per cent, of electrical engineering by 3.2 per cent, of motors and cycles by only 0.1 per cent, and aircraft not at all. On this evidence it would seem preferable to emphasise

> what Strassmann calls the interrelatedness of innovations effect. To explain this: innovations at one stage of production tend by altering the structure of costs at another stage to facilitate innovations there which would not otherwise have been profitable. The degree of interrelatedness is obviously higher in industries with close input-output connections. (Richardson, 1967, p. 95).

Unlike Richardson, my input–output findings here as well as my earlier results on the spillover of productivity change would lead me to pursue much of this effect, too, straight back to the old export staples.

Whether the degree of feed-back (and forward) to the older industries persists into more modern periods remains for future testing. All I am able to do here is collate the input–output coefficients from tables for subsequent years, as in Table 1.9. Transactions between firms but within the industry have been suppressed from this comparative Table, since the basis for collecting such data appears to have altered substantially from year to year. Otherwise the Barna division of industries has been my guide, inasmuch as it produced the kind of results already discussed.

Unsurprisingly, in view of the rapid growth rates of new industries, there was a rise in the proportion of inputs into leading sectors coming from those other new industries, with all of the rise occurring in the period 1935–48. The proportional input from old

TABLE 1.9   *Input coefficients for leading sectors, 1935–68*

	From other leading sectors	*From other new industries*	*From the old staples*	*From old staples plus mechanical engineering*
1935	.0344	.0801	.1102	.1267
1948	.0509	.1397	.1470	.1601
1954	.0466	.1159	.1433	.1721
1963	.0467	.1060	.1318	.1618
1968	.0429	.1232	.1049	.1282

NOTES   So far as the columns are concerned (the *j*'s), the leading sectors are as for Table 1.6 plus gas, electricity and water supply. For rows (the *i*'s) they are Table 1.6 leading sectors plus electricity supply. With these additions new industries are as in Table 1.6. Old staples are also as for Table 1.6 with the addition of coal mining. These plus mechanical engineering (less constructional and mechanical handling equipment and textile machinery and accessories) are shown in a further column because of the significance of mechanical engineering in the linear programming solution for 1935.

SOURCES   1935–based on T. Barna 'The Interdependence of the British Economy', *Journal of the Royal Statistical Society* (Series A) (1952), revised upwards to exclude inter-firm intra-industry transactions.

1948–I. G. Stewart's table, republished with amendments in Ghosh (1954), Supplementary Tables B.

1954, 1963, 1968–Central Statistical Office input-output tables.

staples did not, however, fall notably over the period 1935–68, and was much higher between 1948 and 1963 than in 1935. It is thus not obvious that repetitions of the calculations undertaken in Table 1.8 would yield vastly different results for later years.

III

Aldcroft and Richardson have attempted to reconcile the sustained growth of output of the interwar period with its notoriously poor record for unemployment by hinting that the new industries had much more to offer the former than the latter. As Aldcroft stated in 1967, ' . . . one has to remember that, apart from building, most of the new and rapidly expanding sectors were less labour intensive than the old staples and so their impact on the labour market was less than might be expected' (Aldcroft and Fearon, 1969, p. 53). Richardson agrees with this relative capital intensity of the new industries, for example pointing out that their contribution to the growth of employment 'is likely to be the least impressive consequence of their expansion' (Richardson, 1967, p. 90). There are many difficulties with defining labour or capital intensity, and it is

44   *Applications and Cases, Part II*

compounded here by having to marry differing sources. For what it is worth, in Table 1.10 I have tried to combine C. H. Feinstein's figures for capital in manufacturing industry with employment and net output figures from the 1935 census of production. It may be noted that, with the outstanding exception of chemicals, most new industries assessable on this classification (the classification is

TABLE 1.10   *Capital–labour ratios and labour productivity by industry (S.I.T.C./ Feinstein classification) 1935*

Industry	Fixed capital: labour		Total capital: labour		Net output per employee	
	£000/ man	rank	£000/ man	rank	£	rank
Cotton	0.73	6	0.80	8	116.4	22
Woollen and worsted	0.55	11	0.74	10	179.8	16
Silk and rayon	0.71	7	0.82	7	172.3	18
Linen and jute	1.07	3	1.50	2	143.6	21
Other textiles	0.36	18	0.38	20	170.8	19
Iron and steel	0.66	10	0.71	11	216.0	13
Mechanical engineering	0.54	12	0.65	14	220.2	12
Electrical engineering	0.41	17	0.54	16	231.3	11
Motor and cycle	0.21	21	0.28	21	231.4	10
Nonferrous metals	0.45	15	0.60	15	245.3	8
Drink	1.18	2	1.39	3	658.2	2
Tobacco	0.42	16	1.21	4	662.2	1
Food	0.66	9	0.78	9	283.1	5
Chemicals and allied	1.40	1	1.58	1	456.1	3
Rubber and leather	0.35	19	0.48	18	249.1	7
Textile finishing	0.21	22	0.25	22	151.1	20
Paper	0.78	5	0.92	6	239.8	9
Printing and publishing	0.46	14	0.54	17	284.9	4
Wood and wood products	0.52	13	0.66	13	201.2	14
Brick and cement	0.67	8	0.70	12	251.1	6
China and glass	0.34	20	0.39	19	173.7	17
Miscellaneous n.e.s.	0.82	4	1.12	5	197.8	15

SOURCES Capital – (C. H. Feinstein, *Domestic Capital Formation in the United Kingdom 1920–38* (Cambridge University Press, 1965, Table 8, pp. 102–42). Labour and productivity – Census of Production for 1935. The capital figures are first-cost estimates. If depreciated values are used instead, motor vehicles fall to lowest place for capital: labour ratios, and none of the new industries changes its rank by more than one place.

Feinstein's, based on the 1948 SIC) come well down the list of rankings of capital intensity, with motor vehicles particularly low on the scale. Conversely, many of the old staples – including most of the branches of the textile industry – come quite high up the list. An alternative way of expressing capital intensity would be a relative one, that is relative to manufacturing or the economy as a whole. Figures borrowed from Dowie and aggregated can illuminate this formulation as in Table 1.11.

TABLE 1.11   *Percentage shares in UK employment and capital stock, 1929–37*

	Employment		Capital		Relative capital intensity	
	1929	*1937*	*1929*	*1937*	*1929*	*1937*
4 New industries	5.8	6.6	2.9	3.1	0.50	0.47
3 Old staples	9.9	8.5	6.7	5.4	0.67	0.64
Total manufacturing	35.7	35.2	17.2	15.4	0.48	0.44

NOTE The four new industries are chemicals, electrical engineering, vehicles, and rayon and silk. The three old staples are iron and steel, shipbuilding, and other textiles.

SOURCE A. Dowie, 'Growth in the Inter-War Period: Some More Arithmetic', *Economic History Review* 1968, Table 4. Dowie's capital figures are based on Feinstein (1965).

The categories differ again from those utilised earlier, but the general impression is probably not misleading. The new industries have about the same shares in the national cake of capital relative to employment as manufacturing as a whole, whereas the old staples have a relative capital intensity half as high again as the new industries (or manufacturing generally). Even textiles, packed with female labour and operating at particularly low levels of output per employee (Table 1.10), have a higher capital intensity in 1929 and 1937 than the mean of these new industries.

Leontief himself was first to demonstrate how input–output techniques could throw further light on employment generated. One begins with a vector of labour requirements per unit of output, $l = (l_j)$, representing the number of employees needed per thousand pounds of gross output. Vector l is rewritten as a diagonal matrix L (with zeroes off the diagonal) and post-multiplied by the matrix of input–output coefficients, A^*.[10] The column sums of the resultant matrix represent the coefficient of direct and indirect labour requirements.

46   *Applications and Cases, Part II*

The overall employment effect of the new industries is then calculated in the same way as was output and consumption in Method I of Table 1.8 relying on the usual Leontief assumption of zero elasticities of substitution. The decline in employment between actual-1935 and hypothetical-1935 is 2.9 per cent, the same as in final demand. For secondary industry alone, the decline (5.8 per cent) is only a fraction lower than either final demand or gross output. These results suggest that the new industries were about as good at creating jobs as at increasing output. One or two, like chemicals, are indeed relatively labour-saving with respect to the economy as a whole; but once the indirect employment effects are taken into account, the others more or less compensate for them. As noted in the introduction to this paper, this result is in line with the reservations of Rostow concerning the supposed capital-intensity of electricity supply – his precise point is this very one about the possibilities for indirect employment creation.

The impact on employment may be brought out in another way by considering the magnitudes involved. Employment in the seven new industries considered in Table 1.8 grew by some 170 000 between 1930 and 1935 – a goodly proportion of the 205 000 added to employment in all secondary industry over that quinquennium. So powerful are the labour coefficients, however, that if the gross output of these new industries in 1935 were cut back to 1930 levels, as was done in Table 1.8 then total employment would fall by as much as 513 000. There are grounds for arguing that the benefits conferred by the rise of new industries on the economy lay as much in putting to work factors that would otherwise have been unemployed (at least in the 1930s) as in windfall productivity gains.

IV

The major conclusions are as follows. Over the long run, the 'shift' effect of resource allocation and reallocation among sectors has been much less important in explaining productivity growth in the UK than the 'internal' effect of productivity growth within all sectors. Such shift effect as there was owed most to the relative or absolute displacement of labour from a comparative handful of low-productivity 'old staples', though the recruitment of labour into one or two new industries, especially chemicals, also helped. The internal effect was more evenly shared around among industries, old and new alike (the reasons why productivity growth affected most industries more or less commensurately deserve further attention). With a few obvious exceptions, like rubber and non-ferrous metals, the backward and forward linkages of the leading sectors run consistently to the export staples – it does not seem valid to view the new industries as a 'development block' largely independent of the staple trades. Finally, the belief that a structural shift towards new industries explains the coexistence of high economy-wide growth rates and high unemployment in the 1930s is not supported. The advantage of new industries to the economy emerges not so much as exceptionally rapid technical progress (unless through leading innovation elsewhere) nor as once-for-all productivity gains while they are growing rapidly, but equally as the simple Keynesian effect of employing primary resources in sufficiently large quantities.

NOTES

1. Rostow (1971), pp. 175–6. I am grateful to the Houblon–Norman fund of the Bank of England for financial assistance towards compiling the data herein.
2. Schumpeter (1961) and Svennilson (1954). For an alternative perspective to Rostow's that also anchors itself on these authors see Cornwall (1977).
3. The general tenor of their contributions is perhaps most readily conveyed in the essays published in Aldcroft and Richardson (1969), also Richardson (1967).
4. It should be noted that there is a misprint in this equation in Salter – at least in the edition referred to here (1966).
5. It should be noted that 'net output' is not identical with value-added 'since it contains payments for services rendered by firms, e.g. payments made for repairs, hire of plant, advertising, research work, etc.' (*Historical Record*, 1978, p. xiv). Any corrections on these scores would involve greater errors than the gain in precision.
6. This point will be touched on in what follows but is taken up in more detail in my paper to the Cliometrics Conference at the University of Warwick in 1978 (see the brief summary in the *Journal of European Economic History*, vol. 9:1 (1980), 229–31 from which most of this section derives). My thanks again to the individuals and participants at seminars for their help with that paper.
7. Barna (1952). In using Barna's table hereafter, the one change I have made is in row 34, column 26 – inputs of gas, electricity and water into food processing industries – where Barna has evidently been misled by a misprint in the 1935 census. The figure has been adjusted down from £8.7 to £2.1 millions, and final demands adjusted upwards accordingly.
8. The list of new industries adopted here is that given for the contribution of new industries to output given by Aldcroft in 1967 (see Aldcroft and Fearon, 1969, p. 47). On the following page he gives a quite different list, when discussing their contribution to investment; and then a drastically different list – comprising no less than 71 out of 100 industries! – when talking about

employment. The list given in Aldcroft (1970, p. 177) is similar to that here.

9. The multiplier is accounted for rather perversely, in that the result of the counterfactual is to give most industries other than new industries a higher *share* of 1935 final demand than they actually held in that year. T. C. Thomas' estimate (see Floud and McCloskey, 1981, p. 346) for the public-expenditure multiplier with a cumulative five-year lag is 1.44; which does not indicate a drastic need to amend the results to allow for the multiplier. However, Thomas' figure may be biased downward by ignoring the feedback from British imports (treated as a straight leakage) to British exports (see next footnote).

10. A* is the previous matrix A adjusted by taking account of imports, so that employment generated abroad is excluded; if employment is generated in British exports through Britain accepting a higher level of imports then one can work straightforwardly with the matrix A.

REFERENCES

Aldcroft, D. H., *The Inter-War Economy: Britain, 1919–1939* (London: Batsford, 1970).

Aldcroft D. H., and Fearon, P. (eds), *Economic Growth in 20th-Century Britain* (London: Macmillan, 1969).

Aldcroft, D. H., and Richardson, H. W., *The British Economy, 1870–1939* (London: Macmillan, 1969).

Alford, B. W. E., *Depression and Recovery? British Economic Growth 1919–1939* (London: Macmillan (Studies in Economic History Series), 1972).

Barna, T., 'The Interdependence of the British Economy', *Journal of the Royal Statistical Society* (Series A), 1952.

Brown, B. C., 'Industrial Production in 1935 and 1948', *Bulletin of the London and Cambridge Economic Service*, December 1954.

Business Statistics Office, *Historical Record of the Census of Production 1907 to 1970* (London: HMSO, 1978).

Cornwall, J., *Modern Capitalism: Its Growth and Transformation* (Oxford: Martin Robertson, 1977).

Dahmén, E., 'Technology, Innovations and International Industrial Transformation', in L. H. Dupriez (ed.), *Economic Progress*, Institut de Recherches Economiques et Sociales (Louvain, 1955) pp. 293–306.

Dowie, J. A., 'Growth in the Inter-War Period: Some More Arithmetic', *Economic History Review*, 1968 (reprinted in Aldcroft and Fearon, *supra*).

Feinstein, C. H., *Domestic Capital Formation in the United Kingdom, 1920–38* (Cambridge University Press, 1965).

Feinstein, C. H., *National Income, Expenditure and Output of the United Kingdom, 1855–1965* (Cambridge University Press, 1972).

Floud, R. C., and McCloskey, D. N. (eds), *The Economic History of Britain since 1700*, vol. 2 (Cambridge University Press, 1981).

Ghosh, A., *Experiments with Input–Output Models: an Application to the Economy of the U.K., 1948–55* (Cambridge University Press, 1954).

Mitchell, B. R. with Deane, P., *Abstract of British Historical Statistics* (Cambridge University Press, 1971).

Structural Change in British Manufacturing, 1907–68   49

Mitchell B. R. and Jones, H. G., *Second Abstract of British Historical Statistics* (Cambridge University Press, 1971).

Richardson, H. W., *Economic Recovery in Britain, 1932–9* (London: Weidenfeld & Nicolson, 1967).

Rostow, W. W., *The Stages of Economic Growth*, 2nd edn (Cambridge University Press, 1971).

Rostow, W. W., *The World Economy: History and Prospect* (London: Macmillan, 1978).

Salter, W. E. G., *Productivity and Technical Change*, 2nd edn (Cambridge University Press, 1966).

Schumpeter, J. A., *The Theory of Economic Development*, 2nd edn (New York: Oxford University Press, 1961).

Stone R. and Rowe, D. A., *The Measurement of Consumers' Expenditure and Behaviour in the United Kingdom, 1920–1938*, vol. II (Cambridge University Press, 1966).

Svennilson, I., *Growth and Stagnation in the European Economy* (Geneva: Economic Commission for Europe, 1954).

9 W. W. Rostow: A Selective Chronological Bibliography

BOOKS

1948   *Essays on the British Economy of the Nineteenth Century* (Oxford: Clarendon Press) reprinted (Westport, Conn.: Greenwood Press, 1981).

1952   *The Process of Economic Growth* (New York: W. W. Norton; Oxford: Clarendon Press, 1953) second editions, 1960.

       The Dynamics of Soviet Society, with Alfred Levin and others (New York: W. W. Norton; London: Secker & Warburg, 1953) second edition, 1967.

1953   *The Growth and Fluctuation of the British Economy, 1790–1850*, with Arthur D. Gayer, Anna Jacobson Schwartz, with the assistance of Isaiah Frank, 2 vols (Oxford: Clarendon Press). Second edition (Hassocks, England: Harvester Press, 1975).

1954   *The Prospects for Communist China*, with Richard W. Hatch, Frank A. Kierman, and Alexander Eckstein (New York: Technology Press, MIT, John Wiley).

1955   *An American Policy in Asia*, with Richard W. Hatch (New York: Technology Press, MIT/John Wiley).

1957   *A Proposal: Key to an Effective Foreign Policy*, with Max F. Millikan (New York: Harper).

1960   *The Making of Modern America, 1776–1940: An Essay on Three Themes* (monograph, available in mimeograph, Center for International Studies, MIT, Cambridge, Mass.)

       The Stages of Economic Growth: A Non-Communist Manifesto (Cambridge University Press) second edition, 1971.

       The United States in the World Arena (New York: Harper & Row) second edition, 1969.

1963   *The Economics of Take-off into Sustained Growth* (edited) (London: Macmillan; New York: St Martin's Press).

1964   *View from the Seventh Floor* (New York: Harper & Row).

1971   *Politics and the Stages of Growth* (Cambridge University Press).

1972   *The Diffusion of Power* (New York: Macmillan).

1975   *How It All Began: Origins of the Modern Economy* (New York: McGraw-Hill).

1978   *The World Economy: History and Prospect* (Austin: University of Texas Press; London: Macmillan).

        Getting from Here to There (New York: McGraw-Hill; London: Macmillan).

1980   *Why the Poor Get Richer and the Rich Slow Down: Essays in the Marshallian Long Period* (Austin: University of Texas Press; London: Macmillan).

1981   *British Trade Fluctuations, 1868–1896: A Chronicle and a Commentary*, Ph.D. dissertation, Yale University, 1940 (New York: Arno Press).

        Pre-Invasion Bombing Strategy: General Eisenhower's Decision of March 25, 1944 (Austin: University of Texas Press; Farnborough: Gower).

        The Division of Europe after World War II: 1946 (Austin: University of Texas Press; Farnborough: Gower).

1982   *Europe after Stalin: Eisenhower's Three Decisions of March 11, 1953* (Austin: University of Texas Press).

ARTICLES, REVIEWS

1938   'Investment and the Great Depression', *Economic History Review*, 8, 136–8.

1939   'Investment and Real Wages, 1873–86', *Economic History Review*, 9, 144–59.

1940   'How Money Works', Public Affairs pamphlet, with Arther D. Gayer.

        'James Harvey Rogers as an Economist', in *James Harvey Rogers, 1886–1939: In Memoriam* (Stamford, Conn.: Overbrook Press).

        'Explanations of the "Great Depression" 1873–96: An Historian's View of Modern Monetary Theory', *Economic History* (Supplement of *The Economic Journal*), 4, 356–70.

1941   'Business Cycles, Harvests, and Politics: 1790–1850', *Journal of Economic History*, 1, 206–21.

1942   'Adjustments and Maladjustments After the Napoleonic Wars', *American Economic Review Supplement*, 32, 13–23.

1943   'Bagehot and the Trade Cycle', in *The Economist, 1843–1943* (Oxford University Press).

1946   'The American Diplomatic Revolution', an inaugural lecture before the University of Oxford on 12 November 1946.

1947   'The Political Basis for U.S. Foreign Policy', *Lloyds Bank Review*, October 1947, pp. 39–40.

1950   'Government and Private Enterprise in European Recovery', *Tasks of Economic History*, Supplement X, pp. 105–13.

        'The United Nations' Report on Full Employment', *Economic Journal*, 60, 323–50, review.

1951   'Some Notes on Mr. Hicks and History', *American Economic Review*, 41, 316–24.

        'The Historical Analysis of the Terms of Trade', *Economic History Review*, 4, 53–76.

        'Two Analyses of Britain's Transition', review of Keith Hutchison, *The Decline and Fall of British Capitalism* and Robert A. Brady, *Crisis in Britain: Plans and Achievements of the Labour Government*, *Journal of Economic History*, 11, 55–9.

1953   '*A Note on "The Diffusion of Ideologies"*', *Confluence*, 2, 31–42.

        Review of Sir John Clapham, *A Concise Economic History of Britain, From Earliest Times to A.D. 1750*, *American Economic Review*.

'Notes on a New Approach to U.S. Economic Foreign Policy', *World Politics*, 5, 302–12.

'Toward a General Theory of Action', *World Politics*, 5, 530–54. Review of Talcott Parsons and Edward A. Shils (eds), *Toward a General Theory of Action*.

1954 'Factors in a British Trade Cycle', *Journal of Economic History*, 14, 266–70, review of R. C. O. Matthews, *A Study in Trade-Cycle History, Economic Fluctuations in Great Britain, 1833–42*.

1955 'Marx Was a City Boy, or Why Communism May Fail', *Harper's Magazine*, February 1955.

Review of *History of Peterborough, New Hampshire*, George Abbot Morison, Book One – *Narrative*, Etta M. Smith, Book Two – *Genealogies*.

'Russia and China Under Communism', *World Politics*, 7, 513–31.

'Trends in the Allocation of Resources in Secular Growth', in Leon H. Dupriez (ed.), *Economic Progress* (Louvain: Institut de Recherches Economiques et Sociales).

'Some General Reflections on Capital Formation and Economic Growth', in *Capital Formation and Economic Growth*, National Bureau of Economic Research (Princeton University Press).

1956 'The Take-off into Self-Sustained Growth', *Economic Journal*, 66, 25–48.

1957 'The Fallacy of the Fertile Gondolas', *Harvard Alumni Bulletin*, 25 May 1957.

'Ideas and Reality', *Confluence*, 6, 199–214.

'The Interrelation of Theory and Economic History', *Journal of Economic History*, 17, 509–23.

1958 'Foreign Aid: Next Phase', with Max F. Millikan, *Foreign Affairs*, 36, 418–36.

'The American National Style', *Daedalus*, 87, 110–14.

'The National Style', in Elting E. Morison (ed.), *The American Style: Essays in Value and Performance* (New York: Harper).

1959 'Débats et Combats. Histoire et Sciences Sociales: La Longue Durée', *Annales*, October–December 1959, pp. 710–18.

'The Stages of Economic Growth', *Economic History Review*, 11, 1–16.

'The Stages of Economic Growth and the Problems of Peaceful Co-existence', Lecture at the Institute of World Economy and International Relations, Academy of Sciences of the USSR, Moscow, May 25, 1959, published in *Fortune*.

1960 'The Problem of Achieving and Maintaining a High Rate of Economic Growth: A Historian's View', *American Economic Review*, 50, 106–18.

'Industrialization and Economic Growth', in *Proceedings* of First International Conference of Economic History, Stockholm (Paris: Mouton).

'The Dynamics of American Society', in *Postwar Economic Trends in the United States* (New York: Harper).

'Economics for the Nuclear Age', *Harvard Business Review*, 38, 41–9.

1962 'Some Lessons of History for Africa', in American Society of African Culture (ed.), *Pan-Africanism Reconsidered* (Berkeley and Los Angeles: University of California Press).

1963 'The Third Round', *Foreign Affairs*, 42, 1–10.

1964 'The Challenge of Democracy in Developing Nations', *Department of State Bulletin*, 50, 251–60.

'The Problems of Nuclear Arms', H. V. Hodson (ed.), *The Atlantic Future* (London: Longmans).

'The Planning of Foreign Policy', in E. A. Johnson (ed.), *The Dimensions of Diplomacy* (Baltimore: Johns Hopkins Press).

1965   'The Chapter That Keynes Never Wrote', *Department of State Bulletin*, 52, 454–9.

1966   'The Sharing of the Good Life', *Department of State Bulletin*, May 23, 1966.

1967   'The Great Transition: Tasks of the First and Second Post-War Generations' (Leeds University Press).

1969   'The Anglo-American Situation', in *The American Oxonian*, 56, 105–10.

1970   'The Past Quarter-Century as Economic History and the Tasks of International Economic Organization', *Journal of Economic History*, 30, 150–87.

'The Irrelevance of the Relevant', *The Addendum*, 1, 1–8.

1971   'An Historian Looks at History: 1970', *Southwestern Historical Quarterly*, 74, 385–92.

1972   Review of Ronald D. Brunner and Garry D. Brewer, *Organised Complexity: Empirical Theories of Political Development* (New York: Free Press), in *Political Science Quarterly*, 87, 280–2.

'Stages of Enterprise: The Business of America', in Daniel J. Boorstin (ed.), *American Civilization* (London: Thames and Hudson).

1973   'The Role of the President in a World of Diffusing Power', School for Advanced International Studies, 17, 19–34.

'The Politics of Arms Control or How to Make Nuclear Weapons Wither Away', in William R. Kintner and Robert L. Pfaltzgraff, Jr. (eds), *SALT: Implications for Arms Control in the 1970's* (Pittsburgh Press).

1975   'The Developing World in the Fifth Kondratieff Upswing', *The Annals*, 420, 111–24.

'Is the American Style Viable', *The Educational Forum*, 40, 457–68.

1976   'The Bankruptcy of Neo-Keynesian Economics', *Intermountain Economic Review*, 7, 1–12.

'A Rejoinder', *Intermountain Economic Review*, 7, 61–4.

'The Case for Sectoral Planning', in *National Economic Planning*, (Washington, D.C.: Chamber of Commerce of the United States).

1977   'A National Policy Towards Regional Change', *New England Economic Indicators*, May 1977, pp. 5–11.

'How Close is a Planned Economy?' *The Wharton Magazine*, 2, 32–7. A conversation with Walt W. Rostow and Paul A. Samuelson.

1978   'Food as the Foundation of Civilization', in Gary H. Koerselman and Kay E. Dull (eds), *Food and Social Policy, I* (Ames, Iowa: Iowa State University Press).

'Energy and Full Employment', in Charles J. Hitch (ed.), *Energy Conservation and Economic Growth* (Boulder, Colorado: Westview Press).

'Growth Rates at Different Levels of Income and Stage of Growth: Reflections on Why the Poor Get Richer and the Rich Slow Down', in *Research in Economic History: An Annual Compilation of Research*, 3 (Greenwich, Conn.: JAI Press.).

'The South: Regional Development and National Responsibility', in *Texas Business Review*, 52, 141–4.

1979 'A Fresh Start for the Americas', *Americas*, 31, 39–44.
'The Economic Power of the United States', in Donald W. Harward (ed.), *Power: Its Nature, Its Use, and Its Limits* (Cambridge, Mass.: Schenkman).
'A Simple Model of the Kondratieff Cycle', in Paul Uselding (ed.), *Research in Economic History: A Research Annual* (Greenwich, Conn.: JAI Press) 4, 1–36.

1980 'Energy and the Fate of the Nation', *Chemical Times and Trends*, 3, 25–8.
'Energy Target for the United States: A Net Export Position by 1990', *ORBIS*, 24, 3, 459–89.

Part II
Retardation and the Victorian Climacteric

[3]

THE CLIMACTERIC OF THE 1890's:
A STUDY IN THE EXPANDING ECONOMY

By E. H. PHELPS BROWN *with* S. J. HANDFIELD-JONES[1]

I

1. IT has been known for some time that a check to the rise of real wages, or of productivity, occurred in a number of countries about the end of the nineteenth century.

In his *Wealth and Income of the People of the United States*, in 1915, Dr. Willford I. King found that the real earnings of the American wage-earner, though not real income per head of the whole population, failed to rise between 1900 and 1912, and he attributed this to the closing of the internal frontier while the immigration of unskilled labour continued.

In 1920 A. L. Bowley, in his lecture on *The Change in the Distribution of the National Income 1880–1913*, stated that 'average real wages were very nearly stationary from the late '90's to 1913. . . . It was not uncommonly alleged immediately before the war that real wages had fallen. Though I do not accept the truth of this statement as being demonstrable on the evidence if the average of all wages is in question, yet it is undoubtedly true if we ignore the part of the progress due to the numerical increase of the better-paid occupations' (p. 19). For the population as a whole, 'average incomes were quite one-third greater in 1913 than in 1880' (since it happened that prices were much the same in those two years, Bowley could speak indifferently of money and real income here); 'but the increase was gained principally before 1900, since when it [*sc.* money income] barely kept pace with the diminishing value of money' (p. 26). 'I think . . . that the increase of luxury and the abundance of wealth which many people believe they observed before the war were illusions, fostered by the newspapers. I can find no statistical evidence that the rich as a class were getting rapidly richer in real income. . . . A considerable part of the impression of wealth was, I think, caused by the diversion of expenditure from other objects to motor-cars' (p. 20).

In 1933 G. T. Jones's *Increasing Return* found[2] that 'the 19th century was characterised by a progressive diminution in the quantity of resources consumed per unit of product in British manufacturing industries. By the close of the century, however, this movement had spent its force, so that real costs remained almost constant during the first decade

---

[1] The statistical studies, of which the ground was largely covered by S. J. Handfield-Jones before he went abroad, were completed by Bernard Weber, who in particular revised and extended the calculations of national capital reported in Appendix C. Sheila V. Hopkins carried out the work reported in Appendix A.   [2] pp. 247–8.

[The appendices have not been reproduced here.]

of the 20th century in at least three of the basic industries of Great Britain'—namely building, cotton, and pig-iron.[1] Jones attributed this partly to the balance of diseconomies consequent upon a growth of scale,[2] but more especially to easier working conditions for labour.[3] He further found that the efficiency of the Massachusetts cotton industry resembled that of Lancashire in reaching a maximum in 1900 and falling slightly in the next decade;[4] but real costs in the American pig-iron industry fell throughout 1900–12.[5]

In his *National Income and Outlay*, in 1937, Colin Clark noted a fall in the rate of growth of British real income a head in 1900–13: 'the curve was approaching a very definite ceiling.'[6]

In his *Conditions of Economic Progress*, in 1940, Colin Clark gave estimates of real income per head of the working population (after correction for changes in the length of the working week) which showed a check to the rate of rise appearing about 1900 or later in U.S.A., Canada, Great Britain, Australia, and France, but an unchecked rise in Germany, Switzerland, Sweden, Norway, Russia, and Italy.[7] Of Great Britain he said, 'productivity per worker-hour only increased slowly during the first fourteen years of this century';[8] of the U.S.A., 'productivity per worker per hour, which was rising sharply up to 1900, showed very little increase between 1900 and 1914';[9] of Australia, 'we have the remarkable feature of a very rapid growth of real income between 1886 and 1898 followed by a definite recession. Not until 1920 was the 1898 level of real income per head recovered.'[10]

In 1950 Phelps Brown and Hopkins[11] published estimates of real income per head of the occupied population in five countries. These showed that in Germany and the United Kingdom a rapid rise in real income per head was broken off between 1895 and 1900, after which there was little advance in the United Kingdom, and in Germany even some decline; but no such check was evident in the U.S.A. or in the fragmentary observations for France, and in Sweden a rapid rise was sustained. The same authors gave estimates of product wage-rates (i.e. money wage-rates divided by product prices), which are reproduced in Fig. 1, together with a similar series calculated subsequently for Belgium.[12] This figure gives a stronger impression of a check than do the income series, for in France, the United Kingdom, and the United States the ratio of wage-rates to the average income of the whole occupied population was probably lower in 1913 than in the

---

[1] pp. 93, 118, 143.   [2] pp. 255–6.
[3] See p. 248 for a general statement. There are particular observations at pp. 94, 96, 97, 118–19, 144.   [4] pp. 212, 214.
[5] pp. 238, 240.   [6] p. 271.   [7] Graph opposite p. 147, table opposite p. 148.
[8] p. 147.   [9] p. 158.   [10] p. 162.
[11] 'The Course of Wage Rates in Five Countries, 1860–1939', *Oxford Economic Papers*, June 1950.   [12] See Appendix A of the present article.

268   THE CLIMACTERIC OF THE 1890's

1890's. But such distributive shifts were of minor effect: even had product wage-rates fared no worse than other incomes, they would still have been checked.

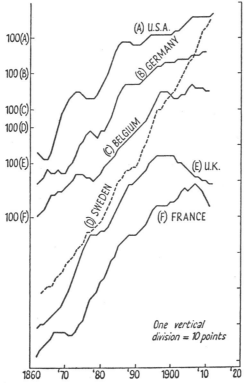

Fig. 1. Product Wage-rates. 5-yr. moving averages (1890–9=100).

II

2. The object of the present paper is to examine the climacteric in the United Kingdom more closely. From the evidence so far cited it appears that the check to the rise in British real wage-rates was due in part to a distributive change,[1] but that even had wage-rates kept pace with average income they would have made little if any net gain between the late 1890's and 1913. This is in marked contrast with the sustained advance of earlier years. Does it arise only from some bias, perhaps, in the index numbers, or does it mark a real check to the economic progress of the country?

3. There are three factors on which the real income of the people of the United Kingdom depends: their efficiency in production; their net receipts of property income from overseas; and the terms on which they exchange

[1] The reasons for this are discussed in Phelps Brown and Hart, 'The Share of Wages in National Income', *Economic Journal*, June 1952.

E. H. PHELPS BROWN AND S. J. HANDFIELD-JONES   269

their produce for that of the outside world. We have taken out estimates of the contributions of the last two factors, to see whether they played any part in the climacteric. The results are shown in Fig. 2.[1] Curve *A* shows total national income per head of the occupied population; income is expressed

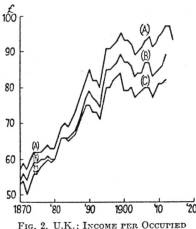

FIG. 2. U.K.: INCOME PER OCCUPIED PERSON, IN 1890-9 £s. (A) Total. (B) Home-produced. (C) (B) at 1881 terms of trade throughout.

in £s of constant purchasing power (that of 1890–9), to which it has been reduced from the original £s by applying an index of the prices of final products. Curve *B* shows the corresponding series for home-produced national income, reckoned by deducting from total national income the amount of property incomes from abroad. This curve of home-produced income shows if anything rather more of a check from 1899 onwards than total income does: property incomes from abroad seem to have made up rather less than 5 per cent. of national income in the 1870's, but from 1908 onwards they made up over 8 per cent., and this rise gave total income a better showing than home-produced. But the difference is not very great.

Then was the check brought on by a change in the terms of trade? Statistically, these lie in controversial ground,[2] but there can be no doubt that they underwent a change of direction about the end of the century. We have used Schlote's[3] indexes of the prices of imports and exports, and the result is shown in Fig. 3. From 1882 to 1900 there was a big fall of import prices relatively to export prices; after 1900 the movement though smaller was on balance the other way. So from 1882 to 1900 the rise in real income was being boosted by a change in the terms of trade, but after 1900 this factor operated in the opposite direction. How much did this contribute to the difference between the earlier rise and the later stagnation of real income a head? We can make a rough estimate by reckoning the value of the goods which would have had to be withdrawn from use at home in order to complete payment for the actual imports of each year, had these been bought at the terms of trade of 1882. The estimate is only rough, because if the terms of trade had been different, no doubt many

---

[1] Data, sources, and methods in Appendix B.

[2] The controversy is surveyed in W. W. Rostow, 'The Terms of Trade in Theory and Practice', *Economic History Review*, iii. 1, 1950. See also his 'The Historical Analysis of the Terms of Trade', ibid. iv. 1, 1951.

[3] *Entwicklung des Englischen Außenhandels*, Table 26.

270   THE CLIMACTERIC OF THE 1890's

other things would have been different too; but it gives us at least the
order of magnitude of the effects on real income which changes in the terms
of trade had from time to time. Deducting this from the figures of home-
produced national income gives us the series which, after reduction to £s of
constant purchasing power, appears as curve *C* of Fig. 2. This shows, as
we might expect, that the changes in the terms of trade made the rise of
real income more rapid than it would probably have been otherwise from

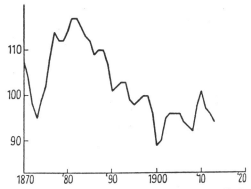

FIG. 3. U.K.: TERMS OF TRADE. Exports per unit of imports (Index, 1890–9 = 100).

1882 to 1900, whereas from 1900 to 1912 their effect was small: so the part
of the rise in real income which depended solely on the efficiency of British
production at home shows less check than real income as a whole, which
felt the impact of things beyond our control in the world market. Yet
when we have allowed for this, by far the greater part of the check remains.
Its causes must still be sought in productivity within the United Kingdom
itself.

4. Here our widest measure of output, short of the whole national
income, is Hoffmann's index,[1] which brings together many records of
physical output, some of them running back into the eighteenth century.
In 1861–1913 it has forty-three or more series, from a wide range of
industries.[2] The weights are proportional to the estimated total 'value
added' of each industry,[3] and if on the whole, at constant factor prices,
this varies from year to year in rough proportion to the physical output
of the industry, the index traces the growth in real terms of aggregate

[1] Walther Hoffmann, *Wachstum und Wachstumformen der englischen Industriewirtschaft
von 1700 bis zur Gegenwart* (Fischer, Jena, 1940). The index is also given in W. Hoffmann,
'Ein Index der industriellen Produktion für Großbritannien seit dem 18. Jahrhundert',
Weltwirtschaftliches Archiv, xl, 1934.

[2] The groups, with the number of series comprised in each in 1861–90, are: mining (7);
iron, steel, and machines (2); metal (non-ferrous) and metal wares (5); ships and vehicles (3);
wood (2); textiles (8); food, alcohol, and tobacco (9); paper (1); leather (2); rubber products
(1); chemicals (3). Three more series are used in 1891–1913.

[3] For 1861–90, estimated as at 1881; for 1891–1913, according to the Census of 1907.

E. H. PHELPS BROWN AND S. J. HANDFIELD-JONES   271

'value added'. Hoffmann reckons that his series during these years represent around 70 per cent. of the value added by all industry, and according to our estimate they cover more than 20 per cent. of the contemporary occupied population of Great Britain.

To arrive at the changes in productivity in this field we took the number of operatives within it from the occupational tables of the Census, and divided the index of this number into Hoffmann's index of output.[1] The

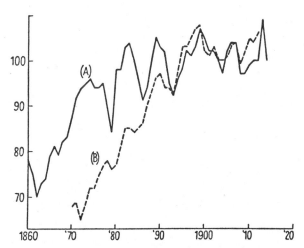

Fig. 4. (A) Output per Operative in Mining and Manufacturing
(B) Home-produced Real Income per Occupied Person, at 1881 Terms of Trade
(A) G.B. (B) U.K. (1890–9 = 100).

upshot is shown in curve *A* of Fig. 4. The *fluctuations* here are those of the trade cycle, for our numbers occupied year by year are obtained simply by linear interpolation between one census and the next, and are not adjusted for unemployment. But what concerns us here is the *trend*, and this shows a marked slowing down after 1880 in the rate of rise, and an asymptotic approach to a level no more than 5 per cent. above the average of the nineties. So marked is the change, indeed, that the trend can be closely approximated by a linear rise from 1860 to 1885, in which output a head rose by nearly a third, and after that a barely rising course down to 1914.

Can this be due solely to bias in our materials? Our numbers are of operatives only, not of all occupied: but the ratio of staff to operatives will have risen rather than fallen in this period. In working on the censuses we have encountered the difficulties of uncertain and changing classifica-

---

[1] Hoffmann's index, and the corresponding index of output a head, are at Table II, and the estimated numbers occupied at Table III, in Appendix B.

tion with which all who use these tables are familiar: the treatment of dealers, and of labourers, is specially liable to mislead, and there are many other points at which a hazardous decision had to be made on what to take in and leave out. But our guiding principle was to take only those series which were continuously comparable, rather than to achieve the fullest count possible at any one time; so though our coverage is sometimes incomplete, the movements of our total between one census year and another should be reasonably representative, save for one source of error. This lies in the attribution to particular industries in later censuses of many who had appeared before only as general labourers. In 1891 there were some 879,000 general labourers recorded in Great Britain, but in 1911, despite the growth of population meanwhile, only 481,000. Let us suppose that the whole of the difference of almost 400,000 was due to labourers getting classified by industry, and that all those so classified appeared as additions to the labour force of Hoffmann's industries: if we corrected for this, we should raise output a head in 1911 from 100 to nearly 110 per cent. of the average of the 1890's. Even on this extreme assumption, the contrast between the earlier and later rates of growth would remain: in the 20 years from 1861 to 1881, a rise of about a third; in the 30 years from 1881 to 1911, a rise of about a tenth.

Alternatively, does the behaviour of our index of productivity arise out of changes in the distribution of the working population between industries, rather than from changes in the productivities of those industries themselves? Since 'value added' per operative differs in different industries, a redistribution of the working force towards industries in which 'value added' per operative was low could lower productivity in the aggregate, even though in each separate industry it had been rising. We have checked this possibility by estimating the effect of the actual redistribution of the working force on average 'value added' per operative, on the assumption that in each industry 'value added' was at its 1907 level throughout, and we find a sustained rise, amounting to about 8 per cent. in all between 1861 and 1911. The check, then, cannot be ascribed to the redistribution of the working force, which worked rather the other way.

There may, however, be a downward bias in our index, because Hoffmann's series make no allowance for the product becoming more highly fabricated as time goes on. Some allowance is due for this; we cannot tell how much.

With some reservations, then, we can accept our index as a check on the evidence of national income; indeed, in one respect it may be more reliable, for it does not depend, as the series for national income must do, upon appropriate representation of the general level of prices. Fig. 4

E. H. PHELPS BROWN AND S. J. HANDFIELD-JONES   273

enables us to compare the movements of our two indexes, that is, real income per occupied person (at constant terms of trade), and output a head in the Hoffmann industries. There is one divergence—between 1885 and 1900 real income a head rose by more than a fifth, whereas in 1885 the rapid rise of productivity in the Hoffmann industries had already come to an end. After 1900, the two series follow remarkably similar courses;

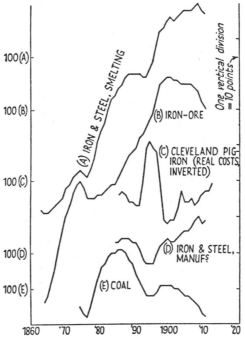

FIG. 5. U.K.: INDEXES OF OUTPUT PER OPERATIVE OR PER UNIT REAL COST.
5- or 7-yr. moving averages (1890–9 = 100).

and if we represented them with 1870 as base, we should see that the same holds for the years on the other side of the divergence, those, namely, from 1870 to 1885. For the most part, then, the two series bear each other out. What of the divergence? In part it was due to the influence on the Hoffmann index of coal-mining, in which output a head began to fall off before 1890; but even when allowance is made for this,[1] much of the divergence remains. It may well be due partly to a fall in our price index which, at a time of sharp movement in commodity prices, was excessive relatively to the less flexible money flows. The main impression remains one of agreement. There is no doubt about the check.

[1] The index of productivity in the Hoffmann coverage less coal is at col. 8 of Table II in Appendix B.

274   THE CLIMACTERIC OF THE 1890's

5. This change in general productivity can be explored by calculating indexes of output a head in those industries where we have records of output, and also can trace the number of operatives in a sufficiently comparable and consistent form. The results[1] appear in smoothed form in Figs. 5 and 6, together with two of G. T. Jones's estimates[2] of real cost per

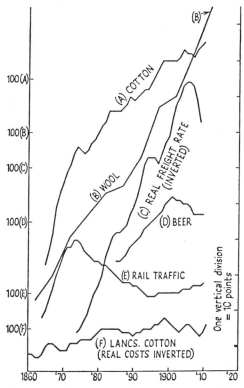

FIG. 6. U.K.: INDEXES OF OUTPUT PER OPERATIVE OR PER UNIT REAL COST.
5-, 7-, or 10-yr. moving averages (1890–9 = 100).

unit of output, which are inverted here so as to appear as indexes of output per unit of real cost. The estimates of the numbers occupied in particular industries are more liable to error than those for industry as a whole, and

---

[1] Data, sources, and methods are in Appendix B. These include estimates for shipbuilding, which are not illustrated in the Figures, because of the unsatisfactory nature of the only unit of output available—the unit of tonnage. Taking these estimates for what they are worth, we find a declining trend of tonnage per man between the 1880's and 1914.

[2] G. T. Jones, *Increasing Return* (1933). Jones's estimates of real cost were made by deflating the product price by an index of factor prices. When inverted, as here, they provide indexes of output per composite unit input of resources of all kinds, whereas our indexes are of output per operative only. Thus where equipment per head is increasing our index will rise more than the inverted G. T. Jones index, and this may account for some of the difference between the two types of index for cotton down to 1899 (Fig. 6). The G. T. Jones type is disturbed when the product price departs from the normal supply price, and this accounts for the peak in the 1890's in the Cleveland pig-iron series in Fig. 5.

E. H. PHELPS BROWN AND S. J. HANDFIELD-JONES   275

the allocation of more labourers to particular industries in 1911 may distort the results for one industry. But the possibilities of error are not so great as to bring marked movements under suspicion.

Two industries stand out as reaching their highest output per operative early on, and considerably declining thereafter. The first of these is transport by rail, though this does not fall within Hoffmann's coverage. The traffic, measured by a combined index of passengers and freight, which the railways carried per operative employed, reached its maximum in the early seventies and then declined for 20 years. This can scarcely have been due to any lack of the economies of scale, for traffics continued to rise faster than the occupied population, even though there was an abrupt stop in 1901 to the rise of passenger journeys a head. The cause must be sought on the opposite side, in diminishing returns; or in the competitive increase of amenities offered to the public; or in improvements in the working hours and conditions of work of the railwaymen. In the coal-mines also there was an early turning-point, in 1886, from which time till 1914 there was a fairly steady decline, which was attributable certainly to the resort to deeper or more difficult seams, and possibly to a shorter working week per man not compensated by higher outputs per man-hour.

The index for shipping is different from the others: we have deflated an index of freights by an index of the general price level, so as to get the quantity of goods required to compensate the ton-mile of sea transport, and then inverted this. In the long run, though by no means in the short, an industry in which costs are falling more rapidly than they are in the aggregate elsewhere, will generally receive a smaller quantity of goods in exchange for the unit of its own product. The sustained fall of 'real freights' therefore suggests a sustained *relative* advance of productivity in sea transport.

Two other industries show no check—iron and steel manufactures, and wool.

This leaves four industries in which output per operative seems to have been checked about the turn of the century: cotton, in both its otherwise very different indexes; beer, in which economies of scale may have been cut back, for consumption a head began to fall from 1900; the mining of iron ore; and iron and steel smelting, in which output per operative continued to rise, but more slowly, though G. T. Jones's real costs of Cleveland pig-iron conflict with this.

In sum, the evidence needs cautious handling, and is by no means unanimous; so far as it goes, it shows a check or reversal of the rise of output per operative in six particular industries, at various dates from the seventies to the turn of the century; and no check in three others. The field surveyed is not wide, but so far as any generalization is warranted, it is that no concentration of effects or causes has been revealed: the rise of productivity was checked in some industries, and not in others; those in which the check appeared were of various kinds.

6. An index of output cannot usually include new industries until they have grown to some size and come of statistical age, and so it gives us no view of technical progress in its early stages. We must take care, therefore, not to read into the later course of productivity within Hoffmann's coverage a general verdict of stagnation. On the contrary, there was much technical development in the United Kingdom in the 20 years before the First World War, and a rapid expansion of still small industries which were to attain a massive development through and after the war.[1]

We may cite three here. The output of motor vehicles trebled between 1907 and 1913, when it was about 34,000—in 1934 it was over ten times as great.[2] The number of operatives whom the Census classified as manufacturing chemists, or as engaged in the manufacture of alkali, in Great Britain, rose by a half between 1901 and 1911.[3] In electricity, the expansion of a still small industry became very rapid at the turn of the century. The output sold by supply undertakings increased fifteenfold between 1899 and 1914.[4] Between 1901 and 1911 the number of operatives recorded by the Census as electricians or as manufacturing electrical equipment in Great Britain nearly doubled.[5]

Yet the rise of these industries, and of others such as rayon, aluminium, and aircraft, was big with promise rather than achievement. In the three we first cited, all the operatives together were less than a quarter of a million in 1911, when there were about $13\frac{1}{2}$ million wage-earners in Great Britain. Hoffmann's index in this period actually includes motor-cars, alkalis, and aluminium. Its omission of the others cannot give it any significant downward bias as a measure of current output: what it leaves out was significant for the future, but too small to make much difference for the time being.

7. We can supplement our study of industrial productivity with the estimates of output a head in agriculture shown in Fig. 7.[6] The more

[1] See R. S. Sayers, 'The Springs of Technical Progress in Britain, 1919–39', *E.J.*, June 1950; A. Plummer, *New British Industries in the Twentieth Century* (Pitman, 1937). In 1907 electrical engineering and contracting accounted for 4·5 per cent., and commercial vehicles and aircraft for 1·2 per cent., of the aggregate value of gross investment in fixed capital; in 1930 the corresponding percentages were 8·5 and 3·4 (Colin Clark, *Investment in Fixed Capital in Great Britain*, London and Cambridge Economic Service, Special Memo. No. 38, Sept. 1934).
[2] *The Motor Industry of Great Britain*, issued by the Statistical Dept. of the Society of Motor Manufacturers and Traders, 1936.
[3] *Census of England and Wales, 1911*, x, Table 26; *Census of Scotland, 1911*, ii, Table D.1.
[4] Garcke, *Manual of Electrical Undertakings*, vol. xvii, 1913–14, p. 6.
[5] *Census of England and Wales, 1911*, x, Table 26; *Census of Scotland, 1911*, ii, Table D.1.
[6] We are indebted for commentary and guidance here to Dr. J. R. Raeburn of the London School of Economics.

E. H. PHELPS BROWN AND S. J. HANDFIELD-JONES 277

steeply rising curve shows the result of dividing Drescher's index[1] of the gross output of agriculture in Great Britain by our own figures for the numbers occupied there.[2] The other curve is E. M. Ojala's estimate[3] of value added (at 1911–13 prices) per person occupied in agriculture in the whole United Kingdom. The difference between the two curves can be accounted for by the first using the gross output of Great Britain alone and

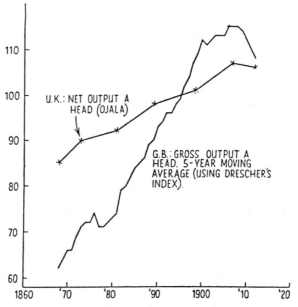

FIG. 7. OUTPUT PER PERSON OCCUPIED IN AGRICULTURE
(1890–9 = 100).

the second the net output of the whole United Kingdom, and subject to this they confirm each other closely.[4] The second is the more closely connected with our estimates of national income a head, and it is also based on

[1] Leo Drescher, 'Die Entwicklung der Agrarproduktion Großbritanniens und Irlands seit Beginn des 19. Jahrhunderts', *Weltwirtschaftliches Archiv*, xli, 1935, p. 270. We use the 'economic index of volume' in his Table 10; it is cited, on a different base, in col. 23 of Table II, Appendix B, of this article.

[2] Series 2, Table III, Appendix B.

[3] E. M. Ojala, *Agriculture and Economic Progress* (Oxford University Press, 1952), Table LV, p. 153, col. 4:

1867–9 = 100. *Output per worker in agriculture in the United Kingdom, averages of groups of years*

1867–9	.	. 100	1886–93.	. 115	1911–13.	. 124	1930–4.	. 140
1870–6	.	. 106	1894–1903.	. 119	1920–2 .	. 116	1935–9.	. 127
1877–85	.	. 108	1904–10.	. 126	1924–9 .	. 125		

In Fig. 7 these are shown as relatives to the average of 1890–9 (taken as 117·3) as base.

[4] (*a*) In Ojala's estimates the ratio of net to gross output falls from 77 per cent. in 1867–9 to about 67 per cent. through 1894–1913 (op. cit., Table XX, p. 215), so if a corresponding

more extensive materials; it suggests that the agriculture of the United Kingdom as a whole did not contribute much to the check to the rise of real income. The first serves to separate gross output a head in British agriculture from that of the very different rural economy of Ireland. Irish gross output a head seems to have been lower at all times than British, and to have risen less rapidly down to 1901, but much more rapidly thereafter.[1] When this element is removed, we are left with a course of change in Great Britain alone which in its set-back after 1900 resembles industrial productivity. Proximately, at least, this resemblance was a mere co-incidence, for the check in agriculture seems to have sprung from the changed course of agricultural prices. The near doubling of gross output a head between 1860 and 1900 came about through a moderate but fairly persistent increase in output being achieved by a rapidly falling labour force. This may have been made possible by continued technical improvement, the contraction of tillage to the best soils, and a general pressure on farmers to save labour, as product prices fell relatively to money wage-rates. In 1896 the price trend was reversed, and soon afterwards the rise in gross output a head came nearly to a stop. But though agriculture seems

correction were applied to the curve from Drescher in Fig. 7 it would be raised by about one-sixth at its start relatively to its end, and rise rather more slowly down to 1900.

(b) Drescher also gives a combined index for the whole United Kingdom and this shows close agreement with an index of gross output which Ojala also gives, except in the first 20 years, when it rises rather more rapidly. Irish output carried about a quarter of the weight of Drescher's combined index. Thus it is probable that Drescher's estimate for Great Britain alone would be borne out by the wider materials used by Ojala. The figures are:

U.K.: gross output of agriculture, at constant prices

1911–13 = 100. Col. (1): Drescher, op. cit., Table 10. Col. (2): Ojala, op. cit., Table XVIII, p. 210

	(1)	(2)			(1)	(2)
1867–9	83	89		1894–1903	95	95
1870–6	87	93		1904–10	102	99
1877–85	85	90		1911–13	100	100
1886–93	93	94				

[1] The numbers occupied in agriculture in Ireland may be obtained by subtracting our estimates of the number occupied in Great Britain (Appendix B, Table III, Series 2) from the numbers occupied in the United Kingdom given by Ojala, op. cit., Table XXXIII, p. 85, the earlier entries here being scaled down to give continuity through 1881. The results can be divided into Drescher's index of physical output in Ireland (average of 5 years centred on census year) to yield an index of productivity:

Col. (1): Numbers occupied in G.B., '000s. Col. (2): Numbers occupied in Ireland, '000s. Col. (3): Index of gross output a head in Ireland, 1871 = 100.

	(1)	(2)	(3)			(1)	(2)	(3)
1871	1,477	1,242	100		1901	979	1,202	118
1881	1,327	1,152	104		1911	1,081	1,102	140
1891	1,205	1,200	110					

Drescher (op. cit.) gives the aggregate value of British and Irish gross outputs (items within his index only) as £m.202 and £m.63 respectively in 1909–13. At this time the numbers occupied in the two areas were about equal, so Irish gross output a head seems to have been much lower than British, even when allowance is made for any relative under-representation of Ireland in the index (e.g. omission of horsebreeding). This seems to have been the position after 40 years of continuous and, latterly, rapid advance in Irish productivity.

E. H. PHELPS BROWN AND S. J. HANDFIELD-JONES   279

in this way to have been governed mostly by the change in its own prices, this in turn was bound up with the changed relation between industry and agriculture, to which we return in paras. 12 and 13 below. If we have interpreted the records of British agriculture rightly, they suggest that the increased scarcity of farm products may have reinforced itself somewhat: there may be a general tendency for productivity to be checked where the product becomes scarcer, because higher prices make life easier for the producer.

III

8. Our estimates are subject to a wide margin of error at some points, but contain enough agreement of independent evidence to make it clear that some checks to the rise of productivity in industry and agriculture underlay the set-backs to real income a head and real wages in the United Kingdom about the turn of the century. Why did these things come about ? We can narrow our search for causes, because we have good reason to believe that the check was not peculiar to the United Kingdom, but was also experienced in some measure by Belgium, France, Germany, and the United States (see Fig. 1). The most likely causes will be those which could have operated in all these countries. When, therefore, we consider the reasons given for the United Kingdom's falling behind other countries at this time, we must ask whether they mark factors common to the other countries but operative with greater intensity in the United Kingdom, or factors peculiar to the United Kingdom but working there to the same effect as different factors in the other countries.

9. To contemporaries these reasons seemed important: it was alleged that both management and labour were less efficient in Britain than they had been.

Criticism was directed against British management by comparison with other countries. Awareness of higher productivity in American industry, and dispatch of teams to find out how it is achieved, go back at least to the 1850's in Britain,[1] but perhaps the first team to contain trade unionists was that of Mr. Alfred Mosely, who in 1902 took twenty-three trade union officers to visit their own industries in the United States.[2] Their observations have a familiar ring to readers of recent reports, whose findings they anticipate in some detail. The special correspondent of *The Times* who accompanied them endorsed the main points of contrast which they drew between British and American management.[3] American managers were chosen for their competence, not their family connexions. 'The American

[1] See D. L. Burn, 'The Genesis of American Engineering Competition, 1850–70', *Economic History*, ii. 6, Jan. 1931.
[2] *Mosely Industrial Commission to the United States of America, Oct.–Dec. 1902. Reports of the Delegates* (Manchester, 1903).
[3] *The Times*, 16, 23, 25, and 26 Dec. 1902.

manufacturer realizes the supreme importance of order and system in the factory, and accordingly sees not only that every operation is simplified and sub-divided to the form in which it can be most efficiently performed, but also that each worker is always fully supplied with the kind of work which he or she can do best.' Probably the American 'has few, if any, machines that are utterly unknown in England, but he is more determined and wholesale in his use of mechanical appliances generally, and runs them for the utmost he can get out of them'. 'In America, employer and workman seem to be closer together than they are in England, and in consequence the former is more able to benefit from the latter's knowledge and experience.'

In the following year, 1903, Marshall noted the loss by Britain of the industrial leadership she had had sixty years before. 'It was not inevitable', he wrote,[1] 'that she should lose as much of it as she has done. The greatness and rapidity of her loss is partly due to that very prosperity which followed the adoption of Free Trade.' The combination of advantages which she enjoyed in those years encouraged 'the belief that an Englishman could expect to obtain a much larger real income and to live much more luxuriously than anybody else, at all events in an old country; and that if he chose to shorten his hours of work and take things easily, he could afford to do it'. Other causes of complacency lay in the distraction of competitors by civil war in America, and the wars which Germany fought in Europe; and in the bounty conferred upon the entrepreneur by rising prices consequent upon the influx of gold. 'This combination of causes made many of the sons of manufacturers content to follow mechanically the lead given by their fathers. They worked shorter hours, and they exerted themselves less to obtain new practical ideas than their fathers had done; and thus a part of England's leadership was destroyed rapidly. In the 'nineties it became clear that in future Englishmen must take business as seriously as their grandfathers had done, and as their American and German rivals were doing.'

The relative decline of British industry was also attributed to an increased enforcement of restrictive practices by trade unionists. This was the contention of eleven articles by E. A. Pratt which *The Times* printed in the winter of 1901–2 under the title of 'The Crisis in British Industry'.[2] 'The "new" unionism, with its resort to violence and intimidation, has in turn been succeeded by a "newer" unionism, which, although working along much quieter lines, is doing even more serious injury'—by enforcing restrictive practices. The articles contained instances of these practices,

[1] Sec. L of *Memorandum on Fiscal Policy of International Trade*, completed Aug. 1903, published as H. of C. No. 321, Nov. 1908.

[2] 18, 21 Nov.; 3, 14, 16, 24, 26, 27, 30 Dec. 1901; 4, 16 Jan. 1902; reprinted in *Trade Unionism and British Industry*, by E. A. Pratt (1904).

E. H. PHELPS BROWN AND S. J. HANDFIELD-JONES   281

but little definite evidence that they had increased of late. The Webbs rejoined[1] that

'the complaints as to diminished quantity or energy of work, and of the tacit conspiracy to discourage individual exertion, occur with curiously exact iteration in every decade of the last hundred years at least. . . . To give one instance only, we have found exactly the same accusation of the bricklayers' limiting the number of bricks, and precisely the same belief that they were only doing "half as much" as they did twenty years before, in the great strikes of 1833, in those of 1853, again in 1859–60, and again in 1871.'

It is probable none the less that the rise in the strength of trade unions between 1889 and 1901 did increase the practical effect of restrictive tendencies which had long been present. There is a distinct, and real, possibility, that wage-earners' standards of achievement were kept down, or even lowered, through emigration taking off many of the most energetic.

Yet with trade unionists as with management, what is well-founded in the charges does not seem enough to account for the severe check to productivity which came about in the 1890's. The fact that great advances in British productivity have been achieved in later years, when similar contrasts have been drawn between British and American management, and British trade unions have been stronger than ever, reminds us that these factors, though important, are not the only ones on which productivity depends. In accounting for the climacteric, moreover, we have to look not for persistent conditions which kept productivity down at all times, but for recent changes which could have halted its previously rising trend, and what change there was at this time in the qualities of management and labour does not seem commensurate with that effect. It was rather that through these factors Britain was denied some energies of industrial advance, which were active in America, and might have sustained the rise of productivity here when a pause came in other kinds of development. British labour generally was not prepared to risk job security and abandon bargaining weapons for the chance of higher earnings. British industrial society had not developed the morale and institutions which would accumulate the practical achievements of management as a doctrine, and impart them as a discipline, so as to maintain a general level of managerial performance not far below that of the best firms in each generation.

These seem to have been continuing deficiencies in the endowment of British industry, rather than the active causes of the check to British productivity in the 1890's, which are more likely to be found in factors affecting Britain in common with the other countries which experienced something of the same check.

[1] *The Times*, 6 Dec. 1901.

10. Such common factors may reasonably be sought in the declining rate of extension at this time of the techniques of power, transport, and machinery comprised beneath the names of Steam and Steel. There is a varying but usually considerable lag between the inventions which first open the way and the massive applications which alone take effect on the productivity of whole peoples. So though the heroic age of the steam-engine lay far back, in the eighteenth century, and Bessemer's invention is usually assigned to 1856, it was not till after the civil war in America, and the Franco-Prussian war in Europe, that the general benefit began to be won of steam-engines driving steel machinery, and of transport by steam-engines on steel rails and in steel ships. Our hypothesis is that the rapid and general extension of these techniques was coming to an end in the 1890's. The supersession of sail by steam at sea is a striking example.[1] In 1860, nearly half a century after the first steamships had been tried, the tonnage of British shipping under sail was still growing, and was nearly ten times as great as the tonnage in steam; in 1880 the ratio was still about 3 to 2. But steam tonnage was now growing very rapidly, and in 1883 it overtook the declining tonnage under sail; by 1895 it was more than twice as great; and in carrying capacity of course the disparity was far wider than this. The replacement of each sailing-ship by a steamship makes a big advance in the productivity of transport, but once the sailing-ships have been replaced, such rapid improvements are no longer possible: only those annual advances remain which can be brought about by gradual improvements in the performance of the steamship itself.

The example brings out another point: the inventions which affect productivity most are those which improve processes common to many industries. All industries depend on power, transport, and the basic techniques of machine-making, and an invention which improves one of these is likely to raise productivity everywhere; unlike the inventions which are specific to particular industries. Even when technical improvements are coming forward fairly steadily, the inventions of widespread application may be made and brought into general use only discontinuously. The times of greatest rise in national productivity are those in which important inventions of widespread application have reached the stage of widespread installation.

Our knowledge of industrial history agrees with this. It shows, first,[2] that in manufacturing generally, about 1850 there was still much hand-work, and outwork, the sailing ships, so to speak, of industry, giving the opportunity for a rapid rise in productivity when they were superseded

---

[1] Tables 58A and 60 in W. Page (ed.), *Commerce and Industry*, vol. ii.

[2] J. H. Clapham, *Economic History of Modern Britain*, vol. ii, chap. ii, 'The Industrial Field in 1851'.

by factory power and machinery. Second,[1] it shows that the advance of power and mechanization in the 40 years after 1850 brought about changes in industrial methods which were widespread, far-reaching, and sometimes revolutionary. Third,[2] it shows some continuing technical progress, and the opening of new possibilities, in the 20 years before the First World War, but no longer the massive application of new equipment to raise productivity throughout industries that were already large. In the previous period, steel had ousted puddled iron; working to gauge on steel had made machine parts interchangeable, and this 'reacted continuously on the older mechanised industries';[3] spinning and weaving had been mechanized in the woollen industry; steel rollers had superseded millstones in the steam mills—the list might be longer. But the 20 years before the First World War do not see such widespread changes. The emphasis lies on 'widespread'. Much development was beginning now, which was to bring about the rise of nearly two-thirds in output per man-hour in British industry, which Rostas[4] has found between 1907 and 1937; but it took most of its effect only in its massive application after the war.

In sum, then, our main explanation of the check to the rise of real income in the United Kingdom about the end of the nineteenth century is that the previous rise had been carried forward by the massive application of Steam and Steel, which now had not much scope for extension; while the new techniques, especially of electricity, the internal combustion engine, and the new chemical processes, did not attain massive application until during and after the First World War.

Of the countries in Fig. 1, only Sweden shows in the aggregate no sign of the check, and this agrees with our theory if in fact the general application of Steam and Steel came later there.

11. The reduced rate of extension of new types of equipment in the United Kingdom suggests a lower rate of capital accumulation, and the great increase in capital export after 1904 also makes this seem likely. But the new estimates of real capital per head which we report in Appendix C show a rise sustained to 1914 along a linear trend. We have used two methods, which have a common base in Stamp's estimate of the capital stock about 1912, but are quite independent in their estimates of the changes through earlier years. The first method is to estimate annual net investment, and after reducing this to £'s of constant purchasing

---

[1] Clapham, op. cit., vol. ii, chap. iii.

[2] Clapham, op. cit., vol. iii, chap. iii, in contrast with chap. iii of vol. ii.

[3] Clapham, op. cit., vol. ii, p. 80.

[4] L. Rostas, *Comparative Productivity in British and American Industry* (National Institute of Economic and Social Research, Occasional Papers, xiii, 1948), p. 49. The coverage is manufacturing, mining, building, and public utilities. In this area output per wage-earner rose by 47 per cent. between 1907 and 1937, by 37 per cent. between 1924 and 1937 (ibid., pp. 42–43).

power, use it to decumulate the stock of 1912 and arrive by difference at the stocks of earlier years. The second method is to capitalize property incomes either (as Stamp did) by applying the appropriate number of years' purchase to each category of property income in the Inland Revenue returns, or by applying an average of years' purchase to profits as a whole. This second method has two drawbacks—the uncertainty of the right number of years' purchase for some property incomes, and the quasi-rent

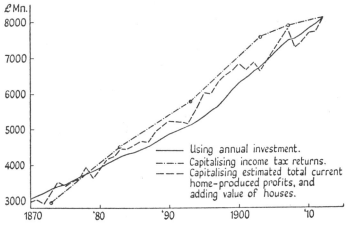

FIG. 8. TOTAL REVENUE-EARNING CAPITAL (EXCLUDING FARM CAPITAL) WITHIN U.K., IN DEC. 1912 £s.

nature of much of the income capitalized, which causes the capital values obtained to swing above or below the current replacement cost of the buildings, equipment, and stocks. The first method avoids these snags of valuation, but has drawbacks of its own: it rests on a relatively small number of series, and involves some rough estimating; any bias in it, or defect of coverage, will take cumulative effect on the estimates of capital stocks. But we can use the two methods as checks on one another, and Fig 8 shows that there is more agreement between the results than we might expect, at least over the whole span; since two independent methods have been used, and different price indexes, the agreement confirms the magnitude of the movement. This magnitude is illustrated in Fig. 9, which shows that real capital a head rose by 60 per cent. during this period. This rise, moreover, appears to have been sustained through the 20 years before the First World War, so that the average man at work in the United Kingdom in 1914 was working with more equipment, even though he was not much more productive, than his counterpart in 1895.

This impression is borne out by Fig. 10, which shows total net home investment each year, in £s whose purchasing power over investment goods is about that of December 1912. So far from the nineties bringing a slackening in home investment, they saw a rapid rise to an average half as great again as that of the seventies and eighties, and except in 1908 a substantial increase was maintained down to the war. It has been generally

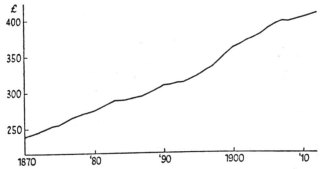

FIG. 9. U.K.: HOME REVENUE-EARNING CAPITAL (EXCLUDING FARM CAPITAL) PER OCCUPIED PERSON, IN DEC. 1912 £s.

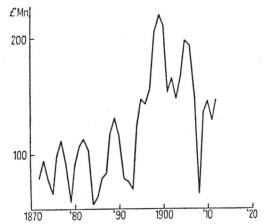

FIG. 10. U.K.: ANNUAL NET HOME INVESTMENT, IN DEC. 1912 £s.

known that a housing boom began in the nineties, but our estimates suggest that investment in industrial equipment rose then even more rapidly than housing.

The continued and indeed accelerated growth of capital a head throws doubt on an explanation of the check to productivity which otherwise would seem likely to have something in it, namely, that the decline in product wage-rates, i.e. the rise in prices of products relatively to money wage-rates in Britain after 1899, relieved firms of the pressure to introduce labour-saving equipment, to which rising product wage-rates had been submitting them throughout the preceding 40 years. Very likely there was some relaxing effect, but it does not seem to have checked the growth of equipment per occupied person.

Our findings do not conflict with the explanation of the check to productivity put forward in para. 10—the tonnage of steamships, so to speak, might continue to increase even faster than the occupied population, but adding one steamship to others would not make so much difference as substituting a steamship for a sailing-ship had done. There was no longer the innovation effect.

12. This working out of the innovation effect of Steam and Steel was the more serious for the British people, because they had been gaining so much from it as importers of food and raw materials.

'It has been said, and it may be with truth', wrote the signatories of Part II of the report of the Royal Commission on Gold and Silver,[1] 'that the development of machinery was as great in the fifteen or twenty years which preceded 1874, as in the subsequent years, and that steam transport had been also largely developed in the earlier period. But not only has the actual extension of railways and the cheapening of land and sea freight been greater in the subsequent years, but the effect of railways which had been previously made has been more felt. . . . . Large new districts of great natural fertility, and rich in minerals, have been opened up, and consequently civilized countries have been furnished with an unprecedented quantity of raw vegetable and mineral products.'

Thus the ever-growing British population drew supplies whose rate of increase was even greater than its own, so long as Steam and Steel were opening new sources up; but when that opening up was done, though supplies continued to rise in total, their rate of increase fell, while that of population went on. The factory-worker's terms of trade with farmers and miners ceased to move in his favour.

This sort of check would have been bound to hold back the standard of living of the British people, even if it had not coincided with a reduced rate of progress in their own industrial productivity. British imports were largely of materials which we may call basic, because some quantity of them is indispensable to subsistence. Inventions and discoveries may be roughly divided into those on the one hand which open up new sources of basic materials, or increase the return to a unit of human work on the existing sources, or make transport from them easier; and those on the other hand which provide more of other materials, or increase our ability to work material up into useful and pleasing manufactures. A first rise in the standard of living above the level of subsistence requires an almost proportional rise in the intake of basic materials: it depends, that is to say, on inventions of the first class. No doubt, if the rise is maintained, and population is constant, the relative importance of the second class rises, and after some point has been passed there is no presumption that the one class is more beneficial than the other. But the population of Britain at

[1] C. 5512 of 1888; Part II, para. 26.

this time was relentlessly increasing, and if only the existing standard of living were to be maintained, supplies of basic materials had to be increased as rapidly as the number of consumers. Sooner or later the ability of an expanding economy to do this is likely to be impaired by decreasing returns at its existing sources of supply, and this obstacle cannot be avoided by however vigorous a development of inventions of the second class. The consequent set-back to real income will generally be felt most by the wage-earners, because their consumption contains a higher proportion of basic materials than does that of the better off.

The relative unimportance in such circumstances of skill in working basic materials up, compared with the availability of those materials themselves, was put with unusual emphasis by Marshall in 1903.[1]

'The progress of the arts and resources of manufacture has benefited England more than almost any other country in one important but indirect way. It has so reduced the cost of carriage by land and sea that raw materials and food can come to her, even from the centres of great continents, at a less cost than they could come from the near neighbourhood of the sea-shores and great rivers of the Continent sixty years ago; and the 300,000 miles of railways which have been built during the last sixty years in America, Asia, Africa, and Australia are rendering greater service to Englishmen than to any other people, except those in whose lands the several railways are placed.'

So far 'the progress of manufactures' as it provides inventions of our first class; now for the second.

'In almost every other respect the progress of the arts and resources of manufacture has benefited England less than any other country. For, even sixty years ago, the excess of the cost of the manufactures needed for her own consumption over that of the raw material by which they were made was small. If it could have been reduced to nothing, she would have gained by the change very much less than she has gained by the lowering of the cost of imported food and raw material for her own use.'

The changed balance between the growth of population and the supply of basic materials seemed ominous to contemporaries. On the eve of the war D. H. Robertson[2] concluded 'that the normal tendency for the ratio of exchange to alter against the manufacturing and in favour of the agricultural communities was in force in the 'seventies, was suspended in the 'eighties and 'nineties, and is now once more on the whole triumphing. This is perhaps the most significant economic fact in the world today.' We know now that those conditions were fostering their own correction, and the balance swung back after the war, so that the years 1896–1914 have fallen into their place in an historical alternation. As W. W. Rostow[3] has said, 'The three famous periods of extensive expansion, with rising

---

[1] See. L of his *Memorandum on Fiscal Policy of International Trade (1903)*, H. of C. No. 321, Nov. 1908.

[2] At p. 169, n. 1, of his *Study of Industrial Fluctuation* (1915). (No. 8 in the London School of Economics series of Reprints of Scarce Works on Political Economy.)

[3] 'The Historical Analysis of the Terms of Trade', *Economic History Review*, iv. 1, 1951, p. 64.

price and interest trends (roughly 1793–1815; 1848–73; 1896–1914) were part of the rough and ready process by which an appropriate balance of world production and a more or less appropriate distribution of population on the earth's land were maintained.' Even the immediate effect, moreover, though it fell specially hard upon the wage-earners, was not so very great in proportion to national income.[1] But since the Second World War we have learned again how an economy may be rapidly increasing the range and efficiency of its manufactures yet be held back by short supplies of foodstuffs, raw materials, and power.

13. In the greater scarcity of basic materials we may find a link between contemporary changes in the trends of productivity and of prices. The upturn of prices was facilitated by the increased supply of gold, but this other factor seems to have been at work to start the rise in prices and carry it on, and may well have made itself felt even without any increase in the output of gold. An initial rise in raw material prices tends to raise requirements of working capital, which in certain monetary conditions will be provided in such increased quantities as to support a general sympathetic rise of product prices and other factor prices. Consumers whose real income is reduced by scarcity of basic materials try to maintain it by getting higher money incomes; again in certain monetary conditions they will succeed, and another round of price rises follows. We have seen in recent years how in the absence of monetary constraint a price rise in one sector can spread outwards, and one set-back to real income can start a spiral of prices and money incomes. These processes, beginning with the greater scarcity of basic materials in the 1890's, may have been at work to draw out the monetary expansion and rise in prices which the increased gold supply made possible.

14. Some inferences may be drawn for the present prospects of Great Britain.

It seems that the substantial and general raising of productivity is brought about by the massive application of technical advances. The phase of massive application may follow that of pathbreaking invention only at a long remove. When it comes, it brings a high rate of advance, which falls off as the field of innovation is worked over. The progress of productivity, and the standard of living, thus appears to be very unstable. We cannot count upon the advance of productivity along a constant growth curve. Should at any time our standard of living not be much raised for 20 years, that would be only what has already happened in the lifetime of many people now living.

The raising of the standard of living generally requires increased supplies of basic materials. Improvements in our efficiency in working

[1] Para. 3 above.

materials up into products of existing types, and fertility in designing new products, can compensate only partially for inability to increase these supplies. Such an increase can be achieved by capital investment which develops new sources of supply overseas, by success in exporting, or by inventions which liberate new sources of energy and basic materials within the country. If advances of these kinds can be made, a limiting factor can be lifted which otherwise will restrict the use of all other technical advances.

IV

15. Summary

1. A number of investigators have detected a check to the rise of real income a head, in several countries, about the end of the nineteenth century. Estimates of real wage-rates show some adverse change of trend about this time, in differing degree, in Belgium, France, Germany, the United Kingdom, and the United States, but not Sweden. (Para. 1.)

2. The check in the United Kingdom was not due to a falling off in property income from abroad. It was increased by the cessation in 1900 of the improvement in the terms of trade which had persisted since 1882. But when allowance has been made for this, the greater part of the check remains, and its causes must be sought in productivity at home. (Paras. 2–3.)

3. Output per operative within the coverage of Hoffmann's index of British industrial output provides independent confirmation of the check shown by real income estimates, but its earlier rise had been more gradual, and its slowing down is marked from as early as 1885. The changes in output a man in coal-mining slowed down the rise of industrial productivity, but the remainder of industry still shows by itself a declining rate of advance. (Para. 4.)

4. Estimates of the course of output per operative in particular industries are hazardous, but contain evidence, which in the aggregate carries some weight, of checks to the rise of output per operative in a number of industries at different dates from the seventies to the turn of the century. (Para. 5.)

5. New industries at this time were significant for the future but still too small to make much difference to current output. (Para. 6.)

6. Output a head in British agriculture shows a similar pattern to that which predominates in industry; proximately, at least, the probable causes were distinct from those affecting industry, but there is a common factor in the changed trend of raw material prices. (Para. 7.)

7. Some shortcomings of management, and some increased enforcement of restrictive practices by labour, probably did hold back British productivity at this time. But it is unlikely that any contemporary growth of these influences was commensurate with the check to productivity, whose

main causes must be sought in conditions common to the other countries which also experienced it. (Paras. 8, 9.)

8. These conditions are probably to be found in the working out towards the end of the century of the massive application and extension of the techniques of Steam and Steel. There now began an interval between the rapid advances in productivity which this had brought, and those brought later, mostly after the First World War, by the wide application of the new techniques of electricity, the internal combustion engine, and industrial chemistry. (Para. 10.)

9. But there was no check to the accumulation of equipment, stocks, and buildings as a whole in the United Kingdom after 1890. Estimates by two independent methods agree in showing that the stock of capital, in physical terms, per head of the occupied population, rose by 60 per cent. between 1870 and 1914, and its growth was roughly linear throughout. (Para. 11.)

10. The working out of the innovation effect of Steam and Steel also affected the United Kingdom, in common with urban and factory workers elsewhere, by ending the rapid rise in supplies of food and raw materials which the railway and steamship had been effecting on their introduction. This kind of set-back was significant for the future, but not of so much immediate effect for the United Kingdom as the check to productivity at home. (Para. 12.)

11. The greater scarcity of raw materials may provide a link between the contemporary changes in the trends of productivity and prices. (Para. 13.)

12. Some inferences are suggested for the present prospects of Great Britain. (Para. 14.)

[4]

SOME RETARDING FACTORS IN THE
BRITISH ECONOMY BEFORE 1914

John Saville

THE recent enquiry by Political and Economic Planning into the performance of the British economy since 1945 summarised their findings with the statement that "the rate of growth of production and of productivity in the United Kingdom has been much slower since the Second World War than in many other countries." [1] The Report noted that the level of investment has been too low compared with what has been achieved elsewhere, and that the rate of growth of productivity could be substantially improved if the level of investment were higher. While the Report says nothing of any period earlier than the Second World War, it is generally accepted that the failure of the U.K. to sustain a high rate of growth in her economy is no new phenomenon and can indeed be dated from the last quarter of the 19th century. Mr. Coppock, of the University of Manchester, has produced the most detailed evidence to date of the climacteric which occurred in the 1870's, and whatever qualifications may be made in the future to the statistical material on which his analysis is based, the break in trend, from the high growth rates of the middle decades of the century to a lower rate of growth from the 1870's on, is now well established. [2] But while the facts of economic development are being increasingly articulated, the explanation of their meaning, and the analysis of their causes, have received much less attention.

I.

Most explanations of the slowing down of technological change and of the failure to effect, in Svennilson's terms, [3] a continuous transformation of the British economy, have their origin in some variant of the theory of the early start. The core of this argument is that Britain has inherited certain structural handicaps as a result of her early pioneering in industrial development, and that the early beginnings in a number of ways have hindered or retarded later progress. Thorstein Veblen, in his fascinating chapter on England in his *Imperial Germany and the Industrial Revolution* [4] was one of the first to discuss some of the reasons why Britain was "paying the penalty for having been thrown into the lead and so having shown the way." Part of his argument related to what he called "a growth of use and wont" and Veblen distinguished between what today we would describe as the carryover of certain cultural aspects of pre-industrial society, on the one hand, and on the other the "broad fringe of usages, conventions, vested rights, canons of equity and propriety" that has grown out of the industrial system itself. The distinction is an important one. Most later discussions have analysed conservative attitudes too narrowly in terms of entrepreneurial characteristics and traditions while ignoring the ways in which these characteristics and traditions have been shaped by the general course of economic, social and political development. The training and scientific knowledge of the managerial class, the technical and general education of foremen and operatives, the willingness or otherwise to experiment with new processes, new materials, new ideas—all such have their origin in the same environment from which the dynamic factors in the British economy have also developed. When the Platt Report [5] remarked that the outlook of American managers was "highly analytical and progressive," comparing them favourably with their counterparts in Britain, it was, in part, an echo of what Matthew Arnold had noted in 1868 as a major defect in our educational system and teaching. This, wrote Arnold, was the lack of "the idea of science and systematic knowledge," an absence, he suggested, which was beginning to threaten the English business class with "practical inconvenience." [6]

The indifference towards education except for the propertied minorities and the steady and growing emphasis upon practicality as the essential guide to material success were attitudes which were central to middle class thinking in Victorian Britain. When the *Economist* wrote a devastating critique of English education in 1850, beginning with the trenchant words: "It is generally agreed that no civilised people are so little and so ill educated as the English," it was just as certain that the failures it so heavily underlined were of small significance. The statements are worth quoting at length. The date of the editorial is March 2nd, 1850:

> "It is generally agreed that no civilised people are so little and so ill educated as the English. Nor can there be any doubt that our school system .... is unworthy alike of an organising government, and of the orderly methodical spirit of the nation. It has never, within our recollection, been examined but to be condemned. It has found innumerable accusers and opponents—not one advocate. Those who have been hopelessly at variance as to the means of improving it, have cordially agreed in saying that it was an intolerable disgrace to the community..."

But, the *Economist* continued, the English as a nation were not behind any other "in either intellect or morality"; and it went on to make the point that "mere school instruction" was a good deal less important in the training of youth than many believed. This judgement it underlined just over a month later, in the issue dated April 20, 1850:

> "To say that our secular education is perfect would be terribly erroneous; but to say that it is unrivalled, judging from its effects by the progress and success of the community, will not be far from the truth. That kind of education which fits men to perform their duties in life is not got in public or parish schools, but at home, in the counting house, in the lawyer's office, or the camp, or on board ship, in the shop or the factory. ..
> What is most wanted in society seems to be a knowledge of our moral duties, in detail, and a general discipline of the minds of all who perform them. ...."

This emphasis upon what a foreign observer once described as "le practical man" derives in business circles both from the divergence between science and industry in 18th century England [7] and the immense technological successes of the industrial revolution. As has often been remarked, the first stage of industrialisation in Britain was carried through without any close alliance between the scientist and the entrepreneur. We have recently been reminded that the gap was never so wide as some earlier commentators have suggested,[8] but the general thesis remains broadly correct. It is a hazardous business to attempt a broad generalisation covering nearly a century's technology, but it is probably true that down to the 1850's, and in some industries a later date would be appropriate, most of the technological innovations and improvements were the work of practical men. The faith of the self-made entrepreneurs in hard facts as against what they believed to be empty theorising hardened into dogma, and the continued success of themselves and of Britain in general served only to buttress their immense complacency. It was the coming of the steel age in the last thirty years of the 19th century that ended the epoch of the practical man. With steel, the new basic material, and electricity, the new and for many purposes the improved source of power, it was increasingly difficult to improvise technical improvements; and when these two innovations came together to provide the possibilities of the mass production age, the scientist moved steadily into the centre of the technological process. Or rather, this was what an increasingly complex technology demanded, and what did in fact take place in both American and German industry before 1914; but not, alas, in Britain.

It was not that an appreciation of the general problem failed to develop, but that the gap between enlightened public opinion and majority attitudes within industry proved unbridgeable. This general problem was not just a matter of technical education *per se* but of a wholesale reshaping of the English attitudes to education on all levels. There had grown up in the first half of the 19th century an indifference to educational opportunity for the labouring classes that merged into downright hostility; and these attitudes have lasted, albeit in some respects in weakened and certainly in changed forms, down to our own time. As the Vice-President of Firth College said in evidence to the 1884 *R.C. on Technical Education*: "...... of course technical education without previous elementary education is an impossibility. The time has come when the scheme of technical education can be formulated and developed." [9] But what was needed was a broadening of what so properly was called elementary education in order to establish a much more adequate grounding for technical training at a later stage; and without a radical alteration in the educational structure at the base of the pyramid there could be no major change of any significance. There was in fact no substantial body of opinion in 19th century England which constantly and continuously argued for a major break through in educational opportunity. Individual prophets continued to cry in the wilderness, but the complacency towards education, of a general kind as well as in its more technical aspects, remained by and large undisturbed. There was, of course, the minor flurry which followed the Paris Exhibition of 1867 and which produced the *S.C. on Scientific Instruction*; and there was the greater upheaval of the 1880's when, for a few years, it began to be borne upon contemporaries that Britain's economic progress was slowing down, and when, as a result of this recognition, the search for the causes of this decline was undertaken. The Fair Trade movement was one result,; an interest in technical education another. This decade saw a quite remarkable pamphlet literature published on the connections between general education, technical education and industrial progress; and there occurred, in addition, the first full scale investigation of the *R.C. on Technical Instruction*. But how much was left undone by later decades was revealed by the Balfour Committee's reports in the 1920's, and by the many reports and the volume of public discussion that have been characteristic, indeed perhaps symbolic, of our own times. For eighty years a stream of information and documentation has underlined the inadequacies of scientific and technical training in a society whose technology has become increasingly complicated, and it is a melancholy fact that the tenacity of the old ways of thinking and doing have proved stronger than the forces making for change. What Tawney described as "the rule of thumb and a nose for money"—a combination that proved extraordinarily successful in

54   SOME RETARDING FACTORS IN THE BRITISH ECONOMY BEFORE 1914

an earlier historical period, has been a motivating influence of considerable size until and including our own day.

II.

At the centre of the problem of retardation are the forces and influences playing upon the level of investment. And what is at issue here is not just the overall level of investment at any given point of time, or within a trend period, but the rate of capital formation in those leading or key sectors of the economy [10] which normally determine overall growth. The complicated question which has to be answered relates to those many factors, economic, social and political, which together determine investment decisions and from which result particular patterns of investment throughout the economy. Veblen, with his theory of 'systematic obsolescence' began to approach the analysis developed so magisterially by Svennilson in his *Growth and Stagnation in the European Economy*. In Veblen's discussion obsolescence is the 'unavoidable' existence of past technological development which no longer suits the requirements of the present, but which only a large scale recasting of whole sectors of the economy would overcome. His well known comment on the transportation problem in England is worth quoting again:

"So, e.g., it is well known that the railways of Great Britain, like those of other countries, are built with too narrow a gauge, but while this item of "depreciation through obsolescence" has been known for some time, it has not even in the most genial speculative sense come up for consideration as a remediable defect. In the same connection, American, and latterly German, observers have been much impressed with the silly little bobtailed carriages used in British goods traffic; which were well enough in their time, before American and German railway traffic was good for anything much, but which have at the best a playful air when brought up against the requirements of today. Yet the remedy is not a simple question of good sense. The terminal facilities, tracks, shunting facilities, and all the ways and means of handling freight on this oldest and most complete of railway systems, are all adapted to the bobtailed car. So, again, the roadbed and the metal, as well as the engines, are well and substantially constructed to take care of such traffic as required to be taken care of when they first went into operation, and it is not easy to make a piecemeal adjustment to later requirements. It is perhaps true that as seen from the standpoint of the community at large and its material interest, the out-of-date equipment and organisation should profitably be discarded—"junked," as the colloquial phrase has it—and the later contrivances substituted throughout; but it is the discretion of the business men that necessarily decides these questions, and the whole proposition has a different value as seen in the light of the competitive pecuniary interests of the business men in control." [11]

An extreme, if marginal, example of obsolescent equipment in Britain that fell almost completely into disuse because of an unwillingness to modernise, is that of the canals in the second half of the 19th century. It has sometimes been argued, notably by Sir William Acworth in the early 20th century and more recently by Mr. Jervis, that the canal system would have been re-equipped had the economic incentives for so doing been apparent.[12] Mr. Jervis' discussion in particular stems from a theory of the firm that is now old-fashioned—the belief that the acceptance of profit maximisation will ensure that "the entrepreneur combines his factors in the optimum manner under the circumstances applicable to him." It is precisely the analysis of what constitutes the "circumstances" within which the entrepreneur finds himself that has led to the introduction, *inter alia*, of the dimension of uncertainty into the modern discussion of the firm. In the case of the canals, the argument that the canals were not re-built because traffic was not expanding—that is, there were no economic incentives encouraging re-equipment—ignores, first, the considerable technical problems involved in modernising the canals because of their early haphazard growth; second, the immense financial burden of rebuilding: and third, the deliberate policy of the railway companies by which the canals were deprived of any real possibilities of growth and expansion.[13] The example of the canals is an excellent if minor illustration of Veblen's thesis whereby the "discretion of the business men," underlined by the "competitive pecuniary interests" of the railway companies which owned the canals, ensured that the canals would fall through obsolescence into almost total commercial disuse.

Since it is to be expected that obsolete or slow growing industries will employ a higher ratio of labour to capital than later, more up-to-date areas of activity, systematic obsolescence, in whatever form it is found, will exercise two main effects. It will, firstly, act as a drag upon the economy as a whole by hoarding an excessive labour force which otherwise would find employment in the growing points of the economy, and it will also depress the demand for capital equipment. Secondly, and this is especially true of a public utility, an obsolescent service industry will exert a conservative influence upon entrepreneurial attitudes and incentives in general. It cannot be too strongly emphasised that a rapidly growing economy is the result of dynamic changes not only within industries and groups of industries, but in the total environment within which industry and the entrepreneurial class find themselves; and this concept of 'totality,' or of overall transformation, includes all those aspects of social and political life which bear directly or indirectly upon economic development.

In the context of the British economy of the last quarter of the 19th century, the 'total' situation was unquestionably in certain respects failing to provide the incentives and encouragement which, other things being equal, entrepreneurs would respond to in their own firms and industries. The transportation system, including dock and harbour installations, was undeniably inadequate, and the demand, among some groups of business men, for railway nationalisation was one reflection of the contemporary exasperation at the poor facilities available. The educational structure was almost totally incapable of encouraging the flow of scientists and technicians into industry which a mass production economy so urgently needed. The absence of social provision, and the high incidence of sickness and premature death among the labour force, discouraged the more rational and efficient use of labour, although there were other, more powerful factors reinforcing its wasteful utilisation.

III.

These are some of the external diseconomies which, in a given environment, influence in a conservative way the policy decisions of the entrepreneurial group. There are, of course, more direct influences upon the rate of capital formation in individual industries or within the economy as a whole. One of these relates to the supply of labour; another to the provision of capital.

Even where technological progress is capital-saving, it is still true that a high rate of long term growth involves a rise in the ratio of capital to labour. Any discussion therefore of retardation in a mature industrial society must examine the capital/labour ratio and the factors affecting it at any given period of time. The PEP Report mentioned above noted the weakness of the incentives to substitute capital for labour, and this was a thesis developed

in historical terms by Erwin Rothbart in a posthumously published article.[14]
The problem he attempted was to account for the differences in productivity
and efficiency between American and British industry. His argument, briefly,
was that the existence of free land in the United States drew off large masses
of labour from the Eastern States, where industry was establishing itself, and
there resulted a constant shortage of labour. The high wage and labour costs
which were the product of this situation acted as a constant encouragement to
the American entrepreneur to economise on his labour force by introducing
labour saving inventions. This, it may be noted, although Rothbart does not
make the point, was only practicable when technology itself had reached a
certain stage of development; but from the 1840's on, and emphatically in the
age of steel, the possibilities of substitution were increasingly offering themselves.
Once established as a tradition, even though the original causes may, and in
the present example certainly did, weaken, the tradition continued. This is
saying the same thing as Professor Arthur Lewis when he remarked, of the
period before 1914, that the "Germans had an irresistible urge to invest in
steel, machinery, chemicals." [15] Once the 'irresistible urge' has been accepted,
then it develops its own momentum and the total environment is itself, with
varying degrees of speed, adapted to the new ways of thinking and practice.
Now this, it needs to be said, is not a psychological theory of growth, since the
origins of tradition are to be found within material circumstances. It is of
course a theory of the momentum but without some such concept it is difficult
to get far in the discussion of British economic history; but it naturally allows
for sharp breaks in tradition, and its transformation under certain conditions.[16]

By contrast the labour market in Britain was never in short supply for any
category of worker. Only in exceptional years was a position of full or near
employment reached and then only for skilled workers or for particular
occupations such as coal mining. The abundance of labour, especially of cheap
unskilled labour,[17] exercised a long term influence upon the industrial structure
and accounted in part for the striking persistence of small scale and domestic
industry in the face of the advancing factory economy. The incentive to alter
the capital/labour ratio was reduced and the rate of technical change correspondingly slowed down. Allied to the other conservative elements in the
economic environment, the overstocked labour market was a powerful factor
encouraging inertia.

IV.

Connected with the structure of the labour market are the income distribution and market demand which confront the domestic producer. In the
high and egalitarian income society of the United States (the terms are relative), the demand for standardised consumer goods appeared much earlier
than in the United Kingdom; and, other things being equal, the possibilities
of mass production of these consumer goods were therefore greater, reinforcing
other factors working in the same direction. This, of course, was a notable
feature of American experience from the mid-19th century onwards, and its
relative absence was just as remarkable in Britain.[18] It is the 20th century which
has seen the massive development of the home market as an essential part of
the continued growth of mature industrial societies. The need to promote an
internal expansion was one of the main tasks of the West European economy
in the inter-war years and such expansion was made the more difficult because

of the high concentration on capital goods production and exports, as well as capital export, in the decades before 1914.[19] As with other aspects of the British economy before 1914 it is not that nothing was achieved in the expansion of the home market but progress was slow and uneven.[20]

V.

The ease or otherwise of raising capital for development is always one of the crucial determinants of entrepreneurial decisions. Professor Arthur Lewis gets the best of both worlds when he argues that capital before 1914 was at least as cheap in Britain as in Germany or the United States at the same time as the financial institutions of the English capital market were "to some extent imprisoned" in the habits of the past.[21] The cheapness or dearness of capital, taken by itself, is not the relevant factor. What matters to business men in the joint stock era is its availability through recognised channels, and the organisational structure of the domestic capital market is therefore of central importance. This was a matter much debated in Britain during the inter-war years, especially following the Report of the MacMillan Committee in 1931. The main differences between English and foreign capital markets are familiar. While elsewhere the connections between banks and industry have usually been close, in Britain the early beginnings of the factory economy were in small scale industrial units with accumulation occurring mainly within the individual firm. The tradition of the family business together with the growth of short term credit facilities assured the independence of industry from any effective control by, or close association with, the deposit banks. The increase in the size of the industrial unit, with its corresponding increased demand for capital was met in part by the introduction of limited liability in the 1850's; but the development of a new institutional framework for long term industrial investment was markedly slow. This tardiness in the emergence of new types of institutions in the English capital market was the product of many factors, of which three may be mentioned here.[22] The first is the long establishment of the London money market as the source of capital for overseas investors, and by the second half of the 19th century investment institutions of first class repute were concerned almost exclusively with the world demand for capital outside the United Kingdom. Down to 1914 there were no comparable houses whose wisdom and experience were at the disposal of the domestic investor or the home producer. From the first days of the limited joint stock company, domestic flotations were left mainly to the company promotor or to the *ad hoc* syndicate. As the scale of capital requirements increased the individualistic traditions of self financing no longer sufficed, but the absence of powerful finance houses as well as what has been called the "entrepreneur" spirit in banking meant that the gap between individual resources, admittedly considerable, and the capital requirements of industry must have been growing before 1914. This, of course, is a complicated question since it is bound up with the relatively small scale nature of much of British industry, and it is widely agreed that what British industry required was a much higher rate of amalgamation and a larger scale organisation than was in fact achieved. It is difficult here to sort out cause and effect, since the small size of the average industrial unit would offer few attractions to the London merchant bankers through whose hands a large part of the capital export was channelled; and at the same time a more adequate institutional provision for domestic capital would itself have encouraged the growth in unit size. As Mr. Dobb has remarked the workable alternatives that confront the entrepreneur are often more circumscribed than pure theory suggests,[23] and just as the shortcomings of the total environment will act in a conservative way upon the policy decisions of the individual entrepreneur so the inadequacies of the domestic capital market will have tended to influence them in the same direction. While the argument here remains a thesis still to be justified for most of British industry, Mr. Burn has emphasised the point for the steel industry before 1914; and steel was above all others the key sector in the whole economy.[24]

There are two other points to be made in this connection. One is the absence of restraint upon company promotion under the English legal code.[25] The laxity of the rules and regulations governing such promotions encouraged fraud and dishonesty, and the bankruptcies and corruption of the decades following 1860 contributed materially to the failure to develop sound financial promoting organisations; and after the failure of the City of Glasgow bank in 1878, the few ventures into the field of company promotion and underwriting by the banks seem to have come to an end.[26] The second point is that the tradition of the family business and the rugged individualism of the industrial managers, sustained until the first World War by the ability of Britain to command a large share of the trade and services of the world, also played a part in lessening from the side of industry the demand for the emergence of new institutions within the capital market; but this is a matter also of small average size to which reference has already been made.[27]

VI.

The question which remains is why did it prove impossible for the British economy to make the change to a higher gear? We have discussed some of the individual factors involved; but taken by themselves, or as acting cumulatively, they do not explain satisfactorily why the economy as a whole was not able to overcome these factors of retardation. A striking example of the breakthrough that can be achieved has been the performance of the French economy in the 1950's. The brief answer, in the case of Britain before 1914, is surely prosperity.

Britain's economy in the first three quarters of the 19th century had been adapted to the supply of goods to countries who were either in their first stage of industrialisation or who were primary producers with cash crops to sell on the world market. Of her exports down to 1870 textiles were by far the most important, and within the textile group, cotton was pre-eminent. With, however, the growing industrialisation of Western Europe and the U.S.A. iron and machinery products, and especially railway materials, became increasingly important in world trade. The beginnings of the steel age in the 1870's coincided with the growing industrial maturity of Western Europe and the U.S.A., and had the world economy been limited to the Atlantic community a very considerable adaptation of her export trade, and therefore of her industrial structure, would have been forced upon the United Kingdom. In the event she found expanding markets for her traditional type exports in the Empire and in the countries of recent settlement which more than took up the slack from the markets bordering on the Atlantic. While the rate of exports slackened, which itself may have had very considerable consequences for the low rate of growth of industrial capital accumulation,[28] the absolute increase in exports between 1870 and 1914 was considerable. The concentration upon her staple industries was thereby confirmed, much assisted by the extraordinarily successful "connections" developed throughout the world by British financial institutions. The weaknesses we can now see—the failure to expand in those sectors of world trade that were growing at the fastest rate—but these were less apparent to contemporaries and they were certainly disguised by the buoyant surplus on the overall balance of payments and the strength of sterling as an international currency.

It was, then, the success of the British economy which in the final analysis confirmed business men in their 19th century attitudes and practices, and the growing criticisms upon individual matters met little response from those in whom entrepreneurial decisions were concentrated. And since the picture was very far from being in sharp black and white colours, criticism was inevitably muffled. For not only did exports grow, so did the economy as a whole. While the rate of increase in steel production fell a good deal short of what was being achieved in contemporary America and Germany, in absolute terms the increase was from a quarter of a million tons in 1870 to nearly eight million tons on the eve of the First World War. Similarly, while the failure of Britain to develop new products in her export list—the motor car is one example; dyestuffs is another; and electrical equipment is a third—in most industries the balance is far from being only a debit one. While in 1901 Germany was exporting around £18 million of chemicals of all kinds, the figure for Britain was as high as £35.5 million, and progress in the heavy branches of the industry was considerable. And so the story could be continued. It is retardation not stagnation that characterizes the economy before 1914. The economy is becoming adapted to the requirements of the mass production era; but the adaptation is lagging and the transformation is as yet only partially completed. This is the legacy which the inter-war generations inherited.

University of Hull.   JOHN SAVILLE.

REFERENCES

[1] *Growth in the British Economy* (1960) p. 52.

[2] D. J. Coppock, "The Climacteric of the 1890's: A Critical Note," *Manchester School*, XXIV, No. 1 (January 1956) pp. 1–31.

[3] Ingvar Svennilson, *Growth and Stagnation in the European Economy*, (Geneva, 1954) esp. Chs. 1–3.

[4] 1939 ed., first published in 1915.

[5] *Report of the Cotton Textile Mission to the United States*, H.M.S.O., (1944) p. 34.

[6] *Higher Schools and Universities in Germany* (2nd. ed. 1882) pp. 191–192.

[7] For a recent discussion of early 18th century England: Margaret 'Espinasse, "The Rise and Fall of Restoration Science," *Past and Present*, No. 14 (November 1958) pp. 71–89.

[8] A. E. Musson and E. Robinson, "Science and Industry in the late 18th Century," *Economic History Review*, XIII, No. 2 (December 1960) pp. 222–244.

[9] *Second Report*, Vol. 3 (1884) Q. 7718.

[10] For the concept of the 'key sector': W. W. Rostow, *The Process of Economic Growth* (N.Y. 1952); and the same author's "Trends in the Allocation of Resources in Secular Growth," *International Social Science Bulletin*, VI, No. 2 (1954) pp. 206–211.

[11] op. cit. pp. 130–1. I say nothing in this article of the associated and relevant questions of complementarity and interrelatedness, for which see: L. M. Lachman, "Investment Repercussions," *Quarterly Journal of Economics*, LXII, (November 1948) pp. 698–713; Marvin Frankel, "Obsolescence and Technological Change in a Maturing Economy," *American Economic Review*, XLV, (June 1955) pp. 296–319.

60   SOME RETARDING FACTORS IN THE BRITISH ECONOMY BEFORE 1914

[12] Sir W. Acworth, "British Canals," *Economic Journal*, XV, (June 1950), pp. 149–155; F. R. J. Jervis, "The Handicap of the Early Start," *Manchester School*, XV, No. 1 (January 1949) pp. 112–122.

[13] For the arguments that the railways 'strangled' the canals, see W. T. Jackman, *The Development of Transportation in Modern England*, II, (Cambridge, 1916) p. 645. ff; and for the general discussion. *R. C. on Canals and Waterways, Final Report*, Cd. 4979 (1909) para. 415; and *R. C. on Transport, Final Report*, Cmd. 3751 (1931), Ch. VI.

[14] E. Rothbart, "Causes of the Superior Efficiency of U.S.A. Industry as compared with British Industry," *Economic Journal*, LVII, (September 1946) pp. 383–390.

[15] W. A. Lewis, "International Competition in Manufactures," *American Economic Review, Proceedings*, XLVII, No. 2, (May 1957) pp. 578–587.

[16] As has happened, for example, in the French economy since 1945.

[17] The excess of women over men in the age group 16–49 in Britain throughout the 19th century is important in this context.

[18] Rothbart, *loc. cit.*

[19] Svennilson, *op. cit.*

[20] One index of what was achieved in the home market was the expansion of the retail trades: J. B. Jefferys, *Retail Trading in Britain, 1850–1914*, (Cambridge, 1954) Ch. I.

[21] Lewis, *loc. cit.*, p. 585.

[22] For an early account of the general problem discussed in the text, see H. S. Foxwell, "The Financing of Industry and Trade," *Economic Journal*, XXVII, (December 1917) pp. 502–22. See also B. C. Hunt, *The Development of the Business Corporation in England 1800–1867*, (Harvard 1936); J. B. Jefferys, *Trends in Business Organisation in Great Britain since 1856*, (London, Ph. D., 1938).

[23] Maurice Dobb, *Studies in the Development of Capitalism* (1946) p. 286.

[24] D. C. Burn, *Economic History of Steelmaking* (Cambridge, 1940) p. 249 ff.

[25] For a comparative account of the legal regulations controlling company promotion in the 19th century: A. B. Levy, *Private Corporations and their Control*, I (1950), Pt. I.

[26] For an example, see W. F. Crick and J. E. Wadsworth, *A Hundred Years of Joint Stock Banking* (1936) pp. 226–7.

[27] For a denial of the thesis put forward in this article, see A. R. Hall, "A Note on the English Capital Market as a Source of Funds for Home Investment before 1914," *Economica*, XXIV (February 1957) pp. 59–66; and the subsequent discussion initiated by A. K. Cairncross, "The English Capital Market before 1914," *Economica*, XXV (May 1958) pp. 142–6.

[28] W. A. Lewis, *Economic Survey, 1919–1939* (1949) p. 74.

[5]

(4) SOME REASONS WHY

It is now time to pull the threads of our story together and ask ourselves why the different nations of western Europe grew and changed as they did. In particular—for lack of space compels us to select our problems—why did industrial leadership pass in the closing decades of the nineteenth century from Britain to Germany?

The larger interest of this question will not escape the reader. It is of concern not only to the student of economic growth but to the general historian who seeks to understand the course of world politics since 1870. The rapid industrial expansion of a unified Germany was the most important development of the half-century that preceded the First World War—more important even than the comparable growth of the United States, simply because Germany was enmeshed in the European network of power and in this period the fate of the world was in Europe's hands.

In 1788 a perceptive French demographer named Messance wrote: 'The people that last will be able to keep its forges going will perforce be the master; for it alone will have arms.'[1] He was somewhat in advance of his times. In subsequent years the Revolutionary armies and then Napoleon were to show what well-directed manpower—a nation in arms—using traditional weapons, could do to traditional armies. By the 1860's, however, Messance's analysis was borne out, first by the American Civil War, and then by the Franco-Prussian War. It was now *Blut und Eisen* that counted, and all the blood in the world could not compensate for timely, well-directed firepower.

It took a long time for people to adjust to this new basis of power. When the Prussian coalition defeated France in 1870, numerous Britons, including the Queen, rejoiced to see the traditional Gallic enemy and disturber of the peace humbled by the honest, sober Teuton. Within fifteen years, however, the British awoke to the fact that the Industrial Revolution and different rates of population growth had raised Germany to Continental hegemony and left France far behind. This was

[1] M. Messance, *Nouvelles recherches sur la population de la France* (Lyons, 1788), p. 128.

one of the longest 'double-takes' in history: the British had been fighting the Corsican ogre, dead fifty years and more, while Bismarck went his way.

In subsequent decades, this shift in the balance of power was the dominant influence in European international relations. It underlay the gradual re-forming of forces that culminated in the Triple Entente and Triple Alliance; it nourished the Anglo–German political and naval rivalry, as well as French fears of their enemy east of the Rhine; it made war probable and did much to dictate the membership of the opposing camps. It has, I know, been fashionable for more than a generation to deny this interpretation. In the reaction against Marxist slogans of 'imperialist war' and 'the last stage of capitalism', scholars have leaned over backwards to expunge the slightest taint of economic determinism from their lucubrations. Yet doctrine was never a valid guide to knowledge, at either end of the ideological spectrum, and this effort to rule out material considerations as causes of the World War betrays *naïveté*, or ignorance about the nature of power and the significance of power relations for the definition of national interests.

These political concerns go far to explain Britain's agitated response to German economic expansion. Germany was not, after all, the only country to compete with Britain in the home and foreign markets. American manufactures, particularly machine tools and other devices that placed a premium on ingenuity, invaded the United Kingdom as early as the middle of the century and continued to trouble British producers to the end of our period. And we have already noted the success of Indian and Japanese cottons in the competition for the potentially bottomless Eastern market.

Yet it was Germany that stuck in John Bull's craw. In the decades preceding 1870, she had gradually turned from one of the best markets for British manufactures to a self-sufficient industrial country; one can follow the process in her diminishing dependence on imports of such tell-tale products as cotton yarn (see above, p. 442) and pig iron ($57\frac{1}{2}$ per cent of consumption in 1843 at the height of the railway boom, 34 per cent in 1857, 11 per cent a decade later).[1] After 1870, with the home market won, German industry began to make an important place for itself abroad. Actually, the process had begun before, but it is from this point roughly that the increase in the volume of manufactured exports picked up and the British began to awaken to their new rival. From 1875 to 1895, while the value of British exports stood still, though volume rose by some 63 per cent, the value of German exports rose 30 per cent and volume correspondingly more. At the same time, where only 44 per cent of German exports were finished products in

---

[1] Beck, *Geschichte des Eisens*, IV, 696; Benaerts, *Origines*, pp. 460–1.

'UNFAIR' GERMAN COMPETITION 555

1872, 62 per cent fell into this category in 1900 (as against 75 per cent for the United Kingdom).[1]

Moreover, the particulars of the trend were more disturbing than the general tide. There was, for example, the export of German iron and steel to areas that Britain had come to look on as a private preserve—Australia, South America, China, Britain herself. There was the marked superiority of Germany in the newer branches of manufacture: organic chemicals from the 1880's, electrical equipment from the 1890's. Above all, there were the 'unfair' methods allegedly employed by the Teuton: he sold meretricious, shoddy merchandise, often under the guise of British articles; he accepted training engagements with British houses in order to spy out a trade; he pandered to the tastes of the natives and seduced them by concessions to their ignorance—to the point of translating sales catalogues into their language. Complaints reached a peak during what Ross Hoffman called the 'midsummer madness of 1896'.[2] Parliamentary orators exercised their eloquence on government purchases of Bavarian pencils, or the importation of brushes made by German convict labour; newspapers denounced the purchase of cheap German garments, many of them produced from reclaimed British woollens. No item was too small to heap on the flames of indignation: playing-cards, musical instruments, buggy whips.[3]

To be sure, it is easy to demonstrate the exaggeration of these alarms. Germany's gains still left her far behind Britain as a commercial power: the volume of her trade in 1895 was perhaps three-fifths as great; the tonnage of her merchant marine only a sixth as large. British commerce was still growing, losses in one market were generally compensated by gains in another, her industry had not forgotten how to meet competition. Moreover, the difference in overall rates of growth between the two countries was considerably smaller than the discrepancy in rates of industrial growth would lead one to expect. Where British output of manufactured commodities (including minerals and processed food) slightly more than doubled from 1870 to 1913, against a German increase of almost sixfold, the ratio between the rising incomes of the

---

[1] Germany, *Statistisches Jahrbuch* (1908), p. 125; Schlote, *British Overseas Trade*, p. 125. The 1872 figure is from France, *Annu. statistique*, XLVIII (1932), *rés. rétro.* p. 408, which gives the 1900 German percentage as 65.

[2] *Great Britain and the German Trade Rivalry, 1875–1914* (Philadelphia, 1933).

[3] On all this, see D. S. Landes, 'Entrepreneurship in Advanced Industrial Countries: the Anglo-German Rivalry', in *Entrepreneurship and Economic Growth* (Papers presented at a Conference sponsored jointly by the Committee on Economic Growth of the Social Science Research Council and the Harvard University Research Center in Entrepreneurial History, Cambridge, Mass., 12 and 13 November 1954).

556   BRITAIN'S SHIFT TO SERVICES

Table 56. *Capital Formation as Share of National Product*
(in percentages)

| | | United Kingdom | | | | Germany[a] | | |
| | | NDCF/NDP | | NNCF/NNP | | NDCF/NNP | NNCF/NNP | |
U.K.	Germany	Current prices	Constant prices	Current prices	Constant prices	Current prices	Current prices	Constant prices
	1851–60					8·4	8·6	7·9
1860–9		7·2	8·6	10·0	11·5			
	1861–70					8·5	9·7	10·6
1870–9		8·2	7·3	11·8	10·9			
	1871–80					11·6	13·5	13·0
1880–9		6·4	3·4	10·9	8·1			
	1881–90					11·2	14·0	14·5
1890–9		7·3	3·0	10·1	6·0			
	1891–1900					13·9	15·4	15·9
1895–1904		8·8	4·8	10·5	6·7			
1900–9		8·2	4·1	11·7	7·8			
	1901–13					15·6	16·5	15·9
1905–14		6·7	1·2	13·0	8·0			

ᵃ 1913 boundaries.

ABBREVIATIONS
    NDCF   Net Domestic Capital Formation.
    NDP   Net Domestic Product.
    NNCF   Net National Capital Formation.
    NNP   Net National Product.

SOURCE. S. Kuznets, 'Quantitative Aspects of the Economic Growth of Nations: VI. Long-Term Trends in Capital Formation Proportions', *Economic Development and Cultural Change*, IX, 4, part II (July 1961), 58, 59, 64.

two countries, whether calculated in aggregate or *per capita*, was of the order of 0·7 or 0·8 to 1.[1]

In part this paradox simply reflected a shift in resources. More mature than Germany, Britain was beginning to develop her service sector (distribution, transport, banking and insurance) at the expense of manufacturing industry; so that the share of the latter in national product diminished steadily. The increase in foreign holdings had similar statistical consequences.[2] In part, however, Britain's relatively good

---

[1] On production of *Sachgüter*, see R. Wagenführ, 'Die Industriewirtschaft: Entwicklungstendenzen der deutschen und internationalen Industrieproduktion 1860 bis 1932', *Vierteljahrshefte zur Konjunkturforschung* (ed. Institut für Konjunkturforschung), Sonderheft 31 (Berlin, 1933), pp. 58, 69.

[2] On the eve of the First World War, Britain earned almost £200 million a year by business services to the rest of the world—just about as much as she derived from her

overall performance was the result of a more efficient allocation of resources. The rapidity of German industrial expansion had left important sectors of the economy behind, protected from the shock of obsolescence and the logic of marginal rationality by human foibles and such institutional devices as protective tariffs. A surprisingly large area of manufacturing, for example, clung tenaciously to hand processes and domestic production;[1] and where Britain had liquidated the less remunerative aspects of her agriculture, a sizable fraction of the German population continued to live on the soil.[2] The German economy, in other words, presented some of those contrasts between advanced and

enormous foreign investments. The two together represented more than a sixth of national income. A. H. Imlah, *Economic Elements in the Pax Britannica: Studies in British Foreign Trade in the Nineteenth Century* (Cambridge, Mass., 1958), table 4, pp. 70–5.

[1] Of 10,873,701 people engaged in mining and manufacture in 1907, almost 30% (3,166,734) were self-employed or worked in enterprises of five persons or less. Dispersed home production was common in clothing and textiles, leather and woodwork, toy manufacture, food processing and a host of minor metal trades. In these areas Wilhelmian Germany was just beginning to go through the process of modernization that Britain had largely traversed by 1870, as the spate of contemporary studies on the problem of the *Hausarbeiter* testifies.

The best brief introduction to the subject is W. Sombart, 'Verlagssystem (Hausindustrie)', in J. Conrad *et al.*, eds., *Handwörterbuch der Staatswissenschaften* (3rd ed., Jena, 1911), vol. VIII. There is a convenient guide to the literature in Belgium, Ministère du Travail, *Bibliographie générale des industries à domicile* [Supplément à la publication: *Les industries à domicile en Belgique*] (Brussels, 1908). Sombart offers a list of materials published in the years immediately following.

[2] How large the discrepancy was between input and output in agriculture, not only in Germany, but throughout Europe, may be inferred from the following table:

Place of Agriculture in Selected Economies, c. 1891–96 (in percentages)

	Share of population dependent thereon	Share of national wealth	Share of national income
Russia	70	43	32
Austria	62	39	27
Italy	52	45	28
France	42	32	21
Germany	39	31	20
United States	35	25	16
Belgium	25	36	14
Holland	22	33	18
Great Britain	10	15	8

SOURCE. M. G. Mulhall, *Dictionary of Statistics* (4th ed., London, 1909), p. 615.

On the winnowing of British agriculture, see T. W. Fletcher, 'The Great Depression of English Agriculture, 1873–1896', *Econ. Hist. Rev.* XIII (1961), 417–32.

558   CAPITAL FORMATION AND FOREIGN INVESTMENT

backward sectors that we have come to call dualism and to associate with rapid, unbalanced growth.[1]

Even so, compound interest is a remorseless arbiter. The difference in the rates of growth cannot be blinked: any projection of the trends constitutes a judgment unfavourable to Britain. And this is the more true in that the discrepancy between the two countries applied not only to national income, that is, the yield of today, but also to capital formation, that is, the yield of tomorrow. Here the contrast was particularly striking: as Britain slowed down, Germany speeded up (see Table 56).

Table 57. *Germany and United Kingdom: Foreign Investment as Percentage of Total Net Capital Formation (at current prices)*

Germany		United Kingdom	
1851/5–1861/5	2·2	1855–64	29·1
1861/5–1871/5	12·9	1865–74	40·1
1871/5–1881/5	14·1	1875–84	28·9
1881/5–1891/5	19·9	1885–94	51·2
1891/5–1901/5	9·7	1895–1904	20·7
1901/5–1911/13	5·7	1905–14	52·9

SOURCES. The German series is from a manuscript kindly furnished by Professor Simon Kuznets and based on information from Professor Walter Hoffman. The series for the United Kingdom is based on Imlah's calculation of foreign balance on current account, *Economic Elements in the Pax Britannica*, pp. 70–5, and on estimates of net domestic capital formation kindly communicated by Miss Phyllis Deane.

At this point, moreover, our aggregate statistics join our qualitative and micro-quantitative data. All the evidence agrees on the technological backwardness of much of British manufacturing industry—on leads lost, opportunities missed, markets relinquished that need not have been. These are themes that have recurred in every official

[1] In this sense, the pre-First World War German economy was comparable to the Japanese. See Henry Rosovsky, *Capital Formation in Japan, 1868–1940* (Glencoe, Ill., 1960), ch. IV, who argues, however, that the persistence of a labour-intensive traditional sector released resources for the costly installations of the modern sector and thereby promoted Japanese growth. The thesis is a provocative one. It does not seem applicable to the German case.

One should carefully distinguish, incidentally, between this dualism of growth, inherent in the inevitable unevenness of development, and the dualism of the colonial economy, in which the modern installations of foreign administration and enterprise contrast sharply with the primitiveness of indigenous life; or the dualism of a semi-stagnant economy like that of Spain or southern Italy (at least until very recently), in which a few gleaming cities, or merely city districts, and other isolated expressions of modern technology are scattered over a countryside little different from what it was two millennia ago.

inquiry, every report of a travelling delegation, for the last two generations. And the very spurts that certain branches have made from time
to time are evidence of an effort to catch up and of previously unexploited potential. There is no doubt, in short, that British industry was
not so vigorous and adaptable from the 1870's on as it could have
been. Why?

Before attempting to answer this question, it may be useful to clear
the ground by ruling out the usual congenial explanations. Thus
Britain's industrial resources were as good as those of any other European country in the late nineteenth century. In the whole world, only
the United States surpassed her in coal output; and no country possessed
better coal for power, metallurgy, or chemical manufacture. One of the
ironies of economic history is that Germany, which almost mono-
polized the production of coal-tar derivatives, drew much of her tar
from the United Kingdom.[1] Much has been made of the great Lorraine iron deposits and their suitability for the production of Thomas
steel; but England had her own large deposits of phosphoric ores in the
East Midlands, far closer to good coking coal than the Lorraine beds
and just as easily mined. As for those industrial materials which had to
come from the outside—cotton, for example, and almost all wool—
England was better situated than her European competitors. No
nation had so wide a commercial network at its command, and it was
no accident that almost all the major primary commodities had their
central markets in Liverpool and London. To be sure, England's
relative importance as a re-exporter of the world's merchandise
declined somewhat as countries like Germany, France and the United
States learned to buy directly from producing areas; but they—and
other countries still less—never learned to by-pass the British entrepôt
entirely, and the absolute value of this re-export trade continued to rise
right up to the war. Actually, commodities like cotton and wool
tended to be a few pennies cheaper in Liverpool and other British ports
than in Le Havre and Hamburg; and though the difference was not
great, foreign industrialists thought it great enough to buy there.

Nor was the smaller size or slightly slower rate of increase of the
British population a disadvantage. From the standpoint of labour
supply, it was Germany rather than Britain who found it difficult to
meet the needs of growing industries toward the end of the century;

---

[1] Marshall, *Industry and Trade*, p. 195. On the advantageous resource position of the
British chemical industry, both for organic and inorganic processes, and Germany's
dependence on imports for a significant fraction of her consumption of things like
pitch, tar, and anthracene, cf. *Parliamentary Papers*, 1901, LXXX, no. 2, 'Report on
Chemical Instruction in Germany and the Growth and Present Condition of the
German Chemical Industries', pp. 42, 68.

among other things, she had to move tens of thousands of people from the villages of Pomerania and East Prussia clear across the country to the mills of Westphalia and the Rhineland. As for demand, although the German home market was no doubt growing faster and was potentially greater, British manufacturers actually had most of the known world for an outlet. Here again, their wide-flung, experienced commercial relations gave them an important initial advantage over potential competitors. Even in certain German colonies, British traders and planters long held a pre-eminent position because of their earlier establishment in these areas, their familiarity with the problems and possibilities of backward regions, and the greater willingness of the British investor to put his money into distant ventures.[1]

Finally, Britain had more capital to work with than Germany. Her role as precursor of industrialization had made possible an unprecedented accumulation of wealth, which spilled over her boundaries in increasing abundance from the late eighteenth century on. The first of a series of booms in foreign funds occurred in the 1820's, and by the middle of the century the London Exchange had taken on that cosmopolitan colour that distinguished it from all others. It was and remained, in spite of the rivalry of the Paris Bourse toward the end of the century, the world's most important international securities market, whether for funds, rails, mining shares, or industrial and agricultural ventures.[2]

Germany, by contrast, was a net importer of capital throughout the first two-thirds of the nineteenth century. And even after, the appetite of her burgeoning industry was such that foreign placements never took more than a small fraction of savings available for investment. For a long time indeed, the government discouraged the export of capital on the explicit ground that domestic needs were urgent and should receive priority. This attitude later yielded to other considerations—the desire to develop an empire and to extend German political influence abroad.[3] Even so, and in spite of the rapid ramification of German bank interests throughout the world, the outflow of funds was sporadic and from the 1890's on represented a diminishing portion of net capital formation (Table 57).

This hunger for money was reflected in a continued gap of one to

[1] Cf. W. O. Henderson, 'British Economic Activity in the German Colonies, 1884–1914', *Econ. Hist. Rev.* xv (1945), 55–66.

[2] The best source remains L. H. Jenks, *The Migration of British Capital to 1875* (New York, 1928). See also Landes, *Bankers and Pashas*, chs. I and II; A. K. Cairncross, *Home and Foreign Investment 1870–1913* (Cambridge, 1953); and Imlah, *Economic Elements in the Pax Britannica.*

[3] The traditional hostility to foreign lending remained strong notwithstanding, and the ministries of Finance and Foreign Affairs were often divided on the issue. See Herbert Feis, *Europe the World's Banker, 1870–1914* (New Haven, 1930), ch. VI.

two points between the rate of interest in Berlin and those rates prevailing in the other markets of western Europe. Short-term funds moved back and forth with the business cycle, but the net balance favoured Germany, even *vis-à-vis* a country like France which discouraged lending to a former enemy. French banks may have been reluctant to entrust their funds to domestic industry, as undeserving of confidence; but they thought German banks a good risk, and these passed the money on to their own entrepreneurs. Financially this procedure was unexceptionable; politically it had the makings of a scandal.

No, the reasons for German success in the competition with Britain were not material but rather social and institutional, implicit once again in what has been called the economics of backwardness.

There were, first, certain disadvantages inherent in chronological priority: not so much, however, the oft-cited costs of breaking the path as the so-called 'related costs' of adjustment to subsequent change. The former have been much overemphasized. Admittedly a pioneer in any field incurs additional expense owing to ignorance and inexperience; and in theory those who follow may profit by his mistakes. Yet this assumes on the part of the imitators a wisdom that historical experience belies. If the pioneer often sins on the side of excessive modesty, the follower often suffers from excessive ambition; if the one does not quite know where he is going, the other knows too well and undoes himself by his eagerness. There is such a thing, as technicians of the late nineteenth century were careful to point out, as machines that are too big, engines too powerful, plants that are too capital-intensive.

Far more serious are the burdens imposed by interrelatedness, that is, the technical linkage between the component parts of the industrial plant of an enterprise or economy. In principle, the entrepreneur is free to choose at any time the most remunerative technique available. In fact, his calculus is complicated by his inability to confine it to the technique under consideration. For one thing—and here we shall stress the point of view of the enterprise—no piece of equipment works in a void: the engine, the machine it drives, and the means by which it transmits its power are all built to fit; similarly the number and kinds of machines employed, as well as the capacity and type of channels for supply, transfer, and removal of raw and finished material are rationally calculated in relation to one another. As a result, the replacement of one unit of equipment by another, or the introduction of a new device, can rarely if ever be considered in isolation. What is more, the decision on a given change does not always lie entirely within the enterprise but will depend rather, in greater or lesser degree, on the co-operation of outside units. New assembly techniques, for example, may require new standards of accuracy, hence new equipment, in the plants of subcontractors; more rapid loading facilities may yield far less than their possibilities if carriers do not adjust their methods to the new tempo. In such cases, the allocation of cost and risk poses a serious obstacle, not only because calculation is objectively difficult but even more because human beings are typically suspicious and stubborn in this kind of bargaining situation.[1]

On the other hand—and here we are considering the problem from the standpoint of the economy—large-scale, mechanized manufacture requires not only machines and buildings, but a heavy investment in what has been called social capital: in particular, roads, bridges, ports, and transportation systems; and schools for general and technical education. Because these are costly, because the investment required is lumpy and far exceeds the means of the individual enterprise, and because, finally, the return on such outlays is often long deferred, they constitute a heavy burden for any pre-industrial economy condemned by its technological backwardness to low productivity. Moreover, the burden has tended to grow with the increasing size of industrial plant, so that today many of the so-called underdeveloped countries are trapped in a vicious circle of poverty and incapacity. The much-vaunted freedom of the latecomer to choose the latest and best equipment on the basis of the most advanced techniques has become a myth.

There are thus two kinds of related costs: the one, micro-economic, falls most heavily on the early industrializer; the other, essentially macro-economic, falls most heavily on the follower country. The relative weights of the two have never been measured historically, nor is it likely that the information at our command will ever permit such a calculation. It would seem, however, that the ratio has varied over time. If the balance today favours the advanced countries, whose lead in output and in standard of living continues to grow, the advantage lay the other way in the middle and late nineteenth century. By that time Germany had built up a more productive stock of social capital than Britain (she was never so far behind as the 'backward' countries of today), while the related costs of growth fell to the enterprises of the unhappy pioneer. All of British industry suffered from the legacy of precocious urbanization; the cities of the early nineteenth century were

[1] On the comparative advantages and disadvantages of priority, see F. R. J. Jervis, 'The Handicap of Britain's Early Start', *The Manchester School*, XVI (1947); M. Frankel, 'Obsolescence and Technological Change', *Amer. Econ. Rev.* XLV (1955), 296–319; and an exchange between D. F. Gordon and Marvin Frankel on the same subject, *ibid.* XLVI (1956), 646–56. Also W. E. G. Salter, *Productivity and Technical Change* (Cambridge, 1960); and C. P. Kindelberger, 'Obsolescence and Technical Change', *Bull. Oxford University Institute of Statistics*, XXIII (1961), 281–97.

not built to accommodate the factories of the twentieth (logistics again !). Steel plants, especially, with cramped, ill-shaped sites, found it difficult to integrate backward to smelting or forward to finishing; and lack of integration in turn inhibited adoption of a number of important innovations, among them by-product coking. Similarly, railways and colliery owners were long unable to agree on the adoption of larger freight trucks; and the electrical industry was crippled for decades by the initial diversity of methods of supply. The very sight of the spacious arrangements of the Homestead plant in the United States made Windsor Richards wish he 'could pull down the whole works at Bolckow's and start afresh'.[1] If wishes were horses, beggars would ride.

Where, then, the gap between leader and follower is not too large to begin with, that is, where it does not give rise to self-reinforcing poverty, the advantage lies with the latecomer. And this is the more so because the effort of catching up calls forth entrepreneurial and institutional responses that, once established, constitute powerful stimuli to continued growth.

The French, among others, have a saying: 'It is easier to become rich than to stay rich' (compare the related apothegm, 'shirtsleeves to shirtsleeves in three generations'). However sceptical those of us who have not had the opportunity to test this aphorism may be of its general validity, it clearly rests on empirical observation of the rise and fall of fortunes. On the one hand, prosperity and success are their own worst enemies; on the other, there is no spur like envy.

Thus the Britain of the late nineteenth century basked complacently in the sunset of economic hegemony. In many firms, the grandfather who started the business and built it by unremitting application and by thrift bordering on miserliness had long died; the father who took over a solid enterprise and, starting with larger ambitions, raised it to undreamed-of heights, had passed on the reins; now it was the turn of the third generation, the children of affluence, tired of the tedium of trade and flushed with the bucolic aspirations of the country gentleman. (One might more accurately speak of 'shirtsleeves to hunting jacket—or dress coat, or ermine robes—in three generations'.) Many of them retired and forced the conversion of their firms into joint-stock companies. Others stayed on and went through the motions of entrepreneurship between the long weekends; they worked at play and played at work. Some of them were wise enough to leave the management of their enterprises to professionals, comparable in privilege and function to the steward of the medieval domain. Yet such an arrangement is at best a poor substitute for interested ownership; at its worst, it is an invitation to conflict of interests and misfeasance. The annals of

[1] In the *J. Iron and Steel Institute*, LI (1897), 106.

history are full of enriched and ennobled stewards, bailiffs, *Meier*, valets, and the like.

Nor were corporate enterprises significantly better. For one thing, family considerations often determined their selection of managing personnel. For another, such scanty and impressionistic evidence as we have indicates that private and public companies alike recruited too many of their executives from the counting room rather than from the shop.[1] And such production men as were elevated to high responsibility were more likely than not to be 'practical' people who had learned on the job and had a vested interest in the established way of doing things.

The weaknesses of British enterprise reflected this combination of amateurism and complacency. Her merchants, who had once seized the markets of the world, took them for granted; the consular reports are full of the incompetence of British exporters, their refusal to suit their goods to the taste and pockets of the client, their unwillingness to try new products in new areas, their insistence that everyone in the world ought to read English and count in pounds, shillings, and pence. Similarly, the British manufacturer was notorious for his indifference to style, his conservatism in the face of new techniques, his reluctance to abandon the individuality of tradition for the conformity implicit in mass production.

By contrast, the German entrepreneur of the late nineteenth century was generally a *novus homo*; he was almost bound to be, given the lateness and rapidity of the country's industrialization. Often he was a technician, formally trained for his work; trained or not trained, however, he was utterly serious. He worked long hours and expected his subordinates to do likewise; he watched every *pfennig*, knew every detail of his firm's operations. The observers of the day join in picturing him as supple, ingenious, aggressive to the point of pushingness, and occasionally unscrupulous. He had no antiquated veneration of quality for its own sake, was skilled in meretricious presentation, accommodating on terms of sale, energetic in prospecting for new customers and tenacious in serving them.

Yet these unflattering comparisons, which ring true and conform to the historical experience of similar rivalries (compare the inflexibility of the declining Italian cloth industry of the seventeenth and eighteenth centuries),[2] also contain a great deal of caricature. For one thing, a

---

[1] Cf. Charlotte Erickson, *British Industrialists: Steel and Hosiery, 1850–1950* (Cambridge, 1959), ch. VIII, esp. p. 194.

[2] See the interesting article by Carlo Cipolla, 'The Decline of the Italian Cloth Manufacture: the Case of a Fully Matured Economy', *Econ. Hist. Rev.* 2nd ser. v (1952), 178–87.

certain amount of exaggeration is built into any contrast of this kind. For another, the evidence is biased, to a degree that is hard to assess. Contemporary observers emphasized the failures of British entrepreneurship and the imminent dangers of German competition much as a newspaper cries up the morbid aspects of the news. That was the way one sold articles or attracted the notice of officials in London. Besides, there is such a thing as fashion in opinions, and this was clearly one of the popular dirges of the day.

The question is a complicated one. Berrick Saul has shown that a number of British enterprises in fields like engineering reacted vigorously and imaginatively to foreign competition in the years before the First World War. He cites an American consular report of 1906: 'No one who has not lived in England during the last seven or eight years can realize how great has been the awakening here nor how changed the British mental attitude is regarding new ways of doing things. There has been much wise and clever adaptation to British cheaper labor of American machinery ideas.'[1]

In certain fields, then, the lag was probably diminishing. Yet there was still a great deal to be accomplished, as the wartime inquiries into these same industries were to show. Moreover, this very irregularity of pace and this uneven distribution of technological advance pose important questions for the economic historian. If many older enterprises were complacent, why did younger units not take advantage of the opportunity to push them aside? In other words, why did not change diffuse more rapidly? And what of new industries like electrical engineering and organic chemicals, where hardening of the arteries had not set in?

A number of considerations suggest themselves. There were the usual market frictions. Macro-economic change is rarely abrupt, simply because the system works imperfectly. The nature of the competitive imperfections of the British economy before 1914 is a subject well worth investigating. This was in principle the freest market in the world—no barrier to outside products and, as we have seen, a limited movement toward formal cartelization. Yet only a close study of actual buying and selling practices will show the extent to which habit, personal ties, and sheer inertia distorted the play of competition.

A second support of conservatism was increasing difficulty of entry. This was most severe in heavy industry, especially in branches like metallurgy, where site and ready access to scarce mineral resources were critically important; but the increase in the scale of enterprise and consequently in initial capital requirements was general, and it was no

[1] S. B. Saul, 'The American Impact on British Industry 1895–1914', *Business History*, III (1960), 28.

longer an easy matter for an individual or even a group of partners to undertake the manufacture of a mass-market commodity.

There were exceptions. Trades like clothing, where taste played a role, the vagaries of fashion limited standardization, and equipment was inexpensive and shop production feasible, continued to beckon to new-comers. And there was a steady proliferation of small repair and maintenance units, not only in the older machine trades, but in new fields like bicycle and electrical repair. A few of these firms became giants—one has only to think of the beginnings of the British or, for that matter, any motor car industry. The bulk, however, performed modestly; economies of scale were limited, and with them the scope for entrepreneurial ability; and while the rate of entry was high, so was the death rate.

All of this was connected with a general turning away of talent from the older branches of manufacture, whose inadequacy of reward at once justified and was aggravated by this abandonment. The area of greatest opportunity for new men lay in catering to the needs of a long-enriched business class freed of the habit and necessity of abstinence, of a labour force enjoying for the first time an income above the minimum of decency, of a growing rentier class reposing on the returns from home and overseas investments. Mass leisure had become a powerful market force, for the first time in European history, and the service sector grew apace—not only banking, insurance and the professions, but the whole range of activities that provide for recreation and travel. It began to look as though Britons would soon be living by transferring back and forth the income received from the work of others. The image was caricature, but it testified to the direction of economic change. The situation offers some interesting analogies to that of eighteenth-century Holland.[1]

Finally, there were two difficulties that afflicted the entire industrial sector, but above all its newest branches: scarcity of skills and scarcity of venture capital.

Skills are learned. And the supply of skills to industry is essentially dependent on education. To observe this, however, is merely to state a truism. To do more, one must begin by breaking down this omnibus word 'education' and relating its content to the requirements of production.

By education we really mean the imparting of four kinds of know-ledge, each with its own contribution to make to economic perfor-

---

[1] Cf. the studies of Charles Wilson: 'The Economic Decline of the Netherlands', *Econ. Hist. Rev.* IX (1939), 111–27; and *Anglo-Dutch Commerce and Finance in the Eighteenth Century* (Cambridge, 1941).

mance: (1) the ability to read, write, and calculate; (2) the working skills of the craftsman and mechanic; (3) the engineer's combination of scientific principle and applied training; and (4) high-level scientific knowledge, theoretical and applied. In all four areas, Germany represented the best that Europe had to offer; in all four, with the possible exception of the second, Britain fell far behind.

The first raises special problems of evaluation. It is not easy to define and assess the relationship of primary education to industrial efficiency. The more obvious connections are probably the least important. Thus, although certain workers—supervisory and office personnel in particular—must be able to read and do the elementary arithmetical operations in order to perform their duties, a large share of the work of industry can be performed by illiterates; as indeed it was, especially in the early days of the Industrial Revolution. Probably the main economic advantages of an extensive, well-run system of compulsory elementary education, therefore, are first, the foundation it provides for more advanced work, and second, its tendency to facilitate and stimulate mobility and to promote thereby a selection of talent to fit the needs of the society. It helps optimize, in short, the allocation of human resources.

Yet it is one thing to point out the significance of this mechanism and another to measure its effectiveness. No empirical studies of the relationships between education and selection on the one hand, between selection and industrial performance on the other, exist for our period. All we have is qualitative observations, plus data on length and generality of schooling and on some of the more elementary cognitive consequences of instruction—notably percentages of literacy. The rest we are obliged to infer.

For what these data are worth—and they are subject to serious caution when used for international comparisons—they show an enormous gap between British and German achievements in this area. On the one hand, we have a nation that until the closing decades of the century preferred to leave schooling to the zeal, indifference, or exploitation of private enterprise. It was not only a question of *laissez-faire*. For every idealist or visionary who saw in education the path of an enlightened citizenry, there were several 'practical' men who felt that instruction was a superfluous baggage for farm labourers and industrial workers. These people, after all, had been ploughing fields or weaving cloth since time beyond recall without knowing how to read or write; not only was there no reason to change now, but in the last analysis, all they would learn in school was discontent. As a result of this indifference and resistance, it was not until 1870 that local boards were empowered to draft by-laws of compulsory attendance; and not until 1880 was primary instruction made obligatory throughout the kingdom.

Under the circumstances, Britain did well to have roughly half of her school-age children receiving some kind of elementary instruction around 1860. At least this was the finding of the Newcastle Commission, which was exceptionally tolerant of hearsay evidence and tended to view the situation with invincible optimism.[1] There was good reason to believe that many if not most of these students honoured their classrooms by their absence more than their presence; and that in some of the large industrial centres, attendance was lower in the 1860's than it had been a generation before.[2] Even granting the accuracy of the Newcastle estimates, one notes that only two-fifths of these children went to schools inspected by the state; and only one quarter of these remained long enough to enter the upper classes, the only ones that were 'reasonably efficient'.

The situation improved considerably in later years. At least attendance increased sharply from 1870 on and the content of elementary education was enriched by the simple act of assimilating the instruction of the generality of schools to the modest standards of the inspected institutions. Even so, the system remained sterilized by invidious prejudice and the constraints of pathological social conditions. Thus it was widely assumed that aptitude for instruction—or more subtly, ability to use instruction—was a function of class, and that the content and level of training should be suited to the student's station in life. 'The Education Act of 1870,' wrote H. G. Wells, 'was not an Act for common universal education, it was an Act to educate the lower classes for employment on lower class lines, and with specially trained, inferior teachers who had no university quality.'[3] In short, it was not intended to find and advance talent. But one could go further: whatever the ostensible aims of compulsory elementary education, its essential function (what Robert Merton might call its latent function) was not even to instruct. Rather it was to discipline a growing mass of disaffected proletarians and integrate them into British society. Its object was to civilize the barbarians; as Her Majesty's Inspector for London put it, 'if it were not for her five hundred elementary schools London would be overrun by a horde of young savages'.[4]

Compulsory elementary education goes back in parts of Germany to

---

[1] See *Parliamentary Papers*, 1861, XXI (Cd. 2794).

[2] Frank Smith, *A History of English Elementary Education, 1760–1902* (London, 1931), pp. 280–1.

[3] In his *Experiment in Autobiography*, cited by G. A. N. Lowndes, *The Silent Social Revolution: an Account of the Expansion of Public Education in England and Wales, 1895–1935* (London, 1937), p. 5.   [4] *Ibid.* p. 19.

PRIMARY SCHOOLING IN GERMANY 569

the sixteenth century; in Prussia, Frederick the Great issued his *General Landschulreglement* in 1763. The quality of the instruction was often poor—teaching posts were long looked upon as excellent places for old soldiers—but improved with time. By the early nineteenth century, the school systems of Germany were famed throughout Europe, and travellers like Madame de Staël and observers like Victor Cousin made it a point to visit and examine this greatest achievement of a knowledge-hungry people.

The obligation of children to attend primary school was enforced—as laws usually are in Germany: in Prussia in the 1860's, the proportion of children of school age attending class was about 97½ per cent;[1] in Saxony, it was actually over 100 per cent.[2] More important than quantitative results, however, were the character and content of the system. To begin with, it was the expression of a deep-rooted conviction that schooling was a cornerstone of the social edifice; that the state not only had an obligation to instruct its citizenry, but found its advantage therein, since an educated people is a moral and strong people. Secondly, the very antiquity of the system obviated the emphasis on debarbarization that marked the first generation of compulsory education in Britain. Observers from abroad were impressed by the neatness and decorum of German schoolchildren, from whatever class; the schools were consequently free to concentrate their efforts on instruction. Thirdly, schooling tended to last longer than in Britain, and the elementary classes were linked to so-called 'middle' and secondary grades in such a way that some selection of talent occurred. The process was only moderately effective; in large areas, particularly rural districts, it was inoperative. Yet even in the middle decades of the nineteenth century, visitors were impressed by the catholicity of recruitment of the continuation (as well as the elementary) schools: 'They are generally very well attended by the children of small shopkeepers,' wrote Joseph Kay in 1850, 'and contain also many children from the poorest ranks of society.'[3]

[1] It had been 43% in 1816, 68% in 1846. Prussia, *Mittheilungen des Statistischen Bureaus in Berlin* (ed. Dieterici), 1847, p. 47.

[2] The excess is to be accounted for by children under six or over fourteen years of age, and by a number of foreign students. France, Min. de l'Agriculture, du Commerce et des Travaux Publics, *Enquête sur l'enseignement professionnel* (2 vols.; Paris, 1865), II, 7f.

[3] J. Kay, *The Social Condition and Education of the People in England and Europe* (2 vols.; London, 1850), II, 227. Kay returns to this theme repeatedly: '...I *constantly* found the children of the highest and of the lowest ranks sitting at the same desk....' *Ibid.* p. 209; also pp. 74–5, 80.

Compare the introduction of universal education in Japan in the 1870's, which was hastened and facilitated by similarly deep-rooted social values. According to

570   GROWING IMPORTANCE OF TECHNICAL TRAINING

It hardly needs saying that the above discussion does some violence to the complexity of the contrast between the two countries. One can find some striking bright spots in the British achievement—certain elementary and grammar schools, for example, which provided excellent instruction to poor scholars and children of well-to-do parents alike; just as one can find among the Junkers of East Elbia instances of a benighted hostility to education to match anything in Britain.[1] Similarly, one could discuss endlessly the merits of the educational philosophies of the two countries, not only because the subject is intrinsically open to contention, but because it is almost impossible to reconcile the contradictory mass of impressionistic evidence. Was one system of elementary instruction more given to 'cramming' than another? one more practical, the other more liberal? one more devoted to facts, the other to ability to think? No categorical answer is possible.

The link between formal vocational, technical, and scientific education on the one hand and industrial progress on the other is more direct and evident. Moreover, it became closer in the course of the nineteenth century, for reasons that can be deduced from our earlier discussion of technology. To begin with, the greater complexity and precision of manufacturing equipment and the closer control of quality, in conjunction with the growing cost of inefficiency and pressure of competition, conduced to higher standards of technical knowledge and proficiency, especially on the upper levels of the productive hierarchy and among the designers of industrial plant. Secondly, the high cost of equipment made on-the-job training increasingly expensive and helped break down an apprenticeship system that had long been moribund. And finally, the changed scientific content of technology compelled supervisory employees and even workers to familiarize themselves with new concepts, and enhanced enormously the value of personnel trained to keep abreast of scientific novelty, appreciate its economic significance, and adapt it to the requirements of production.

It would serve no useful purpose to paint in detail the familiar

Ronald Dore, the acceptance of the Confucian principle that virtue consists in knowledge of one's station and respect for one's superiors, implied the necessity of education for all, but especially for the lower classes, who had that much more virtue to acquire. (See his essay on 'The Legacy of Tokugawa Education', to be published in one of the forthcoming volumes of the Association of Asian Studies Conferences on the Modernization of Japan. I am indebted to Henry Rosovsky for this reference.) The system ostensibly aimed, then, at least before the Meiji period, at reducing ambition and mobility. Yet latent functions are often more important than manifest ones, and history is full of unanticipated consequences.

[1] Cf. R. H. Samuel and R. H. Thomas, *Education and Society in Modern Germany* (London, 1949), pp. 6–7.

chiaroscuro of the late and stunted growth of technical and scientific education in Britain as against the vigorous, precociously developed German system. Briefly, where Britain left technical training, like primary education, to private enterprise, which led in the event to a most uneven and inadequate provision of facilities, the German states generously financed a whole gamut of institutions, erecting buildings, installing laboratories, and above all maintaining competent and, at the highest level, distinguished faculties. Until the middle of the century, Britain had nothing but the young University of London, the good, bad, and indifferent mechanics' institutes, occasional evening lectures or classes, and courses in the rudiments of science in a few enlightened secondary and grammar schools. After that, improvement came slowly, though the pace picked up measurably after about 1880. The first gains came around the middle of the century in scientific education (Royal College of Chemistry in 1845; Government School of Mines, 1851; Owen's College, Manchester, 1851; university degrees in science, 1850's); they came at the highest level and for many years were partially vitiated by the above-mentioned failure of the primary and secondary schools to find and prepare recruits. Technical and vocational training had to wait another generation and suffered right through the inter-war period from the same handicap. On the eve of the First World War, the British system still had a long way to go to catch up with the German—at least from the standpoint of economic productivity. (There were social and psychological aspects of the Teutonic system that gave outsiders pause.) The long chorus of anguish from otherwise sober savants, writing in the press, addressing the public, or testifying before a remarkable series of parliamentary commissions from 1867 on bears witness to the high cost of this educational backwardness.

More important than the lag itself are the reasons. Essentially they boil down to demand, for a free society generally gets the educational system it wants, and demand was once again a function in part of British industrial priority and German emulation.

As we have seen, even elementary education encountered suspicion and resistance in England; *a fortiori*, technical instruction. There were those industrialists who feared it would lead to the disclosure of or diminish the value of trade secrets. Many felt that 'book learning' was not only misleading but had the disadvantage of instilling in its bene-ficiaries or victims—depending on the point of view—an exaggerated sense of their own merit and intelligence. Here management was joined by foremen and master craftsmen who, products of on-the-job apprenticeship, despised or feared—in any case, resented—the skills and knowledge of the school-trained technician. Still other employers

572 PRACTICAL EXPERIENCE VERSUS BOOK KNOWLEDGE

could not see spending money on anything that did not yield an immediate return, the more so as the notions imparted by these classes and institutes almost invariably called for new outlays of capital.

A few were afraid of raising up competition.[1] But most would have snorted at the very idea: they were convinced the whole thing was a fraud, that effective technical education was impossible, scientific instruction unnecessary. Their own careers were the best proof of that: most manufacturers had either begun with a minimum of formal education and come up through the ranks or had followed the traditional liberal curriculum in secondary and sometimes higher schools. Moreover, this lesson of personal experience was confirmed by the history of British industry. Here was a nation that had built its economic strength on practical tinkerers—on a barber like Arkwright, a clergyman like Cartwright, an instrument-maker like Watt, a professional 'amateur inventor' like Bessemer, and thousands of nameless mechanics who suggested and effected the kind of small improvements to machines and furnaces and tools that add up eventually to an industrial revolution. She was proud of these men—listen to Lowthian Bell citing in reply to criticism of British technical shortcomings the names of Darby and Cort.[2]

In many trades there developed a mystique of practical experience. Consider the implications of the following question at the Parliamentary Inquiry of 1885:

You know perfectly well that in every mill there is one man who can spin very much better than anyone else, and if you wanted a finer number, that was the man that was put on. Without a technical school you have always some man of that kind; do you think any technical school would turn out any number of those men in a mill?[3]

And one manufacturer in the tinplate trade, denying the importance of trained engineers, remarked that what was needed was 'practical men who were in sympathy with their rolls and everything else. They could do a lot with their machinery if they were in sympathy with it.'[4]

Moreover, even when employers did come to recognize the need for trained technical personnel, they yielded grudgingly. The underpaid

---

[1] In 1884 Huxley stigmatized this 'miserable sort of jealous feeling about the elevation of their workmen'. Cited in S. F. Cotgrove, *Technical Education and Social Change* (London, 1958), p. 24.

[2] *J. Iron and Steel Institute*, 1878, p. 315.

[3] *Parliamentary Papers*, 1886, XXI: 'Commission...on Depression of Trade and Industry', Q. 5173.

[4] W. E. Minchinton, 'The Tinplate Maker and Technical Change', *Explorations in Entrepreneurial History*, VII (1954–5), 7.

ATTITUDES TO CAREERS   573

'scientists' were put in sheds, reclaimed workrooms, and other improvised quarters that hardly permitted controlled conditions and accurate tests. Their work was one cut above the rule-of-thumb techniques of the skilled workman; it was far below that of the German laboratory researcher.[1]

In sum, job and promotion opportunities for graduates in science and technology were few and unattractive. The most remunerative field, in spite of what has been said, was chemistry, and even there the best positions were often reserved for men trained abroad; undoubtedly the mediocre quality of many British graduates served to reinforce the scepticism of management. There was just about nothing for physicists until the last decade of the nineteenth century. The worst situation was in the lower ranks, on the level of vocational training, where students occasionally suffered for their ambition: a witness before the Committee on Scientific Education of 1868 testified that only one in four of those who attended vocational classes of the Science and Art Department in the 1850's got back into his trade.[2] In 1884 the Royal Commission on Technical Instruction reported:[3] 'We believe that many workmen are disposed to attach too little value to the importance of acquiring knowledge of the principles of science, because they do not see their application.' No wonder. No wonder also that the most gifted of those few young men who had the means to pursue their education beyond the intermediate level followed the traditional liberal curriculum to careers in the civil service, to pursuit of the genteel county life, or to the kind of post in industry or trade—and there were many—that called for a gentleman and not a technician.

The contrast with German attitudes is hard to exaggerate. For an ambitious nation, impatient to raise its economy to the level of the British, vexed if not humiliated by its dependence on foreign experts, an effective system of scientific and technical training was the foundation and promise of wealth and aggrandizement. A veritable cult of *Wissenschaft* and *Technik* developed. The kings and princes of central Europe vied with one another in founding schools and research institutes and collected savants (even humanistic scholars like historians!) as their predecessors of the eighteenth century had collected musicians and composers; or as the courts of the Italy of the *cinquecento*, artists and

---

[1] Cf. J. E. Stead, *J. Iron and Steel Institute*, XLIX (1896), 119; Burn, *Economic History*, p. 178; *Final Report of the Committee on Industry and Trade* (Cd. 3282; London: H.M.S.O., 1929), pp. 214f.

[2] *Parliamentary Papers*, 1867–8, Comm. on Scientific Instruction, pars. 301–28, cited by Cotgrove, *Technical Education*, p. 51, n. 1.

[3] *Parliamentary Papers*, 1884, XXIX: Royal Commission on Technical Instruction, Second Report, 1, 523; cited *ibid*. p. 40.

sculptors. The people came to gape at the *Hochschulen* and universities with the awe usually reserved for historical monuments. Most important, entrepreneurs prized the graduates of these institutions and often offered them respected and often powerful positions—not only the corporate giants with their laboratory staffs of up to a hundred and more, but the small firms also, who saw in the special skills of the trained technician the best defence against the competition of large-scale production.

There is keen irony in all this. We have noted how a British observer of the mid-nineteenth century was impressed by the 'social democracy' of the German classroom; yet this is precisely what had struck continental travellers of the eighteenth century as one of the peculiar virtues of the British society of that period. To be sure, higher schooling in those days was confined to a very small fraction of the population; even the children of wealthy families often received little formal instruction; so that such equality as prevailed was as much or more one of ignorance than of knowledge. But that is the point: it did not make that much difference in the eighteenth century how much instruction a man had received. The recruitment of talent was on other grounds; wide avenues of mobility were open to the unschooled as well as the schooled; and many a man taught himself or learned by experience the knowledge and skills he required for his work.

With industrialization and the proliferation of bureaucracy in business as well as government, however, formal education took on steadily increasing importance as the key to occupational, hence social, preferment. This is not to say that the system or content of instruction was well suited to the requirements of the economy and polity; merely that schooling came more and more to govern recruitment of talent.

This is a task that a school system is in theory ideally equipped to perform. It is of its essence objective, grading and advancing students on the basis of ability and work—except where competition has been deliberately excluded from the classroom. Yet in fact, the selective efficiency of the system depends directly on its own circumstances and principles of recruitment, and these reflect in turn the values and attitudes of its creators and clientele.

Once again, timing and intent are crucially important. In Britain, where technological change came early, a new industrial society had already taken shape by the time the schools were built; so that these embodied not only the prejudices and cleavages of the established order, but the material inequalities. For members of the poorer classes, it was not only presumptuous to covet a more than minimal education; it was pecuniarily impossible—not so much because of the direct outlays required (though these were often a serious deterrent) as because of the earnings that would have to be foregone. It was the opportunity cost of instruction that made it the almost exclusive prerogative of the well-to-do. The school system, in other words, which might have been the great force for social mobility and advancement by talent, became a powerful crystallizer, defending the positions of a newly entrenched Establishment by giving it a quasi-monopoly of such knowledge and manners (including speech pattern) as the society valued.

Some of this was also true of German education, but to a much smaller degree—and differences in history are almost always a question of degree. The Germans developed their schools in advance of and in preparation for industrialization. The system was meant to strengthen the polity and economy not only by instruction, but also by finding and training talent, and while it necessarily fell short of its objectives, the elements of intent and direction were critically important. Hence one of the strangest paradoxes in modern history: that on the one hand, a liberal society standing out from all others in the eighteenth century for equality and mobility of status, should have lost something of these during the very period of its progressive political democratization; while on the other, a far more authoritarian society, characterized in its pre-industrial period by a clearly defined, fairly rigid hierarchy of rank, should have developed a more open structure, without corresponding political change.[1]

Needless to say, this contrast between two forms of social organization is not meant to imply an invidious moral judgement. Education and mobility are not virtuous ends in themselves, but means to ends, and their consequences, intended or not, may as easily be evil as good. One could easily argue that the *élite* produced by the British system— obnoxiously sure at times of its place and prerogatives but endowed with a keen sense of traditional morality and *noblesse oblige*—was in every way to be preferred to the hard, opportunistic, end-justifies-means specimens promoted by the German *cursus honorum*. But such a comparison would take us well beyond the limits of our subject.

Britain's relative lack of skills and knowledge (who could have imagined this eventuality in the first half of the nineteenth century?) was accompanied by, and contributed to, an equally astonishing in-adequacy of venture capital. This statement may well strike the reader as inconsistent with our earlier discussion of Britain's plethora of wealth. But savings are not necessarily investment, and there are all kinds of investment—foreign and domestic, speculative and safe, rational and irrational. The British had the capital. But those who channelled and dispensed it were not alert to the opportunities offered

[1] Cf. Kay, *Social Condition*, II, 74–5; also G. M. Trevelyan, *British History in the Nineteenth Century* (1st ed., London, 1922), p. 353.

by modern technology; and those who might have used it did not want or know enough to seek it out.

The supply side first: the British banking system had grown more or less like industry—step by step, from the ground up, along with its clientele. Its greatest virtue was its remarkable ability to transfer resources from suppliers to demanders of capital through such traditional instruments as the bill of exchange, the open credit, the overdraft. Its greatest weakness, which became apparent only after the middle of the nineteenth century, was its inability to initiate or encourage the kind of industrial enterprise that would call for large amounts of outside capital. It was passive rather than active, responsive rather than creative.

Moreover, in so far as the capital market did direct the flow of funds, habit and predilection combined to give the preference to overseas governments and to public utilities, foreign and domestic. These were London's stock in trade, and London controlled the bulk of the country's liquid capital.[1] Industry was left to local markets: Manchester had its cotton enterprises; Birmingham, arms and hardware; Newcastle, coal and metallurgy. In such fields London itself was no more than a regional centre, trading the shares of shipyards on the Thames, a machine construction firm at Ipswich, local breweries, and the great department stores and hotels of the capital. As a result, the British corporation was often simply a partnership writ large—parochial in resources, direction, control, and scope. It was bigger than its predecessors of the first half of the century; but it was no match for the *Konzerne* and *Interessengemeinschaften* that were mushrooming across the North Sea.[2]

The sharply contrasting structure of German credit and finance is once again understandable only in terms of the economics of priority and backwardness. We have already observed that whereas British industry could build its resources from the ground up, the Germans found it necessary from the start to create institutions to mobilize scarce capital and channel it to a productive system taking its departure on an advanced level of technique and organization. These were the joint-stock investment banks, and their increasingly intimate collaboration with manufacturing enterprise was to have major consequences for the rate and character of German development.

For one thing, it meant planned promotion and development of the individual firm. The banks had to learn to evaluate the possibilities for

---

[1] Cf. John Saville, 'A Comment on Professor Rostow's British Economy of the 19th Century', *Past and Present*, no. 6 (November 1954), pp. 77–8.

[2] Cf. C. W. von Wieser, *Der finanzielle Aufbau der englischen Industrie* (Jena, 1919), pp. 134–5; Lord Aberconway, *The Basic Industries of Great Britain* (London, 1927), p. 346.

profit in a given business situation before undertaking to issue securities. To this end they not only consulted outside technicians, but developed their own specialists to examine and advise on industrial matters. There were some banks, to be sure, which were less careful than others, or less scrupulous. Germany had her *Gründerzeit*, and there were always financiers who felt that the only significant question in any promotion was its speculative potentialities. Yet most banks did not float and unload; they stayed with their creations, held on to some of their stock, kept an eye on their performance, and encouraged their growth as lucrative clients.

For another, bank financing implied continuing expansion of the industrial sector as a whole. If the profitability of *any given* promotional transaction depended on careful appreciation of the elements involved and on influence over later developments, the *total return* of this very important branch of the bank's operations depended on finding or inventing promotions. Thus the specialists in industrial finance were as concerned with discovering possibilities for growth or reorganization as with helping them come about. This was especially true from 1880 on, after the decline in railway construction and nationalization had deprived the market of its most popular staple. In the following years, the banks played an important role in stimulating as well as in supporting the growth of German heavy industry and its integration along vertical and horizontal lines. Throughout, their influence was on the side of a more thorough utilization of resources and a more effective combination of the factors of production.[1]

Yet it is easy to exaggerate the importance of these differences in the structure and behaviour of the capital markets of the two countries. Students of British economic history in particular have offered on occasion a simpler answer: they have assumed a straightforward inverse relationship between domestic and overseas investment; when the one waxed, the other waned.[2] More careful examination of the data has forced the abandonment of this simple model for a more complex, more accurate, but less comfortable analysis.[3] Even so, many scholars have continued to take for granted that, *grosso modo*, the scale of British foreign investment was such as to deprive domestic industry of nourishment.

[1] One of the best studies of this relationship is O. Jeidels, *Das Verhältnis der deutschen Grossbanken zur Industrie* (Leipzig, 1905).

[2] This point of view is implicit in W. W. Rostow's *British Economy of the Nineteenth Century* (Oxford, 1948), though nowhere does he state it so plainly as A. K. Cairncross, who affirms 'that in the *long* run foreign investment was largely at the expense of home investment or vice versa'. *Home and Foreign Investment* (Cambridge, 1953), p. 187.

[3] Cf. S. B. Saul, *Studies in British Overseas Trade*, pp. 90f.

578   HOUSE VERSUS FOREIGN INVESTMENT

I am not persuaded by this thesis. It rests, first, on a misapprehension. Without going so far as Professor Rostow, who saw the period 1873–98 as one of a general shift from foreign placements toward 'intensive investment at home', one may note that there were times during these years when Britain sank large sums into domestic industry. In 1885 Goschen waxed fairly rapturous on the subject:

Never before has there been so keen a desire on the part of the whole community to invest every reserve shilling they may have in some remunerative manner. There is a competition between men who have a few tens of pounds and a few hundreds of pounds to put them into business, and into business they are put. Joint-stock enterprise has swept up all these available resources. Like a gigantic system of irrigation it first collects and then pours them through innumerable conduit pipes right over the face of the country, making capital accessible in every form at every point.[1]

Yet from the macro-economic standpoint, the results were a disappointment. Clearly, it is not money that counts, but what one does with it.[2]

Secondly, there is good reason to believe that capital flows to opportunity, that if there are borrowers who know what to do with it and seek it, there will be lenders to meet their needs. Admittedly such a generalization does violence to the facts of many individual cases and even perhaps to the experience of certain nations. And it slights the contribution that an imaginative, active banking system can make to industrial development—as we have seen. Yet it seems valid on balance for the major sectors, *qua* sectors, of the advanced industrial economies.[3]

This consideration, moreover, is reinforced here by the fact that, barring non-economic deterrents—lack of security, confiscatory exchange controls, and the like—home enterprise has first claim on the resources of an economy. It has all the advantage of the familiar, whereas foreign ventures are difficult to appreciate, relatively immune from verification and control, and intrinsically more speculative. Indeed the differences between the two are sufficient to give rise to a substantial gap in the expectations of return required to attract investment to each of the two sectors—a gap analogous to the cost of moving

[1] *Addresses on Economic Questions* (London, 1905), quoted in Rostow, *British Economy*, p. 70.

[2] In this connection, it is interesting to note that a recent comparison of production functions in different countries shows differences in the efficiency of capital as well as in the better known efficiency of labour. Indeed the two seem to be related.

[3] Cf. Alec K. Cairncross, 'The Place of Capital in Economic Progress', in Leon H. Dupriez, ed., *Economic Progress* (Louvain, 1955), pp. 235–48.

THE RESPONSE TO INNOVATION   579

labour from one job to another. In sum, if Britain sent so much money abroad, it was partly for lack of initiative on the part of lenders, but even more because borrowers at home did not want it.

This brings us to the demand side of the equation, which, given the rough equality of the two economies in material resources, was essentially a function of entrepreneurship, that is, of those human elements—imagination, energy, aspiration—that shaped investment decisions in the two systems. Here again, the contrast is sharp enough to transcend the intrinsic limitations of qualitative evidence. The British manufacturer, strong in his admiration for experience and his preference for empiricist tinkering as against bookish experiment, was inclined to be suspicious of novelty. Riley, describing his finally successful efforts to introduce the use of hot pig in Scottish open-hearth mills to the Iron and Steel Institute in 1900, declared that 'the want of confidence in success and the passive resistance often met with in such cases was perhaps more discouraging than any possible difficulties which might arise in actual working, or in working out practical methods'. The conservatism of the tinplate trade was notorious: 'Generally speaking,' said one manufacturer in the years before the war, 'when anything new is introduced into any work, if it is not right away a success out it goes'. The response to something new was to ask 'if any other fool had tried it yet'.[1] One could cite similar examples from other branches of industry.

In the meantime the German system had institutionalized innovation: change was built in. There was no assurance of major discoveries—it is worth noting, for example, that the great advances in metallurgy in the second half of the century were English (Bessemer, Siemens, Thomas–Gilchrist), French (Martin, Carvès), or Belgian (Coppée). But there was some assurance that inventions of whatever origin would be tested and exploited; and there was within industry itself a steady flow of small improvements which cumulatively constituted a technological revolution.[2] The six largest German firms for coal-tar products took out 948 patents between 1886 and 1900, as compared with 86 by the corresponding English firms.[3] And as Schumpeter put it in his description of the German electrical industry, the variety and frequency of innovation under the impulse of the technical departments of the big

[1] Minchinton, 'The Tinplate Maker', *Explorations*, VII (1954–5), 6.
[2] Cf. the discussion of W. N. Parker, 'Entrepreneurial Opportunities and Response in the German Economy', *Explorations*, VII (1954–5), 27: 'Economic opportunity in Germany has been an opportunity for the technologist of ingenious and limited range, and for the production engineer. It has not been aimed at devising striking new types of machinery....' On p. 29 he speaks of 'German possibilities and their introduction in small and incessant doses into existing technology....'.
[3] Cotgrove, *Technical Education*, pp. 20f.

concerns gave rise to a race which 'though never displaying the formal properties of perfect competition, yet produces all the results usually attributed to perfect competition'.[1]

Furthermore—and again we come up against the complexity and inextricability of multiple factors in historical explanation—these contrasts in receptivity to innovation were strengthened by differences in entrepreneurial rationality. The British manufacturer remained faithful to the classical calculus: he attempted to maximize return by making those investments which, given anticipated costs, risks, and sales, yielded the greatest margin over what existing equipment could provide. He was handicapped, as we have seen, by the burden of related costs, which often made otherwise interesting outlays unprofitable. He often made the mistake of tying investment to current operations and returns rather than to expectations of what the future might reasonably bring. Either his tacit assumption was that tomorrow would be the same as today or, as Kindleberger suggests,[2] he was unconsciously trying to minimize the need to make decisions—as always, the most demanding and disagreeable duty of the entrepreneur. Finally, he was sometimes unreasonable enough to neglect one of the cardinal precepts of economics, that sunk costs are sunk, and cling to antiquated equipment because it worked. The theorist is reluctant to admit that people often behave this way, because irrationality does not lend itself to logical analysis; but they do. The weight of earlier advance and growth lay heavy on many a British producer. As Lowthian Bell put it in a comparison of British and American practice: 'The English ironmaster stood in a somewhat different position, inasmuch as if he spent £25,000 to effect [a] saving, he would have to sacrifice the £25,000 he had already laid out.'[3] And another remarked: 'One wants to be thoroughly convinced of the superiority of a new method before condemning as useless a large plant that has hitherto done good service.'[4] The latter statement, of course, may have been nothing more than an affirmation of the need for accuracy in comparing the profitability of old and new equipment—though one is troubled by the reference to past rather than future returns. Even when the British entrepreneur was rational, however, his calculations were distorted by the shortness of his time horizon, and his estimates were on the conservative side.

[1] J. A. Schumpeter, *Business Cycles: a Theoretical, Historical and Statistical Analysis of the Capitalist Process* (2 vols.; New York, 1939), I, 440.

[2] Kindleberger, 'Obsolescence and Technical Change', *Bull. Oxford Univ. Inst. of Statistics*, XXIII (1961), 296, 298.

[3] *J. Iron and Steel Institute*, LIX (1901), no. 1, p. 123.

[4] Alfred Baldwin, in his Presidential Address to the British Iron Trade Association, as reported in *Engineering*, 6 May 1898, p. 569; cited in Burn, *Economic History*, p. 186. Cf. Kindleberger, 'Obsolescence', p. 295.

The significance of this pecuniary approach is best appreciated when it is contrasted with the technological rationality of the Germans. This was a different kind of arithmetic, which maximized, not returns, but technical efficiency. For the German engineer, and the manufacturer and banker who stood behind him, the new was desirable, not so much because it paid, but because it worked better. There were right and wrong ways of doing things, and the right was the scientific, mechanized, capital-intensive way. The means had become end. The economist, to be sure, considering the situation *ex post*, will simply distinguish between two pecuniary calculations: the German entrepreneur simply had a longer time-horizon and included in his estimates exogenous variables of technological change that his British competitor held constant. But this would miss the crucial difference in *ex ante* motivation that made the German behave as he did.

Given this non-rational motivation, there was of course no *a priori* reason why the German pattern should have paid better. It is clear that there can be such a thing as overmodernization—an excessive substitution of capital for labour—just as there can be overemphasis on one or two branches of economic activity at the expense of the rest. Here, however, Germany was fortunate, in that the long wave of technological change favoured science- and capital-intensive methods and industries, while the nature of her own human and material resources were such as to enable her to take advantage of the opportunities offered. In short, she took the right path, though in part for the wrong, or more exactly, irrelevant reasons.

Here some words of caution are in order. I have rested much of this discussion of Anglo–German economic competition on what sociologists call the analysis of ideal types, in this case, two contrasting types of entrepreneurs. This is inevitably a dangerous technique of historical comparison, because it rests on the averaging of the unmeasurable, hence unaverageable, and does violence to the complexity and variety of human behaviour. The economist would be the first to point out that it does not matter in the long run how backward the techniques or how inefficient the performance of the great majority of entrepreneurs, so long as a few are energetic enough to introduce change and force the rest to follow suit. And this is true enough—of the long run. The observation of Lord Keynes has been so often repeated that it has lost much of its pungency; but its correctness remains: In the long run, we are all dead. In the long run, under the pressure of American and German competition, British industry did change many of its ways. But in the meantime it lost ground; one war and then another intervened; new economic rivals appeared; and much talent and capital flowed in other channels. The world does not stand still for anyone, and the short-run weakness contributes, in ways that we are as yet unable to define and measure, to the long-run lag.

One final point. Even if one grants the importance of this human factor—the success of entrepreneurial and technological creativity on one side, the failure on the other—perhaps it was itself nothing more than a reflection of economic determinants. There is, for example, what we may call the 'feedback approach', which sees the growth of an economy or even an industry in any period as a function of its growth in the preceding period: the rate of expansion itself elicits the material and human responses required to sustain it. A succinct statement of this position is to be found in Svennilson:[1]

It may be assumed that the new capacity added in an expanding industry will be built in accordance with the latest technical knowledge, while the rest of the industry, representing the earlier capacity, will lag behind in modernization. The proportion of modern equipment in an industry will thus increase in proportion to the rapidity of the industry's growth. This leads to the conclusion that, *ceteris paribus*, the efficiency of an industry increases according to the rapidity of its expansion.

This line of explanation has been applied to the Anglo-German rivalry by Professor Habakkuk in his study of *American and British Technology*.[2] To begin with, he is inclined to depreciate the gap between British and German performance: he lays stress, for example, on the British bright spots of open-hearth steel and shipbuilding, the one related to the other. And while he concedes the backwardness of other branches, old and new, he lays great stress on related costs of change, on the burden of established plant and vested interest (for example, the obstacle posed by a widespread gas network to electrification), and above all, on the slow rate of expansion. This last, he feels, explains not only the lack of opportunity to build up-to-date plant, but also such entrepreneurial short-comings as may in fact have existed (here too, Habakkuk feels that the usual indictment is exaggerated): 'Great generals are not made in time of peace; great entrepreneurs are not made in non-expanding industries.' Even the weakness of British scientific training and technical performance (once again, Habakkuk contends that it has been overdrawn) can be largely accounted for in analogous terms: 'the English industry failed to attract or retain the

---

[1] Svennilson, *Growth and Stagnation*, p. 10.

[2] H. J. Habakkuk, *American and British Technology in the Nineteenth Century: The Search for Labour-saving Inventions* (Cambridge, 1962). It would have been desirable to consider this work at a number of other points. Unfortunately, the original manuscript was in the hands of the printer at the time Professor Habakkuk's volume appeared. The present discussion has been added in galley because of the fundamental importance of the general issue.

INADEQUACY OF A 'FEEDBACK APPROACH'   583

available scientific ability, and lacked the desire to train its own scientists, because its prospects deteriorated for reasons independent of the supply of scientific skills'. In sum, 'such lags as there were in the adoption of new methods in British industry can be adequately explained by economic circumstances, by the complexity of her industrial structure and the slow growth of her output, and ultimately by her early and long-sustained start as an industrial power'.[1]

I disagree. Not that the argument is wrong; it is simply incomplete and does justice to the behaviour of neither adversary.[2] In regard to Britain, there is the evidence that even the new investment of older industries was characterized by excessive caution and short horizons; and it is also necessary to account for the generally weak performance of the new science-based branches of manufacture. Moreover, it would be wrong to dismiss as incorrect or irrelevant a great mass of contemporary evidence not only testifying to entrepreneurial and technological shortcomings but attributing them to social values and forces independent of the economic system.

The explanation is equally incomplete for the German side of the rivalry. Here too, the analysis has much truth in it: the economic achievements of the *Zollverein* and then the Reich, in conjunction with the military triumphs of Prussia, promoted an atmosphere of euphoric confidence and thereby reinforced the material stimuli to investment and growth. But this is not all one has to explain. There is the question in particular, why the pattern of German investment deviates from what relative factor costs would lead one to expect. Until the last quarter of the nineteenth century, this was not the case: new German plant was less capital-intensive than British plant; equipment was smaller, often less advanced—and this in spite of a far higher rate of growth than in Britain, from 1850 certainly and perhaps from 1834. There is also the objective evidence of technological fecundity deriving from good and widespread scientific training; nowhere is this more obvious than in organic chemicals, where the opportunities for research are in large measure independent of the character or volume of current production. Finally, there is again an abundance of concurrent contemporary testimony about the influence of entrepreneurial attitudes and technical standards on business performance that one would be ill-advised to dismiss except on the strongest grounds.

[1] The quotations are to be found *ibid.* pp. 212, 216, 220.
[2] Our concern here is specifically with the feedback part of the analysis, that is, the contention that Britain's slower rate of growth 'adequately' (perhaps 'substantially' would be more accurate) accounts for those aspects of her economic performance not explained by such direct limitations on entrepreneurial decisions as related costs. On these, already discussed above (see p. 561), one would find general agreement.

In other words, the feedback approach offers an explanation for one side of economic behaviour, that of the stimulus to economic activity which comes from the side of demand. But it slights the supply side and thereby truncates historical reality. Nothing succeeds like success ...but why do some succeed and others fail? Why do some front runners fade and laggards pick up?

Such questions take us into the most difficult problem of economic history, that of explaining why—not simply how or what—change occurs. This is not the place to undertake a discussion of the causation of development and growth, a subject that has already provoked a library of debate, much of it concerned explicitly with the issue posed by the Anglo-German rivalry, that is, the relative importance of human and non-human determinants. But one brief *wissenschaftsoziologische* observation is worth making: when all is said and done, neither empirical evidence nor theoretical reasoning is likely to settle the dispute. Sharp differences of opinion will always remain. For one thing, so complex is the matter of history and so unamenable to the replicated analysis of the laboratory, that the precise imputation of weights to each of the many determinants of economic development— even in a limited situation, *a fortiori* in general—is impossible and likely to remain so. For another, this very complexity and imprecision precludes demonstration that any given explanation of events, however plausible, is the only possible explanation. And since scholars are human, with many, if not all, of the predilections and biases of other humans, they tend to choose and will no doubt go on choosing those interpretations that they find not only plausible but congenial.

This element of congeniality must not be underestimated. Economic development is a great drama. It is the puberty of nations, the passage that separates the men from the boys. It therefore carries with it, in a world that admires power and covets material prosperity, connotations of success and virility. Now some societies have effected this passage earlier than others and have consequently achieved greater wealth; some, though later starters, have been growing faster than some of their predecessors and promise (or threaten, depending on the point of view) to pass them; others have not yet been able to enter on the path of development at all. Because of the profound implications of this drama for the status of the participants, the explanations offered for success or failure are themselves crucial to the self-esteem of these societies and their members. Under the circumstances, the identification of the scholar with the problem he studies has often been as important a determinant of his approach as the objective data.

[6]

Chapter 5

The British Climacteric

SYNOPSIS: 5.00 The rate of growth of industrial production declined continually in Britain from 1873 onwards. 5.01 This deceleration was only partly offset by the growth of services; it was fully offset after 1899 (but not before) by the growth of income from abroad. This Chapter explores the deceleration of industry.

5.02 Population cannot explain the change since the growth rate of the industrial population was increasing up to 1901, and did not then decline. The main problem was a declining rate of growth of productivity. 5.03 This decline was associated with a very low ratio of domestic investment, due partly to weaknesses in foreign trade, partly to exhaustion of the techno-logical opportunities of the original industrial revolution, and partly to lag in adopting new industries.

5.04 In foreign trade exports grew slowly and imports of manufactures grew rapidly. Britain lost out in competition with Germany and the USA. 5.05 German competition was based on lower wages, faster rising product-ivity and greater energy in selling. 5.06 American competition was based on higher capital intensity which the British could not match, not because of differing relative prices of capital and labour (as is alleged) but because British workers produced less than American workers with the same machines. 5.07 The British also lagged in adopting new industries and new technologies.

5.08 The textbook remedies were all out of reach, being incompatible with Britain's free trade ideology, educational patterns, worker attitudes, and self-chosen role as guardian of the gold standard.

5.00 The growth rate of British industrial production fell after 1873, and declined to 1913. This is now generally accepted. The revision of Hoffmann's index of industrial production, which we report in Appendix I, has raised the rate of growth, but has left the deceleration. Taking only manufacturing and mining, and excluding the much more doubtful figures for construction, the growth rates now run as follows, counting from peak to peak:

1853–73	2·7
1873–83	2·2
1883–99	2·1
1899–1913	2·0

Our task is to explain this deceleration.

[The appendices of statistical material referred to in the text have not been reproduced here.]

GROWTH RATES

5.01   First, was this deceleration of industry offset by acceleration in the rest of the economy? There was indeed considerable expansion of the service trades at this time, especially of shipping and of financial services, which brought in a large income. This can be seen in our calculation of real Gross Domestic Product from 1853 to 1913, which is also reported in Appendix I. Service income accelerated its growth rate from 1·6 per cent per annum between 1853 and 1873 to 2·2 per cent per annum between 1873 and 1913. But this was not enough to offset the deceleration of industry and agriculture, so the growth rate of total GDP also decelerated, as follows:

1853–73	1·95
1873–83	1·90
1883–99	1·85
1899–1913	1·70

Neither was this compensated by income from abroad. Indeed GNP declined faster than GDP between 1873 and 1899. Only between 1899 and 1913 was the rise in income from abroad enough to offset the deceleration of domestic output. The annual percentage growth rates of real GNP were as follows:

1853–73	2·1
1873–83	2·0
1883–99	1·9
1899–1913	1·9

5.02   The next question is whether these growth rate changes merely reflect changes in the rate of growth of population. The answer is that this question is relevant for the last sub-period, 1899 to 1913, but not for earlier periods, since before 1899 the growth rate of the occupied population was rising all the time. The census figures are tricky, for reasons reported in Appendix I, where we have tried to put them on a comparable basis. One of the necessary adjustments is to reduce all occupied population figures for 1871 and before by at least 4 per cent, because these earlier censuses included retired persons, and the later censuses did not. With these adjustments, the figures between corresponding dates ran as follows, for the average annual growth rate of the occupied population of the United Kingdom:

1851–71	0·7
1871–81	0·9
1881–1901	1·1
1901–11	0·9

The occupied population of the UK was rising faster after 1871 than before, so population change cannot explain the deceleration of output, at any rate before 1901.

114 *Growth and Fluctuations 1870–1913*

This acceleration of population growth is compounded of two different factors. One is that the population of Ireland was declining absolutely all this time, but declined faster before 1871 than it did thereafter. The other factor is the simultaneous slight acceleration of the population of Great Britain (England, Wales and Scotland). Shown separately, the occupied populations grew as follows:

	Great Britain	Ireland
1851–71	1·20	−1·10
1871–1901	1·25	−0·55
1901–11	1·10	−0·75

The occupied population of Great Britain was accelerating in the last quarter of the nineteenth century because the birth rate had increased in the middle of the century. The decline in the birth rate did not begin until the end of the 1870s, and this was not transmitted to the occupied population for another fifteen years. The following figures (per thousand of population) illustrate the determinants of the rate of natural increase in England and Wales, over intervals of thirty years:

Averages	Birth rate	Death rate	Natural increase
1845/9	32·6	23·3	9·3
1875/9	35·6	21·2	14·4
1905/9	26·7	15·1	11·6

This establishes so far that population change cannot explain the deceleration of output as a whole between 1870 and 1900. But our main concern is with industrial production and the industrial population.

It is not easy to establish what happened to the industrial population. As was explained in the last chapter, census figures have to be arranged to distinguish between industrial workers and workers in distribution; and we do not know how many 'general labourers' should be assigned to manufacturing. Working with the figures in Appendix I we get the following annual rates of growth of persons occupied in manufacturing (separately) and in mining and manufacturing (together):

	Manufacturing	Manufacturing and mining
1851–71	0·6	0·65
1871–81	0·8	0·95
1881–1901	1·05	1·20
1901–11	0·9	1·20

The mining industry was growing rapidly, so the population in industry as a whole was accelerating to 1901 while industrial output decelerated all the time. A major element in this declining productivity was the declining productivity of mining after the mid-1880s, a phenomenon which was general in Western Europe. If we separate out manufacturing and mining, and assume that the growth of the occupied population between peaks in production was the same as between census dates, we get the following annual rates of growth of productivity per person:

	Manufacturing	*Mining*
1853–73	1·85	3·0
1873–99	1·15	0·05
1899–1913	0·90	− 0·7

While the decline in mining productivity was the more spectacular, there was also a constant decline of the rate of growth of productivity in manufacturing.[1]

We may yet evade the issue: can this decline have been due merely to shorter working hours? Definitely not. The standard working week was still 55 hours in 1913, and many observers doubt that the decline from 65 hours had affected output adversely, except in mining. In any case the orders of magnitude are too dissimilar. The growth rate of productivity fell from 1·85 before 1873 to an average of 1·1 up to 1913. To explain this fall over forty years by a reduction of hours would require hours to have fallen by more than 27 per cent (since output would fall by less than hours). So the question remains: why did the growth rate of productivity decline?

INVESTMENT

5.03 It has often been remarked that to seek the causes of social change is like peeling an onion. Each answer is the occasion for a new question: if *b* caused *a*, then what caused *b*? The problem in hand is no exception. Wherever we begin, we shall have to shift continually as each answer opens up new questions.

Let us begin with investment. Low investment ratios are both a cause and a symptom of malaise. The effects are easy to discern; the causes are more complex.

The British ratio of domestic investment was low throughout our forty years. According to Feinstein's figures, the stock of real capital increased between 1873 and 1913 at an average annual rate of only 1·4 per cent per annum, which is rather low for a country whose occupied population was growing by 1·0 per cent per annum, and is probably an underestimate. The biggest investment boom during this period occurred at the end of the century, peaking in real terms in 1903. The average ratio of gross domestic investment to gross domestic product over 1899 to 1904 was 11·2 (including houses; 9·1 excluding houses). These are very low proportions, but they are the best in four decades, according to Feinstein's count.

While domestic investment lagged, foreign investment mounted. At its peak in the eight years just before the outbreak of the war (1906/13) foreign investment averaged 8·4 per cent of net national product. Even if we write up net domestic investment to say 5 per cent, the contrast is striking.[2]

Why did the British invest so much abroad and so little at home? One view is that overseas investment was very profitable, so the home market was starved of capital. The other view is that the home market had an excess of capital, for lack of investment opportunities, so capital was pushed overseas. There is no evidence that entrepreneurs experienced a shortage of capital in the home market. We have already referred to this topic in analysing the depression of the 1880s, noting that interest rates were falling,

116   *Growth and Fluctuations 1870–1913*

and borrowers scarce. Neither was foreign investment all that profitable. Most of it was on fixed interest terms. One could lend to the British government at 3 per cent or to a fairly reputable foreign government at 5 per cent (less reputable ones or doubtful railways at perhaps 8 per cent). Investment in mortgages at home might bring 5 per cent; in commerce and industry perhaps 8 to 10 per cent. Industry's need for capital was small, in comparison with housing, public works and public utilities. At the peak of 1903 according to Feinstein, 'plant, machinery, vehicles and ships' absorbed only 30 per cent of net capital formation, equal to only 2·0 per cent of net national product. Industry also largely financed itself. It is very difficult to believe that if entrepreneurs had wished to invest more in industry they would have been inhibited by lack of capital. And if industrial investment had been profitable, it is highly likely that associated investment in infrastructure, housing and so on would have been forthcoming. Some of this would have been at the expense of foreign investment, but not all; for faster domestic growth would also bring larger profits and greater savings. This is the consensus of students of this subject, although it is difficult to quantify.

The shortfall of domestic investment contributed to a low rate of growth both directly and indirectly. This distinction is meant to separate the functions of capital as a factor of production, and of capital as a bearer of new technology. The distinction is difficult to sustain because the move from less to more capital almost always involves some change of technology. Yet it is a distinction which the econometricians have decided to pursue, and on which they will for some time be continuing to break their heads.[3] For our purposes it suffices to note that in so far as each generation of machines is more productive than its predecessor, a country with a high investment ratio will, other things being equal, have higher productivity than a country with a low investment ratio, because a greater proportion of its machines will be of the latest designs. So what we are saying is that British productivity was diminished not merely by the small amount of capital, but also by the extent to which its capital was out of date; and both these resulted from the low investment ratio.

There is another connection between a low investment ratio and low productivity. Here the distinction is between new investment which replaces old capital by new capital, and new investment which expands employment in an industry, or transfers workers to industry from other sectors. A new machine should replace an existing machine if the average cost of using the new is less than the marginal cost of using the old; whereas if one is expanding employment in the industry the new machine will be installed so long as its average cost per unit of output is less than the average cost of duplicating the old machine. Moreover, in considering replacement, the issue is more than a comparison of prime cost of the old with average cost of the new, since the cost of adopting the new may be more than simply the average cost of the new equipment. Suppose, for example, that an innovation on the railways requires use of a wider track. To use it on an existing railway system requires that existing tracks be replaced by new ones, tunnels be widened, new and wider bridges be built, and station platforms be relocated. Hence it is cheaper to adopt the new system in a new country than it is in an old country with an existing railway system. This is one of the disadvantages of having been first which the British frequently assert, especially in relation to the layout of their railways, mines, ironworks and roads. The new country has the advantage of not having to begin by tearing down the structures of an old system before adopting a new one.

One consequence of this is that an economy whose industrial population is constant will have more incentive to invest abroad and less to invest at home than an economy whose population is growing rapidly. Given the same investment ratio, the latter country may have less capital per head in industry, but may nevertheless have the same or higher productivity because a larger proportion of its capital will be of the latest designs. The former country will have invested more of its capital in other countries. Now the British industrial population was bound to grow more slowly than the German, since already by 1871 it had reached 35 per cent of the occupied population, and this alone would constrain productivity. However, we must not take this argument too far. Since the Second World War many developed countries with industrial populations growing less rapidly than the pre-1913 British have been investing heavily in increasing capital per head.

Why was the domestic investment ratio so low? Because new investment was not sufficiently profitable. We saw in Chapter 2, looking at the ratio of wages to income, and again in Chapter 4, looking at share prices, that the economy was relatively unprofitable in the eighties and the first half of the nineties. It was being squeezed by a combination of relatively stagnant world trade in manufactures and rising competition, which had brought down prices to levels incompatible with current money wages and productivity.

The ultimate cause was exhaustion of the innovations which had propelled the industrial economy in the century up to 1880. By this time the British railway system was largely completed, though France, Germany and the USA would continue to invest in expanding their systems for much longer. Railways were such a large user of capital goods that the system had to find some substitute propellant if it was to maintain its growth momentum. The old technologies in the basic industries, especially iron and cotton, were also reaching exhaustion, and although the United States was developing new highly capital-intensive methods, yielding twice as much output per head, the British were slow to move in this direction. They were also slow in developing the new science-based commodities, leadership in which had passed to Germany and the United States. Given the inevitable passing of British domination of world trade in textiles and iron, the economy needed a higher input of new technology if it was to maintain a reasonable share of world trade at prices compatible with its now constantly increasing money wages. These two checks – the exhaustion of the old technology and the challenge in foreign markets – were not necessarily connected, since either could have occurred without the other. But in fact they happened together, and one check reinforced the other. The internal and the external were linked because the solution to both was a shift to pioneering new technologies and commodities; or at the very least to adopting with minimal delay the discoveries and inventions of other

118 *Growth and Fluctuations 1870–1913*

countries. If Britain had been pioneering new commodities in her domestic market, she would also have been leading in world trade; or if she had led in world trade, the external demand would have buoyed up domestic investment. So whether one starts with the internal or the external situation, the road will lead back to innovation. Given the importance of foreign trade in the period up to 1880, we will start there.

FOREIGN TRADE

5.04 As other countries industrialised, Britain's proportionate share of world trade in manufactures diminished. There are estimates of the British ratio at various dates,[4] but this ratio does not matter. What mattered to Britain was that its foreign trade should grow fast enough to support domestic needs, including full employment, and this did not happen.

The growth rate of British exports of manufactures in constant prices[5] decelerated very sharply after 1873. Between 1853 and 1873 it was 3·3 per cent per annum; from 1873 to 1899 it was 1·6 per cent per annum. After 1899 the growth rate revived (2·7 per cent per annum to 1913), but the dark side of this revival was the extent to which it was due to a combination of adverse terms of trade and extraordinarily heavy capital export.

In any case what mattered was not exports as such, but exports minus imports. The growth rate of imports was coming into equilibrium; having been 6·6 per cent per annum between 1853 and 1873, it fell to 4·5 per cent per annum from 1873 to 1899, and fell again to 2·3 per cent per annum between 1899 and 1913. But in the period 1873–99 the combination of 1·6 per cent growth of exports and 4·5 per cent growth of imports subjected British manufacturing to a terrible beating, for which the term 'the Great Depression of 1873 to 1896' does not seem to be inappropriate. Here are the figures for exports and imports of manufactures at constant prices (£m.).

	1853	1873	1899	1913
Exports	92·7	179·2	272·5	396·7
Imports	8·5	30·9	97·6	135·1
Net exports	84·2	158·3	174·9	261·6

The figures bring out the painful fact that the volume of net exports grew only at 0·4 per cent per annum between 1873 and 1899. However, the figures look even worse in current prices, falling from £178·3m. to £118·5m.

The fall in the growth rate of net exports of manufactures will have damped industrial production. We can estimate the effects by experimenting with different growth rates for foreign trade. Table 5.1 shows actual trade, production and domestic use of manufactures in 1873 and 1913, at 1913 prices. In column 3 we have the actual annual percentage rates of growth. In column 4 we assume that the growth rate of imports had instead been 2·5 per cent per annum, and the growth rate of exports 2·8 per cent per annum, which is considerably lower than the growth rate of world trade in manufactures as a whole (about 3·5). This leaves two unknowns, the growth

The British Climacteric 119

Table 5.1   UK: Balance Sheet of Manufactures[6]

| | | Actual | | Hypothetical | |
	1873 (£m.)	1913 (£m.)	Growth rates	Growth rates	1913 (£m.)
Imports	31	135	4·8	2·5	83
Exports	179	397	2·0	2·8	536
Production	342	767	2·1	2·8a	1,013a
Domestic use	194	505	2·4	2·7	560

a Residual.

rates of production and of domestic use. If we assume that as a result of greater prosperity the growth rate of domestic use rises to 2·7 per cent, it follows residually that the growth rate of production rises from 2·1 to 2·8 per cent per annum (say 1·2 for labour force and 1·6 for productivity).

A higher growth rate of British exports of manufactures would not necessarily have been at the expense of competitors in other industrial countries. A faster growth rate for Britain would have meant greater imports of food and raw materials. The less developed countries would have produced more, and world trade as a whole, both primary and secondary, would have been larger. Possibly the terms of trade would not then have moved so much against primary products up to 1900, but the extra burden could have been borne, with the higher growth rate of production.[7]

Four factors contributed to Britain's trade difficulties in this period.

In the first place the volume of exports to some extent reflected foreign lending. As we saw in Chapter 2, this varied considerably, being high in 1873, low in 1899 and extraordinarily high in 1913 (10 per cent of net national product). In so far as extraordinary foreign lending reflected a shortage of domestic investment opportunities, the high growth rate of exports associated therewith was a symptom of trouble rather than a cause of prosperity.

Secondly, the volume of exports of manufactures varied inversely with the terms of trade in a ratio of almost one to one. This was true both for world trade as a whole, and for British trade. It shows itself in the statistics of world trade in the form of the constant proportion assumed by manufactures in world trade between 1880 and 1929. This is a curious phenomenon which has not reappeared since the Second World War. We have discussed it elsewhere.[8]

The upshot was that the growth rate of the volume of British exports of manufactures decelerated sharply during the Kondratiev downswing of prices, and accelerated sharply thereafter. From the standpoint of the economy as a whole this downswing had one advantage. The industrial workers especially experienced a rapid rate of growth of real wages, well in excess of the growth rate of their physical productivity. But industry was depressed all the same by low prices and slow income growth, and industrial investment was accordingly restrained.

All this should have come to an end with the price upswing after 1900. The terms of trade improved, and exports and net exports leaped upwards at 2·7 and 2·9 per cent per annum respectively. Manufacturing became

120   *Growth and Fluctuations 1870–1913*

markedly more profitable, but the growth rates of manufacturing (output and persons) again declined.

This is a puzzle. Perhaps the solution lies in the nature of the boom, which was for the traditional commodities bought by the less developed countries of the day, who were the ones benefiting from the terms of trade – especially cotton, pig iron and coal – and not a boom for the modern commodities with a long-term future in international trade – such as automobiles and electrical machinery. At the same time that British exports of pig iron were swelling to the poorer countries, Britain was herself becoming the world's largest importer of steel. As we have just suggested, large exports resulting from large foreign investment are probably more a symptom of domestic unease than an occasion for domestic investment. In this case domestic investment in manufacturing was presumably re-strained by Britain's backwardness in the new commodities, which is our next point.

The two preceding influences on the level of British exports, namely capital export and the terms of trade, were fluctuating and temporary factors. Now we come to two more influences of a more permanent character. These two are related, namely the rise of competitors, and the changing commodity composition of trade, from old to new commodities. We shall begin with the competition.

5.05   In 1850 Britain was the main source of the world's supply of the commodities of the industrial revolution – cotton textiles, coal, pig iron, railway materials and steam engines. Obviously this could not last. As other countries industrialised, the British situation would be eroded in three ways. First, these other countries would make these products for them-selves. Secondly, the most successful industrialisers would begin to compete with Britain in third markets. And thirdly, the British market itself would be invaded. Britain could escape this trap only in two ways: by reducing its propensity to import, and by moving out of the older commodities into new ones. Her failure at both strategies was the major cause of her troubles.

France, Germany and the United States were in the first stage of evolution in the middle and third quarters of the nineteenth century. By 1870 they had freed themselves from dependence on British cottons, and had nearly escaped dependence on British coal. They still used a lot of British iron, but this situation too would change in the 1880s. By then, too, other countries would have discovered import substitution, including Belgium, Russia, India (yarn), Brazil, Canada and others.

Germany entered into the second and third stages in the 1880s, competing in third markets, and invading the British market itself. The USA joined the competition after 1895.

The geographical pattern of German competition is interesting. The industrialising less developed countries (LDCs) of our day are frequently advised to form regional customs unions and concentrate on selling manufactures to each other. Germany did begin by securing the local base. The *Zollverein*, established in 1834 and constantly extended, provided the regional framework for the stage of import substitution. But as soon as the industrial base was established, the Germans launched their trade drive everywhere. An early phase, in the 1880s, was to use Britain's own wholesale exporting firms and their markets overseas, by selling to these firms for re-export. The British were shocked to find that re-exports had jumped from 2·2 per cent of their total exports of manufactures in 1873 to 4·0 per cent in 1882. The British domestic market itself was also feeling the blast in the 1880s, and by 1899 was taking 19 per cent of Germany's exports of manufactures. Simultaneously Germany sought and gained footholds in all the other European markets, and shortly afterwards German trade spokesmen were roaming the world.

Maizels has divided the world into industrial countries, semi-industrial countries, and the rest. Table 5.2 compares the performance of Germany and the United Kingdom in these markets. It will be observed that by 1913 Germany was exporting more manufactures than the UK both to industrial countries and to the rest of the world.

Table 5.2 *Germany and UK: Exports of Manufactures, 1913 ($m.)*[9]

To	From Germany	From UK
Industrial	925	624
Semi-industrial	218	810
Rest	583	526
Total	1,726	1,960

The German total had nearly caught up with the British total (having been somewhat less than half thirty years earlier), and the British position was maintained only in the semi-industrial countries. Most of these were satellites of the British economy in one sense or another, and their adherence to British goods derived from imperial relations, imperial preference or dependence on the British market or on British overseas lending, in which the borrowers frequently had British connections. Maizels's 'semi-industrial' group includes Australia, New Zealand, South Africa, India, Argentina, Brazil, Chile, Colombia, Mexico and Turkey. Britain did not impose discriminatory practices upon her 'non-self-governing' colonies, but the self-governing Dominions themselves imposed discrimination in favour of British goods (Canada in 1897, South Africa and New Zealand in 1903 and Australia in 1907) in the hope of inducing reciprocity. Even this tariff discrimination was of little significance. Dependence on the British market, dependence on British lending, and business connections were the major forces supporting loyalty to British goods, bolstered in the British territories by sentiment, and by the official policy of buying only British goods for the public sector.

What accounts for the tremendous German achievement? The causes may be grouped into three: competitive prices, sales energy and leadership in new commodities.

Germany began with a price advantage over the UK, which it maintained throughout this period. The price advantage was due to the fact that

122　*Growth and Fluctuations 1870–1913*

whereas in 1883 German product per head was about 70 per cent of the British, the German money wage was only about 60 per cent of the British. Money wages grew much faster in Germany than in Britain, but productivity grew much faster too, and as we saw in the preceding chapter, money labour cost per unit of output changed at the same rate. So a gap remained; in 1913 productivity was perhaps 6 per cent lower in Germany, but wages were 14 per cent lower. As can be seen in Table 5.3, prices of manufactures exported fell less and rose more in Britain than in Germany. The figures are not entirely trustworthy, but the general impression they convey is right; prices were falling faster elsewhere than in Britain.

Table 5.3　*Prices of Manufactured Exports*[10]

	1883	1899	1913
UK	113	100	125
Germany	126	100	108
France	110	100	112
USA	127	100	112

Added to this price advantage was a tremendous sales effort. The world was flooded with German salesmen. All kinds of sales organisation were tried: wholesale export houses, manufacturers' representatives selling directly to the foreign buyer, manufacturers' export co-operatives, sales through foreign commission agents, and so on. Numerous consulates were opened at strategic points, and consuls were expected to promote sales of German goods, a decision which shocked British conceptions of diplomatic behaviour. Trade credits were liberalised. The British were masters of the three months trade bill and of the long-term bond; the Germans developed intermediate credits of a year or more, which better suited the kinds of capital goods that they were selling. The British were astonished by the vigour and inventiveness of the German effort, and poured out articles, pamphlets and books on the subject from the mid-1880s onwards. Some of the literature was the occasion for self-flagellation. It was said that German salesmen abroad learnt the native languages and carried catalogues in the native languages, in contrast with British salesmen; that German manufacturers would design to the customer's specifications or (alternatively and in contradiction) derived success from concentrating exclusively on standardised mass-produced commodities. The literature also accused the Germans of every kind of chicanery, including piracy of trademarks. But of course one does not build up a huge trade over thirty years by gimmicks and chicanery.[11]

This kind of successful trade drive is more familiar to us than it was to the late Victorians. The Germans were followed by the Americans, starting in the nineties. Then came the Japanese, especially after 1929 and again after 1960. And now it is Brazil.

American exports of manufactures were growing respectably but not spectacularly in the 1880s. Lipsey's figures in constant prices yield a growth rate for finished manufactures of 3·9 per cent per annum between the two peaks of 1883 and 1891. Then comes an explosion. The growth rate rises to 11·7 per cent per annum between 1891 and 1899 helped, as we have suggested before, by a deflated economy. From 1899 to 1913 the rate is 6·5 per cent per annum, which is no mean achievement. The commodities leading this explosion are machinery and iron and steel products. In 1913 the share of metals, engineering and chemicals is, according to Maizels, 70 per cent of US exports of manufactures compared with 41 per cent of British exports of manufactures. The US also, like Germany, was looking to wealthier markets. It sent 62 per cent of its exports of manufactures to Canada and Western Europe, whereas the British sent only 29 per cent to North America and Western Europe.

The two factors we have so far mentioned, low prices and highly concentrated sales effort, are characteristic of all sales drives. But one must go behind these and ask what causes a country to set out on this road. Such highly unbalanced growth may originate in one or other of three cases. First, the country may be deficient in natural resources, and thus have an inescapably large propensity to import food and raw materials. This was the case of Japan. Secondly, the country may have the natural resources, but be failing to develop them, leaving its farmers and service workers with incomes too low to absorb the surplus of manufactures. This is the case of Brazil. Thirdly, the country may, through its leadership in technological skills, have a comparative advantage in industry which produces a large foreign demand for what it offers. Here Britain was the pioneer before 1880, after which date its mantle was inherited by Germany and the United States.

The entrepreneurial drive to invest in manufacturing is a crucial element. It is compounded partly of those price relations which determine the profitability of investment, partly of the degree of help or hindrance offered by the government, and partly of the dynamism of the entrepreneurial class itself. Germany and the USA had all three: wages low in relation to productivity, governments which accounted industrialisation and foreign trade among their top priorities, and businessmen with unlimited confidence.

PRODUCTIVITY

5.06   When we talk about productivity we must distinguish between the old industries of the industrial revolution, including coal, pig iron, textiles and steam power, and the new industries which grew up after 1880, especially electricity, steel, organic chemicals and the internal combustion engine.

British productivity was much higher than German productivity in the old industries around 1880. Therefore it was easy for German productivity to keep rising. In Britain, however, the old technology had been extended about as far as it could. In the cotton textile industry, and again in the utilisation of coke for making pig iron, productivity moved on to a plateau in the 1880s. Even so, German productivity was still lagging, and had not fully caught up with the British even in 1913.

For British productivity to have increased considerably the British would have had to convert to American methods. This involved using about twice as much horsepower per head, and getting about twice as much product per head. The data relating to comparative productivity are set out in Appendix II; relying mainly on Flux's and Rostas's census comparisons,

124   *Growth and Fluctuations 1870–1913*

we put American productivity at 1·9 times the British in 1913.[12] Rostas also offers figures of horsepower per worker, which are 1·4 for Britain in 1907 and 2·9 for the USA in 1909, and it is generally assumed that capital per head was in the same ratio.[13]

Why did the British not adopt American methods? The favourite answer of some economists is: because wages were lower in the UK. But this will not work. UK wages according to Phelps Brown were 52 per cent of the American in 1913. If twice as much capital per head produced twice as much output, the American technology would have been more profitable in Britain at any (positive) levels of wages. The error springs from making the wrong comparisons.

Let us assume that the cost of a unit of capital is the same in both countries, that the Americans use twice as much capital per head, that the American wage is twice the British, and that the American technology yields twice the British output per head. If

w =   US wage for one day's work
k =   daily cost (including interest and amortisation) of hiring the capital used with one man in the USA
P =   cost of one half day's output in the USA, considered to be one unit of output

then the cost of producing one unit of output in the USA is

$$0·5w + 0·5k = P$$

and the cost of producing one unit of output in the UK with British technology is

$$0·5w + 0·5k = P$$

Cost per unit is the same, so Britain and the USA can compete in the same international market despite their different wages and technologies.

Two propositions which are sometimes deduced from this equality are both false. It is not true to say that because money cost per unit of output is the same, therefore real cost must be the same, the difference in factor proportions being exactly offset by difference in factor prices. Real costs are not the same: one man plus one capital will produce in the USA as much as two men plus one capital in the UK (i.e. two units of output).

Neither is it true to say that the equality of money cost proves that the UK is using the right combination of factors. To find out whether the UK is using the right technology one must compare not Britain using one technology and the USA using another, but the cost in Britain at British factor prices for both technologies. One will then find that when using British technology the British cost per unit is

$$0·5w + 0·5k$$

but when using US technology at British wages (with twice the output and twice the capital), the British cost per unit would be

$$0·5 (0·5w + k) = 0·25w + 0·5k$$

So the American technology would have been cheaper in Britain too. In fact on the assumptions so far made the American technology would be cheaper in Britain at any wage exceeding zero.

The real reason why it did not pay the British entrepreneur to adopt American techniques was that they yielded less in Britain than in America. Whereas twice the capital per head yielded twice the product in the United States, it yielded much less than twice the product in Britain. Given the wage levels and capital costs, the comparative yields determined which technology would be cheaper in Britain. We can calculate the turning point as follows. British cost is the same when the British technology yields the same cost at British wages as the American technology, that is when

$$\frac{0 \cdot 5w + k}{n} = 0 \cdot 5w + 0 \cdot 5k$$

where n is output per man per day. The solution to this equation depends on the ratio of w to k. Assuming that in the USA wages are 55 per cent of output and capital costs are 45 per cent of output, it follows that

$$w = 1 \cdot 2k$$

whence it follows that

$$n = \frac{1 \cdot 61k}{1 \cdot 11k}$$
$$\therefore n = 1 \cdot 45$$

Since the American output per man was two units, the American technology would pay only if the British got from it 72·5 per cent as good a result as the Americans got from it.

If the British were not doing as well as this, they needed a lower wage for the American technology to yield the same cost in Britain as in the USA. Suppose that n is only 1·3. Then we have the same money cost when

$$0 \cdot 5w + 0 \cdot 5k = \frac{xw + k}{1 \cdot 3}$$
$$\therefore x = 0 \cdot 3636$$

The British wage would have to be 36 per cent of the US wage for the American technology to yield the same cost there as in the USA, but at this lower wage the British technology would be cheaper in Britain, and could undersell the American technology both in Britain and in the USA.

The moral of this little exercise is to eschew all econometric calculations in this field which begin with some version of 'let us assume that the two countries have the same technology', in which case all differences in factor combinations have to be explained by relative factor prices. Two countries do not have the same technology when the same combination of inputs yields more output in one than in the other.

As we have seen before, British entrepreneurs were under heavy pressure in the last quarter of the century, since the economy had turned unprofitable. American methods were fairly widely known. If entrepreneurs had expected them to yield the same output in Britain as in the USA, they would most probably have adopted them.

126   *Growth and Fluctuations 1870–1913*

There is no dispute that the difference between British and American productivity from the same inputs was substantial. The best statistical work on this derives from Rostas's comparisons of the two censuses of manufactures in the mid-1930s. We find for example that in boots and shoes, where British and American factories were using almost exactly the same machinery, American output per manhour exceeded the British by about 80 per cent Many companies have factories in both Britain and the United States, using exactly the same machinery Their consensus is that the yield per man is much higher in the United States.

The causes of these differences are also well known. The American pace is faster. The work is organised to produce a faster flow-through. There is greater standardisation, to secure the economies of repetition. Factory discipline is tighter. Work study plays a larger role in setting production norms. In fact, starting from about the 1880s the Americans set out to study the economising of labour in factory operations; their factory is a more 'scientific' place than the British factory.

In contrast Phelps Brown believes that there was actually a slackening of the pace of British factory workers from the 1890s onwards, which he attributes to the rise of trade unionism and the increasing resentment of the working class against the factory system.[14] This cannot be proved, but is not without plausibility.

How did American entrepreneurs get away with increasing the pace? The explanation lies perhaps as far back as the beginning of the nineteenth century, when America led in inventing what would later become the basis of the assembly line, namely the standardisation and bulk production of interchangeable parts – beginning with guns and clocks and moving into engineering. Already in the thirties and forties visitors to America were reporting the working man's fascination with useful gadgets. At any rate he was already accustomed to taking pride in the quantity of his output, whereas the British tradition, descending from the guilds, was rather one of pride in craftsmanship and in the quality of the result. This British suspicion of quantity was more than a little reinforced by the British worker's experience of the effects of innovation on employment, which differed in significant degree from that of the American worker. For while in Britain the new technology had expanded employment in cotton and in iron, it had also played havoc with employment for handloom weavers in wool, as it would also do to the domestic clothing and footwear industries. The American experience was different. In the first half of the nineteenth century the economy was import-substituting. New inventions cut costs, and by reducing imports created more employment at home; the machine was a friend to employment rather than an enemy.

As the century proceeded these explanations became less and less relevant to the contemporary situation. At least from the 1870s onwards American workers were subjected to severe and long bouts of unemployment, by which time import substitution had also ended. Why did they not learn to fear innovation as much as the British workers? Some certainly did, but their fear could not be so easily translated into action. For one thing, there was always that long line of immigrants looking for jobs. The worker had to adjust, or get out. Again the British unions put high on their agenda protection of workers from dismissal without due cause, and would certainly not have permitted the dismissal of workers for falling behind production targets set by time and motion study. But trade unions hardly existed in the USA in the decades when those practices were spreading. And by the time trade unions achieved power in the USA they were so concerned about wages that many maintained their own work-study experts to help the less efficient firms whose methods were restricting their ability to pay high wages. It was inconceivable that a British trade union would specialise in showing the employers how to speed up output.

More surprising, perhaps, is the alleged contrast between the attitudes of British and German or other continental workers. In our day Europeans speak of 'the British disease', by which they mean a combination of a continual tendency to go on strike and a relatively slow work pace. Forty years ago the conventional wisdom was that the German workers' movement, with a high proportion of Marxist leaders, was more militant than the British workers' movement, yet today the British workers seem much more alienated than the German workers. Much has happened over that forty-year interval, including the liquidation of the German Marxist leaders under Hitler and after. But looking back one can also see reasons why the British workers should be more alienated than the German, even before the First World War. One reason is that they suffered more from unemployment. From 1870 onwards the British economy moved from one deep slump to the next, punctuated only by brief booms, while the German evidence is of long periods of near full employment, penetrated by short recessions. The German economy also expanded fast enough to absorb all who wanted industrial jobs, whereas the British economy was expanding so slowly that British people had to emigrate right up to 1913. Moreover, until the triumph of Keynesianism in the 1930s, British leaders, including the economists, took it for granted that the British economy could not be expected to maintain full employment. The workers' natural reaction to this was alienation from the system, and unwillingness to co-operate in any measures which might reduce the demand for labour, coupled with the conviction that the nation's leaders were an enemy, in whom no confidence should be reposed. This 'enemy' also showed itself more callous than its German counterpart, since social insurance was introduced in Germany as early as 1885, and did not find its way across the Channel for another quarter of a century. It is true that Bismarck introduced social insurance not out of the kindness of his heart, but to buy working-class political support against his political enemies. He may have judged correctly. At any rate, the British workers had better reason to be alienated from industrial capitalism than the German workers.

Given the lower work pace of the British workers it is easy to see that the main reason why the British employers did not adopt the American technology was that it was not as productive for them as it was for American employers. No moral judgement. is implied in this. Men who have to work at a fast pace set by their employers are not necessarily better off than other men who set their own pace, even if they are paid twice as much (actually only 33 per cent more in real terms, since the US cost of living was 50 per cent higher: the rest accrued to urban landlords in higher rents, to employers in higher profits, and to the non-industrial sectors of the economy in improved terms of trade). However, the matter is not quite so simple. A slow growth rate of productivity did not matter so much before 1900, because the terms of trade were moving in favour of industry. After 1900 the terms of trade were moving against industry, but the unions had by then become accustomed to an annual rate of growth of real wages which was simply not compatible with their attitude to work and machinery. Thus began that gap between reach and grasp which was to plague British industry in the 1920s, and again in the 1970s.

Given that the American methods were not profitable in Great Britain, the British were also deprived of some techniques which were a part thereof, especially mass production of the cheaper ranges of commodities. Examples of this are to be found in greater concentration on fabrication from steel than on mass production of steel; in specialisation on the finer counts of cotton yarn rather than the coarser counts, for which the more productive ring spindles would have been more appropriate,[15] and in a movement away from the cheaper to the more expensive kinds of textile fabrics. Frustrated in price competition, the British tried, correctly, to build up a reputation for quality and for production to the customer's special design. The reputation for quality was especially relevant not only to textiles, but also in such other fields as shipbuilding, electric cables, steam turbines, bicycles, railway equipment or textile machinery – not all British trades were on the decline.[16] To the extent that the British were upgrading the quality of their product, the index of industrial production, based largely on raw material inputs, understates the growth of British production; and the low volume with high prices revealed by the trade statistics is partly justified. This is not of course the whole answer, since if it were the relative unprofitability of the period 1873 to 1899 would not have occurred, and the average unemployment level would not have been so high.

INNOVATION

5.07 Earlier we named three factors in Germany's success: competitive prices, sales energy and leadership in new commodities. Now we come to the third.

The less developed countries of our day have all learned to enter world trade via the cotton and clothing industries. Germany too began there, but she did not stay there long. By 1913 Germany's exports were much more

Table 5.4   *Germany and UK: Exports of Manufactures, 1913 ($m.)*[17]

	From Germany	From UK
Metals and engineering	695	680
Chemicals	239	119
Textiles and clothing	324	950
Other	468	211
Total	1,726	1,960

advanced than those of the UK. The only one of Maizels's four groups in which the UK exported more than Germany was textiles and clothing; this emerges in Table 5.4.

In the century before 1880 most of the important inventions of the industrial revolution (with the notable exceptions of the cotton gin, some machine tools, the sewing machine and the idea of interchangeable parts) originated in Great Britain. More important, all inventions, wherever they originated, were quickly followed up. After 1880 a very large proportion of the new inventions originated elsewhere. More important, whether they originated in Britain or elsewhere, the British economy lagged in exploiting them. Perhaps the most spectacular case is that of steel whose major innovations (the Bessemer converter, the Siemens' open hearth, and the Gilchrist–Thomas process) were all British; whereas the British were rapidly outdistanced in steel production by both Germany and the USA.

Controversy has raged over whether the British lag in adopting new processes and pioneering new commodities after 1880 was due to entrepreneurial failure or to objective economic circumstances.[18] There is no evidence that British businessmen were any less enterprising after 1880 than their forefathers. There is a general expectation that the third generation will be less enterprising than the first, but there is no evidence that the older firms were ossifying.[19] Indeed in the older industries, where the older firms were – especially cotton, pig iron, steam engines – productivity per unit of input seems to have been as high as anywhere else. Moreover it would not have mattered if the third generation was weak, since new men could have entered industry, just as in the first generation. British industry was less monopolised than any other, and the costs of starting in business were still relatively low.

Yet something was lacking. Britain's competitive weakness was not in the old industries but in the new. These new industries were characterised by a higher scientific level than the old – one exception being the bicycle industry, which tests the rule because Britain was in the forefront of this new trade. But whereas any intelligent and observant person with a stroke of genius could invent the steam engine or the flying shuttle, or the hot blast, innovation after 1880 for the most part needed something more than genius. It required scientific knowledge to develop electrical machinery, organic chemicals or workable internal combustion engines.

To put the matter differently, academic science contributed next to nothing to the industrial revolution, and did not become entwined with industrial progress until after 1880. Between academic science and industry lay a big gulf which had to be bridged. The Germans bridged it in the last quarter of the nineteenth century, but the British failed to do so.

Once the nature of the problem became clear to all, as it did shortly before the onset of the Great War, science and industry blamed each other for the gap. Industry blamed the universities for concentrating on the humanities and neglecting science. The universities retorted that industry would not hire their science graduates, or, if hiring them, misused them in junior and non-scientific positions.[20]

It also became clear that the gap existed not only at the managerial level, but also at the intermediate level of foremen, supervisors and technicians.

130 *Growth and Fluctuations 1870–1913*

Britain lagged far behind Germany in the provision of technical schools. Even more important, perhaps, was the general backwardness of British mass education compared with the American. The big deficiency was in secondary education, which the British reserved for a handful, with the result that the intermediate industrial class was better educated in Germany or the USA than in Britain. This class, being on the shop floor, plays an important role in improving production techniques.

The weakness at the intermediate level probably relates to another puzzle. If British entrepreneurs were not ripe for new scientific commodities, why did German and American entrepreneurs not come to Britain and start the new industries? Exchange of entrepreneurs was an old story. British entrepreneurs had played a hand in starting industries in France and Germany, and French entrepreneurs were to be found throughout the continent.[21] Some foreign entrepreneurs did come, specialising in alkali chemistry and electrical machinery, but their effect was limited. Perhaps they too were inhibited by the restricted education of the intermediate class.

It was not necessary for British entrepreneurs to be scientists; what mattered was that they should be receptive to science, and understand how to use scientists. There is no doubt that British ideology was at this time hostile to science, and even more so to industrial science. This was the great age of the public school (an offshoot of the railway, without which parents could not have moved so many children so many times a year) which, being based on the proposition that the English were the modern descendants of Periclean Athens, found little virtue outside the classics and religion. At this time too, the public service grew enormously, attracting the best brains into Parliament, the home civil service, the Indian civil service and the diplomatic service. Of course there were plenty of brains in the classes from which industrialists had typically been recruited. What gentlemen's sons thought or did is not relevant to us since industrialists had never been gentlemen's sons. What does matter is that the non-gentlemen's sons were going (as they always had) through a school system which held applied science and technology in contempt. This had not mattered in 1830, but it was crucial to industry in 1900, when industry was in need of an increasingly scientific base.

Consequently organic chemicals became a German industry; the motor car was pioneered in France and mass-produced in the United States; Britain lagged in the use of electricity, depended on foreign firms established there, and took only a small share of the export market. The telephone, the typewriter, the cash register and the diesel engine were all exploited by others. When after 1900 the economy was profitable, capital was exported instead of being invested at home. Most tragic was the failure in steel. Temin has rightly emphasised that Britain could not have expected to make more steel than Germany, let alone the United States.[22] But there was no need for her to become the world's largest importer of steel, incapable of meeting Belgian and German prices. An important element in Germany's success was the achievement of heat economies which were surely within the British grasp.

5.08 One can of course dismiss the entire controversy by reducing it to a matter of relative prices and profitability. On this view it was lack of profitability that held up investment. If the gap between wages and prices had been adequate, some entrepreneurs (British and foreign) would have been in the forefront with the new technologies and others would have followed rapidly.

We have seen that the economy was definitely unprofitable in the 1880s and 1890s, and although unprofitability gives some stimulus to the adoption of cost-reducing technologies it is not surprising that domestic investment slowed at that time. However, profitability revived in the second half of the nineties, and was duly accompanied by high investment. What happened between 1900 and 1913 remains uncertain. Exports were booming, but domestic investment declined to its lowest level. Profitability seems to have been reduced, but not by so much as to explain the phenomenal decline of domestic investment. The best conclusion seems to be that the old export industries which were leading this boom were profitable (cotton, iron, steam engines, railway equipment, coal, shipbuilding), but that the new industries were still not sufficiently attractive, given the scientific and technological environment of British industry.

It is then a matter of choice whether one blames prices or the environment. Given the price level, the environment was the source of the trouble. Given the environment, the problem lay in relative prices.

Let us follow the argument through. We shall assume that the environmental deficiencies could have been overcome if the system had been sufficiently profitable, since congenial entrepreneurs would have emerged from somewhere, internal or external. We are saying then that Britain's competitive power would not have declined if Britain's money costs had fallen faster or risen more slowly than German and American costs. The standard solutions for this problem, if there was a problem, would be either a lower level of wages and other incomes, or a devaluation of the pound.

It is first necessary to establish that there was a problem. If devaluation is a remedy only for a shortage of foreign exchange, then there was no problem requiring devaluation, since foreign exchange was abundant. Keynes has, however, taught us not to fall into this trap. The balance of payments can always be brought into equilibrium by varying the level of employment. If there was a case for devaluation, it would be not in order to earn more foreign exchange, but in order to have a higher level of employment.

Did the British economy need a higher level of employment? This question divides into two: a higher level of employment as a whole, or a higher level of employment in manufacturing industry? Britain needed a higher level of employment as a whole. Part of the evidence for this is her relatively high unemployment rates compared with those of Germany (see Table 2.2 and accompanying text). Looking again at Chart 2.1 it is hardly an exaggeration to describe the British picture for 1883 onwards as one of continuing gloom, punctuated occasionally by spurts of prosperity. Another part of the evidence is the continued need for the English to emigrate, long after emigration from France and Germany had dried up. Indeed, more people than ever were emigrating just before the First World War, and

132   *Growth and Fluctuations 1870–1913*

more than ever remaining in rural areas for lack of job opportunities in the towns (see section 2.16). We saw at the beginning of this chapter that the expansion of service industries was not enough to compensate for decelerating income from industry; now we also note that it was not enough to meet the employment needs of the still high rate of natural increase of the population.

If the British had a surplus of foreign exchange, this surplus was due partly to the same factor that produced unemployment, namely the fact that the British had been investing their capital abroad instead of at home. More employment at home might have resulted in a smaller surplus of interest and dividend income from abroad, but one cannot even be sure of this. Lower British prices would both have cut imports and have increased exports, thereby increasing the surplus on visible trade. Total profits and savings would have risen with employment, so home investment would not have been entirely at the expense of foreign investment. Even if it were, one could adopt the moral conclusion that income from employment at home was better than income from dividends abroad, earned at the expense of creating unemployment at home.

Besides, some of the non-manufacturing employment at home would prove to be a poor long-run investment. In particular, Britain built up huge foreign exchange receipts from shipping and from exporting coal. In shipping she was building a near monopoly of world trade, much like her earlier monopolies of cotton textiles and pig iron – with much the same fate in store. British shipping was a headache industry from 1920 onwards. Similarly the coal mining industry grew swiftly. Employment in coal increased at 3·0 per cent per annum, while productivity and the relative price of coal both declined sharply. This was an untenable situation, marked by an ever increasing momentum of strikes and bitter industrial conflict. This industry too was an albatross from 1920 onwards. More steel, electricity or chemicals would have been much sounder bets. This is all hindsight, but is nevertheless true.

If it is agreed that British prices were too high, and if the obstacles to reducing real costs could not be overcome (exhaustion of the old technology, worker resistance to the higher work norms needed to support greater capital intensity, lack of sympathy for industrial science) then the standard solutions would be (a) lower wage income levels or (b) devaluation of the pound.

We have seen that between 1883 and 1899 money wage costs per unit of output (wages divided by productivity) declined by about the same amount in Britain and in Germany (by much less than in France). Since German costs were lower than the British in 1883, the Germans had leeway in which to reduce their prices relative to British prices, as they did. British money wages were not in fact rising very fast: the rate of increase was 0·9 per cent per annum, in comparison with Germany's 2·0 per cent. This was faster than in the first half of the nineteenth century, but conditions had changed. The trade union movement became very militant at the end of the 1880s, and a lower rate of growth of money wages was not feasible. Why was labour so militant at this particular time? Here we have an interesting vicious circle. Labour was restless not because of the wage situation –

thanks to falling import prices real wages were now rising quite fast by contemporary standards (and nearly twice as fast as productivity) – but because of what slow industrial expansion was doing to job opportunities: forcing people to emigrate or to remain in the countryside. But wage increases did not help employment.

Devaluation was unthinkable. Actually, it cannot ever have been far from the minds of Governors of the Bank of England, seeing how difficult they found it to maintain their gold reserves throughout the whole of our period. But it was for them a threat rather than a potential refuge, and was irrelevant to the Bank's difficulties, which arose not from an adverse balance of payments on current account, but partly from a tendency to over-lending in boom years, and mainly from the Bank's own stubborn unwillingness to hold adequate gold reserves.

We cannot be sure what difference devaluation would have made to relative prices. It would presumably have stimulated money wage demands, but we know, especially from French experience, that it is possible to devalue without dissipating all the effect in higher domestic money incomes. Britain's problem would have been greater than France's because of greater dependence on imports entering into the cost of living, but the overseas suppliers depended so largely on the British market that their prices would have fallen somewhat as Britain devalued. More doubtful is the reaction of the competing industrial countries. Would they have permitted Britain to devalue relative to other core currencies? British devaluation in 1931 was followed by US devaluation in 1933, and by French devaluation in 1936; and when the USA wanted to devalue in 1971, it had the greatest difficulty in persuading the Western European nations to permit it to do so. A good date for a British devaluation would have been about 1885; whether the other members of the core would have permitted this we cannot say.

If Britain could neither hold down wages nor devalue, she could have imposed an import tariff. A large school of industrialists and conservative politicians advocated this step, which all other core members had already taken by 1890. But the economic theory of the day did not recognise 'involuntary unemployment', and could easily prove that tariffs were not in the national interest. In any case a tariff is only a half-substitute for devaluation. The other half is a system of export subsidies. This also was unthinkable; the best liberal minds of the day were, on the contrary, devoted to trying to secure international agreement against dumping.

5.09 Thus Britain was caught in a set of ideological traps. All the strategies available to her were blocked off in one way or another. She could not lower costs by cutting wages because of the unions, or switch to American-type technology because of the slower pace of British workers. She could not reduce her propensity to import by imposing a tariff or by devaluing her currency, or increase her propensity to export by devaluing or by paying export subsidies. She could not pioneer in developing new commodities because this now required a scientific base which did not accord with her humanistic snobbery. So instead she invested her savings abroad; the economy decelerated, the average level of unemployment increased and her young people emigrated.

134 *Growth and Fluctuations 1870–1913*

If she could have broken into this succession of negatives at any one point, the whole situation could have been different. We are more conscious than our forefathers were of the importance of spiralling (upwards or downwards) in economic growth. They were aware of the economies of scale, and this was a part of the case then made for an industrial tariff. We are also aware of the relationship between productivity and growth. The higher the ratio of investment, the more up-to-date and productive is the equipment. Costs are therefore lower, competitive power in world markets is increased, demand is stimulated, investment increases still further, and so on. The steel industry, for example, explained that its productivity was lagging because its growth rate was so low. It was not profitable to replace old processes by new ones, but if the industry were growing faster one would have both old and new, thereby raising average productivity. The British relied on the market economy to bring them into equilibrium; but the market pays no heed to external economies; instead it brought them to relative stagnation.

Notes

1 The general tenor of the result is not affected by reasonable and consistent alloca- tions of 'General Labourers' to manufacturing. For example, assume that by 1911 none of the General Labourers belongs to Manufacturing, since by 1911 the census takers had modernised their classifications. Assume further that in all previous censuses the percentage of 1911 (i.e. 2·3) is the 'correct' proportion of General Labourers in the occupied population, and allocate to Manufacturing half the difference between this and the actual number of General Labourers reported by the Census. Then the productivity growth rates for Manufacturing become 1·8, 1·4 and 1·0 instead of the 1·85, 1·15 and 0·9 reported in this paragraph. The main feature that interests us, the continual deceleration, remains.
2 Estimates of foreign investment here and elsewhere relate to long-term lending. Since Britain was already borrowing short (holding other countries' balances) and lending long, they slightly exaggerate the net investment.
3 The subject is surveyed by Murray Brown, *The Theory and Measurement of Technological Change*, Cambridge University Press, Cambridge, 1966.
4 For two such estimates see S. B. Saul, 'The Export Economy 1870–1914', *Yorkshire Bulletin of Economic and Social Research*, May 1965; and W. A. Lewis, 'Inter- national Competition in Manufactures', *American Economic Review*, May 1957. Estimates differ because of different definitions of what to include in manufactures, and also different treatments of the changes in the customs area reported in German statistics.
5 Despite reservations about Schlote's price indexes, we have to use his figures for manufactures at constant prices, because other calculations of British trade at constant prices do not distinguish between manufactures and other commodities.

310

Fortunately the contrasts we are making in this paragraph are so sharp that they would not be much affected by reasonable changes in the price indexes.

6 In order to add trade and production of manufactures either both must be in value added, or both must include the cost of materials and other elements in the wholesale price of manufactures. The solution here is to add 50 per cent to value added in production of manufactures, following Maizels.

7 For an alternative estimate of the potential effect on production of a large growth rate of exports see J. R. Meyer, 'An Input–Output Approach to Evaluating the Influence of Exports on British Industrial Production in the Late Nineteenth Century', *Explorations in Entrepreneurial History*, 1955.

8 See W. A. Lewis, 'World Production, Prices and Trade', *Manchester School of Economic and Social Studies*, May 1952.

9 See A. Maizels, *Industrial Growth and World Trade*, Cambridge University Press, Cambridge, 1969, p. 430.

10 Figures for 1913 are from Maizels; for 1883 UK figures from Schlote, Germany from Hoffmann, USA from Lipsey and France from Lévy-Leboyer. Schlote possibly understates the fall of UK prices to 1900. A major difficulty is that the commodity composition of exports differed; for example the main cause of the relative rise in British prices to 1913 was the rise of the prices of textiles, which were a relatively large component of British exports. Maizels's commodity comparisons of 1913 on 1899 base show the following:

	Germany	*UK*
Metals	126	108
Metal goods	108	104
Machinery	136	106
Transport equipment	70	95
Chemicals	81	127
Textiles and clothing	130	147
Other	103	120
Total	108	125

Britain was holding her own in the important metal and machinery trades.

11 For a full account of British reactions see R. J. S. Hoffman, *Great Britain and the German Trade Rivalry 1875–1914*, University of Pennsylvania Press, Philadelphia, 1933.

12 Flux's analysis of the 1907 UK and 1909 US censuses of manufactures led to the conclusion that American productivity was 2·5 times the British, in terms of value added. However, US prices were higher than British. See Appendix II for evidence leading to the conclusion that US productivity was 1·9 times the British. A. W. Flux, 'The Census of Production', *Journal of the Royal Statistical Society*, May 1924; also 'Industrial Productivity in Britain and the United States', *Quarterly Journal of Economics*, November 1933.

13 L. Rostas, *Comparative Productivity in British and American Industry*, Cambridge University Press, Cambridge, 1948.

14 E. H. Phelps Brown with Margaret Browne, *A Century of Pay*, Macmillan, London, 1968, pp. 185–7.

15 L. G. Sandberg, 'American Rings and English Mules: the Role of Economic Rationality', *Quarterly Journal of Economics*, February 1969.

16 See the useful essays in Derek H. Aldcroft, *The Development of British Industry and Foreign Competition 1875–1914*, University of Toronto Press, Toronto, 1968.

17 A. Maizels, op. cit., pp. 478 and 482.

18 This literature is enormous. Most of it is mentioned in the footnotes of Donald N. McCloskey (ed.), *Essays on a Mature Economy: Britain after 1840*, Methuen, London, 1971. Another source is the bibliographical monograph by S. B. Saul, *The Myth of the Great Depression*, Macmillan, London.

19 Charlotte Erickson, *British Industrialists: Steel and Hosiery, 1850–1950*, Cambridge University Press, Cambridge, 1959.

20 Michael Sanderson, *The Universities and British Industry 1850–1970*, Routledge and Kegan Paul, London, 1972.

311

21   W. O. Henderson, *Britain and Industrial Europe*, University of Liverpool Press, Liverpool, 1954. Rondo Cameron, *France and the Economic Development of Europe*, Princeton University Press, Princeton, NJ, 1967. Also J. P. McKay, *Pioneers for Profit: Foreign Entrepreneurs and Russian Industrialisation 1855–1913*, University of Chicago Press, Chicago, 1970.

22   Peter Temin, 'The Relative Decline of the British Steel Industry 1880 to 1913', in Henry Rosovsky (ed.), *Industrialisation in two Systems: Essays in Honour of Alexander Gerschenkron*, Wiley, New York, 1966.

Part III
Relative Decline: The Inter-War and Post-War Periods

[7]

CAUSES OF THE SUPERIOR EFFICIENCY OF U.S.A. INDUSTRY AS COMPARED WITH BRITISH INDUSTRY [1]

THE theory that the superior efficiency of the U.S. industry is due to the larger size of the market is expressed in each of three different forms. The first form of the theory is that the individual enterprises in the United States enjoy the advantages of larger markets. If the advantage is indeed of this form, it is difficult to see why England should not secure similar advantages by having relatively fewer firms in each industry.

The second form of the theory is that the groups of firms in each industry in the United States enjoy a larger market for the product of the industry. If this is the form of the advantage which the United States enjoy, then England could secure the same advantages if she concentrated her industrial effort upon a smaller number of industries, so that each of these industries would secure a larger world market.

The third form of the theory is that the United States secures greater efficiency of production because of the greater size of her whole economy. This is the only one of the three explanations which indicates a final reason for the United States advantage which England cannot hope to overcome. But an examination of the historical evidence and a study of the variation of productivity between different countries to-day both throw considerable doubt upon whether this third kind of advantage due to the large size of the economy as a whole is really so very important.

Historical Evidence

The superior efficiency of the United States industry is no new phenomenon. Indeed, as long ago as 1870 the superiority in efficiency of the United States industry over the British seems to have been as great as it is to-day. But in 1870, the market for the United States industry as a whole was probably smaller than the market for British industry as a whole. It is therefore difficult to account for the superior efficiency of the United States industry to-day by reference to the larger size of its market to-day.

[1] This article has been compiled from some unfinished notes left by Erwin Rothbarth at his death. Alterations have been reduced to a minimum for fear of misrepresenting the author's original ideas.

It is difficult, of course, to make any precise comparison between the size of the United States market and the British market; one reason for this is that we have to make due allowance for transport costs when we measure the size of the market; we must also make allowance for the average purchasing power of the individuals who compose the market. The question which we have to answer is: How many units could the United States industry sell if the price charged ex-factory were the same as the price charged ex-factory by British industry? But all that we know is the actual number of units sold by United States industry and British industry respectively in various localities. Only when we can find localities with similar purchasing power, but which, owing to different distances from the source of supply, pay different prices for the same product, are we able to isolate and measure the influence of transport costs on the size of the market. We may then estimate the size of the market as being the aggregate amount which can be sold for a given ex-factory price α, say, which will be equal to $P - \gamma\pi$, where P is the price paid at the selling point, π is the transport cost per mile, and γ is the distance of the selling point from the factory.

No such refined calculations are needed in order to show that the United States market in 1870 was less than the British market, for at that time the population of the United States was no larger than that of the United Kingdom, and it was thinly spread over the vast area of the continent. Since transport costs by land were then much higher than transport costs by sea, their effect in reducing the United States market was far more serious than their effect on the United Kingdom market. Moreover, with low marine transport costs, the United Kingdom was able to sell its goods to Belgium, Holland, France and parts of Germany and Italy far more easily than the eastern states of the U.S.A. could sell to the states of the far west. It is therefore clear that the United Kingdom was selling to a larger market than the United States in 1870, so that the relatively higher efficiency of the United States industry at that date cannot have been due to any superiority of the size of the market which they served.

Evidence from Interregional Comparisons

Further doubt is cast on the theory that a large market for the whole economy is the source of the United States efficiency by the fact that the industries of the Southern States of the U.S.A. are not particularly efficient, although they have as easy an access to the large markets as the industries of the rest of the U.S.A. On the other hand, the industries of Australia, Canada, New Zealand and Argentina all show high efficiency without having access to particularly large markets. On these grounds, we are led to reject the theory that the availability of a large market is the explanation of the high efficiency of U.S.A. industry.

Alternative Theories to Explain U.S.A. Efficiency

"Age of Industry" Theory. The superior efficiency of United States industry is sometimes attributed to the fact that it developed more recently than the British industry, and was thus able to adopt more up-to-date techniques. British industry was, on this theory, hampered by the possession of antiquated equipment on which it had to pay overhead charges. It is doubtful, however, whether a detailed comparison of British and American industry would lend much support to this theory.

On the other hand, it is certainly a common belief that American industrialists are always more ready to scrap industrial equipment than are their British counterparts. This may be due to capital being more readily obtainable in the United States, but it may also be due to a psychological difference between the adventurous employers of the United States and the more conservative British employers. It is interesting to speculate how far the superior efficiency of the United States industry may be due to a readiness to take on a venture which is in fact quite irrational from the point of view of the individual employer concerned, although it benefits his country by increasing efficiency and stimulating business.

Availability of Land. In any country where land is readily available in large quantities, labour is likely to be expensive. For the income of the industrial worker must be sufficiently high to present an attractive alternative to his cultivating the land for his own profit. Thus the high productivity of labour in American industry at the beginning of this century can be explained by the fact that industry had to instal labour-saving equipment and to economise in the use of labour until its productivity was sufficiently far higher than it was in agriculture to enable relatively attractive wages to be paid in industry. The same explanation will account for the high productivity of labour in Canadian and Argentinian industry until quite recently. Kaldor has raised an objection to this theory by pointing out that in American industry the proportionate share of labour in the total product has always been lower than it is in British industry. This does not seem to be a valid objection to the theory; for the superficial paradox is explained by the following facts : (1) American industry is more highly mechanised than British industry; (2) the supply of labour is less elastic compared to the supply of capital in U.S. industry than in U.K. industry.

Size of Market for Standardised Products. The ease with which the United States industry has been able to install mass-production methods is probably due as much to the structure of the buying public as to anything else; for the United States public is very ready to buy standard articles which are not differentiated by marked individual features. In the United Kingdom, on the other hand, there remains an aristocracy and a middle class impregnated with aristocratic ideas, who reject mass-produced articles and insist on articles with individual character. These fancy goods cannot be mass-produced conveniently because the process of production differs between all the specialised articles and it pays small firms to specialise in the production of particular products.

If this theory of the successful use of mass production in the United States were correct, it might be expected that the " colonial " countries would have benefited to the same extent, since they also serve a public which is content with standardised goods. The only reason that firms in the " colonial " countries are not in fact found to have grown to the same extent as those in the United States, is that their transport costs are considerably higher, so that no individual firm can grow beyond a certain point without coming up against market limitations.

Both these last two explanations are valid, and account for the superior efficiency of United States industry. On the one hand the availability of large amounts of land and the consequent scarcity of labour have stimulated industry to install labour-saving machinery which has resulted in high efficiency. On the other hand the same plenty of land and scarcity of labour have resulted in a social structure which has put purchasing power in the hands of those who are ready to buy large quantities of standardised goods but who do not favour the purchase of aristocratic goods of high individual quality. Thus the special structure of the market in the United States has resulted in the production of products where the economies of mass production by labour-saving machinery have been particularly high. Both our explanations go back to the ample supply of land in the United States as the fundamental explanation of the superior efficiency of her industry to-day.

Objections to the Last Two Theories

One obvious objection to these theories is that land is no longer a free good in the United States. This is quite true, but it is only claimed that in the first instance the ready availability of land and the consequent scarcity of labour caused the United States industry to become more efficient than that of any other country. Once the tendency towards large-scale production had become established it became self-reinforced and operated independently of its original cause, because it had created a buying public which was predisposed to pay for large quantities of mass-produced goods. In the United Kingdom, where industry never began to become efficient in mass-production methods, the market remained specialised and the forces of market imperfection are much more deeply ingrained, so that the size of the market and mechanisation and output per head all remained limited. The preference for " craftsmanship " in British industry is probably due to this fact of aristocratic buying habits and to the relative abundance of labour much more than it is due to the lack of scientific training of British business men.

Economies of Large Scale

The advantages which the American economy has derived from the large scale of production have been very considerable, although they may in some cases have been exaggerated. They may all be explained in terms of the complementarity of indivisible processes of production.

One example is the large scientific instruments industry in the United States which supplies an industry which consists of large firms. One of the chief reasons for the large size of the firms in the consuming industry is the indivisibility of some of the productive units which they employ. It is only because there is a considerable number of these large consuming firms that the mass production of scientific instruments in the United States is profitable.

During the war a large number of mechanical devices for making measurements and for the operation of quality control were produced and used in the United States. There grew up on this basis a very large industry for the production of these machines. It may be argued even in this case that although the great size of the whole United States economy facilitated the rapid introduction of such machines, their use need not really be confined to large-scale industries, and that the extensive and profitable use of these devices in America was chiefly due to the scientific outlook of the managers of the large American firms. Indeed, the scientific instruments industry in Sweden is also very highly developed although they had to start from small beginnings with a small market and to build up their export connection. In that country the early growth of the industry depended upon the high development of actuarial mathematics and the use of calculating machines by insurance companies.

It would be absurd to suggest that the advantages of large-scale production are solely based on the indivisibility of certain productive processes. The point is that large scale is an advantage whenever there are complementary relations between large-scale productive processes. This may be illustrated by means of an imaginary example. Suppose that the optimum size of a blast furnace is large for reasons connected with fuel economy, and that the products of the blast furnace are used by a rolling mill where the optimum size is also large. Then, unless the capacity of the rolling mill is an exact multiple of the capacity of the blast furnace, it will be necessary to use more than one rolling mill in order to maintain both the blast furnaces and the rolling mills in continuous production. Indeed, if the ratio of the capacity of the rolling mill to that of the blast furnace is some inconvenient fraction, such as 7 to 5, it will evidently be necessary to use quite a large number of rolling mills (5 in our example) to ensure continuous working of both the blast furnaces and the rolling mills.

Too much stress must not be attached to arguments of this kind. For example, it has been argued that the high cost of scientific research gives an advantage to large firms. But theoretically scientific research could be carried on by independent organisations who would sell their results to firms of all sizes. Although small and medium firms could theoretically share the advantages of scientific research in this way for a moderate fee and without incurring the heavy cost involved by carrying out their own research, such a solution is not practicable under present conditions because of the high degree of business secrecy and because of the lack of scientific training amongst the managers of medium and small firms. For these reasons, large firms do secure an advantage under this head, but these advantages depend upon the secretiveness of industrial managers rather than on the large scale of the enterprises.

In general, we find that what at first seems to be an advantage due to large scale frequently turns out to be an advantage contingent on various special features of the present productive system. For instance, the advantage may depend on the character of the buying public, or on the imperfection of the division of labour which is itself due in the last resort to the monopolistic tendencies of a productive system run for private profit. The private ownership of the firms then limits the scope of enterprise and scientific initiative, whereas if there was division of labour that enterprise would obtain fuller scope.

It is still true, on the other hand, that in a large economy like the American economy private enterprise itself will often provide the remedy, whereas in a smaller economy only the State can provide the scientific research or other services needed. Thus private enterprise in the United States provides widespread information based on market research, and there are also firms providing specialists in quality control techniques. The reason for this is the development of the scientific outlook amongst the managements of many large firms in the United States. Once such a service as market research has been provided at all through a market, competition tends to spread it to a far wider circle of firms than the large firms who in the first instance fostered its provision. Where there are a sufficient number of large firms to introduce the service in the first instance, they enable it to be provided eventually for large and small firms alike. This experience in the United States suggests that in smaller countries although public intervention may be necessary for providing such services in the first instance, yet once their use has become widespread the provision of them could be taken over from the State by a number of competing private firms. Experience alone can decide whether this is so, and unless the market proves sufficiently large to allow competition to develop in the provision of the service, the State should continue to provide it.

The Future of the Small Firm

Although under present conditions large firms in large industries certainly do secure several advantages over small firms, these advantages are likely to become less important as scientific training becomes more widespread so that a larger number of competent scientists can be employed at moderate salaries.

The availability of scientifically trained staff will give a new lease of life to the small firms in those industries where production at a small scale can be partially standardised. When the small firm is almost as well staffed with scientists as the large firm, it will have overcome one of its greatest disadvantages, and various advantages of small scale will again be felt.

The chief of these advantages is that the manager of the small firm can devote his individual judgment to every stage of his business both in manufacturing and marketing. There are other advantages also : for example, there is more scope for enterprise in small business than in large business. Another advantage, which largely accounts for the preference of Jewish employers for small business, is that the human relations in small firms are less impersonal than in large firms. Another potential advantage, which will be felt only when technical knowledge has become widespread and trade unions are firmly established in all firms, is that small firms should be able to provide more scope for the workers.

For these various reasons, the spread of scientific training and a reasoned outlook is likely to diminish the purely economic advantage of the large firm, so that men of independence and judgment will more often choose to accept the hazards of small-scale business because of the variety and the interesting opportunities for individual enterprise which it offers them.

E. ROTHBARTH

[8]

THE NEW INDUSTRIES BETWEEN THE WARS

By H. W. RICHARDSON

FROM the vantage point of the sixties, the experience of the new industries[1] in the inter-war years would seem to suggest that in their progress could be discerned the basis of a new industrial future for Britain. Strangely enough, the orthodox view on the subject gives the opposite impression: it argues that the central fact about the new industries' development in this period was not that they were growing at a rapid rate, but rather that they were growing very slowly in relation to their position in other countries. More surprisingly, this judgement has been unanimous; scarcely anyone, overtly at least, has dissented from it. It is the purpose of this article to examine certain aspects in this judgement and to suggest that the expansion of the new industries between the wars was satisfactory, and consequently it is unnecessary to talk of Britain's declining entrepreneurship, her slowness to innovate, or failure to exploit export markets to the full to account for non-existent backwardness. It is believed that the attempt to decry the role of these industries is a misunderstanding to be explained partly by the fact that its protagonists have emphasized the wrong issues and made irrelevant comparisons, but largely because they have ignored (or did not have at their disposal) important evidence in recent books and articles which conflicts with their interpretation.

I

In volume iii of his famous work *An Economic History of Modern Britain*, Sir John Clapham drew attention to the slow growth (aluminium, electrical engineering) or absence (dyestuffs, pharmaceutical products) of new industries in Britain in the period 1887–1914.[2] Possibly here lay the seeds of the orthodox judgement discussed above. What happened was probably this: economists and historians came from reading Clapham to look at the new industries in the twenties and thirties and found ample evidence for a similar trend; without paying too much attention to the significance of the growth potential of the new industries revealed in their absolute increase in output, they merely extrapolated Clapham's argument referring to the period before 1914 into the inter-war years. Certainly, since the thirties economists have repeatedly put forward the view that the new industries' performance could have been better. The first expression of this judgement was probably A. Loveday in *Britain*

---

[1] By new industries, I refer not only to those industries which had their origins in this century such as the motor, wireless, and rayon industries, but also to those which were in existence in the last century but did not show any marked advance until this, such as the electrical, chemical, and rubber industries.   [2] Section III.

H. W. RICHARDSON   361

and World Trade (1931): 'Today what is really important and significant
in England is not the depression of the depressed industries, but the
relatively small progress made by the relatively prosperous' (p. 160). In
the standard work *British Industries and their Organization* (1933), G. C.
Allen took a similar standpoint, reasonable in the period of world depression, but what is surprising is that the same argument remains un-
modified in the fourth edition of the book published in 1959; for example
(p. 24): 'What is significant about the British position is that this country
shared in an exaggerated degree in the depression which existed in some
trades and failed to advance as much as the rest of the world in the
industries which grew most rapidly.' The same point is reiterated again
and again; it reappears, for example, in that stimulating and well-known
book *Great Britain in the World Economy* (1946) by A. E. Kahn (p. 74).
The unanimity of opinion is accentuated by the fact that now that economic
historians have begun to take an interest in the period they have followed
suit without deviation. In his *An Economic History of England 1870–1939*
(1960), W. Ashworth argues (p. 335): 'What seems probable however is
that, in the 'thirties, though many promising and profitable types of production were begun, a large proportion of them were not carried nearly as
far as they might have been, or as far as they were in competing countries.'
The other recent work by an economic historian on the period, A. J.
Youngson's *The British Economy, 1920–57* (1960), throws little light on
the problem at issue, although it contains comments on the new industries in the twenties (pp. 46–49) and the thirties (pp. 107–11). However, one clue which suggests that Professor Youngson perhaps shares the
view that the new industries were not doing as well as they might is given
when he describes the new industries in the thirties as 'uncertain and
struggling' (p. 211).

The above list of authorities is an impressive one and the arguments
which they use to support their view are superficially strong. Upon closer
inspection, however, these arguments contain weaknesses; at this stage
I will discuss only two.

Professor Ashworth (op. cit., p. 344) stated that Britain imported more
of the newer type of goods (or of manufactures for which there was a
growing world demand; which he is referring to is ambiguous) than she
exported. Admittedly, he adds the qualification 'probably', but nevertheless the effect of this statement on someone seeking to denigrate the
new industries is that it gives them another nail for the coffin. Yet Professor Ashworth does not elaborate on the products to which he is referring, nor does he support his claim with statistics. The table given below
seeks to remedy this: it gives details of imports and exports for some
products of the new industries in the thirties. It is easy to see that these

statistics contradict his argument; it would be interesting to know which goods he had in mind, for if his statement has any validity it can only be as the exception rather than the rule. It is evident from the table that the only products which are compatible with his statement are electronic valves and electric lamps—and those for volume only. If value is taken as the criterion the position is reversed, for the exports of both these products were far more valuable than imports. For other products conclusions are similar; for example, in the chemical fertilizer industry imports of superphosphates fell from 114,000 tons to 14,500 tons, 1931–8.[1] Of course there were a few speciality luxury goods to which Professor Ashworth's statement applies, such as watches. British production of watches was small before 1939, exports were negligible and most of the watches in use were imported from abroad. At best, however, the argument is misleading.

All the critics of the new industries stress their relative failure in exports. Moreover, they argue that in so far as they did export it was to a disproportionate extent confined to Commonwealth markets where trade received a stimulus from Imperial preference. The most extreme conclusion to be drawn from this is put forward by A. E. Kahn (op. cit., p. 107), who argues that there was 'no cause for this especially great dependence . . . upon relatively sheltered markets, except competitive weakness'.

The facts are not in doubt. In many cases the proportion of the new industries' exports going to the Commonwealth was three-quarters or more. But it is very naïve to postulate a causal relationship between this fact and the existence of Imperial preference. The argument that the orientation of the export markets for new products towards the Commonwealth was due to competitive weakness is completely unproven. There is indeed a far more feasible explanation. The new goods were in general expensive consumer and capital goods, such as motor-cars and electrical equipment, which are only of use to highly civilized and wealthy societies. Demand was consequently significant only in Western Europe and the United States where it could be satisfied by domestic industry and in the rich and rapidly developing primary-producing countries, pre-eminently in the British Dominions. Apart from these, there were no other countries with a level of income per head high enough to need these products in any quantity. Of the possible suppliers for the Dominions, moreover, Britain was the strongest candidate, for in return she constituted the greatest single market for primary products; it is a commonplace that factors favouring trade in one direction frequently favour trade in another. Thus it was quite logical that the British Dominions should provide the largest market for the exports of Britain's new industries.

[1] Monopolies Commission, *Report on the Supply of Chemical Fertilizers* (1959), p. 21.

H. W. RICHARDSON   363

TABLE I

Relation between Imports and Exports of the Products of some Newer Industries in the Thirties

Product	Period	Imports (annual average)		Exports (annual average)	
		Volume (nos.)	*Value* (£)	*Volume*	*Value*
Motor vehicles	1930–8	10,950	1,666,000	59,400	8,171,000
Pneumatic tires	1930–8	88,060	112,000	1,333,740	2,712,000
Electric lamps	1930–9	50,511,000	224,000	14,028,000	519,000
Insulated electric wires and cables	1930–8	..	479,000	..	2,908,000
Electronic valves	1930–9	1,860,400	216,000	1,292,900	388,000
Electrical machinery and plant	1930–8	..	383,000	..	3,678,000
Rayon piece goods	1933–8	25 million sq. yds.	..	64 million sq. yds.	..
Rayon yarn	1933–8	1·8 million lb.	..	9·5 million lb.	..
Staple fibre and rayon waste	1931–8	negligible	..	8 million lb.	..

Kahn's over-simplification of the question was probably due to an exaggeration of the importance of Imperial preference. His argument would only make sense if the new goods were subject to the ravages of competition in foreign markets but were immune from competition in the Commonwealth because of the security that Imperial preference gave them there. But this was by no means true, for Imperial preference sometimes proved of no avail when British exporters were faced with sales drives from their competitors in Commonwealth markets. Take the Austrialian market for motor vehicles, for example. During the world depression Britain was easily the largest supplier of motor-cars to Australia, but by the middle thirties the United States had taken over the lead; the result was that Britain's share of Australian car imports fell from 61 to 35 per cent., 1932–6. The point was that competition in the products of the new industries was at least a potential danger in Empire, Commonwealth, and foreign markets alike.

II

Those who have stressed the inferior position of the new industries of Britain relative to those in other countries with respect to technical performance have relied upon two types of evidence: comparative productivity (especially Anglo-American) figures and facts indicating a more impressive rate of technological innovation abroad than at home. The reliability of the two will be discussed in turn.

This is no place to pay disrespect to L. Rostas's pioneering work, *Comparative Productivity in British and American Industry* (1948), but it is necessary to point out the limitations of such a study. Changes in productivity over time within a country (particularly within an industry) are far more valuable than comparisons of the productivity of industries at one point of time between countries. If productivity figures are used for the former modest purpose (once the difficulties of measurement have been surmounted), the record is impressive. The rise in output per wage-earner in British manufacturing between 1924 and 1937 was considerable, amounting to 37 per cent. In the new industries the increase was even greater: in the motor industry output per man-year doubled 1924–35, while in the rayon industry output doubled in the short period 1930–5 as a result of an increase of only 18 per cent. in the labour force.

On the other hand, productivity was low in relation to the position in the United States: in the inter-war years the compound annual rate of growth in productivity per man-hour in manufacturing in Britain was only 2·5 per cent., while in the United States the rate was 3·5 per cent. As for the new industries, in 1935 productivity in their motor industry was three times that of the British and in the radio industry four and a half times as large. But the question arises: are these comparisons meaningful? The dangers involved in the use of such statistics have been urged most cogently by W. E. G. Salter in a recent book, *Productivity and Technical Change* (1960).

His main point in this connexion is that if technical progress, and consequently productivity, were greater in the United States than in Britain, this did not imply that Britain was 'inefficient' or that her management in industry was inferior. For technical progress was more widespread in the United States because of the nature of the economic environment there as reflected in standards of obsolescence. In many industries the best plants in Britain compared well with those of the United States; the point was that there were more out-of-date plants in this country—and the explanation of this was not lack of entrepreneurial ability and foresight in Britain but the higher standard of obsolescence in the United States. Why was this standard higher in the United States? The answer is simple—the margin of obsolescence is determined by the level of real wages, that is, 'when labour is an expensive factor of production, an economy must adjust rapidly to new methods which require less labour' (p. 71). Thus the predominance of more efficient plants in the United States and the higher productivity may have been little more than an inevitable consequence of the fact that the level of real wages there was far above that in Britain.

If this argument is sound, in those industries where technical factors necessitated a high ratio of capital to labour American productivity should not have been much greater. There was some evidence for this: in the rayon industry which was particularly capital-intensive the ratio of American to British productivity was only 1·5. The fact that productivity was still higher in the United States was to be explained by another inherent advantage she possessed—her large and stable home market. This meant that American industries were able to take especial advantage, *at an early stage*, of large-scale mass production and distribution methods. This leads on to another point made by Salter. Productivity in the British new industries was relatively low because, being 'new' and therefore of limited size, they had scarcely begun in the inter-war years to explore the possibilities of large-scale production (p. 134). He cites the case of turbo-generators in the electricity supply industry; the capacity of the first was only 1,000 kilowatts but by 1950 units of 200,000 kilowatts were in use. This is an adequate riposte to those who criticize the new industries on the ground that they did not expand quickly enough to absorb the excess labour force from the old staple industries. The growth of the motor and the electronics industries since 1945 illustrates the tendency of the new industries, with the passage of time, to expand continuously to new levels of production. This trend was observable even before 1939, for the development of the new industries was far more rapid in the thirties than in the twenties, and was comparable with growth abroad. Indeed, it has been shown in an important article, 'Investment in Industry— Has Britain lagged ?', *The Banker*, April 1957, by T. Barna, that in the thirties output per head in British industry was increasing faster than in Germany (31 per cent., 1929–38 as against 12 per cent.) while in the United States output per head was stagnant. In view of the fact that the United States, at least, had had a good start in the new industries, these statistics are significant, for they suggest that Britain was rapidly catching up. It is considered that general evidence of this kind is more meaningful than comparisons of productivity between countries at the level of the individual industry.

It is obvious that without the new industries—motor-cars, rayon, household appliances, radio and electrical engineering, for example—the increase in productivity and real income would only have been very small compared with what was actually achieved in the inter-war period. It is important, therefore, to understand how the new industries were able to assert themselves in the economy. Salter presents the following analysis (pp. 148–51). As technology in the new industries improves, and as the economies of scale are realized, their costs fall, and this makes for falling relative prices, rapidly expanding output, and increasing employment. This affects declining industries by means of both demand and cost pressures. The demand pressures operate via the price-reducing activities of the new industries; as the prices of new products fall declining industries are robbed of markets, for many of these products were adequate substitutes for old ones. The replacement of cotton fabrics by rayon and of gas and coal by electricity and oil are obvious examples. The cost pressures are most clearly visible in the case of labour costs, for as the new industries expand they require increasing numbers of workers to whom they are able to offer higher wages. This affects the general level of wages and the declining industries are also affected. The result of all this is to reinforce the decline of the old industries in total output.

It is only by understanding this—the nature of structural change in the economy—that the importance of the new industries in the inter-war years can be appreciated. The new industries are sometimes criticized because their increase in output and employment did not adequately compensate for the decline of the staple industries, but the criticism is hardly fair if it is based on the fact that the substitution of new industries for old was not completed in the inter-war period. This was not achieved by 1939 because of several factors: the old industries were predominantly export industries while the new tended to be home-market industries, and thus Britain was faced with the difficult and laborious problem of diverting a large part of her resources from manufacture for export to manufacture for home use; the sharp contrast in geographical location between the old industries and the new (that is, the old being heavily localized in the north while the new tended to sprout up in the Home Counties and the south) seriously aggravated the transfer problem, especially with regard to labour; the post-war boom of 1919–20 and certain external factors in the twenties masked the decline of the staple industries, and it was not generally realized until the next decade that the solution of Britain's difficulties did not lie in their recovery but in the reallocation of resources to the new. Those critics who point to the heavy unemployment of the thirties or to the small scale of the newer industries as an indication of their failure are drawing attention to irrelevancies. What is important is that the new industries were a potent force making for permanent structural change in British industry, and to place an arbitrary time-limit (such as 1939) for the readjustment to be made is to ignore the difficulties involved.

The admirable theoretical analysis of the relationship between productivity and technical change by Salter suggests that if one wishes to criticize the British industries' technical performance relative to those abroad one will have to find more reliable criteria of evidence than comparative productivity statistics. It is necessary, therefore, to use other sources of information to inquire whether or not the rate of technical innovation in British new industries was low in relation to other countries. This, of course, has been done, but critics of Britain's progress have tended to ignore the evidence in favour of Britain's performance, although a mitigating factor is that most of this evidence is of very recent origin.

A common argument is that research expenditure in British industry was at a low level compared with that of the United States. This fact was pointed out more than 30 years ago by the Committee on Industry and Trade, *Factors in Industrial and Commercial Efficiency* (1927). In the period 1920–6, the research associations of the motor industry spent only £25,000, the rubber industry £28,000, and the electrical industry £50,000; whereas in the United States, in 1924 alone, the General Electric Co. spent $3 million, Du Pont $2 million, and General Motors $1 million (p. 319; pp. 333–4). Of course, this did not necessarily imply a low rate of technical innovation. Although the correlation between research expenditure and technical progress was probably positive, there may be some truth in the argument that the more money an organization has to spend the more it is likely to be squandered. It must also be remembered that the activities of the research associations of individual industries was not the only research under way. The government gave some direct encouragement through various channels: State-owned laboratories, development contracts given out to selected industries, its own manufacturing facilities. Most important of all was the private developmental research of the large firm.

The most quoted example of British failure and inadaptability in this century is the dyestuffs industry. Britain had failed to develop such an industry before the First World War, and although one was stimulated by government intervention in the inter-war period (that is, under the Dyestuffs (Import Regulation) Act of 1920) British backwardness persisted; even by 1937–8 Britain was a net importer of dyestuffs by value (though not by volume, since we exported 97,000 cwt. compared with an import of 45,000 cwt.).[1] But in other industries there was a completely different picture. For the radio industry S. G. Sturmey's *The Economic Development of Radio* (1958) is a testimony to the constant stream of innovations introduced in Britain. The industry took up many technical improvements in the inter-war years such as automatic volume control, press-button tuning, multiple wave bands, static reducing devices, and better calibration of dials; portable radio sets and car radios were on the market from 1933 (pp. 178–9). As a separately housed unit, the Rice-

[1] W. B. Reddaway, 'The Chemical Industry', in D. L. Burn, *The Structure of Industry*, vol. i (1958), p. 247.

Kellog moving coil loudspeaker was on the British market before it reached the American (p. 169). In an article in *Lloyds Bank Review*, October 1957, 'Science and Industry', T. Wilson points out the interesting fact that although the United States was ahead in the work on the television camera Britain had the first fully electronic television service in the world. Rapid technological change also showed itself in techniques of production: in the thirties most of the leading set makers adopted line production methods, in many cases with endless belt conveyors. On the debit side, Sturmey states that technical advance in receiving sets was faster in America before 1939, and that much of the progress recorded here was based on communicated American patents. This was also the case in several other related industries. For example, in the production of electric lamps although Britain was not responsible for any major development, leading British maufacturers were able to acquire United Kingdom patent rights under a series of agreements with the principal American and German companies; from 1912 British-Thomson-Houston, G.E.C., and Siemens had a patents pool. This method of taking up technical advances was not necessarily harmful, for the disadvantages of being the first with an innovation may in some cases outweigh the advantages. There was something to be said for letting other countries make the running and for us to follow, to profit from the mistakes of others and to avoid the risks of investment in research—in other words, to reverse our role of the Industrial Revolution and to allow other countries to pay the penalties of industrial pioneering. As Professor Ashworth reminds us, 'the adoption of technical advances which originated abroad would nevertheless increase the efficiency of production at home' (op cit., p. 415).

In other industries, too, Britain's performance seemed adequate. In the motor industry, the conclusion of the P.E.P.'s *Report on Motor Vehicles* (1950) is that technical development was largely confined to the post-1945 era (p. 55), but in fact there were continuous improvements in the inter-war period: better carburettors, more efficient brakes and combustion chambers, automatic voltage control in electrical equipment, thermostatic control of cooling systems, group lubrication, windscreen wipers, self-starters; besides the more obvious developments such as the diesel engine, pneumatic tires, and generally better coachwork design. In the plastics branch of the chemical industry, as a short but interesting article by P. Morgan, 'The Plastics Industry, 1958', *National Provincial Bank Review*, February 1958, reveals, there were significant technical advances in spite of the fact that the output of plastics was less than 30,000 tons in 1939. The use of cellulose acetate as an injection-moulding material began in the late twenties for producing thimbles, golf tees, and small radio components. Resin M (the forerunner of Perspex) was being

produced in the United Kingdom from 1937. In 1933 Britain was responsible for one development which today seems of almost revolutionary
importance, the discovery of polythene by I.C.I.—just one of the many
results of the research on polyvinyl compounds in the thirties; by 1939
the first polythene unit had begun production. Finally, in electricity,
Britain was the first with the idea of electrical heating for public buildings.

On this question of the tempo of technical innovation there is a danger
in assuming that the conditions operating before 1914 continued in the
inter-war period. There is little doubt that in the quarter-century before
1914, as a generalization, the rate of technological change in Britain was
slowing down—in some of the newer industries as well as in the old
(although S. B. Saul in the article mentioned below warns against overestimating this). Take, for example, the following conclusion on the
electric lamp industry: 'The British manufacturers of incandescent lamps
had dropped far behind the Germans by 1900, as indeed had all the British
electrical industries. . . . The obstacles . . . which largely persisted from
1897 to 1912 were apathy, limited ability and a lack of specialisation. . . .
There was not a single lamp-research laboratory in Great Britain during
all that time, and all important innovations were imported from Germany,
Austria and the United States.'[1] It is very easy to extend this argument
into the inter-war period, but it would be a false step of inquiry. In 1914
many countries of the world were enthusiastically expending the energies
of industrial youth, while Britain appeared to be settling down to a restful
and, perhaps, complacent middle age. Yet, did this necessarily mean that
in the inter-war years she would announce her retirement?

To predict this from pre-1914 experience was to disregard the course
of events. The First World War, of course, intervened and this proved
a stimulus to rejuvenation. Whether the economic consequences of war
are beneficial or not is still a matter for dispute, but it would be difficult
to overlook the boost given by this war to the new industries. This is
brought out in the famous article by R. S. Sayers, 'The Springs of Technical Progress, 1919–39', *Economic Journal*, June 1950. His view that the
effect of the war was 'to accelerate rather than to innovate development'
(p. 278) is probably substantially correct, but (as some of the following
examples illustrate) is not applicable to every case. Moreover, the examples
that Professor Sayers cites—the aircraft, the motor lorry, the rise of
automatic welding and the development of certain plastics—are mainly
the obvious ones. Large-scale production of valves grew up in response to
the demands of the armed forces for large quantities for radio communication, and the commercial production of valves and radio sets was under

[1] A. A. Bright, *The Electric Lamp Industry: Technical Change and Economic Development
from 1888 to 1947* (1949), pp. 161–2.

way as early as 1919–20. The development of cellulose acetate rayon, which by 1930 accounted for 20 per cent. of the world's rayon output, originated in research at a government factory during the war on the use of cellulose dopes for strengthening aircraft wings. It was the realization that dye-making plant is rapidly adaptable to the requirements of chemical warfare which induced the government to give a grant of £2 million for the development of the industry in 1918, and to pass legislation regulating imports in 1920. Similarly, military demand factors were at work in aluminium and alloys research, in insulated cable production and in petroleum chemistry.

The trouble with evidence of this kind, however, is that it is too general and unsystematic. It is very easy to answer an accusation of technical backwardness with an example of technical progress in another industry or even in the same industry. What is required is a more detailed examination of the many factors governing the rate of innovation in each industry. In a recent article, 'The American Impact upon British Industry, 1895–1914', *Business History*, December 1960, S. B. Saul examines the effect of American competition in stimulating individual firms in certain sections of the engineering industry to adopt technical improvements and to introduce innovations during the two decades before the First World War. Until we get more articles of this type on the new industries in the inter-war years, the problem of whether or not their rate of innovation was lower than it might have been is likely to receive no clear solution.

Another problem which deserves more attention is that posed by Salter (op. cit., p. 24) of how far the application of new techniques is due to the acquisition of new knowledge and how far it is attributable to changed factor prices. For if in certain industries Britain was behind in technical innovations in the inter-war period this was not necessarily a sign of lack of initiative, but could have been explained by the fact that it would have been uneconomical to introduce them. For example, because of the heavy unemployment on the one hand and the falling off in the rate of saving with a consequent scarcity of capital on the other, Britain's supplies of labour were plentiful relative to her supplies of investment and this militated against the rapid adoption of new techniques. Thus, *if* Britain was backward technically this may have been a reflection, not of the failure of applied science, but of the economic conditions of the time.

What we really need to know, of course, is how the many factors at issue affected the decisions of the individual entrepreneur. This can be observed not by referring to industries, but only by studying the individual firm—hence the importance of business histories. Two recent publications are concerned with new industries: J. D. Scott, *Siemen Brothers, 1858–1958: An Essay in the History of Industry* (1958), and C. Wilson and W. Reader, *Men and Machines, A History of D. Napier and Sons, Engineers, Ltd., 1808–1958* (1958). Both shed light on how individual firms faced the problems of technological innovation.

Napier & Sons, by the first decade of this century, was a small specialist car firm. At the end of the First World War the firm realized that the future lay with moderately priced cars turned out by large manufacturers. The company therefore changed over to the production of aero engines; in 1919, 300 Lion engines were put into production in spite of the fact that there were no orders for them (pp. 110–11). This suggested that the outlook of the management (if foolhardy) was at least progressive. However, in the twenties the policy paid off; in the period 1924–35 73 types of British aircraft had Napier engines, and in 1928 and 1929 world air-speed records were set up with planes running on Napier engines. The firm did not figure prominently in the export trade, but there was a simple explanation for this—several of its engine designs were on the Secret List. On the other hand, the authors point out that although the firm was very progressive technically, it was not so commercially (p. 120). This distinction is of general importance. For it may possibly be argued that Britain's failings were not due to tardiness in the application of new techniques or in scientific research, but to conservatism in the commercial field. British businessmen tended to be sceptical about the value of market forecasting, paid insufficient attention to the diversity of the demands of consumers (especially those abroad), and relied on rule-of-thumb and outmoded methods in sales policies.

Siemens was a much larger firm, originating as cable-makers but later branching out into other sections of the electrical industry. By the middle thirties it was possible to speak of a team or even of a research and development organization consisting of a dozen or more workers at their branch in Preston (which specialized in lamp production). The firm represents an example of how a manufacturer can do well without making the basic innovations. In 1918 the British cable had a 'world-wide reputation' and was regarded as a sort of prize exhibit, yet all the important technical advances between the wars came from abroad. In spite of this, the methods adopted by Siemens, the leading firm, satisfied their customers. In the field of telephone cables, for example, the G.P.O. was satisfied with the 'minor improvements in the regularity of the product' (p. 139). In contrast with Napier, therefore, this firm was not very go-ahead in development, but the scale of development undertaken reflected the commercial needs of the time in the sense that their customers were content with it. If this was 'backwardness' it did not prevent Siemens from expanding their exports in the late thirties, when the general trend was for international trade to decline. Just as Napier & Sons extended the range of their products by turning to aero engines, so Siemens in the years before the First World War began to manufacture electric locomotives, motors for rolling mills, batteries, telegraph and telephone line material, electrical machinery for use in ships, wireless telegraphy, 'fringe equipment' for the telephone industry, and lamps; the production of these was expanded considerably between the wars, especially in the case of automatic telephone exchanges and electric lamps (pp. 196–204). This willingness of firms to branch out into new lines was in fact typical of the new industries, and because it almost invariably involved new plant and sometimes new processes and techniques of production this characteristic indicates the progressive attitude of these industries towards technical change. In the twenties Dunlop experienced a similar widening of the scope of activities. In 1925 they turned to producing footwear, clothing, belting, and rubber hose; in the next decade other products involving the use of latex were added to their range.

The evidence given in these two histories suggests that it is dangerous to generalize about the technological bankruptcy of British industry. But two swallows do not make a summer, and far more business histories of a reputable standard are required before any firm conclusion may be drawn. The need for them is important, for the individual firm has been responsible for many, perhaps the majority of, technical developments. For example, Courtaulds, the rayon firm, undertook an intensive development of staple fibre in the inter-war period. This culminated in the thirties in the establishment of two experimental and demonstration mills the most important of which, the Arrow Mill at Rochdale, proved to Lancashire cotton manufacturers that staple fibre could be used extensively in Lancashire cotton mills. In the rubber industry, Dunlop's research was very successful: they were first in the field with aeroplane tires (1910), bullet-proof tires (1917), and giant pneumatic tires (1921). They had been the first to use carbon black in the tire tread, and in the inter-war years experimented in the use of rayon for casing.

III

An important source of material on the new industries for this period is the reports of the Monopolies and Restrictive Practices Commission (now the Monopolies Commission). Extensively used, of course, for investigation into monopoly problems, it is not often realized that they are a mine of information on the new industries, containing not only details of amalgamations and trade associations, but also general histories of the industries concerned and statistics of prices, output, and imports and exports. A list of the reports concerned with newer industries is given below.[1] A large part of the information given in these reports is naturally about trade associations and amalgamation, and it is on these aspects that our attention will be concentrated.

In most cases the trade associations were formed in response to increasing foreign competition in the home market. The Tyre Manufacturers' Conference, set up in 1929, was an attempt to override the instability of trading conditions which had been a feature of the twenties. Its main purpose was to maintain prices, but it did not always succeed; in times of depression severe competition again became the rule, and company losses were great. The initiative in the Electric Lamp Manufacturers' Association, a reconstitution in 1933 of the former body of 1919, was taken by G.E.C. and A.E.I.; the members sought to meet by higher quality and by exclusive agreements with distributors the price competition of both imported, especially Japanese, lamps and lamps produced by independent British manufacturers. The B.V.A. (British Radio Valve Manufacturers' Association), constituted in 1926, also had to struggle to maintain agreed list prices in the face of vigorous competition from abroad. The Cable Makers' Association had been formed as early as 1899 with the aim of reducing costs of production by maximum efficiency. By 1931, however, the industry was bedevilled by excess capacity; the Association tried to meet this by promoting rationalization and amalgamation. The National Sulphuric Acid Association was established in 1919 to deal with surplus capacity of acid production, the result of enormous expansion during the First World War to cater for the needs of the explosives industry. Also in 1919 the Fertiliser Manufacturers' Association had been formed: its activities were extensive, including internal discussions on prices and attempts to counter the situation created by the sale of cheap foreign superphosphate in Britain. In 1921 the Association acquired a controlling interest in a Belgium company, Superphosphates Standaert, and agreements were made with foreign firms in Holland, Belgium, and France between 1923 and 1930, under which these firms consented to restrict their exports to the United Kingdom to agreed quotas. There was a severe depression in the production of metal windows in the early thirties, and attempts to standardize the commodity broke down. Consequently, the Metal Window Association was set up in 1933 and by 1939 had restored the industry to full prosperity; in 1937, for example, sales increased by

---

[1] In the electrical industries, *Report on the Supply of Electric Lamps* (1951), *Report on the Supply of Insulated Electric Wires and Cables* (1952), *Report on the Supply of Electronic Valves and Cathode Ray Tubes* (1956), and *Report on the Supply and Export of Electrical and Allied Machinery and Plant* (1957). In the pharmaceutical industry, *Report on the Supply of Insulin* (1952); in the chemical industry, *Report on the Supply of Certain Industrial and Medical Gases* (1956) and *Report on the Supply of Chemical Fertilizers* (1959); and in other industries, *Report on the Supply and Export of Pneumatic Tyres* (1955) and *Report on the Supply of Standard Metal Windows and Doors* (1956).

36 per cent. although the number of houses built increased by only 26 per cent.

The amalgamation movement was also widespread throughout the new industries. In the electrical industry (with particular reference to the valve section) Associated Electrical Industries was formed in 1928 and the company acquired all the ordinary shares of Edison, British-Thomson-Houston, and Metropolitan Vickers. This was partly responsible for the great extension of British valve production from $5\frac{1}{2}$ million to 11 million, 1930–5. In the rubber tire industry Dunlop expanded rapidly during and after the First World War, mainly as a result of internal development rather than of absorption. After 1927, however, the firm followed a policy of controlling distributive outlets; for example, a majority interest was obtained in the firm of C. H. Brittain of Stoke. In 1938 the company began retreading with the acquisition of the Regent Tyre and Rubber Co. In the chemical fertilizer industry in 1928 I.C.I. gained control of a number of Scottish companies and in 1929 three East Anglian producers amalgamated to form Fisons; in the next ten years Fisons acquired twenty-four fertilizer companies and formed five new ones which were registered as subsidiaries. The British Oxygen Company absorbed its greatest rival, the Allen-Liversidge interests, in 1930, and thereafter followed a policy of acquisition at any cost. For example, it attempted to move into south-west England and South Wales by driving out and taking over the Cornish firm of T. W. Ward, Ltd., a manœuvre which was finally successful in 1944. Amalgamations and concentration were not, of course, limited to the new industries examined by the Monopolies Commission; other examples included Courtaulds in rayon, and Joseph Lucas and the Chloride Electrical Storage Company in the electrical equipment branch of the motor industry.

Although this trend towards monopoly and restrictive agreements could also be observed in the old staple industries, it was more prevalent in the new. The question arises whether the tendency to concentration in the new industries was due to the endogenous development of capitalism there or whether it was an exogenous effect of the prevailing economic situation during their period of growth, by which is meant the general depression of the inter-war years. While the depression undoubtedly presented a further incentive to cartelization, it seems clear that this grew up in the new industries out of their normal course of development. This is substantiated by the fact that in the post-war era of prosperity the trend continued and was intensified, except where and until the Monopolies Commission and the Restrictive Practices Court intervened. But history, too, suggests reasons why this was so. Kahn (op. cit., p. 81) contrasts the situation in the old industries, where the psychology was defensive, with the new, where it was aggressive; in his view, the incentive to monopoly profits was strong simply because the new industries were not hampered by having developed into small, vigorously competing units. A. F. Lucas (in the standard work on industrial reorganization between the wars, *Industrial Reconstruction and the Control of Competition* (1937), p. 40) argues that the tendency for the new industries to locate themselves in the newer industrial areas of the south and the midlands struck a double blow at the competitive system. In the first place, it contributed to the general flux of industry which dislodged the British manufacturer from his old ways: secondly, it meant the rise of a group of new producers who were untarnished by the traditions of individualistic enterprise which had from the beginning characterized the staple industries. He concludes that it was this factor, above all, which led to the new industries' early denial of the philosophy of free competition. Both these arguments, while difficult to prove, seem plausible. Today, under the influence of the Restrictive Practices Act, it is too easy to condemn this trend towards monopoly and trade associations; but in the conditions of the inter-war period it was quite reasonable for one of the new industries' representatives to maintain: 'The day of the fixed price has come, and such a development must be considered as a real condition of social and economic progress.'[1]

The term 'fixed price' used in reference to the new industries between the wars may be misleading. Attempts to fix prices, whether by a monopolistic producer or a trade association, were made only at a given level of production—in other words, in the short run. In the longer run, the inter-war years witnessed a continuous reduction in price of all products of the new industries under the influence of technical progress and increasing economies of scale. The price index of motor-cars fell from 100 in 1913 to 51 in 1924 and 42 in 1936. In the electricity supply industry unit revenue derived by authorized undertakings from sales of energy to consumers was more than halved between 1921–2 and 1935–6. In the period 1923–38 the price of rayon viscose yarn fell from 9s. to 2s. 7½d. per lb., and in the thirties the price of viscose staple fibre fell from 3s. to 10d. per lb. The retail prices of electric filament lamps set by E.L.M.A. fell by about a third, 1930–8. In the pharmaceutical industry theprice of insulin fell from 25s. to 1s. 6d. for a standard pack between 1923 and 1935. Finally, in spite of the criticisms of B.O.C.'s price policies, the average price of industrial oxygen by 1939 was less than half what it had been at the outset of the inter-war period. In many cases these price reductions were achieved only at the expense of the profits of large firms and the livelihood of smaller ones. The solution to the paradox of price-fixing agreements

---

[1] British Electrical and Allied Manufacturers' Association, *Combines and Trusts in the Electrical Industry* (1930), p. 22.

and constant price reduction is as follows: the growth of industry is always governed by demand conditions, but in the newer industries where many of the products were 'high-income' goods the influence of demand conditions was even stronger because demand for these goods was very elastic; without technical efficiency and its result in the market, a long-term and significant fall in price, therefore, the new industries simply would not have expanded at all; on the other hand, manufacturers were anxious to maintain prices in the short run. Thus, the extensive price reductions in the new industries were not the consequence of depression but a necessary condition of growth.

Attention was drawn above to Saul's article which shows how American competition in the period before 1914 stimulated British industries to introduce innovations and adopt new methods. The process was taken a step further, particularly in the inter-war years, when Americans actually began to invest in British manufacturing industry and to establish subsidiaries here of firms in the United States. The details of this are told in J. H. Dunning, *American Investment in British Manufacturing Industry* (1958). What is really noticeable about this investment was its concentration on the new industries. In the motor industry Ford and Vauxhall, in tire production Goodyear and Firestone, in the electrical industry Associated Electrical Industries (in which the United States holding varied from 25 per cent. to 40 per cent.): these are obvious examples, but the range was wider. American investments in the United Kingdom were also in telephones, chemicals, gramophones, pharmaceutical products, machinery, and musical instruments. In the thirties American firms established branches in those newer industries in the development of which Britain was possibly falling behind, such as the Hoover Company (1931) in domestic electrical appliances and the Remington Rand Company (1937) in office equipment. Indeed, the United States was responsible for introducing many new methods and innovations into this country. The effect of the establishment of subsidiaries of Bristol Instruments Company in industrial instruments and of Frigidaire and York Shipley in refrigeration was to stimulate British firms to expand in the same field (p. 46).

What was the significance of this development? The impetus was strengthened by tariff protection, and United States subsidiaries were often intended as a means of surmounting tariff barriers. But the causes of the development are not so important as its consequences. Opposition was raised to American investment by firms in the electrical and rubber industries, and this was manifested in stipulations limiting American holdings of shares and voting rights. Yet United States investment in British industry did not necessarily imply a condemnation of British industrial achievements and in fact had two important beneficial results. In the first place, American capital helped to utilize resources previously unemployed; 1919–39, 140 new enterprises were set up employing 60,000 workers (p. 298). Secondly, the fact that most of the American investment was in new industries and also contributed to the further expansion of British firms in these industries was a great advantage because it speeded up the adjustments in the structure of British industry necessary for highly industrialized countries, that is, the transition from old staple industries to the production of newer highly processed goods.

IV

Those who decry the role of the new industries in the inter-war economy stress their export position. Their argument is: first, that the new industries exported a far smaller proportion of their output than the older staple industries, and that this was an unhealthy development in view of Britain's overall balance of payments difficulties; secondly, that most of their exports went to protected Commonwealth markets; thirdly, that the new industries of Britain fared less well in the export markets than those of her competitors. Superficially, the factual basis in support of these arguments is strong, but there is a great danger in interpreting the meaning of these facts.

In the thirties 17 per cent. of the number of motor vehicles produced were exported; in rayon the proportion was smaller, 10 per cent. of yarn being exported and little more than 6 per cent. of piece goods; sales abroad in the electronics industry amounted to less than 10 per cent. of gross output. This formed a strong contrast with the staple industries, where in the most extreme case, cotton piece goods, almost 90 per cent. of output had been exported before 1913 and even in the thirties the percentage of production exported varied between 50 per cent. and 60 per cent. The proportion of output exported by the other staple industries was rather less but the contrast was still noticeable. There were a number of sensible reasons to account for this. The new industries, with huge resources of capital and technical knowledge, adopted the latest methods of large-scale organization and in fact spread round the world far more rapidly than had the old staple industries. This made for a more balanced distribution of new industrial production between countries, and consequently export markets were shared out more evenly. The prevalence of international agreements in these industries made direct inroads into exports, for a common feature in these agreements was the promise to 'reserve' to each member his home market. Moreover, as I. Svennilson points out in *Growth and Stagnation in the European Economy* (1954), the main developments of the period affecting manufacturing were domestic (p. 220). The development of electric power, the extension of the use of motor vehicles and increased town and surburban building were greater demand forces on the new industries than any operating abroad. Another point was that Britain shared in the common objective at this time—what Svennilson calls a 'self-sufficiency boom': in face of falling exports, the accepted policy was to increase tariff protection and attempt to reduce the volume of imported manufactures. In such an international atmosphere the new industries were bound to look more to the home market, just as in the nineteenth century the staple industries, favoured by an insatiable world demand, had expanded mainly by catering for markets overseas. Indeed, it is possible to argue that the home-market orientation of the new industries was a source of stability in a period of declining international trade. Finally, to blame the new industries for the balance of payments diffi-culties of the inter-war years is a distortion of the facts. The problem of the twenties was largely the result of Britain's attempt to retain her position as the world's leading creditor by lending abroad, and when the balance of payments again became negative after 1935 the main factor responsible was increased imports in response to rearmament demand.

The second point of issue, that of the concentration of the new in-dustries' exports upon Commonwealth markets, has been discussed earlier in this article. One observation only will be made here. It is easy to exaggerate the extent of this concentration if certain industries alone are chosen for illustration. In the motor industry, for example, of sales abroad during the inter-war period (apart from during the depression when Empire purchasing power was severely reduced) about 85 per cent. went to the Commonwealth. But taking the new industries as a whole (Kahn's classification) only 54·5 per cent. of their exports in 1929 went to the Commonwealth, and it is likely that this was increased only slightly as a result of the Ottawa agreements. Moreover, it must be remembered that a high proportion (about 40 per cent. in 1929) of staple exports went to the Commonwealth too.

The real attack on the export capabilities of Britain's new industries has been made in relation to their counterparts abroad and in the light of the changing structure of world trade. The best-known example of British deficiency in this respect is that illustrated by a German inquiry (*Der Deutsche Aussenhandel unter der Einwirkung weltwirtschaftlicher Strukturwandlungen* (1932), vol. ii, p. 156, quoted widely by E. Staley, *World Economic Development* (1944), A. J. Brown, *Applied Economics* (1947), W. A. Lewis, 'The Prospect before Us', *Manchester School*, May 1948, and G. C. Allen, op. cit.). This shows that, of a sample covering 80 per cent. of British exports (by commodities), 42 per cent. of our exports in 1929 were of goods which had increased less than 75 per cent., 1913–29, while only 4·3 per cent. were of goods in which world trade had increased more than 150 per cent.; in contrast, 28·6 per cent. of United States exports were in the latter category. A. Loveday (op. cit.) draws similar conclusions from the new industries' performance in export markets in the twenties. In the period 1925–8 the Netherlands increased her exports of wireless apparatus by £1¾ million, whereas British exports declined; in gramophones and records, while British exports increased from £1·44 million to £2·78 million, United States exports soared from £830,000 to £2·26 million (pp. 168–70). These statistics are of doubtful value for 4 years is too short a time for any trends to emerge. More important is the conclusion of the British Economic Mission to the Argentine (quoted by Loveday) that while Britain held on to her position in certain trades, in the new departments of trade—for example, aviation, road construction, and motor transport—she had been completely outdistanced. It is probable, however, that all this evidence relating to the twenties has been given more attention than it deserves. If the new industries were still infant industries in the inter-war period, as is suggested here, it may be conceded that their development in the twenties was slow and argued instead that their achievements between the wars were centred in the thirties. That their export performance by 1929 was limited was only to be expected.

Of more relevance to this question are the statistics given by Svennilson and by H. Tyszinski, 'World Trade in Manufactured Commodities, 1899–1950', *Manchester School*, September 1951, especially as they cover a wider period. Tyszinski points out that Britain's share of world trade in manufactures fell from 29·9 per cent. in 1913 to 22·4 per cent. in 1937, and argues that because this fall would not have been as great if Britain had kept the same proportion of her exports in the old staple industries throughout this period the cause of the decline was not so much changes in the structure of world trade but in her capacity to compete. The indictment is not as well founded as appears on first sight, for in reference to the structure of trade the proportion of British trade in the expanding groups increased from 17·7 per cent. to 31·2 per cent., 1899–1937, while world trade in this group increased from 13·4 per cent. to 34·8 per cent. (pp. 289–92). Thus, in spite of losses in her competitive position Britain did not lag behind the shifts in the structure of world trade to any great extent. This is supported by similar evidence in Svennilson (op. cit., tables, pp. 294–5). He shows that the categories 'Machinery' and 'Transport Equipment' were the expanding ones in world trade. The share of these in British exports increased from 15·9 per cent. in 1913 to 19·5 per cent. in 1928 and 31·6 per cent. in 1938 at the expense of textiles, which fell from 48·2 per cent. to 44·9 per cent. and 28·5 per cent. of exports at the above respective dates—and this change signified a successful adjustment in the structure of Britain's export trade. A. J. Brown in *Industrialization and Trade: The Changing World Pattern and the Position of Britain* (1943) presented statistics showing that the exports of machinery, electrical appliances, vehicles, and chemicals increased in relation to total exports from 14 per cent. to 40 per cent., 1910–38 (p. 60). What are the implications of this? In the first place, the argument that Britain failed to compensate for the fall in staple exports by the expansion of exports of the newer industries is overstated. Secondly, the cause of Britain's decline in world trade and her *apparent* sluggishness in exporting new products in relation to her best competitors and her former predominant station is to be found in her competitive position; by this one means not an absolute deterioration in the power of individual industries to compete effectively in world markets, but a change in international economic relationships unfavourable to Britain consequent upon the industrialization of new countries and the appearance of new competitors. She was no longer a giant among pygmies, but one of many. This did not mean failure, only the inevitable adjustment of British industry to its proper place in the modern world.

In fact, in certain of the new industries Britain was keeping in advance of their importance in world trade. In transport equipment (including motor vehicles) British exports expanded from £7·6 million in 1913 to £29·6 million in 1937, while its share in world trade rose from 3·3 per cent. to only 9·4 per cent. in the same period; similarly for electrical goods Britain's exports rose from £7·7 million to £19·1 million in the same period while the share of electrical goods in world trade increased from 2·4 per cent. to 4·7 per cent. (Tyszinski, loc. cit, pp. 278–83).

The argument that Britain was falling further and further behind in the development of the new industries, particularly with regard to overseas trade, makes nonsense when one looks at their post-war position. For example, by 1956 50 per cent. of the output of motor-cars were exported and the proportion of production sent abroad in electronics rose from 8 per cent. to 15 per cent., 1938–56. Although it was probable that conditions after the Second World War were especially favourable for British exports of those products, nevertheless, this dramatic transformation does not tally with the usual interpretation of the new industries' experience between the wars.

If Britain appeared to be lagging slightly behind, a possible explanation is that the new industries were infant industries in the inter-war years, and that this lag was merely a symptom of growing pains. That the government regarded them as such is suggested by the fact that almost all the new industries had received some form of tariff protection before the fundamental change in British commercial policy. The adjustment was slow but, as the post-war record shows, successful. The reasons for the slow pace of development are easy to find. Britain had come to world supremacy as the producer of common consumer goods. The products of the new industries were of a different nature—usually either equipment for production and communications such as machinery, cars, and communication devices or 'high-income' goods such as radios and gramophones. These were mainly capital goods industries, and it was more difficult for Britain to make the change. Britain also suffered from a lack of the increasingly important cheap hydro-electric power, petroleum, and non-ferrous metals. The United States, on the other hand, was better equipped because of an environment which made for the smooth application of a rapidly progressing technology to industry and because of a highly developed home market which encouraged methods of quantity production at low unit cost. Svennilson makes an important point which throws light on Britain's slow adjustment when he suggests (p. 116) that the prevalence of industrial areas 'based on the direct use of coal, coke and gas' delayed the extension of electric power on which successful production in many of the new industries depended. Another factor of significance (table, p. 241) is that Britain was the most industrialized country, 90 per cent. of the occupied population in 1920 being employed outside agriculture, as against 58·3 per cent. for Europe as a whole. This perhaps made the transition more difficult for Britain, for it is a reasonable hypothesis that the labour transfer problem between old industries and new is aggravated the higher the proportion of manpower already committed to the old manufacturing industries and is alleviated when semi-skilled workers for the new may be recruited from agriculture.

One final point—was it necessarily a criticism of the new industries that their export position was not as strong as that of her best competitors abroad? It is too readily assumed that exports are the sole criterion of industrial achievement. Keynes once said that he saw no special virtue in exports for their own sake which were not required to pay for imports. As A. J. Brown points out (*Industrialization and Trade*, p. 64) exports are not so important if imported goods, for which adequate substitutes can be produced at home at little more than the import prices, are replaced by home-produced goods, in such groups as iron and steel goods, cutlery, instruments, machinery, vehicles, and electrical goods. In fact, in the inter-war period the imports of these goods tended to fall as home production of them increased. Moreover, as Professor Ashworth suggests (op. cit., p. 322), the new products were far more highly processed than the old and consequently the imports of raw materials were likely to grow less proportionately than the production of new goods, and there was thus possibly less need for expansion in exports.

Indeed, the case that the new industries should have exported more than they did between the wars has never been proved.

V

This article in its assessment of recent evidence on the new industries has been able to concentrate on only a few aspects of their development. The solutions offered to the problems raised have not been conclusive; what has been demonstrated, it is hoped, is that the traditional view has been too easily accepted. To take a low view of the new industries' position was possible 20 or 30 years ago under the shadow of unemployment and general depression, but it is scarcely feasible in 1961 now that these former 'new' industries have developed into the staple industries of modern Britain. Because a larger proportion of her resources was involved in the old basic industries of the nineteenth century, Britain's newer industries were later in maturing than those of, say, the United States. It is quite possible, therefore, that even in the inter-war period these industries were still fundamentally infant industries which had not yet benefited from full economies of scale, and on this view the difficulties they incurred can be passed off as inevitable teething troubles. This interpretation, simple though it may be, at least allows one to make sense of the inter-war and post-war experience taken together.

There are a number of unsolved questions hardly touched upon here which will have to be answered before a complete assessment of the new industries' place in the inter-war economy can be made. Did the protection of the new industries act as a deterrent (or perhaps as a stimulus) to technological advance? How great a handicap on the shift to new industries was the fact that Britain was more deeply involved in the fortunes of the old staple industries than her competitors? Was government intervention an obstacle or an aid to development; in other words, did the benefits of tariff protection and the extensive influence of public corporations on certain of the new industries outweigh the restrictions on road transport, the deadweight of the tax-licensing system for motor vehicles and the burden on small producers of the excise duty on rayon yarn? How far did the misplaced faith in the capacity of the old industries to revive in the twenties delay investment in the new? In view of the fact that the new industries generally had a high ratio of capital to labour, was the heavy unemployment of the inter-war years a factor limiting their expansion—because some of the older industries employed more workers per unit of capital invested? As there were obvious links between the new industries (motor-cars and rubber tires, motor-cars and electrical equipment, plastics and radio parts, rayon and chemicals), how far was the fate of one industry bound up with that of another? Most important of all perhaps, what effect did the Second World War have on the new industries, and how many of the elements in their post-war expansion could be discerned before 1939 ? The answers to these questions may well be different for each industry. There is no *a priori* reason why all the new industries should have done well, or all done badly. Indeed, it is more likely that their fortunes were varied and their expansion was uneven. What is maintained here, however, is that if a generalization must be made on the state of Britain's new industries between the wars, the judgement which maintains that they were doing as well as might be expected and were fighting to hold a respectable position in a competitive world is far more realistic and plausible than that which holds that they were falling behind.

University of Aberdeen.

APPENDIX

A SELECT bibliography of works not discussed or mentioned in the text is given below. All the official publications in this list are important, but the rest of the material is not of uniform value. Some works are mainly about post-war developments and the inter-war years receives incidental mention only; others are not directly concerned with the new industries yet contain useful information on them. Those books and articles which are considered of especial importance are marked with an asterisk.*

(i) *Official publications*

Standing Committee on Trusts, Sub-committee, *Report on the Electric Lamp Industry* (Cmd. 622, 1920).

Standing Committee on Trusts, Sub-committee, *Report on the Electrical Cable Industry* (Cmd. 1332, 1921).

Committee on Industry and Trade, *Survey of Textile Industries* (1928).

Committee on Industry and Trade, *Survey of Metal Industries* (1928).

Report of the Dyestuffs Industry Development Committee on the Present Position and Development of the Dyestuffs Manufacturing Industry in Great Britain (Cmd. 3658, 1930).

Third Report of the Dyestuffs Industry Development Committee (Cmd. 4191, 1932).

Annual *Reports of the Department of Scientific and Industrial Research.*

Imperial Economic Committee, 30th Report, *Survey of the Trade in Motor Vehicles* (1937).

(ii) *Books*

D. L. BURN (ed.), *The Structure of British Industry* (1958), 2 vols.*

J. H. DUNNING and C. J. THOMAS, *British Industry: Change and Development in the Twentieth Century* (1961).*

D. C. HAGUE, *The Economics of Man-Made Fibres* (1957).

W. G. HOFFMANN, *British Industry, 1700–1950* (1955).*

J. M. LETICHE, *Balance of Payments and Economic Growth* (1959).

G. MAXCY and A. SILBERSTON, *The Motor Industry* (1959).*

C. L. MOWAT, *Britain between the Wars* (1956).

National Institute of Economic and Social Research, *Trade Regulations and Commercial Policy of the United Kingdom* (1943).

384   THE NEW INDUSTRIES BETWEEN THE WARS

A. PLUMMER, *International Combines in Modern Industry* (1934).
—— *New British Industries in the Twentieth Century* (1937).*
Political and Economic Planning, *Report on the Market for Household Appliances* (1945).
H. A. SILVERMAN, *Studies in Industrial Organization* (1946), 'The Artificial Textile Industry'.*
D. H. SMITH, *Industries of Greater London* (1933).
Society of Motor Manufacturers and Traders, *The Motor Industry of Great Britain* (1939).*
C. H. WARD-JACKSON, *A History of Courtaulds* (1941).

(iii) *Articles*

G. C. ALLEN, 'The Outlook for British Industry', *Westminster Bank Review*, August 1952.
G. R. ALLEN, 'The Growth of Industry on Trading Estates, 1920–39, with special reference to Slough Trading Estate', *Oxford Economic Papers*, October 1951.
A. K. CAIRNCROSS and R. L. MEIER, 'New Industries and Economic Development in Scotland', *Three Banks Review*, June 1952.
J. H. DUNNING, 'Newer British Industries and Increasing Productivity', *District Bank Review*, June 1954.
—— 'The Radio and T.V. Industry: A Post-War Survey', *Three Banks Review*, June 1952.
D. DUXBURY, 'The Role of Man-Made Fibres', *District Bank Review*, March 1957.*
D. W. HILL, 'Man-Made Fibres', *Three Banks Review*, December 1953.
R. HOPE, 'Profits in British Industry from 1924 to 1935', *Oxford Economic Papers*, June 1949.
E. J. JONES, 'Price Leadership in the Rayon Industry', *Manchester School*, vol. xii, 1941.*
C. E. V. LESER, 'Scottish Industries during the Inter-war Period', *Manchester School*, vol. xviii, 1950.
'Oil Refining in Great Britain: A Major New Industry', *Midland Bank Review*, February 1955.
E. H. PHELPS BROWN and S. J. HANDFIELD-JONES, 'The Climacteric of the 1890s', *Oxford Economic Papers*, October 1952.
Planning, 5 Dec. 1947, 'The Agricultural Machinery Industry'.
Planning, 2 July 1948, 'The Motor Industry'.*
Planning, 20 Dec. 1948, 'The Machine Tool Industry'.
Planning, 28 Feb. 1949, 'Commercial Vehicles'.*
Planning, 17 Oct. 1949, 'The Cycle Industry'.*
Planning, 5 Nov. 1951, 'The Gramophone Record'.
G. RAE, 'The Statistics of the Rubber Industry', *Journal of the Royal Statistical Society*, vol. ci, 1938.*
J. M. A. SMITH, 'The British Motor Industry', *National Provincial Bank Review*, May 1958.
W. WOODRUFF, 'Growth of the Rubber Industry of Great Britain and the United States', *Journal of Economic History*, vol. xv, 1955.*
Articles in *The Economist*, particularly:
    'The British Motor Industry, I', vol. cxvii, 1933.
    'The British Motor Industry', vol. cxxi, 1935, pp. 1129–54.*
    'The Electrical Equipment Industry', vol. cxxvii, 1937.
and in *The Statist*:
    'The British Electrical Industries', Supplement, 17 Dec. 1938.*

[9]

BRITAIN'S ECONOMY BETWEEN THE WARS: A SURVEY OF A COUNTER-REVOLUTION IN ECONOMIC HISTORY*

Patrick K. O'Brien

Over the past decade economists and economic historians have been engaged in intense, incomplete and largely inconclusive debate on Britain's economy between the wars. Naturally the diagnosis and cures for the high levels of unemployment which afflicted the work-force from 1918-38 have been at the core of the argument. But economic growth, structural adjustment, foreign competition and the economic and social policies pursued by successive Conservative, Labour and National governments figure as subsidiary and comp-lementary themes. This essay which attempts critically to survey this voluminous and fascinating discussion in terms readily communicated to historians is divided into four sections.

First, there follows an outline of revisionist interpretations of the inter-war years. Secondly, the paper provides some assessment of the performance of the economy in long-run and international perspec-tive. Thirdly, the central problem of unemployment will be con-sidered largely as a symptom of malfunctioning labour-markets. Fourthly, the macro-economic policies pursued by governments to deal with unemployment and cyclical depression will be reviewed in the context of the debate between Keynesian and anti-Keynesian prescriptions for those economic maladies. Finally, the paper will conclude by arguing that this brief and unique period of economic history is best depicted as an interlude in Britain's inevitable decline from its pinnacle of world economic power; and that the emphasis afforded by economists of all persuasions to discussions of policy (which stems largely from their theoretical and ideological commit-ments) lacks historical perspective and is often politically naïve.

* My colleague Nick Crafts and those who participated in his Oxford workshop on the inter-war economy provided the education and stimulus which prompted me to write this paper. I would also like to acknowledge helpful comments on earlier drafts from Nick Crafts, Ross McKibbin, Mark Thomas and Peter Witt.

I

REVISIONIST AND KEYNESIAN INTERPRETATIONS OF THE INTER-WAR YEARS

With unemployment again at record levels and as the post-war boom begins to emerge as a unique and even an inexplicable phase in the development of the British economy, a school of "neo-Conservative" historians now present the years between the wars in a sanguine and altogether more favourable light. Fundamentally, from three perspectives (and with degrees of emphasis naturally varying from author to author) the revisionists have staged a counter-revolution against the pessimistic interpretation of the period by Keynesian and left-wing critics of British capitalism; interpretations which "walked tall" during the long boom and years of full employment from 1948-50 to 1971-3.

In point of chronology, the earliest of these attacks was concerned to place the overall performance of the economy into perspective, in order to gainsay the impression of stagnation. Briefly and categorically stated, the argument concentrated upon statistical evidence to show that rates of growth and productivity change experienced by the British economy in 1921-38 were satisfactory in terms of historical trends and a definite improvement, compared with the long cycle of 1899-1913. Furthermore British industry adapted reasonably well to shifts in consumer demand and to the "inevitable" loss of overseas markets to younger and more favourably endowed foreign competitors. Indeed the continued, even accelerated, advance of new industries ("structural change") helped to regenerate the economy and strongly assisted its recovery from the Great Depression over the years 1932-8.[1]

Turning next to confront the infamous scourge of the period, unemployment (which Keynesians and the left had analysed as a failure of Britain's capitalist market economy to grow without serious oscillations in the demand for labour), the revisionists point out that the two major downswings in economic activity from 1920-1 and from 1929-32 were the concomitant of war and its aftermath in the first case, and that financial mismanagement by the monetary authorities of the United States triggered off and sustained the great

[1] Recent surveys of the period with good bibliographies are: D. H. Aldcroft, *The British Economy between the Wars* (Oxford, 1983); S. Pollard, *The Development of the British Economy, 1914-80* (Bungay, 1983); M. W. Kirby, *The Decline of British Economic Power since 1870* (London, 1981); S. Constantine, *Unemployment in Britain between the Wars* (London, 1980).

depression in the second case. They do not accept estimates for "average" levels of unemployment which include these five years of severe but unavoidable recession. Moreover the abnormal rates of unemployment endured by British workers outside these peculiar years emanated, revisionists argue, in large measure from inescapable shifts of competitive advantages away from the country's staple export industries (textiles, coal, shipbuilding and steel) which suffered in any case from dislocations to international economic relations and from slow recovery of world trade. Furthermore (and at this point directing a provocative assault on the notion that the operation of free markets conspicuously failed throughout the 1920s and 1930s to provide jobs for an unusually high proportion of those seeking work) the revisionists now claim that the unemployment of the period was both exacerbated by rigidities in money wages (supported by the growing power of trade unions) and needlessly prolonged by unemployment benefits, rent subsidies and other governmental impediments to what had been a historically efficient labour-market.

Thirdly, the revisionists have drawn intellectual sustenance from monetarism, new classical political economy, rational-expectations theory and other aspects of the revolution in macro-economic analysis to deride Keynesian critiques of public policies, pursued for over two decades before the war.[2] And the failure of Keynesian policies to arrest the slow-down in productivity growth, to check inflation or stem the advance towards the higher levels of unemployment of 1968-79 have all served to render their perspectives on the years between the wars more acceptable and plausible.[3] Revisionists now maintain that the fiscal, exchange-rate and monetary policies implemented by successive Conservative, Labour and National administrations in 1921-8 exercised neutral or, at worst, moderately unhelpful effects on economic growth and unemployment. They dismiss the alternative policies prescribed by Keynes and his supporters to deal with cyclical unemployment as politically and fiscally unrealistic prescriptions for the problems of the time and as potential (but fortunately latent) restraints upon the structural changes required for the long-term prosperity of the British economy.

Needless to say, Keynesians (old and young) have not allowed this

[2] R. Skidelsky (ed.), *The End of the Keynesian Era* (London, 1977); E. Malinvaud, *The Theory of Unemployment Reconsidered* (Oxford, 1977); R. J. Barro, *Macroeconomics* (New York, 1984); W. H. Buiter, "The Macroeconomics of Dr. Pangloss: A Critical Survey of New Classical Macroeconomics", *Econ. Jl.*, xc (1980).

[3] See *Econ. Jl.*, special issue, xciii (1983); R. C. O. Mathews (ed.), *Slower Growth in the Western World* (London, 1982).

counter-revolution in economic history to become consolidated into a new orthodoxy serving to defend the idea that free markets operated efficiently and benignly even during those troubled years of 1919-39. This essay surveys the recent bibliography and offers an interim report on the state of the argument.

II
THE PERFORMANCE OF THE ECONOMY

Alas, there is no space to evaluate the quality of the basic statistics used to measure the performance of the economy from 1921 to 1938, and perceptions will always depend on the reference points used for comparison. Nevertheless, taking stock of standard indicators for growth and productivity change, it would be difficult not to concur with the view that the advance of the British economy proceeded at a rate which was definitely above trends, established for 1873-1913, and markedly better in almost every respect than its poor record over the cycle from 1899 to 1913 — now referred to as the Edwardian climacteric.[4] The conspicuous exception was exports which actually declined in value between 1920 and 1938.[5] Most of that failure can, however, be attributed to disruptions to international commerce, because Britain's share of the declining volume of world exports did not fall sharply.[6]

But in relation to its rivals, the performance of the national economy appears much less satisfactory. Cross-country tabulations for average annual rates of growth of domestic product and for output per worker employed in manufacturing industry for the years 1913-38 expose the United Kingdom languishing close to the foot of the league tables. For the period 1922-9 the country's record was dismal indeed, but it moves closer to the average performance for major industrialized

[4] Basic data sources are: C. H. Feinstein, *National Income Expenditure and Output of the United Kingdom* (Cambridge, 1972); R. C. O. Mathews, C. H. Feinstein and J. Odling-Smee, *British Economic Growth, 1856-1973* (Oxford, 1982); C. H. Feinstein (ed.), *The Managed Economy: Essays in British Economic Policy and Performance since 1929* (Oxford, 1983).

[5] B. R. Mitchell and P. Deane, *Abstract of British Historical Statistics* (Cambridge, 1962).

[6] W. A. Lewis, "The Rate of Growth of World Trade, 1830-1973", in S. Grassman and E. Lundberg (eds.), *The World Economic Order: Past and Prospects* (London, 1981); R. A. Batchelor *et al.*, *Industrialization and the Basis for Trade* (Cambridge, 1980).

countries over the years 1929-37.[7] Such comparisons are difficult to interpret simply because nations possess different capacities for development over time and slow-growing economies such as Britain may have grown closer to some indefinable potential than, say, high flyers from Scandinavia.[8]

International comparisons still help to highlight Britain's long-standing economic problem: namely the need to alter the composition of industrial output in order to bring it into line with changes in consumer demand and, more important, to compensate for the persistent decline in the competitive position held by its staple industries built up during the Industrial Revolution.[9] This central concern with structural change, discussed for several decades before 1914, became a preoccupation during the world boom from 1899 to 1914, remained in abeyance during the war, but reappeared as a malady from 1921 to 1938.[10]

Primary production, not only agriculture and forestry but also mining, continued to decline in relative terms over the inter-war years when the share of manufacturing industry rose to reach 40 per cent of national output.[11] Within the economy's leading sector a slight acceleration in the pace of structural change prompted some historians to make exaggerated claims for the significance of "new" industries experiencing rapid growth during these troubled years.[12] Their importance for the long-term regeneration of the economy and for Britain's recovery from the Great Depression depends upon what is meant by "new" industries, and the time-spans allowed for their influence to materialize. Definitions vary from author to author.[13] Clearly they should not be synonymous with expanding industries,

[7] J. Cornwall, *Modern Capitalism* (Oxford, 1977); A. Maddison, *Phases of Capitalistic Development* (Oxford 1982).

[8] A. Maddison, "Economic Policy and Performance in Europe, 1913-70", in C. Cipolla (ed.), *The Fontana Economic History of Europe*, 6 vols. in 9 (Glasgow, 1972-6), v (ii).

[9] M. Beenstock, *The World Economy in Transition* (London, 1964).

[10] C. K. Harley and D. N. McCloskey, "Foreign Trade: Competition and the Expanding International Economy", in R. Floud and D. N. McCloskey (eds.), *The Economic History of Britain since 1700*, 2 vols. (Cambridge, 1981), i; F. Crouzet, *The Victorian Economy* (London, 1982); P. Friedman, *The Impact of Trade Destruction on National Incomes: A Study of Europe, 1924-38* (Gainesville, 1974).

[11] J. A. Dowie, "Growth in the Inter-War Period: Some More Arithmetic", *Econ. Hist. Rev.*, 2nd ser., xxi (1968).

[12] Mathews, Feinstein and Odling-Smee, *British Economic Growth*; D. H. Aldcroft, "Economic Growth in Britain in the Inter-War Years: A Reassessment", *Econ. Hist. Rev.*, 2nd ser., xx (1967).

[13] H. Richardson, *Economic Recovery in Britain, 1932-39* (London, 1967); D. Aldcroft and H. Richardson, *The British Economy, 1870-1939* (London, 1969).

but even when properly confined to vehicle-building, electrical engineering, rayon, non-ferrous metals, chemicals, paper, printing and publishing the overall significance of this particular group of "virile" industries is not easy to isolate over a short and abnormal span of time.[14] For example, their share in industrial output rose from 7 per cent in 1907, to 14 per cent in 1924 and to 21 per cent by 1935. Their work-forces and capitals stocks also expanded at rates conspicuously above average for industry as a whole. But from 1924 to 1937 the new industries did not achieve rates of productivity growth that were outstanding.[15] In terms of their scale of production, capital intensity, forms of organization and technology, they replicated advances occurring in other industries, including the declining staples.[16] Their purchases of inputs and raw materials from traditional industries such as iron and steel, coal, shipbuilding and railway rolling-stock did not generate exceptional "feedback" or "linkage" effects to the rest of industry.[17] Finally, the argument that new industries mitigated the impact of the Great Depression on the British economy and played a leading role in the recovery of 1932-7 has been severely qualified by careful quantification which showed that deceleration in the growth of consumer expenditure in 1929-32 adversely affected profits and investment in almost all industries, new and old alike. Investment in new industries from 1932 to 1937 formed but a tiny proportion of total expenditure on net capital formation during the 1930s, and the reallocation of labour and capital from old to new industries proceeded at comparable rates in 1925-9 and 1932-7.[18] New industries remained too small to lead the economy forward either in the 1920s or during the recovery of the 1930s. Their progress was steady but nothing remarkable, and the impact of structural change within industry on the economy at large was less important than more broadly based productivity changes. The growth of new industries cannot be compared, at least in its medium-term effects, to investment in housing, which accounted for nearly three-quarters of net capital formation from 1924 to 1937.[19]

[14] B. W. Alford, "New Industries for Old?: British Industry between the Wars", in Floud and McCloskey (eds.), *Economic History of Britain*, ii.

[15] Dowie, "Growth in the Inter-War Period"; N. Buxton, "The Role of the New Industries in Britain during the 1930s: A Reinterpretation", *Business Hist. Rev.*, xciv (1975).

[16] Alford, "New Industries for Old?".

[17] N. von Tunzelman, "Structural Change and Leading Sectors in British Manufacturing, 1907-68", in C. P. Kindleberger and G. Di Tella (eds.), *Economics in the Long View*, 3 vols. (London, 1982), iii.

[18] Buxton, "Role of the New Industries".

[19] C. H. Feinstein, *Domestic Capital Formation in Britain, 1920-38* (Cambridge, 1965); S. Howson, *Domestic Monetary Management in Britain, 1919-38* (Cambridge,

(cont. on p. 113)

III
UNEMPLOYMENT AND THE LABOUR-MARKET

Since no definitions of unemployment or labour force are widely accepted, it is extremely difficult to measure the degree to which the economy failed to provide jobs for all those seeking work during the inter-war years.[20] Perhaps the most acceptable estimate for the average annual rate of unemployment from 1921 to 1938 is just under 11 per cent. Of course that percentage conceals considerable yearly dispersion, with peaks in 1921 and 1931-3.[21] Feinstein's estimates have, moreover, been criticized for both under and overstating the scourge which was, in any case, compounded by rapid growth in the population of working age, in the rate of household formation and by the decline in emigration compared to the decades before the war.[22]

Given two abnormally severe cyclical downswings in economic activity for 1920-1 and 1929-32, as well as the problem of measuring the unemployment, underemployment, seasonal and short-time working experienced by the labour force in the years before 1914, it may well prove impossible to say whether or not the incidence of "unemployment" among men, women and juveniles seeking work increased "markedly" or "moderately" over the 1920s and 1930s.[23]

Fortunately, the information for these two decades is good enough to reveal the degree to which the incidence of unemployment was unequally distributed across locations and industries, among occupations and between sexes and age groups. Unemployment was concentrated among the young, the elderly and those who remained out of work for more than one year.[24] Female participation rates

---

(n. 19 cont.)
1975); D. H. Aldcroft and H. W. Richardson, *Building in the British Economy between the Wars* (London, 1968); Pollard, *Development of the British Economy.*

[20] G. D. N. Worswick (ed.), *The Concept and Measurement of Involuntary Unemployment* (Oxford, 1980).

[21] Feinstein (ed.), *Managed Economy*; S. Howson, "Slump and Unemployment", in Floud and McCloskey (eds.), *Economic History of Britain*, ii.

[22] W. R. Garside, *The Measurement of Unemployment* (Oxford, 1980); T. Hatton, "Excess Demand in the Labour Market, 1861-1939" (paper delivered to cliometrics conference, Warwick, 1977); N. von Tunzelman, "Britain, 1900-45: A Survey", in Floud and McCloskey (eds.), *Economic History of Britain*, ii.

[23] J. A. Garraty, *Unemployment in History* (New York, 1978); Garside, *Measurement of Unemployment*; J. Harris, *Unemployment and Politics: A Study of English Social Policy, 1886-1914* (Oxford, 1972).

[24] Constantine, *Unemployment in Britain between the Wars*; S. Glynn and A. F. Booth, "Unemployment in the Interwar Period: A Multiple Problem", *Contemporary Hist.*, x (1975); Howson, "Slump and Unemployment".

(which varied across regions) reverted to pre-1914 levels, which suggests that unfavourable economic circumstances discouraged women from seeking work outside the home.[25] The data also reveal rates of unemployment well above the national average among the work-forces of "Outer Britain", engaged in large part in old staple export industries such as coal, cotton, steel, shipbuilding and mechanical engineering — industries which had dominated the regional economies of Wales, Scotland and Northern Ireland, as well as the north-east and north-west of England for decades before the Great War.[26]

These broad patterns of unemployment and the interpretation of regional and other variations which appear in the data are not particularly controversial.[27] Keynesians and their critics might also agree that unemployment among the work-force was certainly "higher" than before the war and (the United States and Germany apart) above the modal rates for industrialized countries as a whole.[28] They cannot agree on how much of the unemployment of the period should be classified as cyclical or how much was structural and thus not amenable to the inflation of the economy by governmental action; and the mix varied year by year.[29] It was both, and studies of the development of the British economy over spans of time which transcend the years between the wars have made historians aware that the country's industrial base was adjusting all too slowly to the accelerated erosion of its comparative advantages on world markets.[30] In the wake of global war and the failure of the great powers to reconstruct international economic institutions which might have facilitated a resumption in world trade at traditional rates of growth, Britain's structural problems intensified. Of course there remains a legitimate debate on how far the diplomatic policies pursued by the government of the world's senior trading nation were conducive to the reconstruction of an efficient international economic system.[31] It

[25] S. Constantine, *Social Conditions in Britain, 1918-39* (London, 1983).

[26] S. Glynn and A. F. Booth, "Unemployment in Interwar Britain: A Case for Relearning the Lessons of the 1930s", *Econ. Hist. Rev.*, 2nd ser., xxxvi (1983).

[27] S. Glynn and J. Oxborrow, *Interwar Britain: A Social and Economic History* (London, 1976).

[28] Maddison, *Phases of Capitalistic Development.*

[29] Howson, "Slump and Unemployment"; Glynn and Booth, "Unemployment in the Interwar Period"; W. R. Garside and T. Hatton, "Keynesian Policy and British Unemployment in the 1930s", *Econ. Hist. Rev.*, 2nd ser., xxxvi (1985).

[30] R. S. Sayers, *A History of Economic Change in England, 1880-1939* (Oxford, 1967); W. Ashworth, *An Economic History of England, 1870-1939* (London, 1960).

[31] S. Strange, *Sterling and British Policy* (London, 1971); I. Drummond, *British Economic Policy and Empire* (London, 1972); D. H. Aldcroft, *From Versailles to Wall Street, 1919-29* (London, 1977).

may not be enough to blame the weakness and eventual breakdown of that order on the government of the United States for failing to assume a role in its management commensurate with the increasing power of the American economy.[32]

But that inconclusive discussion will not be reviewed in this paper, which will move on to consider the virulent controversy provoked by the revival of suggestions (made at the time by Pigou and other economists) that a "considerable" share of unemployment during the inter-war years can be blamed on the failure of labour-markets to adjust (as efficiently as they had before 1914) to changes in relative prices and to the continued loss of comparative advantages on world markets.[33] Nominal and real wages became, it is argued, more inflexible after the war and this "wage stickiness" precluded redundant workers from pricing themselves into jobs, eroded profits, discouraged investment and created unemployment. The main legal and institutional changes which are perceived to have constrained labour-markets from operating closer to traditional standards of efficiency include the (war-induced) rise in the share of employees organized in trade unions, rent controls and, above all, the extension of social insurance to provide increasingly generous cover against the vicissitudes of unemployment to over 60 per cent of the work-force.[34] No social historian would deny that pressures on workers seeking employment to accept jobs at lower wages were steadily diminished by state and trade-union action between 1911 and 1920, but the precise influence of these institutional changes upon the record levels of unemployment from 1921 to 1938 remains in dispute.[35]

The posited mechanisms through which increased state "interference" might, in theory, have constrained the capacity of supposedly free labour-markets to achieve higher levels of employment seem familiar enough. First, the dole set a floor, or reference base, for wage bargaining. Secondly, and before the National Insurance Act of 1911 and its amendments altered the basis of labour relations, benevolent employers had been more reluctant to lay off workers in recessions or to experiment with short-time working. As a conse-

[32] C. P. Kindleberger, *The World in Depression, 1929-39* (London, 1973); F. C. Costigliola, "Anglo-American Financial Rivalry in the 1920s", *Jl. Econ. Hist.*, xxxvii (1977).
[33] M. Casson, *Economics of Unemployment: A Historical Perspective* (Oxford, 1983); K. Hancock, "Unemployment and Economists in the 1920s", *Economica*, xxvii (1960).
[34] The argument is set out by D. N. Worswick, "Economic Recovery in the United Kingdom in the 1930s", *Bank of England Panel Paper*, xxiii (1983).
[35] J. Tomlinson, *Problems of British Economic Policy, 1870-1945* (London, 1981).

quence of welfare legislation, union officials (particularly those who managed contributory unemployment insurance on behalf of skilled workers) became less inhibited from pushing wage demands to a point which jeopardized the jobs of their members. Thirdly, and with the spread of national and more aggressive wage bargaining, the traditional function of wage differentials in the reallocation of labour from declining industries and regions, characterized by excess supplies of labour, to expanding sectors of the economy became more attenuated.[36] Price incentives to labour mobility were further weakened by the emergence of rent controls and subsidized housing which cheapened the relative cost of accommodation in depressed areas. Fourthly, unemployment benefits encouraged people of working age both to register themselves as members of the labour force and to spend more time in searching for "acceptable" jobs and rates of pay. Prolonged search activity mitigated the downward pressure of potential labour supplies upon established wage rates and expanded the proportion of workers who fell within the category of what the revisionists now call the "voluntary unemployed".[37]

By far the most important question to investigate is how far institutionally supported stability in wage levels and wage differentials prevented the economy from absorbing a far higher share of the registered work-force from 1921 to 1938. But a secondary (although related) argument which endeavours to link unemployment with social security benefits has certainly captured the headlines. Unfortunately, the data do not permit us to explore this extremely contentious connection over pre-war cycles. Unemployment insurance covering large numbers of workers came on to the statute-book in 1911, and eligibility and benefits under the law were extended during the war and demobilization period.[38] To estimate the initial or even the lagged impact of liberal legislation on labour participation rates and workers' propensities to look longer for acceptable work might well be impossible. But starting from a base-point in 1920, two American economists have asserted that their econometric tests established a positive and significant correlation between changes in the rate of unemployment

---

[36] S. Glynn and S. Shaw, "Wage Bargaining and Unemployment", *Polit. Quart.*, ii (1981).

[37] These arguments are modelled by T. Hatton, "Unemployment Benefits and the Macroeconomics of the Interwar Labour Market", *Oxford Econ. Papers*, xxxv (1983), and discussed by J. Wright, "Britain's Inter-War Experience", in W. A. Eltis and P. J. N. Sinclair (eds.), *The Money Supply and the Exchange Rate* (Oxford, 1981).

[38] N. Buxton and D. I. Mackay, *British Employment Statistics: A Guide to Sources and Methods* (Oxford, 1976).

and the upward movement in the ratio of unemployment benefits to wages for male, female and juvenile employees.[39] But under the critical examination of other econometricians, their claim that *if* 1913 proportions of benefits to wages had been maintained between the wars, then *average* rates of unemployment would in all probability have been reduced by up to one-third has hardly survived as a hypothesis which merits further historical investigation.[40] Furthermore, in dealing with basic facts and with changes in the rules affecting unemployment benefits, Benjamin and Kochin also stand indicted by historians on charges of overestimating the proportion of benefits to wages for a majority of the unemployed, failing to comprehend changes in eligibility affecting female employees from 1929-31 and exaggerating the supposed liberality of the laws and administration of social insurance compared with the years after 1945, when similar ratios of benefits to wages were associated with rates of unemployment of a totally different magnitude.[41] They also failed to understand the special nature of the market for juvenile workers before and after the war.[42] Above all, the direction of causation posited by this assertion — running from the provision of more generous benefits to higher levels of unemployment — probably moved the other way. For example, there can be no mistaking the concern of successive governments with law and order in the 1920s and 1930s, and the high levels of unemployment of those years at the very least precluded serious revisions to the liberal welfare programme

[39] D. K. Benjamin and L. A. Kochin, "Searching for an Explanation of Unemployment in Interwar Britain", *Jl. Polit. Econ.*, lxxxvii (1979); D. K. Benjamin and L. A. Kochin, "Unemployment and Unemployment Benefits in the Twentieth Century: A Reply to our Critics", *Jl. Polit. Econ.*, xc (1984).

[40] S. Broadberry, "Unemployment in Interwar Britain: A Disequilibrium Approach", *Oxford Econ. Papers*, xxxv (1983); P. A. Omerod and D. N. Worswick, "Unemployment in Interwar Britain", *Jl. Polit. Econ.*, xc (1982); M. Collins, "Unemployment in Interwar Britain: Still Searching for an Explanation", *Jl. Polit. Econ.*, xc (1982).

[41] T. Hatton, "Unemployment in Britain between the World Wars", *Univ. of Essex Economics Department Discussion Paper*, cxxxix (1980); D. Metcalf *et al.*, "Still Searching for an Explanation of Unemployment in Interwar Britain", *Jl. Polit. Econ.*, xc (1982); R. Cross, "How Much Voluntary Unemployment in Interwar Britain", *Jl. Polit. Econ.*, xc (1982).

[42] Hatton, "Unemployment Benefits"; Hatton, "Unemployment in Britain between the World Wars"; W. R. Garside, "Juvenile Unemployment and Public Policy between the Wars", *Econ. Hist. Rev.*, 2nd ser., xxx (1977); D. K. Benjamin and L. A. Kochin, "What Went Right with Juvenile Unemployment Policy between the Wars", *Econ. Hist. Rev.*, 2nd ser., xxxii (1979); W. R. Garside, "Juvenile Unemployment between the Wars: A Rejoinder", *Econ. Hist. Rev.*, 2nd ser., xxxvi (1979).

established between 1906 and 1920.[43] Keynesians continue to remark that the dole helped to boost effective demand and thereby contained unemployment within tolerable and politically manageable limits.[44]

The extension of social insurance in the period 1911-20 shifted the problem of unemployment from the domain of household, family and poor law into the realms of public policy and concern.[45] How far the liberal welfare programme seriously exacerbated the problem by giving workers encouragement to malinger, to engage in token registration for employment in order to secure the dole, to substitute leisure for work and to engage in more prolonged search activity remains to be established. At present there is no evidence that anything but a tiny share of unemployment in 1921-38 could have been eradicated, even if British politicians had been prepared to contain the ratio of benefits to wages at 1913 levels. Perhaps "voluntary unemployment" should only appear on an agenda for historical research when the relationship between total numbers of unemployed and registered job vacancies is quite different from the kind of figures now indicated for the inter-war years?

Wage "stickiness" is surely a more important matter. At the time, and again recently, economists argued that high and inflexible wage rates reduced demand for labour. But the wage and price evidence for "stickiness" remains ambiguous, and interpretation depends upon the time-spans selected for detailed analysis. For example, from 1920 to 1923 money wages declined (by what were extraordinary percentages by historical standards) in response to falling prices and the emergence of mass unemployment.[46] But this interlude has been represented as a once-and-for-all adjustment to war and post-war inflation facilitated by the direct and demonstration effects of sliding-scale wage agreements.[47] Britain's experience with wages and prices during and after the war was, moreover, replicated in numerous other industrial countries also moving (via a "restocking" boom and slump)

[43] R. Skidelsky, *Politicians and the Slump: The Labour Government, 1929-31* (London, 1970); F. M. Miller, "The Unemployment Policy of the National Government, 1931-36", *Hist. Jl.*, xix (1976).

[44] Hatton, "Unemployment Benefits"; G. C. Peden, *British Economic and Social Policy: Lloyd George to Margaret Thatcher* (Oxford, 1985).

[45] Tomlinson, *Problems of British Economic Policy*; Peden, *British Economic and Social Policy*.

[46] S. Broadberry, "Nominal and Real Wage Adjustment in Interwar Britain" (paper delivered to cliometrics conference, Oxford, 1984); Wright, "Britain's Inter-War Experience".

[47] J. Dowie, "1919-30 Is in Need of Attention", *Econ. Hist. Rev.*, 2nd ser., xxviii (1975); E. V. Morgan, *Studies in British Financial Policy, 1914-25* (London, 1952).

from war to peacetime economies, and had its historical antecedents in similar adjustments from 1815 to 1819.[48] If we focus upon manufacturing industry for the "true" post-war period (1924-38) and compare annual movements in money wage rates and average annual earnings on the one hand, with the available (but rather unsatisfactory) indices for the prices of manufactured goods and the cost of living on the other, the prima-facie case for "inflexibility" still appears convincing. The impression is one of rather stable nominal wage rates and earnings in a period of falling prices.[49] For those with jobs, standards of living rose throughout the period. Wage "costs" for the industry as a whole also increased steadily, particularly in the 1920s. Finally, the highly skewed distribution of unemployment by region and by industry did not lead to any visible widening of published wage differentials between depressed and prosperous regions or between expanding and contracting industries.[50]

Until far more historical knowledge of how late nineteenth-century labour-markets actually functioned becomes available, it will not be clear how far the "apparent inflexibility" of wages from 1924 to 1938 represented a break with tradition which can be blamed upon the rise of trade unions and the extension of social welfare to a majority of working people.[51] (In any case the share of the work-force in unions declined from 40-45 per cent in 1920 down to 25-30 per cent in 1922 and remained roughly constant for most of the inter-war period.[52]) It is not the case that either the frequency or the amplitude of declines in wage rates and earnings differed from the pre-war cycles from 1885 to 1913 — a period when workers' living standards also rose during conditions of intensified foreign competition.[53] As far as we can generalize from business history, late Victorian and Edwardian firms did not lightly respond to recessions and falling prices by lay-offs and the substitution of cheaper unemployed workers

[48] W. Galenson, "The Labour Force and Labour Problems in Europe, 1920-70", in Cipolla (ed.), *Fontana Economic History of Europe*, v (i); Maddison, "Economic Policy and Performance in Europe".

[49] Broadberry, "Nominal and Real Wage Adjustment"; Worswick, "Economic Recovery in the United Kingdom in the 1930s".

[50] Hatton, "Unemployment Benefits"; Glynn and Booth, "Unemployment in Inter-war Britain".

[51] N. Whiteside, "Welfare Insurance and Casual Labour: A Study of Administrative Intervention in Industrial Employment, 1906-26", *Econ. Hist. Rev.*, 2nd ser., xxxii (1979).

[52] A. G. Hines, "Trade Unions and Wage Inflation", *Rev. Econ. Studies*, xxxi (1964).

[53] Wright, "Britain's Inter-War Experience"; Worswick, "Economic Recovery in Britain in the 1930s".

for their established and trained work-forces.[54] And it could well be that the revisionist view of a labour-market equilibrating historically through changes in wage rates refers (if indeed it encapsulates the experience of any known period) to far earlier phases of British industrialization, to decades well before the rise of trade unions, paternal employers and the emergence of social welfare. For historians, wage behaviour in the inter-war years may have been more normal and perhaps even more flexible than many "neo-classical" theorists suspect.[55] The latter might, however, prefer to occupy safer ground by arguing that the persistent erosion of Britain's traditional competitive advantages and the unusual amplitude of the deflations and recessions witnessed from 1920-1 and again from 1929-32 called for even greater flexibility to slow down the rise of unemployment. Future discussion will then doubtless turn upon the extent of possible and potential demand from firms for workers, compared with hypothetical declines in wage costs. Although some of the more simplistic assertions about the malfunctioning of the labour-market in the inter-war years have been undermined, it would be myopic to reject the revisionist view that lower and more flexible wages might have raised demand for labour and stimulated higher rates of investment, particularly during the 1920s when the share of profits in the net value of industrial output declined.[56] Nevertheless the counterfactual decline in wage rates required to restore the competitiveness of Britain's staple industries to a position where their work-forces expanded and made serious inroads on regional unemployment is probably too unrealistic to contemplate. Finally, no historian has argued that the expansion of new industries or the building boom were impeded by shortages of labour and high wages.[57] On the contrary, the obstacles to even higher rates of expansion in these industries continue to be identified as the relatively slow growth of mass consumer demand.[58] At the moment, the most that should be conceded to the wage-stickiness hypothesis is first, that rather high wages contributed to the deterioration in the competitive position of

[54] D. Baines, "Labour Supply and the Labour Market, 1860-1914", in Floud and McCloskey (eds.), *Economic History of Britain*, ii.
[55] M. Beenstock *et al.*, "Economic Recovery in the United Kingdom in the 1930s", *Bank of England Panel Paper*, xxvii (1983).
[56] Hatton, "Unemployment Benefits"; Broadberry, "Unemployment in Interwar Britain".
[57] B. W. Alford, *Depression and Recovery: British Economic Growth, 1918-45* (London, 1972).
[58] Glynn and Booth, "Unemployment in the Interwar Period".

British industry, 1924-9; and secondly, that a detectable moderation in the growth of money wages provided some but probably minor assistance towards Britain's recovery in the 1930s.[59]

IV

MONETARY, EXCHANGE-RATE AND FISCAL POLICIES

Were the economic policies pursued by British governments for two decades after 1919 more realistic and potentially superior to the prescriptions inspired by Keynes and other critics? Keynesians have long maintained that the monetary and exchange-rate policies implemented between 1921 and 1931 produced an overvalued exchange rate, higher rates of interest, deflation and stringency in money markets, but considerable room remains for debate about the short- and longer-term impact of these policies on output and employment.[60] Moreover recent interpretations of governmental actions during the period's first major boom and slump, 1919-22, are inclined to follow Pigou, who analysed it in terms of an understandable but over-optimistic reaction by businessmen to their perceptions of the scale of pent-up demand for investment and consumer goods.[61] In the aftermath of a major war governments everywhere lacked the power to cut back rapidly on public expenditure or to restrain access to bank credit in order to ensure a more orderly transition to peacetime economies.[62] Nevertheless the experience of high rates of inflation followed by comparable rates of deflation in prices and wages, severe industrial unrest succeeded by rocketing levels of unemployment and an alarming depreciation in the exchange rate, all served to reinforce the predilection of politicians for a speedy return to gold, and strengthened their resolve to persist with restrictive monetary policies, bolstered by historically high real rates of interest over the 1920s.[63]

---

[59] N. H. Dimsdale, "Employment and Real Wages in the Inter-War Period", *National Inst. Econ. Rev.* (Nov. 1985); Beenstock *et al.*, "Economic Recovery in the United Kingdom in the 1930s".

[60] Howson, *Domestic Monetary Management*; S. Pollard (ed.), *The Gold Standard and Employment Policies between the Wars* (London, 1970).

[61] A. C. Pigou, *Aspects of British Economic History, 1918-25* (London, 1974); Dowie, "1919-20 Is in Need of Attention".

[62] S. Howson, "The Origins of Dear Money, 1919-20", *Econ. Hist. Rev.*, 2nd ser., xxvii (1974); C. P. Kindleberger, "Banking and Industry between the Two Wars: An International Comparison", *Jl. European Econ. Hist.*, xiii (1984); Cipolla (ed.), *Fontana Economic History of Europe*, vi (i); W. W. Rostow, *The World Economy: History and Prospect* (London, 1978).

[63] Tomlinson, *Problems of British Economic Policy*; Howson, *Domestic Monetary Management*.

How far their policies restrained the growth of output and employment or inhibited the pace of structural change from 1921 to 1929 is difficult to gauge. In retrospect, the interest rates of that decade are hard to depict as a particularly serious deterrent to domestic investment and, it has been argued, they were necessary in order to attract short-term foreign balances to London, which provided conditions for the resumption of long-term investment overseas, and supported the revival of world trade — upon which Britain's exports and her staple industries ultimately depended.[64] There is, moreover, no good evidence that the availability (as distinct from the price) of bank loans constituted a serious problem for industry, although such evidence is often impossible to pin down.[65]

Was the much-publicized overvalued exchange rate far more of a real handicap? For industries which catered basically for the home market and for industries where a high component of imported raw materials entered into the sales prices of their final outputs, the answer is clearly "no". Even for industries producing exportable goods, the handicap may have been exaggerated and was surely not comparable to persistent decline in the international efficiency of iron and steel, shipbuilding, heavy engineering, coal, textiles and other industries.

Following Keynes, several calculations have been made by economists, which purport to measure the extent of overvaluation implicit in Churchill's 1925 return to gold at the pre-war parity.[66] Their estimates (which essentially compare movements in American and British prices from 1913 to 1925) naturally depend on the indices selected for comparison and not only offer a range of answers but are predicated on the assumption that sterling's parity with the dollar, *circa* 1913, was somehow right for the long-term growth of the economy. The relevant facts seem to be: while sterling definitely appreciated in nominal terms from 1920 to 1929, the "real" exchange rate (that is, the nominal rate adjusted for movements in domestic and foreign prices) went up far less, from 5 per cent to 7 per cent.[67] And this "somewhat over-valued" exchange rate apparently had some advantages. According to the revisionists it operated to restrain upward pressures on wages and prices, intensified competition for British industry at home

[64] Wright, "Britain's Inter-War Experience".

[65] D. K. Shepard, *The Growth and Role of U.K. Financial Institutions, 1880-1962* (London, 1971); D. H. Aldcroft, *The Inter-War Economy, 1919-39* (London, 1970).

[66] D. Moggridge, *British Monetary Policy, 1924-31* (Cambridge, 1972); Howson, *Domestic Monetary Management*.

[67] N. H. Dimsdale, "British Monetary Policy and the Exchange Rate, 1920-38", in Eltis and Sinclair (eds.), *Money Supply and the Exchange Rate*.

and abroad, and may have forced the pace of necessary structural adjustments.[68] They add that Keynesian-style calculations which seek to measure possible losses of exports, of total output and employment, contingent upon an overvalued exchange rate are statistically insecure, do not take into account potential benefits flowing from structural changes, from the substitution of non-tradable for tradable production, nor do they allow for favourable effects on consumption and the growth of the home market, upon which the recovery of 1932-7 was largely based.[69] Given that economists are now a long way from agreement upon what an "efficient" exchange rate for this period might have been, it is becoming more difficult to castigate the policies pursued during the 1920s as being anything other than mildly unhelpful and unimaginative responses to the problem of unemployment.

No sustained arguments have appeared to suggest that the world depression of 1929-32 could have been avoided by well-designed monetary and exchange-rate policies.[70] But the downswing in the United Kingdom was almost certainly exacerbated by its government's decision to maintain the exchange rate (while reducing the bank rate all too gradually — from 6½ per cent in October 1929 to a low point of 2½ per cent in May 1931).[71] In September 1931 (following a run on the pound) the Bank of England abandoned the gold standard. Thereafter the monetary authorities, freed from the obligation to maintain a fixed rate of exchange, attempted to iron out fluctuations in the value of sterling and pursued policies which liberalized credit and reduced nominal interest rates below the levels maintained from 1920 to 1931. Real interest rates fell sharply down to 1933 and the monetary policies of the 1930s have been credited with stimulating and sustaining rapid growth in the British economy from 1932 to 1937.[72] Although the decision to leave gold hardly constituted a policy, and historians agree that cheap money was helpful, there is an unresolved debate on the precise significance to be attached to the government's manipulation of exchange and inter-

---

[68] Wright, "Britain's Inter-War Experience".

[69] D. Moggridge, *The Return to Gold, 1925: The Formulation of Economic Policy and Its Critics* (Cambridge, 1969); Alford, *Depression and Recovery*; Dimsdale, "British Monetary Policy and the Exchange Rate"; T. Thomas, "Aggregate Demand, 1918-45", in Floud and McCloskey (eds.), *Economic History of Britain*, ii.

[70] P. Fearon, *The Origins and Nature of the Great Slump, 1929-32* (London, 1979).

[71] Dimsdale, "British Monetary Policy and the Exchange Rate".

[72] Worswick, "Economic Recovery in the United Kingdom in the 1930s"; S. Howson, "The Management of Sterling, 1932-39", *Jl. Econ. Hist.*, xc (1980).

est rates as factors in Britain's recovery.[73] Compared to 1929-31, the nominal value of sterling certainly fell against the dollar but the "effective rate of exchange" (calculated with reference to a basket of twenty-eight currencies) shows that the pound (after an abrupt fall in 1931) rose to within a few percentage points of its original gold parity.[74] No doubt the government's curbs on long-term investment overseas helped to maintain it at that level. Export prices also declined slightly compared with the prices of Britain's major competitors, and the country's export performance stopped deteriorating in the sense that on falling markets her shares of both total world trade and of trade in manufactured goods ceased to decline.[75] But this "improved" record may be attributed more to imperial policy, bilateral trade agreements and changes in the composition of exports than to any marked increase in the competitiveness of British exports.[76] In any case, the growth of exports was too weak to lead the economy out of recession. Furthermore imports of manufactured goods (which had increased by nearly two-thirds from 1920 to 1929) fell away, but until trade flows are analysed in detail it is difficult to separate out the effects of tariffs, import substitution and the relocation of trade from exchange depreciation *per se*.[77] That particular influence on recovery was almost certainly minor.

While similar judgements do not pertain to cheap money, the Treasury and Bank of England deserve no approbation for pursuing more liberal monetary policies during the 1930s. They were, after all, "forced" off gold, and increases in the money supply and lower interest rates flowed basically from the build-up of foreign-exchange reserves by the banking system and that following in turn from the general decline in interest rates in New York, Paris and other financial centres. Debt conversion operations initiated by the Treasury exercised negligible effects on interest rates.[78] Against that negative view of the Treasury, it can be argued that the insistence on balanced

[73] Beenstock *et al.*, "Economic Recovery in the United Kingdom in the 1930s".

[74] J. Redmond, "An Indicator of the Effective Exchange Rate of the Pound in the Nineteen Thirties", *Econ. Hist. Rev.*, 2nd ser., xxxiii (1980).

[75] Dimsdale, "British Monetary Policy and the Exchange Rate"; Wright, "Britain's Inter-War Experience"; Worswick, "Economic Recovery in the United Kingdom in the 1930s".

[76] I. Drummond, "Britain and the World Economy, 1900-45", in Floud and McCloskey (eds.), *Economic History of Britain*, ii.

[77] F. Capie, *Depression and Protectionism* (London, 1983); A. Cairncross and B. Eichengreen, *Sterling in Decline* (Oxford, 1983).

[78] Beenstock *et al.*, "Economic Recovery in the United Kingdom in the 1930s"; Howson, *Domestic Monetary Management*.

budgets (which precluded government competition for scarce inves-
tible funds) held down interest rates and encouraged rather than
crowded out private capital formation.[79]

Cheaper and more accessible supplies of credit surely formed one
of the conditions for the revival of the economy in 1932-7, but the
econometric evidence now available does not suggest any significant
role for changes in monetary policy.[80] Economists agree that lower
interest rates exercised more positive effects upon investment in
house-building than upon industrial and other forms of capital formation, which remained less responsive to the variations in the costs of
borrowing.[81] Expenditure on the construction of new houses and
related facilities certainly increased sharply some two years before
other forms of investment revived. But the stock of houses had
already grown rapidly over the 1920s and construction had only been
checked, not arrested, by the Great Depression of 1930-2.[82] Four
and a half million new dwellings were erected in Britain between the
wars, and a complete explanation for the observed long swing and
short cycles in house-building would have to include a long list of
"real" supply-side variables such as the price of land, construction
costs and charges for complementary inputs (utilities, furniture and
utensils) and increased competition among building societies; as well
as changes in income, tastes, occupations, social and geographical
mobility on the demand side. The building boom cannot be accounted
for in simple terms as the product of more favourable conditions in
financial markets.[83] Government subsidies and local authority housing programmes were probably at least as important as variations in
interest rates.[84] The pre-eminence of house-building is not in dispute,
but its direct and indirect effects upon the overall growth of employment and output can be exaggerated. In the early 1930s, when
building amounted to only 4-5 per cent of gross domestic product,
the expansion of house-building and related activities probably accounted for no more than 20 per cent of the rise in total employment

[79] Worswick, "Economic Recovery in the United Kingdom in the 1930s"; Beenstock
et al., "Economic Recovery in the United Kingdom in the 1930s".
[80] Thomas, "Aggregate Demand"; T. Thomas, "Econometric History and the
Inter-War Period" (unpublished paper, 1976); but see D. N. Worswick, "The Sources
of Recovery in the U.K. in the 1930s", *National Inst. Econ. Rev.* (Nov. 1985).
[81] Dimsdale, "British Monetary Policy and the Exchange Rate"; Worswick, "Economic Recovery in the United Kingdom in the 1930s".
[82] Aldcroft and Richardson, *Building in the British Economy between the Wars*.
[83] S. Broadberry, "Housebuilding in the 1930s" (paper delivered to the workshop
on the economic history of the inter-war years, Oxford, 1984).
[84] Pollard, *Development of the British Economy*.

in 1932-7. Recovery embraced services, distribution trades and new industries and became too broadly based to be subsumed under a building boom which had, in any case, petered out by 1937.[85]

Finally, the argument that whatever gains accrued to the economy from cheap money simply served to offset the deflationary budgetary policy pursued by successive chancellors from 1929 to 1937 has again been implicitly stated and challenged in recent studies of fiscal policy. Britain seems untypical among major industrial countries in not resorting to public works financed by budget deficits in order to promote recovery from the Great Depression.[86] Of course it has been easy to demonstrate that this particular "Keynesian panacea" for a restoration of "full employment" implied politically unacceptable and economically implausible increases in government expenditure — equivalent according to one calculation to 70 per cent of public revenue for 1932.[87] Other ostensibly more viable schemes for public-works expenditure (proposed at the time by Lloyd George) were not carried out and (even if implemented) would probably have reduced unemployment by rather modest percentages.[88]

The small surpluses (as well as deficits for 1930 and 1931) which appear in the public accounts for the period have led many historians to depict the budget as exercising "fairly neutral" effects on output and employment. That view has, however, been questioned by recent calculations of "full employment surpluses" or "constant employment balances" which are counterfactual concepts designed to reveal what the state's receipts and expenditures would have been if full employment had been maintained. These estimates show that *if* government revenue and expenditure had remained unaffected by unemployment and falls in national income, then its fiscal policies "would have" generated large surpluses, increasing rapidly throughout the Great Depression, but diminishing gradually into deficits associated with rearmament in 1937-8. In terms of these Keynesian indicators, the government's "fiscal stance" for a decade after 1927 emerges as contractionary and (in the circumstances of the time) perverse.[89]

---

[85] Beenstock *et al.*, "Economic Recovery in the United Kingdom in the 1930s".

[86] Maddison, "Economic Policy and Performance in Europe"; E. Lundberg, *Instability and Growth* (New Haven, 1968).

[87] S. Glynn and P. G. A. Howells, "Unemployment in the 1930s: The Keynesian Solution Reconsidered", *Austral. Econ. Hist. Rev.*, xx (1980).

[88] R. Middleton, *Towards the Managed Economy: Keynes, the Treasury and the Fiscal Policy Debate of the 1930s* (London, 1985); Peden, *British Economic and Social Policy*.

[89] R. Middleton, "The Constant Employment Budget Balance and British Budgetary Policy, 1929-39", *Econ. Hist. Rev.*, 2nd ser., xxxvii (1984); S. Howson and D. Winch, *The Economic Advisory Council, 1930-39* (Cambridge, 1977).

Both the indicators themselves and the inferences that might be drawn even from more acceptable measures of the overall effects of budgetary policy have come under attack. First because economists cannot define a single and unambiguous measure of "fiscal stance". Even balanced budgets (actual or counterfactual) are not necessarily "neutral". The impact of fiscal policy depends upon underlying tax and expenditure multipliers as well as variations in the allocation of government expenditures and the composition of its tax revenues.[90] Although fiscal stance might be quantified, the actual impact of changes in taxation and expenditure (fiscal leverage) upon employment and national income is difficult to expose, has not and probably cannot be measured. Bolstered by recent revisions in economic analysis, historians writing about the 1930s are nowadays more wary of dismissing the Treasury view during the period — which maintained that balanced budgets were required to restore business confidence, to attract foreign capital to London, to support cheap money at home and the stability of sterling abroad.[91] To head off tedious reruns of arguments well rehearsed at the time, economic historians will be compelled to construct and to quantify the implications of alternative budgetary policies — with the advantages of counterfactual deficit-financed public works on one side, counteracted in some "specified" degree by higher interest rates, exchange depreciation, and some crowding-out of private investment on the other. At this distance in time they should be historians enough to resist the temptation to cast discussion in terms of a Treasury or Conservative conspiracy to resist the logic and inherent correctness of Keynesian prescriptions.[92]

That line of work is under way and if recent and carefully quantified reassessments of the effects of rearmament in 1936-8 are correct, the case for deficit finance long before 1936 will prove hard to resist.

[90] R. A. Musgrave, *Fiscal Systems* (New Haven, 1969); S. Broadberry, "Fiscal Policy in Britain during the 1930s", *Econ. Hist. Rev.*, 2nd ser., xxxvii (1984); R. Middleton, "The Measurement of Fiscal Influence in Britain in the 1930s", *Econ. Hist. Rev.*, 2nd ser., xxxvii (1984).

[91] Middleton, *Towards the Managed Economy*; G. C. Peden, "The Treasury View on Public Works and Employment in the Interwar Period", *Econ. Hist. Rev.*, 2nd ser., xxxvii (1984).

[92] Middleton, *Towards the Managed Economy*; A. Booth, "The Keynesian Revolution in Economic Policy Making", *Econ. Hist. Rev.*, 2nd ser., xxxvi (1983); G. C. Peden, "Keynes, the Treasury and Unemployment in the Later Nineteen-Thirties", *Oxford Econ. Papers*, xxxii (1980); R. Middleton, "The Treasury in the 1930s: Political and Administrative Constraints for the Acceptance of the New Economics", *Oxford Econ. Papers*, xxxiv (1982).

Approximately one million jobs were created by defence expenditures in the late 1930s, and the major beneficiaries included workers in steel, coal and engineering, who, by and large, resided in depressed areas. Other public-works programmes may not have been nearly as acceptable to business confidence and the employment multipliers for proposed alternative packages of civil construction might have been lower. Nevertheless deficit-financed expenditure on armaments stabilized the economy during the recession of 1937 and reduced unemployment in 1938 by anything up to 40 per cent. Its success (albeit in the short term) establishes a strong presumption that a considerable share of the unemployment in the 1930s was cyclical, not structural, that private investment may not (as the Treasury was prone to assume) have been subject to crowding-out by public-works expenditures and that the budgetary policies pursued from 1927 to 1936 were, to say the least, misconceived.[93]

V

CONCLUSIONS: THE INTER-WAR ECONOMY IN HISTORICAL PERSPECTIVE

Economic history is distinguished from economics by a predisposition to focus upon the long run. When looking at the inter-war years (which for purposes of debate should be defined as the period succeeding the transition to a "normal" peacetime economy but preceeding rearmament for the Second World War), the time-span (1921-37) is short and punctuated by a uniquely severe depression (1929-32). Thus in arguments about the efficacy of governmental policies, inspired by Keynesian and anti-Keynesian conceptions of the period, historians are inclined to bring Britain's structural problems to the fore. The origins of these problems can be traced back to the 1870s and they became serious during the last great international boom of the Liberal era, 1899-1914, when the productivity of British industry failed to grow at all. Britain entered the First World War with an economy specialized upon a narrow range of staple industries, under intensifying threat from foreign competition.

War delayed necessary structural adjustments, promoted industrialization among rival economies and, above all, weakened the institutional and monetary foundations upon which the development of

---

[93] M. Thomas, "Rearmament and Economic Recovery in the Late 1930s", *Econ. Hist. Rev.*, 2nd ser., xxxvi (1983); Garside and Hatton, "Keynesian Policy and British Unemployment in the 1930s"; but cf. Middleton, *Towards the Managed Economy*.

international commerce had prospered for several decades before 1914. At the same time, changes in the age distribution of the population and in participation rates maintained the growth of the work-force well above rates observed for 1911-21. Thus the long-run decline in the natural rate of increase of the population offered little by way of immediate relief from an ever-growing demand for jobs, while emigration ceased to provide anything like as effective a safety-valve for the British labour-market as it had done from 1900 to 1913.

Overcommitment to staple industries rapidly losing their traditional competitive strength on world markets, together with a long-term neglect of investment in the skilled and professional manpower required to establish new comparative advantages in science-based industries, was bound to make growth with full employment difficult to achieve at the best of times. Obviously the times were anything but propitious, yet stagnation was not in evidence. The economy managed to grow and adapt at rates that seem respectable by historical standards. Sadly, its performance was not good enough to arrest the relative decline of manufacturing industry or to provide jobs for much more than 90 per cent of those seeking paid employment over a dozen or so years which fell either side of the Great Depression.

Revised classical notions that trade unions and unemployment benefits prevented the normal operations of competitive labour-markets from securing full employment, albeit at lower and more flexible money wage rates, represent theoretical, even ideological, assertions that seem difficult to pursue into serious historical research. No doubt trade unions prevented some workers from pricing themselves into jobs, and pressures to accept work at any wage had surely been reduced by the liberal welfare legislation of 1911-20. But the supposition that more flexible wages and greater mobility of labour could have raised employment by a substantial percentage has no evidence behind it and is politically naïve.

Other economies blessed with more competitive labour-markets did not provide higher rates of employment than Britain and to focus on labour-markets is surely one-sided.[94] Why are detailed investigations into the rather unimpressive movement of capital and enterprise towards pools of underutilized labour not receiving comparable attention?[95] Furthermore, once in place, social welfare legis-

[94] R. Gordon, "Why US Wage and Employment Behaviour Differs from that in Britain and Japan", *Econ. Jl.*, xcii (1983).
[95] C. H. Lee, *Regional Economic Growth in the United Kingdom since the 1880s* (London, 1971); and C. Heim, "Industrial Organization and Regional Development in Interwar Britain", *Jl. Econ. Hist.*, xxxxiii (1983).

lation and the extension of collective bargaining could not be radically reformed in the politically unstable circumstances of the 1920s and 1930s. Some of the new classical counterfactuals may not be interesting to discuss!

Finally, historians will be struck by how often both Keynesian and anti-Keynesian interpretations of government policies (which nowadays represent the transposition of modern controversies in macro-economics back to the troubled years between the wars) are detached from the political and administrative context of policy-making. Many are also prone to assume a certain omnipotence on the part of a state operating within a highly unstable international economy, which was dislocated in the 1920s by the effects of global war and which failed in the 1930s to escape from the greatest recession in modern history. Given that the present unsettled and contentious status of macro-economic theory makes it far more difficult to analyse and evaluate the impact of monetary, exchange-rate and fiscal policies pursued from 1919 to 1939, historians may be tempted to conclude that actions taken by governments of the day (with the possible exception of their fiscal stance) exercised neither a particularly benign nor (as Keynesians used to maintain) a particularly malign influence on economic growth and employment from 1919 to 1939. Britain's economic problems were historical and deep-rooted. The depressed and unstable state of international commerce implied that liberal economies might stage "recoveries" but could not hope to achieve full employment until they mobilized for war.

St. Antony's College, Oxford   *Patrick K. O'Brien*

266-93

(90) ₅₂₄

8250

0442-N34 ₁₃₂

6310-L60

U.S.   D₂₄

U.K.

[10]

OXFORD BULLETIN OF ECONOMICS AND STATISTICS, 52, 4 (1990)
0305-9049 $3.00

EXPLAINING ANGLO-AMERICAN PRODUCTIVITY DIFFERENCES IN THE MID-TWENTIETH CENTURY*

S. N. Broadberry and N. F. R. Crafts

I. INTRODUCTION

The productivity gap between Britain and other countries, notably the United States, has been much studied for the postwar period (Davies and Caves, 1987; Paige and Bombach, 1959; Prais, 1981; Pratten, 1976). Despite the pioneering work of Rostas (1948a) relatively little systematic attention has been given to Britain's interwar productivity gap with the United States, although it is well-known that there was a large difference in performance.

In this paper we assemble the evidence which is available both on productivity levels and potential determinants of the productivity gap for sectors in which the measurement of relative interwar Anglo-American productivity is likely to be reasonably accurate. In effect, we seek to extend Rostas' original work in two ways, both by quantifying factors likely to be important in explaining inferior British performance and by looking at the movements over time in sectoral productivity ratios.

The data set we have constructed permits a preliminary analysis of the causes of Britain's interwar productivity gap set against the background of standard criticisms of British companies prominent in the business and economic history literature. Inevitably a fuller account will require detailed investigation at the industry level but the approach followed here nonetheless enables a number of conventional beliefs to be shown to be half-truths at best.

II. LABOUR PRODUCTIVITY 1907–48

1. Data

There are a number of existing studies of comparative US/UK labour productivity levels in manufacturing industry. However, since they cover different products, different levels of aggregation and even different concepts

*The authors are grateful to seminar participants at Warwick, Oxford, Essex, Cambridge, Lancaster and York for helpful comments. The usual disclaimer applies.

of labour productivity, it is difficult to establish comparability between studies. In this section we seek to establish comparative productivity levels for 31 industries moving both backwards and forwards in time from the widely accepted estimates of Rostas (1948a) for 1937–35.

Rostas' estimates of comparative productivity levels for 1937/35 are based on a careful matching of information from the UK Census of Production for 1935 and the US Census of Manufactures for 1937. The US Census for 1937 was preferred to the 1935 Census because of the low level of capacity utilization in 1935 (which would have biased the results in favour of the UK), and because it was closer to the much more detailed 1939 Census, which provided additional information. The concept of productivity used where possible by Rostas was physical output per operative, thus avoiding problems of price deflation.

Once we have a reliable base year comparison for 1937/35, it is possible to extend the comparison back in time. We present results for 1929/30, 1925/24 and 1909/07 by extrapolating from 1937/35 using information from the UK Census of Production and from Fabricant (1940, 1942) for the US. The years of comparison are those used by Flux (1933), who compared net output per worker converted at the official exchange rate, now generally regarded as an unacceptable basis of comparison (Paige and Bombach, 1959).

For the UK, indices of real gross output and the number of operatives in 1924 and 1930 based on 1935 are presented in the 1935 Census. For the US, indices of real gross output and the number of operatives for 1925 and 1937 based on 1929 are taken from Fabricant (1942). For the US, extension back further to 1909 used Fabricant's indices of gross output and employment for 1909 based on 1919. Fabricant checked that the indices over the whole period 1899 to 1937 were consistent with the spliced indices. For the UK, extension back to 1907 was achieved by making estimates of physical output per operative for a number of industries, using the 1907 Census, and relating them to 1935 quantities in index number form. Thus we have checks on the end-points for both the US and the UK.

Moving forward in time from 1937/35 to 1947/48, the basic information is taken from Brown (1954) for the UK and Kendrick (1961) for the US. The study by Brown presents indices of real gross ouput and employment for 1948 based on 1935, while the study by Kendrick presents an extension of many of Fabricant's indices for real gross output and employment from 1937 to 1947. In both cases some minor alterations had to be made because of different trends in the number of operatives compared with total employment.

Fortunately, for 1947/48 there is a reliable check for our calculations, since Frankel (1957) presents estimates of physical output per employee for 34 industries for the same years. Frankel used essentially the same methods as Rostas, except that he used output per employee rather than output per operative. However, since adjustments from a per operative to a per

EXPLAINING ANGLO-AMERICAN PRODUCTIVITY DIFFERENCES   377

employee basis are small, Frankel's study provides a useful check. Where figures exist for both studies, we find a high degree of agreement (see Table 2).

We also include in Table 2 the estimates of Paige and Bombach (1959) for 1950, which were based on extrapolations from the UK Census of Production for 1948 and the US Census of Manufactures for 1947. However, Paige and Bombach used net output deflated by purchasing power parity relative prices calculated on a sectoral basis, rather than physical productivity. These estimates are included to show that the use of physical productivity, even at this comparatively late point in time, does not lead to seriously misleading conclusions.

2. RESULTS

In Table 1 we set out our estimates of US/UK comparative labour productivity over the period 1907–48. Industries have been ordered according to the UK 1948 SIC. Clearly there is a great deal of diversity, but nevertheless a number of patterns emerge. First, for most industries there was a widening of the productivity gap across both world wars, as noted by Broadberry (1988). Second, we note that the gap was generally much larger in the heavier industries (numbers 1–15 in our sample) than in the lighter industries (16–31). Using UK employment weights, the average productivity ratio was 2.50 in the heavy industries and 1.67 in the light industries, while using US employment weights the corresponding ratios were 2.57 and 1.72. The finding of a smaller productivity gap in the lighter industries has its counterpart in the trade data used by Crafts and Thomas (1986) to calculate Britain's revealed comparative advantage. In Table 3 we present data on Britain's world market share. We see that on this measure, five of the top six sectors are in the lighter industries (16–31).

Finally, we present in Table 4 figures on the relative productivity of capital, where capital is measured by available horse-power (HP of prime-movers plus that of electric motors driven by purchased electricity).Note that the data here refer to the period 1929–30, since the question on HP was discontinued in the UK after the 1930 Census. Our purpose here is to indicate that a labour productivity gap of this scale cannot be explained by differences in capital. In over half the industries in our sample, capital productivity was higher in the US. This indicates that higher US labour productivity was accompanied by higher multi-factor productivity.

III. RESOURCE CONSTRAINTS AND PRODUCTIVITY DIFFERENCES

1. The Role of Economic Fundamentals

Differences in relative productivity performance in a cross-section of industries can arise in a number of ways. The simplest possibility is that

TABLE 1
Physical Output Per Operative US/UK

	1909/07	1925/24	1929/30	1937/35	1947/48
1. Bricks	2.05	2.34	2.11	1.32	1.77
2. Glass containers		2.07	2.28	2.64	2.15
3. Cement	1.78	2.37	1.67	0.99	1.24
4. Coke & by-products		2.81	3.15	2.36	2.20
5. Soap	2.02	3.12	3.23	2.85	2.92
6. Matches			3.08	3.36	
7. Seedcrushing	1.01	1.82	1.60	1.05	1.00
8. Blast furnaces		4.27	4.80	3.62	4.31
9. Steelworks		2.72	3.25	1.97	2.93
10. Iron foundries		2.10	2.21	1.54	
11. Machinery				2.68	
12. Radios				3.47	
13. Electric lamps				5.43	
14. Motor cars	1.51	5.34	5.69	2.94	2.60
15. Tin cans				5.77	
16. Cotton spinning and weaving		1.59	1.87	1.50	1.87
17. Woollen and worsted	1.34	1.41	1.71	1.31	1.77
18. Rayon		1.68	1.49	1.85	1.93
19. Hosiery		1.55	2.00	1.56	2.17
20. Boots & shoes		1.49	1.55	1.41	1.52
21. Grain milling	1.98	2.01	2.14	1.73	2.35
22. Biscuits		2.99	3.28	3.45	1.98
23. Beet sugar	0.63	1.42	1.22	1.02	0.98
24. Margarine				1.52	
25. Fish curing		0.91	0.66	0.50	1.87
26. Manufactured ice	1.35	2.30	1.83	2.19	0.98
27. Brewing	1.51			2.01	2.73
28. Tobacco	0.59	1.07	1.26	1.60	2.50
29. Paper	2.65	2.47	2.83	2.47	2.41
30. Rubber tyres & tubes		5.52	3.47	2.85	2.76
31. Linoleum & oilcloth				1.70	

adopted as a maintained hypothesis by the early neoclassical analyses of late Victorian Britain (e.g. McCloskey, 1970). In the strictest version of this view it would be supposed that any differences between labour productivity levels in Britain and America in a given industry arose from factor inputs rather than total factor productivity, particularly in capital and material resources to labour ratios. Thus we have for the *i*th industry:

$$\text{RELPROD}_i = f(\text{RELCAP}_i, \text{RELMAT}_i) \qquad (1)$$

EXPLAINING ANGLO-AMERICAN PRODUCTIVITY DIFFERENCES   379

TABLE 2

Ouput Per Operative 1947/48 US/UK

	This study	Frankel	Paige and Bombach
1. Bricks	1.77	1.66	1.97
2. Glass containers	2.15	2.87	2.74
3. Cement	1.24	1.15	1.16
4. Coke & by-products	2.20		
5. Soap	2.92	2.81	2.49
6. Matches		2.48	3.76
7. Seedcrushing	1.00		
8. Blast furnaces	4.31	4.17	4.08
9. Steelworks	2.93		2.69
10. Iron foundries			2.02
11. Machinery			2.21
12. Radios		3.36	4.00
13. Electric lamps			3.56
14. Motor cars	2.60	2.84	4.66
15. Tin cans		4.96	5.61
16. Cotton spinning and weaving	1.87	1.62	2.49
17. Woollen and worsted	1.77		1.85
18. Rayon	1.93		2.26
19. Hosiery	2.17		1.87
20. Boots & shoes	1.52	1.51	1.71
21. Grain milling	2.35	1.94	1.83
22. Biscuits	1.98	2.04	
23. Beet sugar	0.98	1.28	1.48
24. Margarine		1.21	
25. Fish curing	1.87	0.95	
26. Manufactured ice	0.98	0.75	
27. Brewing	2.73	1.98	3.00
28. Tobacco	2.50	3.63	2.51
29. Paper	2.41		3.38
30. Rubber tyres and tubes	2.76	1.76	2.41
31. Linoleum & oilcloth			2.56

where in industry i RELPROD is $(Y/L)_{US}/(Y/L)_{UK}$, RELCAP is $(K/L)_{US}/(K/L)_{UK}$ and RELMAT is $(M/L)_{US}/(M/L)_{UK}$.

A more sophisticated extension of this argument which would still suppose no X-inefficiency or lags in the application of economically profitable production methods might allow for variations in the use of human capital and in home market size. Attention has been drawn to the former by attempts to produce a plausible empirical version of the Heckscher–Ohlin theory of international trade flows (Leamer, 1984). The potential role of the accumula-

TABLE 3
Britain's Revealed Comparative Advantage 1935
UK World Market Share

1. Bricks	
2. Glass containers	0.0709
3. Cement	0.1440
4. Coke & by-products	
5. Soap	0.2462
6. Matches	0.0282
7. Seedcrushing	
8. Blast furnaces	
9. Steelworks	
10. Iron foundries	
11. Machinery	0.2177
12. Radios	
13. Electric lamps	
14. Motor cars	0.1717
15. Tin cans	
16. Cotton spinning and weaving	0.3767
17. Woollen and worsted	0.5832
18. Rayon	0.0842
19. Hosiery	
20. Boots & shoes	0.2192
21. Grain milling	
22. Biscuits	
23. Beet sugar	0.0479
24. Margarine	
25. Fish curing	
26. Manufactured ice	
27. Brewing	0.1218
28. Tobacco	0.3546
29. Paper	
30. Rubber tyres & tubes	0.2569
31. Linoleum & oilcloth	

tion of human capital is also suggested by modern versions of neoclassical growth theory which seek to allow for the observed persistence of different levels and rates of growth of per capita income in the world (Lucas, 1988). Differences in the length of production runs are widely held to allow higher productivity in America than in Europe (Pratten, 1976) and market size can be expected to affect plant size and proximity to minimum efficient scale (Scherer *et al.*, 1975). This augmented version of the first hypothesis results as:

$$RELPROD_i = f(RELCAP_i, RELMAT_i, RELHUMCAP_i, RELMKT_i) \ (2)$$

with definitions of variables analogous to those in (1).

TABLE 4
Relative Productivity of Labour (Y/L) and Capital (Y/K), US/UK

	Y/L 1937/35	Y/K 1929/30
1. Bricks	1.32	0.67
2. Glass containers	2.64	1.25
3. Cement	0.99	0.38
4. Coke & by-products	2.36	0.67
5. Soap	2.85	2.00
6. Matches	3.36	0.83
7. Seedcrushing	1.05	0.45
8. Blast furnaces	3.62	{1.25}
9. Steelworks	1.97	
10. Iron foundries	1.54	0.71
11. Machinery	2.68	1.43
12. Radios	3.47	2.00
13. Electric lamps	5.43	3.33
14. Motor cars	2.94	1.00
15. Tin cans	5.77	2.00
16. Cotton spinning and weaving	1.50	1.11
17. Woollen and worsted	1.31	0.67
18. Rayon	1.85	0.91
19. Hosiery	1.56	0.55
20. Boots & shoes	1.41	0.83
21. Grain milling	1.73	1.00
22. Biscuits	3.45	1.67
23. Beet sugar	1.02	0.50
24. Margarine	1.52	
25. Fish curing	0.50	0.13
26. Manufactured ice	2.19	1.25
27. Brewing	2.01	
28. Tobacco	1.60	
29. Paper	2.47	1.00
30. Rubber tyres & tubes	2.85	2.00
31. Linoleum & oilcloth	1.70	

2. Data

In Table 5 we present data on economic fundamentals. Dealing first with material resources, we use the US/UK ratio of fuel costs per operative from the UK Census of Production for 1935 and the US Census of Manufactures for 1937 converted at a purchasing power parity of £1 = $4.94 (Rostas 1948a, Table 2). Frankel (1957) and Melman (1956) both estimate that for the 1940's the ratio of unit fuel costs to average hourly wage rates was substantially higher in the UK than in the US.

TABLE 5

Fundamentals and the Productivity Gap

	Relative productivity US/UK 1937/35	Fuel costs per operative US/UK 1939/35	HP per operative US/UK 1929/30	Average annual earnings of operatives US/UK 1937/35	White collar share of employment US/UK 1939/35	Size of industry US/UK 1939/35	Growth of output 1924–35 UK (% pa)	Growth of output 1925–37 US (% pa)
1. Bricks	1.32	2.19	2.0	1.40	1.93	0.4	4.1	−3.9
2. Glass containers	2.64	2.70	2.0	2.14	1.05	4.8	4.4	5.7
3. Cement	0.99	1.20	2.4	1.59	0.82	2.2	5.2	−2.7
4. Coke & by-products	2.36	3.03	3.0	2.06	1.50	3.8	0.6	0.6
5. Soap	2.85	2.64	1.6	2.53	1.09	2.7	3.3	2.0
6. Matches	3.36	3.91	4.0	1.76	0.85	4.8	0.6	
7. Seedcrushing	1.05	2.23	2.6	0.96	1.18	1.4		
8. Blast furnaces	3.62	3.27	{1.3}	2.08	1.41	4.4	−1.3	0.4
9. Steelworks	1.97	1.72		2.11	1.16	3.9	0.7	1.4
10. Iron foundries	1.54	2.58	2.2	2.01	1.22	2.5	3.2	1.4
11. Machinery	2.68	2.36	2.0	2.23	1.38	4.9	1.1	1.4

Continued overleaf

#	Industry								
12.	Radios	3.47	1.90	{1.7}	1.85	{1.00}	5.6	{5.6}	1.9
13.	Electric Lamps	5.43	2.35		1.94		6.8		6.3
14.	Motor cars	2.94	2.57	2.9	2.17	1.01	9.2	8.2	
15.	Tin cans	5.77	5.01	2.8	2.43	1.58	10.1		
16.	Cotton spinning and weaving	1.50	2.43	1.6	1.83	1.29	2.8	−2.2	0.5
17.	Woollen and worsted	1.31	2.28	1.9	2.21	1.13	1.0	0.8	0.5
18.	Rayon	1.85	1.27	1.6	1.52	0.76	2.2	15.8	18.6
19.	Hosiery	1.56	2.27	3.0	1.96	0.90	3.2	3.3	4.5
20.	Boots & shoes	1.41	1.62	1.8	1.71	1.15	2.9	1.8	2.4
21.	Grain milling	1.73	0.23	3.4	1.50	1.28	1.9	1.2	−1.4
22.	Biscuits	3.45	3.04	2.2	2.19	1.11	2.9	5.9	1.8
23.	Beet sugar	1.02	1.59	2.4	1.56	1.35	2.9	6.7	1.5
24.	Margarine	1.52	2.03		2.15	1.83	1.0		
25.	Fish curing	0.50	2.94	8.0	1.61	0.61	0.2	−3.4	4.8
26.	Manufactured ice	2.19	3.07	1.9	1.36	3.77	24.9	0.1	−1.3
27.	Brewing	2.01	1.94		2.14	1.92	1.5	−1.9	22.6
28.	Tobacco	1.60	1.25		1.24	0.53		2.9	3.1
29.	Paper	2.47	1.38	2.5	1.77	1.85	5.2	4.9	4.0
30.	Rubber tyres & tubes	2.85	1.86	1.5	2.64	1.11	8.5	9.2	−0.6
31.	Linoleum & oilcloth	1.70	1.61		2.27	1.16	1.6	3.1	1.0

If we assume a fixed capital stock, we might expect high fuel prices in the UK to lead to substitution of labour for fuel, and thus to lower measured labour productivity. The effect of high fuel prices on labour productivity would not be unambiguous if we relaxed the assumption of a fixed capital stock and allowed substitution of capital for fuel. However, we do not regard this as an important effect here, since capital per worker was also much higher in the US.

We have already indicated in Section II that the labour productivity gap is too large to be explained by capital. Nevertheless we may expect capital per worker to play some role in explaining the productivity gap. Thus in Table 5 we present data on horse-power per operative for 1929/30. In fact, it is possible to calculate HP per operative for the US in 1939 as well as 1929. Rostas (1948a) notes that it makes little difference whether the 1929/30 or 1939/30 estimates are used. The capital/labour ratio was substantially higher in the US, but the capital/output ratio (the inverse of capital productivity, given in Table 4) was not.

Turning to human capital, research at the NIESR, particularly since the work of Prais (1981) has shown that in recent years deficient education and training of workers on the shopfloor, from foremen downwards, has had a major impact in holding back British productivity levels relative to those in Germany and America. The differences in approaches to technical and vocational training highlighted by the NIESR are longstanding, and as recent critics have noted (Barnett, 1986, Ch. 11; Sanderson, 1988) the interwar British economy seems to have been poorly served despite the rapid growth of provision in the quarter century before the First World War.

In practice, measuring human capital is difficult, and neoclassical studies have typically taken the short cut of assuming that factors are paid their marginal products, so that higher wage rates can be taken as indicative of higher levels of human capital. This is the procedure used by Denison (1967) and Matthews *et al.* (1982). Thus we present in Table 5 data on US/UK relative earnings per operative from the UK Census of Production for 1935 and the US Census of Manufactures for 1937. The data have been converted to a common currency using a purchasing power parity of £1 = $4.94 from Rostas (1948a, Table 2). Note that a stock measure of human capital would only differ from our flow measure if there was a difference in the discount rate between the two countries. Earnings may well be an imperfect measure of human capital, affected by distortions in the labour market. Therefore, in addition, we provide data on the white collar share of employment on a relative US/UK basis. This includes administrative, scientific and clerical workers, and hence is far from an ideal indicator of human capital. Data are from the Census of Production and the Census of Manufactures.

Data on relative market size, measured by gross output, are taken from Rostas (1948a, Table 18). Frankel (1957) argues that making an adjustment for net exports does not make much difference for the period 1947/48, and it seems likely that this would be even more true for the 1930's, when trade was severely restricted by tariffs. US market size was larger in most industries, and substantially so in many.

Growth in demand might also be expected to affect productivity levels. This point is emphasized by Frankel (1957, Ch. 7) who elaborates an 'early start' explanation for Britain's relative economic decline. With slower growth of demand in the UK, the capital stock grew more slowly, thus raising the average age of capital. As well as age and quality differences in the capital stock, Frankel also emphasizes technical interrelatedness. Without fast growing demand, investment occurs only as replacement rather than expansion, and if only part of a plant is being replaced, it may not be possible to use the most modern technology. Data on annual growth rates for UK industries over the period 1924–35 are calculated from the 1935 Census of Production. In addition we provide in Table 5 data on US growth 1925–37 from Fabricant (1942). The slower growth in a large number of US industries reflects the severity of the Depression of the 1930's.

IV. COMPETITION, CONTROL AND THE ANGLO-AMERICAN PRODUCTIVITY GAP

1. Britain's Response to the Second Industrial Revolution

By 1929, measured on a purchasing power parity basis, real GDP per hour worked in the United States is estimated to have been 58 percent above that in Britain, having been roughly equal to the British level some 50 years earlier (Feinstein, 1988, p. 4). As Section II established, the labour productivity gap in industry was considerably wider than this and it is in this sector that any British 'failure' is likely to have been mainly located. The immediate reason for relatively poor industrial productivity in Britain appears to be closely related to a failure to achieve a comparable acceleration in productivity growth in the years when the advances of the 'Second Industrial Revolution' came to full fruition. While for the UK TFP growth in manufacturing rose from 0.6 percent per year in 1873–1913 to 1.9 percent in 1924–37 (Matthews *et al.*, 1982, p. 229), in the United States TFP growth in manufacturing rose from 0.7 percent in 1889–1909 to 5.3 percent in 1919–29 and 2.0 percent in 1929–37 (David, 1989, Table 2).

A number of factors have been identified in the literature as contributing significantly to American manufacturing productivity pre-eminence in the interwar period. First, Chandler (1980) has stressed the American lead in the development of large, vertically-integrated, multi-unit firms using large batch and continuous-process technologies of mass production culminating in new modes of internal management organization and hierarchy such as the multi-divisional company.

Second, there is a widespread tendency to be critical of the quality of British management across the economy as a whole and not just in cases where Chandleresque gains were to be obtained. For example, Gourvish in his recent survey of business histories concluded that 'training for management was rare and recruitment could be astonishingly casual' (1987, p. 26) while 'the "club" atmosphere of most boardrooms was a key factor influencing attitudes to organizational change ... even large companies retained a cosy amateurishness' (1987, p. 34). Keeble documents the lack of interest in business studies graduates and the preference for 'good chaps' in management recruitment (1984, pp. 140, 146, 196). Hannah (1983) points to a substantial number of cases of poor managerial response to strategic and organizational needs between the wars, including Associated Electrical Industries, Cadbury-Fry, Distillers, GKN, Morris Motors, Tube Investments and Vickers. Detailed productivity studies from the early postwar years tend to confirm this picture. The reports of the Anglo-American Council on Productivity summed up in AACP (1952) found unsatisfactory management practices lowering productivity in virtually all the industries they studied and found American managers on average to be more vigorous, much more cost-conscious and methodical. Dunning found American managed companies operating in the UK to be superior to their British managed counterparts in each of the ten industrial groups by 34 percent on average (1958, p. 181).

Third, the United States productivity surge was based to a considerable extent on an imaginative and relatively flexible approach to the possibilities of the electric unit drive in factory layout and materials handling (Devine, 1983, pp. 363–65). Factory electrification may have accounted for as much as nearly half of the 1920's productivity surge in the United States (David, 1989, p. 27).

Fourth, British firms appear to have been less committed to R & D than American ones. For example, relatively few large British manufacturing firms had their own research laboratories (Mowery, 1986, p. 192). In fact the British R & D effort appears to have been heavily skewed to relatively few firms doing a few relatively large projects. For example, in 1930 ICI appears to have done around 30% of all British R & D and spent half their total on oil-from-coal (Edgerton, 1987, pp. 89, 100). Relatively few British firms developed the in-house competence fundamental to technological success in a world of firm-specific cumulative developments (Patel and Pavitt, 1988).

Fifth, it has been emphasized in much recent labour history that British firms tended to exercise less management control of work practices and to concede a relatively large part of job control to workers, suggesting a different outcome to bargaining over work effort in the two countries. Particularly in the engineering sector, characterized by family firms and fragmented employers' organizations, managerial strategies with regard to job control steered away from large scale investment, deskilling and systematic management (Zeitlin, 1983, pp. 25–26; 1987, pp. 173–75). Similarly, Lewchuk (1987) argues that British motor manufacturers, anticipating a non-cooperative strategy on the part of their workers if they incurred the high sunk costs of following the Fordist capital intensive, high-throughput labour intensive methods with payment by day rates, adopted low-throughput labour intensive methods with payment by piece rates.

The contrast between Britain and America should not be overdone. Thus, by 1939 some 250 British firms had adopted Bedaux techniques of managerial control (Littler, 1982, p. 114) and the general movement towards the bureaucratization of employment and full development of control within an institutionalized internal labour market came only in the years after 1935 in the United States (Jacoby, 1986). Nevertheless the overall outcome seems to have been a relatively large degree of overmanning in the UK — more than half the Anglo-American Council on Productivity reports found such problems.

This catalogue of alleged failings in Britain leading to the interwar productivity gap raises the question 'why were the problems so persistent?' In other words, if there was a failure in terms of potentially avoidable productivity shortfall, persuasive reasons must be found for the inability of market forces and/or governments to eliminate them. Several factors appear likely to have played an important part in preventing the rapid elimination of poor performers in British industry.

First, as already noted in Section IV competitive pressures were often rather weak in interwar Britain and market sharing and pricing agreements were encouraged rather than resisted by Government. By 1943 there were 2,500 Trade Associations compared with 500 in 1919 and up to 60 percent of manufactured output may have been produced in cartels (Gribbin, 1978, p. 24). Market sharing agreements are widely perceived to have allowed inefficient plants to remain in production and indeed the role of the cotton yarn spinners' cartel in retarding structural rationalization was cited as a major reason for its abolition by the Restrictive Practices Cour in its landmark decision following the 1956 Restrictive Practices Act (Scherer *et al.*, 1975, p. 169).

Second, capital market disciplines on company management were still very weak. As Hannah (1974) points out, the hostile takeover bid did not really emerge until the 1950's and the asymmetries of information (inherent in the companies legislation of the period) between incumbent management and others meant that shareholder monitoring of management performance was a very weak constraint at best. Ownership and control of firms in Britain generally remained in the hands of founding families and mergers tended to lead to loose federations of autonomous family enterprises (Chandler, 1980).

Third, in many sectors there were still quasi-rents to be earned on old equipment, particularly in declining industries, as Salter emphasized in his famous (1960) study. The process of exit of old-vintage plants could therefore be rationally slow and the proportion of output not produced with best-practice techniques could remain high for lengthy periods. In terms of the Salter model (1960, pp. 58–60), fast growth of demand in America, prior to the Great Depression, would have tended to reduce the average age of the capital stock. Relative factor prices would also have influenced the standard of adolescence, and as Salter pointed out (1960, pp. 67–73) the high level of real wages in the United States would be expected to have reduced the extent of the tail of low productivity plants. In addition, it has been suggested that in the steel industry, in particular, British wage bargaining institutions, by in effect lowering wage costs for the least efficient, seriously slowed down the exit of high cost producers (Wilkinson, 1989). This is consistent with the findings of Rostas (1948b, pp. 35–36) for a number of other industries. Given the existence of long tails of relatively high cost plant in a given sector, the scope for cartels to harm productivity was probably significantly enhanced.

Fourth, government motivations were frequently such as fatally to flaw attempts at rationalization as producer interests realized the weaknesses of the government's strategic position in bargaining with the industries concerned. Studies of government or government agency policy in cotton (Bamberg, 1988), coal (Supple, 1987) and steel (Tolliday, 1987) have seen politicians as lacking the incentive to promote productivity improvement. Indeed, the macroeconomic strategy of the Treasury — which involved raising prices relative to wages on a once and for all basis by depreciation of the pound, cartel-pricing and tariffs whilst signalling fiscal rectitude and a long-run non-inflationary monetary policy (Booth, 1987) — was conducive in general to shifting bargains over work effort towards lowered productivity outcomes (Broadberry and Crafts, 1990). The industrial climate was rather different from that of the Thatcherite 1980's.

To the extent that product and/or capital market conditions were such as to allow the persistence of failure, we may expect barriers to entry, collusion and strong unions to be important determinants of relatively weak productivity performance in British industry. In practice it would be difficult to argue that factor endowments are totally unimportant, which leads us to the more eclectic equation (3), in which the arguments of both the market failure and factor endowments schools are subsumed:

$$RELPROD_i = f(RELCAP_i, RELMAT_i, RELHUMCAP_i, RELMKT_i, \\ CR3_i, TARIFF_i, UNION_i) \tag{3}$$

where CR3 is the three-firm concentration ratio, TARIFF is the tariff rate and UNION is union density. Such a specification is inevitably *ad hoc* and may well fail to do justice to a failure of competitive forces hypothesis. Market power depends on barriers to entry or the degree of contestability of the market, which we can expect to depend on the existence of sunk costs on precommittments by incumbent producers rather than on market structure *per se*. This suggests that a regression approach to relative productivity is likely to require augmentation by case studies if the role of obstacles to competitive forces is to be adequately understood. This is indeed our research strategy in what follows.

2. Data

To complement Table 5, we present in Table 6 data relating to Britain's weak response to the challenge of the Second Industrial Revolution in America as a determinant of labour productivity. One reflection of this might be the use of suboptimal plants in the UK. Rostas (1948a) presents data on the distribution of plant size between small (< 100 employees), medium (100–999) and large (≥ 1,000), as well as average plant size. However, we simply report in Table 6 summary information on the US/UK ratio of average plant sizes, from Rostas (1948a, Table 18).

Building on popular belief, Elbaum and Lazonick (1986) have recently emphasized the persistence of small-scale production in Britain despite the switch-over to large-scale high-throughput production methods in America. However, as can be seen from Table 6, this picture is very misleading outside the unrepresentative sample of industries examined by Elbaum and Lazonick. Indeed, in some sectors such as soap, seedcrushing, grain milling, manufactured ice, average British plant size was four or five times the average American plant size.

The rest of our variables attempt, albeit imperfectly, to quantify distortions to the competitive environment in Britain, and are therefore collected on a UK-only basis rather than on a comparative basis. We would expect these variables to be detrimental to productivity only in particular historical circumstances, as suggested in Section IV.1.

Perhaps the most obvious quantitative measure of product market power is the three-firm employment concentration ratio, taken from Leak and Maizels (1945, Appendix 3). However, we would not expect this to be a good measure of the impact of market power on productivity, firstly because in the interwar period collusion was more important than concentration (Rees, 1922; Levy, 1927; Lucas, 1937) and secondly because recent work in industrial organization has stressed that we cannot assume that a high degree of concentration necessarily implies a high degree of market power.

In an open economy such as Britain, the level of protection can also be used as an indicator of barriers to competitive pressures for efficiency. The basic source for tariff levels is Hutchinson (1965, Appendix A). In general, the evidence of Table 6 suggests that protection was geared more to the poor-performing heavy industries. This appears to be consistent with the most recent work on effective protection (Kitson *et al.*, 1989).

Our final column in Table 6 attempts to capture the bargaining power of labour, using figures on trade union density from Bain and Price (1984). Although an attempt has been made by Burkitt (1973) to disaggregate the metals and engineering sector, it is clear that members of multi-industry unions have been assigned to sectors arbitrarily, so these estimates have been disregarded (Bain and Price, 1980, pp. 17–18).

TABLE 6
The Challenge/Response Mechanism

	Relative productivity US/UK 1937/35	Average plant size US/UK 1939/35	3-Firm employment concentration UK 1935 (%)	Nominal rate of protection UK 1935 (%)	Trade union density UK 1935 (%)
1. Bricks	1.32	0.48	14		10.7
2. Glass containers	2.64	1.37	39	20	21.7
3. Cement	0.99	1.17	66		10.7
4. Coke & by-products	2.36	1.70	17		⎫
5. Soap	2.85	0.24	70	20/30	⎬ 13.6
6. Matches	3.36	1.72	89		⎪
7. Seedcrushing	1.05	0.18	79		⎭
8. Blast furnaces	3.62	0.80	35	33 1/3	⎫
9. Steelworks	1.97	3.78	22	33 1/3	⎪
10. Iron foundries	1.54	0.71	18	33 1/3	⎬ 26.9
11. Machinery	2.68	0.48	26	20	⎪
12. Radios	3.47	0.66	41	20	⎪
13. Electric lamps	5.43	0.89	67	20	⎭

Continued overleaf

14.	Motor cars	2.94	1.49	24	33 1/3	26.9
15.	Tin cans	5.77	0.74	45		
16.	Cotton spinning and weaving	1.50	2.11	13	20	51.2 }
17.	Woollen and worsted	1.31	1.74	6	20	25.1 }
18.	Rayon	1.85	0.90	80	20	14.5
19.	Hosiery	1.56	1.01	10	20	58.2
20.	Boots & shoes	1.41	1.52	9		
21.	Grain milling	1.73	0.26	34		
22.	Biscuits	3.45	0.22	37		
23.	Beet sugar	1.02	0.49	72		
24.	Margarine	1.52	0.31	72		19.1
25.	Fish curing	0.50	0.81	10		
26.	Manufactured ice	2.19	0.19	26		
27.	Brewing	2.01	0.64	16	20	17.9
28.	Tobacco	1.60	0.38	66		
29.	Paper	2.47	0.85	20	20	30.9
30.	Rubber tyres & tubes	2.85	1.41	76	20	13.9 }
31.	Linoleum & oilcloth	1.70	1.45	64		13.9 }

V. RESULTS

In Table 7 we list and describe the variables which we use to explain Britain's productivity gap. In addition, we report simple correlation coefficients between relative productivity and each of the explanatory variables. However, simple correlations may be misleading, so in Table 8 we present results

TABLE 7
Simple Correlation with US/UK Productivity Level

Variable	Description	r
RELMAT	US/UK fuel per worker	0.55
RELCAP	US/UK HP per worker	−0.25
RELHUMCAP	US/UK average earnings	0.47
RELMANAGE	US/UK white collar share of employment	0.04
RELMKT	US/UK gross output	0.41
RELPLANT	UK/UK plant size	−0.041
CR3	UK 3 firm employment concentration	0.19
TARIFF	UK nominal tariff	0.18
UNION	UK union density	0.074

TABLE 8
US/UK Productivity Level Regressions
All Variables Measured in Natural Logarithms
Dependent Variable: RELPROD
Estimation Method: OLS

	Equation 1		Equation 2		Equation 3	
	Coefficient	(Standard error)	Coefficient	(Standard error)	Coefficient	(Standard error)
RELMAT	0.090	(0.13)	0.11	(0.13)		
RELCAP	−0.11	(0.20)	−0.067	(0.20)		
RELHUMCAP	0.77	(0.35)	1.04	(0.37)	0.99	(0.32)
RELMKT	0.33	(0.082)	0.26	(0.090)	0.30	(0.078)
RELPLANT			−0.11	(0.099)		
CR3			0.18	(0.11)	0.17	(0.090)
UNION			0.14	(0.20)		
CONSTANT	−0.12	(0.30)	−1.33	(0.95)	−0.80	(0.37)
$\bar{R}^2$	0.591		0.619		0.648	
SE	0.354		0.342		0.328	
N	27		27		27	
					$F(4, 19) = 0.364$	

of regression of the US/UK relative productivity level on the set of variables listed in Table 7. All reported equations are in logarithmic form, which ensures that the fitted values of the dependent variable remain positive.

It is clear that the simplest neoclassical model, using only fuel and capital would not be sufficient to explain the variation in the productivity gap observed in our sample. In fact, we see from equation 1 in Table 8 that market size and human capital (proxied by earnings) are the key ecomomic fundamentals. If the white collar share of employment is used as the human capital proxy, although market size remains important, human capital becomes statistically insignificant and wrongly signed. The important role for market size would be expected on the basis of the emphasis in the existing literature (e.g. Frankel, 1957).

The correct interpretation of the human capital (relative earnings) variable merits further discussion. First, it might be argued that the earnings variable merely picks up the extra rewards given to employees in recognition of high productivity outcomes (what might be called the reverse causality argument). We believe the balance of evidence allows us to reject this claim. Salter himself was unequivocal on this point (1960, pp. 156–57), noting that wage changes were a general phenomenon, not correlated with productivity changes in the period 1924–50. The inference is that industries competed in the market for labour and that different average earnings levels reflected the different composition of the labour force by industry with respect to human capital. Second, it is possible that the effects of trade union bargaining distort our measurement of human capital. However, in general we would expect there to be two effects, which tend to offset each other, working through movements along the demand curve for labour (through the union wage differential leading to higher capital/labour ratios) and also through an inward shift of the labour demand curve if trade union presence leads to restrictive practices. Both these claims are frequently advanced in the historical literature. Third, the finding that inputs of human capital are a reason for America's superior labour productivity would be consistent with the Crafts and Thomas (1986) finding that Britain's comparative advantage lay in goods which required relatively little human capital. On balance, it seems to us to be reasonable to accept the human capital interpretation of the regression results, but it would be as well to keep the above qualifications in mind.

The second equation in Table 8 adds the variables relating to organization, including plant size as well as the competition variables. Note that we cannot report results for the inclusion of tariffs in a logarithmic specification, since tariffs were zero in some industries. However, in a linear specification, the tariff variable was insignificantly negative. The addition of these organizational variables improves the performance of the equation in terms of reducing the standard error and increasing the adjusted coefficient of determination. However, a number of the variables have very little explanatory power.

Hence we also report a third equation in Table 8, removing variables with little explanatory power. This is our preferred equation, which explains the variation in the productivity gap across our sample in terms of human capital, market size and concentration. The F-test for equation 3 against equation 2 is easily satisfied.

As has been argued in Section IV, regression analysis cannot be expected to reveal the sources of productivity failures arising through obstacles to the elimination of high cost producers. For example, we have emphasized that market power may be damaging to productivity, but recent work in industrial organization has stressed that a high concentration ratio does not necessarily imply a high degree of market power. In looking for evidence of the weakness of competitive forces we have been guided by the pattern of the residuals from equation 3 in Table 8. A large positive residual (more than one standard error of the equation) indicates an unexpectedly poor UK performance, given the values taken by the explanatory variables. We found large positive residuals for blast furnaces, tin cans, electric lamps, bricks and biscuits. A large negative residual indicates an unexpectedly, good UK performance, which we found in cement, beet sugar, and rubber tyres and tubes.

VI.   CASE STUDIES

It was noted in Section II that Britain's productivity performance around mid-century varied substantially across sectors with a general tendency for the worst results to be found in the heavier industries. More precisely the raw data suggest food, drink and tobacco and textiles/clothing as the least bad performers relative to the United States. Broadberry and Fremdling in their contribution show that a broadly similar pattern exists when comparisons are made with Germany. The variability of industrial performance potentially provides useful information and also sets an important research agenda where, if the roles of competitive pressures and factor endowments are to be understood, detailed case studies will be required — as has become more apparent since the retreat from the structure-conduct-performance paradigm in industrial economics. In this section we present some initial observations arranged into industrial sub-divisions.

1. Non-Metalliferous Mining Products

Performance in this sector was highly variable, whether seen in terms of the raw data or guided by the regression results. Cement appears as a very good performer, with productivity slightly higher than that in the United States and with a negative residual of more than one standard error. Bricks, although not having an obviously weak performance on the raw data, has a large positive residual in the regression and from Tables 5 and 6 we note that this comes from the relatively large size of the British output levels in the mid-1930's, the low value of CR3 and lowish relative earnings ratio. Both cement and bricks

EXPLAINING ANGLO-AMERICAN PRODUCTIVITY DIFFERENCES   395

had high output growth in Britain in 1924–35 while suffering big output falls in the United States in 1925–37 reflecting the very different situation in housebuilding and construction in the two countries. In cement in Britain costs fell by about 40 percent between 1925–35 in a period of rapid technical change and intense competition which resulted in the elimination of old vintages of capital (Cook, 1958, p. 93). A collusive agreement fixing prices and quotes was made in 1934 with adverse long-term consequences (Scherer *et al.*, p. 169) but was made at a point where there was no long tail of low productivity firms, as Rostas' data on prime costs in the industry makes clear (1948b, p. 188).

2. Chemicals and Allied Industries

In chemicals, concentration levels were very high except in coke, relative human capital is unhelpful to coke and soap and market size is relatively small in matches. Soap is an interesting case (with a substantial secondary literature) where the productivity gap narrowed somewhat during the 1930's. At this time entry by the American firm Procter and Gamble seems to have put pressure on the dominant home firm Lever's which embarked on a major rationalization programme cutting out by 1939 38 of the 49 factories operating in 1929 (Cohen, 1958, p. 257).

3. Metals and Engineering

The metals and engineering sector perhaps comes closest to confirming the traditional picture of small scale British firms producing at much lower productivity levels than abroad. Here, in particular, market size in the United States was generally much larger than in Britain and earnings levels were also relatively high. Electric lamps, tin cans and blast furnaces are all cases where the regression results indicate 'unusually' bad performance and in each case collusion and barriers to entry appear to have played an important part. In tin cans competition was essentially suppressed by Metal Box which in 1931 successfully forced the American Can Company out of the British market aided by an agreement with the Continental Can Company of America to use their processes, equipment and methods. Dominance was enforced through long term leasing for can closing machines. In steel, high tariff protection was granted and government hoped for rationalization under the auspices of the British Iron and Steel Federation. Worries about unemployment meant that elimination of the tariff was never a credible sanction for the Government against the producers while the existence of the cartel provided the credible threat of a price-cutting war against best practice producers seeking to undercut. The implication was the survival of a tail of inefficient plants with a wide range of costs (Tolliday, 1987, pp. 326–27). Half the production of the blast furnace (pig iron) industry was used in integrated iron and steelworks (Rostas, 1948b, p. 113). Electric lamps were produced under the auspices of a highly anti-competitive trade association, one of the first cases to be investigated by the Monopolies and Restrictive Practices Commission (1951). The Electric Lamp Manufacturers' Association enforced strict cartel arrangements which protected high-cost producers. In addition, the metals and engineering sector tended to be highly unionized and has been singled out in the history of industrial relations as a group of industries where British managers conceded substantial areas of job-control to workers (Zeitlin, 1987).

4. Textiles and Clothing

The traditional picture of the UK tetile industry is of inefficient small scale production, lagging behind the US in terms of both technology and organization. In the much quoted case of cotton (e.g. Lazonick, 1986) the mule and powerloom remained important in Britain, where the industry remained vertically specialized, in contrast to the dominance of the ring spindle and automatic loom in vertically integrated American companies. The fact that, in terms of relative productivity levels, the UK cotton industry performed well is perhaps surprising. Thus we echo the comments of Saxonhouse and Wright (1987) that the glorification of the American cotton industry in Anglo-American comparisons should be tempered by the fact that it never attained international competitiveness for any sustained period. Despite losing world market share, the British cotton industry still retained a strong revealed comparative advantage.

Woollen and worsted is another industry that remained highly competitive and performed well in terms of relative labour productivity and revealed comparative advantage. The industry was characterized by absence of economies of scale, small size of capital, slow technological progress, and the survival of a very large number of small firms, while CR3 was only 6 percent in 1935. In such circumstances it is perhaps not surprising that attempts at collusion were generally unsuccessful (Rainnie, 1965).

5. Food, Drink and Tobacco

Food, drink and tobacco (FDT) does not fit easily into the traditional picture of British industry between the wars. Productivity performance was relatively good, and the FDT sector featured heavily in the merger boom of the 1920's (Hannah, 1983, Ch. 8), achieving a high degree of concentration and plant sizes often much larger than in America (Table 6). Despite the high degree of concentration, however, the FDT sector does not appear to have been very highly collusive.

Until recently, relatively little has been written about the British food processing industry, which has fallen between the two disciplines of agricultural economics and industrial economics (Burns *et al.*, 1983). One industry that has nevertheless received some attention is margarine, which was dominated by Unilever from 1929. Unilever was formed from Lever Bros. and their major competitor the Margarine Union, itself the product of a merger between Jurgens and Van den Bergh, the two major Dutch producers (Wilson, 1954, Vol. II). However, under strong competition from butter during the agricultural depression of the 1930's, Unilever were forced to rationalize their margarine operations, closing half of the ten factories between 1929 and 1937 (Reader, 1960, p. 43). Unilever has been relatively well regarded by business historians as a well-managed company, among the first to move towards a modern divisional structure under overall central control (Gourvish, 1987; Wilson, 1977). UK productivity performance in margarine was thus above average.

6. Miscellaneous

There is clearly some diversity of performance in this sector. The most interesting case is rubber tyres and tubes, which despite being a below average performer on the raw data, has a large negative residual, indicating an unexpectedly good performance. This is because the regression predicts a very poor UK performance due to small market size and a high level of concentration. After the imposition of a tariff in 1927, a strong multinational presence was established in Britain (Goodyear, Michelin, Firestone, Pirelli and India Tyre and Rubber). Although the dominant British producer, Dunlop, took the lead in establishing the Tyre Manufacturers' Conference in 1929, it seems likely both that the new entry increased pressures for efficiency in Dunlop, and directly improved productivity (Jones, 1984; Prais, 1981).

VII. CONCLUSIONS

Although Britain's productivity gap *vis-à-vis* the United States since the Second World War has been much studied, it is less widely known that US productivity levels were already more than twice their British counterparts by the mid-1920's. Although his gap has remained large and pervasive, performance has varied across industries. Our data set and case studies for the mid-1930's suggest that the traditional reasons offered for British failure often have validity for particular industries, but cannot be generalized to the whole manufacturing sector. One way to restate our results would be to emphasize that the much studied engineering sector is not typical of the whole of manufacturing industry. In the neglected and far more favourable lighter industries, textiles performed far better than is generally acknowledged, while food, drink and tobacco in general emerge as an underappreciated success story. Similarly, it is clear that a number of commonly held beliefs are invalid. In particular, British plant sizes in the 1930's were generally larger than those in America.

Regression analysis revealed surprisingly strong patterns of association in the data. Taken at face value, the results suggest that market size and human capital were the major reasons for the American productivity lead in the 1930's, while physical capital per worker was unimportant. It would be unwise, however, to place too much emphasis on these results or to curtail the analysis at this point. As the case study material suggests, obstacles to the rapid elimination of inefficient producers are likely to have played an important part in the productivity gap, but the impact of these factors cannot readily be captured by regression methods. We believe, therefore, that the regression equations as they stand probably exaggerate the role of market size and human capital in the British productivity problem.

An important but neglected part of the variation in productivity levels between industries is the variation in the ability of poor performers to survive. During the 1930's, external pressures to remove poor performers were weakened by tariff protection and government industrial policy, including the encouragement of cartels. Thus in many cases, pressures to remove poor performers had to come from within firms in the form of managerial reform and rationalization, yet British management has been severely criticized by most business historians for its failure to match American management in these areas. The industrial case studies which we have examined emphasize that new entry on occasions served to discipline incumbent management (rubber tyres, soap) while high barriers to entry could permit the protracted survival of weak management and low productivity (tin cans).

Market sharing arrangements were a prominent feature of British manufacturing industry between the wars, and were viewed extremely critically by American commentators. The case studies suggest that there are important examples where cartels allowed high cost producers to remain in the industry indefinitely (blast furnaces, steel, electric lamps). Indeed, the reports of the Monopolies and Restrictive Practices Commission during the 1950's suggest that this was a common outcome of such arrangements. Nevertheless, we do not wish to argue that all cartelized industries exhibited sub-standard productivity performance. Indeed, cement is a case of cartelization in the British industry but extremely strong productivity performance. This particular case indicates the importance of the industry's evolution prior to cartelization and the importance of the extent of productivity variation when cartelization occurred.

Obviously, an important implication of our discussion is that further and more detailed case studies focusing on 'barriers to exit' of the high cost producers are fundamental to a fuller understanding of the relatively low productivity of interwar Britain. It must also be recognized that a more formal analysis of cartel behaviour in this period would be highly desirable. In particular, it would be useful to know precisely what prevented the low cost firms in the market sharing agreements from engineering the exit of high cost firms and plants and why the conduct of interwar British cartels seems to

EXPLAINING ANGLO-AMERICAN PRODUCTIVITY DIFFERENCES 399

have been much less favourable to productivity advance than that of the much praised cartels in pre-1914 Germany.

University of Warwick

REFERENCES

Anglo-American Council on Productivity (1952). *Final Report*, London.
Bain, G. S. and Price, R. (1980). *Profile of Union Growth: A Comparative Statistical Portrait of Eight Countries*, Oxford, Blackwell.
Bamberg, J. H. (1988). 'The Rationalisation of the British Cotton Industry in the Interwar Years', *Textile History*, Vol. 19, pp. 83–102.
Barnett, C. (1986). *The Audit of War: The Illusion and Reality of Britain as a Great Nation*, London, Macmillan.
Booth, A. (1987). 'Britain in the 1930's: A Managed Economy?', *Economic History Review*, Vol. 40, pp. 499–522.
Broadberry, S. N. (1988). 'The Impact of the World Wars on the Long-Run Performance of the British Economy', *Oxford Review of Economic Policy*, Vol. 4, pp. 25–37.
Broadberry, S. N. and Crafts, N. F. R. (1990). 'The Implications of British Macro-economic Policy in the 1930's for Long-Run Growth Performance', *Rivista di Storia Economica*, (forthcoming), (Also CEPR Discussion Paper).
Broadberry, S. N. and Fremdling, R. (1990). 'Comparative Productivity in British and German Industry 1907–37', *BULLETIN*, Vol. 52, pp. 403–21.
Brown, B. C. (1954). 'Industrial Production in 1935 and 1948', *London and Cambridge Economic Bulletin*, Vol. 12, pp. 5–6.
Burkitt, B. (1973). 'The Calculation of the Degree of Unionisation', *British Journal of Industrial Relations*, Vol. 11, pp. 449–58.
Burns, J., McInerney, J. and Swinbank, A. (eds.) (1983). *The Food Industry*, London, Heinemann.
Chandler, A. D. Jr. (1980). 'The Growth of the Transnational Industrial Firm in the United States and the United Kingdom: A Comparative Analysis', *Economic History Review*, Vol. 33, pp. 396–410.
Cook, P. L. (1958). *Effects of Mergers: Six Studies*, London, Allen and Unwin.
Crafts, N. F. R. and Thomas, M. (1986). 'Comparative Advantage in UK Manufacturing Trade, 1910–35', *Economic Journal*, Vol. 96, pp. 629–45.
David, P. (1989). 'Computer and Dynamo: The Modern Productivity Paradox in a Not-Too-Distant Mirror', (unpublished, Stanford University).
Davies, S. W. and Caves, R. E. (1987). *Britain's Productivity Gap*, Cambridge, Cambridge University Press.
Denison, E. F. (1967). *Why Growth Rates Differ*, Washington, DC, The Brookings Institution.
Devine, W. Jr. (1983). 'From Shafts to Wires: Historical Perspective on Electrification', *Journal of Economic History*, Vol. 42, pp. 347–72.
Dunning, J. H. (1958). *American Investment in British Manufacturing Industry*, London, Allen and Unwin.
Edgerton, D. E. H. (1987). 'Science and Technology in British Business History', *Business History*, Vol. 29, pp. 84–103.

Elbaum, B. and Lazonick, W. (eds.) (1986). *The Decline of the British Economy*, Oxford, Oxford University Press.

Fabricant, S. (1940). *The Output of Manufacturing Industries 1899–1937*, New York, National Bureau of Economic Research.

Fabricant, S. (1942). *Employment in Manufacturing, 1899–1939: An Analysis of its Relation to the Volume of Production*, New York, National Bureau of Economic Research.

Feinstein, C. H. (1988). 'Economic Growth Since 1870: Britain's Performance in International Perspective', *Oxford Review of Economic Policy*, Vol. 4, pp. 1–13.

Flux, A. W. (1933). 'Industrial Productivity in Britain and the United States', *Quarterly Journal of Economics*, pp. 1–38.

Frankel, M. (1957). *British and American Manufacturing Productivity*, Urbana: University of Illinois.

Gourvish, T. R. (1987). 'British Business and the Transition to a Corporate Economy: Entrepreneurship and Management Structures', *Business History*, Vol. 29, pp. 18–45.

Gribbin, J. D. (1978). 'The Postwar Revival of Competition as Industrial Policy', (Government Economic Service Working Paper No. 19).

Hannah, L. (1974). 'Takeover Bids in Britain Before 1950: An Exercise in Business Pre-History', *Business History*, Vol. 16, pp. 65–77.

Hannah, L. (1983). *The Rise of the Corporate Economy*, (2nd edition), London, Methuen.

Hutchinson, H. (1965). *Tariff-Making and Industrial Reconstruction*, London, Harrap.

Jacoby, S. M. (1986). *Employing Bureaucracy: Managers, Unions and the Transformation of Work in American Industry, 1900–1945*, New York, Columbia University Press.

Jones, G. (1984). 'The Growth and Performance of British Multinational Firms Before 1939: The Case of Dunlop', *Economic History Review*, Vol. 37, pp. 35–53.

Keeble, S. P. (1984). 'University Education and Business Management from the 1890's to the 1950's: A Reluctant Relationship', (PhD Thesis, University of London).

Kendrick, J. W. (1961). *Productivity Trends in the United States*, Princeton: Princeton University Press.

Kitson, M., Solomou, S. and Weale, M. (1989). 'Effective Protection and Economic Recovery in the UK During the 1930's', (unpublished, University of Cambridge).

Lazonick, W. (1986). 'The Cotton Industry', in Elbaum, B. and Lazonick, W. (eds.), *The Decline of the British Economy*, Oxford, Oxford University Press.

Leak, H. and Maizels, A. (1945). 'The Structure of British Industry', *Journal of the Royal Statisical Society*, Vol. 108, pp. 142–99.

Leamer, E. E. (1984). *Sources of International Comparative Advantage: Theory and Evidence*, London, MIT Press.

Levy, H. (1927). *Monopolies, Cartels and Trusts in British Industry*, London, MacMillan.

Lewchuk, W. (1987). *American Technology and the British Vehicle Industry*, Cambridge: Cambridge University Press.

Littler, C. R. (1982). *The Development of the Labour Process in Capitalist Societies*, London, Heinemann.

Lucas, A. F. (1937). *Industrial Reconstruction and the Control of Competition: The*

British Experiments, London, Longmans, Green & Co.

Lucas, R. E. Jr. (1988). 'The Mechanics of Economic Development', *Journal of Monetary Economics*, Vol. 22, pp. 3-42.

McCloskey, D. N. (1970). 'Did Victorian Britain Fail?', *Economic History Review*, Vol. 23, pp. 446-59.

Matthews, R. C. O., Feinstein, C. H. and Odling-Smee, J. C. (1982). *British Economic Growth 1856-1973*, Oxford, Oxford University Press.

Melman, S. (1956). *Dynamic Factors in Industrial Productivity*, Oxford, Blackwell.

Monopolies and Restrictive Practices Commission (1951). *Report on the Supply of Electric Lamps*, London, HMSO.

Mowery, D. C. (1986). 'Industrial Research, 1900-50', in Elbaum, B. and Lazonick, W. (eds.), *The Decline of the British Economy*, Oxford, Oxford University Press, pp. 189-222.

Paige, D. and Bombach, G. (1959). *A Comparison of National Output and Productivity of the United Kingdom and the United States*, Paris, Organisation for European Economic Cooperation.

Patel, P. and Pavitt, K. (1988). 'The Technological Activities of the UK: A Fresh Look', in Silberston, A. (ed.), *Technology and Economic Progress*, London: MacMillan, pp. 113-54.

Prais, S. J. (1981). *Productivity and Industrial Structure*, Cambridge: Cambridge University Press.

Pratten, C. F. (1976). *Labour Productivity Differentials Within International Companies*, Cambridge, Cambridge University Press.

Rainnie, G. F. (ed.) (1965). *The Woollen and Worsted Industry*, Oxford: Clarendon Press.

Reader, W. J. (1960). *Unilever: A Short History*, London: Unilever.

Rees, M. (1922). *Trusts in British Industry 1914-21*, London, King.

Rostas, L. (1948a). *Comparative Productivity in British and American Industry*, Cambridge, Cambridge University Press.

Rostas, L. (1948b). *Productivity, Prices and Distribution in Selected British Industries*, Cambridge, Cambridge University Press.

Salter, W. E. G. (1960). *Productivity and Technical Change*, Cambridge, Cambridge University Press.

Sanderson, M. (1988). 'Education and Economic Decline 1890 to the 1980's', *Oxford Review of Economic Policy*, Vol. 4, pp. 38-50.

Saxonhouse, G. and Wright, G. (1987). 'Stubborn Mules and Vertical Integration: The Disappearing Constraint?', *Economic History Review*, Vol. 40, pp. 87-94.

Scherer, F. M. *et al.* (1975). *The Economics of Multi-Plant Operation*, Cambridge, Mass., Harvard University Press.

Supple, B. E. (1987). *History of the British Coal Industry, Vol. 4, 1913-46*, Oxford, Oxford University Press.

Tolliday, S. (1987). *Business, Banking and Politics: The Case of British Steel 1918-39*, Cambridge, Mass., Harvard University Press.

Wilkinson, F. (1989). 'Industrial Relations and Industrial Decline: The Case of the British Iron and Steel Industry, 1870-1930', (DAE Working Paper No. 8915, University of Cambridge).

Wilson, C. (1954). *The History of Unilever: A Study in Economic Growth and Social Change*, (2 vols.), London, Cassell.

Wilson, C. (1977). 'Management and Policy in Large-Scale Enterprise: Lever

402   BULLETIN

Brothers and Unilever, 1918–38', in Supple, B. E. (ed.), *Essays in British Business History*, Oxford, Oxford University Press.

Zeitlin, J. (1983). 'The Labour Strategies of British Engineering Employers, 1890–1922', in Gospel, H. F. and Littler, C. R. (eds.), *Managerial Strategies and Industrial Relations*, London: Heinemann.

Zeitlin, J. (1987). 'From Labour History to the History of Industrial Relations', *Economic History Review*, Vol. 40, pp. 159–84.

[11]

The Economic Implications of North Sea Oil Revenues

P J Forsyth and J A Kay

I

The growth of North Sea oil revenues is the most important fiscal development in the British economy in the 1980's. Yet it is one which does not impinge directly on individuals—we do not see the activity which yields these returns nor are we direct recipients of them. Perhaps it is for this reason that there is little understanding or analysis of the impact of North Sea oil on the British economy.

The purpose of this article is to set out a framework for such understanding and analysis. It is not concerned with the development of the oil sector itself, nor with directly oil-related activities—there are already several substantial discussions of these topics (e.g. Page, 1977, Robinson and Morgan, 1978, Gaskin, 1978). Our concern is to elucidate the effects of the growth of the oil sector on the non-oil economy.

We shall show that the benefits of North Sea oil are very large, and generally underestimated. It is realistic to suppose that by the middle of this decade they will have raised the national income of the UK by at least ten per cent. But this windfall arises in a highly unbalanced form. A consequence is that it demands extensive structural change in the UK economy. The adverse effects on manufacturing industry have been recognised, and deplored as 'the Dutch disease' or 'deindustrialisation'. But it is not the case that pressure on manufacturing is an adverse side effect of an undesirable, and perhaps temporary, over-reaction by the foreign exchange market to Britain's newly acquired oil self-sufficiency. Rather the contraction of manufacturing output, and an increase in domestic absorption of imported manufacturers, are—whether desirable or not—the only means by which the British economy can benefit from the North Sea. The rise in the exchange rate is simply the market's mechanism for bringing this about, and if it were suppressed some

Peter Forsyth is Senior Lecturer in Economics at the University of New South Wales, Australia, John Kay is Research Director of the Institute for Fiscal Studies. The authors are grateful to Alastair Ulph for comments and to David Morrison of Wood McKenzie and Co for advice and information on prospective oil revenues. A fuller and more technical version of this paper is available as IFS Working Paper No. 10.

[The appendices have not been reproduced here.]

alternative means of achieving the same result would emerge and would be required. However, we shall argue that the rise in the exchange rate is a beneficial mechanism for achieving this outcome, and one which confers significant indirect gains on the economy over and above the direct value of oil revenues.

It follows from these observations that the benefits from oil are uneven in their incidence—that although the net effect is substantially favourable many sectors of industry and many individuals will be net losers. While efficiency demands that structural change should not be discouraged, equity demands that its consequences be made more tolerable for those directly involved. It is not only equity, but prudence that demands this; for without it—and indeed even with it—there will be political pressure from those whose existing interests are adversely affected or who misunderstand the nature of the economic future which oil offers to dissipate this future by inappropriate policy responses.

II

How large are the benefits of oil, and what form do they take? Peak production levels, which will be attained in the mid 1980's, will be slightly in excess of one billion barrels per year. In 1979, UK consumption (inland deliveries plus refinery use) was 0.68 billion barrels and production 0.58 billion barrels: self-sufficiency is likely to be reached late in 1980. Estimated reserves are in the range 18 – 32 billion barrels. Although we shall continue to talk about North Sea oil, it is likely that future major discoveries will be in other areas of the British continental shelf.

TABLE 1

UK Oil Reserves (billion barrels)

	Minimum	Maximum
Production to end 1978	0.8	0.8
Current discoveries—proven	10.3	18.6
Future discoveries, from present licences	2.6	5.9
Other reserves	4.1	7.4
	17.8	32.7

Source: Department of Energy (1979).

What are the economic implications of a shift from a position when we import the whole of our oil requirements to one where we produce around one billion barrels per year? There are several measures of the benefits, each of which has relevance for particular purposes. We discuss their relationship and derivation further in the appendix. The first measure, and the largest, is the gross value of oil output. At a price of $35 per barrel, peak production is worth between $35 and $40 billion per year. Converting this to sterling at a rate of $2.25 implies a value of £16 billion. The benefit to the balance of payments is somewhat less than this, because of imports required for North Sea operations and the remittance of profits and interest overseas. These may amount to £3bn, implying a balance of payments gain of £13bn. The direct value of oil to the British economy (value added from oil) is less than this because we need to subtract domestically incurred operating costs (including a return on capital which British companies have employed in exploration and development which might otherwise have been used elsewhere). These may be £2bn, leaving a balance of £11bn. Virtually all of this will accrue to the government as tax revenue; the balance is the profit earned by British companies over and above what they could have expected to earn from alternative investments. This is unlikely to be more than £1bn, consistent with an annual tax yield of £10bn. All these figures are at 1980 prices, and can therefore be compared with 1980 gross national income of around £180bn and total tax revenue of £70bn.

It is easy to calculate the effect on gross revenue from oil of changes in the real price of oil or the real exchange rate. We can then estimate the consequences of such changes for tax yields, since almost all the change in the value of output will be reflected in a change in government revenues. A complete model of the North Sea tax system is very complex, because of the interactions between the various taxes. Such a model has been developed by Wood McKenzie & Co, and we discuss its conclusions in the appendix. But it is both simpler and more realistic to estimate long run revenue by describing government behaviour rather than the tax system. This is because, as the Inland Revenue has acknowledged in evidence to the Select Committee on the Treasury, it is the revenue secured which determines the tax system rather than the tax system which determines the revenue secured.

The current target is 80 per cent of net revenue at the 1980 exchange rate and oil price. The estimates in Table 2 assume that the government achieves this target and imposes a marginal tax rate of 90 per cent on revenue changes resulting from variations of exchange rate or oil price. Since the marginal tax rate is now about 87 per cent, this assumes that (as has happened rather too frequently in the past) changes in the oil price lead to changes in tax rates. The

TABLE 2

Long Term Estimates of North Sea Oil Revenue

(£bn, annual rates, 1980 prices)
Real Oil Price

		$25	$35	$40	$50
Real Exchange rate	$1.75	9.3	14.4	17.6	22.2
	$2.00	7.7	12.2	14.4	18.9
	$2.25	6.4	10.4	12.4	16.4
	$2.50	5.4	9.0	10.8	14.4

Source: Own calculations.

3

range of figures shown in the table is quite wide; but this exaggerates the degree of uncertainty because it is unlikely that a high oil price will be associated with a low value for sterling, or a low oil price with a high exchange rate. A revenue projection in the range £9bn – £12bn is therefore reasonably robust. This is only slightly less than the yield from value added tax, and is equal to half the revenue from income tax.

The figures we have presented are essentially illustrative in nature, but they do indicate the order of magnitude of revenues from oil, and their considerable size—whether we compare oil output with national income or tax yield with public expenditure. The degree of uncertainty about these projections, especially of oil prices, is such that any precise numbers quoted should be distrusted. Moreover, our calculations relate to peak production, and for many purposes it is more appropriate to ask what is the size of a corresponding flow of revenue which is permanently sustainable. We return to this issue in Section V. But for our analysis in Section III we shall assume that oil production adds £10bn to net output in the UK. This is not intended to be our best estimate of the gains from oil. It is simply the figure which we have chosen to illustrate the economic effects of a development of this kind, which is our principal objective. We believe we have said enough to demonstrate that it is of a realistic order of magnitude.

III

We begin by examining the basic structure of the pre-oil economy. Table 3 shows how production is distributed over the various sectors. The data refers to 1976—the last year before domestic oil production had significant effects on the British economy—but we have brought it to 1980 prices by using a general price index on all items. There have been important changes in relative prices since 1976, partly as a result of the influence of oil, but we defer discussion of these until Section IV.

The second and third columns of Table 3 also show exports and imports by producing sector. This indicates that manufacturing has a much greater role in relation to the traded sector than it does to the domestic economy. Manufactures account for well over half of both imports and exports, but little more than a quarter of domestic output. The comparison between column one and columns two and three is in some degree misleading, however. Column one records net output by sector, while exports and imports are measures of gross output. It is not surprising that most exports take the physical form of manufactured goods, but the tangible export usually includes the contributions of several different sectors. For example, there is little international trade in electricity, but refined aluminium is in a sense congealed electricity and Norway and Canada, with considerable supplies of cheap electricity, are the major exporters of aluminium. More generally, although many services cannot be exported directly they are exported indirectly by contributing value added to the goods which are exported; and Britain imports raw materials not only in their crude form but also as part of the manufactured goods which we buy from abroad.

4

TABLE 3

The Structure of the UK Economy, 1976 (£bn, 1980 prices)

	Production	Exports	Imports
		(as gross output)	
Primary production	9.3	0.8	11.5
Manufacturing	50.6	39.8	34.7
Construction and housing	23.3	0	0
Distribution and services	91.2	16.5	12.8
Public administration	14.0	0	0
Residual	– 6.5	1.3	1.7
	181.9	58.5	60.7

So we need to look behind exports and imports at the various production sectors which contribute to them. This we can do using input-output analysis, and Table 4 shows the composition of imports and exports in terms of value added.

The picture presented is somewhat different. Both imports and exports are considerably smaller than in Table 3. This is because a high proportion of UK imports—some £13bn—are ultimately re-exported after further processing in Britain. The approach we have adopted counts only the value added in the UK as an export, while the conventional trade accounts include the whole value of the export. Since the goods in question are not finally consumed in the UK, they are also excluded from imports.

The second difference is that the contribution of distribution and services to exports is significantly increased, reflecting the inclusion of indirect as well as direct imports. Services account for 28 per cent of exports by commodity but 41 per cent of exports by value added. It remains true, however, that manufacturing

TABLE 4

The Structure of the UK Economy, 1976 (£bn, 1980 prices)

(residuals allocated pro rata)

	Production	Exports	Imports	Consumption
		(by value added)		
Primary production	9.0	– 1.2	+ 8.0	15.8
Manufacturing	48.9	– 24.9	+ 22.0	46.0
Construction and housing	22.5	– 0.2	+ 0.3	22.6
Distribution and services	88.1	– 18.8	+ 16.9	86.2
Public administration	13.5	—	—	13.5
	181.9	– 45.1	+ 47.3	184.1

Source: Our calculations, see IFS working paper for details.

features much more in trade than do other sectors. Almost half of manufacturing value added is exported as against 20 per cent for services and less for other sectors.

This approach enables us to derive the fourth column of Table 4, which we have headed 'consumption'. This shows the composition, by producing sector, of the goods consumed in the UK. It is what the structure of the UK economy would be if we were self-sufficient (assuming, implausibly, that we could take over from abroad the technology required to produce domestically the goods which we currently import). Consumption is slightly higher than production, reflecting the balance of payments deficit which occurred in 1976. In that year, and in general, Britain consumed more primary products and fewer manufactures and services than it produced. We exported manufactures and services to buy primary products. It should be noted that although we have called this column 'consumption' it would be more accurate to call it domestic resource utilisation. It includes not only private consumption but private and public investment as well.

Now we shall assume that the development of oil output creates £10bn of additional value added in the primary sector. Assuming that other primary production remains constant, this will raise primary output to £19bn. However, there is no reason to expect that demand for primary output will rise by this amount. An additional £10bn of income raises total output from the UK economy by 5.5 per cent. If we increase domestic resource utilisation in line with this increase in income, the resulting increases in demand will be spread over all sectors. The simplest assumption is that demand for value added in each sector rises by 5.5 per cent. In that case, consumption of primary output would be £15.8bn and a deficit of £6.8bn would have become a surplus of £2.3bn.

If domestic resource use is to rise in line with national income, it follows that we must maintain a broad overall balance on external trade. This implies that the move from deficit to surplus on primary account must be reflected in a move from surplus to deficit in other accounts. If there were no change in the net payments position, then the non-primary balance of payments would deteriorate by £9.1bn. As a preliminary assumption, suppose this change is reflected in an equal percentage increase in all non-primary imports and reduction in all non-primary exports.

Table 5 works back from these assumptions to the new levels of production which are implied. We start from consumption figures in which all items are increased by 5.5 per cent. We then impose the 11 per cent change on all imports and exports which is needed to avoid any change in the overall balance. And while in Table 4 we worked forward from the known production data by adding the net effects of trade, in Table 5 we work back from estimated consumption data by subtracting the net effect of trade to find implied production by sector.

Table 6 compares this production sector with the original pre-oil figures. In the two non-traded sectors—construction and public administration—output expands in line with the overall growth of national income. In the primary sector, output grows much faster—it doubles. This is compensated for, however, by less

6

TABLE 5

The Post-oil Economy (£bn, 1980 prices)

	Production	Exports	Imports	Consumption
Primary production	19.0	(− 2.3)		16.7
Manufacturing	46.1	− 22.2	+ 24.6	48.5
Construction and housing	23.7	− 0.2	+ 0.3	23.8
Distribution and services	88.9	− 16.9	+ 18.9	90.9
Public administration	14.2	—	—	14.2
	191.9	(+ 2.2)		194.1

Source: As Table 4.

rapid growth in the remaining traded sectors—services and manufacturing. Much the largest effect is on manufacturing, which not only declines in relative terms but suffers an absolute contraction of 5.7 per cent.

The essentials of what is happening are very simple. North Sea oil adds considerably to the growth of the UK economy. However, this growth takes a highly unbalanced form; all of it occurs in a single sector whose size is, even then, small in relation to the overall economy. To use the additional resources which it makes available to us, it is necessary to convert them to a form in which they can be exploited domestically. But there is simply no way in which oil can be converted into houses, or restaurant meals, or retail and distributive services, either directly or through trade: and it is largely on items of these kinds that we shall want to spend our increased income. All we can do is to exchange oil for trade goods—predominantly manufactures—and redeploy the resources released from these sectors into the other, non-tradeable, sectors of the economy. *There is no mechanism for deriving benefit from North Sea oil which does not, sooner or later, require this structural change.*

The model we have presented is heavily over-simplified, and we shall discuss many qualifications to it in subsequent sections. But none of them will fundamentally alter the simple arithmetic logic of the argument. The discovery of

TABLE 6

Production Changes by Sector (£bn, 1980 prices)

	Pre-oil	Post-oil	% Change
Primary production	9.0	19.0	+ 111.1
Manufacturing	48.9	46.1	− 5.7
Construction and housing	22.5	23.7	+ 5.5
Distribution and services	88.1	88.9	+ 0.9
Public administration	13.5	14.2	+ 5.5
Total	181.9	191.9	+ 5.5

North Sea oil involves a large expansion of the traded sector of the economy. Since, in the long run, the balance of payments must balance, that implies a contraction of the remainder of the traded sector, in which manufacturing is disproportionately represented.

It may seem paradoxical to those who see manufacturing as the heartland of the economy that economic growth should involve a contraction in its role. But what is the source of the common belief in the central role of manufacturing? Doubtless there are some people who think that large cars represent real wealth in a way that the plays of Shakespeare do not, but their views do not deserve much attention. The serious point is that because tradeables are predominantly manufactures, the import of raw materials requires the export of manufactures in return and other sectors of the economy cannot substitute in this role. But the corollary to this is that when, as is now the case, Britain emerges as a significant primary producer, the role of manufacturing is to decline. Traditionally, Britain has exported manufactures and services in return for primary inputs. In the future, this will be substantially less true and may even be reversed.

IV

The analysis of the previous section was conducted in terms of physical quantities and we did not discuss the prices of the outputs of the various sectors. The mechanism which brings about the structural changes is, in a market economy, a rise in the real exchange rate. Externally, this reduces the competitiveness of British exports and increases the attractiveness of imports, thus restoring the balance of payments to equilibrium. Internally, it reduces prices, profits and wages in the tradeable sector—principally manu-facturing—relative to those in less tradeable sectors and so brings about pressure for the reallocation of resources in the domestic economy.

These changes in relative prices have important implications in themselves. They also feed back into our earlier analysis. One simple way of seeing the problem they pose is this. Peak production of UK oil will, at current world prices, be worth perhaps $35bn. At £1 = $2.25, this is worth £16bn. At £1 = $1.85, this same output would be worth £19bn; and if there were no oil the exchange rate might well be $1.85 rather than $2.25.

At first sight this suggests that as oil pushes up the exchange rate so its value to the British economy falls. But in reality the reverse is the case. A shift in the exchange rate from $1.85 to $2.25 is equivalent to a revaluation of 22 per cent. This reduces import prices in sterling terms. Primary product prices (other than food) will fall by the full amount of the revaluation. The prices of imported manufactures will also fall, although by rather less, if Britain is a large importer relative to the size of the world market, or if foreign exporters can raise their profit margins on sales to the UK. Suppose import prices are 15 per cent lower than they would otherwise have been, and sterling export prices remain constant. On an import bill of £60bn (Table 3), this implies a saving of £9bn, equivalent to five per cent of national income. The gain from the reduction in the cost of imports is of the same order of magnitude as the direct gain from oil itself, and this much more than offsets the fall in the direct value of the oil. How do we actually receive these benefits? Because imports are around one-third of domestic consumption, a 15 per cent fall in import prices reduces domestic prices by around five per cent. The gain takes the form of lower prices at a given level of money incomes. The benefit is most obvious to those who travel abroad and find the pound buys more; but similar gains are being made by everyone who buys goods which are imported or contain imported components.

It is therefore important to estimate what the effect of oil revenues on the exchange rate is. We go on to consider how this affects relative prices in the domestic economy, and to estimate the size of the gains from exchange rate appreciation. We illustrate how the rising exchange rate shifts revenue from oil away from government tax receipts and directly into the pockets of the people; and that the amount of this indirect gain is substantially more than the amount of direct loss. We shall describe the difference between the equilibrium exchange rate with North Sea oil and without it as the 'oil premium'. If the current exchange is \$2.25, but would have been \$1.85 without oil, that implies that the current oil premium is 22 per cent. There are two ways of estimating the oil premium. One is to analyse the recent behaviour of the exchange rate in order to see how its trend has been affected by oil. As shown in the Appendix (Table A2), the real exchange rate rose by around 20 per cent between 1976 and January 1980. It has since strengthened further. There are many other factors at work, and without oil there would have been some movement in one direction or the other, but this is one indication of the order of magnitude of the oil premium.

An alternative approach to assessing the oil premium is to ask what rise in the exchange rate is needed in order to worsen the non-oil balance of payments by the value of oil output. For this purpose, oil output includes domestically incurred operating costs as well as net value added, since these costs also represent a shift of domestic resources into the tradeable sector. Set the value of oil output at \$25bn. Exports and imports of manufactures in the pre-oil economy (measured in terms of gross output, since it is on this basis that export and import elasticities are normally estimated), are between £35bn and £40bn at 1980 prices (Table 3), equivalent to \$70bn at a tentative pre-oil exchange rate of \$1.85. Some deterioration of the trade balance follows automatically from the growth in national income and associated increase in demand for imports. If net imports rise by 10 per cent, the import bill rises by \$9bn. This leaves some \$16bn of adjustment, of which say \$13bn might fall on manufacturing, equal to just under 20 per cent of import or export volume. Central estimates of demand elasticities suggest that this might require a change in relative prices of 12 per cent to 15 per cent.

This figure cannot immediately be translated into an exchange rate change, however. Although the real exchange rate has risen by more than 20 per cent since 1976, the export price of manufactures relative to the import price of manufactures has risen by somewhat less, as Table 7 shows. This is because

9

TABLE 7

UK Terms of Trade in Manufactures

	Export Prices (£)	Import Prices (£)	Terms of Trade
	(1970 = 100)	(1970 = 100)	(1976 = 100)
1970	100	100	97
1971	110	107	100
1972	118	112	102
1973	128	127	98
1974	153	147	101
1975	194	184	102
1976	238	232	100
1977	287	265	105
1978 1	309	278	108
1978 2	315	289	106
1978 3	325	296	107
1978 4	334	304	107
1979 1	340	306	108
1979 2	340	296	112
1979 3	346	293	115
1979 4	352	304	113
1980 (Jan)	358	306	114

Source: Monthly Digest of Statistics
   1970 – 6, machinery and transport equipment series
   1976 – 80, finished manufactures series
   Terms of trade = ratio of export prices to import prices.

domestic exporters have been forced to absorb part of the impact of revaluation while foreign exporters to the UK have been able to increase their margins somewhat. The change in the exchange rate needed to produce a 15 per cent improvement in the terms of trade in manufactures is probably in the range 20 per cent – 25 per cent. However this 15 per cent reflects the change in the price of gross output: since the import content of exports is substantial the terms of trade for value added have improved by an amount closer to the extent of the revaluation.

These calculations suggest that our preliminary assessment of the oil premium at 22 per cent, based on the difference between a non-oil exchange rate of $1.85 and a post-oil rate of $2.25, is a realistic order of magnitude. Tentatively adopting this figure, we now examine the implications of the oil premium for the analysis of Section III. In converting 1976 data to 1980 prices, we assumed that all prices increased at the same rate; but the oil premium ensures variability in prices. The prices of some primary products (such as oil) are set internationally, so that when the real exchange rate rises the prices of these items fall in terms of domestic currency by the amount of the revaluation, i.e. to 83 per cent of their previous level. Most agricultural goods are an exception because of the way in which Britain has operated the CAP, which has led partly to a diversion of oil income to domestic farmers and partly to its transfer to the EEC. The sterling price of imported goods and services will fall by most of the amount of the revaluation. The sterling price of exported goods and services will fall somewhat, because British exporters are unable to pass on the whole of the revaluation to their customers. Import competing goods and services will also fall in relative price. We have illustrated these possibilities in Table 8. Primary products are assumed to fall in price by 15 per cent, and the same assumption is made for imports. Manufacturers absorb some of the revaluation by reducing profit margins: we have assumed four per cent for exporters and two per cent for domestic producers (who suffer intensified competition from imports). Smaller price reductions occur in domestically produced services. These precise numbers are not intended at all seriously; they are simply chosen to enable us to illustrate qualitative effects.

TABLE 8

Relative Output, Import and Export Prices

	Production	Exports	Imports	Implied price of Consumption
Primary production	0.85	0.85	0.85	0.850
Manufacturing	0.98	0.96	0.85	0.923
Construction and housing	1.00	—	—	1.000
Distribution and services	0.99	0.98	0.85	0.963
Public administration	1.00	—	—	1.000
Implied average price	0.976	0.969	0.850	0.951

The final row and column of Table 8 represent implied average prices, given the structure of production described in Table 5. A feature of this is that the price of imports falls much more than the price of exports. This has the consequence that although trade as in Table 5 appears to cause a balance of payments deficit, if it took place at the prices implied by Table 8 the outcome would in fact be a balance of payments surplus. The difference results from a change in the ratio of export prices to import prices (the terms of trade). This means that the change in prices consequent on North Sea oil itself produces a gain in real income for the UK; activities which would previously have yielded a loss are now profitable. An alternative way of making the same point is to see that the price of goods which Britain consumes has fallen more than the price of goods which Britain produces. The value of British output has risen, measured in terms of its purchasing power for the goods Britain wants to buy. This change is itself equal to an increase in real income of about four per cent.

11

TABLE 9

The Post-oil Economy with Changed Relative Prices

(a) At changed prices

	Production	Exports	Imports	Consumption
Primary production	16.2	(− 1.6	)	14.6
Manufacturing	43.8	− 20.0	+ 22.2	46.0
Construction and housing	24.3	− 0.2	+ 0.3	24.4
Distribution and services	88.4	− 15.6	+ 17.1	89.9
Public administration	14.6	—	—	14.6
	187.3	(+ 2.2	)	189.5

(b) At constant (pre-oil) prices

	Production	Exports	Imports	Consumption
Primary production	19.0	(− 1.9	)	17.1
Manufacturing	44.7	− 20.8	+ 26.1	50.0
Construction and housing	24.3	− 0.2	+ 0.3	24.4
Distribution and services	89.3	− 15.9	+ 20.1	93.5
Public administration	14.6	—	—	14.6
	191.9	(+ 7.7	)	199.6

Such a rise in income allows a further rise in total domestic resource utilisation. A possible final outcome is shown in Table 9. In Table 9, consumption is allowed to expand until the balance of payments deficit is at its initial level of £2.2bn, as shown by the current price figures in (a). Table 9(b) shows that this deficit would have been £7.7bn without the improvement in the terms of trade, but the higher exchange rate means that this is a purely hypothetical calculation. In Table 9(b), the outcome has been converted back to original pre-oil relative prices using the prices in Table 8 so that Table 9(b) can be compared with the pre-oil economy of Table 4. The impact on production is shown in Table 10. Alternatively, Table 9(b) figures can be interpreted as physical volumes of goods.

There are two principal points to note. First, overall production still rises by only 5½ per cent, although national income increases by more. This is because the *value* of UK production has increased with the rise in the exchange rate. This effect is comparable in size to the immediate gain from the oil production itself. Second, the structural changes which are implied for the UK economy are now even larger. When we examined the direct impact of oil (Table 6) the difference in experience of non-oil sectors ranged from minus 5.7 per cent for manufacturing to plus 5.5 per cent for housing and construction. Now the range is from minus 8.9 per cent to plus 8.1 per cent. The reason is that again the increase in real income has occurred entirely in the traded sector. This implies a

TABLE 10

Output Changes, by Sector

	Pre-oil	Post-oil	% Change
Primary production	9.0	19.0	+ 111.1
Manufacturing	48.9	44.7	− 8.9
Construction and housing	22.5	24.3	+ 8.0
Distribution and services	88.1	89.3	+ 1.4
Public administration	13.5	14.6	+ 8.1
	181.9	191.9	+ 5.5

further expansion of the non-traded sector, compensated for by a further contribution in tradeables—the magnitude of the required structural change is increased.

Table 7 showed the very considerable change in the terms of trade which has occurred since oil production began. (The overall terms of trade do not display the same trend, but these are dominated by commodity prices which fluctuate for reasons unconnected with the UK domestic economy). The terms of trade in manufactures have improved by around 14 per cent since 1976. This figure underestimates the true effect, because export prices are those of gross output, which as we showed in Section II have a substantial import content. The corresponding rise in the relative price of exported manufacturing value added is around 20 per cent. Of course, oil was not responsible for precisely 14 per cent of the change, though it has been the major positive influence on the terms of trade during the period.

Many people will find it surprising that we should ascribe large benefits to what others would think a worrying decline in the competitiveness of British exports. But the proper attitude depends on the reason for the decline in competitiveness. A manufacturer is properly concerned if his prices rise because his costs rise relative to those of his competitors, and happy if they rise because market demand for his product forces them up. The flaw in this analogy is that in the case of British exports it is the demand for one product—oil—which raises the price of another product group—manufactures—but from the viewpoint of the British economy as a whole the effect is the same.

We have shown that the indirect gains from the improvement in the terms of trade are potentially large and it is appropriate now to consider how large they are. As the exchange rate rises, the direct gains fall. This is because the sterling value of British oil is lower, and so is value added in the North Sea and government tax revenue from oil. But as the exchange rate rises, the indirect gains rise; and we can show that it is virtually certain that the increase in indirect gain more than offsets the fall in direct gain. It follows that the larger the effect of oil in pushing up the exchange rate the greater the overall gain to the UK economy. The answer to the question 'should one assess the value of oil using a

13

TABLE 11

Gains from North Sea Oil

Oil premium	Implied current exchange rate	Gain to (£bn)		
		Companies and government	Consumers	Total
0	$1.85	10.0	—	10.0
10%	$2.04	9.0	3.4	12.4
20%	$2.22	8.3	6.8	15.1
30%	$2.41	7.6	10.1	17.1
40%	$2.59	7.1	13.5	20.6

Base assumptions: value added from oil $18.5
non-oil economy exports and imports £45bn
non-oil exchange rate $1.85
¾ of exchange rate gain reflected in *value added* terms of trade

pre-oil or a post-oil exchange rate?' is therefore that in general the higher of these two figures—the pre-oil exchange rate calculation—will underestimate the total value of oil.

These points are illustrated in Table 11. In this Table, we have assumed a non-oil exchange rate of $1.85, implying an oil premium of 22 per cent in a current exchange rate of $2.25. The value added directly attributable to oil is assumed to be $22.5bn. The Table shows the gains derived as government revenue and rents to oil companies, and as gain on the terms of trade, for various values of the oil premium. It implies that if the oil premium in the current exchange rate is indeed 22 per cent, the gain to consumers from the terms of trade improvement will actually be as large as the revenue directly attributable to the North Sea: the total gain is equal to 10 per cent of 1980 national income.

Table 12 approaches the same question from a slightly different angle. It asks: starting from a current exchange rate of $2.25, what is the gain for alternative

TABLE 12

Gains from North Sea Oil

Oil premium	Implied non-oil exchange rate	Indirect gain (£bn)	Total gain (£bn)
0	$2.25	0	8.2
10%	$2.05	3.4	11.6
25%	$1.80	8.4	16.6
40%	$1.61	13.5	21.7
50%	$1.50	16.9	25.1

Base assumptions: value added from oil $22.5bn
non-oil economy exports and imports £45bn
current exchange rate (including oil premium) $2.25
¾ exchange rate gain reflected in *value added* terms of trade

assumptions about the level of oil premium which this exchange rate incorporates? Under this assumption, the direct value of oil value added of $18.5bn is £8.2bn (since $2.25 is the actual exchange rate), but the indirect value depends on the assumed level of implicit oil premium.

We have shown that a major part of the gain from North Sea oil is incorporated in the terms of trade, and already has been. As the exchange rate rises, the benefits of oil are transferred from government revenue directly to domestic consumers of imported goods; and the higher the exchange rate the larger the total benefit and the proportion of it which is enjoyed immediately by consumers. On reasonably conservative assumptions, the total gain is nearly twice the direct gain and 10 per cent of current national income.

V

WHAT HAPPENS WHEN THE OIL RUNS OUT?

Britain's oil reserves will not last for ever. It would probably be a mistake to blow them all on raising current consumption during the limited period when oil production is flowing on a large scale. This argument gains particular force when the need for major structural change in response to North Sea oil is recognised. It would be very costly to make these structural adjustments only to be forced to unwind them again and restore the initial structure when oil production starts to fall.

The appropriate response is to invest sufficient of Britain's oil revenues to transform their windfall nature into a permanent increment to national income. We should consider how large such a permanent increment might be. Suppose we can earn a real rate of return on investment of three per cent. Suppose we can anticipate a production flow of one billion barrels a year for 17 years, followed by 17 years of production at ½ billion barrels per year, after which UK oil production ceases. This implies total reserves recovered of about 25 billion barrels, which is a central estimate of available reserves (Table 1). At a real oil price of $35 per barrel, the present value of this production is, at a real interest rate of three per cent, some $600bn. Investing this at three per cent yields $18bn per year—just over half the value of peak production. If we consumed half of oil revenues and invested the rest, we could maintain that boost to our consumption level indefinitely.

This calculation is quite sensitive to the real interest rate assumed. At one per cent real interest, we should invest three-quarters of the revenue. At five per cent, we can afford to consume nearly all of it. It is also sensitive to the real price of oil. If oil reserves are currently being depleted at an efficient rate, oil prices would rise at the real rate of interest—by three per cent per annum, on our central assumption. If they did, the present value of the depletion plan described would be $900bn and we could consume three-quarters of initial peak revenues. If oil is being depleted too rapidly, then the real oil price will rise faster and the value of UK reserves will be greater; conversely if depletion is too slow.

WHY DO WE STILL HAVE A BALANCE OF PAYMENTS DEFICIT?

It is important to be aware that the foreign exchange market anticipates future developments. If Britain were likely to produce large quantities of oil in 1985, which would push the exchange rate up in that year, then people will buy sterling now in anticipation of exchange gains: so that even if Britain were not now producing a single drop of oil the exchange rate would incorporate an oil premium. It follows that this would imply a balance of payments deficit at *current* levels of oil production. It is sometimes found paradoxical that Britain at present combines near self-sufficiency in oil, a current balance of payments deficit, and a high exchange rate; but for so long as oil output is increasing that is precisely what one can expect to observe. The experience of Norway illustrates this clearly; in 1976 and 1977, when growth in oil production was expected but had not fully occurred, its balance of payments deficit was more than 10 per cent of national income. This was equivalent to a deficit of over £20bn in the UK and was probably the largest deficit relative to GNP ever incurred by a developed country. Yet the Norwegian kroner strengthened before and during this period, as the foreign exchange market anticipated the prospective elimination of the deficit through oil (as has, in fact, subsequently happened).

WHY CAN'T WE RUN A BALANCE OF PAYMENTS SURPLUS?

We can, and we shall suggest below that when peak oil production levels are reached we should. A balance of payments surplus on current account implies that Britain is acquiring assets abroad. There are two methods of doing this. One is by official intervention in the foreign exchange market, in which the Bank of England moderates the rise in the exchange rate by selling sterling and obtaining foreign currencies in return. By convention, such investment is limited to the short-term money market. The alternative mechanism is by straight forward acquisition of overseas assets, either through portfolio investment or by direct investment with British companies constructing factories or other property abroad.

We can avoid any requirement for structural change in the domestic economy by reinvesting oil revenues overseas, and by reinvesting the interest on this reinvestment, and the interest on the interest, and so on *ad infinitum*. The price of doing so is that we never raise the rate of domestic resource utilisation above its pre-oil level. If we are ever to derive any benefit from oil revenues, it is necessary to reimport these assets, or the interest on them; and this we can only do by reducing domestic output of traded goods accordingly. Running a balance of payments deficit or surplus is a means of advancing or retarding the date at which structural change becomes necessary, but it is not a means of avoiding it; the only way of avoiding it is to throw North Sea oil revenue away.

WHAT KIND OF INVESTMENT?

We have suggested that it is appropriate for Britain to invest a substantial fraction of its oil revenues—perhaps £5bn – £10bn per annum. What forms should such investment take? There are investment opportunities both in the domestic economy and overseas.

Investment in the domestic economy poses a number of problems. It is obvious that we cannot use oil directly for investment. It is therefore necessary to convert oil into investment goods. The simplest way of doing this is to export oil and import resources for investment goods. If the material for investment is to be domestically generated, it would be necessary to contract the domestic tradeable sector further and divert resources to the investment sector. This change would be imposed on top of the contraction already occurring and would be essentially temporary in nature. This might be easy if the sectors whose export markets were disappearing were those equipped to produce items for investment; but it is much more likely that manufactured exports will be hit most in semi-finished and homogeneous products such as steel while more sophisticated products will continue to make sales at higher prices. It is therefore desirable to expand domestic investment via imports. This is certainly possible for plant and machinery; but investment makes heavy demands on construction and construction is the least tradeable sector of all.

It is widely suggested that North Sea oil revenues should be used to support investment in manufacturing industry. We have seen that an inevitable result of these revenues is that growth prospects for UK manufacturing are worsened and those for other sectors are improved. It seems a perverse response to this change in relative fortunes to use the proceeds for investment in manufacturing. The effect of oil is to increase, over the long-term, output of tradeable goods relative to non-tradeable goods, while it has little effect on demand for the two sectors. The ideal form of investment is one which uses tradeables to produce non-tradeable goods; imported machinery for use in service industries, for example. Manufacturing investment, which tends to use non-tradeables to produce tradeables, achieves precisely the reverse.

The same point can be made more forcefully in terms of prices and rates of return. North Sea oil implies a higher exchange rate and a lower rate of return in UK manufacturing than would otherwise be the case. Investment in manufacturing will therefore be unequivocally less profitable with oil than without it. Support for increased investment must therefore rely on the view that otherwise such investment would offer very high rates of return which are not obtained because of constraints on the availability of resources for investment. We know of no serious evidence to support such a proposition, and data on realised rates of return suggests the reverse—that investment is low because returns are low. Certainly it is hard to believe that any substantial fraction of the £5bn – £10bn per year we have suggested should be available for investment could be added to the existing level of £7bn per annum without driving returns down to nugatory levels. As past experience with British Steel and British Leyland has shown, there is no guarantee that investment in unprofitable industry will produce any return at all.

Investment abroad would seem to have considerable attractions. Firstly it reduces the requirement for temporary structural adjustments and readjustments in the UK economy. Secondly, financial investment responds more easily and more flexibly than physical investment, and this is important when there is considerable uncertainty about the future of the real oil price and the equilibrium level of the oil premium in the real exchange rate. Thirdly, there is no serious doubt that the world economy can absorb these funds and yield a reasonable real rate of return on them; the capacity of the British economy to use an additional £10bn of investment at acceptable real yields is much less clear.

DEPLETION POLICY

An alternative method of investing North Sea surpluses, and of spreading North Sea benefits into the future, is to retard depletion of North Sea reserves. This can be done by slowing depletion of existing fields, or by discouraging further exploration or development either through tax policy or through licensing. British policy has so far been close to pursuing the maximum attainable production levels (the restrictions on flaring gas in the Brent field are the most important departure from this), while Norway has proceeded rather cautiously. The rate of return on conservation as an investment depends on the anticipated rate of appreciation of the real oil price. We have used a three per cent real rate of return as an illustration of what Britain might hope to earn on foreign investment. If oil prices are expected to rise more rapidly than this, then slowing depletion will be a profitable investment strategy. If they will rise more slowly, then the right investment decision is to deplete as quickly as possible and invest the revenues elsewhere.

It should therefore be recognised that two quite separate investment decisions are required. One is to ask what proportion of potential oil revenues should be exploited now, and what proportion deferred to the future. The second question is what form the investment implied by the answer to the first should take: domestic investment, capital export, or conservation. It is the second of these issues, rather than the first, which should govern depletion policy.

WHAT ABOUT PROTECTING MANUFACTURING INDUSTRY?

We have painted a gloomy picture of the prospects for British manufacturing industry, especially for import competing sectors. This will lead to pressure for protection against the 'cheap' imports which result from the 'unrealistic' exchange rate implied by the oil premium. We began our analysis by looking at volumes of imports and exports and saw that oil necessarily implied the reduction and perhaps elimination of Britain's trade surplus in manufactures. The rise in the exchange rate is not the fundamental cause of this change; it is simply the market's mechanism for bringing it about.

It follows that one cannot stop this change by tariff or quota protection. What protection can do is to transfer the burden of adjustment from one sector to another. One reason why manufacturing will bear the brunt of the difficulties facing producers of tradeable goods is the government policies effectively insulate agriculture and coal mining from these problems. Import controls ease matters for the protected sector but by pushing the real exchange rate up still further increase the pressure on the unprotected sector. This is why industries will lobby for protection and it is also why such lobbying should be resisted. If the whole import-competing sector is protected by universal import controls, the burden of adjustment is transferred to the exporting sector. The rise in the exchange rate can only be prevented by capital export, but capital export would protect manufacturing industry anyway whether one imposed import controls or not. Alternatively, one might seek to restrain the rise in the exchange rate by 'some complex combination of official sales of sterling, relation of fiscal and monetary policy and inspired rumour' (CEPG, 1980, p. 31).

Why we should see by these means artifically to reduce the value of UK assets and output relative to those of other countries is hard to understand. The proposal is about as sensible, and as rewarding, as a major shareholder spreading unfounded rumours of the imminent bankruptcy of his company. The primary effect of generalised import controls is to favour import-competing sectors at the expense of exporting sectors. This policy cannot succeed in its objectives and can only reduce industrial efficiency.

NORTH SEA OIL AND EMPLOYMENT

What are the effects of North Sea oil on employment? In recent years, the British economy has operated at increasingly high levels of unemployment and the gap between actual and potential output levels has probably increased steadily. It is sometimes suggested that this reflects a balance of payments constraint which North Sea oil will relieve. With floating exchange rates, such a constraint could only reflect a policy of depressing domestic demand in order to push up the external value of sterling. Although the gains from improvement in the terms of trade are large, they are not so large as to make sense of such a policy; nor do we think it is an accurate description of what British governments thought they were doing. Demand has been depressed for other reasons of macroeconomic policy outside the scope of our present discussion.

Our principal concern in this paper has been with microeconomic effects and we return to these. Manufacturing is a relatively labour intensive sector. Value added per worker in manufacturing is around £7,000 in 1980 and about £10,000 in the rest of the economy. If these ratios remain unchanged, each one per cent shift of total output from manufacturing to other sectors would imply a reduction in manufacturing employment of 250,000 and an increase in jobs elsewhere of 180,000, with a net loss of 70,000 jobs.

These structural adjustments will be difficult, and the reduction in wages in manufacturing relative to other sectors which they imply will be resisted. This makes it likely that there will be increases in structural unemployment. We might offset against these factors the small employment creating effects of North Sea activity itself; against this, however, is the probability that labour intensive industry will suffer particularly severely from the rise in the exchange rate. The overall effect of North Sea oil on domestic employment is almost certainly to reduce it.

PROBLEMS OF STRUCTURAL CHANGE

Our simple model assumed that demand for the output of all sectors expanded in the same proportion when incomes did. This led to the largest requirement for increased output from the construction and public administration sectors.

However, these demands are largely determined politically rather than in the market, and expansion of them seems unlikely in present circumstances. Thus the main requirement for structural change is a shift from manufacturing towards services.

The incorporation of an oil premium in the exchange rate implies that British prices will seem high in relation to those of other countries. This will be particularly serious for industries where Britain has no cost advantage and where there is little difference between British output and that of other countries; steel is a good example of an industry whose future is permanently blighted. The more successful manufacturing industries will be those where goods are little traded—food manufacturing for example—or where products are strongly differentiated—such as defence equipment. Britain's exports will move 'up-market', as has happened to other industrial countries, such as Japan, Germany and Switzerland, which have experienced substantial changes in their real exchange rates. Some exporting service industries will also suffer—tourism is one; but financial services may be protected by inelastic demand for their product and shipping and aviation may not suffer too severely because their value added in the UK is relatively small.

These adjustments will be difficult. The greater pace of structural change will imply an increasing level of unemployment, and as a result the full benefit to potential output of North Sea oil will not be realised. Moreover, although it is certain that some contraction in the size of manufacturing output is required, uncertainty about the oil price implies uncertainty about the magnitude of the reduction; and the current oil premium simply represents the foreign exchange market's guesstimate of the real exchange rate appreciation required to achieve it, which may ultimately turn out to be too high or too low.

There is little cost to the foreign exchange market in an oil premium which oscillates around its ultimate equilibrium level, but these oscillations can have substantial adjustment costs for the domestic economy. There is therefore some case for damping initial movements toward equilibrium. The principal mechanism for doing this is capital export. It would seem wise to err in the early years of oil production on the size of excessive balance of payments surpluses and capital export, since it will be easier to move further in the direction of domestic structural change in future than to retreat from initial over-reaction.

CHANGES IN THE REAL OIL PRICE

What is the effect on Britain of a change in the real price of oil? In 1981, Britain will probably be for the first time a net exporter of oil: and it would appear that a further rise in oil prices would be of positive benefit. However, it is probably unlikely that Britain will be a net exporter of oil indefinitely. We conjectured that British oil reserves might, at the current real oil price have a value equivalent to $18bn per annum, which is a little less than the current cost of buying Britain's oil consumption at the current price. This level of consumption has not increased since the first oil crisis of 1974. It is reasonable for Britain to be more or less indifferent to the real price of oil.

But we should look here also at the effect on the terms of trade. Rising oil prices do, in fact, seem to be associated with an increase in the real exchange rate for sterling. This is reasonable since Britain's principal trading partners are net importers of oil, and so a rise in the price of oil tends to depress the values of their currencies relative to those of countries which are self sufficient or exporters of oil. Even if a rise in the real price of oil is of no direct benefit to Britain, the improvement in the terms of trade to which it leads will be of indirect benefit.

It is appropriate at this point to note an important qualification to our earlier analysis. In 1976, the oil price was around £7 per barrel, or £12 at 1980 prices; in 1980 it is £15 per barrel but this would, assuming a pre-oil exchange rate of $1.85 be £19. On these assumptions Britain would have needed to export an additional £4bn – £5bn to pay for the increased cost of primary imports. Thus part of the contraction of the tradeable sector which we have described is not an actual contraction but an escape from an expansion which in a non-oil economy would have had to occur. But if we think through the implications of this the assumption of a 22 per cent oil premium in the current exchange rate may seem relatively modest.

WHERE HAS THE MONEY GONE?

We have argued that the benefits of North Sea oil are larger than is generally realised. Moreover, a major part of growth in real incomes which they yield has already occurred; oil production is well over half its ultimate level and the terms of trade have already improved considerably. Yet many people would be surprised to be told they were experiencing a bonanza.

The answer to this is in several parts. First, a significant element of the benefit is not something which makes us positively better off but something which prevents us from being as much worse off as we would otherwise have been. Real incomes in Britain have been protected from the oil price rise in 1979 – 80, and without indigenous oil they could not have been. Second, real disposable incomes did increase sharply in 1978 – 80: earnings rose by 35.4 per cent between January 1978 and January 1980 while the GED, which shows the rise in earnings required to maintain their purchasing power, rose by only 26.0 per cent.

The change is not properly reflected in aggregate statistics of economic growth. For technical reasons, national income accounting conventions do not cope well with major changes in relative prices and very little of the benefits of North Sea oil will ever be reflected in the national accounts. Thirdly, although the growth of production and the rise in oil prices means that major gains from the North Sea are now starting to be reflected in oil company profits, the structure of the tax regime means that it is not until 1983 – 5 that these receipts are fully reflected in government revenues.

21

EXPERIENCE ELSEWHERE

There are very few precedents for the explosive growth of the primary sector in an already industrialised economy. The experience of the Netherlands is widely quoted. The analogy with the growth of mineral industries in Australia is less commonly recognised, but it has perhaps more to teach us, because of the widespread discussion of the need for structural change in the Australian economy which has resulted. This debate was inaugurated by Gregory (1976), and the arguments put forward by him have been an important influence on the thesis of this paper.

There are two aspects to the development of oil production in Britain which taken together mean that our experience is unique. There are no other commodities where the gap between costs of production and selling prices is so large as it is for oil. Hence the gain to income, and tax revenue, from the growth of output of oil is wholly exceptional. Gold is, at current price levels, the only comparable case. South Africa, as the principal gold producer, and Norway, benefitting from oil, are therefore likely to undergo similar changes. However, neither of these countries is as Britain is, a major exporter of manufactured goods in relation to the world economy as a whole; and it is therefore principally in Britain that the further twist to the spiral implied by the appreciation of the terms of trade is fully effective.

VI

The method we have adopted in this paper is to propose a stylised model of the British economy and consider how that model is affected by oil. It is not intended for, or capable of, forecasting—there are many changes occurring in the British economy, and the growth of oil revenues is only one of them, albeit an important one. But this approach does, we believe, enable us to describe the effects and the policy options which result from this development. What are these policy implications? Perhaps the most urgent requirement is for a fuller public understanding of the main issues. The government is not contributing to such understanding by failing to publish realistic estimates of North Sea oil revenues or to state its plans for dealing with them. The present position is disconcerting to many people. The current level of the sterling exchange rate seems absurd in terms of purchasing power, or to the manufacturers of traded goods. Yet it is probably not a temporary aberration; it is the market's mechanism for imposing a cutback in Britain's output of manufactured goods. It is possible to argue whether this is desirable, but to do so is no more sensible than to argue whether it is desirable that the sun should set in the evening; no doubt it would be more convenient if it did not, but that is neither here nor there. There is no other way in which we can benefit from North Sea oil revenues. The only serious alternative is to throw them away.

This should perhaps be considered as a serious alternative, and it seems to be what—consciously or unconsciously—the advocates of import controls or large programmes of manufacturing investment have in mind. It is possible that the costs of structural change are so high, and the capacity of the UK economy to

22

adapt to new patterns of production is so low, that it is better to sustain the existing structure of output so long as national income does not actually decline. If we reduce the efficiency of manufacturing industry sufficiently, we can go on using the resources—labour and capital—presently employed there to produce a lower level of output. We are confident that a programme framed and justified in these terms would be unhesitatingly rejected. We are much less confident that a series of individual policy options which in aggregate amount to such a programme would be rejected.

If we do discard this alternative, then the most important policy implications are negative ones. We should accept the need for structural change in the British economy and while we might try to ameliorate its social consequences we should not seek to retard or reverse it. This means resisting inevitable pressure to support or protect declining sectors of manufacturing industry.

We have argued that a substantial proportion of North Sea oil gains should be used for investment, and that the bulk of this investment should be abroad. Domestic manufacturing is the least likely area to provide profitable scope for such investment. What kinds of policies are likely to stimulate capital outflows of the size required? It is clearly not desirable to encourage capital movement *to* the UK by maintaining relatively higher interest rates than other countries; or by actively stimulating inward investment. Outward investment—both direct and portfolio investment—has already been encouraged by the ending of exchange controls and the high exchange rate will continue to make it more attractive. A policy which uses a major part of North Sea oil revenues to reduce the PSBR, and so puts the cash flows received into the hands of financial institutions, is likely both to encourage the use of a large proportion of these cash flows for portfolio investment and to facilitate their transfer overseas.

We are sceptical of the government's ability to outguess the foreign exchange market as to the appropriate long term level of the oil premium, and would prefer to see foreign assets acquired by the private sector rather than by large scale official intervention in currency markets. Nevertheless, there are costs to the economy if the market initially overestimates the oil premium, imposing excessive pressure on manufacturing which is ultimately relieved, which are greater than the costs imposed on the market itself. Speculators lose money equally from overestimation and underestimation; the economy stands to lose more from overestimation. There is therefore a case for some damping of the initial movement towards the new equilibrium by using official sales of sterling to reduce the rate of appreciation. But this pressure should in due course be phased out—which involves recognising that it is an operation on which the Bank will lose money. It is, in fact, probably already too late for such a policy to make much sense. A considerable oil premium has already emerged, and this must be regarded as the market's assessment of its ultimate level.

We recognise that the approach and the arguments presented in this paper are ones which many people will find difficult to accept, although the logic of them is simple and hard to dispute effectively. We see two principal reasons for this. First, it has become all too common to believe that the end of economic activity is production rather than consumption. This seems to be born of spurious moralising and the power of interest groups of producers. It is no doubt difficult to believe that one can become better off as a result of events which imply no merit of one's own and a reduction rather than an increase in hard and unpleasant labour; but the mineral royalties which once enriched undeserving landowners now enrich an undeserving population. It is worth stressing that there is no *a priori* moral or economic argument for preferring one industrial activity or structure to another; the appropriate pattern of production is the one best adapted to the needs of the society of which it is part and the trading opportunities open to it.

Second, much economic debate in the UK is conducted in terms which were set in the 1950's and 1960's. It is an oversimplification to contrast 'demand side' and 'supply side' approaches to economic policy, but it is certainly true that our analysis is motivated by a view that the principal constraints on economic growth in the UK are to be found on the side of supply rather than demand. Fifteen years ago, it was plausible to argue that Britain suffered from a fixed and overvalued exchange rate and that the level of domestic demand was depressed in order to sustain equilibrium at this level. But although the current exchange rate may appear overvalued in terms of its international purchasing power, there is no reason to regard it as other than an equilibrium rate. Loss of competitiveness is a serious matter when it results from a rise in domestic costs at a fixed exchange rate; but it has wholly different implications when it results from a rise in the exchange rate at a given level of domestic costs. De-industrialisation, as Sir Alec Cairncross, has defined it, "is a matter for concern if it jeopardises our eventual power to pay for the imports we need" (Blackaby, 1979) but when it is the product of an increased capacity to pay for these imports it is just the reverse.

APPENDIX

HOW LARGE ARE THE BENEFITS?

It is necessary to derive two central measures of the impact of oil. One is the increase in net output which results from it—the additional value added in the UK economy. The second is the net effect on the balance of payments of oil; this requires us to see how the increase in net output is divided between the traded and non-traded sectors. Because (non-traded) domestic resources are sucked into the (traded) oil sector, the direct effect is that the balance of payments effect is larger than the increase in net output and the non-traded sector contracts.

If we start with gross revenue from oil, it is appropriate to subtract remittances overseas, whether for the purchase of related imports or as the earnings of overseas companies. The balance consists of domestic operating costs, the profits of UK companies, and tax paid to the British government. All of this reflects an improvement in the balance of payments (an expansion in the output of the tradeable sector) except to the extent that the resources involved would otherwise have been used for exports. Some of the domestic costs are spent on items which might otherwise have been exported but the bulk of them represents net balance of payments gain. A major part of the capital invested by UK companies in the North Sea would otherwise have been used for oil production elsewhere in the world, and would therefore have formed part of the UK export sector in any event; only the return on the remainder represents net gain to the balance of payments.

In computing the net addition to national income, we begin by subtracting domestically incurred operating costs, which simply reflect the costs of transferring resources to the oil sector from the rest of the economy. Parts of oil company profits fall into this category also: the *net* gain to the economy is only the amount by which North Sea profits exceed the returns which could have been earned by investing the capital and other resources devoted to the North Sea elsewhere. The measure of benefit is the difference between the return which they are earning and the return which they would have earned by deploying the funds in alternative uses—the 'economic rent' which they are earning. It is clear that the returns in the North Sea are much higher than would have been obtained from investment in the British domestic economy—the safeguard provisions of petroleum revenue tax (PRT) remit the tax if the rate of return should fall below 30 per cent. It is less clear that these returns are higher than oil companies could have earned from investment in other parts of the world. It is impossible to make any scientific calculation of the rent earned by British companies, but it is unlikely that it would be more than £1bn per annum. There is also some rent earned by those working in the North Sea or in onshore operations who are earning more than they would expect in alternative occupations, but this amount is quite small in aggregate. These items apart, the direct increment to national income which results from North Sea oil is equal to the tax receipts of the British government.

Thus the direct increase in national income which results from North Sea oil is a little larger than government revenue from North Sea taxes—larger by the amount of 'economic rent' earned there. The gain to the balance of payments is a little larger than that—larger by the value of domestic resources drawn into North Sea operations from non-exporting sectors. Precise computation of either of these figures depends on comparison with an unknown, and unknowable, hypothetical outcome.

Table A1 gives estimates of the growth of oil revenues over the period to 1985 and their allocation. The calculations underlying such estimates are complex. This is largely attributable to the complexities of the tax system, which includes three different charges—royalties, based on output, PRT, which is calculated on a field-by-field basis, and corporation tax, which is levied on a company by company basis. These estimates of revenue, like all figures in this paper are at 1980 prices, so that they can validly be compared with 1980 national income and 1980 tax revenues. But it is necessary to spell out what this means. We have assumed that the real price of oil is constant. By this we mean that the oil price rises from that level at the same rate as prices in Western economies generally. We have also assumed that the real exchange rate is constant. By this we mean that the effective international value of sterling depreciates by the amount by

25

which British inflation exceeds the average of other countries. It would be convenient if there were a single international currency in which such prices could be quoted, but although artificial constuctions exist there is none which will mean much to many people. We therefore quote both prices in dollars, so that we start from a real oil price of $35 per barrel and a real exchange rate of $2.25.

Table A2 shows the behaviour of the real oil price since oil became available from the North Sea by comparing the price of oil (in $). The real price was roughly constant in 1975 – 7, fell in 1978 and rose considerably in 1979 – 80. The Table also shows the movement of the real exchange rate over the same period by comparing the movement of UK prices (in sterling) with the cost of buying the consumer goods of OECD member countries (in sterling).

The tax yield also depends on the rate of domestic inflation. This may seem paradoxical when we are making calculations in constant prices, but the reason is that inflation reduces the real value of allowances which are given on past capital expenditure. Thus rapid inflation increases government revenue at the expense of company profits. The six per cent rate implicit in Table A1 is clearly too low but this effect is not very large.

Yield is also sensitive to production levels. In the past, the growth of production has tended to fall below expectations, and if this is true in future then the growth of revenue both in aggregate and to the government will be slower than Table A1 implies. But unless peak production is substantially cut back in order to delay depletion this makes no difference to ultimate revenues—indeed it is likely to increase them slightly.

TABLE A1

Allocation of Oil Revenues, 1980 – 5 (£bn)

		1980	1981	1982	1983	1984	1985
Operating costs		3.1	3.2	2.9	2.6	2.1	1.9
Earnings:	UK companies	2.3	1.6	1.5	1.0	1.1	1.6
	foreign companies	2.8	3.4	2.5	2.7	3.2	2.5
	Total profits	5.1	5.0	4.0	3.7	4.3	4.1
Taxes:	royalties	0.9	1.2	1.4	1.5	1.6	1.6
	PRT	1.7	3.5	4.8	6.4	6.5	6.7
	corporation tax	0.4	1.0	1.6	2.1	2.8	3.0
	Total tax	3.0	5.7	7.8	10.0	10.9	11.3
Total revenue		11.2	13.9	14.8	16.3	17.2	17.3

Source: Wood McKenzie & Co

All figures are at 1980 prices and assume a constant real price of oil, a constant real exchange rate and six per cent domestic inflation.

The revenue projections presented in the text are designed as long-run 'steady state' estimates. They reflect basic assumptions of production of one billion barrels per year and annual operating costs of £2.5bn (at 1980 prices). We assume that the tax system claims 80 per cent of net revenue at a price of $35 per barrel (this is to present target) and imposes a marginal tax rate of 90 per cent. The marginal tax rate in the existing system is 87 per cent (Table A3); this implies that tax rates will be raised or lowered in line with oil price changes.

TABLE A2

The Real Exchange Rate and the Real Price of Oil, 1975 – 80 (1975 = 100)

	Real exchange rate			Real oil price		
Year	OECD consumer prices, in sterling	UK consumer prices	UK prices ÷ OECD prices	North Sea oil price ($)	OECD prices ($)	Oil price ÷ OECD prices
1975	100	100	100	100	100	100
1976	129	117	91	110	104	106
1977	147	135	92	121	114	106
1978	156	146	94	119	136	88
1979	164	166	101	203	154	132
1980 (Jan)	166	182	110	256	167	153

Sources: Prices: OECD Economic Outlook
                 Exchange rates: IMF Financial Statistics
                 Oil price: UK Offshore Operators Association

TABLE A3

The Marginal Rate of Tax on North Sea Oil Revenue

	Rate	Amount
		100.0
Additional revenue		
Royalty	12½ %	12.5
		87.5
Petroleum Revenue Tax	70%	61.3
		26.2
Corporation Tax	52%	13.6
		12.6
Implied marginal tax rate	87.4%	

Notes (1) Where the safeguard provision for marginal fields is operating, the marginal rate of PRT is 80% and the implied marginal tax rate higher.
         (2) Additional revenue may allow more rapid utilisation of allowances against PRT and/or corporation tax: this would reduce the effective marginal tax rate.
         (3) Many companies with North Sea operations would otherwise be unable to offset ACT against any liability to mainstream corporation tax. Where this is true it reduces the effective rate of corporation tax and also reduces the net gain to the UK Exchequer from North Sea activities.

Fiscal Studies

References

Blackaby, F (ed) (1979). *De-industrialisation.* NIESR/Heinemann, London
CEPG (1980). *Economic Policy Review,* Gower Press
Gaskin, M (1978). *The Impact of North Sea Oil on Scotland,* HMSO, London
Gregory, R G (1976). 'Some Implications of the Growth of the Mineral Sector', *Australian Journal of Agricultural Economics*
Page, S A B (1977). 'The Value and Distribution of the Benefits of North Sea Oil and Gas', *National Institute Economic Review*
Robinson, C and Morgan, J (1978). *North Sea Oil in the Future,* Trade Policy Research Centre/Macmillan, London.

[12]

De-industrialization in the UK: three theses

Introduction

In this chapter we take up some of the themes explored in general terms in Chapter 1. We examine what has happened to manufacturing and other forms of industrial employment in the UK since the Second World War. We show how the UK has experienced an enormous reduction in manufacturing employment over the past thirty years – greater than that in almost any other advanced capitalist country. And we consider various hypotheses which might explain why this has occurred. Three possible explanations are identified, namely, the 'Maturity Thesis', the 'Specialization Thesis' and the 'Failure Thesis'. All three theses, it turns out, have *prima facie* evidence to support them. However, this is only a provisional conclusion and a final judgement must wait until the next chapter.

Britain's post-war employment record in an international context

Fig. 10.1 shows what has happened to employment in the major sectors of the British economy since the war. There has been an almost continuous fall in the number of people employed in agriculture, from around 1.8 million in 1946 to under 1 million in 1983. Over the same period, employment in the service sector rose dramatically, from just under 10 million to over 14 million. In the so-called 'production' industries – manufacturing, mining, construction and public utilities – the picture is more complex. Immediately after the war, under the impetus of post-war reconstruction and the export drive, the number employed in these sectors increased rapidly. Then, in the 1950s, the pace of expansion slackened. Employment continued to rise in manufacturing and construction, though at a slower pace than before, whilst coal mining began to shed labour as pits were closed because of competition from oil. For a time, the new jobs created in manufacturing and construction more than offset those lost in mining, with the result that industrial employment, as a whole, continued rising right through into the 1960s. However, this expansion came to an abrupt halt in 1966 when, following a major sterling crisis, the Labour government

208   **De-industrialization in the UK**

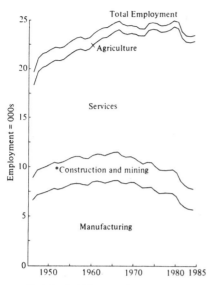

* includes electricity, gas and water

Fig. 10.1 Employment in the UK by sector 1946–83 (millions)

of the day imposed a severe deflationary budget on the economy. Since that time, industrial employment of all kinds – in mining, construction and manufacturing alike – has fallen irregularly at what seems like an accelerating pace. From an all-time peak of 11.5 million in 1966, the total number of industrial workers in employment had fallen to well under 8 million by 1984. Over the same period, manufacturing employment alone has fallen from 8.5 million to well under 5.7 million. About half of this enormous decline took place before the present Thatcher government took office in 1979, whilst the rest has occurred since.

The story is much the same if we look at relative shares rather than absolute numbers, although the timing of events is somewhat different (see Fig. 10.2). After rising strongly immediately after the war, the share of industry in civil employment reached a peak in 1955 of around 48%. In that year, approximately one-third of the entire population between the ages of 15 and 64 were employed as industrial workers, whilst most of the rest were students, housewives and service workers. These figures for industry's share in total employment have rarely been equalled and certainly never surpassed in the whole of British history. Moreover, they are almost without equal in the experience of other capitalist countries. This last point can be verified from Table 10.1, which compares Britain's employment structure in 1955 with that of other highly industrialized economies at an equivalent stage in their development. In the entire history of world

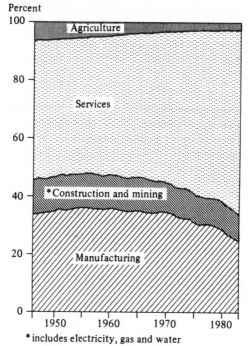

*includes electricity, gas and water

Fig. 10.2 Employment in the UK by sector 1946–83 (percentage shares)

Table 10.1. *Comparative employment structure in the West's most industrialized economies*

	Industrial employment as % of		Manufacturing employment as % of	
	Civil employment	Population aged 15–64	Civil employment	Population aged 15–64
Belgium (1957)	47.0	26.9	36.0	20.6
Germany (1970)	48.5	33.1	37.7	25.8
Luxemburg (1966)	46.9	28.8	35.8	22.0
Switzerland (1963)	47.6	n.a.	38.5	n.a.
UK (1955)	47.9	32.8	36.1	24.7

Source: OECD. The dates in parenthesis refer to the year in which industrial employment reached its all-time peak as a share of civil employment

capitalism, the all-time peak of industrialization (in employment terms) was probably achieved by Germany in 1970 or Switzerland in 1963. In each case, industry accounted for 47–8% of civil employment'– which is virtually identical

210   De-industrialization in the UK

to the figure reached in Britain in 1955. Thus, in employment terms, the British economy in 1955 was one of the most highly industrialized economies the capitalist world has ever seen. Never before, nor since, in any capitalist country at any time has industrial employment been significantly more important than it was in Britain in 1955.

Yet, no sooner had this pre-eminence been achieved, than the process went into reverse. Industrial employment began declining in importance, at first slowly and then with gathering speed. By 1983, the share of industry in total employment had fallen to 34% and that of manufacturing alone to under 25%. To illustrate the scale of the transformation which has occurred since 1955, consider the relationship between industry and the services. In 1955 there were more workers employed in industry than in all of the services combined, both public and private. By 1983 there were almost two service workers for each industrial worker, and the public services alone employed about three-quarters as many people as the whole of the manufacturing industry put together (4.3 million as compared to 5.8 million). Under ideal conditions of prosperity and full employment, such a transformation over such a short period of time would have been disruptive. Under the actual conditions of stagnation and unemployment, it has been traumatic.

Let us now consider the experience of other countries over the past thirty years. We shall concentrate on the manufacturing sector, but our remarks apply with only minor qualifications to the industrial sector as a whole, including mining and construction. Tables 10.2 and 10.3 show what has happened to manufacturing employment in the advanced capitalist countries. Wherever possible the figures go back to 1955 or even before, although in some cases there are gaps caused by a lack of reliable information.

Let us first consider Table 10.2. This shows the rate of growth of manufacturing employment during three distinct periods: 1956–66, 1966–73 and 1973–83. Looking at these growth rates, the following points stand out. In the first period, manufacturing employment increases in every single country shown in the table, often at extremely high rates. In the second period, the pace of expansion slows down, and there are even a few countries in which manufacturing employment starts to fall. Finally, in the third period, 1973–83, there is an almost universal decline in manufacturing employment, with only three minor exceptions: Finland, Iceland and New Zealand. Thus, the first period (1956–66) is one of general expansion in manufacturing employment, the second (1966–73) is one of transition and the third (1973–83) is one of general contraction.

Comparing Britain's performance with that of other countries, we find that between 1956 and 1966 manufacturing employment grew more slowly in Britain than in any other country shown in the table; between 1966 and 1973, it fell by more than in any other country, with the exception of Sweden; and between

Table 10.2. *Manufacturing employment in the advanced capitalist countries*

	Annual percentage change			Cumulative percentage change	
	1956–66	1966–73	1973–83	1956–66	1966–83
Italy	1.0	2.0	−0.9	10.3	5.3
Japan	3.9	2.9	−0.4	47.3	18.3
Finland	n.a.	1.6	0.5	n.a.	17.5
Austria	n.a.	n.a.	−0.6	n.a.	n.a.
Iceland[a, b]	1.5	2.1	2.8	15.6	52.1
France	0.8	0.6	−1.9	8.7	−14.0
Norway	n.a.	n.a.	−0.9	n.a.	n.a.
Denmark[b]	2.2	−1.2	−1.9	24.5	−24.4
Canada	2.4	1.4	−0.4	26.5	6.7
Luxemburg[a]	1.3	0.9	−2.3	14.3	−15.5
Germany	1.2	0.2	−1.9	12.2	−16.2
Sweden[a]	1.0	−1.3	−1.2	10.7	−18.8
Switzerland[a]	1.7	−0.2	−2.0	18.5	−19.9
New Zealand[b]	n.a.	1.9	0.4	n.a.	18.9
Netherlands	1.0	−0.8	−2.4	11.0	−25.7
Australia	n.a.	1.7	−2.7	n.a.	−14.3
Belgium[b]	0.6	−0.3	−3.4	7.1	−30.8
USA	1.3	0.7	−0.4	13.5	0.6
UK	0.4	−1.2	−3.1	+4.1	−33.2

Notes: [a] the initial date is 1957, and the estimate for cumulative change over the period 1955–66 is based on the average annual growth rates for the years 1957–66;
[b] the terminal date is 1981, and the estimate for cumulative change over the period 1966–83 is based on the average annual growth rates for the periods 1966–73 and 1973–81
Source: See notes to Table A7.1 of Appendix 7

1973 and 1983, it fell by more than in any other country, with the exception of Belgium. Taking the period 1955–83 as a whole, or even the subperiod 1966–83, Britain has experienced the greatest percentage decline in manufacturing employment of any Western country.

Table 10.3 shows what has happened to the relative share of manufacturing in total employment. Here the picture is not quite so clear as in the case of absolute numbers. Between 1955 and 1981, the share of manufacturing in civil employment in the UK fell by 9.7 percentage points (from 36.1% to 26.4%). This is certainly a much greater reduction than occurred in most of the countries shown in the table. However, enormous though it is, even greater reductions were recorded in Australia and Belgium, where manufacturing's share fell by 10.2 and 10.6 percentage points respectively. Thus, if we take the share of manufacturing in total employment as our index, the extent of de-industrialization over the last thirty years has been much greater in Britain than in most other advanced capitalist countries, although slightly less than in Australia and Belgium.

212   **De-industrialization in the UK**

Table 10.3. *Share of manufacturing in civil employment, 1950–81*

	Percentage share					Change
	1950	1955	1966	1973	1981	1955–1981
Italy	n.a.	20.0	25.8	28.5	26.1	+6.1
Japan	n.a.	18.4	24.4	27.4	24.8	+6.4
Finland[c]	n.a.	21.3	22.8	25.4	26.1	+4.8
Austria[a]	n.a.	29.8	29.8	29.7	29.7	−0.1
Iceland[b]	21.5	23.7	25.5	25.2	26.3	+3.3
France	n.a.	26.9	28.7	28.3	25.1	−1.8
Norway	22.0	23.1	23.7	23.5	20.2	−2.9
Denmark	n.a.	27.5	29.0	24.7	21.3	−6.2
Canada	24.9	24.1	23.9	22.0	19.4	−4.7
Luxemburg[b]	n.a.	33.2	35.8	33.8	27.4	−5.8
Germany	n.a.	33.8	35.2	36.7	33.6	−0.2
Sweden[b]	n.a.	31.7	31.2	27.5	23.3	−8.4
Switzerland[c]	n.a.	36.1	37.8	35.0	32.0	−4.1
New Zealand[c]	n.a.	23.7	25.4	25.7	24.0	+0.1
Netherlands	29.3	29.3	28.9	25.7	21.1	−8.2
Australia[c]	n.a.	29.6	28.6	25.6	19.4	−10.2
Belgium	35.0	35.3	33.6	31.8	24.7	−10.6
USA	27.9	28.5	27.8	24.8	21.7	−6.8
UK	34.8	36.1	34.8	32.3	26.4	−9.7

Notes: [a] Figure in second column is for 1956; figure in the final column refers to 1956–81
[b] Figure in second column is for 1957; figure in the final column refers to 1957–81
[c] Figure in second column is for 1959; figure in the final column refers to 1959–81
Source: Divers OECD publications and Bairoch (1968)

Three theses

Whether one considers relative shares or absolute numbers the decline in industrial employment in the UK has been spectacular. What accounts for it? Why did this decline begin so much earlier in the UK than in most other countries and why has it been so great? From the general discussion in Chapter 1, we can identify three potential explanations for what has happened.

The Maturity Thesis

The first thesis locates Britain's own historical experience within a more general theory of economic development and structural change. In Chapter 1, we saw how economic development is accompanied by an almost continuous rise in the share of services in total employment, and how the impact of this on industrial employment depends on the stage of development that an economy has reached. In the early and intermediate stages of development, services grow at the expense of agriculture and their share in total employment rises, whilst that of agriculture falls. Meanwhile, the share of industrial employment generally rises. However, at a later stage of development, once an economy has reached 'maturity', the situation is quite different. In such an economy, only a small fraction of the labour force is employed in agriculture and any major increase in the share of services in total employment must be at the expense of industry, whose share must fall. This, in a nutshell, is the Maturity Thesis. It explains why, in a mature economy, the share of industry in total employment falls in the course of time. One cannot lay down general rules which determine exactly when any particular economy will reach the point of maturity, as there are many different factors which can influence the turning-point. However, from the regression analyses of Chapter 1, it seems that the typical capitalist economy reaches maturity when per capita income is in the region of 4,000 US dollars (at 1975 prices). At this stage, agriculture normally accounts for between 5 and 10% of total employment, although the figure may be higher depending on the economy concerned and its pattern of trade speicalization. Before considering how the Maturity Thesis applies to the UK, there are several points which should be noted. The first point concerns employment.

The Maturity Thesis is primarily about employment shares and not absolute numbers. The absolute number of people employed in the industrial sector depends on the behaviour of total employment. Where total employment is growing rapidly, the relative share of industry may fall a considerable amount without there being any reduction at all in the absolute number of people employed in this sector.[1] On the other hand, where total employment is increasing slowly, any major reduction in the relative share of industry will be accompanied by an absolute fall in industrial employment. The second point concerns economic performance. The Maturity Thesis asserts that, at a certain stage in development, the share of industry in total employment will start to fall. In a successful mature economy this fall in industry's share of employment will be accompanied by a rapid growth in output and labour productivity in the industrial sector. The growth in service employment will be enough to provide work for virtually all who require it, including people displaced from the industrial sector through automation and other labour-saving measures. In Chapter 1, we used the term 'positive de-industrialization' to describe the kind of dynamic change in employment structure which occurs in a successful mature economy. In an unsuccessful mature economy, a similar shift in employment structure occurs, but the mechanism is different. In such an economy, industry is in a state of crisis, industrial output is rising very slowly or even falling, and industrial employment may be falling absolutely. Although service employment may be increasing, it is not doing so fast enough to prevent a considerable rise in unemployment. In Chapter 1, we used the term 'negative de-industrialization' to describe this kind of shift in the structure of employment. Thus, in a mature economy, no matter how good or bad is the performance of the industrial sector, the share

214   **De-industrialization in the UK**

of industry in total employment will normally fall in the course of time. Depending on what happens to total employment, this fall in the share of industry may or may not be accompanied by an absolute fall in industrial employment. This, at least, is the claim made by the Maturity Thesis and, as we have seen in Chapter 1, there is considerable evidence in its favour.

The Maturity Thesis is of obvious relevance to the UK. In the 1950s, the UK was still one of the richest countries in the world, and her economy was on the verge of maturity. Per capita income in 1955 was $3,305 (at 1975 prices), which is not far short of the turning-point at which the share of industry in total employment starts to fall. Moreover, agriculture accounted for only 5% of total employment, so that any substantial rise in the share of services could only come about at the expense of industry. The situation was very different in most other capitalist countries. Some were still relatively poor and still had enormous reserves of labour in agriculture. These countries were nowhere near mature, and there was still ample room for services to increase their share of employment at the expense of agriculture without reducing the share of industry. Other countries had a higher per capita income than the UK, but even in these countries the share of agriculture in total employment was much greater than in the UK and so, in this respect, their economies were less mature.

The contrast in experience between the UK and other countries can be seen from Table 10.4, which shows what has happened to the structure of employment since 1955. Countries have been divided into three groups, depending on the share of agriculture in total employment in 1955. At one extreme are the 'immature' economies in group A, all of which were still highly agrarian in 1955, having more than 21% of their employed labour force in agriculture. At the other extreme is the UK which stands on its own, being the least agrarian economy in the world in 1955, with just over 5% of its labour force in agriculture. Between these two extremes are the 'transitional' economies of group B, all of which were still moderately agrarian in character in 1955, with agriculture accounting for between 9 and 18% of total employment.

From Table 10.4 and the supporting data given in Appendix 9, we can see how the share of services in total employment has risen dramatically throughout the advanced capitalist world. In the group A (immature) countries, this increase has been matched by an almost equal reduction in the share of agriculture; as a result industry's share has hardly altered. This can be seen from Table 10.5 which summarizes some of the information given in Table 10.4. Between 1955 and 1981, the share of services in total employment rose by 19.2 points in the immature countries of group A (from 36.0% to 55.2%). Over the same period, the share of agriculture fell by 21.1 points (from 31.0% to 9.9%). Meanwhile the share of industry actually rose, though only slightly, from 33.0% in 1955 to 34.9% in 1981. At the other extreme is the UK, where the relative

Table 10.4. *Employment structure and stage of development*

	Percentage share of civil employment				Absolute change in % share		
	1955	1966	1973	1981	1955–73	1973–81	1955–81
	Agriculture						
Group A	31.0	20.6	14.1	9.9	−16.9	−4.2	−21.1
Group B	14.6	9.3	7.0	5.8	−7.6	−1.2	−8.8
UK	5.4	3.6	2.9	2.6	−2.5	−0.3	−2.8
	Manufacturing						
Group A	23.8	26.2	26.6	25.0	+2.8	−1.6	+1.2
Group B	30.5	30.8	28.9	24.7	−1.6	−4.2	−5.8
UK	36.1	34.8	32.3	26.4	−3.8	−5.9	−9.7
	Industry						
Group A	33.0	36.6	37.2	34.9	+4.2	−2.3	+1.9
Group B	40.7	41.2	38.6	33.7	−2.1	−4.9	−7.0
UK	47.9	46.3	42.6	35.7	−5.3	−6.9	−12.2
	Services						
Group A	36.0	42.8	48.7	55.2	+12.7	+6.5	+19.2
Group B	44.7	49.5	54.4	60.5	+9.7	+6.1	+15.8
UK	46.7	50.1	54.5	61.7	+7.8	+7.2	+15.0

Note: The group figures refer to an unweighted average of the countries concerned. Group A contains those advanced capitalist countries in which the share of agriculture in civil employment was at least 21.8% in 1955: Italy, Japan, Finland, Austria, Iceland, France, Norway and Denmark. Group B contains those countries in which the agricultural share was between 9.7 and 18.0% in 1955: Canada, Luxemburg, Germany, Sweden, Switzerland, New Zealand, Netherlands, Australia, Belgium, USA. The UK, with an agricultural share of 5.4% in 1955, is the only advanced capitalist country not in one of these groups
Source: See Table A1 of Appendix 7

expansion of services has been almost entirely at the expense of industry. Between 1955 and 1981, the share of services in total employment rose by 15.0 points in the UK (from 46.7% to 61.7%). There was some decline in agriculture, whose share fell by 2.8 points, but the vast bulk of service expansion was at the expense of industry, whose share fell by 12.2 points. This is hardly surprising. Given the small size of agriculture's share at the begining of the period (5.4%), it was mathematically impossible for this sector to provide the labour required to meet a 15.0% rise in the share of services. As a matter of arithmetic, such a rise in the share of services could only be at the expense of industry, whose *share* was bound to fall.

So, at one extreme are the immature, agrarian economies of group A where, as a rule, services have increased their employment mainly at the expense of agriculture, leaving industry largely unaffected.[2] At the other extreme is the UK, where the share of agriculture was already very small in 1955, and where the relative expansion of service employment has been almost entirely at the expense of industry. Between these two extremes lie the transitional economies

216　　**De-industrialization in the UK**

Table 10.5. *Summary of employment changes, 1955–81*

| | Absolute change in percentage share | | |
	Group A (immature)	Group B (transitional)	UK (mature)
Agriculture	−21.1	−8.8	−2.8
Industry	+1.9	−7.0	−12.2
Services	+19.2	+15.8	+15.0
Total	0.0	0.0	0.0
cf. manufacturing	+1.2	−5.8	−9.7

Source: last column of Table 10.4

of group B. These economies were moderately agrarian in 1955, and the increase in the share of services since then has been at the expense of both agriculture and industry, in almost equal proportions (see Table 10.5).[3]

To explore this point a little further, let us go back to Tables 10.2 and 10.3. In these tables, countries are ranked according to the share of agriculture in total employment in 1955. Thus, at the top of the list is Italy, where the share of agriculture was 40.8% in 1955; at the bottom of the list is the UK, where agriculture's share was only 5.4%. Looking at these tables, we find a clear pattern in the behaviour of employment. In the more agrarian economies, towards the top of the list, manufacturing employment has in general grown faster (or fallen less) than in the least agrarian countries towards the bottom of the list. This relationship is illustrated graphically in the scatter diagrams shown in Figs. 10.3 and 10.4. Along the horizontal axis in these diagrams is measured the share of agriculture in total employment in the relevant base year (1955 in Fig. 10.3 and 1966 in Fig. 10.4).[4] Along the vertical axis is measured the change in manufacturing employment since the base year. Looking at these diagrams, we notice immediately a positive association between the variables concerned. This is particularly clear in Fig. 10.3, which shows how manufacturing share has changed since 1955. It is also true of Fig. 10.4, which shows how the absolute numbers employed in manufacturing have changed since 1966. In each case, the least agrarian economies at the beginning of the period have experienced the greatest fall in manufacturing employment, either absolutely or as a share of total employment.

Quite apart from the light they throw on structural change in general, Figs. 10.3 and 10.4 also tell us something about the British economy. As the least agrarian economy, the UK lies well to the left in each diagram, and this in itself helps to explain why the fall in manufacturing employment in the UK, both absolutely and relatively, has been so great. Here, then, we have an explanation for why the decline in industrial employment began so early in the UK and why it has been so great. By the early 1950s, the UK was already approaching economic

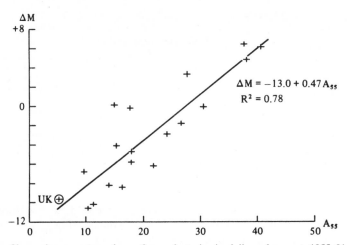

ΔM = Change in percentage share of manufacturing in civil employment, 1955–81.
A_{55} = percentage share of agriculture in civil employment in 1955.

Fig. 10.3 Manufacturing employment and stage of development, 1953–83

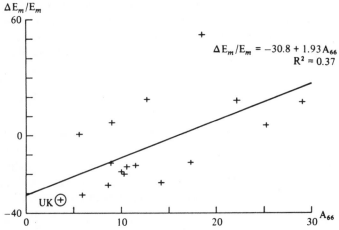

$\Delta E_m/E_m$ = percentage change in manufacturing employment over the period 1966–83.
A_{66} = percentage share of agriculture in civil employment in 1966.

Fig. 10.4 Manufacturing employment and stage of development 1966–83

maturity, and the pattern of employment was bound to shift away from industry
towards the services. By contrast, many other currently advanced capitalist countries were nowhere near maturity in the early 1950s: many of them still had
a large proportion of their labour force employed in agriculture, and they had

simply not yet reached the stage of development at which economic growth involves an absolute or relative decline in industrial employment.

Thus, from the evidence we have examined so far, the Maturity Thesis looks quite convincing as an explanation for what has happened in the UK. It certainly helps to explain why the fall in industrial employment began earlier in the UK and has been more extensive than in most other countries. Further evidence is provided by the fact that many other capitalist countries began to experience a similar decline in industrial employment in the 1960s and 1970s, once their reserves of agricultural labour were depleted and they had reached the stage of maturity at which the service sector increases its share of total employment at the expense of industry.

The Specialization Thesis

A second potential explanation for the decline in manufacturing employment in the UK is concerned with foreign trade, with the huge changes which have occurred in the structure of UK trade over the past thirty years. These changes have been described at length in preceding chapters, so here we outline only their main features. By the time post-war recovery was complete, Britain had once again become a highly specialized 'workshop' economy, importing vast amounts of food and raw materials, as well as oil, in return for manufactured exports. This can be seen from the balance of payments figures. In 1950–2, the surplus on UK manufacturing trade averaged 10.5% of GDP whilst, on non-manufacturing trade, the average deficit was 13.3% of GDP.[5] These are truly remarkable figures, which have never been equalled, before or since, in British history. The reasons for such a remarkable situation are briefly as follows. On the non-manufacturing side, global scarcities in the aftermath of the Second World War had forced up to unprecedented levels the real cost of items which Britain had always imported in bulk, such as food and raw materials. Moreover, Britain's previously massive income from service activities, such as shipping and the City of London, had fallen, whilst receipts from coal exports, which had earlier been enormous, had almost vanished. This combination of inflated import prices and reduced earnings from service and coal exports explains why the deficit in non-manufacturing trade was so large in the early 1950s. To cover this deficit, the UK had no alternative but to export manufactured goods. Her profits from overseas investment had been greatly reduced by the enforced war-time sale of assets in the US and elsewhere, and the scope for overseas borrowing was limited. So, to finance her huge deficit on non-manufacturing trade, the UK required a surplus of almost equal magnitude in her manufacturing trade. This surplus was achieved through a vigorous combination of industrial protection and export promotion.

The early 1950s mark the high point of the UK's role as a 'workshop' economy. Since then, the picture has been transformed beyond recognition. In non-manufacturing trade, the old deficit has disappeared completely, to be replaced by a small surplus averaging 1% of GDP in 1981–3. Meanwhile, in manufacturing trade the opposite has occurred, and the old surplus has been replaced by a small deficit. This transformation is often seen as a symptom of Britain's industrial decline and of the failure of her manufacturing sector to compete successfully in international markets. However, as we have argued in earlier chapters, such an interpretation in unfounded. Certainly, the performance of manufacturing industry has been very poor during the past thirty years, but this is not a major factor explaining why there has been such a dramatic transformation in the structure of UK trade. The cause of this transformation lies mainly in events largely unrelated to the country's industrial performance. Since the early 1950s, there has been a whole stream of autonomous developments whose cumulative impact on Britain's trade structure and pattern of specialization has been enormous. It is these autonomous developments which explain why Britain is no longer a workshop economy, why she no longer has a large deficit on her trade in non-manufactures or a large surplus on her manufacturing trade.

Since the early 1950s, imports of food and raw materials have become much cheaper in real terms; increased domestic food production has reduced the need for food imports; new methods of production and a changing composition of output have reduced the need for imported raw materials; service exports, in such areas as civil aviation, consultancy and finance have risen; finally, the discovery of North Sea oil has turned Britain into a major oil producer. Between them, these developments explain why the UK's balance of trade in non-manufactures has improved so dramatically since the early 1950s. They also explain why the balance of trade in manufactures has deteriorated so dramatically over this period. In the early 1950s, the UK was a 'workshop' economy because she had to be. To finance the huge deficit in non-manufacturing trade, the country required a huge surplus in manufacturing trade. There was simply no other way to remain solvent. Nowadays, however, the situation is quite different. The UK no longer has a huge deficit in non-manufacturing trade and, as a result, she no longer requires a huge surplus in her trade in manufactures. The UK is no longer a massive net exporter of manufactures, because she no longer needs to be, and her poor industrial performance has only a marginal bearing on the matter. The dramatic decline in the UK's manufacturing surplus during the past thirty years is not primarily a symptom of industrial failure but is mainly a response to developments elsewhere in the economy. Autonomous developments in non-manufacturing trade have led to a new pattern of specialization, a new role for the UK in the world economy, of which the loss of her formerly huge manufacturing surplus is but one expression.

220   **De-industrialization in the UK**

Now, for reasons explored in Chapter 1, a country's internal pattern of employment depends on its pattern of specialization, on its role in the international division of labour. *Ceteris paribus*, a 'workshop' economy, such as the UK in the early fifties, with a large trade surplus in manufactures, will have a much larger manufacturing sector than a country with a more balanced trade structure. Moreover, when an economy ceases to be a workshop economy and acquires a less specialized foreign trade structure, its manufacturing sector is likely to contract relatively, if not absolutely.

Here, then, is a potential explanation for what has happened to manufacturing employment in the UK over the past thirty years. In the early 1950s, the UK was a highly specialized manufacturing exporter, perhaps the most extreme example of a workshop economy the world has ever seen. This, in itself, helps to explain why such a large fraction of her labour force was employed in manufacturing industry. Since those days, because of developments in non-manufacturing trade, the British economy has become much less specialized. The country no longer requires such a large surplus in manufacturing trade and, as a result, no longer needs to employ anything like such a large fraction of her labour force in manufacturing. Moreover, no other country has experienced such a massive transformation in its foreign trade structure during the past thirty years. No other country, not even Austria or Norway, has experienced such a vast improvement in its non-manufacturing balance over the period, nor such a deterioration in its manufacturing balance. This may help to explain why the decline in manufacturing employment has been so much greater in the UK than in most other countries.

The Failure Thesis

So far we have considered two explanations for the decline of manufacturing employment in the UK. First, there was the Maturity Thesis, which located this decline within the framework of a general theory of development and structural change. The UK, it argued, was the first country to reach the stage of development known as 'maturity', in which the share of manufacturing in total employment starts to fall. This, in itself, helps to explain why the decline in manufacturing employment began so much earlier in the UK than elsewhere and has been so much greater. A very different explanation was put forward by the Specialization Thesis. According to this thesis, the decline in manufacturing employment is merely an internal consequence of the UK's changing external relations with other countries, in particular of the huge improvements which have occurred in the realm of non-manufacturing trade since the early 1950s. Thus, one thesis argues that a fall in manufacturing employment was inevitable, given the stage of development which the UK had reached by the 1950s, whilst the other argues that improvements in non-manufacturing trade are responsible for this decline.

There is, however, a third possible explanation – the 'Failure Thesis'. As its name suggests, this thesis sees the decline of manufacturing employment as a symptom of economic failure: the growing failure of manufacturing industry to compete internationally or to produce the level of output required for a prosperous and fully employed economy. The Failure Thesis can be summarized in the following set of propositions:

(1)   The UK's economic record in the realm of incomes and employment has been poor;

(2)   This is largely due to the weak performance of UK manufacturing industry;

(3)   If the performance of UK manufacturing industry had been much stronger, UK manufacturing output would have been much greater;

(4)   This would have stimulated the non-manufacturing side of the economy and led to the creation of more employment in services and other non-manufacturing activities;

(5)   Finally, if UK manufacturing output had been higher, neither the absolute number of people employed in manufacturing, nor this sector's share in total employment, would have fallen anything like as fast as they have done.

Many of these propositions are quite uncontroversial and are universally accepted by economists of all persuasions. Even so, let us examine them briefly.

Consider the question of Britain's economic record. Here the evidence of failure is overwhelming. By international standards, real per capita income has risen slowly in the UK, particularly since 1973. Moreover, growth in GDP since 1973 has been entirely the result of North Sea oil production; indeed, between 1973 and 1983, non-oil GDP actually fell by 2% (Fig. 10.5). The cumulative effect of slow growth on the UK's position in the international hierarchy can be seen from Table 10.6. In 1953, the UK was amongst the half dozen richest countries in the world. By 1983, of all the advanced capitalist countries, she was amongst the poorest. In the realm of employment, the UK's record is equally dismal. In the 1950s, there was almost full employment in the UK, and the bulk of her population had never enjoyed greater economic security. However, by 1984, well over three million people were out of work and, of all the advanced capitalist countries, only Belgium and the Netherlands had a greater fraction of their labour force without employment (see Table 10.7). Not since the 1930s have so many British people faced such a bleak and insecure future.

So much for economic welfare. What about the role of manufacturing industry in all of this? Here again the evidence is overwhelming. By international

222   **De-industrialization in the UK**

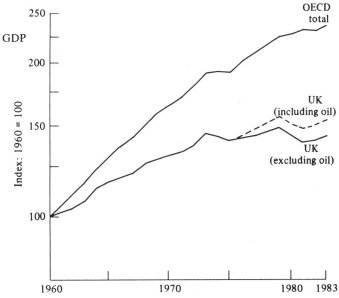

Fig. 10.5 GDP in the UK and OECD, 1960–83

Table 10.6. *GDP per head in selected countries ($US 1975)*[a]

	(1)	(2)	(3)	(4)	Percentage growth per annum
	1953	1963	1973	1984	1953–84
Canada	3896	4688	7030	7970	2.3
USA	4946	5503	7371	8511	1.8
Japan	1054	2245	4974	6314	5.9
Australia	3074	3884	5337	6126	2.2
Austria	1735	3031	4785	5752	3.9
Belgium	2499	3384	5253	5959	2.8
France	2432	3476	5437	6362	3.2
Germany	2319	3866	5628	6473	3.4
Italy	1814	2903	4363	4721	3.1
Netherlands	2694	3639	5502	5836	2.5
Norway	3067	4058	5716	7562	3.0
Sweden	3536	4993	6769	7567	2.5
Unweighted average	2756	3806	5680	6596	2.9
UK	3080	3834	5053	5616	2.0

[a] Exchange rates are based on purchasing power parity
Source: OECD, Kravis (1982)

Table 10.7. *Unemployment rates in selected OECD countries[a] (percentage of total labour force)*

	1964–73	1974–79	1980	1981	1982	1983	1984
US	4.4	6.6	7.0	7.5	9.5	9.5	7.4
Germany	0.8	3.2	3.0	4.4	6.1	8.0	8.6
France	2.2	4.5	6.3	7.3	8.1	8.3	9.7
Italy	5.5	6.6	7.4	8.3	9.0	9.8	10.2
Canada	4.7	7.2	7.5	7.5	10.9	11.8	11.2
Australia	1.9	5.0	6.0	5.7	7.1	9.9	8.9
Belgium	2.2	3.8	9.0	11.1	12.6	13.9	14.0
Netherlands	1.4	3.8	4.9	7.5	11.4	13.7	14.0
Japan	1.2	1.9	2.0	2.2	2.4	2.6	2.7
Norway	1.7	1.8	1.7	2.0	2.6	3.3	3.0
Sweden	2.0	1.9	2.0	2.5	3.1	3.5	3.1
Austria	1.5	1.6	1.9	2.5	3.5	4.1	4.0
Unweighted average	2.5	4.0	4.9	5.7	7.2	8.2	8.1
UK	3.1	5.0	6.9	11.0	12.3	13.1	13.2

[a] Standardized to accord with the ILO definition of unemployment. Figures given here for the UK differ slightly from those used elsewhere in this book
Source: OECD *Economic Outlook* and *Main Economic Indicators*

standards, the performance of British manufacturing industry has been very poor, especially since the oil crisis of 1973. Prior to 1973, British manufacturing output and productivity rose quite fast compared with the country's previous historical experience. However, in many other countries they rose even faster. As a result, despite moderately fast industrial growth, Britain was overtaken by many of her foreign rivals during this period and, by the time the world crisis broke at the end of 1973, she was no longer a first-rank industrial power. Thus, up to 1973, the decline of British manufacturing was relative rather than absolute. Since then, however, industrial decline has become absolute and manufacturing output is now lower than it was in 1973. Meanwhile, manufacturing output has continued to rise in other countries, albeit irregularly (see Fig. 10.6). Between 1973 and 1982, manufacturing output fell by 18% in the UK, whilst in the six major OECD countries it rose by 15% on average.[6]

In the realm of labour productivity, Britain's performance has also been poor by international standards since 1973. Despite a spectacular shakeout in vehicles, steel and certain other industries in the period since 1979, output per person per hour in British manufacturing rose by only 22% in the decade 1973–83, compared to an average of 34% in the six major OECD countries. Although accurate comparisons in this field are notoriously difficult, available statistics establish beyond doubt that labour productivity in manufacturing industry is

224   **De-industrialization in the UK**

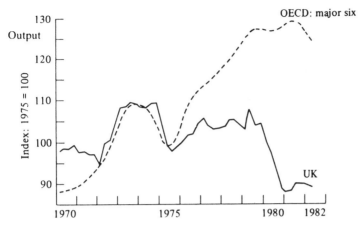

Fig. 10.6 Manufacturing output in the UK and OECD, 1970–82

now much lower in the UK than elsewhere in the advanced capitalist world (see Table 6.15).

The weakness of manufacturing industry is certainly the main reason why the UK has become a relatively poor country and why per capita incomes in the UK are now the lowest in Northern Europe. It also helps to explain why the unemployment rate is so high.

Consider what it would mean if Britain's manufacturing industry were much stronger and more competitive than it is at present, having more equipment, using more advanced methods of production and producing a wider range and higher quality of output. For a start, manufacturing output would obviously be much greater. Part of this additional output would go directly to meet domestic requirements, and part would be exported to pay for imports from foreign countries. Some of these additional imports would be non-manufactures, such as raw materials and services, but there would also be a large increase in manufactured imports. Taking account of additional supplies from both domestic industry and foreign producers, the total amount of manufactured goods available for use in the UK would be much greater than it is at present. Since the production and distribution of manufactured goods involves a wide range of complementary activities, output would be greater in areas such as construction, mining, consulting, transport and retail distribution. Moreover, real incomes would be higher and, consequently, consumers' expenditure of almost every kind would be greater, as would public expenditure on items such as health and education. Thus, with a stronger manufacturing sector, there would be more output in almost every sector of the economy.

What about employment? Would it also be greater? In answering this question,

De-industrialization in the UK   225

we must distinguish between employment in the economy as a whole and employment in particular industries or sectors. Taking the economy as a whole, total employment would certainly be much higher than it is now, if Britain's manufacturing industry were much stronger and had performed much better over the past thirty years. The weakness of manufacturing industry has been largely responsible for the inflation and balance of payments problems which have plagued the UK for many years. In the face of these problems, successive governments, Tory and Labour alike, have imposed deflationary measures which both reduce employment in the short term and inhibit its longer-term growth. If manufacturing industry had performed better, there would have been less need for such measures. Inflationary pressures would have been weaker, because more output would have been available to meet the rival claims of workers, employers and the state; meanwhile, the balance of payments would have been stronger, because British industry would have been more competitive in home and overseas markets. Thus, governments could have pursued more expansionary policies without jeopardizing their targets for inflation and the balance of payments; as a result, the overall level of employment would have been much higher. How would this increase in total employment have been distributed between one sector of the economy and another? In particular, how would employment in the manufacturing sector itself have been affected, and what would have happened to the share of manufacturing in total employment? To answer these questions by means of a priori argument is not easy, and specific numerical estimates are required if one is to go beyond the most general of observations. In the next chapter we will provide such estimates, but for the present we will limit ourselves to a few general remarks.

As we have just argued, if manufacturing industry had performed much better over the past thirty years, then total employment in the UK would by now be much greater than it is. Given such a large addition to total employment, we can assume that almost every major sector of the economy, including manufacturing itself, would have gained extra jobs: either new jobs would have been created or old jobs saved. As a result, more people would now be employed in construction, in the services and, of course, in manufacturing itself.[7] Thus, employment would be greater than it now is, in both manufacturing and non-manufacturing alike. However, this still leaves open several possibilities. Suppose the stronger performance in manufacturing industry had been accompanied by a large increase in labour productivity; in this case, relatively few additional jobs would have been created in the manufacturing sector itself, despite the large increase in manufacturing output, and most of the additional employment would have been in non-manufacturing, especially services. In this case, the *share* of manufacturing in total employment would have fallen as fast or even faster over the past thirty years than it has done. Conversely, suppose a stronger

226   **De-industrialization in the UK**

performance in manufacturing industry had been accompanied by only a modest increase in labour productivity – an unlikely, but logically conceivable combination. In this case, many of the additional jobs would have been in the manufacturing sector itself. As a result, the *share* of manufacturing in total employment would be much greater than it is now and over the past thirty years this share would have fallen much less than it has done. Both these scenarios are logically conceivable and, on a priori grounds alone, there is no way of choosing between them.

All we can say with complete certainty is that if the UK's manufacturing sector had been much stronger, then manufacturing output would have been much higher. It is also likely that more people would now be employed in this sector than at present. However, at this stage, we cannot say how the *share* of manufacturing in total employment would have behaved. We cannot even say whether this share would have fallen more slowly or more rapidly than it has done over the past thirty years. To answer such a question we require something more than a general a priori discussion. We need a specific, quantitative assessment of the various factors involved. In the next chapter we will attempt such an assessment, but for the moment we must leave open the question of how economic performance has affected relative shares.

Conclusions

In this chapter, we have considered three potential explanations for what has happened to manufacturing employment in Britain: the Maturity Thesis, the Specialization Thesis and the Failure Thesis. There is no need to summarize these theses, as their names speak for themselves – and besides they have already been fully described. From the evidence considered in this chapter, there is *prima facie* support for all three theses, and it seems likely that all of them can play some role in explaining what has happened to manufacturing employment during the past thirty years. However, this is only a provisional conclusion, and a more definite answer will have to wait until the next chapter.

11

Towards a better past

Introduction

In this chapter we take up in a more systematic way some of the themes just considered in Chapter 10. Our aim is to quantify the influence of the various factors which have affected manufacturing employment in the UK since the early 1950s, in particular the influence of poor macro-economic performance and the country's changing role in the international division of labour. Our method is that of counterfactual history. We consider various hypothetical scenarios under which the observed, historical behaviour of certain key variables is modified, and we then estimate how such a modification affects other variables in the economy. By its nature, such an exercise is rather speculative in character and may involve considerable guesswork, especially when long periods of time or large variations in the key variables are being considered. Even so, this method can be extremely useful in quantifying the role of individual factors and in providing a rough indication of their relative importance. Indeed, such information is often impossible to obtain except by the counterfactual method. In the present case, for example, there is no other way to assess the relative importance of the major factors which have influenced manufacturing employment in the UK over the past thirty years.

The chapter is organized as follows. It begins with a brief description of several hypothetical scenarios for the period 1946–83. (Further information on this subject is given in Appendix 10.) It then goes on to consider, in detail, what happens to the level and structure of employment under each of these scenarios. By comparing one hypothetical scenario with another – as well as with the actual behaviour of the economy over the period in question – we are able to estimate numerically how far employment in both manufacturing and non-manufacturing has been affected by the UK's poor macro-economic performance and her changing role in the international division of labour.

Our principal conclusions are as follows. If the UK economy had performed much better since 1950 and had remained close to full employment right up to the present, then by 1983 there would have been around 3 million more people in employment than was actually the case. Of these extra jobs, perhaps three to four hundred thousand would have been in the manufacturing sector and some in construction, but the vast majority would have been in the service sector. As a result, the *share* of manufacturing in total employment would have been lower by 1983 than it was in reality. Thus, compared to their peak values in the fifties and sixties, both the level of manufacturing employment and its share would still have fallen dramatically, even if industrial performance had been much stronger. A dramatic fall in manufacturing employment was inevitable for two reasons: (a) because of the massive shift which has taken place in the UK's role in the international division of labour since 1950 and (b) because of the fact that, thirty years ago, the UK economy was already on the brink of 'maturity'. Thus, of the various explanations advanced in the previous chapter to account for falling manufacturing employment, our results in the present chapter strongly support both the 'Specialization Thesis' and the 'Maturity Thesis'. However, they provide ambiguous support for the 'Failure Thesis'. A vast number of manufacturing jobs were lost through factory closures, layoffs and the like. However, virtually as many manufacturing jobs would have been lost through higher productivity, if industry had been dynamic. Thus, the *net* impact of industrial failure on manufacturing employment was rather small. In practice, Britain has been an example of 'negative de-industrialization', due to the weakness of manufacturing, but she would have experienced just as much, if not more de-industrialization of a 'positive' kind, if her manufacturing performance had been stronger. In this sense, most of the loss of manufacturing jobs over the past few decades was unavoidable. These, briefly, are our principal conclusions. Let us now see how they were reached.

Hypothetical scenarios

In this chapter we shall consider two hypothetical scenarios covering the period 1950–83. These will be called Scenario I and Scenario II. Each scenario is defined by specifying the behaviour of four key variables: GDP per capita measured in constant 1975 US dollars (Y), the percentage unemployment rate (U), total employment (E) and net manufactured exports as a percentage of GDP at current market prices (B_m). The behaviour of these variables under the hypothetical scenarios is as follows.

Scenario I
Under this scenario per capita income (Y) starts at its actual level in 1950 and then grows at a uniform rate of 3.0% p.a. right through to 1983. This compares to an actual growth rate over the period 1950–83 of 2.1% p.a. By 1983 GDP

per capita under Scenario I is equal to $7,732 (at 1975 prices), which is some 40% higher than the level actually achieved in the UK in that year. With such a per capita income, the UK would have been one of the richest countries in the world, second only to the USA. Note that most of this additional growth occurs after 1973 (see Fig. 11.1a).

Under Scenario I the unemployment rate (U) falls from its actual level of 1.5% in 1950 to 1.0% in 1955. It then remains at this level until 1966, after which time it rises slowly to reach 3.5% in 1983. The general rise in unemployment towards the end of the period under this scenario accords with the experience of successful economies like Austria or Japan. In such economies, unemployment has been creeping upwards over the past decade or more, despite their high rates of growth. We assume the same phenomenon occurs under both hypothetical scenarios (see Fig. 11.1b). Note our assumption that unemployment remains low under Scenario I is merely a working hypothesis. No one can be sure exactly what the impact of faster growth on unemployment would have been in practice. With the faster rate of output growth assumed under Scenario I, we can be sure that total employment would have risen faster than it did in reality, and that unemployment would not have reached the level actually witnessed in the early 1980s. But whether this would have been enough to keep unemployment down to 3.5% is an open question.

The behaviour of total employment under Scenario I is illustrated in Fig. 11.1c. As can be seen from the diagram, total employment rises strongly from 1950 right through to 1983, apart from a brief hiatus in the late 1960s when it drops back for a few years.[1] Comparing the actual and hypothetical curves for total employment, we see that they almost coincide up to 1966. However, from then onwards these curves diverge by an increasing amount. By 1983, total employment under Scenario I is nearly 3 million greater than in the actual economy. This is reflected in a much lower figure for officially registered unemployment: less than 1 million as compared to 3 million in the actual economy. Moreover, there is also much less hidden unemployment in the hypothetical economy, for nearly a million of the extra jobs in this economy are filled by people not officially classified as unemployed: school leavers, housewives, retired persons, and possibly new immigrants from abroad. The formula used to estimate total employment under Scenario I is given in Appendix 10.

In the realm of foreign trade, Scenario I assumes that the ratio of net manufactured exports to GDP (B_m) falls from its actual value of 11.2% in 1950 to 1.3% in 1983. The assumed values for intermediate years are shown in Fig. 11.1(d). These values are baded on the assumption that under normal conditions the surplus on manufacturing trade must be just sufficient to cover the deficit on non-manufacturing trade. In Chapter 7 and Appendix 8, we considered how faster growth would have affected the UK's balance of trade in non-manufactures.

230   **Towards a better past**

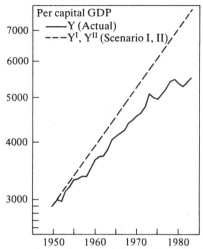

Fig. 11.1a Per capita GDP (Y) (1975 US dollars)

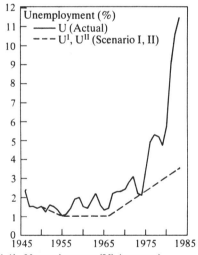

Fig. 11.1b Unemployment (U) (per cent)

Our conclusions were as follows: if the UK economy had grown at the rate assumed under Scenario I during the period 1950–83, then non-manufacturing trade (including services) would have been in deficit to the tune of 1.3% of GDP by 1983 (the 'Intermediate' Scenario in Chapter 7). It is because of the need to cover this deficit that Scenario I assumes a surplus on manufacturing trade equal to 1.3% of GDP in 1983. The manufacturing surplus for earlier years is derived by means of the simple formula described in Appendix 8. With

Towards a better past

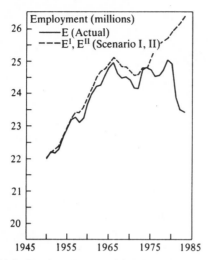

Fig. 11.1c Total employment (E) (millions)

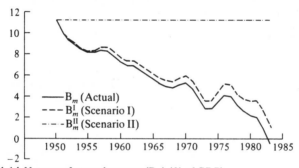

Fig. 11.1d Net manufactured exports (B_m) (% of GDP)

the exception of the abnormal years 1951 and 1973–5, the surplus on manufacturing trade under Scenario I is on average just sufficient to offset the deficit on non-manufacturing trade. Note that the deficit in non-manufacturing trade falls both absolutely and relative to GDP during the course of time under Scenario I. This reflects the influence of the various autonomous factors described in Chapter 6: cheaper food and raw materials; greater domestic food production; economies in the use of raw materials and their replacement by synthetics; the exploitation of North Sea oil and gas; and, finally, the development of new service exports. All of these autonomous factors have been at work in the actual UK economy, and they are assumed to continue operating under Scenario I. This explains why the deficit on non-manufacturing trade gradually falls under this scenario. It also explains why net manufactured exports fall both absolutely and in relation to GDP under this scenario. Such exports are used to finance

232   **Towards a better past**

the deficit on non-manufacturing trade and, as this deficit falls, so too does the required amount of net manufactured exports.

To conclude this description of Scenario I, let us consider briefly the role of the manufacturing sector under this scenario. In a well-known paper, Ajit Singh has given the following definition of what he calls an 'efficient manufacturing sector':

The evolution of the structure of the U.K. economy over the last century has rendered it a net importer of food and raw materials, which have to be paid for largely by exports of manufactures. . . . given this historical evolution, an efficient manufacturing sector for the U.K. economy may be defined as one which, given the normal levels of other components of the balance of payments, yields sufficient net exports (both currently, but more importantly, potentially) to pay for import requirements at socially acceptable levels of output, employment and the exchange rate.[2]

Under Scenario I, the UK's manufacturing sector is efficient in the sense just described. Since there is rapid economic growth and unemployment is relatively low, we can presume that output and employment are at 'socially acceptable' levels. We can also assume that the exchange rate is at a socially acceptable level, although its behaviour has not been explicitly described here.[3] Finally, net manufactured exports are normally sufficient under Scenario I to finance the deficit in trade in non-manufactures. However, there is one rider to add. Because of autonomous improvements in the realm of non-manufacturing trade, the role of an 'efficient' manufacturing sector gradually changes during in the course of time under Scenario I. In the early 1950s, there is a huge deficit in non-manufacturing trade and in order to achieve external balance British industry must generate a huge export surplus in trade in manufactures. However, at the end of the period in 1983, the situation is radically different. The deficit on non-manufacturing trade has shrunk to around 1.3% of GDP and so, too, has the required surplus on manufacturing trade. Thus, although the manufacturing sector still needs to be competitive internationally, it no longer needs to generate a huge surplus of *net* exports. Whilst gross exports of manufactured goods may be considerable, most of the revenue from such exports will be spent on imports of manufactures, so the volume of net manufactured exports will be quite small. Thus, under Scenario I, the trading role of an efficient manufacturing sector gradually alters during the course of time. Initially, it provides manufactured exports primarily in order to pay for imports of food, raw materials and the like. In the course of time, however, this role becomes less important, and the main function of manufactured exports becomes increasingly that of paying for manufactured imports. This is, of course, just what has occurred in reality during the course of the past thirty years. It is also what happens under Scenario I.

Scenario II

Under this scenario, GDP, the unemployment rate and total employment all behave exactly just as they do under Scenario I. However, net exports behave very differently. Under Scenario I, the ratio of net manufactured exports to GDP (B_m) falls dramatically between 1950 and 1983, as the economy becomes less specialized. Under Scenario II, by contrast, there is no change at all in the pattern of specialization. The UK continues to be a specialist 'workshop' economy throughout the entire period, and the ratio of net manufactured exports to GDP remains constant at 11.2% from 1950 right through to 1983 (see Fig. 11.d).

Scenarios I and II compared

The above scenarios can be summarized as follows. Both scenarios assume that the economy grows much faster over the period 1950–83 than it did in reality; both assume that it remains relatively close to full employment and that total employment rises strongly right through to 1983. However, in their assumptions about foreign trade, the two scenarios differ radically. Under Scenario I, the UK gradually abandons her role as a specialist 'workshop' economy, just as she has done in reality. As a result, her trade surplus in manufactures shrinks dramatically in the course of time. Under Scenario II, by contrast, the UK remains a highly specialized 'workshop' economy throughout the period, exporting a huge surplus of manufactured goods in return for food, raw materials and oil. Thus, the UK's experience under Scenario I is just a more successful version (in terms of growth and employment) of actual history. By contrast, under Scenario II, it is as if the whole range of autonomous improvements in non-manufacturing trade described in Chapter 6 had never occurred. Table 11.1 compares output and employment under the two scenarios with actual experience.

The structure of employment

To determine what happens to the structure of employment under the hypothetical scenarios, we shall use the following equation:

$$M = -1619.8 + 395.81 \log Y - 23.71 (\log Y)^2$$
$$- 0.56 U + 0.70 B_m + v$$

where M is the percentage share of manufacturing in total employment and v is a residual disturbance term. The functional form is of the same general type as was used in Chapter 1 to anaylse international data on the structure of employment. However, the method of estimation is different in the present case. Previously the coefficient (and the residual) were estimated using annual time-series data for the UK alone. After consulting UK input–output tables and the evidence provided by the regression analyses of Chapter 1, the coefficient on B_m (the ratio of net manufactured exports to GDP) was set equal to 0.70. The remaining coefficients and the residual were thus estimated from UK time-series data using the method of restricted least squares. Full details of the estimation procedure are given in Appendix 10, together with alternative estimates and a discussion of their implications.

234   **Towards a better past**

Table 11.1. *Summary of UK economic history and hypothetical alternatives*

	Actual						Hypothetical	
	1950	1955	1966	1973	1979	1983	1983I	1983II
Employment and population ('000)								
Manufacturing employment	7657	8270	8678	7977	7378	5791	6164	7989
Non-manufacturing employment	14345	14638	16260	16719	17631	17607	20170	18345
Total employment	22002	22908	24938	24696	25009	23398	26334	26334
Unemployment	327	239	353	557	1235	2986	995	995
Total labour force	22329	23147	25291	25253	26244	26382	27289	27289
Population	50150	50946	54500	55913	55881	56187	56187	56187
Output (1975 US$)								
GDP per head	2915	3305	4173	5097	5475	5506	7732	7732
GDP per civilian worker	6644	7350	9120	11540	12234	13222	16497	16497
Other statistics								
Share of manufacturing in total employment (%)	34.8	36.1	34.8	32.3	29.5	24.7	23.4	30.3
Unemployment (%)	1.5	1.0	1.4	2.2	4.7	11.3	3.5	3.5
Net manufactured exports (% of GDP)	11.0	8.7	5.9	3.0	1.8	−0.5	2.0	11.0

The behaviour of M under the hypothetical scenarios is shown in Fig. 11.2, whilst the absolute number of people employed in the major sectors of the economy is shown in Figs. 11.3a–b. Using these diagrams, let us now consider what happens to employment under each of the hypothetical scenarios.

Scenario II [fast growth but no change in trade specialization]
Under this scenario manufacturing employment increases rapidly during the 1950s. However, this expansion comes to an end in the 1960s and, from then onwards, this kind of employment falls almost continuously, both absolutely and as a share of total employment. By 1983, the number of people employed in the manufacturing sector has fallen to 8 million, which as a share of total employment is just over 30%. It is interesting to compare the UK under Scenario II with the situation in other countries. This is done in Table 11.2. By 1983, the UK under Scenario II has an economic structure midway between the two great 'workshop' economies, West Germany and Japan. Like these economies, the UK has a massive trade surplus in manufactures, whilst the share of its workforce employed in manufacturing is lower than in West Germany but greater than in Japan. In terms of per capita income, however, the UK is more prosperous than either of them.

Towards a better past

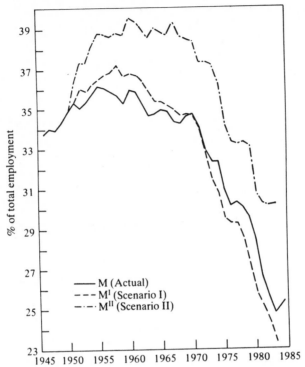

Fig. 11.2 Manufacturing share (M) (% of total employment)

There are several reasons why the share of manufacturing in total employment rises during the 1950s under Scenario II. Of these perhaps the most important is concerned with the agricultural sector. In the 1950s the UK economy is not yet completely 'mature', and there is still room for the manufacturing sector to increase its share of total employment by a fair amount at the expense of agriculture, whose share is falling. (The same is also true under Scenario I and in the actual economy.) However, the potential for this kind of transformation is soon exhausted and, by the 1960s, the economy is fully mature. Once this stage is reached the dominant factor is no longer the shift in employment from agriculture to manufacturing, but rather the shift from manufacturing to the services. The fate of manufacturing in later years under Scenario II is an example of the 'crowding-out' which occurs in all successful economies once they reach maturity. When this stage is reached, service employment begins to crowd out manufacturing employment and, as growth continues, the share of services rises, whilst that of manufacturing falls. What happens under Scenario II is also an example of what we have called elsewhere 'positive de-industrialization'.[4] Under

236   **Towards a better past**

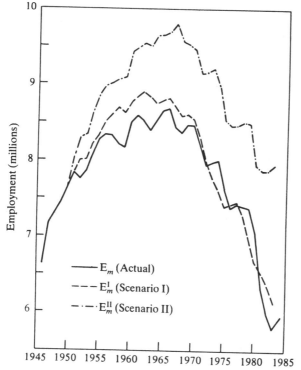

Fig. 11.3a Manufacturing employment (E_m) (millions)

this scenario, manufacturing output rises quite fast in later years, but output per worker rises even faster, with the result that employment in the manufacturing sector falls. However, increased output in the manufacturing sector is able to sustain a high level of output of services and, to provide these services, more workers are taken on by the service sector. Indeed, sufficient new jobs are created in the service sector to keep the economy fairly close to full employment, despite a large increase in the total labour force. This is in stark contrast to experience in the actual economy, which has been beset by 'negative de-industrialization' on a spectacular scale: millions of workers have been shed by an ailing manufacturing industry, and too few new jobs have been created elsewhere in the economy to absorb them, with the result that unemployment has risen dramatically.

Scenario I [fast growth, changing trade specialization]
Let us now consider Scenario I. Under this scenario, the economy grows at the same rate as under Scenario II and, hence, all of the growth-induced shifts

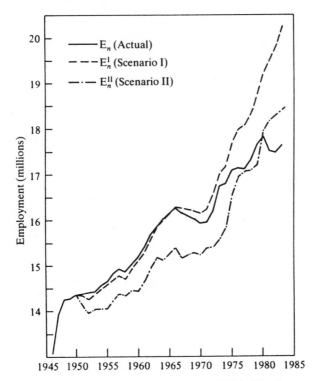

Fig. 11.3b Non-manufacturing employment (E_n) (millions)

in the structure of employment just described also occur under Scenario I. However, superimposed on these are other structural shifts which arise from events in the sphere of foreign trade. Under Scenario II, changes in the UK's pattern of trade specialization were ignored, and the trade surplus in manufactures was assumed to remain constant as a proportion of GDP. Under Scenario I, by contrast, such changes are taken into account and, as a result, the manufacturing trade surplus falls almost continuously. As the surplus falls, there is a transfer of labour from manufacturing to the services, and the result is a growing divergence in the structure of employment between Scenarios I and II. Comparing the two scenarios, we find that, in each case, the share of manufacturing in total employment rises during the 1950s and then undergoes prolonged decline (Fig. 11.2). However, the initial rise is less pronounced under Scenario I and the subsequent decline is much greater. By 1983, the number of people employed in manufacturing is 1.8 million less under Scenario I than Scenario II (see Fig. 11.3a), which is equivalent to 7% of total employment in the economy as a whole (Table 11.1). These figures give some indication of the enormous

238

Table 11.2. *Some international comparisons in 1983*

	United Kingdom			Other countries					
	Actual	Scenario I	Scenario II	Norway	Canada	USA	Sweden	Japan	Germany
Per capita GDP[a]	5506	7732	7732	7347	7701	8037	7311	6010	6291
Unemployment rate[b]	11.4	3.5	3.5	3.3	11.8	9.5	5.5	2.6	8.0
Net manufactured exports[c]	−0.5	1.3	11.2	−5.7	−2.3	0.9	5.5	11.8	10.1
Share of manufacturing in total employment[b]	24.7	23.4	30.3	19.7	19.8	20.4	22.4	24.8	33.1

Notes: [a] 1975 US dollars
[b] Percent of civilian labour force; all figures are standardized to accord with the ILO definition of unemployment, except for those for the UK which are not standardized
[c] Percent of GDP at market prices; figures for countries other than the UK refer to 1981; for these other countries f.o.b. figures for imports are estimated by multiplying the c.i.f. figures by 0.92
[d] Figures for countries other than the UK refer to 1982

impact which changing trade specialization has had on the UK's internal structure of employment since 1950.

Table 11.2 compares the UK economy in 1983 under Scenario I with the situation in other economies at around the same time. From this table we see that the UK economy under this scenario is rather similar to the Swedish economy. Per capita incomes are somewhat higher in the UK than in Sweden, but the unemployment rate is identical and the share of manufacturing in total employment is much the same. Thus, if the UK had grown as envisaged under Scenario I, her economy would by now be similar to that of Sweden. By international standards a relatively low share of her workforce would be employed in manufacturing (23.4%), although this share would still be greater than in Canada, Norway and the US, where manufacturing now accounts for 20% or less of total employment.

Scenario I and the actual economy compared

Scenario I differs from actual history in one respect only: it assumes that UK industry is more dynamic and that as a result the rate of economic growth is higher, and the economy remains fairly close to full employment right through to 1983. Apart from this difference in macro-economic performance, Scenario I and actual history are identical. (In particular, the same autonomous changes in trade specialization occur in both cases.) Thus, by comparing what happens under Scenario I with what actually happened, we can see how the level and structure of employment were affected by the UK's poor economic performance over the period in question. Perhaps the most striking thing to emerge from this comparision is how small was the net impact of poor industrial performance on manufacturing employment (i.e. over and above any loss which would have occurred if industrial performance had been stronger). Under Scenario I manufacturing employment rises a little faster during the 1950s than in the actual economy, but its subsequent decline is just as dramatic (Fig. 11.3a). By 1983 there are around 6.2 million people employed in manufacturing industry under Scenario I, as compared to an actual figure of 5.8 million – which in each case is over $2\frac{1}{2}$ million below the peak number achieved in the 1960s. Looking at relative shares, the picture is much the same. Under Scenario I, just as in the actual economy, the share of manufacturing in total employment rises up to the mid- or late 1950s and then undergoes a prolonged and massive decline. Indeed, so great is this decline that, by 1983, the share of manufacturing is even lower under Scenario I than in the actual economy: 23.4% as compared to 24.7% (Fig. 11.2). Thus, under Scenario I, the absolute number of people employed in the manufacturing sector in 1983 is somewhat greater than in the actual economy, whilst the share of this sector in total employment is somewhat less. This discrepancy between relative shares and absolute numbers is explained

240   **Towards a better past**

by what happens total employment under Scenario I. Under this scenario, non-manufacturing employment grows extremely fast – mainly in service activities – and by 1983 there are 20.2 million people employed in the non-manufacturing sector as a whole (Fig. 11.3b). In the actual economy the corresponding figure for 1983 is 17.6 million. As result of this massive increase in non-manufacturing employment, the share of manufacturing in total employment is lower under Scenario I than in the actual economy, even though slightly more people are employed in this sector than was actually the case.

As we have just seen, the long-term evolution of manufacturing employment is much the same under Scenario I as in the actual economy. However, the timing of events is rather different. From its peak in the mid-1960s through to 1979, manufacturing employment falls more rapidly under Scenario I, but afterwards the opposite is the case and the fall is greatest in the actual economy (see Fig. 11.3a). The explanation for this difference in timing is as follows. Under Scenario I manufacturing employment declines at a fairly uniform pace during a prolonged period lasting from the mid-1960s right through to 1983. The uniformity and pace of this decline reflect the influence of continuous and rapid structural change. In the actual economy, by contrast, the pace of structural change is slower and fewer manufacturing jobs are lost because of it. This explains why, prior to 1979, manufacturing employment falls more rapidly under Scenario I than in the actual economy. After 1979, however, a new factor enters the situation. In the actual economy, the manufacturing sector is hit by a severe crisis, in which output slumps and there are widespread closures and layoffs. Under Scenario I the economy avoids this slump and output continues to expand without interruption. Of course, even after 1974, manufacturing jobs are still lost under Scenario I as a result of structural change, but the scale of these losses does not compare to the wholescale destruction of manufacturing employment which occurs in the actual economy after 1979 as a result of the industrial crisis. It is this industrial crisis which explains why, after 1979, the fall in manufacturing employment is so much greater in the actual economy than under Scenario I.

Output and productivity under Scenario I: some illustrative figures

The foregoing discussion may be summarized as follows. If Scenario I is any guide, faster economic growth would have had only a minor impact on the long-term decline in manufacturing employment. At most, it would have altered the timing of events and made the pace of this decline more uniform: more manufacturing jobs would have been lost before 1979, and the wholesale collapse of the 1980s would have been avoided. Over the long term, the main impact of faster growth would have been on non-manufacturing employment. With

Towards a better past   241

Table 11.3. *The impact of faster growth: an illustrative example*

	(a) Percentage increase[a]		
	Output per worker	Civil employment	Output
Non-market services	0	20	20
Market services	29	15	49
Other non-manufacturing	15	5	21
Non-manufacturing	18	14.5	35
Manufacturing	46	6.5	55
Total	25	12.5	40.5

	(b) Civil employment (millions)[b]		
	(1) Actual	(2) Scenario I	(3) Difference (2)–(1)
Non-market services	4.3	5.2	+0.9
Market services	10.5	12.1	+1.6
Other non-manufacturing	2.8	2.9	+0.1
Non-manufacturing	17.6	20.2	+2.5
Manufacturing	5.8	6.2	+0.4
Total	23.4	26.3	+2.9

Notes: [a] The hypothetical situation in 1983 (under Scenario I) is compared to the actual situation in 1983
[b] Total may not add because of rounding errors
Source: see Appendix 10

the kind of growth envisaged under Scenario I, there would have been an enormous increase in this type of employment and by 1983 an extra 2½ million people would have been employed in the non-manufacturing sector than was actually the case. The vast majority of these extra jobs would have been in service activities.

To explore further the impact of economic growth on employment, we will now consider a simple numerical example. This example illustrates the kind of output and productivity changes which could account for the behaviour of employment under Scenario I. The main features of this example are displayed in Table 11.3 As can be seen, a finer classification of activities is used here than was used in constructing the original scenarios. As before, manufacturing is taken as one sector, but non-manufacturing is now divided into three subsectors: non-market services (public administration, health, education), market services (transport, distribution, finance, etc.) and other non-manufacturing activities (agriculture, construction, extractive industries, gas, electricity and water). Information on how faster growth affects these sectors is given in a comparative form in the table. For each sector, Table 11.3 compares output,

242   **Towards a better past**

employment and productivity under Scenario I with the corresponding magnitudes in the actual economy. The year chosen for comparison is 1983, so the numbers shown indicate the cumulative impact of faster growth over the entire period 1950–83. In constructing this table the numbers have been chosen so as to be consistent with what we already know about Scenario I. Thus, total output in 1983 is 40% greater than in the actual economy, whilst employment in manufacturing and non-manufacturing is respectively $6\frac{1}{2}\%$ and $14\frac{1}{2}\%$ greater. The remaining numbers are consistent with this information. However, these numbers are not, it must be stressed, formal estimates; they are merely informed guesses whose purpose is to indicate the orders of magnitude involved. The example should not, therefore, be taken too literally. Even so, despite this qualification, the example does, in our opinion, provide a reasonably accurate picture of what might have happened to output and productivity if the economy had grown at the pace envisaged under Scenario I. It also lends support to our claim that, over the long term, faster growth would have had only a marginal impact on manufacturing employment.

Looking at Table 11.3, the following points stand out:

(1)   There is a huge increase in manufacturing output, which is 55% higher than in the actual economy as a result of faster growth. There is also a 49% increase in the output of market services and some increase in the output of other sectors.

(2)   There are considerable intersectoral variations in productivity growth. Output per worker in manufacturing is 46% greater as a result of faster growth, whilst in market services the figure is 29%. Elsewhere in the economy the increase in productivity is considerably less. Indeed, there is no increase at all in non-market services. This last assumption is in line with normal accounting conventions.

(3)   Over half of the additional employment resulting from faster growth is in market services, whilst most of the rest is in non-market services, although there is some increase elsewhere in the economy.

Let us consider some of these points in more detail. Take the increase of 55% in manufacturing output. This may seem excessive, given that GDP increases by only 40%, but there are special factors which explain it. In most advanced economies, the long-run income-elasticity of demand for manufactures is around unity (including relative price effects). *Ceteris paribus*, this implies that any given rise in GDP is accompanied by a roughly equal proportionate rise in manufacturing output. In the present case, however, there are a number of reasons why manufacturing output should rise by more than this amount. To start with, the faster growth envisaged under Scenario I provides work and, therefore, additional income for millions of people who would otherwise be unemployed. Since they spend much of this additional income on consumer durables and other manufactured goods, the demand for such goods receives a disproportionate stimulus. Moreover, with a faster rate of growth, the share of investment in GDP is greater, and this too implies a relative increase in the demand for manufactures. Finally, there is foreign trade to consider. In the actual economy Britain had a surplus on her non-manufacturing trade in 1983 and a deficit in her manufacturing trade. However, with the faster growth assumed under Scenario I, this situation is reversed. Net imports of food, raw materials, fuels and services increase, and as a result the non-manufacturing balance goes into deficit.[5] To cover this deficit requires an increase in net manufactured exports and hence an increase in manufacturing output. In view of the special factors just listed, it is clear why faster growth involves such a large increase in manufacturing output.

The second point concerns labour productivity. In Table 11.3, there is a clear correlation between output and labour productivity: activities which experience the greatest increase in output as a result of faster growth also experience the greatest increase in labour productivity. For this reason, the impact of faster growth on employment is more uniformly distributed than the figures on output alone would suggest. Even so, major differences remain, and faster growth has an appreciable effect on the structure of employment. In particular, the increase in manufacturing productivity is so great that the share of this sector in total employment falls despite an above average rise in output.

This concludes our discussion of Scenario I. Before leaving this topic, may we repeat our warning that this example is intended for illustration only. It shows the kind of structural changes which are implied by faster growth and indicates what might have happened had the economy grown at the rate envisaged under Scenario I. The numbers used in the example have been chosen so as to be consistent with estimated values – where these exist – but most of them are not formal estimates and should not be treated as such. They are merely plausible 'guesstimates' designed to indicate the orders of magnitude involved.

The numerical example just considered points to an interesting paradox. The main employment effects of industrial weakness in the UK are to be found not in the manufacturing sector itself, but in other sectors of the economy, especially the services. With a stronger and more dynamic manufacturing industry, there would still have been a precipitous decline in manufacturing employment over the past twenty years or so. However, manufacturing output would have been much greater than it is now and so too would per capita incomes. As a result, there would have been a much greater demand for services (both market and non-market services), and sufficient jobs would have been created in the service sector to absorb the workers displaced from manufacturing. In the present context, the difference between industrial strength and weakness is not measured by the capacity of the manufacturing sector itself to provide employment. Rather, it is measured by the capacity of this sector to generate the material output required to support a prosperous and growing service sector, in which sufficient jobs are available to provide work for all who need it.[6]

Given the stage of development reached by the UK in the early 1950s and the massive changes in trade specialization which have occurred since then, a considerable fall in manufacturing employment was sooner or later inevitable. In actual history, this fall was accompanied by stagnating output and rising unemployment. It was, to use our earlier ternminology, a case of 'negative de-industrialization'. In a more dynamic economy, with a stronger industrial base, much the same fall in manufacturing employment would still have occurred. However, because of higher productivity, this fall in employment would have been accompanied by a rapid growth in manufacturing *output*. This rise in output would in turn have generated sufficient demand for services, and for service employment, to absorb the workers displaced from manufacturing. It would have been a case of 'positive de-industrialization'. In actual history, the decline in manufacturing employment was accompanied by widespread factory closures, rationalizations and layoffs in the face of stagnant or falling demand. In a more dynamic economy, an almost equal fall in manufacturing employment would still have occurred as a result of automation and other measures designed to save labour whilst simultaneously increasing output. Either way, manufacturing jobs would have disappeared, but the implications for real incomes and employment in other sectors of the economy would have been radically different.

The three theses: a quantitative assessment

In the preceding chapter three potential explanations for the decline in UK manufacturing employment were considered. They were as follows: the Maturity Thesis, the Specialization Thesis and the Failure Thesis. Using the hypothetical scenarios developed in the present chapter, we shall now evaluate the explanatory power of these various theses.

Table 11.4 shows what has happened to UK manufacturing employment since 1950, both in absolute terms and as a share of total employment. In this table, changes in manufacturing employment during selected periods are broken down into a number of distinct components. There are three major components, which correspond to the three theses listed above. There is also a catch-all term which measures the effect of miscellaneous factors. The breakdown given in the table is based on the hypothetical scenarios described earlier in the present chapter. Full details of this breakdown are given in Appendix 10, and here we shall merely indicate the main principles involved. The individual components shown in Table 11.4 are defined as follows:

Table 11.4. *Analysis of manufacturing employment since 1950*

	(a) change in relative share of manufacturing in total employment (percentage points)		
	1950–83	1955–83	1966–83
Net failure effect	1.3	1.9	1.4
Maturity effect	−5.5	−7.6	−8.5
Specialization effect	−6.9	−4.8	−3.1
Effect of miscellaneous factors	1.0	−0.8	0.1
Total (= actual change)	−10.1	−11.3	−10.1
	(b) change in manufacturing employment (thousands)		
Net failure effect	−373	−253	−312
Maturity effect	−193	−929	−1830
Specialization effect	−1825	−1344	−859
Effect of miscellaneous factors	525	47	114
Total (= actual change)	−1866	−2479	−2887

(1)   *The Net Failure Effect*. This measures the *net* impact of poor economic performance on manufacturing employment. By definition, it is equal to the actual change in manufacturing employment during a given period minus the change which would have occurred during the same period (for whatever reason), if UK industry had performed better and the economy had grown more rapidly. The net failure effect is evaluated by comparing what happens to manufacturing employment in the actual economy and under Scenario I (see Fig. 11.2 and Fig. 11.3a).

(2)   *Unavoidable job losses: The Maturity Effect*. This effect indicates the extent to which the fall in manufacturing employment during a given period was inevitable simply because the UK economy was already relatively mature at the beginning of the period concerned. The maturity effect is evaluated by considering what happens to manufacturing employment under Scenario II, after allowing for the effect of miscellaneous factors (see below). Note that much of the fall in manufacturing employment – ascribed here to the maturity effect – was, in practice, the result of layoffs, factory closures and the like. In a proximate sense, therefore, most of the fall in employment under this heading was the result of poor industrial performance. However, these jobs would still have been lost even if UK manufacturing industry had performed better, though the causal mechanism would have been different. With a more dynamic and successful manufacturing industry, the jobs in question would have been eliminated through automation and other

246   **Towards a better past**

labour-saving measures. Thus, given the stage of development reached by the UK economy, the loss of manufacturing jobs indicated by the maturity effect was inevitable. The only question was, how would this loss come about? In practice, it came about through factory closures and the like. In a more dynamic economy, it would have come about through automation and similar measures.

(3)   *The Specialization Effect.* This indicates the extent to which autonomous changes in the structure of UK foreign trade have affected manufacturing employment. (These changes were described in Chapter 6.) The specialization effect is evaluated by comparing what happens to manufacturing employment under Scenarios I and II (See Figs. 11.2 and 11.3a). Note that this effect measures the purely 'structural' impact of foreign trade on manufacturing employment. In evaluating this impact, total output and employment in the economy as a whole are taken as given, and any macro-economic effects resulting from changing trade specialization are ignored. Note also that the 'specialization effect', as measured in Table 11.4, is 'performance adjusted', i.e. the figures embody a correction to eliminate the effect of slow economic growth on the structure of UK trade.

(4)   *The Effect of Miscellaneous Factors.* This is a catch-all item which takes into account a variety of factors, such as errors in specification, random disturbances and interaction effects.

After this preamble, let us now examine Table 11.4. As can be seen, three time periods are shown: 1950–83, 1955–83 and 1966–83. The justification for choosing these periods is as follows: 1950 was the year in which the UK economy achieved its largest-ever trade surplus in manufactures (as a percentage of GDP); 1955 was the year in which the share of manufacturing in total employment reached an all-time peak; whilst the absolute number of people employed in the manufacturing sector reached its all-time peak in 1966. Looking at the numbers shown in Table 11.4, perhaps the most striking features is the minor importance of the *net* failure effect. Depending on the time period concerned, this effect accounts for between one-tenth and one-sixth of the absolute fall in manufacturing employment. Moreover, in the case of relative shares, this effect is actually positive and hence accounts for none of the fall in manufacturing's share in total employment.

From the table, it is clear that virtually all of the decline in manufacturing employment, both absolute and relative, is accounted for by two components: the maturity effect and the specialization effect. It is also clear that the relative importance of these two effects depends on the time period concerned. Over the entire period 1950–83, taken as a whole, the specialization effect is the

most important: it accounts for most of the absolute fall in manufacturing employment and over half of the fall in this sector's share in total employment. However,
if a later starting-point is chosen, the picture is rather different. As the starting-
point moves closer to the present, the maturity effect becomes increasingly
important, until eventually it supplants the specialization effect as the major
component. For example, over the period 1966–83, manufacturing employment
fell by 2.9 million. Of this fall, the maturity effect accounts for around 1.8
million and the specialization effect for around 900 thousand.

From the figures shown in Table 11.4, the following points emerge concerning
the three theses. The Failure Thesis explains very little of the absolute or relative
decline in manufacturing employment. Most of this decline is explained by the
other two theses we have considered: the Maturity Thesis, which stresses that
Britain was already on the brink of economic maturity in the 1950s, and the
Specialization Thesis, which stresses the huge changes that have occurred in
the UK's pattern of trade specialization since 1950. Given the stage of development already reached by the British economy in 1950 and the changes in trade
specialization which have taken place since then, manufacturing employment
was bound to fall dramatically over the coming decades no matter how good
or bad the performance of UK manufacturing industry. This is the first and
most important point.

Our second point is concerned with the relative importance of the maturity
effect and changing trade specialization in explaining what has happened to
manufacturing employment. Over the entire period 1950–83, changes in trade
specialization have been the major factor. They account for most of the absolute
decline in manufacturing employment over the period as a whole, as well as
for most of the decline in manufacturing's share in total employment. However,
if we take a more recent starting-point, the picture is more complex. In 1950,
the UK economy was approaching maturity but had not yet reached it. By the
1960s, the economy was fully mature and, for this reason alone, the share of
manufacturing in total employment was bound to fall by a considerable amount
in the coming years. Moreover, given the underlying trends in labour supply,
this fall in manufacturing's relative share would inevitably be accompanied by
a considerable fall in the absolute number of people employed in the manufacturing sector. The extent of this unavoidable fall is indicated by the maturity effect
in Table 11.4. According to the figures shown, manufacturing employment was
destined to fall by at least 1.8 million between 1966 and 1983, simply because
the UK was already a fully mature economy at the beginning of the period
in 1966. This fall would have occurred even if there had been no changes in
trade specialization during these years and even if UK manufacturing industry
had been more dynamic and output had grown more rapidly. Of the 2.9 million
manufacturing jobs lost between 1966 and 1983, approximately 60% were bound

248   **Towards a better past**

to go simply because the economy was already mature in 1966, and another 30% were eliminated by changes in the pattern of trade specialization (North Sea oil, greater food self-sufficiency, etc.). The remaining 10% represent the jobs that were lost as a result of poor economic performance and would have been saved if UK manufacturing industry had been more dynamic and the economy had grown more rapidly.

Conclusions

The main conclusions of this chapter are as follows. The post-war decline in manufacturing employment in Britain has been an example of 'negative de-industrialization' (resulting from poor industrial performance), compounded by the effect of changes in trade specialization. However, almost as many manufacturing jobs would have been lost and manufacturing's share would have fallen even further if industrial performance had been more successful. If this had happened, Britain would, instead, have been an example of 'positive de-industrialization'. Thus, a large reduction in manufacturing employment was unavoidable in post-war Britain, since the country was already on the verge of economic maturity in 1950. Manufacturing employment was bound to decline over the coming decades, no matter how good or bad the performance of British industry. Thus, in the last analysis, the number of manufacturing jobs lost as a result of industrial failure was relatively small. The fact is, in a 'mature' economy, the behaviour of manufacturing employment is not always a good indicator of industrial performance. In such an economy, a dynamic manufacturing sector may be shedding labour yet, at the same time, contributing indirectly to the creation of employment elsewhere in the economy as steady increases in industrial production lay the material foundations for a prosperous and expanding service sector.

Notes

10   De-industrialization in the UK: three theses

1 For example, in the USA, the number of people employed in manufacturing rose by 5.2% between 1970 and 1981. However, total employment rose by 27.6% over the same period, so the share of manufacturing fell considerably, despite an increase in the absolute number employed in this sector. The USA is unusual in this respect. In most other countries a falling share of manufacturing in total employment has been accompanied by a decline in its absolute number of people working in this sector.
2 An exception to this is Denmark, which belongs to group A but has also experienced a big fall in the share of industry (see Table A9.1 in Appendix 9).
3 The principal exception in this group is Germany, where the industry's share hardly changed at all between 1955 and 1981.
4 In Fig. 10.3 the base year is 1955 because this is the year in which the share of manufacturing in total employment began to fall in the UK. In Fig. 10.4 the base year is 1966 because this is the year in which the absolute number of people employed in UK manufacturing begun to fall.
5 As always, in the present work, the term 'non-manufactures' includes services.
6 The six major OECD countries referred to here are: the USA, Canada, Japan, France, Germany and Italy.
7 Amongst the exceptions are agriculture, coal-mining and the railways. In none of these activities would a stronger manufacturing performance have created additional employment. On the contrary, by improving job opportunities elsewhere, it might have accelerated the long exodus of labour from these activities.

11   Towards a better past

1 The hiatus in employment growth in the late 1960s occurs both in the actual economy and under the hypothetical scenarios. It is caused by a hiatus in the growth of labour supply due partly to demographic factors and partly to a sharp fall in the proportion of young people leaving school at the age of 15 years.
2 Singh (1977) p. 128.
3 We take the term 'socially acceptable exchange rate' to be a reference to the distribution of income associated with a particular real rate of exchange.
4 See Chapter 1 for a definition of this term.
5 See p. 271 above.
6 'Support' in the sense of providing the manufactured inputs and manufactured consumer goods used by those working in the service sectors and/or the manufactured exports used to pay for imported inputs or wage goods.

Bibliography

Bairoch, P. *et al.* (1968), *La Population active et sa structure* (Brussels, Free University).

Kravis, I.B., Heston, A.W. and Summers, R. (1982), *World Product and Income,* UN International Comparison Project, Phase III, London.

Singh, A. (1977), 'UK Industry and the World Economy: a Case of De-industrialization', *Cambridge Journal of Economics,* Vol. 1, No. 2, 113–36.

[13]

Cambridge Journal of Economics 1980, **4**, 85–102

COMMENTARY

This section is designed for the discussion and debate of current economic problems. Contributions which raise new issues or comment on issues already raised are welcome.

On the nature of industrial decline in the UK

Andrew Kilpatrick and Tony Lawson*

I. Introduction

In the past few years a considerable body of literature has focused on the relatively poor competitive performance of the UK economy since the second world war (Blackaby, 1979; Singh, 1977), and in particular has highlighted its relatively low productivity growth (Maddison, 1977). These studies however have tended to ignore workplace conflict over the organisation of production, although the resolution of this conflict significantly influences overall factor productivity. (This point has also been made by Mason (1979).)

The labour process has also been largely neglected in those studies which have recognised that the relative industrial decline of the UK economy has been underway for over a century. The supply side of the economy has of course by no means been completely ignored: many studies have detailed how since at least 1870 Britain has been systematically slow at widely adopting new products and processes even when these were invented (and sometimes even manufactured) in Britain, while others have drawn attention to relatively high manning levels in the UK.† Even so, the focus of attention has usually been on 'entrepreneurial failure'‡ or on so-called 'institutional' factors such as Britain's failure to develop a comprehensive technical education system in the nineteenth century.§ While the importance of factors such as the educational infrastructure is not disputed we shall argue that Britain's industrial performance cannot be understood without some analysis of the labour process.

The role of collective bargaining and the strength of job-based worker organisation are factors which must be carefully considered. In the UK, collective bargaining over all aspects of work takes place at local as well as at national level. However, the ability

---

* University of Cambridge.

† Among the most widely cited examples are major inventions such as the Bessemer, the Gilchrist Thomas and the Solvay Processes; Mauve Dyes; the Parsons Steam Engine and Ring Spindles. In fact Payne (1978) refers to 'a formidable list of new inventions, ideas, and developments more quickly put to practical use by Americans and Europeans than the British . . . compiled in 1916 by Gray and Turner' (p. 679). Many historical accounts of the UK's slow rate of adoption of new techniques and of comparatively high manning levels exist. Among the most well-known studies are those of Habakkuk (1967) and Landes (1969). For more recent evidence on high manning levels see, for example, Pratten (1976), and for evidence on slow rates of diffusion see OECD (1970) and Ray (1979) and references provided.

‡ A recent survey of these views is given in Payne (1978).

§ See, for example, Musgrave (1967). For more recent evidence on the educational and other 'deficiencies' of UK management see Channon (1973), Granick (1972) and Peck (1968).

0309-166X/80/010085+18 $02.00/0

of workers to bargain with management at the plant level is essentially a defensive strength: workers attempt to maintain working conditions and living standards. Through the bargaining process workers can only check management's intentions to reorganise production. Even so the highly decentralised structure of bargaining which exists in the UK is not without significance. It tends to inhibit long-term planning and co-ordinated decision-making (ILO, 1974; Clegg, 1979), and works against quick responses to changes in the organisation of work, and generally restrains productivity growth. Bargaining over conditions in the workplace can delay the adoption and diffusion of new techniques and/or lead to manning levels above what they would otherwise have been. Disagreement in negotiations often leads to disruptions which give rise to unmet delivery dates and generally affect availability, while the resulting slow productivity growth usually means low quality or poor reliability.

Section II of this paper looks at the relatively early acceptance of mass trade unionism and the evolutionary nature of industrial relations in the UK and draws some comparisons with the experiences of other industrial countries. The main intention of this section is not to explain the development of the highly decentralised structure of bargaining in the UK, but to indicate its present day economic significance. The nature of collective bargaining cannot be regarded as unchanging, of course, but neither should the influence of job-based worker organisation on economic development be seen as a temporary 'aberration' which can be easily undermined by government strategies designed to restore competitiveness.

Section III draws some implications of this analysis for certain policy proposals currently advocated. In particular, in this section we question the view that import controls can prevent the long-run industrial decline of the UK economy.

II. The Labour Process

2.1. Early 'acceptance' of trade unionism in the UK

The end of suppression of organised collective resistance by the military and the courts occurred in Britain in the nineteenth century. Between 1867 and 1875, a series of acts were passed which made it easier for workers to strike without being imprisoned (Master and Servant Act, 1867; Employers and Workman Act, 1875); which helped secure the legal status of trade unions (Trade Union Act, 1871); and which legalised peaceful picketing (Conspiracy and Protection of Property Act, 1871).

Partly as a result, there was a rapid growth in the number of trade unions, with membership of those affiliated to the newly formed Trades Union Congress (TUC) more than doubling from 250,000 in 1869 to 510,000 in 1873. At first, these were organisations of skilled workers only, defending acquired customs and their privileged status as craftsmen. However, by the 1880s unskilled workers were also able to form stable organisations. These 'new' unions of unskilled workers started out critical of the older craft unions for their inward-looking nature and elitism, and tended to concentrate their energies on national issues. But, by the turn of the century, they too had adopted craft union practices and were possessive of past gains and acquired customs (Clarke and Clements, 1977, p. 12).

This establishment of customs or standards has been an important element in the development of the labour process. As soon as any situation has been regarded as the norm—whether it refers to levels of pay or conditions of work—then efforts by management to reduce the standard, to erode past gains, have, where possible, been resisted.

This last qualification is important: if the interests of similar groups are the same everywhere, then differences in ability to further or to defend those interests partly explain systematic divergences in paths of development. It is therefore significant that, unlike in other countries, trade unions in the UK were legalised and experienced a sharp increase in membership well before the turn of the twentieth century. Thus, growth of real power by workers to resist changes and to defend standards coincided with customs and norms that existed before the introduction of mass production techniques. It appeared when the forms of organisation and bargaining took place on a craft-type basis. The system of industrial relations which evolved was thus highly decentralised, uncoordinated and relatively unsuited to the later needs of mass production.

Of course changes in the organisation of production were continually enforced by management, although worker resistance reduced the speed of change. Where management had accommodated itself to workers' organisations, through the establishment of procedures and the recognition of norms and customs, these procedures and standards were not easy to overcome. Confrontations did occur and workers' organisations were not always able to maintain even the pretence of 'skill' status. As Penn (1978) illustrates, in a comparison of the development of cotton and engineering workers' organisations, the ability to maintain craft status was largely 'a direct function of the relative strength of labour prior to the development of mechanised factory production' (p. 27). However, while the strength of resistance within Britain was unevenly distributed, it remains the case that the relative strength of labour prior to these developments tended generally to be greater everywhere in Britain than in other countries, so that craft-union practices were better able to survive.

2.2. Britain's evolutionary system of industrial relations

(i) Some international comparisons
While early development is an important factor in explaining the unique degree to which trade unionism has penetrated the workplace in the UK,† the latter phenomenon is also due to the fact that 'Britain has had the most evolutionary system of industrial relations in the twentieth century' (Thompson and Hunter, 1978, p. 85). Indeed, Britain's experience contrasts sharply with events that occurred in other countries which also industrialised in the nineteenth century. Not only did these countries undergo upheavals due to more rapid industrial transformation, but they also experienced political traumas, sometimes associated with (defeats in) war and with strong state, or legal, influence over development.

In Germany, for example, the labour movement was suppressed by the Nazis, with unions being abolished in 1933 and unable to re-form until 1945. By this time organisational impediments to industrial unionism had disappeared. Moreover, the Western forces supervising the German reconstruction favoured total centralisation. This latter objective was only dropped following strong opposition from the British TUC. German trade unionists aimed to create a unified structure to avoid the ideological, religious and craft divisions of the Weimar period, with the result that the present day structure is highly centralised (Gunter and Leminsky, 1978, pp. 168, 169, 179).

† Although the structures of workers' organisations outside the UK are more suited to the needs of twentieth century mass production, they are not all equally so. Legal unions which developed in the 1930s in the USA, for example, are much more effective at resisting changes to the work structure than are relatively unorganised workers in South Korea or Taiwan with no tradition of resistance, and with customs established in the second half of the twentieth century.

The suppression of the 1871 Paris commune effectively broke up the French unions (Clegg, 1976, p. 34). Although legal recognition was granted in 1884, it implied only the right of association; there was no obligation on the part of employers to negotiate. Unlike in Britain, no system of collective bargaining arose to give legitimacy to existing customs or procedures. 'The very notion of the obligation to bargain has always met with strong opposition from the courts, and it was only in 1971 that a law was enacted providing for penalties against the party that would not answer a demand for bargaining' (Sellier, 1978, p. 220; see also pp. 217 and 218).

In Italy, Mussolini replaced the Confederation of Labour by government-controlled syndicates, which persisted until the overthrow of fascism in 1945. Moreover, the state-controlled unions which he set up were never properly dismantled in the postwar period, so that the centralised nature of organisation has continued. Indeed, for most of the postwar period there has been no direct union presence in factories in Italy or in France. Only since 1970 in Italy and since 1968 in France has this begun to change (Carew, 1976, pp. 31, 32, and 60–64).

The growth of collective bargaining was also a slow process in the USA. The major development came in the 1930s with the passing of the National Labour Relations (Wagner) Act, and the subsequent expansion in union organisation. Even so, federal government employees are denied the right to strike and, in practice, the right to bargain is limited. A number of union practices have been banned since 1947, when employers successfully challenged the Wagner Act on the basis that it conceded too much to unions (Labor/Management Relations Act [Taft-Hartley]). The legal framework of collective bargaining has remained essentially unchanged since 1947 (Galenson and Smith, 1978, pp. 40–44).

(ii) The conciliatory approach to industrial relations in the UK

The development of industrial relations in the UK stands in sharp contrast to some of the experiences of other old industrial economies. As British management in the late nineteenth century came to accept the reality of workers' power in many industries, it took a more conciliatory approach to workers' organisation than its overseas counterparts and attempted early on to institutionalise current practices, customs and the resolutions of disputes into workplace or firm 'procedures'. In this way management sought to minimise the number of disruptions, not through challenging the basis of worker resistance, but rather by attempting to limit its effect. Friedman (1977), in discussing the use of procedure and 'other forms of conciliation' from 1870 onwards, suggests that 'the most crucial development of the capitalist mode of production in Britain during the 1870s to 1914 was the acceptance by many employers of organised worker resistance as a permanent reality in their day-to-day dealings with workers (American acceptance came somewhat later)' (p. 97).† Unions were an active party to forming agreements with employers for they saw in them a means of defence against further losses of control over the organisation of work. Moreover, there were sectional gains to groups of workers, as procedures were established which related to promotion and discharge. In this way, although many of the workers were relatively unskilled, they gained some protection from the competitive forces of the 'external' labour market.

† See also Friedman, p. 96 or Elbaum and Wilkinson (1979, pp. 286–288, and 297). Moreover, nor did the British employers wish the state (which they distrusted) to intervene on their behalf, for they were 'as much in favour of voluntarism as an ideology for industrial relations as the unions' (Dunlop and Galenson, 1978, pp. 111–112).

Thus the structure of decentralised decision-making and internal 'collective' bargaining was further reinforced.

The conciliatory approach to industrial relations adopted by management must also be set alongside the existence of formal and informal imperial markets, which reduced the necessity for prolonged confrontation with workers over the restructuring of work. Thus, at the turn of the twentieth century, British firms sought to make profits through foreign investment in, and exports to, semi-protected regions, rather than to embark on a path of continuous confrontation with British workers over large-scale modernisation and integration of British industry.†

(iii) *Contracting*

The maintenance of a decentralised structure of bargaining seems also to have been partly due to the existence of systems of internal labour contract that were widespread in the nineteenth and early twentieth centuries. Many of the early British trade unions were primarily associations of subcontractors and it seems likely that the internal contract acted as a means of job control, and structural support of craft-type organisations (Hobsbawm, 1964, p, 299; Elbaum and Wilkinson, 1979, pp. 290–293). In so far as the subcontractor controlled hiring and firing, this power could be utilised to maintain exclusiveness and control of access to jobs. This structure of control may have been preserved because the elimination of contracting was brought about by unskilled workers rather than by employers. In the steel industry, for example, the end of subcontracting was brought about by underhands in separate unions opposed to contracting, but who 'retained much of the contractors' control over the pace of work. Scientific management made little or no impact and employers were unable to easily adjust manning levels and were obliged to take disputes through the disputes procedure where unions were as successful in establishing precedence over manning and work rules as they were over wage rates' (Elbaum and Wilkinson, 1979, p. 300).‡

(iv) *The experience of war*

The experience of two world wars is yet a further consideration. Unlike the continental industrial countries Britain was neither occupied nor defeated, and it seems that the experience in the second world war reinforced resistance to centralisation, and actually strengthened job-based worker organisation in the UK. For example, the 'spirit of co-operation' which the 'war effort' demanded led to the establishment of Joint Production Committees, particularly in the engineering industries. These committees were factory-based, with the union members (often shop stewards) elected by ballot, and were concerned with all aspects of wartime production within the factory. These committees spread in factories throughout Britain, including in those with no previous tradition of shop stewards (Pelling, 1976, p. 220). Thus, while temporarily performing a major role in 'national interest corporatism', these committees formalised and reinforced the institution of shop-floor trade unionism. Moreover they gave workplace-based organisation an even greater independence from trade union officials than had previously been the case and eventually came to be regarded by workers as the custom or norm.

† See evidence in section 3.3.
‡ 'In the US by contrast the interests of management appear to have been chiefly responsible for the abolition of the contracting system' (Elbaum and Wilkinson, 1979, p. 292). This at least partially explains why the 'British unions succeeded in maintaining control of the labour process where the American unions failed' (p. 294).

2.3. The labour process and industrial decline

Factors such as those outlined above all played a role in the maintenance of a highly decentralised structure of bargaining in the UK. That the Donovan Report (HMSO, 1968) found 'that the craft system is deeply rooted in much of British industry' (p. 87) is testimony to the early strength of British unions and to the active role workers' organisations have played in shaping the technical and social conditions of production. And although amalgamations have greatly reduced the total number of unions in the twentieth century—from 1269 in 1913 to 488 in 1975—it remains the case that they have done very little to simplify the overall pattern, or to centralise control (Clegg, 1976, pp. 31–32). In section 2.4 we detail examples from case studies of how decentralised bargaining has constrained productivity growth in the UK, compared with elsewhere. In particular, it has tended to lead to higher manning levels and slower rates of adoption and diffusion than would otherwise be the case.

The reorganisation of production continually took place, of course, but where resistance—or the threat of resistance—was strong, concessions were obtained, concerning either pay or the conditions of work in general. Frequently these concessions provided the basis for further resistance so that one way or another industrial change proceeded more slowly than it would have done in the absence of resistance; and proceeded much more slowly than in other countries.

We have concentrated at length on the active role of workers' resistance in shaping the labour process because this is an important element in understanding the uneven development of the structure of production across countries. The role of management has not been, and cannot be, ignored—although management designs are not the only important factor, as some American radicals are apt to imply.† By the same token it is not obvious that the relatively weak competitive position of the British economy can be seen to be the result of 'entrepreneurial failure'. For example, if British management, when faced with increased competition in certain export markets, choses to exploit protected markets rather than to modernise the methods of production, then the role played by its awareness of workers' ability to resist cannot be ignored. Rather, the outcome must be seen as the resolution of conflicting interests at all levels of society; certainly conflict over the reorganisation of production cannot be neglected.

2.4. Some findings of case studies and other research

The preceding account of developments is somewhat schematic. However, it is broadly corroborated by other more detailed studies such as that of Friedman (1977). The analysis does not lend itself to statistical testing; developments depend on the particular industry, geographical region and a host of 'conjunctural' factors including product market conditions and the recent history of conflict. However historical case studies show clearly that, although structural changes do persistently take place, the emergent broad 'picture across all industry indicates the persistence . . . of themes of workplace resistance despite the multiple transformations in the techniques and organisation of work' (Berg, 1979, p. 15). These studies reveal how workers have defended, or at least have bargained over, conditions of work, including terms of adoption of new technology and manning levels throughout the past century.

† See, for example, Braverman (1974) and Edwards (1979). (The fact that English writers tend to emphasise the role of worker resistance while American authors play it down may reflect the different experiences of worker organisations in the two countries.)

As an illustration, some findings of a recent study by Lazonick (1978) are instructive. In a comparative study of the USA and the UK, Lazonick explores the reasons for the relatively slow adoption of the 'ring frame' in textile production in the UK—an invention which started to replace the outdated 'mule' from the 1880s onwards. Although they were mainly supplied by British textile machinery manufacturers, by 1907 ring spindles comprised less than 15% of total spindles in the UK, compared with 40% in Germany, 38% in France, 36% in Austria, 65% in Italy, 56% in Russia and about 80% in the USA. Lazonick found that, unlike their British counterparts, American 'employers retained virtually complete control over the labour process throughout the 19th century . . .' (p. 50). By contrast, owing to

. . . the longer tradition of union organisation in England and the power of the English mule spinners union to perpetuate a division of labour which had arisen in an earlier era . . . the English mule spinners were able to protect their particular positions within the labour process and to exercise control over the pace of work until the 1960's . . . (p. 45).

. . . any large scale attempt to replace mules by rings [in the UK] would have resulted in a large scale confrontation which capitalists could by no means be sure of winning. The emphasis of the era was on industrial conciliation. If there was 'entrepreneurial failure' in the Lancashire cotton spinning industry, the effective (if not always explicit) constraints which the sharing of control over work with strong unions placed on the possibilities for redivision of labour and the introduction of new technology had a lot to do with it (p. 60).

A second example is provided by comparing the early British and American steel industries. Elbaum and Wilkinson (1979) found that, while different product market conditions were partly responsible for the different outcomes in the labour process in the two countries, the 'direction of causation is by no means one way' (p. 302). In Britain the 'success of the steel unions in maintaining the degree of control of tonnage rates and the labour process exercised by their iron industry predecessors made a significant contribution to the British industry's lack of competitiveness. The strength of union organisation in Britain in the world of emerging monopoly capitalism can be thus regarded as a major contribution to the country's uneven development' (p. 302; see also p. 300).

Further supportive material is contained in a collection of over fifty documents on the organisation of work in British industry written by different people in the nineteenth century (Berg, 1979). Generalising on the basis of this material, Berg outlines how 'the desire of management to gain control over all the functions of the production process was met by working class militancy' (p. 14). Resistance to new technology was found among type-setters and spinners, for example, and in the cutlery trades, the forge workers, file-making labourers, pattern makers, silk workers and farriers (p. 14). In the US shoe industry, mechanical techniques were introduced 'early on', while in the UK 'the sharp resistance of shoemakers to mechanisation and a reasonably successful outworking system meant that the process took over fifty years' (p. 169). Craft union practices were also found to be extremely durable even with major changes in both product and process technology. For example, with the transformation from wood to iron shipbuilding in the UK, 'neither the scale nor the new materials of the industry changed the basic organisation of work, which was still carried on along craft lines' (p. 169). A further example of resistance is provided by the British engineering industry where:

. . . craft orientated engineers were able to slow down . . . the transformation taking place under the system of Taylorism in the United States and on the continent.

92   A. Kilpatrick and T. Lawson

The struggle within all these industries over the rationalisation of production was soon reflected in Britain's comparative industrial performance. Other nations now took the technological lead. In Britain . . . workers resistance met the automation, division of labour, novel flow techniques, speed-up and productivity incentives which Marx had predicted would form the characteristics of the higher phases of modern industry (p. 170).

More recent illustrations can be found, for example, in Rubery (1978, p. 32) and McKersie and Hunter (1973, especially pp. 86–160). For example, the latter examined the influence of collective bargaining procedures on technical change in various UK industries over the postwar period. They found that, whether

. . . referring to the use of containers for cargo on the docks, larger trunk capacities in distribution, 'liner trans' on railways, or a variety of new devices in printing, the road towards the introduction and utilisation of new equipment has been long and tortuous. Even where technical change has taken place, it does not appear universally to have swept away outmoded practices. Indeed it would appear that these are precisely the industries where problems have arisen in the greatest intensity (p. 358).

They found elsewhere that:

The strongly prevailing craft system in many production industries in Britain has exercised a major influence on the allocation of labour and the operation of the production process. As a result [and unlike in the USA] technical innovations have been retarded . . . (p. 370).

While detailed historical case studies have yet (to our knowledge) to be carried out concerning the application of microprocessor or silicon chip technology, it is interesting to note that one factor slowing the adoption of new micro-electronic process technology in the motor vehicle industry is the combination of procedures and norms that have arisen, whereby workers of different real skills have achieved equal skill status and are thus attached to the same payments structure (McLean and Rush, 1978, p. 37). In order to maintain these new technologies in working order, management need to train electronics technicians to a higher level of skill, necessitating higher wages for those receiving the training. While management is 'unwilling to increase wages for the entire grade . . . wage divisions cannot be made within the skilled grade to accommodate a highly trained maintenance staff' (McLean and Rush, 1978, p. 37). By contrast, in other contries, firms which have adopted the same micro-electronic technologies have been able to train a highly paid maintenance 'elite' (p. 37).

There are many other well-documented examples which must be neglected through shortage of space. However, it is clear from the preceding outline that the labour process cannot be omitted from the de-industrialisation debate. While we can still agree with Landes (quoted in Gomulka, 1979, p. 189) that: 'All the evidence agrees on the technological backwardness of much of British manufacturing industry—on leads lost, opportunities missed, [and] markets relinquished', it is clear that this outcome cannot be interpreted as a series of 'mistakes', but as the logical result of the opportunity for change being constrained by organised resistance and obviated by the existence of relatively protected markets, among other factors.

However, this history has given rise to attitudes, structures of organisations and procedures for decision making, which work to inhibit rapid adjustment to changing trends. The social and institutional factors which make for a relatively slow rate of growth of productivity are now deeply rooted in the social structure of British society.

2.5. Uneven development

This discussion should not, of course, be seen as implying criticism of worker organisation. Rather, it is a comment on the nature of the competitive system and its uneven development. Worker resistance can usually only check management intentions; it cannot control developments. Nor are unions opposed to new technology *per se*. It is clear from the TUC's position on technological developments, as set out in 'a programme for action' (TUC, 1979), that it accepts the need for, and indeed wishes to encourage, the adoption of new technology. Understandably, the programme is also concerned to avoid redundancies and to improve conditions of work. The important point is that it takes for granted the right of workers to bargain and to negotiate over all aspects of investment (see TUC, 1979, especially p. 31). Indeed, it argues that '. . . full agreement on negotiating issues should be a precondition of technological change' (p. 32).

The ability to achieve collective bargaining is essentially a defensive strength. Workers bargain to maintain living standards and working conditions, or at least to be partly compensated for detrimental changes to work conditions, skill status, and so on. However, negotiations can take time, and the likely opposition of workers may even deter management from taking up the potential for change. Of course, the defence of standards or 'norms' is carried out by all members of all societies. The important factor in the sphere of international competition is the relative ability to achieve these aims. If UK workers achieve the ability to bargain over the conditions of introduction of a new process, where in another country it is brought in without negotiation, the latter country will tend to experience faster productivity growth. Of course, contrasts are never so sharp, but on the other hand nor are conditions everywhere equal. Development across countries has been uneven.

III. The Role of Demand

3.1. Worldwide expansion

So far we have concentrated on the supply side of the economy. Factors have been identified which tend to restrain productivity growth and generally to limit the competitiveness of UK industry. Industrial performance, however, is also dependent on the nature of, and variations in, demand. An expansion of demand facing UK industry would, other things being equal, provide at least the potential for a reorganisation of the structure of production. If gains in labour productivity could be achieved in this manner, then this in turn might improve the competitiveness of UK industry.

It is clear that this line of argument has to be heavily qualified. While increasing production might be conducive to raising productivity, improving competitiveness depends on obtaining faster rates of productivity growth than those achieved in other countries. But we have seen in section II that it is impossible to divorce considerations of changes to the technical structure of production from social factors, and in the UK these are such as to hold back productivity growth compared with elsewhere. Thus a rapid expansion in world demand—even if it occurred—would not in itself be sufficient to restore UK competitiveness. Indeed during the period of postwar boom, 1950–1973, British industry suffered a relative decline. Output and productivity expanded, but at a slower rate than in the other industrial countries, as Britain's major industries— engineering, shipbuilding, textiles and vehicles—suffered a declining share of world trade. Yet this was the longest and most rapid period of capitalist expansion that the world has ever experienced.

94   A. Kilpatrick and T. Lawson

Clearly, if a demand-oriented strategy is to have any effect on improving UK competitiveness—or at least on maintaining the current rate of output growth—it must be largely concentrated on industry in the UK. A worldwide expansion in demand would be mainly met by Britain's more productive competitors; and the same would be true with internal reflation.

Two policy measures which attempt to meet this requirement are a sterling devaluation and some form of import controls. Devaluation is not really a long-term strategy for raising productivity growth. Essentially, it is a disguised form of incomes policy designed to reduce unit costs by squeezing the real wages of workers. And, as with an incomes policy, the evidence suggests that there are only short-term benefits to this effect, since workers are able to defend themselves from permanent cuts to their normal standard of living (Tarling and Wilkinson, 1977). Labour costs in the UK are already lower than in other more productive industrial countries (Ray, 1979, p. 74, Table 3.5). Strategies aimed at reducing them further, while unlikely to succeed, appear increasingly to be misdirected: there is ample evidence that relative prices are now but one of a variety of characteristics that determine overall competitiveness (Stout, 1977). Customers are also concerned about obtaining high quality, reliable goods that can be delivered on time—hardly factors likely to be provided by an increasingly alienated workforce.

3.2. Import controls and the 'extent of the market'

In the light of this situation, some economists have turned towards supporting a policy of import controls (e.g. Beckerman, 1979). Of course, the UK economy cannot be isolated from the world economy. It must import raw materials, food and some industrial products, and in order to maintain national solvency it must retain the capacity to export. It will be affected by world slumps, international shortages of raw materials, crop failures and so on, and in order to export it must respond continuously to the technological imperative. We discuss import controls as part of a package for full state planning in section 3.5. In this section we consider proposals for temporary import controls accompanied by fiscal reflation, a policy advocated by the Cambridge Economic Policy Group, for example, and recently outlined by Cripps and Godley (1978).

Cripps and Godley claim that their package will stimulate accumulation and improve competitiveness by increasing the general level of activity in the domestic economy. Their argument is that a 'higher level of activity has a beneficial net effect on productivity and innovation' since 'all historical evidence, whether cross-section or time series suggests [this]' (p. 330).

While the first part of the statement is sometimes correct, at least in certain contexts, it is certainly not always true.† More important, and as we have already argued, if UK industry is to become competitive in world trade, not only has productivity to be raised, but it must also be made to grow permanently faster than elsewhere. We have seen throughout this paper how 'supply side' factors have constrained productivity growth which, through its effect on all facets of competitiveness, has in turn influenced output growth. The import controls strategy presupposes that any relation between output growth and productivity growth involves the opposite direction of causation—a view which stems from Adam Smith's famous dictum that 'the division of labour is limited by the extent of the market'. Yet, as a constraint, the 'extent of the market' may be non-operative. As we have seen, the division of labour may already be restricted by

† For example, Kindleberger (1964) puzzles over the fact that, following the Great Depression, technical

(continued on page 95)

the history of conflict at the level of production; certainly this is at least another constraint on the division of labour.

The relative importance of such conflict compared with the 'extent of the market' can be highlighted by considering the success currently being achieved in world trade by some of the newly industrialising countries. In general, being relatively unconstrained by the supply side factors identified earlier—mainly because of the availability of cheap, relatively unskilled labour, which was previously largely rural and with no tradition of union organisation—industries† in some of these countries are producing competitively-priced manufactured goods and are capturing an ever increasing share of world trade in some of these products.‡

Moreover, this invariably involves the use of capacity in excess of the needs of the domestic market. Thus South Korea, for example, has constructed a profitable steel industry capable of supplying both its own needs and demands for steel from overseas, at a time when world steel production is fairly stagnant; and there exists spare capacity (Korea, 1979, pp. 555–557; and *Financial Times*, 1979).

This example makes it clear that the extent of the market for any product is ultimately the world's current needs; and, in a geographical sense, this is as available to the UK as it is to South Korea. It is not so much the 'extent of the market' but the supply-side constraints identified above which vary from country to country and are partly responsible for differing economic performances. Thus, if a strategy of import controls is to be effective, it must be through its effect on these supply-side factors. And the important point concerning these factors is that they are the result of each country's particular path of development. Therefore, the effect of any proposed policy will depend on the particular situation in which it is imposed. The outcome is unlikely to be easily discernible from simple correlations between statistical variables such as output growth and productivity growth, for example. The historical context is crucial, and the policy must be examined in this light.

(continued from page 94)
progress failed to be stimulated by the increased activity after 1896. British cotton, textiles, building, coal, steel and railway industries all failed to respond to the abundance of new processes available at that time due to invention and innovation abroad: 'these industries undertook impressive programs of expansion, especially in cotton textiles and steel, but without modernisation. The challenge of demand met no response, even in the application of available technology' (p. 138). Kindleberger also cites Cole's findings that, despite rapid demand growth after 1906, there appears to have been no improvement in the technical design of locomotives until 1945. Minchenton (1957) notes that the British tin plate industry failed to change its scale or technique throughout the nineteenth century (pp. 24, 29). Yet during this period there was a 150-fold expansion of demand. A more recent example is the British motor vehicle industry which has for years faced an excess of demand. This has led Lord Stokes to attribute the high import penetration, in the UK, to 'lack of availability at least as far as British Leyland Motor Corporation is concerned' (HMSO, 1975, p. 115). Moreover, while statistical support for the relationship between output growth and pro-ductivity growth (the Verdoorn 'Law') has been found for the manufacturing sector, the relationship is not always strong (see, for example, George and Ward (1975) who find little support for the hypothesis in a cross-section analysis of West German manufacturing industry (p. 69)). Moreover, even where statistical support is found, this says nothing about the direction of causation. It may work either way: the context is crucial. We can also note that the statistical relation between productivity growth and employment growth (Kaldor's 'Law'), which is usually supposed to reflect 'economies of scale', has 'broken down' (at least since 1965—see for example Rowthorn (1975) and Cripps and Tarling (1973)).

---

† Including subsidiaries of transnational corporations.
‡ For example, between 1970 and 1977 the following rises in the developing market economies' share of world exports of certain products were recorded: TVs, 3·9% (1970) to 7·1% (1977); radio broadcast receivers, 10·4% to 22·2%; microphones, loudspeakers, and amplifiers, 1·0% to 9·2%; sound recorders, 0·6% to 8·3%; transistors, valves, 6·0% to 21·1%; electrical space heaters, 0·8% to 7·5%; measuring and controlling instruments, 0·7% to 4·7%; watches, etc., 5·7% to 20·4%; and so on. For further examples, see UN (1979).

96   A. Kilpatrick and T. Lawson

3.3. Import controls and worker resistance

Britain is an old industrial country with a highly decentralised system of collective bargaining. The job-based strength of worker organisation is such that management has often only embarked on confrontations over restructuring production when alternative strategies have appeared more costly than the ensuing disruptions (usually in terms of lost sales). In fact, in the face of international competition, a typical management strategy has been to use this situation to threaten a plant's closure unless such a restructuring is accepted. With a domestic market partly sheltered from such competition this argument loses force; and, indeed, the management incentive to restructure production is reduced, as the result of import controls plus fiscal reflation, with the consequence that productivity growth will tend to be lower than it would otherwise have been. This latter tendency will be partly or wholly offset in the short run, if there is spare capacity in the economy which can be utilised to raise the level of productivity. However, in the longer run, given the nature of worker resistance and the relatively monopolistic position in which firms operating in the domestic market would find themselves, the temptation to increase profits through raising prices, rather than through introducing new technology and restructuring work, would be large. Moreover, these factors would also provide the temptation for exporters to switch from producing for the competitive export market to producing for the protected domestic market—a move which again would reduce the incentive for producers to adopt the latest techniques and raise productivity growth. Indeed, the situation would be not unlike that facing Britain in the late nineteenth century, when competition was increasing in domestic and export markets after 1880, while protection was afforded by the markets of the Empire. In this situation, UK exporters found it to their advantage to avoid conflict with workers over an accelerated remoulding of the structure of production, and instead redirected sales to the new or protected markets often with the aid of capital exports.†
There is little reason to believe that the use of import controls will produce a very different outcome, especially if fiscal reflation is the only accompanying measure.

Thus, although demand will increase within the domestic market, the conditions by which it is brought about appear to militate against increasing the long-run rate of productivity growth and, in fact, suggest that the latter will be lower than it would otherwise have been without import controls. Yet with developments taking place which

† For example, the expansion of exports to Empire and protected markets between 1880 and 1914 postponed the necessity to improve productivity in many of Britain's main industries, including cotton, textiles and railways (Kindleberger, 1978, p. 224). Another example is provided by the Ottawa agreements in 1932, when British colonies were instructed to give preferential treatment to British exports, and to apply restrictive quotas to others, especially to Japanese textiles, and when similar demands for preferential treatment were made on a number of other countries. Although trade increased, many economists doubt the long-run benefits of these actions. As Lewis (1949) noted, the 'reason for this is that the effect of the protection for Britain in these markets was to deflect foreign competition into other markets where on the whole, the British position was in any case less favourable. It seems likely that Britain would have fared better elsewhere if she had not fared so well in protected markets' (p. 84). In other words competitiveness was held back through Britain's access to protected markets. This view is also borne out, for example, by the experience of the British motor vehicle industry which had been protected since 1915. Although it was successful abroad, this was mainly due to tariff preferences (Youngson, 1960). By 1937, 85% of exported cars went to Empire countries and 'the industry did not do much, nor did it try to do much, in European markets which it left chiefly to French and German producers' (p. 107). Thus, in the postwar period when tariffs were reduced, UK producers found it difficult to succeed in the more competitive European markets. A further example is the protected steel industry which 'showed little signs of reducing the discrepancy between its costs and those of its rivals . . . lip service only was paid to the ideal of economy through more concentrated production . . . [and] there was still a dearth of modern blast furnaces in 1937' (Youngson, 1960, p. 106).

are 'revolutionising' communication technology and giving rise to many new products and processes, any policy which further reduces the incentives for industry to keep abreast of such developments can only accelerate Britain's declining competitiveness.

3.4. Some opposing views

While our analysis leads to the view that the import controls package discussed above is most unlikely to restore competitiveness in the UK, it is surprisingly difficult to find a study which attempts a reasoned argument to the contrary. Indeed, as with Cripps and Godley, the argument for import controls usually goes by default as other options are shown to be ineffective by comparison:

> We are making no strong claim that protection will necessarily make UK industry sufficiently competitive in the long run, only that deflation will not do so and the effects of import controls on industrial efficiency are at least superior to those of deflation (p. 330).

References are sometimes made to the beneficial effects of past experience of protectionism, but to our knowledge no historical study has been produced which draws conclusions for present day policy. Kaldor (1978) has pointed out that, when controls were imposed in 1932, the following 5 years witnessed an increase in manufacturing output of 8% per annum, 'something unprecedented in a 5-year period of history'. However, productivity growth in this period was no faster than in the early 1920s, while most historians of this period seem to draw the same conclusion as Lewis (1949) that, 'As so many different domestic policies were pursued in the thirties, it is doubtful whether recovery is to be attributed to any particular national policy' (p. 69). Thus the effect of import controls in the UK must be disentangled from the effects of the sterling depreciation as Britain left the Gold Standard in 1931; movements in the terms of trade; the bilateral arrangements agreed in Ottawa in 1932; the fall in interest rates and the building boom of 1932 and after; government industrial reorganisation and rationalisation schemes; plus various events taking place elsewhere in the world.

The context in which a policy is to be implemented is crucial. To point, as some do, to the successful use of tariffs by newly industrialising countries to nurture their infant industries, is not to make an adequate or valid comparison.† Among many other factors, workers in such countries do not have the tradition of resistance to structural change. Certainly currently industrialising countries are not constrained by customs or bargaining practices similar to those currently existing in Britain.

There appears to be little reason for believing that import controls plus fiscal reflation will succeed. There is no guarantee that a stimulus to demand will mean substantial gains to productivity growth in the UK (under any state of competition), and indeed there is evidence to suggest that protectionism would lead to lower productivity growth and to a loss of competitiveness as domestic firms are shielded from the full severity of international competition.

3.5. Import controls plus increased state planning

In the preceding sections we have addressed the discussion to the Cambridge Policy Group's import controls package, because it is around this that most of the discussion

---

† Moreover, even here there were failures. For example Gerschenkron (1955) notes that 'Tariff policy isolated France and accounted more than anything else for the economic stagnation in France in the first half of the 19th century'(p. 376). Similarly Luethy (1955) notes that the same occurred at the turn of the twentieth century when tariffs caused France to isolate itself from 'progressive and competitive' tendencies.

in recent years has revolved. However, there has also been a growth of support for a more comprehensive package along the lines of the so-called 'Benn', or 'Alternative', strategy. There are two distinct strands to this strategy which distinguish it from the Cripps/Godley package outlined in section 3.3. First, certain vagaries of the market system are to be removed, including the temptation for firms to meet the increased domestic demand with price rises rather than new investment. Instead there is to be state-directed investment and price and income controls. The second strand is actively to enlist the support of workers (in the name of 'industrial democracy', or 'increased workers' participation' or even 'workers' control'). Basically it is a programme designed to reform the UK economic system into state capitalism, incorporating workers' support in the 'national interest'.

The two parts of the strategy distinguished are of course mutually dependent. If state-directed investment is to restore Britain's international competitiveness, then, as with private investment, workers' participation is required to achieve high productivity on that investment. Competing nations, including some of those newly industrialising, are by far out-performing Britain in investing in capital-intensive high technology.† Thus if Britain is to regain competitiveness and halt its long-run industrial decline, not only must investment be introduced and diffused as rapidly as elsewhere, but manning levels and the conditions and speed of work must be matched. As we have seen, factors such as these are, in the UK, matters of workplace collective bargaining. Indeed the very existence of workplace bargaining has tended to slow the adoption rate of new technology. In order to ensure low manning levels, high machine running rates and rapid rates of innovation and diffusion of new technology, then workplace collective bargaining must be severely curtailed. Thus, workers are effectively being asked to forfeit norms, practices and traditions that they have defended throughout the history of trade unionism: they are expected to relinquish their job-based power to participate effectively in the determination of all conditions of work (Benn, Morell and Cripps, 1975, pp. 3 and 4).

The strategy clearly relies on the incorporation of workers (as opposed to just union officials), yet it is also clear that, before time-honoured traditions will be relinquished, more than promises and talk of the 'national interest' must be offered. This point is illustrated by the experience of the past forty years when both of the major political parties have attempted to acquire labour's co-operation and so increase productivity by associating labour's interests with those of the nation. These attempts have failed when workers have 'realised' that there were no real benefits from such co-operation (Tarling and Wilkinson, 1977). Take, for example, the most recent crisis in 1975 and 1976 when inflation and unemployment were both rising. The Labour Party and the union officials together attempted to achieve workers' co-operation through the 'Social Contract'. With no obvious material benefits from the strategy, and indeed with a loss of real wages over 1976 and 1977, the reactions of job-based worker organisations gave the lie to any idea that they were sold on national interest corporatism. Following large wage demands and successful strike action, by mid-1979 real wage rates were almost restored to their early 1975 level. Significantly, the pressure for wage increases was opposed by union officials and some senior shop stewards (e.g. British Leyland), and

† In the case of industrialised nations, a recent OECD report (1979) estimated that 'the average life of total plant and machinery assets [in the UK] is almost double that of countries like France, Sweden, Germany and the U.S.' (p. 9). Moreover, some newly industrialising countries have (recently) experienced high rates of accumulation and employ both very young vintages of capital stock and the very latest techniques.

successful strikes (e.g. the lorry drivers against the Road Haulage Association) were invariably outside the control of union officials. Pressure for strikes came from the workplace: union officials and senior shop stewards were either forced to support shop floor demands, or bypassed.

This example illustrates both the need for and the difficulty of enlisting the support of rank and file workers for any national economic strategy. Although a Benn-type alternative is essentially a long-run strategy, the example also demonstrates that, in order to acquire worker co-operation, it is at least necessary that there be immediate gains to real wages. Voluntary corporatism must in a sense be 'bought', and with 'payment today' rather than 'tomorrow'. Immediate benefits from the strategy would be the prevention of increased redundancies, a move towards 'full' employment and some real wage gains if existing spare capacity were quickly utilised,† effecting an increase in the level of productivity. However, while such perceived gains may persuade workers to support electorally an import controls strategy, by themselves they would hardly be sufficient to induce workers to give up their traditional bargaining power and practices.‡ Indeed, without further accompanying measures, the outcome for long-run productivity growth is unlikely to be significantly different from that which would be achieved through the Cripps/Godley package discussed in section 3.3.§ The Benn strategy seems to recognise this through its proposal of increased 'workers' control', although what precisely is meant by this has not, to our knowledge, been made clear. A salutory indication that this sort of proposal is also not without difficulties is provided by submissions to the Expenditure Committee's Enquiry into the Motor Vehicle Industry (1975, p. 80).

It is clear that the vast majority of disputes are about specific issues, and demand specific solutions. In most strike situations it is the immediate problem that has to be solved; 'jam tomorrow' rarely suffices. Mr. Moss Evans said 'If I went to a meeting of workers who were out on strike for an increase in shift differential and suggested that workers' control was the solution to their problem, they would throw me in the canal. Some people make suggestions that the best way to resolve an industrial problem . . . is a political solution, but . . . our members . . . would not accept this as a solution to their particular immediate problem.'

It is thus not clear that the Benn strategy can incorporate workers' support to the degree necessary to achieve a long-run improvement in competitiveness. It is clear, however, that in order to entertain any hope of this being achieved, significant 'control' would indeed have to be obtained by workers. It is difficult in such circumstances not to anticipate a strike by capital, particularly by multinationals—refusing, for example,

---

† Clearly the gains would be larger, the greater the extent of spare capacity in the UK. If the policy were introduced in a period of world recession when spare capacity is high among competitor countries, there might also be some improvement in UK competitiveness.

‡ Indeed, workers may well consider the offer of work a right rather than a gain. Moreover, these short-run benefits to workers may to some extent be offset by certain counteracting tendencies. In particular, as a result of protection there may be offsetting real income losses, due to the use of more expensive intermediate products and through consumers being forced to purchase high-cost inferior substitutes. Furthermore, even with price and income controls, there would be difficulties involved in preventing prices from rising: under protectionism, once certain price increases are viewed as justifiable, the operation of a pricing policy becomes difficult as firms exploit the situation to increase their profit margins. The combination of fuller capacity utilisation and higher prices may not just reduce the share of wages in the national income but, in the short run, may make it difficult to maintain the planned increase in real wages as well. In addition, there is the problem of persuading the workers that they would be worse off with a different strategy. Certainly no-one 'knows' this, even if all governments claim it.

§ In other words the main 'problem' remains. The reduced prospect of redundancy due to a diminished threat of international competition is likely to both strengthen worker resistance to change and weaken management incentive to embark on confrontation over restructuring.

100   A. Kilpatrick and T. Lawson

to invest—resulting in a situation of deadlock. We cannot, of course, refute the proposition that such a strategy will succeed in regenerating British industry; but there do seem to be problems which so far have largely been ignored, if only because the labour process has been left out of the analysis.

IV. Final Comments and Conclusion

We have concentrated on historical factors which have influenced Britain's (relatively poor) competitive performance in international trade. As each region of the world develops its social and political institutions and attitudes under different circumstances, performances everywhere will vary. Differences in economic performance over long periods may be systematic—as for example between the UK and other western industrial countries over the past century—depending on the nature of development.

In a competitive market situation the more constrained countries will face balance of payments problems for which traditional policies offer no obvious long-run solutions. We have discussed how problems will also remain under certain import controls packages and other state planning measures. However, given that these policies at least set out to improve short run UK employment and real wage conditions (compared with what might be expected from traditional policies), we may well see a movement towards increased state planning in the future.† The arguments of this paper suggest, however, that such a strategy will have problems achieving long-run improvement to productivity growth and competitiveness in the UK, with the possible implication that if increasing unemployment is to be avoided through this policy, then, once introduced, import controls may have to be increasingly raised.

However, the precise outcome will depend on the nature and resolution of many struggles in all branches of all societies. The one definite point which emerges from the analysis is that without large scale social and institutional reorganisation of some form, the British economy will continue along an uneven path of industrial decline.

Bibliography

Beckerman, W. (ed.) 1979. *Slow Growth in Britain: Causes and Consequences*, Oxford, OUP

Benn, T., Morrell, S. and Cripps, F. 1975. *A Ten Year Industrial Strategy for Britain*, Nottingham, Institute for Workers' Control

Berg, M. (ed.) 1979. *Technology and Toil in Nineteenth Century Britain*, London, CSE Books

Blackaby, F. (ed.) 1979. *De-industrialisation*, NIESR Economic Policy Papers 2, London, Heinemann

Braverman, H. 1974. *Labour and Monopoly Capital*, New York, Monthly Review Press

Cambridge Economic Policy Group, 1975. *Economic Policy Review* Nos. 1–5, Cambridge, Department of Applied Economics, University of Cambridge

Carew, A. 1976. *Democracy and Government in European Trade Unions*, London, George Allen and Unwin

Channon, D. F. 1973. *The Strategy and Structure of British Enterprise*, London, Macmillan

Clarke, T. and Clements, L. (eds) 1977. *Trade Unions under Capitalism*, Glasgow, Fontana/Collins

Clegg, H. A. 1976. *Trade Unionism under Collective Bargaining*, Oxford, Basil Blackwell

Clegg, H. A. 1979. *The Changing System of Industrial Relations in Great Britain*, Oxford, Basil Blackwell

† Tendencies in favour of state capitalism in Britain may at some stage give way to the idea for the formation of a state-planned bloc involving other—most likely EEC—countries. Together with present experiments in setting up protected trading zones throughout the world economy (which so far have been unsuccessful) (Morton and Tulluch, 1977, pp. 302–325), this may give rise to a world system of separate state-planned blocks.

Cripps, T. F. and Godley, W. A. H. 1978. Control of imports as a means to full employment and the expansion of world trade: the UK's case, *Cambridge Journal of Economics*, September

Cripps, T. F. and Tarling, R. J. 1973. *Growth in Advanced Capitalist Economies 1950–1970*, Cambridge, CUP

Dunlop, J. T. and Galenson, W. (eds) 1978. *Labor in the Twentieth Century*, New York, Academic Press

Edwards, R. E. 1979. *Contested Terrain*, New York, Basic Books Inc.

Elbaum, B. and Wilkinson, F. 1979. Industrial relations and uneven development, a comparative study of the American and British steel industries, *Cambridge Journal of Economics*, September

Financial Times 1979. South Korea: a survey, 2 April

Friedman, A. L. 1977. *Industry and Labour*, London, Macmillan

Galenson, W. and Smith, R. S. 1978. The United States, in Dunlop, J. T. and Galenson, W. (eds) *Labor in the Twentieth Century*, New York, Academic Press

George, K. D. and Ward, T. S. 1975. *The Structure of Industry in the EEC*, Cambridge, CUP

Gerschenkron, A. 1955. Comment on Hoselitz, B. F. (ed.), *Entrepreneurship and Capital Formation in France and Britain since 1700*, in NBER *Capital Formation and Economic Growth*, Princeton, Princeton University Press

Gomulka, S. 1979. Britain's slow industrial growth: increasing inefficiency versus low rate of technological change, in Beckerman, W. (ed.), *Slow Growth in Britain*, Oxford, OUP

Granick, D. 1972. *Managerial Comparisons of Four Developed Countries: France, Britain, United States and Russia*, Cambridge, Massachusetts, MIT Press

Günter, H. and Leminsky, G. 1978. The Federal Republic of Germany, in Dunlop, J. T. and Galenson, W. (eds) *Labor in the Twentieth Century*, New York, Academic Press

Habakkuk, H. J. 1967. *American and British Technology in the Nineteenth Century*, Cambridge, CUP

HMSO 1975. *The Motor Vehicle Industry*, Fourteenth Report from the Expenditure Committee, London

HMSO, Royal Commission on Trade Unions and Employers' Associations 1968. *The Donovan Report*, London

Hobsbawm, E. J. 1964. *Labouring Men*, London, Weidenfeld and Nicolson

International Labour Office (ILO) 1974. *Collective Bargaining in Industrialised Market Economies*, Geneva, ILO

Kaldor, N. 1978. Productivity and job opportunities, speech to House of Lords on Monday, 3 July 1978

Kindleberger, C. P. 1964. *Economic Growth in France and Britain, 1851–1950*, Cambridge, Massachusetts, Harvard University Press

Kindleberger, C. P. 1978. *Economic Response: Comparative Studies in Trade, Finance and Growth*, London, Harvard University Press

Korea 1979. *A Handbook of Korea*, Seoul, Korean Overseas Information Service

Landes, S. 1969. *The Unbound Prometheus*, Cambridge, CUP

Lazonick, W. 1978. *The Division of Labour and Machinery: The Development of British and US Cotton Spinning*, Discussion Paper No. 620, Cambridge, Massachusetts, Harvard University

Lewis, W. A. 1949. *Economic Survey 1919–39*, London, George Allen and Unwin

Luethy, H. 1955. *France against Herself*, New York, Praeger

McKersie, R. G. and Hunter, L. C. 1973. *Pay, Productivity and Collective Bargaining*, London, Macmillan

McLean, J. M. and Rush, H. J. 1978. *The Impact of Microelectronics on the U.K.: A Suggested Classification and Illustrative Case Studies*, SPRU Occasional Paper Series, No. 7, Sussex

Maddison, A. 1977. Phases of capitalist development, *Banca Nazionale del Lavoro Review*, June

Mason, N. 1979. *De-industrialisation in the UK: A Comment on Singh's Approach*, unpublished mimeo, Cambridge

Minchenton, W. E. 1957. *British Tinplate Industry*, Oxford, Clarendon Press

Morton, K. and Tulloch, P. 1977. *Trade and Developing Countries*, London, Overseas Development Institute

Musgrave, P. W. 1967. *Technical Change, the Labour Force, and Education*, Oxford, Pergamon Press

OECD, 1970. *Gaps in Technology: Comparisons between Member Countries in Education, Research and Development, Technological Innovation, International Economic Exchanges*, Paris, OECD

OECD, 1979. *United Kingdom*, OECD Economic Surveys, Paris, March

102 A. Kilpatrick and T. Lawson

Payne, P. L. 1978. Industrial entrepreneurship and management in Great Britain, in Mathias, P. and Postan, M. M. (eds), *Cambridge Economic History of Europe*, Vol. VII, Part I, Cambridge, CUP

Peck, M. J. 1968. Science and technology, in Caves, R. E. *et al.*, *Britain's Economic Prospects*, Washington, DC, Brookings Institution

Pelling, H. 1976. *A History of British Trade Unionism*, London, Macmillan

Penn, R. 1978. *Skilled Manual Workers in the Labour Process*, presented at Nuffield Conference on the Labour Process, unpublished

Pratten, C. F. 1976. *Labour Productivity Differentials Within International Companies*, Cambridge, CUP

Ray, G. F. 1979. Comment on Freeman, C., *Technical Innovation and British Trade Performance* in Blackaby, F. (ed.), *De-industrialisation*, London, Heinemann

Rowthorn, R. E. 1975. What remains of Kaldor's Law?, *Economic Journal*, March

Rubery, J. 1978. Structured labour markets, worker organisation and low pay, *Cambridge Journal of Economics*, March

Sellier, F. 1978. France, in Dunlop, J. T. and Galenson, W. (eds), *Labor in the Twentieth Century*, New York, Academic Press

Singh, A. 1977. UK industry and the world economy: a case of de-industrialisation, *Cambridge Journal of Economics*, June

Stout, D. K. 1977. *International Price Competitiveness, Non-Price Factors and Export Performance*, London, NEDO

Tarling, R. J. and Wilkinson, F. 1977. The Social Contract: postwar incomes policies and their inflationary impact, *Cambridge Journal of Economics*, December

Thompson, A. W. J. and Hunter, L. C. 1978. Great Britain, in Dunlop, J. T. and Galenson, W. (eds), *Labor in the Twentieth Century*, New York, Academic Press

TUC 1979. *Employment and Technology*, Interim Report, London, TUC

UN, 1979. *Yearbook of International Trade Statistics*, New York

Youngson, A. J. 1960. *The British Economy 1920–57*, London, George Allen and Unwin

Part IV
Entrepreneurship, Management and Technical Change

VI

TECHNOLOGY AND GROWTH IN BRITAIN IN THE LATER NINETEENTH CENTURY

In the first half of the century, the problem was to explain why America's technical progress should have been more rapid than Britain's in certain industries. The industries concerned were few, and the problem attracts attention only because it is, on the face of it, surprising that even in a small number of industries a country so predominantly agricultural should have been superior. The absolute contributions of Britain to technological progress in the period must have been much greater.

From the 1870's on the problem is a more general one. What needs to be explained is the widely held impression that in the forty years or so before 1914, advance in technology over industry as a whole was slower in Britain than in the U.S.A., and also than in Germany; her own contributions were fewer, and technical developments of foreign origin were less widely and less promptly adopted in Britain than British developments were adopted elsewhere. There was a technological lag in the most important of the basic industries: the efficiency of British iron and steel plants was thought to be far behind that of their competitors in the U.S.A. and Germany. And there was also a lag in the new industries which were becoming prominent in the closing decades of the century, as shown by the excess of English imports over her exports of cars, electrical equipment and certain types of chemical.

The extent to which the U.K. was falling behind by relevant economic criteria has still to be established, but some lag in technology is reasonably well attested by contemporary comment and requires explanation.[1] There is a widespread impression that this lag represents the onset of deep-seated and persistent deficiencies. The changes are frequently presented in terms of rigidity and ossification, the characteristics of an old economy,

---

[1] For a balanced account of Britain's technological performance from the 1880's on see J. H. Clapham, *op. cit.* III, ch. III.

190   TECHNOLOGY IN THE NINETEENTH CENTURY

and when the explanation is not anthropomorphic it is sociological in character. The form which the sociological explanation most often takes is to attribute these technical deficiencies
wholly or in part to British entrepreneurs. This explanation is
applied to all the British basic industries but most conspicuously
to the heavy industries.

There is a general argument, to which we have referred in a
previous section, that the English social structure and English
public opinion were less favourable than the American to
entrepreneurship, less favourable both to the recruitment of
ability and to full exertion of ability once recruited.[1]

In the United States, there was no long-established class
system to impede social mobility. The possibility of rising to the
top was believed to be greater than anywhere else in the world,
and probably was so in fact. This belief in an open avenue to
wealth was one of the main reasons for the amount of ability
devoted to entrepreneurship in the United States. Moreover,
in the United States, there were few competitors to business
success as a source of social prestige. There was no large and
powerful bureaucracy, no hereditary aristocracy. There was no
professional military class and soldiers were not held in high
esteem. Horatio Alger, the hero of the American success story,
wanted to be a business man, not a general or a civil servant
or a great landowner. The men of ambition and ability turned
naturally to business, not only because of the gains which might
be made there—though they were sometimes certainly enormous—but because business men, a Rockefeller or a Pierrepont
Morgan, were the leading men of the country. Morgan himself, in his early middle age, nearly decided to give up business
and become a gentleman; but he did not do so, and later
American business men did not even consider the possibility.

In England, as, of course, in other countries of Western
Europe conditions were more complicated. There existed a
strongly entrenched social system which limited social mobility,
a social system inherited from pre-industrial times when landowners were the ruling groups. Moreover, there were sources
of power and prestige besides business. Landownership,
bureaucracy, the army and the professions were all powerful
competitors of business for the services of the able men. There
was therefore a haemorrhage of capital and ability from

[1] See pp. 111–15 above.

industry and trade into landownership and politics. Robert Peel and Gladstone both came of entrepreneurial families, but their abilities were devoted to politics not to industry and trade.

In particular the high social standing of the professions drew off a large number of the ablest men. One of the most successful British entrepreneurs of the twentieth century, Lord Nuffield, is said to have entered business only because his father was unable, for economic reasons, to fulfil his original intention of making him a surgeon.[1] In England in the first forty years or so of the century, the professions attracted too many able people and business too few. After 1902, there was a vast increase in educational opportunities in England, but of those who profited from such opportunities up to 1939 many more became teachers or lawyers, doctors or architects than business men. Why were the professions more attractive? Certainly not because they yielded higher incomes; it was partly because, for a person with no personal contacts in business, the professions were more accessible, and partly because business in general lacked the social prestige of the professions. Moreover in the present century a business career and the acquisition of profit became actively disapproved of among the many people who were influenced by socialist ideas about capitalism and the profit motive. In England, therefore, as in Western Europe generally, business has had to face greater competition for the able men than it has had to face in the U.S.A. The wider the circle from which a country draws its business men, the more likely it is to produce great entrepreneurs.

Moreover, much the same circumstances which facilitated the recruitment of entrepreneurs in America were also favourable to the performance of men once they had become entrepreneurs. In the United States, almost from the beginning, birth and hereditary status were of small influence in determining a man's social standing as compared with the highly efficient performance of a specific and limited function. There the man who concentrated his energies on a single goal and achieved success in his occupation was the man who commanded respect; the accepted ideal was that he should rise as far in terms of wealth as his abilities could carry him. A man's

[1] P. W. S. Andrews and E. Brunner, *The Life of Lord Nuffield* (Oxford, 1955). p. 37.

success in his occupation was not invariably judged by the amount of money he made. Some occupations were very highly regarded which did not yield very high rewards, for example, membership of the Supreme Court, but income was certainly an important criterion of occupational success. The signs of social standing could more easily be acquired with money. In England, on the other hand, birth and family, education, behaviour, manners, accent, played the dominant part in determining social standing. The ideal of the 'all-round man', the man of well-developed but non-professional competence in many fields, the ideal of Renaissance Europe, was still strong; and, within the limits left by birth and family, social standing was influenced by the whole range of a man's achievements and abilities, his physical strength or weakness, the way in which he ordered his life, his capacity to paint, or to play instruments, his whole character and personality. A society in which the main emphasis is placed on success in one's job as measured by income is more favourable to the full exercise of business abilities, and for this reason England was less favourably placed than the U.S.A.[1]

These are general characteristics of English society which might militate against English entrepreneurship (and even more against that of continental European countries) at all times. But there are additional reasons which apply with particular force to the later nineteenth century. There are two assertions which need to be distinguished: the first is that English entrepreneurs were apathetic, by comparison with their American and German contemporaries, that is were men of less general capacity and force: the second assertion is that, though still able, they were men of abilities which had ceased to be relevant. Because England industrialised earlier, English entrepreneurs were more likely to be second- and third-generation entrepreneurs; as such they had less need and incentive to exert their full effort, and were more likely to be distracted from concentration on business by the possibilities of social life, which are open to the man who has arrived but not to those who are still climbing. The drive inside the individual entrepreneur to expand his concern, to make the most of

---

[1] For a discussion of this problem see F. X. Sutton, 'Achievement Norms and the Motivations of Entrepreneurs' in *Entrepreneurship and Economic Growth* (Harvard University Research Center in Entrepreneurial History, 1955).

opportunities, is greatest in the early stages of industrialisation and loses some of its force once an industrial society has been created. This, it is argued, is true whatever the form of industrial organisation, but it applies with most force to the members of a family concern, which was probably still the principal form of organisation at this time: the impetus in the first generation is very great but it loses force with succeeding generations. Second- and third-generation business men tend to be less energetic (an argument, however, which is rarely applied to second- and third-generation Professors).

The second assertion is that, quite apart from any decline in the quality of the entrepreneurs, their virtues were not the relevant ones in the later nineteenth century. In some industries the course of technical and economic change called for the exercise of qualities different from those by which the entrepreneurs had established themselves. In the iron and steel industry, for example, the founders of the older British firms succeeded by the operation of qualities which were not those most required in the 1880's and '90's. The ability most evidently absent was technical expertise. The later innovations embodied more technical knowledge than the early ones, that is there were fewer within the scope of the ingenious artisan. Furthermore, many more of the later technical innovations consisted in applying the techniques of one industry to another, in the cross-fertilisation of the techniques of different industries. In such cases even an entrepreneur who had acquired from experience considerable technical mastery, was at a disadvantage compared with someone whose technical training had been more formal and so more general. Altogether therefore British industrialists tended to be less well equipped than their rivals, 'to judge the commercial prospects of innovations while these were in their experimental change' and 'to forecast the trend of technical change'. The English employer was, contemporaries said, more of a commercial man and took less interest in the technical part of the work than those of France and Germany. There was, said Siemens, 'more prejudice against innovations'.[1]

That in late nineteenth-century England there were entrepreneurial deficiencies of a social origin few students of the period would be disposed to deny, but exactly how important

[1] D. L. Burn, *op. cit.* pp. 296–306, has a discussion of the personal factors.

194 TECHNOLOGY IN THE NINETEENTH CENTURY

they were it is very difficult to say. There is no reason to believe that the English business man, though he may have been less well equipped technically than the German, was less well-qualified than the American. Moreover, in general the argument ignores, or at best does not explain, the curious patchiness of English business performance in this period. The rapidity of technical advance in shipbuilding and in the open-hearth sector of the steel industry, for instance, show that the second generation of entrepreneurs in family firms could be conspicuously successful. And many of the deficiencies can be explained in more narrowly economic terms and with less recourse to sociological influences.

Part of the contrast in technology can be accounted for by differences in factor-endowment on lines similar to those already discussed in earlier sections.

In the later decades of the century, it is true, the course of technical change was less subject to this influence. Scientific knowledge became more important as a source of invention, compared with empirical, artisan trial and error, than it had been earlier; and though scientific invention is, of course, often guided by the need to cope with particular bottle-necks, the scientist, even when searching for new methods as deliberately as the artisan or professional inventor, is likely to be more sensitive to the technical possibilities of particular lines of investigation, and to give them priority in his search. Since science is also pursued for its own sake, the autonomous accumulation of scientific knowledge is much more likely to throw off accidental inventions which are not tailored to fit the needs of particular factor-endowments. For the same reason, scientific invention is more likely to produce sudden jumps, discontinuities in the spectrum of existing techniques, which reduce the scope of the influence of factor-supplies on the choice of techniques.

Moreover, there was probably less difference in this period between the labour supplies available in the U.S.A. and in England. The stream of immigrants into the U.S.A. supplemented the supplies of native-born labour; and, with the increase in the size of the industrial sector and improvements in transport and in the labour-market, industrial labour became much more readily available. And if American labour was, except in the remoter parts of the country, no longer scarce, in

England it was no longer as abundant as it had been earlier in the century. The fact that industrial real wages were rising in the middle decades of the century is perhaps evidence that the demand for labour was out-running the expansion of the labour force. In the peak of the 1868–73 cycle, there was a very rapid rise of wages, and this is the first boom of which it might be argued that labour shortage acted as a ceiling.[1] The rise of real wages of English agricultural labour in the 1880's and '90's certainly suggests that the surplus of agricultural labour had been absorbed in English industry or by emigration.

Not only was English labour less abundant than it had been earlier. In the middle decades of the century there was a rise in its productivity as a result of technical progress, capital investment and improvements in quality. Commentators sometimes explained differences between England and continental Europe in terms of dear English labour. Agricultural tasks which on the Continent were performed by labour—the controlling of cattle and the carriage of crops—were in England imposed on fences in the first case and on horses in the second.[2] Contrasting the manufacture of guns in England and Belgium the chairman of the Birmingham Small Arms Company wrote in 1866 that the English had an advantage over the Belgians in that 'more extended use of machinery, the use of which in Liège is discouraged by the cheap rate at which hand labour can be maintained'.[3] 'The cheap labour at the command of our competitors' thought Brassey, 'seems to exercise the same enervating influence as the delights of Caphua on the soldiers of Hannibal'.[4]

All these were significant developments. But on the other hand though science became a more important source of technology in the later nineteenth century, both American and British technology remained predominantly pragmatic until

[1] The difficulties of obtaining labour for puddling were so great that something like the American labour situation was produced. 'It would be to the interest of iron manufacturers' said one of their number 'to adopt a machine (for puddling) even if the cost of it should be greater than that of hand-labour. It seemed, indeed, that unless mechanical puddling could be achieved, they would not be able to get the necessary puddling done at all' (*Journal of the Iron and Steel Institute*, 1871, II, p. 268).

[2] Nassau Senior, *Industrial Efficiency and Social Economy*, ed. S. L. Levy, I, p. 218.

[3] Timmins, *op. cit.* p. 396.

[4] Thomas Brassey, *Work and Wages* (1872), p. 142. Chapter v of this work, 'Dear Labour Stimulates Invention', contains several instances of its theme.

196   TECHNOLOGY IN THE NINETEENTH CENTURY

well into the twentieth century. Over most of industry there
was still a range of choice sensitive to relative factor-prices.

Moreover there were still important differences in labour
supplies between Britain and the U.K. It is easy to exaggerate
the change in conditions in Britain; between the boom of
1869–73 and the height of the 1914–18 war there was never a
general shortage of labour. The disappearance of the rural
surplus was to some extent misleading, for much of it had
merely been shifted as surplus labour to the towns, in response
perhaps to the building boom of the 1870's. 'Has there ever',
asked one observer in 1914 'in the big towns at least been a
time when employers could not get practically at a moment's
notice all the labourers they required?'[1]

More to the present point, the cost of labour continued to
be higher in the U.S.A. than in England. Though returns in
agriculture had ceased to act as a floor to American industrial
wages except in the far west, this function had been taken over
by those sectors of industry which had most successfully adopted
labour-saving equipment, and made technical progress. The
rise in productivity of American industrial labour (more rapid
than the English) reflected itself in the terms on which labour
was available to new industries and undertakings; it meant that
unless these could pass high labour-costs on to the consumer,
they had to adopt the techniques which would raise the productivity of their labour sufficiently to enable them to pay the
high American wages.[2]

There were moreover marked regional differences. The
extreme imperfections of the labour- and product-markets had
disappeared, but the labour-market was still probably less

---

[1] W. Beveridge, *Unemployment* (1930), p. 62.

[2] Brassey (*op. cit.* p. 136) estimated that wages were twice as high in America
as in England. B. Weber, 'The Rate of Economic Growth in the U.S.A. 1869–1939',
Oxford Economic Papers, v (June 1954). Rising productivity, without a commensurate
increase in money wages, lowered the cost of labour in the industry which enjoyed
the rising productivity. But it raised the cost of labour to industries where productivity had not been increased. The effect on a new industry can be seen in the
case of tin-plate. Attempts to establish this very labour-intensive industry in the
U.S.A. were not successful until the 1890's and then only under the protection
of the McKinley and Dingley tariffs and partly as a result of the previous emigration of skilled Welsh workers in the depressions of the preceding period. Once
the industry was established, the American makers sought to improve the efficiency
of the pack-mill equipment, their improvements later being adopted in South
Wales. W. E. Minchinton, *The British Tinplate Industry* (Oxford, 1957), p. 69.

perfect than the product-markets. Wages were higher in the mid-west than in the east and the labour-supply was less abundant,[1] so that it paid mid-western manufacturers as they expanded to import machines made with the cheaper labour of manufacturers further east. Some parts of the story we have told about America and England in the first half of the century can be retold for the mid-west and east of America in the second half, with the difference, of course, that there was no internal tariff.

For these reasons American manufacturers were still under a more compelling need than the English to raise the productivity of their labour. The principal method of doing this was to equip the labour with superior machines, and by the later decades of the century these were generally cheaper, in relation to simpler machines, in America than in Britain. In some types of machine, it is true, the Americans were markedly inferior to the English. At the end of the century the machinery for preparation, spinning and weaving of cotton cost about 50 or 60 per cent more than in Lancashire; and carding engines, cotton combers, drawing frames and other kinds of English textile machinery found a market in the United States despite a 45 per cent tariff.[2] Even in textile machinery, however, the disparity of costs between the two countries was smaller than it had been in the 1830's and '40's. And probably over the whole engineering field, machines in America were cheaper in relation to labour, and in some cases absolutely cheaper as well. This provided an additional reason for the American entrepreneur to replace labour by machines to a greater extent than did his English counterpart.

But the entrepreneur's choice of techniques was influenced by inherited attitudes as well as by contemporary labour conditions. The direction in which technical progress is made depends on the type of problem that inventors and manufacturers are most alive to, and the sort of ways of tackling it which are thought appropriate. Americans had acquired the habit of concentrating on those problems which lent themselves to a solution by the invention of labour-saving equipment, and on labour-saving (as opposed to other factor-saving) solutions to common problems. For this reason it is quite

[1] Report on Cost of Living, American Towns, Cmd. 5609, 1911.
[2] Young, *op. cit.* p. 8.

198   TECHNOLOGY IN THE NINTEEENTH CENTURY

possible that invention in the second half of the century was more responsive to a given degree of labour-scarcity than it had been in the first.

In England on the other hand both employers and workers were still conditioned by attitudes engendered by abundant labour, and reacted to problems in mechanisation in ways that cannot be fully explained by contemporary factor-proportions. The workers still feared the introduction of more mechanical methods as a threat to their jobs. Disputes no longer arose, as they had done earlier in the century, on whether machinery should be introduced, but centered on the conditions of its introduction.[1] In the 1840's and '50's workers in the engineering industry had opposed the introduction of planers and lathes; in the 1890's they attempted to impose conditions on the use of the capstan, turret lathe, miller and borer which rendered the profitability of their introduction uncertain.[2] When employers in the 1890's extended the use of machines in the manufacture of boots and shoes, the workers attempted to maintain the cost of production by machines on a par with the cost of hand methods.[3] Thus the attitudes of labour still imposed a restriction on the choice of technique in England which was not present to the same extent in the U.S.A.

But for his part the English employer too had traits acquired from long experience of cheap labour. As a spokesman of the English boot and shoe manufacturers said in 1901: 'For years labour (in England) has been so cheap and has been content to work under such conditions as to render it a matter of small importance as to the mechanical assistance with which it should be furnished. ... Men have been cheaper than machines. Today ... men are getting dear and machines are getting cheap. The whip of dear labour was applied to the backs of American manufacturers years ago'.[4] Because English employers had been so long accustomed to cheap labour their inclination was apt to be to get more work at the same money wage. 'Nothing is more frequent', wrote one group of American observers of British industry, 'than the remark that the

---

[1] Webb, *op. cit.* p. 295.

[2] James B. Jeffreys, *The Story of the Engineers, 1800–1945* (1946), pp. 35–42, 142.

[3] A. Fox, *A History of the National Union of Boot and Shoe Operatives, 1874–1957* (Oxford, 1958), pp. 206—7.

[4] John Day, *Shoe and Leather Record*, 27 March, 1891, quoted in Fox, *op. cit.* p. 206.

working-man does not need more than so many shillings a week. . . . This view among employers has prevailed for so long and is so nearly universal that their every effort is to obtain more work for a traditional wage rather than to decrease the cost of production by means which will justify a higher wage. . . . Working-men have come to accept the view widely too and it is the acceptance of this theory of status which is at the bottom of the deadlock in British industry'.[1]

Even when labour-saving devices were introduced, many English employers were so habituated to the idea of low money wages that they were not prepared to concede to their labour the higher money earnings which the new devices warranted and which would have reconciled labour to their introduction. When steam was introduced into the Coventry ribbon trade in the 1850's, and machinery into the making of boots and shoes in the 1890's, the difficulties which arose were partly due to the unwillingness of employers to 'view with equanimity the prospect of paying their workmen any larger amount per week than that to which they are accustomed'.[2] American manufacturers by contrast, compelled from the start by dearness of labour to mechanise, were less concerned with money- than with efficiency-wages.

It was not only the attitudes of workers and employers which were influenced by abundant labour. In the 1850's a leading English engineer commended the use of reaping machines in England *not* because they saved labour, but because they enabled the farmer to secure his crops in the worst of seasons. 'In a variable climate . . . where a whole harvest may be lost or seriously damaged unless rapidly cut . . . the machine reaper becomes invaluable'.[3] Herman Merivale, a leading English economist wrote in a memorandum for the Commission on Trade Unions that 'properly considered, piece work is strictly analogous to machinery. It is a mode of obtaining the execution of more work, or better work, at less cost to employers than by the ordinary method of daily wages'.[4] Whatever the formal correctness of this observation an American would have been quicker to see the difference between making the labourer work harder and giving him better tools.

[1] Quoted by Saul, *op. cit.* p. 27.
[2] Webb, *op. cit.* p. 400.
[3] W. Fairbairn, *Useful Information for Engineers*, Third series (1886), p. 202.
[4] P.P. 1868–9, xxxi, p. 357.

14

200   TECHNOLOGY IN THE NINETEENTH CENTURY

How far the choice of techniques was the product of contemporary cost-conditions and how far of inherited attitudes
moulded by the cost-conditions of the past it is impossible to
say, but both influences were certainly at work in the English
coal and steel industries and in some measure explain the
technical differences between the English and American industries. In the coal industry in 1913 more than 40 per cent
of the American coal output was mechanically cut, as against
only 8½ per cent of the British. The reasons for this disparity
were partly geological: conditions in British mines were less
favourable to mechanisation. Something, moreover, was due
to deficiencies in the British electricity industry and something,
no doubt, to entrepreneurial deficiencies. But a major obstacle
was certainly that the profitability of the improvements which
were available after 1880—the coal-cutter and the conveyer—
was very sensitive to the cost of labour, and that in England
the saving of labour did not appear to warrant the costs of the
machines. 'Generally speaking', said the official spokesmen of
the mine-owners before the Samuel Commission in 1925, 'the
saving in labour charges at the face is absorbed by the capital
charges on, and the running costs of, the machine. . . .' Whether
this view was correct it is quite impossible to say. But what is
clear is that sufficient labour was available on terms which
deprived mine-owners of the need to put the matter to the
test. Between 1883 and 1913 there was a very large increase
in the labour-force in the industry, accompanied it is true by a
rise in wage rates, but by a rise which was easily passed on to
consumers; indeed, as Mr A. J. Taylor says, 'it was advancing
coal prices which carried mining wages upwards rather than
vice-versa'. 'There seems . . . to have been no lack of recruits
coming forward [from the land and from the large national
pool of unskilled workers] at wage rates corresponding to
prices which the consumer was already offering for coal'. Even
at the height of the boom the coal industry was not 'handicapped by a shortage of labour at wage rates which it was both
able and, in the last resort, prepared to pay'.[1] Moreover,
because the supply of labour was abundant in the long run,
the workers did not feel sufficiently secure of their prospects
to co-operate during the booms, when demand for labour was

[1] A. J. Taylor, 'Labour Productivity and Technological Innovation in the
British Coal Industry, 1850–1914', *Econ. Hist. Rev.*, vol. xiv, No. 2 (August 1961).

strongest and therefore the incentive to the mine-owner to mechanise was greatest; and since mechanisation in this industry, more than in most, involved considerable reorganisation of working schedules, it could not easily be carried out in face of worker's opposition.

In the steel industry, the improvements in American technique were, initially at least, primarily labour-saving. When the Bessemer plant, a British development, was introduced into America, American improvements took the form we have noticed earlier, that is labour-saving equipment and measures designed to speed up the work and increase output per unit of capital. Cheap labour cannot be the main reason why British makers failed to make and were slow to adopt the improvements made in America. For Germany and Belgium, where labour-costs were lower, adopted labour-saving devices more widely in the 1890's than did Britain.[1] But it must have reduced the effort which British steel-makers devoted to the matter. And the attitudes of workers, which were in part a product of the fear of unemployment, were also unfavourable to mechanisation.[2]

Moreover the fact that manufacture with interchangeable parts was a practice of long standing in America gave her an advantage in the production, not only of machines, but of complicated mechanisms of most kinds. As a result of long preoccupation with labour-saving methods Americans had developed types of engineering skill which were a prerequisite for the development of new methods wherever they arose and whatever factor they saved. At the end of the century, mechanical engineering was often still sufficient by itself to develop a new idea, and even where it was not sufficient it was still generally essential. Many of the ideas came from abroad. 'Until well into the twentieth century' it has been said, 'Americans have been content to let most of the basic discoveries in science and technology originate in Europe, while they themselves have followed a policy of adapt, improve and

[1] D. L. Burn, *op. cit.* pp. 47, 172ff, 184.

[2] The American Journal *Iron Age* in 1874 put forward the case that British ironmasters had enjoyed pauper labour and had for that reason not found it economically desirable to afford 'encouragement to inventive talent to devise labour-saving machinery'. (Quoted, in order to deny it, by Lothian Bell, 'Notes of a Visit to Coal and Iron Mines and Iron Works in the United States', *Journal of the Iron and Steel Institute*, 1875, p. 139.)

apply'.[1] This was particularly the case with inventions which resulted from the application of advanced scientific principles. The central idea behind an invention of this kind was easily borrowed, and where its further development into a practical commercial proposition depended upon mechanical ingenuity, it might be developed more successfully in the U.S.A. than elsewhere. In electricity, for example, the early dynamo improvements which preceded the efforts of Edison and Bush were the work of Gramme, a Frenchman, and Von Hefner Alteneck, a German. In electric traction the important initial steps were taken by Julien, a Belgian. Garz and Company of Budapest were the first firm to perfect the transformer, and it was from them that Westinghouse got his ideas. Many American inventors in this field were Europeans born and trained. E. Weston, an important figure in early electric lighting and C. P. Steinmetz, one of the best electrical engineers at the end of the nineteenth century, went to the U.S.A. in their twenties. But, though the big inventions originated mainly in Europe, their technological development was carried furthest in the States.

The internal combustion engine was another borrowed idea which was most successfully developed by America. There is no mystery about the rapid growth of this industry in a country of great distances and high incomes. More illuminating for the present purpose are the difficulties of the early development of the industry in England, for they show how ill-adapted were the craft traditions of English engineering to the mass production of motors-cars. The first petrol-driven car was produced by Daimler in 1887, but it was not until 1896 that motorcars were assembled in Britain, and not until 1903 that they were completely built here. The necessary mechanical knowledge was widely spread in the English general engineering industry and this was the obvious source of enterprise, but general engineering firms were slow to enter the field. Possibly the domestic boom at the end of the 1890's so fully occupied the industry that there was little incentive to branch out into anything else; several engineering firms, it is true, did go into electricity in these years, but they did it rather as a side show and got out again when prospects clouded. But in the 1880's there must have been plenty of slack in the industry, and the

---

[1] J. B. Rae, 'The "Know-How" Tradition: Technology in American History', *Technology and Culture*, vol. I, No. 2 (1960), p. 141.

failure to exploit the possibilities of the internal combustion engine at this stage perhaps reflects a lack of initiative. Furthermore British engineering firms did not turn to making motorcar parts as readily as American machine shops: the earliest English pioneers in the motor-car industry were handicapped by the need to make a high proportion of their own parts. In 1899 when F. W. Lanchester started to manufacture cars 'no ancillary trades had then developed and we had to do everything ourselves, chassis, magnets, wheels, bodywork, everything except the tyres'. Lanchester's experience is illuminating because he decided to manufacture the components of his car on a system of interchangeable parts. His insight into what was needed had a touch of genius, but his idea was not practicable in British circumstances. He had, for example, to produce his own range of standard threads, and the individualistic craftsmen upon whom he had to draw were reluctant to work to standard instructions. 'In those days' he wrote later, 'when a body-builder was asked to work to drawings, gauges or templates, he gave a sullen look such as one might expect from a Royal Academician if asked to colour an engineering drawing'.[1] The attempt by an individual to create independently a system of interchangeable parts proved, in the short run at least, intolerably expensive. The limitations of English methods showed themselves again later when William Morris decided to buy his main components from the specialist makers instead of making them himself. The specialists proved unable to take orders as large as he wished to place, and 'could not, or would not, at this time (1913) meet him by expanding'.[2] Morris therefore turned to America for components.

Thus the technology and attitudes shaped by the experience of dear labour in the past, as well as dear labour at the time, account for some of the difference in technical progress in Britain and America in the later nineteenth century. But after 1870 there was another influence—the amount of new capacity created. In this period the absolute volume of new investment was greater in America than in England for reasons

[1] P. W. Kingsford, *F. W. Lanchester* (1960), pp. 40, 47–8.
[2] Andrews and Brunner, *op. cit.* pp. 59–60, 71. For the American experience see J. B. Rae, *American Automobile Manufacturers: the First Forty Years* (New York, 1959).

204   TECHNOLOGY IN THE NINETEENTH CENTURY

which, initially at any rate, had little if anything to do with the relative efficiency of the industries of the two countries; because more capacity was created, the Americans had more opportunity to incorporate new technical knowledge, to acquire know-how and so to make further advances.

To clarify the argument it is necessary at this point to consider the long-term changes in the market for Britain's industrial products. Britain was the first country to industrialise and for a surprisingly long time she remained, in absolute volume of production, the leading industrial country. Even as late as 1870 the United Kingdom still had 31.8 per cent of the world's manufacturing capacity, compared with 23.3 per cent for the U.S.A. and 13.2 per cent for Germany.[1]

That Britain's lead was sustained for so long a period was partly due to institutional features in other countries which impeded their attempts to take over the British technology. But, quite apart from this, England's early start gave her certain continuing advantages. Because the British made the first important improvements in cotton textiles, in the primary iron industry and in steam, they were in a favourable position to make the subsequent improvements. In particular, they were able to build their railway system before other countries: demand conditions were more favourable—railway building in England merely involved joining up existing centres of population and industry, not building ahead of demand as in continental Europe and the U.S.A.; and capital for railway building was more plentiful. Britain was therefore the first to enjoy the great external economies of a railway system; she was also in a favourable position to supply other countries with their railway equipment when they started to build.

In an earlier chapter we considered the possibility that the demand for manufactures between 1815 and the 1840's did not expand so rapidly, in relation to total factor-supplies, in Britain as in America. But there is no doubt that the expansion of the market was sufficient to warrant very large absolute increases in English industrial capacity. Quite apart from any increase in the efficiency of any sector, a considerable increase in income was achieved simply by shifts from less productive to more productive sectors. Even an industry without technical progress could therefore expect an increase in demand for

[1] *Industrialisation and Foreign Trade* (League of Nations, 1945), p. 13.

its products. Over and above any increase in total income, there was an increase in the demand for the products of factory industry at the expense of English domestic industry. But English factory industry also expanded at the expense of the domestic systems of other countries, that is foreign demand for English goods increased even in the absence of an increase in foreign incomes.

By the 1840's it was becoming increasingly difficult to expand exports further by these means; the net barter terms of the trade were turning against the United Kingdom. Hence the demand for free trade as a measure to increase the income of the foreign customers of England. But at the end of the 1840's—just when the possibilities of expanding exports at the expense of continental domestic industry were dwindling—a major boom started in several parts of the world associated with the gold discoveries, wars, and above all, railway building. This meant a very rapid increase of incomes in the countries to which Britain exported and, since Britain had very marked advantages as a producer of the consumer and capital goods they required, there was a spectacular expansion of British exports right down to the early '70's. The 1850's and '60's were a period in which incomes abroad were increasing much more rapidly than in the first half of the century, and when the marginal propensity of foreign countries to import from Britain was still very high; indeed, in the case of countries with heavy programmes of railway building, it may have been rising. The fears about British exports which had begun to be entertained in the '40's disappeared, and did not revive again until the later 1870's and '80's.

Thus for the first six or seven decades of the nineteenth century market prospects in England were favourable to the creation of new capacity; there were vigorous sources of demand for U.K. goods. This increased demand was not, of course, independent of the technical efficiency of English industry, but given the initial English superiority it proceeded even in the absence of technical progress, and it warranted an increase in capacity which gave English manufacturers excellent opportunities of adopting new methods and gaining experience.

After the 1870's the market prospects for British goods were less favourable to the creation of new capacity. In the first place, once England had become an industrial state, the possibilities of an increase in income from intersectoral shifts within the English economy were much more limited. In the second place, so far as foreign markets were concerned, though the increase in their real income was considerable, particularly in the U.S.A. and Germany, there was a decline in their marginal propensity to import from the U.K. The propensity would in any case have declined as these countries developed their own manufacturing industry, but the speed of the decline was accelerated by the tariffs which these countries imposed, and also by the fortuitous incidence of technical discovery in the key industry of the period—steel.

It is true that in certain regions of recent settlement the marginal propensity to import British goods remained very high. In some of these areas market goodwill probably retained for British goods a stronger position than was warranted by the price of British manufactures compared with those of other industrial exporters, for example in Australasia, S. America and India. But the rate of increase in income in the primary producing regions between the 1870's and the '90's was probably less than it had been in the '50's and '60's and certainly less rapid than it was in those economies which were industrialising.[1] Moreover, in S. America the preference for British goods was weaker than in most other primary-producing regions; in the 1880's when both Australia and the Argentine had development booms, the latter drew a smaller proportion of her additional imports from Britain. The Canadian preference for British goods was also weaker, and during the boom in the first decade of the twentieth century, a large part of her increased imports came from the U.S.A. These development booms in the Argentine and in Canada redounded to the advantage of British exports less directly than the early development booms in primary-producing regions. Though, directly and indirectly, they increased the demand for British exports, a significant part of the income which they created was probably employed (particularly by Americans) in repaying former borrowings from Britain, and from the point of view of British exports was dissipated. In the closing decades of the century, therefore, English industry as a whole was less assured of an increase in demand which would warrant the creation of a large amount of new capacity.

[1] A. J. Brown, *Industrialisation and Trade* (1943), pp. 60-61.

In Germany and the U.S.A. market prospects were much more favourable in the later decades of the nineteenth century than they were in England. In both there were large reserves of unexploited natural resources which had been developed rapidly as soon as the areas were supplied with railways. In Germany, too, simply because her industrialisation was late, the possibilities of increasing income by intersectoral shifts were still considerable. And the tariffs, which curtailed British exports of certain goods, concentrated the increase in domestic demand in Germany and America on local production. The fact that their total capacity was growing more rapidly meant that these countries had more opportunity of trying out new ideas, at a time when there were many to be tried out.

The argument applies most clearly to iron and steel where an inevitable long-term decline in foreign demand for British bulk products was greatly accelerated by technical and geographical discoveries and by foreign tariffs. The Gilchrist–Thomas process sharply altered the comparative advantages against Britain as a manufacturer of steel. It was more suited to German than to British ores because Britain's phosphoric ores (especially those of Cleveland) proved not to have *enough* phosphorous. Even if British ores had been just as suitable, the Gilchrist–Thomas process would still have produced a shift in comparative advantage; Britain's advantages for the production of acid steel had been very great, since it could import non-phosphoric ores so much more easily than Germany. Up to the Thomas–Gilchrist discovery Britain could produce acid steel and Germany could not; after the discovery Britain was, at best, no worse off as a steel producer and Germany was a great deal better off. The discovery of the Mesabi ores in the U.S.A. had a comparable effect; however enterprising English steel masters had been, there was bound to be a decline in the American demand for English iron and steel products.

This decline was very greatly accelerated by the imposition of tariffs in the 1870's and '80's. No doubt England's exports of the bulk iron and steel products would, in any case, have sooner or later declined, simply because the market for rails was declining, and other countries were becoming more efficient rail producers. The point about the tariffs was that they greatly accelerated the process. The British iron and steel industry had been heavily dependent upon exports—in the

208   TECHNOLOGY IN THE NINETEENTH CENTURY

boom of the early '70's about half the British production of pig-iron was exported, either as pig-iron or as semi-manufactures—and particularly on exports to the U.S.A. and to Europe. The tariffs reduced two large markets for crude iron and steel products (especially rails). They also accentuated the cyclical fluctuations in the British industry. When, despite this tariff, the U.S.A. had to import steel rails—as in the boom of the early 1880's—the American industry made very high profits. Once the U.S. market fell off for cyclical reasons, British steel was virtually excluded from the American market. Conversely, the tariffs ensured that the expansion of American and German demand mainly benefited their own industries, and that they also enjoyed a steadier market than the British.

The net effect of these changes was to make new investment in iron and steel less profitable in Britain than in Germany and America during a period when many new technical methods were available to be incorporated. The effect is most clearly seen in the case of pig-iron production where the capacity in existence in Britain at the end of the 1870's was almost large enough to produce the output which was called for over the next twenty years; the output of 1882–3 was not surpassed until 1895. The British iron industry therefore had few opportunities of introducing new methods and the steel industry had a technologically backward base. Furthermore many of the improvements in steel were associated with improvements to the blast furnace, siting it in relation to the converters, making use of waste gases; and the fact that market prospects warranted the building of few new blast furnaces curbed the adoption of new methods in steel, at least in the Bessemer section which concentrated on rails. In the U.S.A. and Germany market prospects warranted a high rate of investment which facilitated the invention and adoption of new techniques. 'The up-to-date character of many American (steel) works is as much an effect as a cause of the expansion of the industry in America'.[1]

Market prospects are a less plausible explanation of the

---

[1] S. J. Chapman, *Foreign Competition, op. cit.* p. 92. There was undoubtedly some investment in the English industry, which in retrospect, can be seen to have been ill-advised: the heavy investment in malleable iron, in the boom of the early 1870's which made it more difficult later for steel to make headway; the over-concentration on railways, especially in the Bessemer section. But these mistakes were not the result of apathy or lack of technical skills. I am indebted for ideas on this industry to discussion with Mr J. F. Wright.

British lag in the new industries. But in the most important of these industries—electricity—differences in demand do seem to explain a good deal of the difference between the British and American experience.

In the first place, at the time when lighting by electricity first became a practicable proposition, there were more people in the U.S.A. than in Britain who were installing lighting for the first time, and whose choice between gas and electricity was therefore based upon a comparison of the total costs of the two methods. This was partly because, on the eve of the introduction of electric lighting, England was better lit than America; the English gas industry was much more efficient than its American counterpart and, before the coming of electricity, had tapped a larger part of the existing market for light. Furthermore, the demand for lighting was principally an urban demand, and the urban population of America in the later decades of the nineteenth century was growing more rapidly than that of Britain. For these reasons the total demand for lighting grew more rapidly in the U.S.A. than in Britain.

In the second place, in competing for the market in lighting, electricity was in a stronger position *vis-à-vis* gas in America than in Britain, because of the high price of American gas in relation to electricity, due principally to the high cost of American coal, the greater degree of monopoly in the American than in the English gas industry and the technological backwardness of the American industry. Nor was electricity the only case in which a new product and process had to make headway in England against competition from close substitutes produced by older industries or processes.[1]

There is another circumstance, more directly related to Britain's early start, which made it difficult for British manufacturers to incorporate new techniques. Much of the industrial capacity of England in, say, the early 1870's, had been built up gradually and there was therefore no particular reason why it should be well adapted for the absorption of new techniques. Many improvements available in steel in the 1880's and '90's depended on the concentration on a single site and in the same ownership of coking ovens, blast furnaces and rolling mills; but much of the English industry had been

[1] I am greatly indebted for enlightenment about electricity to Mr Ian Byatt who is writing a history of the industry before 1914.

210 TECHNOLOGY IN THE NINETEENTH CENTURY

created before the need for such concentration was evident. Similarly the introduction of the automatic loom in the cotton-textile industry involved considerable changes in the structure of the industry. The point has been well put by Mr Marvin Frankel. 'Real capital, especially in the later stages of industrialisation, may be made up of a number of components such that they cannot be replaced separately, but only on an all or nothing basis'.[1]

It is probable also that in certain industries the nature of the market for English manufactures—as distinct from its rate of growth—was unfavourable to the introduction of new techniques, since the purchasers of English goods demanded less homogeneous and standardised products than did American customers. The orders for English rails, for example, were mostly small and they involved many different sizes. This meant that, in some cases, the individual concern's output of a particular line of product fell below the minimum necessary for the economic installation of the latest techniques. Thus the fact that the English steel manufacturer needed a larger stock of rolls and had to make frequent changes was held to preclude the adoption of such innovation as three-high mills.[2] Moreover, in the iron and steel industry, because demand was unhomogeneous, each concern tended to have its separate goodwill market, and this made it easier for high-cost producers to resist elimination. We have already considered some of the effects of imperfection in the product market in the case of the U.S.A. in the early nineteenth century. But the effects are very greatly influenced by the rate of growth of the total market. Because of the slow growth of English industrial capacity in the last three decades of the nineteenth century, the adoption of new techniques was much more dependent than in America on re-equipment by existing firms and the expansion of the more—at the expense of the less—efficient, and it was precisely this process which was impeded by market imperfections.

The unhomogeneity of demand for British goods, though mainly due to the geographical diversity of our markets, was

[1] M. Frankel, 'Obsolescence and Technological Change in a Maturing Economy', *American Economic Review*, June 1955, XLV, pp. 296–319, together with the *Comment* by D. F. Gordon, and Frankel's reply in *Am. Ec. Rev.* September 1956, XLVI, pp. 646—56.
[2] D. L. Burn, *op. cit.* p. 192.

also related to the rate of growth of demand. It was pointed out in the discussion of American development, that new demand is more readily standardised than demand diverted from other suppliers or products. In England a substantial part of demand was of the second type.[1] Thus, in the first half of the century, factory production of cotton textiles increased partly by invading markets already served by industry organised on a putting-out system, that is by serving customers whose tastes were already formed. In the second half of the century, a good deal of the steel output went to replace malleable iron, so that many of the imperfections in the market for iron products were perpetuated in the market for steel products. But there is the further point that it was easier for manufacturers (or merchants) to impose uniform standards on customers in a sellers' market, when demand was increasing rapidly in relation to capacity. In the English cotton-textile industry, capacity usually responded very promptly to demand, since the units of operation and ownership were small and entry into the industry was relatively easy. The customers of a Massachusetts cotton-textile industry in the early nineteenth century had sometimes to take what they could get; the English industry almost always faced a buyers' market, and manufacturers and merchants were more often anxious to attract demand by meeting consumers' tastes than they were able to impose standard types of product upon the market. This was particularly the case in the last quarter of the century when the output of the industry grew more slowly than it had done previously. Similarly if, in the later nineteenth century, there had been a very rapidly growing new demand for English steel products, English producers would have more easily been able to standardise their products, and by producing standard products at lower prices they might have been able to condition the old demand.

---

[1] This situation, of course, occurred in all European countries with a tradition of mechanical crafts. Emil Rathenau, in an autobiographical sketch on his visit to the Philadelphia Exhibition of 1876, commented on the lack of standardisation of German machines compared with the American, and ascribed it to the character of demand in Germany. The German purchaser of machines was usually better informed than the seller about his precise requirements, and he made his order dependent on the carrying-out of his demands. He sought, by paying extra, to obtain machines specially adapted to his circumstances and this necessitated very careful construction of individual machines. It would be better, Rathenau thought, to come to an agreement about a standard type of machine. A. Riedler, *Emil Rathenau* (Berlin, 1916), pp. 28–9.

212   TECHNOLOGY IN THE NINETEENTH CENTURY

Some of the reasons we have given for England's smaller increments of new investment in the later nineteenth century, compared with America's, arise from England's early and long-sustained start. It is not argued that England was on balance a loser from her early start. Because of this start England's income in the 1870's was higher than it would otherwise have been (and higher than that of other countries except the U.S.A.) and her savings were much larger. Because she had already a large industrial plant she was able to use her savings to build more and better houses and to provide the regions of overseas settlement with their complement of public utilities. But because she already had a large industrial plant which in many branches was adequate to the demands made upon it in the '80's and '90's, the incentive to install new capacity and the opportunity of trying out new methods were circumscribed. And in explaining the different rates of technical progress this fact is of crucial importance.

The same circumstances may also account in large part for the quality of British entrepreneurial performance in the same period. The entrepreneurial deficiencies to which the performance of the British economy is attributed can plausibly be explained as a consequence of that performance. The slow rate of expansion of British industry affected the performance of business men. Great generals are not made in time of peace; great entrepreneurs are not made in non-expanding industries. Because the market was growing slowly, the risks of adventure were much greater than in Germany and America, as may clearly be seen from the fate of those who showed enterprise in the electrical industry in the early '80's, and came croppers as a result.

But the slow expansion must also have affected the recruitment of business men. An Englishman's choice of career was, it is true, very much influenced by tradition, convention and inertia, and no doubt in England these tended to channel talent away from business towards the professions. But it was also responsive to changes in reward,[1] and after the 1870's several purely economic circumstances combined to divert men of ability away from business. The high profits of the 1850's and

---

[1] That the supply of recruits to professions and trades as a whole was responsive to changes in reward was assumed by the opponents of differentiation in the income tax. F. Shehab, *Progressive Taxation* (Oxford, 1954), pp. 95–6.

'60's had attracted an unduly large number of entrants into business so that even had the rate of profit been sustained in the following decades, the rewards of individuals would have fallen. But, over and above this there was a fall in profits, a decline in the ability of firms to offer attractive salaries; in periods of falling prices business was at a disadvantage *vis-à-vis* the professions in competing for talent. The overflooding of an occupation which in any case was becoming less popular meant that business was very much less attractive for men who were making their choice of profession from the 1870's on. Where there was lack of growth there were few new firms, the average age of men at the top of existing firms was high and nepotism was most likely to occur.

The more able men there are in an industry the more chance the industry will throw up an entrepreneur of genius. A country where several industries throw up a genius, gives the impression of being endowed by nature or by its social order with an exceptionally large amount of entrepreneurial talent. And this was the impression which the U.S.A. gave. But the abundance of entrepreneurial talent in the U.S.A. was the consequence rather than the cause of a high rate of growth; and it was the slow expansion of English industry which accounted for the performance of English entrepreneurs in the later nineteenth century not vice versa. Where market conditions were favourable to the expansion of capacity British business men were just as venturesome and dynamic as the American. Charles Parsons in marine engineering, Alfred Jones, the master-spirit of Elder Dempster, who acquired control of the West African carrying trade and brought the banana to the British breakfast table, William Lever, who exploited the mass market in soap, Harmsworth, who exploited the coincidence of literacy and technical changes in printing: these men are the equal in enterprise and achievement of any American entrepreneurs. They were all operating in fields where circumstances quite independent of their own initiative were favourable to expansion. In the provision of merchant shipping and financial services there was considerable entrepreneurial achievement, to judge from the expansion of the U.K.'s income from invisible exports. But perhaps the best instance of the relation of investment to entrepreneurial ability comes from the steel industry. For while the Bessemer section was backward, the open-hearth

214   TECHNOLOGY IN THE NINETEENTH CENTURY

section, which was expanding because it serviced the ship-building industry, was technologically vigorous.[1]

There were, of course, differences in entrepreneurial ability and performance which cannot be explained in these terms. At the start of the electrical industry the leading names were American and continental European. There was no one in England to equal Brush and Edison. This was an entrepreneurial and not primarily a technical deficiency; it was not so much that the Americans were better engineers as that they had greater insight into the nature of the market for electric light, and employed their technical skill in perfecting a system which met the requirements of the market. It is possible also that a difference in pure entrepreneurial ability is reflected in the comparative history of the motor-car in the two countries. In the cotton-textile industry, as an English expert observed in 1902, 'when every allowance has been made for the differences in their situations the conclusion is hard to resist that the average English manufacturer is more cautious—more timid if you will and more liable to reject a good thing because it happens to be new and hitherto untried, than the average American manufacturer'.[2] The slow adoption of the automatic loom in England cannot be explained entirely by factor-proportions, for it was made and worked, not only in America, but in Germany, Austria, France and Belgium.

But was the difference of entrepreneurial ability all that great? In electricity, the men who developed the industry in England, Swan, Crompton and Siemens, were all men of considerable ability and very little behind the Americans technically. The difference in the development of the internal combustion engine was greater: there was more experiment in America than in Britain. But it may be doubted whether this kind of disparity in 'pure entrepreneurial ability' mattered a great deal in the later nineteenth and early twentieth centuries. Where there were no other impediments, it did not prevent the rapid adoption of methods pioneered elsewhere. The absence of the higher forms of inventive and entrepreneurial ability represented by Brush and Edison in the electrical industry was not a major handicap to the development of the

[1] W. A. Sinclair, 'The Growth of the British Steel Industry in the Late Nineteenth Century', *Scottish Journal of Political Economy*, VI, No. 1 (February 1959).

[2] Young, *op. cit.* p. 137, XV.

British industry, since the Brush and Edison systems were very rapidly imported. Where advanced technology of foreign origin was not incorporated, the explanation is probably more often the limitations of economic circumstances rather than the inertness of British entrepreneurs.

If, as we have argued, technical progress in England was retarded by the slow growth of demand for British exports in the last three decades of the century which afforded relatively few opportunities for the growth of new capacity, why, it may be asked, did the boom in exports after 1900 not stimulate technical development? In certain industries the answer is probably that the British lag was, by then, too substantial to be made up easily, because of the lack of the know-how which would have been accumulated by keeping more continuously in touch with new methods. Partly also the explanation may be that the increase in export demand was principally for those goods where the possibilities of technical progress were slightest. It was in the new industries that the possibilities were greatest. Their methods were more elaborate than those of the older industries, and the potentialities of these methods had been less fully exploited. They were the industries with the best long-term demand prospects, and the least stereotyped labour-force.

We shall now attempt to sum up the influences on the technological history of the U.S.A. and Britain in the later nineteenth century, and particularly those most directly responsible for the contrasts between them.

There was no significant difference in the stock of fundamental ideas available to technologists. In this period, Britain and the U.S.A., along with Germany and France and some of the smaller European countries, shared a common stock of such ideas in the sense that there were many people in each country who were intellectual masters of the notions underlying the new developments in technology. From this point of view, these countries form a common group clearly distinguished from most of the rest of the world.

There was certainly some difference in the stimulus to derive new processes from the common stock of fundamental ideas. The rapid growth of the American economy provided incentives to search for new methods in all directions and dear American labour an incentive to search especially for labour-saving

15

216   TECHNOLOGY IN THE NINETEENTH CENTURY

improvements. Possibly too American entrepreneurs were more responsive to a given stimulus for non-economic reasons, for example because society at large attached greater prestige to technological achievement. It may be, that is, that where the Americans drew more readily upon the common stock of ideas it was because they were more anxious than the British to adopt new methods. But much more important than differences in the desire to adopt new methods were differences in the ability to do so, and the essence of the argument of this chapter has been that it was easier to adopt new methods in America than in England.

There is not much force in the argument that the English entrepreneur in this period was hampered by the absence of the scientific skills required by the new technological developments. He was no worse off (indeed he may have been better off) than his American counterpart, and even in comparison with the Germans his disadvantages on this score are commonly exaggerated. It is often said that a shortage of chemists—the result of deficiencies in the English educational system—was responsible for the failure of the English dye-stuffs industry, after a promising early start, to make progress in the 1880's and 90's. No doubt there is something in this. But even in this case, a major part of the explanation is that the English industry failed to attract or retain the available scientific ability, and lacked the desire to train its own scientists, because its prospects deteriorated for reasons independent of the supply of scientific skills. The English patent law did not compel a patentee to work his patent, and this enabled the Germans to deny to English manufacturers the use of the most important German inventions in this field. The English, being thus restricted to a narrow range of dyes, were more vulnerable to change and less likely to make new discoveries than their German counterparts; and under a free-trade regime, once German manufacturers had established even a slight margin of superiority, there was no reason why English customers should not buy their dyes from Germany.[1] Thus a lead once lost was extremely difficult to recover. In other industries I do not believe that the ability of the English entrepreneur to innovate, in comparison with that of his rivals,

[1] L. F. Haber, *The Chemical Industry during the Nineteenth Century* (Oxford, 1958), pp. 198–204.

was seriously limited by the terms on which he could obtain the appropriate scientific and technical expertise.

Where there were serious limitations on innovation they arose principally from the market facing the English entrepreneur. There is first of all the question of the size of the market. It has often been argued that the extent of the American domestic market, unimpeded by tariff barriers, made methods profitable in the U.S.A. which would not have been profitable elsewhere: the greater the total volume of production in a country, the greater the specialisation of products and the greater the inducement to mechanise their production.[1] But while it may be true that the larger economy can more easily avail itself of the advantages to be derived from specialisation and mass production, there is no reason to believe that the differences between Britain and the U.S.A. at the end of the nineteenth century were significant from this point of view. The important difference was not in the size of the market but in its rate of growth.

For reasons we have already explored, American industrial capacity grew more rapidly than the English, and thus American industrialists had more opportunities of trying out new methods. And this consideration does not apply only to America. All the countries who followed the English into industrialisation in the later nineteenth century grew more rapidly than the English because there was a large back-log of technology for them to absorb and a great volume of resources to be shifted into modern industry from agriculture and domestic industry. In the case of some of the late industrialisers, for example Japan, most of their effort was absorbed in copying existing technology; and where technical and scientific skills were very scarce it was probably more economic to devote them to imitation and adaptation rather than to technical innovation. But the rapid growth of capacity among the late-comers, even where it was principally imitative, afforded opportunities for testing new methods; and in the U.S.A. and Germany there were sufficient supplies of technical skill to allow them to make indigenous improvement *pari-passu* with the absorption of existing techniques.

This was the first serious limitation on the comparative

---

[1] A. Young 'Increasing Returns and Economic Progress', *Economic Journal*, XXXVIII (1928), 540.

218   TECHNOLOGY IN THE NINETEENTH CENTURY

ability of British entrepreneurs: the slower rate of growth of the economy. The slower rate of growth was the more important because the structure of industry imposed more severe restraints on the choice of techniques in Britain than in the U.S.A. British industry was longer established and the entrepreneur more limited by history and by the need to shape his investments 'to fit the inherited structure of complementary assets'.[1] Difficulties arose on this score even when a particular improvement was within the power of the individual entrepreneur to adopt. For example, the size and layout of an old textile mill imposed restrictions on the choice of techniques which were not present in one newly built in knowledge of the most recent techniques. But many improvements were profitable for the individual concern only if complementary changes were made in other concerns; for example, an increase in the size of ships might be worth undertaking only if docks were enlarged. This type of change was particularly difficult to effect in later nineteenth-century Britain because of the complex division of labour between processes and industries which had developed during the long period of British industrial supremacy. Division of labour, it has often been observed, promotes mechanisation because the more specialised, and hence simpler, processes which result lend themselves more easily to the use of machinery than a group of complicated, because undifferentiated, processes. But there is another side to the coin. The fact that division of labour had been carried so far in English industry, and that the structure of inherited assets was so complicated, reduced the number of improvements which were within the ability of a single concern to introduce.

There are other reasons why such complementary improvements were easier to bring about in the U.S.A. For one thing American industries were under a common pressure to standardise their production and shared traditions of standardisation. Then again the strength of the merger movement in America was favourable to adoption of improvements which cut across firms. Mergers and amalgamations are ways in which an entrepreneur can assure that such improvements are made; and, because the merger movement in the later nineteenth century was weaker in Britain than in America, the opportunities for securing

---

[1] G. B. Richardson, *Information and Investment* (Oxford, 1960), p. 114.

complementary improvements were more limited. For this weakness of the merger movement there are, of course, many reasons; but one was certainly that mergers were more difficult to arrange in long-established industries and between firms with a complicated and deeply-entrenched specialisation of market and product.

Besides such economic reasons for differences in technical progress, there were no doubt social and psychological reasons. A society in which existing habits and institutions were widely accepted and freedom slowly broadened down from precedent to precedent found it easier to maintain political and social stability; but it was also likely to grow more slowly than a society where individuals were bent on rising in the world and were ready to break with old ties and customs in order to do so. The restlessness of American life was favourable to economic achievement.

There is another consideration of a similar kind. Societies are more likely to grow rapidly, it is often argued, if they feel they require growth for more than purely economic reasons, that is if they are moved by an ideology which gives their leaders a strong emotional commitment to the task and shakes up the feelings and routines of the population as a whole. Various beliefs have served this purpose at different times. Thus it has been suggested that Calvinism provided an ideological reinforcement to economic effort in the sixteenth century. And in the nineteenth century, among countries that lagged behind Britain in industrialisation, the tension between their existing state and their potentialities—the desire to catch up—generated ideologies favourable to development, such as Saint-Simonism in France, or turned existing currents of feeling to this end, for example nationalism in Germany. In our own day, the need to restore economies shattered by war has fired Europeans with a fervour for the task—a fervour which, together with the disruption of old routines by the war, goes some way to explain why, since 1945, France and Germany have grown more rapidly than countries like Britain and the U.S.A. which have not had to meet the challenge of rebuilding large parts of their industrial capacity from scratch.

In the period in which we are particularly interested in this chapter, ideological influences were more favourable to growth in the U.S.A. than in Britain. In the U.S.A. the need to open up

220   TECHNOLOGY IN THE NINETEENTH CENTURY

the vast natural resources of the country had roused general feelings of buoyancy and optimism. In addition immigration provided an emotional dynamism. For the Europeans who had taken the momentous step of tearing up their roots and migrating to America had an immensely strong incentive when they got there to prove their decision right by ensuring, through hard work, that they did in fact better themselves. In Britain, on the other hand, the mid-Victorian pride in her industrial leadership —a pride which had its basis in fact, but which developed a life of its own and acquired an ideological character—was blighted by doubts in the depressions of the 1870's and '80's; and such ideological movements as there were in Britain in the decades before 1914—imperialism and socialism for example—were not particularly favourable to economic effort.

I know of no way of forming more than a general impression of the relative importance of these non-economic influences. There are some contrasts which are best interpreted in such terms. But I do not believe that this is true of Britain and the U.S.A. in the later nineteenth century. The differences in their technical progress, though significant enough to require explanation, were relatively small if we take a broad view of economic history; and there were, of course, fields in which Britain was ahead. Such lags as there were in the adoption of new methods in British industry can be adequately explained by economic circumstances, by the complexity of her industrial structure and the slow growth of her output, and ultimately by her early and long-sustained start as an industrial power.

[15]

C H A P T E R 7

TECHNOLOGY

The Harrod-Domar model is one in which growth gives rise to growth, as increased income leads to more savings, more investment, more income, more savings, and so on. The marginal propensity to save may fall in the long run and stabilize the process, or it may slow it down. But, as a rule, where investment is the key to growth, the front runner is likely to win. The head start opens up a gap that widens.

In models that depend on technological change for economic growth (called here for convenience the Abramovitz-Solow models, after two writers who have emphasized this feature in statistical investigations), the rate of growth is a function of the rate of technical change and its application in industry. Where technical change is indigenous, innovation is the key. With innovation elsewhere in the world, growth requires imitation.

The first question to ask about a leading country is whether the rate of technical change is independent of growth and, if so, whether it tends to move along at a constant rate or to vary in some systematic or random fashion. If technology is a dependent factor, on what does it depend — the overall demand for output, the age of a given industry or economy, the price of labor, or what? Second, there arises the question of how rapidly technological inventions developed at home in a leading industrial economy, or in others developed abroad, are applied. Here a particular question arises for Britain, the value of the head start. Technical progress leaves the pioneer with obsolescing equipment.[1] Gerschenkron believes in the value of starting last, shortcutting the technical stages at which earlier developers rest.[2] Long-lived equipment is said to be a particular handicap, whether in railroads, steel, canals, or early motor roads.

There is, however, dissent from this view: the existence of capital, however obsolete, is said to be a help or nothing — in any case, no hindrance. It is a free gift of the past, which the present has freedom

[1] Veblen, *Imperial Germany*, p. 128: "The British have not sinned against the canons of technology. It is only that they are paying the penalty for having been thrown into the lead and so having shown the way."
[2] Gerschenkron, "Economic Backwardness" (1952), p. 7.

[The appendices have not been reproduced here.]

to scrap or use, but the country is in no way worse off than if it has no capital stocks.[3] The issue is particularly relevant to Britain, which began as the innovator in 1760 and found itself after 1880 or so falling behind other countries, even in imitation.[4]

No such clear-cut issue exists for France, though there is a variety of smaller questions. There is the frequent allegation that the French are good at invention but poor at innovation, or that French inventions partake of a universal quality because of the scientific and deductive character of their thought, while those of Germany or Britain have a much more localized application.[5] The first part of this statement has also been applied to Britain.[6] And finally, the most impressive question to consider, there has been the high technological content in France's economic recovery after World War II, led by the government and nationalized agencies.

THE DEVELOPMENT OF TECHNOLOGY IN BRITAIN

The relations between technical change and growth are complex. Although it is true that technical change — increased productivity not accounted for by capital and labor inputs — has been found by Abramovitz and Solow to be responsible for perhaps two thirds of growth in the United States, and similar results have been obtained for other countries, it is also true that technical change depends in part on economic growth. Or it may. The growth may offer an opportunity to take advantage of new inventions — but the response must be forthcoming.

[3] See, e.g., Jervis, "The Handicap of Britain's Early Start" (1947).

[4] *The Economist,* "Rostow on Growth" (1959), p. 413, states: "Several factors combined to slow down the relative rate of Britain's development; but one is especially significant. It is one thing to be a mature economy, out at the margin of technology, having available each year only a rough approximation to the new technology created in, say, the previous year; it is quite a different thing to be a latecomer with a big unapplied backlog of technology available.

"Once the United States and continental western Europe had completed their take-off, much of the British lead was gone; for they could bring the backlog of technology to bear more rapidly than it had been created."

This is a possible model of relative growth, but one which does not apply. After 1875 British growth slowed down absolutely as well as relatively. In addition, the country was slow in applying existing technology as it developed at home and abroad, and in new industries. In these areas it had room to develop as rapidly as any country.

[5] Parker, "Comment," p. 189.

[6] Wilson, "Electronics" (1958), p. 143: "It is frequently said that the British are quick to invent but slow to develop. No doubt the French and many other people say the same of themselves!" A variety of writers, e.g., Carter and Williams, *Technical Progress,* p. 28, believe that the distinction between invention and innovation is virtually impossible to make today, since inventions represent continuous changes, largely realized in applications rather than in discontinuous steps.

Technology   137

Schumpeter's theory of economic development was connected with business cycles and rested on the observation that innovations occurred in the depth of business depression as business firms sought to cut costs.[7] In the early phases of Britain's growth, however, it was expansion that led to new processes. Two reasons account for this: in the first place, there is the pressure for additional supplies, which leads entrepreneurs to seek new and cheaper methods of production; second, the risk of loss is very much reduced with a briskly expanding demand.[8] Two outstanding waves of British innovation — in the cotton textile industry in the 1770s and in iron and steel in the 1850s and 1860s[9] — were supported by rapidly expanding markets, which happened to be for export.

One can go further and suggest that the decline in British inventive activity was associated with the Great Depression. Its timing is debatable, as noted in the discussion of the Climacteric in Chapter 1. Phelps Brown and Handsfield Jones attach it to the 1890s; Coppock, to the 1870s. These views derive from statistical examination. But the historian's view reaches back before the Great Depression. W. H. B. Court has noted that, whereas the Great Exhibition of 1851 demonstrated that Britain led the world, the Paris Exhibition of 1867 suggested that Britain was falling behind, a mere sixteen years later.[10] The timing is debatable, but the fact that it occurred is not.[11] The slowdown was experienced in cotton textiles, building, coal, steel, and, as we shall see, with some interruption in railroads.[12] But while the rate of technical progress slowed down during or after the depression, the most striking fact is that it did not pick up when business did after

---

[7] Schumpeter, *Theory of Economic Development* (1934), chap. vi; *Business Cycles* (1939), I, 159.

[8] See Sheahan, "Government Competition and the French Automobile Industry" (1960), who suggests that the structure of the market may be less important for technological change than its rate of growth.

[9] Smelser, *Social Change in the Industrial Revolution*, p. 62; Habakkuk, "Commercial Expansion," p. 802.

[10] See Young, *Portrait of an Age*, pp. 159–160: "After the age of the great producers, Armstrong, Whitworth, Brassey, comes the age of great shops and great advertisers. Famous names still kept our station in a world which had no naturalist to equal Darwin and no physicist to surpass Clerk Maxwell, but the springs of invention are failing, and, for the successors of the Arkwrights and the Stephensons we must look to America, to France and even to Italy."

[11] Saville notes ("Retarding Factors in the British Economy," 1961, p. 53) that a minor flurry of interest in scientific and technical education followed the Paris Exhibition and produced the Select Committee on Scientific Instruction, whereas a greater upheaval occurred in the 1880s and led to the Royal Commission on Technical Instruction.

[12] Jones, *Increasing Returns* (1933), parts 2, 3; Taylor, "Productivity and Innovation in British Coal" (1961); Burn, *History of British Steelmaking* (1940), chap. x. On the first four of these industries, see Dobb, *Development of Capitalism* (1947), p. 317.

138   Economic Growth in France and Britain

1896. By this time invention and innovation abroad had made a variety of new processes available to the British in the industries just listed. These industries undertook impressive programs of expansion, especially in cotton textiles and steel, but without modernization. The challenge of demand met no response, even in the application of available technology.

According to this interpretation, there was a major slowdown in the rate of British technological progress in the last quarter of the nineteenth century. There is evidence in support of the contrary. R. S. Sayers has pointed out that technical progress during the 1920s and the growth of real income in Britain have been consistently understated because of the deflationary character of the period.[13] Monetary income did not grow markedly, but real income gained as a result of the application of foreign innovations — American and German, in particular — in new industries. British innovation was not needed to achieve a rapid rate of technological progress, in view of the backlog of existing innovations to be applied — in motor cars, airplanes, radios, electrical appliances, artificial silk, plastics, the internal-combustion engine, ball-bearings, metal alloys, stainless steel (especially), and the mechanical industries. The old industries — textiles, iron and steel, coal, and, to a lesser extent immediately after the war, shipbuilding — failed to share in this advance.[14] Their great weight in the production indexes held down the overall averages.

But I cannot accept the view that technical change proceeds at a pace of its own, or at two paces, in the older and the newer industries. The classic statement that technological change proceeds in fits and starts is that of Schumpeter in Volume One of *Business Cycles*. For our period the evidence of the railroad industry lends support. Cole notes that changes in locomotive design for the Great Western Railway were concentrated in the Brunel period of the 1830s and 1840s, and again in a brief span between 1891 and 1906, when new types of locomotives were produced under Churchward every three years. After 1906 there was no improvement in design until 1945.[15] Both periods happened to coincide with brisk demand. But it seems evident that it was more the personalities of the managing directors than economic conditions which determined the rate of technical progress. Saunders, the general secretary, retired in 1886; Tyrell, the superintendent of lines, in 1888; Gooch, the chairman, died in 1889. Between 1889 and 1893 ten out of nineteen directors remaining after the loss of the three officers listed either died

[13] Sayers, "Technical Progress" (1950).
[14] Kahn, *Great Britain in the World Economy* (1946), emphasizes the distinction between the expanding electrical, automobile, and chemical industries and the declining staple trades.
[15] Cole, "Locomotive Replacement," part 2, p. 38.

Technology 139

or retired.[16] The boom of 1885–1889 produced a shortage of loco-motives, to be sure, but the extent and duration of the response were matters of personality. Declining industries may fail to attract energetic people and leave promotion to seniority.[17] When this happens, the industry will neither innovate nor invest in the inventions of others.

THE APPLICATION OF EXISTING TECHNOLOGY

The problem of the application of up-to-date technology is posed by Frankel in terms of choice between an existing and a new technology, when a substantial amount of capacity is needed to replace capital stock that suddenly wears out, like the one-horse shay.[18] He has devised a formula involving, for each process, the rate of interest, the ratio of fixed to variable cost, the amount of fixed cost, the durability of capital, the elasticity of demand, and the number of components which have to be altered. The impact of most of these variables is obvious. The number of components, however, represents what he calls "interrelatedness": the possibility that a change in one element in the economic process — in production, transport, raw-material supply — will entail other changes elsewhere in the system, because of complex physical interrelations, and will require complementary capital changes. In his view, this technological interrelatedness makes for difficulty of technical progress in complex economies and represents one disadvantage of the head start.

A slightly different formulation is offered by Salter, who holds that the decisions to scrap old capacity and invest in new are theoretically distinct.[19] An old technique using capital that wears out over time will be scrapped when it is unable to cover variable costs. New investment involving a new process will be undertaken only if it is able to earn superprofits. In equilibrium, the price of an output will equal average variable costs in the old method, which in turn are equal to average full costs, including normal profits, on the new. Salter is not concerned with interrelatedness. To him factor prices are the critical variables determining when it is useful to undertake new investment using new techniques. The existence of outmoded capital equipment is an indication not of inefficiency but of relatively cheap labor, which keeps variable costs low in the old technique (assumed to be labor-intensive), or high interest rates, which make for high fixed costs in the new technique.[20]

---

[16] *Ibid.*, p. 33.
[17] Carter and Williams, *Technical Progress*, p. 157.
[18] Frankel, "Obsolescence and Technical Change" (1955).
[19] Salter, *Productivity and Technical Change* (1960), chap. iv, sec. 3, pp. 55ff.
[20] Note that wage rates influence the application of existing technology rather

140   Economic Growth in France and Britain

A number of other economic factors are relevant. One is competition. Under less than perfect competition, old techniques can cover variable costs by means of high prices so long as entry is limited and the super-profits available to the new technique do not lead to expanded output. Another is the rate of gross investment, required either by a widening market as population grows or by high rates of physical depreciation, which would keep physical output falling and prices rising, with a stable population. A high rate of gross investment permits a choice among techniques along the lines of Frankel's model. When such choice is offered, the more efficient technique will be chosen without the margin in favor of the older one, since each process must cover fixed costs if capacity is to be sustained.

Still another factor is the secondhand value of old equipment, which can be regarded as a subtraction from the capital cost of the new technique or as an increase in variable cost — to the extent of interest and normal profit on the secondhand value — which the old technique must earn to be kept going.[21] Salter does not pay much attention to the secondhand value of old equipment; but in some markets, as in the automobile market in the United States today, it clearly plays an important part. The British shipping industry may have been enabled to maintain technological leadership longer than coal, textiles, steel, and locomotives by its brisk secondhand market in ships. At the peak of second-hand sales, in 1911, Britain built a million tons of new shipping, of which 93,000 tons were sold to foreign customers. Another 487,000 tons were sold abroad secondhand.[22] The net expansion of 215,000 tons was much smaller than the 487,000 modernized by selling off the old and building new.

Finally, there is the antieconomic possibility that investment decisions are taken, or are altogether evaded, by rote or habit. In economic terms it might be said that decision makers are a scarce input, decision making has a high cost, and the total return to the firm would be maximized in some sense under a standard other than economic calculation.

---

than, as in some analyses, the production of inventions. (See, e.g., Dobb, *Development of Capitalism*, p. 276.) In discussing the decline in growth in the British economy in the last quarter of the nineteenth century, which "unquestionably failed to provide incentives and encouragement" to transformation, Saville ("Retarding Factors in the British Economy," pp. 55–56) refers to a PEP report which mentions the weakness of incentives to economize labor and states that the British labor market was never in short supply, but without indicating what changes in relative wage rates occurred between the third and fourth quarters of the century. Salter (p. 45) states that the relative price of capital and labor is strongly affected by the cheapening of capital goods relative to wages as a consequence of technical progress in the capital-goods industries, which was occurring rapidly, at least abroad, in this period.

[21] Salter, *ibid.*, p. 54.

[22] *Statistical Abstract for the United Kingdom, 1911–1925*, p. 275.

Technology   141

This might be physical life of equipment, or an arbitrary accounting life as laid down in an office, or merely some traditional number. Frankel's and Salter's models may call for more rationality than the system is prepared to provide. Rules of thumb may substitute for calculation, and these rules of thumb may embody more or less technical change, favoring scrapping or retention of old equipment and adoption or rejection of new.

INTERRELATEDNESS

Frankel's discussion does not make it completely clear whether, by interrelatedness, he means merely physical input-output relations, involving the complementarity of investment decisions at different stages of production, or something more. That something more might be the lumpiness of investment in social-overhead capital, which would inhibit technical change if capital markets were imperfect and small investors had better access to capital than large investors. Or it may be the failure of the market to coordinate investment decisions in different firms — a form of external diseconomy.

Let us take the size of British freight cars on which Frankel quotes Veblen's remarks of 1915 (he could have cited the 1885 authority of Hadley).[23] It has long been understood that small cars are inefficient. To enlarge them from 10 to 20 tons' capacity would raise earning capacity 100 percent, but tare weight only 33 to 50 percent and capital cost only 50 percent. Current maintenance could be reduced 25 percent per ton mile, shunting requirements would fall, and locomotives could haul payloads up to 25 percent greater.[24] The most efficient size for coal wagons has been estimated at 24.5 tons capacity (plus 10.5 tons tare), which would stay within the critical limitations of size — 9 feet in width, 12 feet 10 inches in height, and two axles, limited to 17.5 tons of load per axle.[25]

Two reasons have been advanced for the failure of British railroads under private ownership to move to a more efficient freightcar size. I restrict the discussion to coal cars, since there is the further complication with miscellaneous merchandise that the average load per car has been well below capacity; haul has been short; and, in the absence of an organization like the American Railway Express Agency, speed for numerous small retail shipments has been furnished by the railroads themselves, often assigning a whole car to a single relatively small

[23] Mentioned by Savage, *An Economic History of Transport* (1959), pp. 76–77.
[24] Fenelon, *Railway Economics* (1932), p. 172.
[25] Parkhouse, "Railway Freight Rolling Stock" (1951), p. 214.

142   Economic Growth in France and Britain

shipment.[26] In coal, the retention of the ten-ton car is sometimes said to have been due to the impossibility of changing it without also modifying "terminal facilities, tracks and shunting facilities," [27] which made the cost prohibitive. On the other hand, the major impediment is said to have been the fact that the coal wagons were owned by the coal mines and not by the railroad companies.[28]

The technical aspects of interrelatedness do not seem to have held up the movement to more efficient size, either through making such a change uneconomic because of the enormity of the investment required or by adding amounts too great for any one firm to borrow. The sums involved were not large, and railway finance was rarely a limiting factor in the period up to 1914.[29] Private ownership of the coal cars by

[26] Sherrington, *Economics of Rail Transport* (1937), I, 214; Williams, *Economics of Railway Transport* (1909), p. 134. The question is debatable. British average loads run about 50 percent of capacity, but so do those of other countries with larger wagons.

[27] Veblen, *Imperial Germany*, pp. 126–127. It is wrong to mention track, since there is no necessity to strengthen roadbeds or bridges or to modify tunnels, so long as car size is kept within the limits cited in the text. With bogies or trolleys, much heavier cars are possible with increased construction cost. Fenelon in 1932 mentioned a 70-ton transformer wagon and a London and Northeastern Railway wall-trolley wagon built to carry 110 or, in special circumstances, 150 tons (*Railway Economics*, p. 56). The primary problem for coal would be to re-equip collieries and ports to take larger wagons, and in particular to modify coal screens, weigh-bridges, and sidings (where curves have to be altered to accommodate the greater length of wagon) in collieries, and hoists and tips at ports, along with the work sidings of certain large-scale coal consumers (*ibid.*, p. 172). Fenelon estimated the cost of all alterations at about £8,750,000 in 1932, and the net saving at £2 million per annum.

[28] Of the 1,320,000 freight cars in Britain in 1930, 630,000 were privately owned and 90 percent of these were used for coal. The advantage of direct ownership of cars by a colliery was that it could be assured a supply of cars. The overall economic loss to the country, apart from any inhibition of technical change, was the necessity to haul empty cars back to their owner, rather than to pool them, with an increase in shunting and in empty running. Pearson points out that the change from private to National Coal Board ownership has raised the proportion of productive to total miles from 66.8 percent in 1938 to 71.3 percent in 1952 ("Developments in British Transport," 1953 p. 123).

[29] The problem of inefficient freight-car size may have been affected by an old Railway Clearing House specification for private wagons, forbidding carrying capacities above 10 tons, which was modified "belatedly" in 1902 (Williams, *Economics of Railway Transport*, p. 136). But it was not likely that such prohibitions, which did not bind the railways themselves, were very powerful. The adoption of the Gauge Act by Parliament in 1846 induced the Great Western Railway to abandon its 7-foot gauge only in 1892, under the pressure of competition. Three major conversions took place in 1869, 1872 and 1874, but a new merger in 1876 raised the broad-gauge track from 8 to 293 miles. This was worked down to 183 miles by 1889 and finally converted in 1892. (See Cole, "Locomotive Replacement," part 2, pp. 14–15, 28.) This slow move to modernize and standardize provides an instance of technical interrelatedness. The necessity for new or reluctance to scrap old rolling stock was the main cost of the conversion, apart from labor to shift the rails, since new track was needed only at bends, points and crossings, and very little roadbed. Locomotives had long been built on a convertible basis,

Technology 143

the collieries, on the other hand, posed a type of interrelatedness that was institutional rather than technical.

A decision to change the size of rolling stock involves investment by the railroads, on the one hand, and by the collieries, on the other. Even if the rolling stock had been owned by the railroads, there might have been reluctance on the part of the collieries to alter their screens, weigh-bridges, and sidings. They could insist that they were under no obligation to undertake investment to benefit the railroads. And the railroads in turn would have difficulty in effecting an adequate distribution of the gains from the new investment, especially with uncertainty as to what those benefits would be.

For the railroads to guarantee new low rates on larger wagons would have been to take all the risk of the new investment, and that of the collieries, on themselves. To indicate that they would consider new and lower rates only if these were justified by operating economies would assign the risk to the collieries. An attempt to apportion the risk between the two would have been equitable but not likely to arouse much enthusiasm. The Great Western and the Great Eastern railways adopted twenty-ton wagons for their own use for locomotive coal as early as 1897;[30] and the Northeastern had used twenty-ton bottom-discharge mineral wagons for iron ore and forty-ton bogie coal wagons since the beginning of the century.[31] These wagons were all owned by the railroads, not the coal or iron companies. The Great Western Railway failed, however, to persuade colliery owners to change to a larger wagon when it offered a rebate of 5 percent on freight cars for coal in fully loaded twenty-ton wagons in 1923 and, in 1925, reduced charges on tipping and weighing these wagons. Only 100 came into use.[32] Colliery owners gave the excuse that the bigger wagons resulted in increased coal breakage. But neither ancient example, rebate, nor exhortation by Royal Commission[33] proved of avail until nationalization of the collieries.

---

with wheels outside the frame for broad-gauge work brought in for standard. Part of the slowness was due not to the investment problem, nor to reluctance to scrap rolling stock and traction that could not be converted, but to management's firm belief that the broad gauge was superior to the standard. In Australia the standardization of gauge is held back partly by the lumpiness of the investment problem involved and partly, despite frequent Royal Commissions, by the difficulty of getting agreement among the states. But interstate traffic is more in passengers than in goods.

[30] Sherrington, *Economics of Rail Transport*, p. 214.

[31] Fenelon, *Railway Economics*, p. 171. The London, Midland and Scottish Railway also used 40-ton bogie wagons to carry coal to its own power station.

[32] Sherrington, p. 218.

[33] The Reid Report recommended the establishment of a Standing Committee on Mineral Transport. In its report this latter characterized the system of private wagons as defective and recommended that the railroads ultimately take over the

Institutional interrelatedness inhibiting technical change can be compared to pecuniary economies that are external to the firm. Investment is required of two or more firms. Uncertainty attaches to the yield. A commitment as to the division of the benefits may create such a skewness in the distribution of risk and benefit, or such uncertainty, that one or more parties refuses to participate. An investment is not undertaken because of the possibility that the return will accrue to others. Where the railroad owns the cars and serves its own purposes — locomotive fuel, fuel for power, or even the delivery of iron ore for hire — the more efficient technology is used. Like Rosenstein-Rodan's classic example of external economies in production in underdeveloped countries, vertical integration converts the external to an internal profit and makes the technical change feasible.

The same analysis applies to the equipment of freight cars with automatic brakes. These were fitted to passenger cars after 1878 in response to public and governmental demands for safety, on the one hand, and the need for higher speeds, on the other.[34] Higher speed was partly a response to pressure of competition for passengers.[35] But it was also economical, permitting more traffic to move over a given way. Required were bigger and more powerful locomotives and automatic brakes; these were forthcoming for passenger trains and for a few special commodities which rode in special cars on passenger trains, like flowers and fish. But not for general or coal goods-traffic. In 1903 the Great Western Railway fitted some freight cars with automatic brakes and designed a special locomotive, the Mogul, to pull them — such a nuisance was the short, slow freight train. By and large, however, little was done to fit automatic brakes to freight wagons, and the question of whether to do so, and to what extent, is still under debate.[36] After

wagons. In the meantime it recommended pooling. The Report of the Royal Commission on Transport (Cmd 3751, 1931) scolded the railways, except the Great Western, for not having moved to larger wagons. Sherrington attacks the Act of 1921, consolidating the 130 prewar lines into four major companies, for its failure, *inter alia*, to eliminate private traders' wagons (p. 262).

[34] See Eversley, "The Great Western Railway" (1957), p. 177; Cole, "Locomotive Replacement," part 2, p. 41.

[35] Eversley, *ibid*. It is misleading to think of the railroads as monopolists in this period, since there was intense competition for passengers to different resorts, as well as alternative company facilities on a number of main routes, such as Birmingham to London.

[36] See Hunter, "Freight Rolling Stock" (1954), who claims that fitting brakes to 500,000 cars would be too costly and who would limit them to the new 24.5-ton cars and to mainline wagons. Parkhouse criticizes this limitation and comes out in favor of all cars (p. 364). In rebuttal Hunter suggests that Parkhouse has oversimplified the problem and neglected the extra costs of shunting in marshaling yards, what with all the coupling and uncoupling of vacuum hoses. While this seems absurd to people acquainted with the practice elsewhere, it may not be for Britain, given its greater volume of shunting per ton-mile because of the shortness of average haul.

Technology 145

setting forth estimates of cost and benefits which favor the adoption of brakes on British freight cars, to match those of every other major country, S. E. Parkhouse expresses the opinion that the government would have directed the equipment of freight trains with brakes long ago — "probably before the beginning of this century" — had it not been for the existence of a large fleet of privately owned wagons.[37]

This is where wholesale destruction would have helped — and why a country that loses a large proportion of its capital equipment in a war may thereby gain over the enemy, which emerges with its fixed capital relatively intact. Destruction permits a fresh start. No nation normally has the option of destroying or scrapping existing equipment and starting again. Private owners clinging to their privileges inhibited the railroads from acting as if the old cars, or freight cars without brakes, had no value. Until the coal wagons were nationalized, the British railroads were handicapped by the fact that in the 1830s they had the example of canals and roads in mind, and sought to act as common carriers on which individual traders would provide both rolling stock and motive power.[38] This early proved unworkable for locomotives; but, when it came to freight cars, the unsatisfactory results in inhibiting technical change were recognized too late or were blocked by the tradition of laissez faire. Sherrington says that the policy of private ownership of wagons would have been tolerated in no other country.[39] A later start, governmental intervention of great authority, or wholesale destruction permitting a fresh start would have been required to achieve a more workable basis. In the end it was nationalization.

The same historical issue of the difficulty of change in industries which may be called disintegrated, with separate firms responsible for separate processes or components, can be found elsewhere in Britain. Frankel mentions steel, with its separate stages of smelting, rolling, blast-furnace size, and so on, all technologically interrelated; and cotton textiles, where the adoption of ring spindles and automatic looms was held back by the separation of firms for separate processes and the fact that automatic looms require yarn spun a slightly different way.[40] Frankel discusses the externality of the interrelatedness only for cotton textiles and puts his faith in the purely technical indivisibility of

[37] Parkhouse, "Railway Freight Rolling Stock," pp. 216–218, 242. A truly technological indivisibility is that many private wagons are unsuitable for accelerated running, especially those with grease lubrication instead of oil. For a discussion of lack of standardization in freight cars, see Ministry of Reconstruction, *Standardization of Railway Equipment*, which mentions that there were at least 200 different types of axle boxes and 40 different types of hand brakes.

[38] Sherrington, *Economics of Rail Transport*, p. 213.

[39] *Ibid.*, p. 214.

[40] Frankel, "Obsolescence and Technical Change."

146   Economic Growth in France and Britain

technological change in steel. But the retention of beehive coke ovens
for so long in Britain, when the far more efficient by-product recovery
oven had come into use in 1880, may well have been due to the separate character at that time of coal and coke firms, on the one hand, and
iron and steel, on the other.[41] Other possible reasons for the retention
of beehive ovens: Frankel's interrelatedness; Salter's cheap labor and
high capital cost;[42] simple economic irrationality, which made steel
mills incapable of taking advantage of profit opportunities. But it is
likely that steel firms were both uncertain of the costs and profits of
the existing beehive ovens and fearful that a lower price might reduce
the profitability of by-product ovens if they invested in them. Later,
when vertical integration occurred, by-product coke ovens came into
general use.[43]

A further striking example is furnished by shipbuilding. This industry grew to world supremacy between about 1870 and 1900 on the basis
of a highly disintegrated and specialized industry. There were separate
industries for shipbuilding, marine engineering, marine hardware, and
so on; and big ships were built in big yards, little in little. A host of
distinct innovations was developed, largely by trial and error, and
fitted into ships by the market mechanism. British efficiency was higher
than anywhere else in the world: in 1890 its productivity was 12.5 tons
per man employed, compared with 1.8 tons in French shipyards. This
lead was achieved through the great craftsmanship of the British
worker, through an enormous amount of specialization, and in spite
of comparatively backward equipment. Shipyards lacked electric lighting on the ways, electric motors, pneumatic tools. But the degree of
specialization was carried much further than anywhere else.

After World War II, however, the industry could be held up by
Andrew Shonfield as an outstanding example of what was wrong with
British industry — its failure to grow or to adopt new methods.[44] Shonfield blasts the industry for its failure to keep up with the changes that
had taken place in Germany, for example, or in Japan. But he does not
consider the notion that the organization of the industry into separate
firms dealing with each other at arm's length may have impeded tech-

---

[41] Burnham and Hoskins, *Iron and Steel in Britain*, p. 39, point out that by 1900
no one of the steel companies was fully integrated.

[42] See Burn, *Economic History of Steelmaking*, pp. 250ff, who believes that inadequate access to capital handicapped the British steel industry. See above,
Chapter 3, note 124.

[43] See Andrews and Brunner, *Capital Development in Steel*, p. 146. Just before
the big amalgamations of 1929–1931, pig-iron producers controlled 54 percent of
their coke needs.

[44] Shonfield, *British Economic Policy since the War* (1958), pp. 41ff.

Technology   147

nological change because of the possibility that part of the benefits of that change would have been external to the separate firms.[45]

There is of course no magic in vertical integration. It can lead to a "false sense of balance."[46] More important, it may fail to be combined with sufficient cost accounting and thereby perpetuate inefficient operations. The Ministry of Reconstruction was convinced of the necessity of investigating the costs of construction of locomotives and rolling stock by the separate railways in Britain, persuaded that the companies were making inadequate provision in their costs for rates and taxes, ground rent, and depreciation, though they might save a private builder's profits and advertising costs.[47] But it seems likely that technological change can proceed faster under vertical integration, unless the separate departments seek a quiet life.[48] Integration of the technological changes in one component into the process of another unit can be effectively organized and supervised in many ways which the market alone cannot effect.[49]

[45] Carter and Williams, *Technical Progress*, also fail to test technical change against the degree of integration. They furnish, however, an excellent example of external economies in citing shell moldings as an example of product-user reluctance to accept an innovation (p. 78). Accurate casting of these moldings saved machining, which used to be done by the buyer. The producer hesitated to introduce the casting process, however, because of concern over whether the buyer would be willing to pay the higher price for an improved product.

[46] Jewkes, "Is British Industry Inefficient?" Jewkes believes that the advantages of integration are normally very limited, and that the firms equipped with automatic looms suffered a heavy mortality during the war (p. 7, note). In general, the answer he gives to his question is no.

[47] Ministry of Reconstruction, *Standardization of Railway Equipment*.

[48] Cole observes that in the Great Western Railway there was no interdepartmental pressure for innovation during the superintendency of Tyrell from 1864 to 1888, with his interest in safety and in slowing down trains ("Locomotive Replacement," part 2, p. 30).

[49] This is an inadequate treatment of a complex problem, and it may be that the only effective means of maintaining interest in technical change is to alternate the organization between smaller separate independent units, dealing at arm's length through a market, and a larger integrated entity, subject to central direction. This would be analogous to a discovery made during my own government experience: there is no single system of organization of a bureau designed to keep up with what is going on in the world — whether by geographical units with functional subgroups or by functional units with geographic components. The only guarantee of alertness is the periodic reorganization which shifts to the other system. By the same token, Burton H. Klein of RAND has recently concluded that the organization of weapon development by "systems" (single companies responsible for the design of an entire weapon, with its component systems and subgroups) may be inherently (or currently?) inferior to a disintegrated system under which there is competition among producers of separate components to develop the most efficient possible subunits, and only at the end does an assembler undertake to produce a finished weapon out of competitively improved components. The analogy with the British shipbuilding industry of 1890 is striking.

148   Economic Growth in France and Britain

The Merchant System

A particular form of disintegration is the division of functions of producing and selling between separate firms. This is clearly an efficient system under a fixed state of the arts, allowing separate managements to concentrate on essentially different tasks and to obtain the benefits of specialization and exchange. This is the basis on which Alfred Marshall defends it as the best system for advancing British export trade, despite an occasional yielding by merchants to the temptation to sell non-British goods to their customers.[50] But the separation of selling from production may have the drawback of slowing down technical change by interposing barriers of communication between the ultimate customer and the producer;[51] it may render external to consumer, merchant, or producer the benefits of changed products, or a changed process entailing some alteration in product, or merely increase the possibility that the benefit of change will be external to the firm. In the cotton-textile trade the merchant was partly responsible for the unnecessarily high number of separate qualities of product, since he lacked incentive to induce the customer to change the specifications, however arbitrarily fixed, and had the power to transfer orders from one manufacturer to another. Robson cites a case of fifty-four orders for thirty different varieties of low-grade poplins, differences among which were unimportant to the ultimate user, who could distinguish at best three grades.[52] The advantages of standardization were lost by preventing the producer from sharing his benefits with the customer. It may be significant that the woolen industry, which did much better than cotton in maintaining its rate of technical change (with the help of French competition), moved to direct trading.[53]

Beeseley and Throup point out that in machine tools the selling agents are more concentrated than the producers, which inhibits entry by the latter into new fields. The agents want noncompeting products, and to add a new line, a producing firm may have to change agents — which occurs infrequently.[54] Moreover, the merchant system lacks the capacity to develop new tools through close liaison between producer

[50] Marshall, *Industry and Trade*, pp. 616–618.
[51] Cf. Nicholas Kaldor's defense of advertising as a means of enabling the producer to overcome the stultifying effects of the wholesaler on product change in "Economic Aspects of Advertising" (1950–51), pp. 17–18.
[52] Robson, *Cotton Industry*, pp. 92–95. Robson concludes, however, that the advantage of longer runs of standardized specifications were not of great consequence (p. 100).
[53] Allen, *British Industries*, p. 260. Allen notes that woolens were not sold in the tropics, but only in countries with cultures and legal systems akin to the British, which may have eased the task of replacing the merchant system.
[54] Beeseley and Throup, "The Machine-Tool Industry" (1958), pp. 380ff.

Technology 149

and consumer. After nationalization, for example, Renault established its own machine-tool plant to effect the changes in design it wanted — there were no competent firms at that time in France — and owes the brilliant tooling of its Flins plant to vertical integration.[55]

It is difficult to know how far the merchant system inhibited technical change in tinplate production, where no major change in technology took place for two hundred years.[56] It probably had little to do with it, given the readily satisfied character of the Welsh manufacturers. Complaints leveled by the manufacturers against the merchants dealt with upgrading of produce, passing off seconds as standard sheets, and earning the difference in addition to normal brokerage, all of which hurt the long-run interests of the industry.[57] But it may be significant that when bigger companies emerged from the mass of small producers — Richard Thomas, Stewart and Lloyds, Guest, Keen and Nettlefolds, and Baldwins — they set up their own sales agencies.[58]

The institutional literature on foreign trade devotes a great deal of attention to the choice between direct selling by the manufacturer and indirect selling through merchants. Writers like Allen attribute British losses in foreign trade to the established position of the merchant, in particular to the fact that merchants occasionally substituted cheaper foreign products for British goods.[59] Lewis puts it that the merchant system is fitted to sell consumer goods to agricultural countries, not capital equipment to industrial.[60] But there is the distinct possibility, whose complete demonstration would require a separate book, that the merchant system bears a significant share of the responsibility for slowing down technical change because it renders a large proportion of the benefits of technical change external to the firms that must effect or sell it.

STANDARDIZATION, TECHNICAL EDUCATION

A special form of external economy in technology exists in standardization. Where a single firm has several types of equipment for the same job, it pays to scrap the nonstandard ones first, especially since these are limited in number. In locomotives and buses, odd types acquired in mergers are eliminated ahead of older standard models to save the

[55] See the quotation from Pierre Bézier, *ibid.*, p. 386.
[56] Minchenton, *British Tinplate Industry*, p. 35.
[57] *Ibid.*, pp. 105–107, 148ff.
[58] *Ibid.*, p. 246. See also Chandler, " 'Big Business' in American Industry," p. 26, where the shift from regional to national companies is said to involve above all the assumption of the marketing function.
[59] See Allen, *British Industries*, pp. 18–19, 311. See also Burnham and Hoskins, *Iron and Steel in Britain*, pp. 210–211.
[60] Lewis, "International Competition in Manufactures" (1957), p. 578.

additional operating expense of servicing an unnecessarily heteroge-neous stock of buses or locomotives.[61] Replacement with a modern model may be discouraged by the diseconomy in servicing more than one model while the stock of equipment is being turned over at the depreciation rate. And here durability slows down technological change by lengthening the period of higher operating costs for varied equip-ment.

Standardization within the firm is of minor importance when com-pared to standardization among firms where the industry has been slow to perceive its value.[62] This is illustrated by the holdout of the Great Western Railway on the standard gauge; by the resultant necessity to tranship Midland freight for the southwest in Gloucester; and by the two hundred types of axle boxes and forty different handbrakes for rolling stock, already mentioned. Examples in Britain are legion. Dif-ferent railroads in Britain adopted different automatic brakes for passenger cars, whereas the choice of a common standard would have lowered capital costs by £400,000,[63] quite apart from the gain in oper-ating efficiency. Parkhouse doubts whether this standardization could have been achieved under company management. The Ministry of Reconstruction blames the companies for failing to adhere to the regu-lations laid down by the Railway Clearing House for privately owned cars, and finds its cause in the fact that most railroads built their own stock.

There is no need to restrict examples to the railroads. I was told dur-ing the war, but have been unable to verify it, that there were two hundred sizes and designs of manhole covers produced for current use in Britain to specifications laid down by various local boards and authorities.[64] Plummer notes that the organization of electricity genera-tion and distribution was found inadequate in World War I, with no fewer than seventy generating stations, fifty different systems of supply, twenty-four voltages, and ten different frequencies: "It was the old story of numerous parochial undertakings during the early experimental stages when nobody had enough vision to think in terms of planned development on a national scale." [65] But surely it is too much to de-mand national vision of private enterprise. The average individual firm cannot standardize until some extra-firm unit — a dominant firm or

[61] See Cole, "Locomotive Replacement," *passim;* and Holland, "The Replace-ment of Busses in Bristol" (1961), p. 39.
[62] Carter and Williams, *Technical Progress,* p. 171.
[63] Parkhouse, "Railway Freight Rolling Stock," p. 211.
[64] Burn points out that the big steel firms in the United States and Germany rammed through standardization (*Economic History of Steelmaking,* p. 199); even the French industry adopted set standards (p. 200), but the British did not. See also Burnham and Hoskins, *Iron and Steel in Britain,* p. 43.
[65] *New British Industries* (1937), p. 21.

Technology

oligopoly, the industry, or government — has adopted standards. It is sometimes suggested that the electric companies were obstructed by gas concerns. The alternative view is that Parliament acted too little and too late, without the need for encouragement in this course of inaction. As every British householder knows, some of the results of lack of standardization remain in evidence.

The failure to standardize can be regarded as a penalty of the head start. Latecomers can observe the costs of heterogeneity and take steps to adopt a practical standard.[66] Or it may be regarded as a shortcoming of the intransigent attitude of laissez faire. Government may fail to think about standards (as on the vital question of weights and measures), or its attempts at standardization may be rejected by industry.[67] Government standards may be ignored in practice, as in the Gauge Act of 1846, or the standards may not be worked out thoroughly because of the opposition of those affected (brakes for freight cars) or because of incompetence (possibly in electricity). And it is not only necessary to adopt standards — as technology improves, standards must be changed. Here is a particularly difficult task for industry and government. Results are achieved not only by legislation, but also by specification for government purchases or in extreme instances by nationalization.[68]

Pollard has set out a fascinating account of the impact of the Admiralty in improving ship design throughout the nineteenth century, both in supporting education for governmental designers, by paying for experiments and trials, and in adopting progressive specifications.[69] Iron was adopted, for example, by the navy before the mercantile community — as were steel boilers, water-tube boilers, coal, oil. Progress might have been faster, however. The navy exhibited great reluctance

[66] Jervis seems to protest unduly ("Handicap of Britain's Early Start," p. 118) over the unimportance of standardization in British canals on the grounds that through traffic is more appropriately left to railroads. Savage, *Economic History of Transport*, p. 24, thinks that a uniform lock size would have helped. But see the impassioned Gravier, *Paris et le désert français*, p. 150, who asserts that canals with large locks are of no assistance in economic development: "Birmingham has never seen a barge, nor the Ardennes any large factories."

[67] It is interesting to observe today, as Pakistan and South Africa have converted to a decimal coinage and Australia and New Zealand contemplate the step, that the florin was introduced after 1847 as the first step in such a measure, which was to have had coins of one tenth and one hundredth of a pound. The Society of Arts recommended decimal coinage, weights, and measures in 1853, but the measure to appoint a committee to investigate the question won by only a small majority in the House of Commons, and the move lapsed. See Levi, *History of British Commerce*, p. 474.

[68] Nationalization of the railways was widely discussed in the 1860s, and Walter Bagehot, who once said that an age of great cities requires strong government, recommended nationalization before the Royal Commission, which considered it in 1865 (Cole and Postgate, *The British People*, 1961, p. 341).

[69] Pollard, "Laissez-Faire and Shipbuilding" (1952).

152   Economic Growth in France and Britain

to specify basic steel, so much cheaper than acid.[70] The conversion from coal to oil was delayed, moreover, by an (intentionally?) ill-designed experiment in which an oil-burner naval vessel emitted large clouds of black smoke to make itself unduly conspicuous.[71]

A more familiar type of external economy relevant to technical change, and widely discussed in the development literature, is the provision of technical education — whether by the state, other governmental bodies, or private institutions. Much has been made of the comparative neglect of technical education in Britain,[72] after an early flowering of scientific societies in the course of the Industrial Revolution. The weakness of Oxford and Cambridge in science has been mentioned, as well as the lack of people with scientific education in business. Although there is some skepticism toward all generalizations about technical change,[73] including the one that progress could be made for a time by empiricists and amateurs but that late in the nineteenth century it required trained technical personnel, there seems to

[70] Andrews and Brunner, *Capital Development in Steel*, p. 77, state that with World War I "even buyers so notoriously conservative as the Admiralty had to accept basic steel." This, however, was basic open-hearth steel, not basic Bessemer, which Andrews and Brunner regard as good only for tube and strip (p. 98). Acid Bessemer was largely used for rails, but declined because of the dwindling of hematite iron ore (see above, Chapter 2). All basic steel was distrusted initially, because of the difficulties of controlling its quality and its consequent variability. In 1878 Lloyds Institute of Insurance Underwriters withdrew a 20 percent reduction in premiums accorded to steel ships over iron from Bessemer steel. But with the basic process, German and French metallurgists learned how to control the quality of basic Bessemer. In time, the demand favored basic steel. To what extent the British industry remained more dependent on acid than on basic, and on open-hearth than on Bessemer, because of conservatism on the part of consumers, slowness of the industry to achieve the appropriate skills, or unwillingness to adapt, is a question on which it is difficult to make judgments. Burnham and Hoskins attach importance to the consumer predilection against basic steel, but note that European supplies were imported (*Iron and Steel in Britain*, pp. 35, 118). Contrast the French enthusiasm for Bessemer which, after its invention in 1856 was demonstrated at the London exhibition of 1862 and said by Michel Chevalier to be the greatest thing since the discovery of steel (Labrousse, *L'Évolution économique*, III, 89). For a contemporary account of Bessemer's encouragement by Napoleon III and discouragement by Woolwich arsenal, "the enemy of inventors," see *Fortunes Made in Business* (1883), I, 226. This source also comments ironically on shipbuilding with Bessemer steel in 1862 as follows: "Few will be surprised to learn that this made no impression whatsoever on the Lords of the Admiralty" (I, 233).
[71] Seminar, Nuffield College, November 28, 1960.
[72] See, e.g., Cotgrove, *Technical Education and Social Change* (1958). The general historian puts it much along the following lines: "It was becoming doubtful how long the personal energy of the manufacturer, even the high quality of his wares, would make up for an ignorance of chemistry and the metric system and a lordly indifference to the tastes and requirements of his customers. The age of pioneers was over, and for an age of close cultivation we were imperfectly equipped" (Young, *Portrait of an Age*, p. 164).
[73] Jewkes, Sawers, and Stillerman, *The Sources of Invention* (1958).

Technology   153

be little doubt that British universities and public bodies were slow in responding to the widely recognized need for more technological education.[74] A big push in science began after the Crystal Palace exhibition, under the patronage of the prince consort, with the establishment of the South Kensington museums, the Cavendish laboratory in 1860, and the practical provincial universities. But the National Laboratories for standards were not begun until 1900, and the Division of Scientific and Industrial Research not until 1915. After World War I, a number of industries formed research associations, with government prodding. The failure in higher technical education was matched on the lower levels: technical colleges for artisans were not started until after 1900.

Sponsored research and scientific education are not enough to induce rapid technological progress. There must be general acceptance of the value of the scientific approach to industrial problems at all levels. Education must be widespread instead of just for the elite, and education plus intelligence must be accorded some prestige in business, along with experience on the shop floor.[75] Business leadership must make room for technically competent people. Government cannot provide technical education until the value system is ready to accord it place. When the public is ready to receive it, moreover, there will be a lag before science and technology can be taught, while teachers are being readied.[76]

This interest in technical change and the readiness to take chances on new processes are emphasized by Carter and Williams, especially when they write of a firm's lack of secrecy and willingness to communicate with the outside world and within the plant.[77] In the early phases of the Industrial Revolution, continuous interest and excitement were felt over solutions to technical problems; and work took place on them by people outside of industry. This implies communication. In the third quarter of the nineteenth century, the three major inventions in the steel industry came from nonindustrial sources. By the end of the century, however, interest had turned away from the rapid advance

[74] Carter and Williams, *Technical Progress*, p. 100. Cotgrove (p. 27) believes that the need was not widely recognized, despite the Royal Commission on Technical Instruction of 1882, and he stresses the complacency of the Commission on the Depression of Trade and Industry, in 1885, and the neglect of science and apathy toward technical education bred by fifty years of industrial pre-eminence. Marshall, *Industry and Trade*, p. 95, states that British businessmen awoke to the need for improved education for technical efficiency in 1904.

[75] See Erickson, *British Industrialists*, p. 43: "Workshop training produced men with a supreme contempt for theory and science."

[76] The point was made by Faraday before the Royal Commission (Young, *Portrait of an Age*, p. 97). Young adds that the reason for the classical curriculum was that classically trained teachers were available.

[77] *Technical Progress, passim*, esp. pp. 7, 117, 179.

of Germany that had given concern in the 1890s: it was too easy to sell the old goods to the Commonwealth.

NONECONOMIC BEHAVIOR

Given sufficient demand, lack of technological progress may not stem solely from external economies, whether from a high degree of vertical disintegration, independent marketing arrangements, lack of standardization, or gaps in technological education. Some integrated industries are slow to imitate; and some inventions that can raise productivity within the specialized firm are not adopted. Although the earlier explanations may be valid for the failure of British industry to add brakes on its freight cars, convert its spinning mills from mule jennies to ring spindles and its weaving mills from hand to automatic looms, or adopt mechanical means of cutting and transporting coal underground, they may not explain the whole lag. Another reason is available. It is that British business became increasingly irrational in economic terms, or — to use less pejorative language — more and more economic decisions were made by habit or rote, rather than by calculation, and that the bases chosen did not always lead to profit maximization as implied by the Frankel and Salter models.

Cole states that the routine element in replacement has definitely been underestimated in most studies and theories of replacement.[78] Barna mentions that some firms automatically spend their depreciation allowances on relacement, noting that it is generally easier to obtain approval for replacement decisions than for new investments.[79] Other forms of "uneconomic" behavior are to regulate replacement by the physical life of an asset, or by its "accounting life" as determined in advance. In his study of the replacement of Bristol buses, Holland notes that replacement typically occurred after the end of the accounting life and shortly before the end of the physical life.[80] It was a tragedy to be required to scrap equipment "with money on its back," equipment that had not been fully depreciated on the books; and such action demanded full explanation to the accounting office. On the other hand, a few years of "depreciation-free" running constituted an accounting success. Still other irrationalities or over-rationalized modes of behavior are to govern investment by present profits rather than by future returns on the investment, or by the firm's cash position. These factors affect the availability of capital to the firm, to be sure, and enter into the equation of investment–demand and savings–supply. But dif-

[78] Cole, *Locomotive Replacement*, part 2, p. 156.
[79] See Barna, *Investment and Growth Policies*, p. 31.
[80] Holland, "The Replacement of Busses in Bristol," p. 67.

Technology 155

ferences in the availability of internal and external funds are not likely to be critical for really profitable investments and are more likely to serve as a rationalization for inertia.[81]

These practices are irrational unless the costs of decision making are high and it is cheaper in the long run to be governed by routine and habit. Where decision-making capacity is very scarce, and habits are necessary, the degree of technical change will depend in large measure on the nature of the habits built into the system. Does standard operating procedure favor the new process or the old; writing off obsolescent equipment or keeping it in operation until it collapses, in order to avoid capital expenditure, no matter what the effect on operating outlays? Old equipment is a free gift of the past and need not interfere with profitable investment, provided that one is prepared to take a detached view of it as a bygone to be tolerated only so long as it can cover its out-of-pocket expenses. That this is difficult to do is illustrated time and again. The Anglo-American Council on Productivity finds it remarkable that one American manufacturer scrapped a considerable investment in plant with "years of useful life still left" because the management was convinced that the plant had no future.[82] Cook reports that Pilkingtons was handicapped in plate glass by the fact that it did not need a new machine and that most modern machines tend to be somewhat more economical.[83]

Irrationality can lead to too much innovation and to concern for physical efficiency rather than economic. At the turn of the century, railroad racing led to heavy investment not only in locomotives and passenger rolling stock but also in straightening curves and grades, which was uneconomic in terms of its contribution to earning capacity. Prior to the Railway Companies (Accounts and Return) Act of 1911, which prevented the adjustment of depreciation each year to what the directors wanted to spend on investment, much of this could be disguised from inquisitive stockholders by being paid for out of depreciation funds, or expenses, and not regarded as net investment. After 1928 the establishment of depreciation reserves in a fund, rather than their use to write down capital, provided the basis for another irrationality, strengthening the hand of the engineers who wanted to spend a certain amount on gross investment, but weakening their position if they wanted to spend more.

[81] See Andrews and Brunner, *Capital Development in Steel*, pp. 144, 187, 209, etc., arguing that United Steel would not undertake investment in the early part of the interwar period for lack of cash, on the one hand, and because it might have interfered with the profitable working of Appleby-Frodingham, on the other.

[82] Anglo-American Council on Productivity, *Management Accounting* (1950), p. 17, para. 13.

[83] Cook, *Effects of Mergers*, p. 305.

156 Economic Growth in France and Britain

Excellent reasons exist to reduce replacement and process decisions to a habit. Decision making is expensive; but habits can differ, as well as the approach to technological innovation. The response to suggestions for change can be either "What does it save?" or "What does it cost?" [84] Excess of either courage or caution can lead to disaster, the former more rapidly. Still, habits of receptivity to change, to write-offs, to new processes and new products, can, with appropriate safeguards, yield income and ultimately economize even the most painful decision making.

[84] Burn, *Economic History of Steelmaking*, p. 208. See also p. 296 for the comment to the young men making suggestions, who were told to teach their grandmothers to suck eggs, and that that was tried fifty years ago. See, finally, Minchenton, *British Tinplate Industry*, p. 195, for the Welsh tinmaker's response, "Has any other fool tried it yet?"

BIBLIOGRAPHY

Allen, G. C. *British Industries.* London. Longmans Green, 2nd ed.,1939.

Andrews, P. W. S., and Elizabeth Brunner. *Capital Development in Steel.* Oxford, Blackwell, 1951.

Anglo-American Council on Productivity. *Productivity Report on Management Accounting.* London, New York, November 1950.

Barna, Tibor. *Investment and Growth Policies in British Industrial Firms.* Cambridge, Eng., Cambridge University Press, 1962 (National Institute of Economic and Social Research, Occasional Papers 20).

Beesley, M. E., and G. W. Throup. "The Machine-Tool Industry," in Burn, ed., *The Structure of British Industry,* vol. 1.

Burn, D.L . "British Steelmaking and Foreign Competition, 1870–1914," Appendix 1 in C. R. Fay, *English Economic History, Mainly since 1700.* Cambridge, Eng., Heffer, 1940.

———, *Economic History of Steelmaking, 1867–1939.* Cambridge, Eng., Cambridge University Press, 1940.

———, ed. *The Structure of British Industry,* 2 vols. Cambridge, Eng., Cambridge University Press, 1958. (Burn's essays are "Steel," I, 260–306, and "Retrospect," II, 455–457.)

Burnham, T. H., and G. O. Hoskins. *Iron and Steel in Britain, 1870–1930.* London, Allen and Unwin, 1943.

Carter, C. F. and B. R. Williams. *Industry and Technical Progress.* London, Oxford University Press, 1957.

Chandler, A. D., Jr. "The Beginning of 'Big Business' in American Industry," *Business History Review,* vol. 33, no. 2 (Spring 1959), pp. 1–31.

Cole, G. D. H., and Raymond Postgate. *The British People, 1746–1946.* London, Methuen; reprinted as a University Paperback by Barnes and Noble, 1961.

Cole, Humphrey. "Great Western Railway Locomotive Replacement." Unpublished manuscript, Oxford Institute of Statistics, about 1957.

Cook, P. Lesley. *Effects of Mergers.* London, Allen and Unwin, 1958.

Cotgrove, Stephen E. *Technical Education and Social Change.* London, Allen and Unwin, 1958.

Dobb, Maurice. *Studies in the Development of Capitalism.* New York, International Publishers, 1947.

Economist, vol. 192, no. 6051 (August 15, 1959): "Rostow on Growth– A Non-Communist Manifesto," pp. 409–416.

Erickson, Charlotte. *British Industrialists, Steel and Hosiery, 1850–1950.* Cambridge, Eng., Cambridge University Press, 1959.

Eversley, D. E. C. "The Great Western Railway and the Swindon Works in the Great Depression," *University of Birmingham Historical Journal,* vol. 5, no. 2 (1957), pp. 167–190.

Fenelon, K. G. *Railway Economics.* London, Methuen, 1932.

Frankel, Marvin. "Obsolescence and Technical Change in a Maturing Economy," *American Economic Review,* vol. 45, no. 3 (June 1955), pp. 298–319.

Gerschenkron, Alexander. "Economic Backwardness in Historical Perspective," in Bert F. Hoselitz, ed., *The Progress of Underdeveloped Areas.* Chicago, University of Chicago Press, 1952, pp. 3–29.

Gravier, Jean-François. *Paris et le désert français.* Paris, Flammarion, 2nd rev. ed., 1958.

Habakkuk, H. J. "Free Trade and Commercial Expansion, 1853–1870," in *The Cambridge History of the British Empire,* vol. 2. Cambridge, Eng., Cambridge University Press, 1940.

Holland, David. "The Replacement of Busses in Bristol," *Bulletin of the Oxford Institute of Statistics,* vol. 24, no. 4 (November 1962), pp. 413–436.

Hunter, A. P. "Freight Rolling Stock," *British Transport Review,* vol. 3, no. 3 (December 1954), pp. 179–201.

Jervis, F. R. J. "The Handicap of Britain's Early Start," *Manchester School,* vol. 15, no. 1 (1947), pp. 112–122.

Jewkes, John, David Sawers, and Richard Stillerman. *The Sources of Invention.* London, Macmillan, 1958.

—— "Is British Industry Inefficient?" *Manchester School,* vol. 14, no. 1 (1946), pp. 1–16.

Jones, G. T. *Increasing Return,* ed. Colin Clark. Cambridge, Eng., Cambridge University Press, 1933.

Kahn, A. E. *Great Britain in the World Economy.* New York, Columbia University Press, 1946.

Kaldor, Nicholas. "The Economic Aspects of Advertising," *Review of Economic Studies,* vol. 28, no. 1 (1950–1951), pp. 1–27.

Labrousse, Ernest. *Aspects de l'évolution économique et sociale de la France et du Royaume Uni.* Paris, Les Cours de Sorbonne, 1954 (in three parts).

Levi, Leone. *The History of British Commerce.* London, Murray, 2nd ed., 1880.

Lewis, W. Arthur. "International Competition in Manufactures," *American Economic Review, Papers and Proceedings,* vol. 47, no. 2 (May 1957), pp. 578–587.

Marshall, Alfred. *Industry and Trade.* London, Macmillan, 1920.

Minchenton, W. E. *The British Tinplate Industry.* Oxford, Clarendon Press, 1957.

Ministry of Reconstruction, Advisory Council. *Report on the Standardization of Railway Equipment,* Cd 9193. London, H.M. Stationery Office, 1918.

Parker, William N. "Comment," on Kindleberger, "Resources, International Trade and Economic Growth," in J. J. Spengler, ed., *Natural Resources and Economic Growth.* Washington, Resources for the Future, Inc., 1961.

Parkhouse, S. E. "Railway Freight Rolling Stock," *Journal of the Institute of Transport,* vol. 24, no. 6 (September 1951), pp. 211–218, 242.

Pearson, A. J. "Developments and Prospects in British Transport, with Special Reference to Railways," *Journal of the Institute of Transport,* vol. 25, no. 4 (May 1953).

Plummer, Alfred. *New British Industries in the Twentieth Century.* London, Pitman, 1937.

Pollard, Sidney. "Laissez-Faire and Shipbuilding," *Economic History Review,* 2nd ser., vol. 5, no. 1 (August 1952), pp. 98–115.

Robson, R. *The Cotton Industry in Britain.* London, Macmillan, 1957.

Royal Commission on Transport. *Report,* London, HMSO (Cmd 3751), 1931.

Salter, W. E. G. *Productivity and Technical Change.* Cambridge, Eng., Cambridge University Press, 1960.

Savage, Christopher I. *An Economic History of Transport.* London, Hutchison, 1959.

Saville, John. "Some Retarding Factors in the British Economy before 1914," *Yorkshire Bulletin of Economic and Social Research,* vol. 13, no. 1 (May 1961), pp. 51–60.

Sayers, R. S. "The Springs of Technical Progress in Britain, 1919–1939," *Economic Journal,* vol. 60, no. 238 (June 1950), pp. 275–291.

Schumpeter, Joseph A. *Business Cycles.* New York, McGraw-Hill, 1939.

—— *Theory of Economic Development,* Cambridge, Harvard University Press, 1934.

Sheahan, John. "Government Competition and the Performance of the French Automobile Industry," *Journal of Industrial Economics,* vol. 8, no. 3 (June 1960), pp. 197–215.

Sherrington, C. E. R. *The Economics of Rail Transport in Great Britain,* I: *History and Development.* London, Arnold, 2nd ed., 1937.

Shonfield, Andrew. *British Economic Policy since the War.* Harmondsworth, Penguin Books, 1958.

Smelser, Neil J. *Social Change in the Industrial Revolution: An Application of Theory to the Lancashire Cotton Industry, 1770–1840.* London, Routledge and Kegan Paul, 1959.

Taylor, Arthur J. "Labour Productivity and Technological Innovation in the British Coal Industry, 1850–1914," *Economic History Review,* 2nd ser., vol. 14, no. 1 (August 1961), pp. 48–70.

Veblen, Thorstein. *Imperial Germany and the Industrial Revolution.* New York, Macmillan, 1915.

Williams, S. C. *The Economics of Railway Transport.* London, Macmillan, 1909.

Wilson, Thomas. "The Electronic Industry," in Burn, ed., *The Structure of British Industry.*

Young, G. M. *Victorian England, Portrait of an Age.* London, Oxford University Press, 2nd ed., 1936; reprinted 1960, paperback edition.

[16]

The Decline of the British Economy: An Institutional Perspective

BERNARD ELBAUM AND WILLIAM LAZONICK

This paper attributes the relative decline of the British economy in the twentieth century to rigidities in its economic and social institutions that had developed during the nineteenth-century era of relatively atomistic competition. Inherited and persistent constraints impeded British firms from acquiring the market control, authority in labor relations, or managerial hierarchy necessary to avail themselves fully of modern mass production methods. At the societal level there was an interrelated failure to transform the character of British educational and financial institutions, labor-management relations, and state policy in order to promote economic development. By performing better in these respects late-industrializing countries were able to surpass Britain in economic growth.

THE British economy, once the workshop of the world, seems to have fallen victim to some century-long affliction. For lack of an adequate generic diagnosis, many observers have termed this affliction the "British disease."[1] There are signs, however, that the disease may be spreading, and the recent competitive reverses of American industry in the face of Japanese and European challenges have sparked renewed interest in explanations of economic growth and decline. The Japanese success in particular has recently received most of the attention from economists and policy makers, but there is yet, we would argue, much to be learned from Britain's economic failure.

In Britain itself, the ideology directing current government policy assumes that the nation's decline has been due to the obstruction of the self-regulating market economy by trade union power and state intervention. This ideological perspective finds intellectual reinforcement in orthodox economic theory that, in both its liberal and conservative variants, views the capitalist economy as fundamentally an atomistic market economy. According to economic orthodoxy, the perfection of market competition and economic prosperity go hand in hand.

Although this proposition goes back to the time of Adam Smith, it has

Journal of Economic History, Vol. XLIV, No. 2 (June 1984). © The Economic History Association. All rights reserved. ISSN 0022-0507.

Bernard Elbaum is Assistant Professor of Economics, Boston University, Boston, Massachusetts 02215, and William Lazonick is Associate Professor of Economics, Harvard University, Cambridge, Massachusetts 02138. This paper synthesizes new research on British industrial decline, much of which will appear in a forthcoming Oxford University Press volume edited by Elbaum and Lazonick. They wish to thank the participants at the Anglo-American Conference on the Decline of the British Economy (held at Boston University on September 30-October 1, 1983) for their help in shaping the perspective presented here, and to Lance Davis and Michael Edelstein for their comments at the 1983 Economic History Association meetings.

[1] See, for example, G. C. Allen, *The British Disease* (London, 1976).

never been adequately supported by comparative examination of the historical experiences of capitalist economies. In particular, the issue of Britain's decline has largely been avoided by neoclassical economic historians who have been preoccupied with demonstrating that turn-of-the-century British managers "did the best they could" by optimizing subject to given constraints.[2] Neoclassical economists who have confronted the problem of explaining national decline simply assume that the mainspring of the wealth of nations is free market competition and proceed as a matter of course to blame Britain's economic misfortunes on either market imperfections or "noneconomic" factors such as the cultural peculiarities of businessmen or workers.[3]

By contrast, the historical perspective presented below attributes the decline of the British economy to the rigid persistence of economic and social institutions from the nineteenth-century era of relatively atomistic competition. In such countries as the United States, Germany, and Japan, successful twentieth-century economic development has been based on mass production methods and corporate forms of managerial coordination. But in Britain adoption of these modern technological and organizational innovations was impeded by inherited socioeconomic constraints at the levels of the enterprise, industry, and society. Entrenched institutional structures—including the structures of industrial relations, industrial organization, educational systems, financial intermediation, international trade, and state-enterprise relations—constrained the ability of individuals, groups, or corporate entities to transform the productive system.

Britain's problem was that economic decision makers, lacking the individual or collective means to alter prevailing institutional constraints, in effect took them as "given." In failing to confront institutional constraints, British businessmen can justifiably be accused of "entrepreneurial failure."[4] But the cause of the failure was not simply cultural conservatism, as some historians have implied. If British society was pervaded by conservative mores, it was in this respect certainly no worse off than Japan or continental European countries that were precapitalist, tradition-bound societies when Britain was the workshop of the world. The thesis of entrepreneurial failure casts no light on why Britain, the first industrial nation, should have been less

[2] Donald N. McCloskey, ed., *Essays on a Mature Economy: Britain After 1840* (London, 1971); Donald N. McCloskey and Lars Sandberg, "From Damnation to Redemption: Judgments on the Late Victorian Entrepreneur," *Explorations in Economic History*, 9 (Fall 1971), 89–108; R. C. Floud, "Britain 1860–1914: A Survey," and L. G. Sandberg, "The Entrepreneur and Technological Change," both in *The Economic History of Britain since 1700*, ed. Roderick Floud and Donald McCloskey, vol. 2 (Cambridge, 1981).

[3] See, for example, Richard E. Caves, "Productivity Differences among Industries," in *Britain's Economic Performance*, ed. Richard E. Caves and Lawrence B. Krause (Washington, D.C., 1980).

[4] David Landes, *The Unbound Prometheus* (Cambridge, 1969), chap. 5; Martin Wiener, *English Culture and The Decline of the Industrial Spirit, 1850–1980* (Cambridge, 1981).

successful than later industrializers in shedding customary attitudes that encumbered economic performance.

Britain's distinctiveness derived less from the conservatism of its cultural values per se than from a matrix of rigid institutional structures that reinforced these values and obstructed individualistic as well as concerted efforts at economic renovation. In our view, the causes and consequences of such institutional rigidities remain central to understanding the long-term dynamics of economic development as well as the current crisis of the British economy.

THE CONSEQUENCES OF COMPETITIVE CAPITALISM

In the third quarter of the nineteenth century, the British economy experienced a "long boom" that represented the culmination of the world's first industrial revolution. After three centuries of international conflict for the control of world markets and after seven decades of intense capital investment in productive capacity, Britain emerged unchallenged in the world economy. On the basis of national domination of world markets, there was much in the way of opportunity for aspiring merchants and manufacturers. As they entered into commerce and industry, the structure of British industry became extremely competitive. By today's standards, Britain's major nineteenth-century staple industries—textiles, iron and steel, coal mining, shipbuilding, and engineering—were all composed of numerous firms with small market shares. Their industrial structures were also characterized by a high degree of vertical specialization: distribution of intermediate and final products relied upon well-developed market mechanisms, often involving specialized merchant firms.

The managerial organization and technology employed by nineteenth-century British firms were comparatively simple. Characteristically, firms were run by owner-proprietors or close family associates. Managerial staffs were small, and methods of cost accounting and production control were crude or nonexistent. The development of industrial techniques typically relied upon trial and error rather than systematic in-house research. Most enterprises were single-plant firms that specialized in particular lines of manufacture of intermediate or final products. Industries exhibited a high degree of regional concentration based upon geographical advantages as well as external economies provided by local access to skilled labor supplies, transport facilities and distribution networks, capital, and product markets.

Up to the 1870s the long-term financing for these business ventures came from country banks, personal family fortunes, and retained earnings. After the collapse of the country banks in the Great Depression of the 1870s, financial institutions had little involvement in the long-term finance of British industry. The purchasers of share capital tended instead to be individuals—among them many shopkeepers and skilled workers—who invested their savings locally. With British firms able to tap local as well as internal sources of long-term financing, there is no evidence that they were short of capital in the decades prior to World War I. The last decades of the nineteenth century also saw the extension of national banks and the development of a highly liquid national capital market. But industrial firms were reluctant to risk loss of control by issuing equity on the national market or incurring long-term debt. Financial institutions provided only short-term working capital to British industry (mainly through overdraft accounts), and as a result never developed the institutional expertise to serve the demand for long-term capital that did arise. Instead they exported most of their capital, usually in exchange for fixed-interest bonds, to finance large-scale (typically government-backed) foreign projects such as railroads. A consequence of these arrangements was the separation of provincial industrial enterprise from national financial institutions based in the City of London, a characteristic feature of the British economy well into the twentieth century.[5]

Another outcome of British capitalism as it developed in the last half of the nineteenth century was the consolidation of job control on the part of many groups of workers in industry. During the "long boom," individual capitalists, divided by competition, opted for collective accommodation with unions of skilled and strategically positioned workers rather than jeopardize the fortunes of their individual firms through industrial conflict while there were profits to be made. The labor movement also made important legislative gains that enhanced the ability of workers to organize unions, build up union treasuries, and stage successful strikes.

A distinguishing feature of the British labor movement was its two tiers of bargaining strength. Workplace organizations enjoyed substantial local autonomy in bargaining, backed by the leverage that national unions could exert on employers during disputes. From the fourth quarter of the nineteenth century, as intermittent but often prolonged recessions occurred and as foreign competition began to be felt by many industries, capitalists were unable to replace the job control of shop-floor union organizations by managerial control. Despite the introduction of many skill-displacing changes in technology, the power of the union organizations that had developed earlier had simply become too great. Attempts by Parliament and the judiciary to undermine the trade union movement—most notably by means of the Taff Vale decision—resulted in the emergence of a distinct political party representing the interests of labor.

---

[5] Michael Best and Jane Humphries, "The City and the Decline of British Industry," in *The Decline of the British Economy*, ed. Bernard Elbaum and William Lazonick (Oxford, forthcoming).

THE CHALLENGE OF CORPORATE CAPITALISM

Elsewhere, from the late nineteenth century (notably in Japan, Germany, and the United States) corporate capitalism was emerging to become the dominant mode of economic organization. Corporate capitalism was characterized by industrial oligopoly, hierarchical managerial bureaucracy, vertical integration of production and distribution, managerial control over the labor process, the integration of financial and industrial capital, and systematic research and development.[6]

Oligopoly, by helping to stabilize prices and market shares, facilitated long-run planning, particularly where large-scale capital investments were involved. Managerial coordination of product flows within the vertically integrated enterprise permitted the achievement of high-speed throughputs that reduced unit costs. Vertical integration of production and distribution provided the direct access to market outlets that was a precondition for the effective utilization of mass production methods. Managerial control over the labor process in turn facilitated the introduction of new, high-throughput technologies. Integration of financial and industrial capital, along with managerial bureaucracy, made possible the geographic mobility of capital and the rapid expansion of capacity to produce for new or growing markets. Systematic research and development, particularly in such science-based industries as electrical and chemical manufacturing, provided the mainspring of technological innovation. Across countries, the degree of coordination of economic activity by the state and large financial institutions varied, with significant implications for economic performance. But the experience of successful capitalist economies in the twentieth century demonstrates the ubiquitous importance of the visible hand of corporate bureaucratic management.

In order to compete against the corporate mass production methods being developed in Germany, Japan, and the United States, British industries required transformation of their structures of industrial relations, industrial organization, and enterprise management. Vested interests in the old structures, however, proved to be formidable (if not insurmountable) obstacles to the transition from competitive to corporate modes of organization. Lacking corporate management skills and opportunities, British industrialists clung to family control of their firms. Even where horizontal amalgamations did take place, the directors of the participating firms insisted on retaining operational autonomy.[7] In any case, very few of these managers had the broader

---

[6] Alfred D. Chandler, Jr., *The Visible Hand* (Cambridge, Massachusetts, 1977); Alfred D. Chandler, Jr., and Herman Daems, eds., *Managerial Hierarchies* (Cambridge, Massachusetts, 1980).

[7] Leslie Hannah, *The Rise of the Corporate Economy: The British Experience* (Baltimore, 1976); Alfred D. Chandler, Jr., "The Growth of the Transnational Industrial Firm in the United States and the United Kingdom: A Comparative Analysis," *Economic History Review*, 2nd ser., 33 (Aug. 1980).

entrepreneurial perspectives or skills needed to develop modern corporate structures.[8]

The British educational system hampered industry by failing to provide appropriately trained managerial and technical personnel. On the supply side, the existing system of higher education was designed almost explicitly to remove its "aristocratic" students as far as possible from the worldly pursuit of business and applied science.[9] On the demand side, there was comparatively little pressure to transform this system as highly competitive businesses could not afford to hire specialized technical personnel and were further reluctant to support industry-wide research institutes that would benefit competitors as much as themselves.[10] Given the lack of interest of business and the educational establishment in fostering managerial and technical training, it is not surprising that the British state, rather passive towards industrial development in any case, took little initiative to make education more relevant to economic development.

Nor was leadership for industrial transformation forthcoming from other sectors of the British economy. The financial sector kept its distance from direct involvement in industry, preferring instead to maintain its highly liquid position by means of portfolio investment, mostly abroad. The orientation of Britain's bankers towards liquidity and protection of the value of the pound sterling was reinforced by the undisputed position of the City of London as the financial center of the world. The concentration of banking in the City also gave rise to a relatively cohesive class of finance capitalists with much more concerted and coherent power over national policy than industrial capitalists, who were divided along enterprise, industry, and regional lines.

In the absence of a shift to corporate enterprise structure, British industrialists also had little incentive or ability to challenge the shop-floor control of trade union organizations. In the United States and Germany a critical factor in the development of high-throughput production was the ability of management to gain and maintain the right to manage the utilization of technology. In most of Britain's staple industries, by contrast, managers had lost much of this "right to manage," reducing their incentive to invest in costly mass production technologies on which they might not be able to achieve high enough throughputs to justify the capital outlays. During the first half of the twentieth century, British unionism was able to consolidate its positions of control at both the national and workplace levels, aided by the

---

[8] William Lazonick, "Industrial Organization and Technological Change: The Decline of the British Cotton Industry," *Business History Review*, 57 (Summer 1983), 195–236.

[9] Julia Wrigley, "Seeds of Decline: Technical Education and Industry in Britain," in *The Decline of the British Economy*.

[10] David Mowery, "British and American Industrial Research: A Comparison, 1900–1950," in *The Decline of the British Economy*.

growing strength of the Labour Party and the emergency conditions of two world wars.

Lacking the requisite degree of control over product and input markets, British managers confronted severe obstacles in adapting their enterprise structures to take advantage of new market opportunities. As a result, in the late nineteenth and early twentieth centuries firms continued for the most part to manufacture traditional products using traditional technologies.

How these firms structured production depended very much on the prospects for selling their output. Contrary to typical textbook theory, Britain's competitive firms did not as a rule assume that the market could absorb all the output they might produce at a given price. Indeed they produced few manufactures in anticipation of demand: Almost all production was to order, much of it for sale to merchants for distribution to far-flung international markets.

In the heyday of British worldwide economic dominance, these arrangements proved advantageous to British firms. Unlike many of their international competitors, who had access only to much more confining markets, Britain's international marketing structure meant that British firms could get enough orders of similar specifications to reap economies of long production runs, and had a large enough share in expanding markets to justify investment in (what were then) up-to-date and increasingly capital-intensive plant and equipment. But the tables were turned by the spread abroad of tariff barriers and indigenous industrialization. Because Britain had already industrialized, its domestic market for such staple commodities as textiles or steel rails had reached a point of at best moderate growth potential. Under these circumstances, British firms could not find at home a market that could match the dramatic rates of expansion of the foreign markets foreclosed to them. Indeed, given its dependence on international markets, British industry was severely constrained to keep its own domestic markets open to the products of foreign firms.

Taking advantage of their more secure and expansive domestic markets, foreign rivals, with more modern, capital-intensive technology, attained longer production runs and higher speeds of throughput than the British. By virtue of their reliance on the corporate form of organization—in particular on vertical integration of production with distribution and more concentrated market power—Britain's rivals were better able to rationalize the structure of orders and ensure themselves the market outlets required for mass production. From secure home bases these rivals also invaded market areas and product lines where the British should have been at no comparative disadvantage.

Forced to retreat from competition with mass production methods, British firms sought refuge in higher quality and more specialized

Elbaum and Lazonick

product lines where traditional craftsmanship and organization could still command a competitive edge—in spinning higher counts of yarn and weaving finer cloth, making sheets and plates of open hearth steel, and building unique one-off ships. Unfortunately for the British, in a world of expanding markets, the specialized product of the day all too often turned out to be the mass production item of tomorrow. The arrival of mass production methods and the pace and timing of decline varied among the major staple industries, with British shipbuilding, for example, still holding a commanding competitive position as late as World War II. But all eventually met a similar fate.[11]

INSTITUTIONAL RIGIDITY

From the standpoint of the neoclassical model of competition, these developments would lead one to expect a British response to competitive pressures that would imitate the organizational and technological innovations introduced abroad. In fact, the British only adapted patchwork improvements to their existing organizational and productive structure. Facing increasingly insecure markets and lacking the market control requisite for modern mass production, the British failed to make the organizational renovations that could have allowed them to escape competitive decline.

With the massive contractions of British market shares that occurred in the 1920s and early 1930s, firms in the troubled staple industries alternated between scrambling for any markets they could get and proposals for elimination of excess capacity and concentration of productive structure. In a period of contraction the market mechanism was anything but an efficient allocation mechanism, in part because existing firms remained in operation as long as they could hope for some positive return over variable costs, their proprietors living, so to speak, off their capital. Coordinated attempts to eliminate excess capacity were confounded by numerous conflicts of interest between owner-proprietors, outside stockholders, management groups, customers, banks and other creditors, and local union organizations. In particular the involvement of the national banks in the attempts to rationalize industry was aimed more at salvaging their individual financial positions than at developing a coherent plan for industry revitalization. In light of the failure to achieve coordination the rationalization programs that were implemented in the interwar period were half-hearted and of limited effectiveness.

During the interwar period and beyond, the rigid work rules of British

---

[11] Edward Lorenz and Frank Wilkinson, "Shipbuilding and British Economic Decline, 1880–1965"; Bernard Elbaum, "British Steel Industry Structure and Performance before World War I"; William Lazonick, "The Decline of the British Cotton Industry"; Stephen Tolliday, "Industry, Finance, and the State: Steel and Rationalization Policy"; all in *The Decline of the British Economy*.

unions remained an impediment to structural reorganization. Entrenched systems of piece-rate payment often led to higher wage
earnings in more productive establishments, deterring firms from scrapping old capacity and investing in new. Union rules also limited
management's freedom to alter manning levels and workloads, which in
mechanical, labor-intensive industries such as textiles had particularly
adverse effects on the prospective benefits of new technology.[12] In
general, management could be sure that the unions would attempt to
exact a high price for cooperation with any plans for reorganization that
would upset established work and pay arrangements. On the other
hand, amidst industrial decline the strong union preference for saving
jobs even at low wage levels was an additional conservative influence
on a generally unenterprising managerial class.

Given this institutional structure, Britain's staple industries were unable
to rationalize on the basis of the profit motive. They relied too much—not
too little—on the market mechanism. To be sure, there were some highly
successful enterprises such as Imperial Chemical Industries and Unilever
that emerged in new industries during the interwar period.[13] But in terms
of our perspective on capitalist development, these firms are the exceptions that prove the rule: success was ultimately based on control over
product and input markets and the ability to transform internal managerial
and production structures to maintain control. Furthermore, even the new
industries were not immune to the wider institutional environment. The
slow growth of demand in new product market areas hampered the
emergence of large firms and created a need for consolidation of industrial
structure. In chemicals, fabricated metals, and electrical machinery, newly
amalgamated firms suffered from a dearth of appropriately trained managerial personnel and, initially, experienced serious difficulties in overcoming
vested interests and in establishing effective coordination of their enterprises. In automobile manufacturing, competitive performance was undermined after World War II by a long-established management strategy of
using labor-intensive techniques that helped breed control of shop-floor
activities by highly sectionalized union organizations.[14]

THE IMPACT ON GROWTH

If difficult to quantify precisely, the overall impact of these institutional rigidities on British economic performance was undoubtedly

[12] Lorenz and Wilkinson, "Shipbuilding and British Economic Decline," and Lazonick, "The Decline of the British Cotton Industry."

[13] William Reader, *Imperial Chemical Industries: A History*, 2 vols. (Oxford, 1972); Charles Wilson, *The History of Unilever: A Study of Economic Growth and Social Change*, 2 vols. (London, 1954), and *Unilever 1945–1965: Challenge and Response in the Post-War Industrial Revolution* (London, 1965).

[14] Wayne Lewchuk, "The British Motor Vehicle Industry: The Roots of Decline," in *The Decline of the British Economy.*

576 *Elbaum and Lazonick*

considerable. Throughout the pre-World War I years, the staple industries remained economically preponderant. According to the 1907 Census of Production, the largest of these industries—coal, iron and steel (including non-electrical machinery and railway equipment), textiles, and shipbuilding—alone made up roughly 50 percent of total net domestic industrial production and 70 percent of British exports. During the long boom of the third quarter of the nineteenth century there was a rapid increase in British output per head that drew important impetus from growth and technological advance in the staple industries.[15] Subsequently, from 1873 to 1913 a marked slowdown in aggregate productivity growth occurred, with some evidence that growth was particularly sluggish from the late 1890s to World War I.

Detailed industry-level evidence is useful for assessing the accuracy of the aggregate data and the reasons for the prewar productivity slowdown. British cotton enterprises, for example, did not reorganize the vertical structure of production in order to adopt more advanced technologies. Instead they chose to compete on the basis of traditional organization and techniques by cutting raw material costs and intensifying workloads.[16] The resultant cost-savings, augmented by the benefits of well-developed external economies, enabled the cotton industry to expand its output and exports despite stagnating labor productivity in the 15 years or so before World War I. In the British steel industry there was significant ongoing productivity advance in the newer sectors of open hearth steelmaking. Bessemer practice, however, was comparatively stagnant after 1890 as firms were deterred from investing in new, large-scale facilities by a sluggish domestic market, overseas protection, an increasing threat from foreign imports, and fragmented industrial structure.[17]

British growth in output per head not only slowed in the last quarter of the nineteenth century, but also began to lag relative to latter-day industrializing economies that were developing the institutional bases for corporate capitalism. British growth rates first fell behind those of other countries in the 1870s and 1880s. Serious losses in international competition were first sustained between 1899 and 1913 and were interlinked with the failure of British industry to match the productivity advances achieved abroad by fully availing itself of the benefits of mass production methods. With the exception of wartime intervals, the gap in relative productivity growth performance between Britain and most of its competitors has remained substantial ever since.

During the interwar period the competitive weaknesses of the staple

---

[15] R. C. O. Matthews, C. H. Feinstein, and J. C. Odling-Smee, *British Economic Growth, 1856–1973* (Stanford, 1982), p. 26.

[16] William Lazonick and William Mass, "The Performance of the British Cotton Industry, 1870–1913," *Research in Economic History*, 9 (Spring 1984).

[17] Elbaum, "British Steel Industry Structure and Performance."

industries became evident, while the productivity performance of the British economy as a whole remained poor by international standards. There remains, however, considerable controversy over the connection between the performance of the staple industries and that of the aggregate economy. According to one influential perspective, the weak performance of the interwar economy was largely due to the relative lack of mobility of resources from the "old" to the "new" industries.[18] This argument, however, is open to criticism on several grounds. It assumes that the old industries imposed effective supply constraints on the growth of the new—a rather dubious proposition given the high unemployment levels, ongoing capital export, and the housing boom that characterized the interwar period. If there were supply constraints on the growth of the new industries it was because of the failure of financial and educational institutions to infuse industry with sufficient long-term venture capital and the types of personnel required.

This argument also implies that the basic problem of the British economy was one of structural adjustment out of industries in which comparative advantage had been lost and possibilities for technical advance had for the most part been exhausted. Yet there is little evidence that shifts in comparative advantage were the root of the competitive problems of Britain's staple industries. Some international competitors in these industries, facing prices for labor and resources greater than or equal to the British, were nonetheless more successful because they adopted major technical advances. Recent evidence also indicates that interwar productivity gains in Britain's staple industries were comparable to those in the new industries (although much of the measured gains in productivity reflect the closure of obsolescent capacity).

The staple industries contributed significantly to Britain's relatively poor interwar growth performance mainly because they still bulked large in the economy and lagged behind seriously in international standards of technological and managerial practice. In 1924 staple manufacturing industries still accounted for 45 percent of all manufacturing net output. By 1935 this figure had fallen to 35 percent but remained at roughly that proportion into the late 1940s.[19] With persistent excess capacity in the staple industries, firms that had long ago written off their plant and equipment always stood ready to "ruin the market" for firms that might otherwise have invested in the modernization of plant and equipment and enterprise structure. Divided by competition, the firms of Britain's staple industries were unable on their own to rationalize capacity.

[18] Derek H. Aldcroft and H. W. Richardson, *The British Economy, 1870–1939* (London, 1969).
[19] G. N. von Tunzelmann, "Structural Change and Leading Sectors in British Manufacturing, 1907–1968," in *Economics in the Long View*, ed. Charles P. Kindleberger and Guido di Tella (New York, 1982), vol. 3, pp. 28–30.

578   *Elbaum and Lazonick*

THE BARELY VISIBLE HAND

What British industry in general required was the visible hand of coordinated control, not the invisible hand of the self-regulating market. Given the absence of leadership from within private industry, increasing pressure fell upon the state to try to fill the gap. Even before World War I, calls were made for greater state intervention. By the interwar period the British state had assumed a distinctly more prominent role in industrial affairs, macroeconomic regulation, and provision of social and welfare services.[20]

With further growth of state intervention after World War II— extending to nationalization of industry and aggregate demand management—critics have pointed accusing fingers at the government for failing to reverse, and even for causing, relative economic decline. At various times and from various quarters the state has been blamed for undermining private-sector incentives and the natural regenerative processes of the free market economy, for absorbing resources that would have been employed more productively in manufacturing, or for failing to provide British industry with a needed environment of macroeconomic stability and a competitively valued exchange rate.

In historical perspective, however, state activism must be absolved from bearing primary responsibility for Britain's relatively poor economic performance. In the late nineteenth century, at the outset of relative decline, the most singular features of the British state were its small size and laissez-faire policies. Even in the post-World War II period, British levels of government taxes, expenditures, and employment were not particularly high by European standards. Indeed, a distinctive feature of British state policy throughout recent history has been its reluctance to break from laissez-faire traditions. It is only in the second instance that state policy is implicated in British decline, by virtue of its failure to intervene in the economy more decisively in order to take corrective measures. The consequences of this failure of state policy first became evident in the interwar period.[21]

THE LIMITS OF INTERWAR INTERVENTION

The Irrationalities of Rationalization Policy

State intervention between the wars included programs aimed at rationalizing the depressed staple industries in order to rid them of excess capacity and facilitate modernization. The problem of excess capacity had been exacerbated by the vast and imprudent expansion of

[20] Charles Feinstein, ed., *The Managed Economy* (Oxford, 1983).
[21] Peter Hall, "The State and Economic Decline in Britain," in *The Decline of the British Economy*.

Decline of the British Economy   579

investment and overdraft borrowing during the short but frenetic boom of 1920/21. The prolonged state of depressed trade that followed in the 1920s placed the banks' loans in serious jeopardy. At that time the Labour government was also considering direct intervention as a means of reorganizing the failing industries and alleviating industrial depression. This combination of circumstances prompted the Bank of England to step in.

For the Bank, rationalization was an economically viable and politically desirable alternative to more far-reaching forms of government intervention that threatened to go as far as nationalization and "encroaching socialism." Bank of England Governor Montagu Norman conceived of intervention as limited, temporary, and exceptional. The Bank's approach was highly consensual and "quasi-corporatist." Firms were encouraged to form trade associations and develop their own plans for industry rationalization. Within the trade associations, firms were authorized to negotiate common pricing policies, mergers, and production quotas. Even then individual firms were reluctant to have the Bank of England intervene, and it was only the stick of bankruptcy and the carrot of support for tariff protection that enabled it to do so.[22]

When the Bank intervened more directly, it was as a merger promoter rather than as an investment bank. Where the market did not respond, the Bank was unwilling to put up its own funds. With the Bank and Treasury allied in keeping a tight hold on the public purse strings, the public funds devoted to backing rationalization schemes were negligible. Yet the Bank found that its efforts at voluntary persuasion had little influence over the allocation of market sources of finance.[23]

As for the government, its interwar industrial policies were confined largely to monitoring industrial affairs through the Import Duties Advisory Committee, established under the 1932 tariff legislation, and to legislative schemes aimed at reducing excess capacity in industries such as textiles. Like the Bank of England, the Advisory Committee pursued influence through conciliation and suasion, seeking no powers of centralized control over industry. Lacking the requisite authority to shape industrial development, the committee found itself overseeing a process of industrial quasi-cartellization that ensured profits for weak and strong firms alike. Government legislation generally responded to the wishes of industry trade associations with similar results.

Public attempts at rationalization left British industry with the worst aspects of both competitive and monopolistic worlds. Productive structure remained highly fragmented and inefficient, while quasi-cartellization and tariff barriers (or imperial preference) protected existing producers from competitive pressure. Rather than achieving its objec-

[22] Best and Humphries, "The City and the Decline of British Industry"; Lazonick, "The Decline of the British Cotton Industry"; Tolliday, "Industry, Finance, and the State."

[23] Tolliday, "Industry, Finance, and the State."

tive of promoting industry rationalization, interwar policy inadvertently reinforced preexisting institutional rigidities.

The Underdevelopment of Industrial Research

State policy initiatives in the area of research and development originated at the onset of World War I with concern over the inability of British industry to supply technologically sophisticated materials of strategic military importance. Major policy initiatives included the establishment of a state-owned corporation (British Dyestuffs) and state-subsidized industrial research associations for the promotion of cooperative research and development by firms in the private sector. British Dyestuffs, however, was handicapped by a lack of trained chemists in top management positions and a reliance on chairs in universities for research efforts.

Government promotion of industrial research associations reflected a concern that few firms in Britain were large enough to undertake their own in-house research and development programs. As many as 24 Research Associations were established in industries ranging from woolen textiles to laundering. But firms often lacked the in-house technical expertise required to evaluate and employ the results of extramural research. As a result, Research Associations failed to gather the anticipated financial support from the private sector, and their impact on innovative performance was modest. Government-sponsored cooperative research proved to be an inadequate replacement for the in-house research capabilities of modern corporations.[24]

The Ruin of the Regions

Industrial decline in the interwar period created severe problems of regional unemployment and decaying infrastructure because of the high degree of local concentration of the staple industries. Interwar regional policies were, however, a limited and ad hoc response to diverse political pressures for regional aid, rather than a coherent attempt to deal with the social costs and benefits of relocation of economic activity. The most consistent element in regional policy was the reluctance of the government to become directly involved in industrial development. Instead, the state sought to alleviate regional disparities by policies directed towards improving the operation of labor and capital markets.

The effectiveness of these policies was constrained by macroeconomic conditions, the limited size of the programs, and the underlying assumption that facilitating the operation of market mechanisms would suffice to combat regional problems. Initially, the government promoted labor transference by providing assistance for individual workers or

---

[24] Mowery, "British and American Industrial Research."

households to move to more prosperous regions. But the unemployed workers in the depressed regions were mainly adult males, who were heavily unionized, whereas many of the expanding industries sought primarily new entrants to the labor force, particularly women and juveniles.

By 1937 the emphasis had shifted to moving jobs to unemployed workers by providing businesses with special sources of finance and subsidized factory rentals. Provision of capital to firms in the depressed areas, however, could not overcome the limits on investment demand posed by depressed regional markets. Nor could it overcome the inability of the single-industry family firms that predominated in interwar Britain to manage diversified industrial and regional operations. Expanding industries, which had already begun to develop in the South prior to the stagnation of the 1920s, continued to grow in these more prosperous areas during the interwar period.[25]

The Protection of the Pound

Following the lead of Keynes, a long line of economists have argued that interwar macroeconomic policies had seriously adverse effects on the British economy. A contrast is often drawn between the industrial depression of the 1920s, when restrictive policies preceded the 1925 resumption of the gold standard at the prewar parity, and the relatively strong performance of the economy in the 1930s, when devaluation and protectionism were forced upon the government. Yet if the deflationary impact of the macroeconomic policies of the 1920s seems beyond dispute, there has been a lively debate about its significance for the trend in growth of output per head. Detailed examination of the staple industries, which were the most seriously affected by the 1920s depression, indicates that slack domestic demand, intensified international competitive pressure, and high interest rates *exacerbated* rather than caused problems of excess capacity, shrinking profit margins, and a heavy debt burden. The problems of the staple industries were structural and long-term in character, and if dramatized during the low waters of recession, were also an increasingly evident undertow during the high tides of prosperity before and after the interwar period.

THE LEGACY OF HISTORY

The British economy of the post-World War II period inherited a legacy of major industries too troubled to survive the renewed onslaught of international competition that began in the 1950s. As competitive pressure mounted, the state began to nationalize industries such as coal,

[25] Carol Heim, "Regional Development and National Decline: The Evolution of Regional Policy in Interwar Britain," in *The Decline of the British Economy*.

steel, and automobiles that were deemed of strategic importance to the nation, and (with the exception of steel in 1951) that were in imminent danger of collapse. But nationalization, however necessary, was by no means a sufficient response to Britain's long-run economic decline. Public ownership overcame the problem of horizontally fragmented private ownership, but not inherited problems of enterprise productive structure, managerial organization, and union job control. Nationalized enterprises still had to confront these problems while attempting to overcome the technological leads already established by competitors.

Although the British government was called upon willy-nilly to play an increased role in industrial affairs, the basic theoretical and ideological framework guiding public policy has remained that of the self-regulating market economy. The rise of Keynesianism has led to widespread acceptance of interventionist fiscal and monetary policies, but for the most part has left unchallenged the neoclassical belief in the inherent dynamism of unfettered market competition.

The monetarist policies of the Thatcher government have taken the neoclassical perspective to its extreme. Invoking laissez faire ideology, Thatcher has attacked the power of the unions and sought revival through the severity of market discipline. But the supposition that there are forces latent in Britain's "free market" economy that will return the nation to prosperity finds little confirmation in historical experience. The only foundation for the free-market perspective appears to be the tradition of orthodox economic theory itself.

There is considerable irony in the neoclassical focus on free market competition as the engine of economic dynamism. The focus derives from the fundamental assumption of neoclassical theory that firms are subordinate to markets. History suggests, however, that successful development in the twentieth century has been achieved by markets being made subordinate to firms. The main thrust of the perspective presented here is that the British economy failed to make a successful transition to corporate capitalism in the twentieth century precisely because of the very highly developed market organization of the economy that had evolved when it was the first and foremost industrial nation.

By now, Britain's relative economic decline has persisted through enough ups and downs in the business cycle to indicate that its roots lie deeper than inappropriate macroeconomic policies. If contemporary economic discussion nonetheless is usually preoccupied with obtaining the right monetary and fiscal policies, it is because there has been comparatively little criticism of the microfoundations of neoclassical theory and related versions of laissez faire ideology. Despite the prominence of mass production methods in corporate economies, conventional economic theory has failed to analyze the associated developmental process of productivity growth and technological change.

If existing institutional arrangements seriously constrained the actions of individual British industrialists and rendered impotent intervention by the state, the example of late-developing nations suggests that a purposive national program can enjoy considerable success in adapting institutions to meet growth objectives. The task for political economy is to identify those elements of the prevailing institutional structure that will promote and those that will hinder alternative strategies of socio-economic development. The argument presented here contends that planning at the levels of the enterprise, financial institutions, and the state has become increasingly important for international competitiveness and economic growth, even within the so-called market economies. To elaborate and modify this perspective will require historical studies of the interaction of planning and market forces in economic activity and the resultant impact on performance. Thus far we have only begun to research this perspective, and to test the various hypotheses generated by it. But we view the synthesis presented here, as well as the research upon which it is based, as important foundations for understanding modern economic development.

[17]

Peter L. Payne

Entrepreneurship and British Economic Decline

'It is now conventional wisdom that, for some hundred years or so, British growth and especially productivity performance have been deeply disappointing when compared with that of other advanced countries. More contentious, but nevertheless widely held, is the belief that the failures of the post war economy are deeply rooted in the past, presenting successive governments both with an unenviable legacy and a most daunting task in their aspiration to remedy Britain's relative economic decline.'[1] With these words, Nick Crafts introduces a valuable collection of articles concerned with the long-run economic performance of the economy of the United Kingdom. If they do nothing else, these papers reveal the sheer complexity of the causes of Britain's relative economic decline. The object of this essay is to examine just one of the inter-related factors involved: the role of entrepreneurship, but in discussing this factor a conscious attempt has been made to consider a number of cultural and institutional influences bearing upon it.

I

Let us be quite clear at the outset, criticism of the British entrepreneur is no new phenomenon: it goes back to the closing decades of the last century when Britain's international economic dominance, once so obvious, especially in manufacturing, was seen to be passing to the United States and to Germany. But the modern debate, and its relevance to explaining the *relative* decline of Britain's rate of economic growth, essentially dates back to the appearance of David Landes' paper on 'Entrepreneurship in Advanced Industrial Countries: The Anglo-German Rivalry', which was presented at a conference at Harvard in November, 1954, and which, extended and elaborated, was reborn as his contribution to the sixth volume of the *Cambridge Economic History of Europe* in 1965.[2] Meanwhile, there had appeared Habakkuk's seminal essay on *America and British Technology* in 1962, and Derek Aldcroft's essay on 'The Entrepreneur and the British Economy, 1870–1914'. This was published in the *Economic History Review* in 1964, and it provoked a counterblast by Charles Wilson in the following year.[3]

There followed a number of general assessments of entrepreneurial performance, of which perhaps the most well known is A. L. Levine's *Industrial Retardation in Britain, 1880–1914* (1967). There was also the curiously neglected essay by Eric Sigsworth, 'Some Problems in Business History, 1870–1914' (1969), a remarkably perceptive synthesis which, like Francois Crouzet's much later study on *The Victorian Economy* (1982), made considerable use of the collection of essays assembled by Derek Aldcroft on the responses of a wide variety of British industries to foreign competition between 1875 and 1914.[4] Not the least interesting of the findings which emerged from these essays – the commissioning of which, it was always understood, was to give greater credence to Aldcroft's criticisms of the British entrepreneur – was that the various authors found all too little to condemn. Furthermore, additional industrial studies, like those of Roy Church (on boots and shoes) and A. E. Harrison (cycles, 1969), reached similar conclusions, as did the papers presented to the Mathematical Social Science Board Conference on the New Economic History of Britain held at Harvard University in 1970 and Theo Barker's contribution to *The Twentieth Century Mind*.[5]

But these were, essentially, negative findings: the majority of British authors of case studies of industries and individual firms – ever growing in number and sophistication – could find little or no *evidence* of entrepreneurial failure. Their conclusions were unsatisfactory to a number of American econometric historians. To them, the measures of performance previously employed were inadequate on theoretical and methodological grounds. To Donald McCloskey and Lars Sandberg, foremost among the American cliometricians, the only legitimate way to arrive at a proper conclusion concerning the relative importance of entrepreneurial failure – if such proved to exist – was by quantitative methods, the selection of which should be determined by the application of explicit economic models.[6] Utilizing this more rigorous approach, McCloskey found that British iron and steel masters exploited the potentialities of world technology before the First World War as well as, if not better than, their much lauded American competitors: 'Late nineteenth-century entrepreneurs in iron and steel did not fail. By any cogent measure of performance, in fact, they did very well indeed'.[7] Similarly, Sandberg, after examining Britain's lag in adopting ring-spinning and in installing automatic looms in cotton manufacture, concluded that 'under the conditions then prevailing with regard to factor costs, as well as the technical capabilities of the ring spindles then being built, the British may well have been acting rationally'. He could, moreover, find no evidence that firms installing automatic looms at the time the cotton industry was beginning to be criticised for ignoring them expanded faster or made larger profits than their more conservative competitors'.[8] On the basis of these and other studies, McCloskey expressed the belief that there was 'little left of the dismal picture of British failure painted by historians'.[9]

Essentially, this seemed to represent the state of play, especially concerning what I labelled 'the critical period' between 1870 and 1913, when I attempted to survey the debate on British entrepreneurship from c1815 to 1970 for the seventh volume of the Cambridge Economic History and, a little later, for the nineteenth century alone, for the pamphlet series of the Economic History Society.[10] Yet, however convincing the evidence for abandoning the concept of entrepreneurial failure (and hence the relevance of this possible explanation of British economic decline), I could not resist expressing certain doubts, imprecise and imperfectly articulated though they were.[11] To obscure my ignorance, I adopted the craven – though academically respectable – tactic of posing a series of questions to which further answers were required. These included the yardsticks necessary for the measurement of success or failure, and the desirability of determining the significance of the entrepreneurial factor in

28   *British Culture and Economic Decline*

Britain's manifestly accelerating relative decline *since* the First World War.

II

In the last ten years or so, much new material has appeared and, partly as a consequence, it has been possible more clearly to interpret evidence that even by the mid-seventies was already available but whose significance had wholly or partially escaped me. It is unnecessary, indeed impossible, comprehensively to survey the new information. I must confine myself to touching upon a number of relevant issues.

Let me begin by confessing that in observing that the authors who contributed to Derek Aldcroft's collection of essays had discovered little hard evidence of British entrepreneurial failure in the half century preceding the First World War, I was greatly influenced by my own belief that it was extremely difficult to perceive glaring errors from the records of individual firms. It can be done, of course. Roy Church has demonstrated as much by his masterly investigation of Kenricks;[12] but all too often the inquirer is forced to conclude that, with the information apparently available to the firms themselves, major decisions seem to have been perfectly *rational* in the context of future profitability, although the attainment of such an objective was frequently tempered – even compromised – by social considerations, a point most recently emphasized by Jonathan Boswell and Harold Perkin.[13]

I have always believed that the correctness or ineptitude of entrepreneurial decisions must be assessed within the context of the firm. This means that if, for example, innovations 'do not yield reductions in average unit costs, then it would be irrational for a businessman to introduce them even if the innovations would benefit the future growth of the economy'.[14] It also means that decisions are sometimes arrived at which deliberately eschew maximum profitability because of a conscious awareness that the social cost would be too great; that, in Samuel Courtauld's words, 'the highest rate of profit should not be the over-riding consideration'.[15]

It will be clear that, like McCloskey and Sandberg, I have envisaged businessmen as neo-classical managers optimizing profits subject to given constraints. Not surprisingly, as Leslie Han-

Entrepreneurship and British Economic Decline   29

nah has observed, it has not been difficult to give them 'a clean bill of health'.[16] And yet, as he says, one cannot ignore the fact that between, say, the 1880s and the inter-war years Britain's rate of economic growth was relatively slow[17] and that her international position was deteriorating, mainly because other nations were either making more efficient use of existing resources or shifting resources into new industries and new markets when we remained wedded to well-tried ways in old industries.

In explaining this failure, Lazonick has appealed to us to abandon neo-classical concepts and to embrace a Schumpeterian definition of the entrepreneur as one who fundamentally changes his industrial environment by bursting out of the organizational constraints that narrow his feasible technological choices and profitable opportunities.[18] Looked at in this way, clearly there was – and still is – entrepreneurial failure. Taking Lazonick's own field of research, for example, 'the vast majority of businessmen in the British cotton industry ... had neither the incentive to participate nor the ability to lead in the internal transformation of their industry. The competitive and specialized organization of the industry had developed a breed of managers with specialized skills and individualistic attitudes who were not only ill-suited for involvement in a transition from competitive to corporate capitalism but also by their very presence obstructed such a transition ... The result was prolonged technological backwardness and industrial decline'.[19]

In this, as in the other industries considered by Elbaum, Lazonick and their associates, British businessmen are accused of entrepreneurial failure because they failed 'to confront institutional constraints innovatively'.[20] Only by the replacement of the atomistic, competitive organization of British industry by a corporate, concentrated, managerial structure capable of superseding the market as an allocative mechanism could British decline be halted or even reversed. Adam Smith had to give way to Alfred Chandler: the invisible hand of the self-regulating market to the visible hand of co-ordinated control.[21] Leaving aside the major question of whether this *would* have achieved a higher rate of economic growth, why did this not occur? Elbaum and Lazonick feel that it cannot be adequately explained by reference to 'cultural conservatism'; more significant was the matrix of rigid institutional structures that 'obstructed individualistic as well as collective efforts of economic renovation ... Entrenched

30   *British Culture and Economic Decline*

institutional structures – in industrial relations, enterprise and market organizations, education, finance, international trade, and state-enterprise relations – constrained the transformation of Britain's productive system'.[22] All economic historians are indebted to Elbaum and Lazonick for focusing attention on the question of institutional adaptation. They have, in effect, given substance to the generalities of Mancur Olsen,[23] and one cannot help believing that much future work will necessarily be involved with illustrating, refining and assessing their approach, which represents a major advance in understanding Britain's relative economic decline.

Just how far it will further our knowledge of the role of the entrepreneur in this decline, I remain uncertain. It seems to me that on this score, their arguments and the definitions they employ – however convincing their case for clarification in this regard – take us less further forward than my initial exposure to their ideas led me to believe. If neo-classical theory is inappropriate in the assessment of entrepreneurship, the use of Schumpeterian concepts also contain a definitionally determined answer.[24] Let me ask a question. In the current take-over mania, there can be little question that institutional rigidities are being seriously eroded. Are we then witnessing a belated upsurge in British entrepreneurship? Will British industry be revitalized by the massive restructuring currently underway? It remains to be seen, but it requires the exercise of considerable optimism to believe that the present ferment of leveraged buy-outs, 'junk bonds' and unbundling will necessarily lead to the regeneration of the British economy. To achieve this, the visible hand requires to be actuated by a Schumpeterian brain, not one motivated simply by the desire to achieve short-term financial advantage.

One cannot but be concerned by the evidence that only rarely do mergers lead to increased efficiency (and hence real economic growth).[25] Lazonick's belief in the beneficial consequences of the large corporation – while receiving some support from Hannah – seems to ignore the danger implicit in the larger firm that bureaucratization and adherence to routine and tradition might stifle – rather than promote – innovation.[26] It is indeed part of the folklore of monopoly capitalism that patents have sometimes been purchased and suppressed: the visible hand may throttle the goose that lays the golden eggs. Big is *not necessarily* beautiful (or growth-inducing), a point to which I drew attention in 1978.[27] In the context of my present argument, it might be

added that if the growth of the firm has been achieved by acquisition by shares, the share price has to be maintained, and for
this reason there is a tendency to disperse profits rather than
retain them within the enterprise.[28] Furthermore, there is growing evidence that mergers do not result in synergistic increases
in profitability, but have an averaging effect: companies with
above normal profits have their profits lowered by mergers; companies with initially sub-normal profits have them raised. The
consequence may or may not be increased net real investment.[29]
The post-merger structure of a giant firm or of an industry may
have Schumpeterian *potential* but only time will reveal whether
that potential is exploited: the example of GEC under Lord
Weinstock is not encouraging.[30]

III

Be that as it may, if the work of Elbaum and Lazonick and
the authors assembled by them represents a major contribution
to the continuing debate on British entrepreneurship, perhaps
the most interesting, certainly the most eloquent, of the recent
explorations of the causes of British industrial decline has been
that by Martin Wiener.[31] He argues that from the middle of
the nineteenth century 'Businessmen increasingly shunned the
role of industrial entrepreneur for the more socially rewarding
role of gentleman (landed if possible)', and that the consequence
was a dampening of industrial energies. 'Social prestige and
moral approbation were to be found by using the wealth acquired
in industry to escape it'. By returning to an older, pre-industrial,
agricultural and craft-based countryside, the industrialist became
gentrified, thus 'discouraging commitment to a wholehearted
pursuit of economic growth'.[32] In turn, his children, educated
in revivified public schools and ancient universities, were dis-
suaded from following in father's footsteps. Instead, they found
employment in the civil service, the army, the church and the
liberal professions, resulting in a haemorrhage of talent – often
to the empire – from which the British economy was never to
recover.

Wiener's beautifully written thesis is extremely seductive but
basically flawed. It is not that the evidence that he has marshalled
is wrong, it is partial and inadequate. His explanation of British
economic decline has achieved a remarkable popularity because

32   *British Culture and Economic Decline*

it tells people what they want to hear. By clutching at the belief that Britain's decline can be ascribed to some general cultural miasma and the diminution of 'the industrial spirit', business-men, politicians and trade unionists can each evade blame for Britain's poor economic performance, for this was due to some intangible factor beyond their control. As Coleman has said, such a notion has all the fascination of Max Weber's 'spirit of capitalism' and only a little more evidence that it exists.[33]

A number of specific criticisms may be outlined. The first is concerned with Wiener's chronology. 'There is ample evidence of hostile attitudes towards businessmen in the later eighteenth century. They can be found not simply in those well-known rude remarks by Adam Smith but much more widely in novels, stories, moral tales and other sorts of popular fiction'[34] current, it is worth noting, during the very period during which the industrial revolution occurred.[35] As Professor T. S. Ashton observed in the very first issue of the journal *Business History*, 'The business-man has never been a popular figure. Dislike of him runs, a continuous thread, through nineteenth century literature, show-ing up most strongly in the writings of Ruskin and his followers, but visible also in those novelists and essayists, who much pre-ferred the ways of gypsies and tramps'. Not the least of the reasons for the widespread acceptance of such ideas was that 'the business-man has not had much to say for himself. His taci-turnity is, indeed, one of the counts against him: evidently he must have a good deal to be silent about'.[36]

But while it is possible to accept the argument that the social prestige of business was low during the nineteenth century, there is no evidence that it *declined* after 1850. The social prestige of business has been, and continues to be very low. For re-empha-sizing this 'central truth' – to use Leslie Hannah's words[37] – Martin Wiener has placed us all in his debt. And perhaps too Wiener should be thanked for provoking others, such as Neil McKendrick, to look anew at the evidence which suggests 'a far more complex and subtle interaction of business, literature and society than a simple graph of the rise and fall of literary Luddism'.[38] To McKendrick, the economic consequences of cul-tural responses to industry require much more careful treatment. Peaks of hostility to the businessman could reflect times when his place in society, his power and his influence are seen to be at their zenith; troughs of apparent indifference, times when his power and influence are in eclipse. Wiener's lack of attention to the implications of the relative literary neglect of businessmen in the last fifty years, it is argued, further weakens his case.[39]

But there are other problems too with Wiener's aetiology. As Harold Perkin has recently emphasized, Wiener is incorrect in assuming – albeit with a wealth of superficially convincing examples – that aristocratic values were in fact anti-industrial. A veritable library of monographs reveals that the British aristocracy and gentry during the industrial revolution were the most economically progressive and profit-oriented ruling class in Europe. 'They invested eagerly in agricultural improvement and enclosure, in trading ventures, mining, roads, river navigation and canals, docks, early railways, urban development and even, where circumstances permitted, in manufacturing such as brick-making, iron-founding, and textiles'.[40] They may not always have managed such enterprises directly, but the vast majority encouraged the exploitation of the resources to be found on, near, or under, their estates. And they continued to do so throughout the nineteenth century and beyond.

And what of those early middle class industrialists, traders, financiers and bankers who, being successful in their original pursuits, sought to secure acceptance into upper class society by the acquisition of a landed estate, the purchase or the building of a great house, the pursuit (as Coleman has commented) of foxes instead of profits? Did this buccolic emulation portend the beginning of the end of the British economy? Of course not. It was always so, before, during and after the Industrial Revolution.[41] Certainly, it was not a phenomenon peculiar to the period after 1850. The pursuit of non-economic ends did not involve any *net* haemorrhage of entrepreneurial talent. Quite the reverse. Many new thrusting firms would not have come into existence, or small established companies grown, had not their founders or owners seen or been aware of the tangible results of commercial or industrial success.[42] What was wrong with British industry after (indeed, before) 1850 was not a poverty of entrepreneurial (or industrial) spirit, but a surfeit. There were *too many* fiercely independent, aggressively competitive firms coming into existence,[43] hence the domestic industrial structure of which Lazonick properly complains, and the proprietors of the great majority of them were totally unaffected by public schools and classical liberal education. Furthermore, there is no evidence that the sons of businessmen were *increasingly* deflected to the lifestyle of the landed gentry. Nor, for that matter, 'is it clear that

34   *British Culture and Economic Decline*

the traditional professions absorbed an *increasing* proportion of the labour force'.[44]

One last, more speculative point may be made. What Wiener has discovered is not so much a decline in industrial spirit as a reaffirmation of the stratified and hierarchial nature of British society. From an economic point of view, the significance of this is that the market confronting British manufacturers was similarly stratified. Recognizing this, many of them established themselves and survived by exploiting these differences and, by concentrating on lines that exhibited craftsmanship and individual character, consciously differentiated their products in order to secure a degree of monopoly power which permitted them to reap high profits on a relatively small capital and turnover.[45] This, in turn, strengthened their resolve not to increase the scale of their operations beyond that which would have involved the recruitment of managerial talent and financial resources outside the family circle. This policy of product differentiation, sustained as it was by the lack of homogeneity in the domestic market, depressed the national rate of economic growth and was partially responsible for the longevity of the small family firm and the slow adoption of corporate capitalism 'characterized by industrial oligopoly, hierarchical managerial bureaucracy, vertical integration of production and distribution, managerial control over job content and production standards, the integration of financial and industrial capital, and systematic research and development'.[46]

But even when it appeared that British companies were on the same evolutionary trajectory as the great American corporations; even when British firms – advised by such management consultants as McKinsley & Co – seem to have adopted the multi-divisional form of organization apparently required for the diversification of corporate strategy by region and/or by product, something was lacking. The giant British firms hesitated to embrace *all* the features of the American model.[47] Such deviations may have been the result of a characteristic British slowness to accept an important innovation and hence to employ it properly. Alternatively, they may reflect a rational response to a different economic and social environment.

Certainly, Chandler himself explains the gradual nature of organizational change in Britain in these terms. By the time the United States had entered the First World War, management decisions had already replaced co-ordination by market forces in many of the most critical sectors of the economy, but in Britain – where existing market mechanisms were more efficient than in the United States – businessmen were under far less pressure to integrate forward and backwards, to create managerial hierarchies and to centralize their administrations.[48] Many British firms may have grown to impressive size, usually by merger, but the holding company form of organization which almost invariably was adopted simply permitted the perpetuation of family firms, albeit now loosely grouped into federations.[49] Derek F. Channon, who investigated the post-Second World War strategy and structure of British enterprise found that although the number of family controlled companies fell between 1950 and 1970, just over one third of the hundred largest manufacturing firms in Britain still possessed significant elements of family control by the latter date.[50] Such companies were consistently less diversified than the others and were more reluctant to adopt the multi-divisional form. But even those British companies that had re-structured themselves on the American pattern possessed less sophisticated overall control and planning mechanisms and procedures than their transatlantic counterparts.[51] For the multi-divisional form to be effective, 'it is essential that all divisions adopt a uniform set of accounting conventions in order to generate comparable cost and revenue data. By this criterion, multi-divisionalization in Britain was, with some major exceptions, only marginally effective and certainly different from the USA in the 1960s and early 1970s'.[52] There are further differences. Many British holding companies adopting the multi-divisional form 'often did little more than insert another layer of management between the operating units/subsidiaries and central functions, thus making a cosmetic rather than a fundamental change in their internal organisation'.[53]

As Channon found, 'many of the internal characteristics of the corporations adopting a multi-divisional structure reflected prior structural forms. In particular there was little evidence of change in the reward system, especially as a mechanism to apply *internal* competition for divisional performance'.[54] And Lazonick, in an exceptionally valuable paper, concluded that:

the implementation of a bureaucratically integrated managerial structure in late postwar Britain may have faced severe institutional and cultural obstacles, such as (1) a system of higher education that had been shaped in part by the prevalence of bureaucratically segmented

36 *British Culture and Economic Decline*

managerial structures, (2) the control of technology by shop-floor and shop-culture interest groups, and (3) the persistence of aristocratic values and social class distinctions in the hierarchical ordering of the managerial structure. In the face of these obstacles, insightful executives and experienced management consultants may not have been sufficient to transform the system of incentives, the lines of communication, and the loci of control within a large bureaucratic enterprise to permit managerial structure to make a success of the new organizational form.[55]

Lazonick clearly perceives the British inability fully to replicate American organizational practices as being yet another failure to confront institutional constraints innovatively, but Clark and Tann see it as a rational response conditioned by cultural differences between the two countries. To Clark, the British have appropriated from the Americans only those elements that are compatible with a distinctive British culture. Thus, he argues, in Britain there has been a persistent tendency towards loose-coupling – achieved by permitting a high degree of autonomy between sub-units of the enterprise and by a conscious decision not to preplan and specify the relationship between them – and the devolution of certain areas of decision-making. The consequence has been a considerable degree of that local autonomy which is deeply rooted in so many aspects of British society. Clark's emphasis is significant: 'high degrees of loose-coupling and of devolvement can be quite consistent with degrees of paternalism and with strong social control by a particular strata who themselves handle co-ordination in a personal way'.[56]

Wherever the truth may lie, it is impossible to ignore either the evidence that the largest British multi-divisional firms seem to have performed less well than their American counterparts in similar product markets,[57] or that the British subsidiaries of foreign multi-national companies have been more efficient and profitable than comparable indigenous enterprises.[58] These differences are not readily explicable, but it is difficult to avoid the suspicion that the quality of management was at least partially responsible.

This suggests a further important and relevant issue. The pioneering researches of Mira Wilkins on the multinational company have revealed that although there were many British multinationals operating in the same way as their American counterparts before the First World War, there were, in addition,

Entrepreneurship and British Economic Decline 37

'thousands of companies registered in England and Scotland to conduct business overseas, most of which, unlike the American model, did *not* grow out of the domestic operations of existing enterprises that had their headquarters in Britain ... most were what [Wilkins has] called free-standing companies'.

The limited size of the typical head office was ultimately the crucial feature that distinguished these companies from contemporary US multinationals. American businessmen of this era learned at home about multi-regional operations over the vastness of the United States; American companies became large, multi-functional, multi-regional enterprises that developed management talents. Domestic business was a training ground for multinational enterprise, whereas the compact, geographically small domestic market in Britain provided an unsuitable basis for developing skills in business administration comparable with those learned by American managers. The free-standing company, therefore, served as an alternative in many instances to the extension of the British home-based operating enterprises abroad, though the need to manage the business overseas was still there and provided a formidable challenge, and one that the free-standing companies often failed to meet.[59]

There is little question that the mortality rate of these overseas companies greatly exceeded that of their purely domestic counterparts largely because they failed to create satisfactory managerial organizations. The consequence was that in many cases the holders of the companies' securities suffered losses and the firms were either formally wound up or were simply allowed to wither away.[60] Once again, the root cause of such failures appears to have been the paucity of effective managerial skills and this was, Wilkins implies, a function of the persistence in Britain of the family firm.[61]

IV

The foregoing discussion indicates that while the *central* thrust of Wiener's argument is erroneous, it would be foolish to ignore the importance of certain cultural elements in Britain's relative economic decline, however difficult it may be to determine their exact significance or the manner in which they have operated.[62] Let us return to fundamentals. Many of those who have sought

38   *British Culture and Economic Decline*

to diagnose the basic cause of Britain's economic malaise have concluded that it stems largely from productivity problems.[63] For decades the rate of productivity growth has lagged behind that of most other countries.[64] There have been several hypotheses put forward to explain this disquieting phenomenon. Crude explanations focused upon the greater productivity potential of manufacturing as compared with agricultural activities, with the corollary that where Britain had led others could follow (while avoiding Britain's 'mistakes'), and have been superseded by increasingly sophisticated interpretations dependent upon the analysis of statistical data, the range and variety of which were only recently undreamed of.

What is intriguing here is that several of the factors that have been identified as major influences on Britain's relatively low and slow-growing productivity possess a cultural component. A number of the more simplistic of these may rapidly be discounted, if only because they are mutually inconsistent. Richard Caves provides illustrations:

Britain's productivity is said to be low because an elaborate class structure with wide income disparities denies economic harmony – and because egalitarian measures to redistribute income have dampened the incentives of managers and savers ... Growth and productivity may be stalled by institutions that are too resistant to change – or by public policies that change all too often as the party in power embraces a new policy fad, or a party newly in power jettisons its opponents' pet devices to install its own.[65]

Nevertheless, it is impossible to deny the baneful effects on productivity of British industrial relations and work practices.

The influence of the trade unions on the introduction of new, productivity-enhancing techniques is a much debated topic. The evidence is overwhelming that from the very onset of industrialization the members of the labour force regarded the adoption of new inventions with acute suspicion. New machines were thought of as a means of diminishing labour's bargaining power, reducing wages, eroding the status of those possessing craft skills, and adversely affecting established work patterns.[66] It may be conjectured that the fate of the handloom weavers made an indelible impression on employees in all branches of manufacturing, not simply those in textiles. The workers' conviction that new methods of organization and improvements in physical plant were detrimental to their interests was strengthened by the

Entrepreneurship and British Economic Decline   39

knowledge – originally surmised, but later in the nineteenth century partially confirmed by formal discussions among representatives of the employers and employees – that employers
consistently regarded new techniques primarily as labour-saving
devices. Indeed, it is arguable that many innovations were
directly stimulated by the recalcitrance of the workers.

In the context of the present discussion, the significance of
such attitudes is that much of the return on capital expenditure
was offset by enhanced labour costs consequent upon the
compromises necessary to secure the acceptance of new machines
by the work-force. All too frequently this made itself manifest
in overmanning and a far lower increase in labour productivity
than was technically feasible. Case after case could be cited from
the records of the Board of Conciliation and Arbitration for
the Manufactured Steel Trade of the West of Scotland to illustrate
this argument.[67] One will suffice. In 1902 Colvilles installed new,
more powerful engines in their plate mills at the Dalzell Works.
These greatly accelerated the speed of rolling, and the time taken
to convert a ton of steel slabs into steel plates was considerably
shortened. Ancillary equipment was also fitted in order to reduce
the severity of the physical effort involved in moving these heavy
products. Colvilles therefore appealed to the Board to permit
them to reduce the men's wages, arguing that 'the earnings of
the men have gone up, although the exertions from doing the
work has gone down'.

The operatives saw things differently. Their statement to the
Board emphasized that in accelerating the conversion process,
the introduction of new rolling mill engines had so enhanced
Colvilles' output that prices had fallen and hence their wages,
regulated as they were by a sliding scale based on the selling
price of ship plates. Furthermore:

The improvements referred to have changed the individual labour of
the men, [making] their work more exacting and laborious and [involv-
ing] more exertion and strain, both physically and mentally ... The
increased output and quick speed, coupled with the thinness of the
gauges and larger lengths and wider widths require much greater vigilance and more intense mental strain on the men than formerly. If
[the employers'] claim is admitted by the Board, it means that the more
a workman produces by his extra vigilance, skill and exertion the less
remuneration will he receive. The increased output is equally good
for Employer and workman, but is no reason for reducing the wages

40   *British Culture and Economic Decline*

of the men on the one hand, while increasing the profits of the Employers on the other hand. The present wages do not give adequate remuneration for work performed.

Lengthy discussion of these issues led to a complete deadlock and the case went to arbitration. The arbiter was Sheriff Davidson, the men's choice, part of whose lengthy statement of award reads:

The determination to adopt new machinery was the Employers', the cost was theirs and the risk ... I consider that, giving the workmen all that is fairly due to them for increased responsibility and the fact that they are dealing with material of greater value, and taking into account as well the gain to the Employers from increased output and a certain saving of labour, there is still a clear balance of earnings due in no way to the workmen themselves, but to the action of the Employers. I think, however, that the workmen are entitled to some portion of this balance. Where Employers and workmen come to a voluntary agreement such as was arrived at in 1884 in the Dalzell Steel Works, especially when a Sliding Scale is part of the agreement, it really means that a modified kind of profit-sharing or partnership is established between them, and an arbiter is bound to consider their respective positions in that light. Therefore I do not make the increase of output per day the measure of the reduction in wages, even after making allowance for the claims of the workmen ... The wages of the roller should, in my opinion, be reduced by 12.5 per cent on the present rate. Those of the breaker-down, chipper-in, and back of rolls men should be reduced by 7.5 per cent, and those of the winching-away man, sweeper, and screwer by 5 per cent.

The award gave rise to considerable argument. Certain facts were disputed, and the establishment of the principle of profit sharing and partnership was denounced by the employers. Nevertheless, the recommendations were accepted and the new rates came into effect.[68]

What is interesting about this case – and it is typical of many encountered in the iron and steel trades – was that it was settled reasonably amicably and that it appears not to have given rise to smouldering resentment. The men were conscious that the introduction of improved machinery and the minimization of costs were unavoidable if the industry was to survive the onslaught of competition from Germany, the United States and

Belgium. Yet their representatives tried always to get the best possible bargain for their constituents. As John Hodge, the secretary of the British Steel Smelters' Association, always claimed, his policy was to 'advise the men not to work against the machine ... provided we get a fair share of the plunder'.[69]

Now what is true of the iron and steel trades at the turn of the century is not necessarily true of other branches of industrial activity or of other periods. So much depended on the power of the workers and the determination of the employers to impose agreements upon their employees; and the relative influence of these factors varied over time. It has been suggested that the prevalence of restrictive practices ebbed and flowed with the trade cycle and the relative scarcity of skilled labour; that a general improvement was 'interrupted and reversed between the 1890s and 1920, and not continued in the post war period'.[70] Be that as it may, from the 1880s it is possible to detect a growing tolerance among masters and men, an increase in mutual accommodation. 'Ours wasn't a hating trade', one unionist said of his life-time in the steel industry,[71] and similar observations have been made by those in other industries. But the price paid by British industry for this social cohesion was a sub-optional exploitation of the technical possibilities of innovation, either because of an implicit acceptance of 'profit sharing' or because, as in the car industry, the employers surrendered their right to manage, believing themselves to be – as Lewchuk has so brilliantly demonstrated[72] – unable to convert labour time into labour effort. In such industries, the pace of work came to be determined by the work-force itself. In either case, the result was relatively low investment and low productivity.

How much significance may be attached to such factors is difficult to determine. Williams, Williams and Thomas[73] discuss some of the issues with great care without arriving at a definite conclusion. Suffice it here to say that it is arguable that until the 1970s the mutual accommodation between management and men evident in some branches of economic activity may have played an important role in Britain's sluggish productivity record. With the politics of confrontation associated with the Thatcher government, the absolute decline of manufacturing industry and a high level of unemployment, there has been a remarkable rise in labour productivity.[74] There has also been an ugly erosion of the tolerance once so characteristic of British society.

V

To return to the assessment of the role of entrepreneurship in Britain's economic decline. Recent explorations have strengthened my belief that it is difficult to condemn British businessmen for the way they behaved *within the context of their individual firms*. I would subscribe to Lazonick's verdict that on the whole they 'performed admirably as neo-classical managers – they took the conditions facing them as given and tried to do the best they could'.[75] I experience great difficulty in accepting his corollary that to merit the use of the appellation 'entrepreneur', they *should* have transformed their industrial environment. I ask myself how could they and equally, if not more important, why should they? Empirically to answer these questions involves a more intimate knowledge of many fields of economic activity than I possess. I can only say that my own researches into the Scottish iron and steel industry[76] suggest that the problems confronting those who tried – and I refer specifically to Sir John Craig – were all but insuperable, and the benefit from so doing was so long in arriving that had it been possible to foresee what restructuring the Scottish steel industry was to cost – in profits forgone and the horrendous physical and mental strain incurred – even Craig might have hesitated.[77] As it was, the attainment of his 'grand design' was made possible only by the intervention of Sir James Lithgow for whom – in this instance at least – private and public advantage coincided, a conjuncture which was quite fortuitous and, I would guess, extremely rare.[78] Even then, what was achieved fell short of what hindsight indicates should have been done, and even an ideal solution would have possessed but a limited term.

If I were to summarize what seems to be the current state of the debate on the British entrepreneur, I would be forced to say, albeit epigrammatically, that British entrepreneurs did not fail, but that there was a failure of industrial entrepreneurship.[79] It is undeniable that the rate of British economic growth would have been greatly enhanced had *more* businessmen developed new technologies or new industries possessing high potential levels of productivity.[80] One of the reasons why the British economy failed to generate this desirable response was, it has repeatedly been argued, not the fault of the entrepreneur as such, but stemmed from the British educational system. Certainly, this was the belief of Herbert Gray and Samuel Turner writing in

1916, and echoed most recently by Correlli Barnett and R.R.Locke.[81] By emphasizing the needs of technologically-based industries (and it was here that the British lagged so grievously[82]) and the nature of the new business organizations that the growth of the large-scale firm demanded, Locke shows that higher education in Germany – and to a lesser extent in the United States – met these requirements far more successfully than did the British and French systems.

There are a number of major difficulties involved in this important issue. Against Locke's highly persuasive argument must be set Sanderson's vigorous defence of British education[83] and Pollard's detailed comparative examination which reveals the remarkable 'capacity of the educational sector of the British economy to respond to the challenges facing it' in the period before the First World War.[84] Perhaps, after all, it was a question of demand? Sanderson is convinced that 'the more lasting problem was not so much the provision of technical education as the willingness of employers to receive its products'.[85] And, speaking of scientists, Pollard believes that there was 'no sign of unfilled need'. Even the decline of the Mechanics Institutes can be explained by a lack of demand.[86]

Certainly, there was little demand by the business community for educational provisions for professional management personnel. Lazonick ascribes this to the persistence in Britain of family firms and the reluctance of their owners to share control with qualified outsiders.[87] But there was more to it than this. The fact was that the vast majority of British businessmen were unaware of their own inadequacies and unconscious of the poverty of the information upon which they based their decisions. As Locke makes plain, British accountants – obsessed by the accuracy of the balance sheet and the profit and loss statement – provided little or no guidance for beleaguered management; British neo-classical economists despised and neglected the empirical study of the firm, their theories rarely had operational significance; British engineers knew little of economic realities.

In effect, the owners and directors of so many British firms did not realize what they were missing. It took the reports of itinerant productivity teams after the Second World War to bring home to them just how far the British were behind, just what could have been learned had the British business community shown even minimal interest in what had been going on in

44   *British Culture and Economic Decline*

Germany (let alone America), and had British academics made any attempt to understand, evaluate and disseminate the work of German business economists and cost accountants.

Meanwhile, training for management in Britain was, and to some extent still is, regarded as the responsibility of the firm itself. But, as Ackrill has observed:

Training is best suited to large companies who find it worthwhile to set up [appropriate] courses and whose organisation is big enough and diverse enough to provide recognisable pathways for its new recruits. The longer persistence of the family firms in Britain probably had something to do with a lesser provision of training since firms tended to be smaller in size than corporations in the United States, Germany and Japan, and also because it might be assumed that the sons and grandsons of the owners knew a good deal more about the general nature and indeed the particular details of a firm than outside entrants.[88]

No one knew this better than Lyndall Urwick, who observed in a paper to the Institute of Public Administration in 1927:

Broadly speaking, in ninety-nine hundredths of British industry there is no system of promotion. Family connections, ownership of capital, toadyism, seniority, inertia, or luck decide which men shall be selected to rule their fellows ... it is a fact that in the majority of our great enterprises there is no analysis of the factors which constitute 'fitness' for most of the managerial positions and no methods of measuring or assessing those factors whatever.

Indeed, Urwick reported that one speaker had only a few years ago told an Oxford business conference that 'the only principle of organization he had been able to discover in English industry was "myself, my father, my son, and my wife's sister's nephew"'; and that even more recently a 'friendly American' had written that 'In England the fact that you are the husband of the daughter of the Managing Director is apt to mean more than the fact that you have discovered a new process for smelting steel that cuts a quarter off the price of production'.[89]

Perhaps the most damaging consequence of the prevalence of these attitudes was that until very recently there was little or no 'pressure for the creation and expansion of social institutions for the development of professional managerial personnel'.[90] Is it merely chance that the more rapid growth of productivity in British industry has coincided with the preferment and growing seniority of the products of the feverishly created business schools and the postgraduate business courses mounted in British universities in the 1960s?

But if there was a paucity of training provisions for management, it is plausible that the British labour force was, paradoxically, too well trained (as opposed to too well educated), too disciplined and skilled to encourage their employers to abandon handicraft techniques, which in any case were consistent with the tactics of product differentiation.[91] The long-run economic significance of skilled labour, initially postulated by C.K.Harley,[92] has received powerful support from W.Lewchuk, who in his studies of the British motor vehicles industry has emphasized the importance of the associated tradition of labour independence on the shop floor which led British employers to exercise only partial control over labour effort. Instead, they depended upon motivation provided by piece rates to secure relatively high and acceptable profits despite low productivity, the malign consequences of which were not fully exposed until the 1960s.[93]

It was the skill of the British labour force, combined with the workers' appreciation of the 'rules of the game',[94] that inhibited and continues to inhibit innovation.[95] This, in turn, has contributed to the relatively low level of investment in Great Britain which, perhaps as much as any other factor, has retarded British economic growth.[96] But additional reasons for the low level of investment in *manufacturing* activity were undoubtedly the relative attractiveness of the service sector which, it is plain, did not fail to recruit new entrepreneurs,[97] and the fact, demonstrated by William Rubinstein, that money could be made so much more easily in finance than in industry.[98] Clive Lee's work shows that the expansion of the service sector *during the late Victorian period* possessed highly beneficial consequences for economic growth and that much of this expansion was neither directly nor in spatial terms immediately dependent upon manufacturing.[99] Thus, the movement into services, to which Charles Wilson drew attention in 1965,[100] provides positive evidence of entrepreneurial perspicacity and vigour in the closing decades of the nineteenth century, and this verdict has recently been strengthened by a number of specific illustrations, among the more notable of which have been those provided by Edwin Green and Michael Moss, T. R. Nevett, Asa Briggs, Clive Trebilcock and Charles Wilson himself.[101]

In the context of this exploration of entrepreneurship and

46   *British Culture and Economic Decline*

British economic decline, this movement into services is of the utmost importance. If the British entrepreneur is to be criticized for failing constructively to confront the organizational constraints that were progressively strangling him in the staple industries (industries which were so labour-intensive that Lee has described them collectively as the apogee of proto-industrialization, rather than the products of an Industrial Revolution); and if he is to be criticized for failing more vigorously to enter new manufacturing industries, then surely this same British entrepreneur deserves some praise for moving into the service sector, whose relatively rapid rate of output growth and high productivity, certainly between *c* 1870 and 1913, was so much superior to the old staples that its expansion provided what little buoyancy there was in Britain's aggregate economic growth?[102]

It was not until the twentieth century that the persistent movement into services could have become detrimental to aggregate economic growth. Why is this? The reason appears to reside in the fact that whereas productivity in the tertiary sector was initially greater than that of the waning staple industries, subsequent productivity in services may have increased only slowly, if at all.[103] It is admitted that there are innumerable problems of measurement and interpretation of service output change,[104] but it would seem probable that since the turn of the century higher rates of economic growth might have been achieved by manufacturing *goods*, particularly articles embodying a high technological and scientific component; the products of the sort of industries that Locke has argued that the British – with their 'inferior' or inappropriate educational system – were singularly unfitted to develop.[105] Having belatedly recognized the cost of this neglect – made particularly manifest, as Correlli Barnett has so strikingly revealed, during the Second World War[106] – those businessmen who sought to exploit previously neglected opportunities were confronted with a complex of difficulties. Many of these stemmed, first, from the inability of the British educational system to supply suitably trained middle management skills, applied scientists, production engineers and cost accountants; and second, from a labour force reluctant to accept and accommodate to change, the inevitable consequences of unimaginative labour-management relations over past decades, coupled with motivational problems apparently far greater than those confronting Britain's competitors in the United States and, later, in Japan.[107]

VI

Although several of the themes that have been touched upon in this brief survey undoubtedly deserve more intensive investigation, it should be apparent that some of the problems that have inhibited – and continue to inhibit – growth in the British economy are of a nature and magnitude that make them insoluble by entrepreneurial initiatives alone. An earlier version of Elbaum and Lazonick's argument, presented at the 1983 meeting of the Economic History Association,[108] seemed to point to necessity of state intervention, but as Lance E.Davis observed on that occasion, 'the African ground nut scheme, the Concorde, and the decision to "go with coal"',[109] do not inspire confidence in state ownership or state planning. Nor does the recent series of reflections by Aubrey Jones, who emphasizes that in his own experience as Minister of Fuel and Power and Minister of Supply, 'whatever the government's macro-economic policy, industrial structure was always the Cinderella'.[110] Certainly, governments cannot produce instant breakthroughs. The democratic state may take action which *may* accelerate the erosion of baneful institutional arrangements, but little more. As some of the growth-retarding factors are reduced in number and power (and it may be observed that the present government's attitude towards the universities reveals a lamentable ignorance of the significance of basic research in achieving this objective[111]), then a new generation of entrepreneurs, some of them graduates of the belatedly established business schools,[112] may contribute to the revival of the British economy, but the omens are not propitious.[113]

NOTES

1. Nick Crafts, 'The Assessment: British Economic Growth over the Long Run', in *Oxford Review of Economic Policy*, Vol. 4, No. 1 (Spring, 1988), p. i.
2. David Landes, 'Entrepreneurship in Advanced Industrial Countries: The Anglo-German Rivalry', in *Entrepreneurship and Economic Growth: Papers presented at a Conference sponsored jointly by the Committee on Economic Growth of the Social Science Research Council and the Harvard University Research Centre in Entrepreneurial History, Cambridge, Mass., November 12 & 13, 1954*; David Landes,

48 *British Culture and Economic Decline*

'Technological Change and Development in Western Europe, 1750–1914', in *The Cambridge Economic History of Europe, VI, The Industrial Revolution and After*, Part 1, edited by H. J. Habakkuk and M. M. Postan (Cambridge: CUP, 1965); subsequently reprinted and extended as *The Unbound Prometheus* (Cambridge: CUP, 1969).

3. H. J. Habakkuk, *American and British Technology in the Nineteenth Century* (Cambridge: CUP, 1962); Derek H. Aldcroft, 'The Entrepreneur and the British Economy: 1870–1914', *Economic History Review*, 2nd series, xvii (1964); Charles Wilson, 'Economy and Society in Late Victorian Britain', *Economic History Review*, 2nd ser., xviii (1965).

4. A. L. Levine, *Industrial Retardation in Britain, 1880–1914* (London: Weidenfeld & Nicolson, 1967); Eric Sigsworth, 'Some Problems in Business History, 1870–1914', in *Papers of the Sixteenth Business History Conference* (ed.) Charles J. Kennedy (Lincoln, Nebraska: University of Nebraska, 1969); Francois Crouzet, *The Victorian Economy* (London: Methuen, 1982); Derek H. Aldcroft (ed.), *The Development of British Industry and Foreign Competition, 1875–1914* (London: Allen & Unwin, 1968).

5. Roy Church, 'The Effect of the American Export Invasion on the British Boot and Shoe Industry, 1885–1914', *Journal of Economic History*, xxviii (1968); A. E. Harrison, 'The Competitiveness of the British Cycle Industry, 1890–1914', *Economic History Review*, 2nd ser., xxii (1969); D. N. McCloskey (ed.), *Essays on a Mature Economy: Britain After 1840, Papers and Proceedings of the MSSB Conference on the New Economic History of Britain, 1840–1930* (London: Methuen, 1971); T. C. Barker, 'History: Economic and Social', in C. B. Cox & A. E. Dyson (eds.), *The Twentieth Century Mind, Vol. 1: 1900–1918* (Oxford: OUP, 1972).

6. Donald N. McCloskey and Lars G. Sandberg, 'From Damnation to Redemption: Judgments on the Late Victorian Entrepreneur', *Explorations in Economic History*, ix (1971).

7. Donald N. McCloskey, *Economic Maturity and Entrepreneurial Decline: British Iron and Steel, 1870–1913* (Cambridge, Mass.: Harvard UP, 1973), p. 127.

8. Lars Sandberg, *Lancashire in Decline* (Columbus, Ohio: Ohio State University Press, 1974), pp. 82–4.

9. Donald N. McCloskey, 'Did Victorian Britain Fail?', *Economic History Review*, 2nd ser., xxiii (1970), p. 459.

10. P. L. Payne, 'Industrial Entrepreneurship and Management in Great Britain, *c* 1760–1970', in *The Cambridge Economic History of Europe, VII, The Industrial Economies: Capital, Labour and Enterprise*, Part I, ed. Peter Mathias and M. M. Postan (Cambridge: CUP, 1978); *British Entrepreneurship in the Nineteenth Century* (London: Macmillan, 1974).

11. See for example, Payne, *Entrepreneurship*, p. 50. For a critical evaluation of the cliometric revision, see R. R. Locke, 'New Insights from Cost Accounting into British Entrepreneurial Performance, *circa* 1914', *The Accounting Historians Journal*, vi, Part I (1979); and

Entrepreneurship and British Economic Decline   49

the same author's 'Cost Accounting: An Institutional Yardstick for measuring British Entrepreneurial Performance circa. 1914', *The Accounting Historians Journal*, VI, Part 2 (1979).

12. Roy Church, *Kenricks in Hardware: A Family Business, 1791–1966* (Newton Abbot: David & Charles, 1969).

13. P. S. Andrews and E. Brunner, *Capital Development in Steel* (Oxford: Blackwell, 1952), pp. 208, 362–3; D. C. Coleman, *Courtaulds* (Oxford: Clarendon Press, 1969), Vol. II, p. 218; P. L. Payne, *Colvilles and the Scottish Steel Industry* (Oxford: Clarendon Press, 1979), p. 144; Jonathan Boswell, 'Hope, Inefficiency or Public Duty? The United Steel Companies and West Cumberland, 1918–39', *Business History*, xxii (1980); Jonathan Boswell, 'The Informal Social Control of Business in Britain, 1880–1939', *Business History Review*, LVII (Summer, 1983); Jonathan Boswell, *Business Policies in the Making* (London: Allen & Unwin, 1983); Harold Perkin, *The Rise of Professional Society. England since 1880* (London: Routledge, 1989), p. 364.

14. H. W. Richardson, in Aldcroft (ed.), *op. cit.*, p. 216.

15. Coleman, *Courtaulds*, II, p. 220.

16. Leslie Hannah, *Entrepreneurs and the Social Sciences: An Inaugural Lecture* (London: LSE, 1983), p. 12.

17. Growth in GDP per man-year was less than 1 per cent per annum in the period 1873–1924, lower than that of the first three-quarters of the nineteenth century, and subsequent periods: 1924–51, 1 per cent; 1951–1973, 2.4 per cent. R. C. O. Matthews, C. H. Feinstein and J. C. Odling-Smee, *British Economic Growth, 1856–1973* (Oxford: OUP, 1982), p. 22.

18. William Lazonick, 'Industrial Organisation and Technological Change: The Decline of the British Cotton Industry', *Business History Review*, LVII (Summer, 1983), pp. 230–6.

19. *Ibid.*, pp. 229–30. See also *Lancashire and Whitehall: The Diary of Sir Raymond Streat, 1931–1957*, ed. by Marguerite Dupree (Manchester: MUP, 1987).

20. Bernard Elbaum and William Lazonick (eds.), *The Decline of the British Economy* (Oxford: Clarendon Press, 1986), p. 2.

21. The work of Alfred Chandler is considered later.

22. Elbaum & Lazonick, *op. cit.*, p. 2.

23. Mancur Olson, *The Rise and Decline of Nations: Economic Growth, Stagflation, and Social Rigidities* (New Haven and London: Yale University Press, 1982), see especially pp. 77–87. Olsen stresses the importance of 'special interest' groups in reducing Britain's rate of growth. He cites Peter Murrell, 'The Comparative Structure of the Growth of West German and British Manufacturing Industry' in D. C. Mueller (ed.), *The Political Economy of Growth* (New Haven: Yale University Press, 1983.)

24. *cf.* Burton Klein: 'Even before he wrote *Socialism, Capitalism and Democracy*, Schumpeter had turned his entrepreneur into an innovator who put daring ideas into practices (as in the opening of the railroads). However, because he could not explain why some entrepre-

50 *British Culture and Economic Decline*

neurs acted upon a good idea and others did not, his theory became, in effect, a theory in which those who reached great success were destined to do so, which is to say, it became a more deterministic concept of entrepreneurship than the one set forth in his doctoral thesis'. Burton Klein, *Dynamic Economics* (Cambridge, Mass.: Harvard University Press, 1977), p. 135.

25. See K. Cowling, P. Stoneman et al., *Mergers and Economic Performance* (Cambridge: CUP, 1980). 'Any view that the alleged retardation of the British economy before 1914 was due to a lack of business concentration, while the subsequent improved growth performance in the interwar years and again after 1945, was due to increased merger activity, would clearly need to be qualified [by the conclusions of this book on the welfare cost of monopoly]. If the social cost of mergers was indeed high, then the sources of industrial growth would clearly need to be found elsewhere' (G. Jones reviewing the book in *Business History*, xxxiii (1981), p. 365).

26. W. J. Baumol & K. McLennan (eds.), *Productivity Growth and US Competitiveness* (New York: OUP, 1985), p. 203. See also Lance E. Davis and Susan Groth, 'Industrial Structure and Technological Change', *Caltech. Soc. Sci. Working Papers*, No. 57 (1974); Burton H. Klein, *Dynamic Economics*. In looking at invention Klein could find no case in which significant advances in relatively static industries came from major firms (p. 17), and Jacob Schmookler, 'The Size of Firm and the Growth of Knowledge', in his *Patents Inventions and Economic Change* (Cambridge, Mass.: Harvard UP, 1972), pp. 36–46, found that smaller firms 'used' more of their patents than larger firms (p. 39), quoting a report compiled at Harvard.

27. Payne, 'Industrial Entrepreneurship', p. 229. A recent study by George F. Ray, *The Diffusion of Mature Technologies* (Cambridge: CUP for the National Institute of Economic and Social Research, 1984), p. 90, concludes that 'size has less to do with the diffusion of new technologies in the mature phase than was believed some ten or twenty years ago. It is not denied that large companies have certain advantages ... Nevertheless, there are plenty of examples of medium-sized or smaller companies pioneering'.

28. Aubrey Jones, *Britain's Economy, The Roots of Stagnation* (Cambridge: CUP, 1985), p. 126.

29. Dennis C. Mueller, *Profits in the Long Run* (Cambridge: CUP, 1986).

30. The story of GEC told by John Williams, in Williams, Williams and Thomas, *Why are the British Bad at Manufacturing?* (London: RKP, 1983), pp. 133–78. 'The combination of a company having a billion pounds of free cash with a manufacturing output which has not expanded strongly seems obvious. At the least it provokes the suggestion that the company has not been successful in finding and seizing strategic opportunities in new processes, new products and new marketing arrangements where resources could be profitably and productively used' (p. 157). However, in discussing his recent bid, jointly with Siemens, for Plessey, Lord Weinstock observed 'We built a cash

Entrepreneurship and British Economic Decline   51

mountain because we were efficient and we saw no justification for investing more than we have invested ... Had we had opportunities, we would have taken them but when we tried to use the money to buy other companies (EMI, British Aerospace, Plessey) we were not allowed to do it'. He also said: 'I keep reading surveys by learned academics, who presumably have never had to run businesses, in which they say there is overwhelming evidence that mergers do not produce any improvement in efficiency. My own experience with one small merger, two very large ones and a fairly large one is that we have enormously increased efficiency'. *The Times*, 5 August 1989, p. 19.

31. Martin J. Wiener, *English Culture and the Decline of the Industrial Spirit, 1850–1980* (Cambridge: CUP, 1981).
32. *Ibid.*, pp. 97, 127.
33. Donald Coleman, in a letter to the author, 14 January 1986; and see D. C. Coleman and Christine MacLeod, 'Attitudes to New Techniques: British Businessmen, 1800–1950', *Economic History Review*, 2nd series, Vol. xxxix, No. 4 (November, 1986), p. 599.
34. *Ibid.*, based on J. R. Raven, 'English Popular Literature and the Image of Business, 1760–1790' (Unpublished PhD thesis, Cambridge, 1985). See also, John McVeagh. *Tradeful Merchants. The Portrayal of the Capitalist in Literature* (London: RKP, 1981), and the stimulating essay by Neil McKendrick, '"Gentlemen and Players" revisited: the gentlemanly ideal, the business ideal and the professional ideal in English literary culture', in Neil McKendrick & R. B. Outhwaite, *Business Life and Public Policy* (Cambridge: CUP, 1986), pp. 98–136.
35. *cf.* Olsen, *op. cit.*, p. 78: '... until nearly the middle of the nineteenth [century], Britain was evidently the country with the *fastest* rate of economic growth ... This means that no explanation of Britain's relatively slow growth in recent times that revolves around some supposedly inherent or permanent feature of British character or society can possibly be correct ...'
36. T. S. Ashton, *Business History*, Vol. 1, No. 1 (December 1958), p. 1.
37. Hannah, *Inaugural*, p. 25.
38. Neil McKendrick, '"Gentlemen and Players" revisited', *loc. cit.*, p. 102.
39. J. M. Winter, 'Bernard Shaw, Bertold Brecht and the businessman in literature', in McKendrick & Outhwaite, *op. cit.*, pp. 185–204.
40. Perkin, *op. cit.*, pp. 365–6.
41. D. C. Coleman, 'Gentlemen and Players', *Economic History Review*, 2nd ser., xxvi (1973).
42. Payne, *Entrepreneurship*, pp. 25–6.
43. Again and again, this is emphasized by studies of individual industries. See, for example, Coleman and MacLeod, *op. cit.*, pp. 600–1, and appended notes 77–87; Correlli Barnett, *The Audit of War* (London: Macmillan, 1986), among others, assembles numerous examples. Taking two technological industries, the Report of the Official Sub-Committee on Post-War Resettlement of the Motor Industry, refers to the division of the industry into 'too many, often small-scale units,

each producing too many models' (CAB 87/15, R(1)(45)9, 21 March 1945), pp. 58, 274; on aircraft (cites Wier Papers 19/10–11, Aircraft Factories on Air Ministry Work, April 1935; and M. M. Postan, D. Hay and J. D. Scott, *Design and Development Weapons: Studies in Government and Industrial Organisation*, London: HMSO & Longmans, 1964, pp. 36–7), p. 130. For the cotton industry, Sir Raymond Streat's diaries are invaluable; see Marguerite Dupree (ed.), *Lancashire and Whitehall: The Diary of Sir Raymond Streat, 1931–1957* (Manchester: Manchester University Press, 1987).

44. Matthews, Feinstein and Odling-Smee, *op. cit.*, p. 115. See also David Jeremy, 'Anatomy of the British Business Elite', *Business History*, xxvi (1984), p. 20.

45. See Payne, *Entrepreneurship*, pp. 41–2. As Ackrill has pointed out, 'British managers knew that in Britain they faced differentiated markets, a fact borne out by the adverse experiences of German and US electrical firms which set up in Britain before 1914 but could not reap the same advantages of large-scale identical ordering on which success in their countries of origin had depended in large part'. Margaret Ackrill, 'Britain's Managers and the British Economy, 1870s to the 1980s', *Oxford Review of Economic Policy*, Vol. 4, No. 1 (Spring 1988), pp. 61, 64. It is significant that Mira Wilkins has found that 'the British ... excelled in trademarked consumer products', Mira Wilkins, 'European and North American Multinationals, 1870–1914; Comparisons and Contrasts', *Business History*, xxx (1988), p. 21.

46. Elbaum and Lazonick, in Elbaum and Lazonick (eds.), *op. cit.*, p. 4.

47. I am grateful to Dr Peter A. Clark, of the Work Organization Research Centre of Aston University, for first drawing my attention to certain implications of this point and for kindly supplying me with data. See Peter Clark, *Anglo-American Innovation* (Berlin: de Gruyter, 1987), p. 297.

48. A. D. Chandler, 'Introduction', in A. D. Chandler and Herman Daems (eds.), *Managerial Hierarchies* (Cambridge, Mass.: Harvard University Press, 1980), p. 6.

49. See P. L. Payne, 'The Emergence of the Large-scale Company in Great Britain', *Economic History Review*, 2nd Series, xx (1967), pp. 528–9, 533–5; L. Hannah, 'Visible and Invisible Hands in Great Britain', in Chandler & Daems, *op. cit.*, pp. 53, 55.

50. Derek F. Channon, *The Strategy and Structure of British Enterprise* (London: Macmillan, 1973), p. 76; see also P. L. Payne, 'Family Business in Britain: An Historical and Analytical Survey', in A. Okochi and S. Yasuoka (eds.), *Family Business in the Era of Industrial Growth* (Tokyo: Tokyo University Press, 1984), pp. 176–8.

51. A. D. Chandler, commenting on Channon's study, in 'The Development of Modern Management Structure in the US and UK', in Leslie Hannah (ed.), *Management Strategy and Business Development* (London: Macmillan, 1976), pp. 25–6. See also Peter Clark, *op. cit.*, pp. 306–40.

52. Peter Clark and Jennifer Tann, 'Cultures and Corporations: the

Entrepreneurship and British Economic Decline   53

M-form in the USA and in Britain', Paper to the International Academy of Business, 1986, p. 18.

53. *Ibid.*
54. Channon, *op. cit.*, pp. 213–14.
55. W. Lazonick, 'Strategy, Structure, and Management Development in the United States and Britain', in K. Kobayashi and H. Morikawa (eds.), *Development of Managerial Enterprise* (Tokyo: Tokyo University Press, 1986), p. 139.
56. Clark, *Anglo-American Innovation*, p. 299.
57. Channon, *op. cit.*, p. 221.
58. See, for example, Neil Hood and Stephen Young, *Multinationals in Retreat. The Scottish Experience* (Edinburgh: Edinburgh University Press, 1982), pp. 11–13; Perkin, *op. cit.*, pp. 512–13.
59. Mira Wilkins, 'The free-standing company, 1870–1914': an important type of British foreign direct investment', *Economic History Review*, 2nd series, XLI (1988), pp. 261, 264.
60. P. L. Payne, *The Early Scottish Limited Companies, 1856–1898* (Edinburgh: Scottish Academic Press, 1980), Table 23, pp. 101*ff.*
61. Wilkins, 'The free-standing company', pp. 274–7.
62. Martin Daunton has come to similar conclusions. His discussion of '"Gentlemanly Capitalism" and British Industry, 1820–1914' forces him to accept Wiener's contention that 'the question of the causes of British economic decline remain beyond the sole grasp of the economists'. M. J. Daunton, *Past and Present*, No. 122 (February, 1989), p. 157, quoting Wiener, *op. cit.*, p. 170.
63. See, for example, Richard E. Caves and Lawrence B. Krause (eds.), *Britain's Economic Performance* (Washington, D.C.: The Brookings Institution, 1980), p. 19 and *passim.*
64. Many of the relevant statistics for the period 1870–1914 have been collected by Sidney Pollard, *Britain's Prime and Britain's Decline: The British Economy 1870–1914* (London: Arnold, 1989), pp. 8–17; for the same and for later periods, see Charles Feinstein, 'Economic Growth since 1870: Britain's Performance in International Perspective', in N. Crafts and D. Morris (eds.), 'Long Run Economic Performance in the UK', *Oxford Review of Economic Policy*, Vol. 4, No. 1 (Spring, 1988), pp. 1–3.
65. R. E. Caves in Caves and Krause, *op. cit.*, p. 139; based upon Samuel Brittan, 'How British is the British Sickness', *Journal of Law and Economics*, Vol. 21 (October, 1978), pp. 245–68.
66. For a recent compendium of evidence see Coleman and MacLeod, *op. cit.*, pp. 605*ff.* See also M. Berg (ed.), *Technology and Toil in Nineteenth Century Britain* (London: CSE Books, 1979).
67. *The Minute Books of the Board of Conciliation and Arbitration of the Manufactured Steel Trade of the West of Scotland* were discovered by the author in 1959 among the archives of the Steel Company of Scotland. These were subsequently deposited in the British Steel Corporation's Scottish Regional Records Centre. The general context

54   *British Culture and Economic Decline*

may be found in P. L. Payne, *Colvilles and the Scottish Steel Industry* (Oxford: OUP, 1979), pp. 103–15.

68. The 'Dalzell Plate Mill Case' formed the subject of several meetings of the Board between January and July 1902. The quotations are taken from this source.

69. John Hodge, *Workman's Cottage to Windsor Castle* (London: Sampson Low, Maston & Co., 1931).

70. Matthews, Feinstein and Odling-Smee, *op. cit.*, pp. 114–15.

71. Patrick McGeown, *Heat the Furnace Seven Times More* (London: Hutchinson, 1967), p. 116.

72. Wayne Lewchuk, *American Technology and the British Vehicle Industry* (Cambridge: CUP, 1987).

73. Karel Williams, John Williams and Dennis Thomas, *Why are the British bad at Manufacturing?* (London: RKP, 1983), pp. 34–47. They take as their starting point the article by Andrew Kilpatrick and Tony Lawson, 'On the nature of industrial decline in the UK', *Cambridge Journal of Economics*, Vol. 4 (1980), pp. 85–102, which argues that poor control of the labour process is a major contributory factor.

74. See C. Feinstein, 'Economic Growth since 1870: Britain's Performance in International Perspective', *Oxford Review of Economic Policy*, Vol. 4, No. 1, pp. 4–7.

75. Lazonick, 'Industrial Organisation', p. 236.

76. Payne, *Colvilles*, pp. 151–216.

77. *cf* Sir Eric Geddes on the superhuman difficulties confronting the founders of the Lancashire Cotton Corporation. Leslie Hannah, *The Rise of the Corporate Economy*, 2nd edition (London: Methuen, 1983), p. 76.

78. Steven Tolliday, *Business, Banking and Politics. The Case of British Steel, 1918–1939* (Cambridge, Mass.: Harvard University Press, 1987), pp. 111–23, puts a different interpretation on this episode, but the evidence – the whole of which I was unable to present in my *Colvilles* – does, I believe, support my case.

79. This is somewhat similar to the findings of Robert C. Allen, 'Entrepreneurship and Technical Progress in the Northeast Coast Pig Iron Industry: 1850–1913', in *Research in Economic History*, Vol. VI (1981), pp. 35–71.

80. A number of recent studies – some of them as yet unpublished – have revealed that technological innovation was not *invariably* sluggish (for example, Peter Wardley, 'Productivity, mechanization and the labour market in the Cleveland ironstone industry, 1873–1914', paper for the Cliometrics Congress, 1985; Gordon Boyce, 'The Development of the Cargo Fleet Iron Co., 1900–1914: A Study of Entrepreneurship, Planning and Production Costs in the Northeast Coast Basic Steel Industry', Mimeo, 1985), nor was there *always* a failure to attempt to exploit the new. See Payne, *The Early Scottish Limited Companies*.

81. H. B. Gray and Samuel Turner, *Eclipse or Empire?* (London: Nisbet, 1916); C. Barnett, *op. cit.*; R. R. Locke, *The End of the Practical*

Entrepreneurship and British Economic Decline   55

Man: *Entrepreneurship and Higher Education in Germany, France and Great Britain, 1880–1940* (Greenwich, Conn. and London: JAI Press, 1984). See also Julia Wrigley, 'Technical Education and Industry in the Nineteenth Century', in Elbaum and Lazonick (eds.), *op. cit.*, pp. 162–88.

82. See, for example, William P. Kennedy, *Industrial structure, Capital Markets and the Origins of British Economic Decline* (Cambridge: CUP, 1987), pp. 6, 37, 57, *passim*.

83. Michael Sanderson, *The Universities and British Industry 1850–1970* (London: RKP, 1972); 'The Professor as Industrial Consultant: Oliver Arnold and the British Steel Industry, 1900–14', *Economic History Review*, 2nd ser., xxxl (1978); 'The English Civic Universities and the "Industrial Spirit", 1870–1914', *Historical Research*, LXI (1988), pp. 90–104; 'Education and Economic Decline, 1890–1980s', *Oxford Review of Economic Policy*, Vol. 4, No. 1 (Spring 1988), pp. 38–50.

84. Sidney Pollard, *Britain's Prime and Britain's Decline*, Chapter 3, pp. 115–213. The quotation is from p. 213.

85. Sanderson, 'Education and Economic Decline', p. 38; *cf.* his observation that 'the more insidious evil has not been anti-industrial attitudes in the universities so much as anti-intellectual, anti-academic attitudes in industry', 'The English Civic Universities', p. 102. See also Joan Woodward, *Industrial Organisation – Theory and Practice* (London: OUP, 1965), p. 14, and Michael D. Stephens in Michael D. Stephens (ed.), *Universities, Education and the National Economy* (London: RKP, 1989), pp. xiii, 129, 135.

86. Pollard, *Britain's Prime*, pp. 179, 198.

87. Lazonick, 'Management Development', p. 120.

88. Margaret Ackrill, 'British Managers and the British Economy, 1870s to 1980s', *Oxford Review of Economic Policy*, Vol. 4, No. 1 (Spring, 1988), p. 69.

89. L. Urwick, 'Promotion in Industry', *Public Administration*, Vol. V (1927), p. 185. I owe the reference to Lazonick, 'Management Development', pp. 121–2.

90. Lazonick, 'Management Development', p. 121. See also Robert Locke, 'Educational Traditions and the Development of Business Studies after 1945 (An Anglo-French-German Comparison)', *Business History*, XXX, No. 1 (January, 1988), pp. 88–103.

91. As Pollard has said 'The manual skill of the British workman was never in question; it was his attitude to innovation, his adaptability, and the use he might make of pure science, which were in doubt …' Pollard, *Britain's Prime*, p. 139.

92. C. K. Harley, 'Skilled Labour and the Choice of Technique in Edwardian Industry', *Explorations in Economic History*, xi, No. 4, (Summer, 1974), pp. 391–414.

93. W. Lewchuk, *American Technology*, especially Chapter 9, pp. 185–220; 'The Motor Vehicle Industry', in Elbaum and Lazonick (eds.), *op. cit.*, pp. 135–61, and 'The Return to Capital in the British Motor Vehicle Industry', in *Business History*, xxvii (1985), pp. 3–25.

56   *British Culture and Economic Decline*

See also J. Walker, 'Markets, Industrial Processes and Class Struggle: The Evolution of the Labour Process in the UK Engineering Industry', *Review of Radical Political Economy*, xii (1981), pp. 46–69; J. Zeitlin, 'From Labour History to the History of Industrial Relations', *Economic History Review*, 2nd ser., XL (1987), pp. 159–84. M. Edelstein, 'Realised Rates of Return on UK Home and Overseas ... Investment', *Explorations in Economic History*, xiii (1976), pp. 294, 304, 314, shows that such industries as mechanical equipment, coal, iron and steel, which have been criticized for their technological backwardness, were also among the most profitable.

94. Eric Hobsbawm's expression. See his 'Custom, Wages and Work-load in Nineteenth-century Industry', in *Labouring Men* (London: Weidenfeld & Nicolson, 1964), pp. 344–70.

95. D. C. Coleman and Christine MacLeod, *op. cit.*; William H. Lazonick, 'Production Relations, Labor Productivity and Choice of Technique: British and US Cotton Spinning', *Journal of Economic History*, XLI (1981), pp. 491–516. And see Correlli Barnett, *op. cit.*, pp. 66*ff.*

96. The importance of the level of capital investment to productivity growth has repeatedly been emphasized in such works as Baumol & McLennon, *op. cit.*, pp. vii–viii, 9, 36, 47, 67. Peter Wardley, in a forthcoming work, has estimated the (very low) capital/employee ratios for the largest (and invariably heavy) British industrial firms.

97. The importance of this recruitment was originally suggested by Charles Wilson, *op. cit.*

98. W. D. Rubinstein, 'The Victorian Middle Class: wealth, occupation and geography', *Economic History Review*, 2nd ser., xxx (1977), and 'Wealth, elites and the class structure of modern Britain', *Past and Present*, 76 (1977). The point has been vividly exemplified by R. P. T. Davenport-Hines in his masterly study, *Dudley Docker: The Life and Times of a Trade Warrior* (Cambridge: CUP, 1984); and in numerous entries in David J. Jeremy (ed.), *Dictionary of Business Biography*, 5 volumes (London: Butterworths, 1984–6). The overall picture will doubtless be clarified by the subsequent analysis of the data provided by the various authors and not fully utilized in their entries.

99. C. H. Lee, *The British Economy since 1700* (Cambridge: CUP, 1986), *passim*; 'The service sector, regional specialization, and economic growth in the Victorian economy', *Journal of Historical Geography*, x (1984), pp. 143, 148, 153; 'Growth and Productivity in Services in the Industrial Economies, 1870–1913', forthcoming.

100. Charles Wilson, *op. cit.*

101. Edwin Green and Michael Moss, *A Business of National Importance: The Royal Mail Shipping Group, 1902–1937* (London: Methuen 1982); T. R. Nevett, *Advertising in Britain: A History* (London: History of Advertising Trust, 1982); Asa Briggs, *Wine for Sale: Victoria Wine and the Liquor Trade, 1860–1984* (London: Batsford, 1985); Clive Trebilcock, *Pheonix Assurance and the Development of British Insurance*, Vol. I: *1782–1870* (Cambridge: CUP, 1986);

Entrepreneurship and British Economic Decline 57

Charles Wilson, *First with the News: The History of W. H. Smith, 1792–1972* (London: Cape, 1985).

102. In addition to sources mentioned in note 99, see C. H. Lee, 'Regional Growth and Structural Change in Victorian Britain', *Economic History Review*, new series, xxxiv (1981), pp. 438–52; R. M. Hartwell, 'The Service Revolution: The Growth of Services in Modern Economy, 1700–1914', in Carlo M. Cipolla, *The Fontana Economic History of Europe*, Vol. 3 (London: Collins/Fontana, 1973), pp. 358–96. In the UK in 1870 manufacturing labour productivity was only 71 per cent of that in services, in 1913, only 46 per cent. Note too, although in 1913 service productivity in both Germany and the USA was higher than that in manufacturing, the *growth* of manufacturing productivity in both countries had been much greater (in Germany, double) than in services over the previous forty years. This characteristic was true of *only* Germany and the USA among the six countries considered by Lee, 'Growth and Productivity', Tables 1 and 2.

103. This is certainly an accepted view. An early and influential article is William J. Baumol, 'Macroeconomics of Unbalanced Growth', *American Economic Review*, Vol. 57, No. 3 (1967), pp. 415–26.

104. These problems have been surveyed by Anthony D. Smith, *The Measurement and Interpretation of Service Output Changes* (London: NEDO, 1972).

105. Locke, *The End of the Practical Man*, and his articles in the *Accounting Historians Journal*, see above, note 11.

106. C. Barnett, *The Audit of War, passim*.

107. Concerning this second group of difficulties, some telling examples are provided by Peter Pagnamenta and Richard Overy, *All our Working Lives* (London: British Broadcasting Corporation, 1984), *passim*. In a detailed analysis of the restraints on greater productivity related to problems of industrial relations in the United States, Robert McKersie and Janice A. Klein found 'worker or supervisor resistance to change' to be the area of greatest concern. See Baumol & McLennan, pp. 120*ff*. See also N. Crafts, *op. cit.*, p. ix.

108. B. Elbaum and William Lazonick, 'The Decline of the British Economy: An Institutional Perspective', *Journal of Economic History*, XLIV (1984).

109. Lance E. Davis, *ibid*, p. 597.

110. Aubrey Jones, *Britain's Economy: The Roots of Stagnation*, p. 79. While fiercely critical of the fuel industries – whose nationalization was, he feels, 'abundantly justified' – Aubrey Jones' observations on the nationalized coal, electricity, nuclear power and gas industries indicate their development to have been haphazard and unco-ordinated (pp. 64, 90). He remarks (p. 29) that when he was Minister of Fuel and Power (1955–56) 'the Ministry [lacked] technical expertise in all the industries sponsored by it, a lack which has continued to the present day'. In Scotland it is arguable that in intervening (often for the best of motives), the politicians and the State have all too often succeeded only in perpetuating many of the features of the Scot-

tish economy that stultify growth. See P. L. Payne, 'The Decline of the Scottish Heavy Industries, 1945–1983', in R. Saville (ed.), *The Economic Development of Modern Scotland* (Edinburgh: John Donald, 1985), pp. 79–113. See also Paul Hare, 'Planning a Market Economy: Problems and Lessons', *Royal Bank of Scotland Review*, No. 147 (September, 1985), pp. 46–50.

111. The importance of basic research is emphasized by Baumol and McLennan (eds.), *op. cit.*, pp. 198–200, and see the plea made by Tom Stonier, 'Technological Change and the Future', in Maxwell Gaskin (ed.), *The Political Economy of Tolerable Survival* (London: Croom Helm, 1981), pp. 140–51. See also Maurice Preston, 'Higher Education: Financial and Economic Aspects', *Bank of Scotland Review*, No. 148, December 1985: 'Higher education is, therefore, central to the process of economic advance.' (p. 17).

112. For the business schools, see Payne, *Cambridge Economic History*, VII, Part I, p. 224; Barnett, *op. cit.*, p. 294; Sanderson, *The Universities and British Industry*, p. 377; Hannah, *Inaugural Lecture*, p. 31. It is possible that the increasing number of non-executive directors being appointed to boards of quoted companies may have beneficial results, but even here the operation of the old-boy network may diminish the potential value of this promising development. See *Bank of England Quarterly Bulletin*, Vol. 19, No. 4 (December, 1979), pp. 392–3; Vol. 23, No. 1 (March, 1983), pp. 66–8; Vol. 25, No. 2 (June, 1985), pp. 233–6. And see *The Times*, 25 June 1986.

113. See, for example, the points recently made by Michael Heseltine, *The Challenge of Europe* (London: Weidenfeld & Nicolson, 1989). See also Sir Alan Cook on the industrial applications of scientific discoveries in universities, in Michael D. Stephens (ed.), *Universities, Education and the National Economy*, pp. 120–1; and C. Handy, *The Making of Managers* (London: NEDO, 1987), who reveals continuing gross deficiencies in management education.

[18]

"GENTLEMANLY CAPITALISM" AND BRITISH INDUSTRY 1820-1914*

"Manufacturers and merchants", claimed Richard Cobden in 1863, "as a rule seem only to desire riches that they may be enabled to prostrate themselves at the feet of feudalism". Cobden, the spokesman of the northern industrial middle class, the leading proponent of free trade, seemed to be admitting defeat. Rather than the bourgeois triumph which he desired, he feared that "feudalism is every day more and more in the ascendant in political and social life".[1] Even Marx and Engels, whose theories presupposed a triumphant bourgeoisie, were not clear how to portray Victorian Britain. In 1852 Marx felt that Cobden and the free traders formed "the official representatives of modern English society" and would soon achieve "the complete annihilation of Old England as an aristocratic country"; he could refer to "aristocratic representatives of the bourgeoisie", suggesting a delegation of power to aristocrats who acted on behalf of the bourgeoisie.[2] But by 1889 Engels was less certain, and he pointed instead to "the political decline and abdication of the bourgeoisie".[3]

The apparent failure of a self-confident industrial middle class to emerge and seize political power and social prestige is in danger of becoming a new orthodoxy among historians, attracting a surprising degree of support across the ideological spectrum. The emphasis is upon the continuity of important elements in the economic and social structure of Britain: the Industrial Revolution no longer seems to be such a sharp break; and the bourgeois revolution no more took place in the nineteenth century than in the seventeenth. Jonathan Clark has recently argued for the strength of the *ancien régime* in the

---

* This article originated in a paper delivered at the University of North Carolina at Greensboro, and I am grateful to Ronald Cassell for the invitation. I also wish to thank J. H. Hoppit for his comments. I owe much to conversations with Y. Cassis; this article is a poor recompense.

[1] J. Morley, *The Life of Richard Cobden*, ii (London, 1908), pp. 480-90, quoted by P. Anderson, "The Figures of Descent", *New Left Rev.*, no. 161 (1987), p. 24.

[2] K. Marx, "The Chartists", in *Collected Works*, xii (London, 1979), pp. 332-3, cited by Anderson, "Figures of Descent", p. 22.

[3] F. Engels, "Die Abdankung der Bourgeoisie", in *Werke*, xxi (Berlin, 1962), pp. 383-7, cited by Anderson, "Figures of Descent", p. 23.

eighteenth century, and the conclusion of much recent work on the nineteenth century is that his case might be extended up to 1914.[4] Although there have been differences of emphasis within the emerging orthodoxy, the main themes may be drawn together, without too much distortion, to provide a coherent account of the economic and social structure of nineteenth-century Britain. Once the case for the subordination of the industrial bourgeoisie has been summarized, it may then be asked whether such an argument is convincing.

I

A major problem in recent British history has been the explanation of relative economic decline since the later nineteenth century.[5] The answer, in the eyes of some historians, is to be found in the social structure which emerged in the nineteenth century. Anderson, for example, has pointed to "The agrarian and aristocratic stamp of English rulers in the era of the Pax Britannica, the subordination of bourgeois manufacturers and mill-owners to them, with all the consequences — economic, political and cultural — that followed from the cadet role of industrial capital in the Victorian age".[6] Similarly, Wiener has argued that the process of change during the nineteenth century "entrenched premodern elements within the new society, and gave legitimacy to antimodern elements". A conception of "Englishness" emerged which virtually excluded industrialism, and bourgeois culture was "gentrified", leading to a dampening of

---

[4] N. F. R. Crafts, *British Economic Growth during the Industrial Revolution* (Oxford, 1985); E. A. Wrigley, *People, Cities and Wealth: The Transformation of Traditional Society* (Oxford, 1987); J. C. D. Clark, *English Society, 1688-1832: Ideology, Social Structure and Political Practice during the Ancien Regime* (Cambridge, 1985); J. C. D. Clark, *Revolution and Rebellion: State and Society in England in the Seventeenth and Eighteenth Centuries* (Cambridge, 1986).

[5] Another major problem is imperialism, which has similarly been explained in terms of the approach to British society outlined in this section. For an explanation of imperialism as an expression of the structure of British society, see P. J. Cain and A. G. Hopkins, "Gentlemanly Capitalism and British Overseas Expansion, i: The Old Colonial System, 1688-1850", *Econ. Hist. Rev.*, 2nd ser., xxxix (1986), pp. 501-25; P. J. Cain and A. G. Hopkins, "Gentlemanly Capitalism and British Overseas Expansion, ii: New Imperialism, 1850-1945", *Econ. Hist. Rev.*, 2nd ser., xl (1987), pp. 1-26. The consequences of imperialism for social groups within Britain have been analysed within the same framework by L. E. Davis and R. A. Huttenback, *Mammon and the Pursuit of Empire: The Political Economy of British Imperialism, 1860-1912* (Cambridge, 1986), pp. 211-18, 251-2, 313-14; and P. K. O'Brien, "The Costs and Benefits of British Imperialism, 1846-1914", *Past and Present*, no. 120 (Aug. 1988), pp. 185, 195.

[6] Anderson, "Figures of Descent", p. 20.

economic endeavour as businessmen shunned industrial entrepreneurship for the more socially acceptable role of a gentleman. Industrialists were held in low esteem, lacked confidence and suffered from a political system which was permeated by the values of the gentry counter-revolution against industry.[7]

The notion that the European *ancien régime* survived at least to 1914 has been made most forcefully by Mayer, but his argument that landed or aristocratic political power and cultural prestige were general phenomena throughout Europe cannot explain the peculiarities of *British* industrial decline.[8] It is therefore necessary to stress certain features specific to the British aristocracy. It was "the landowning elite with the longest consecutive history as a capitalist stratum proper", so that capitalism and the bourgeoisie were not identical terms. The aristocracy was capitalist rather than feudal, yet it was still an aristocratic capitalism, "*rentier*, not entrepreneurial or productive". This aristocratic *rentier* capitalism maintained a cultural dominance, and reshaped the industrial bourgeoisie. It was, moreover, the wealthiest landowning class in Europe, with an unusually high concentration of land in its hands. This agrarian élite left farming in the hands of tenants and so could devote itself to politics more than its counterparts in other countries; and this involvement with parliament was associated with "the absence of any long-standing militarism". The *Junkers* in Prussia were less wealthy, and "had to continue to struggle ruthlessly to protect and develop their economic and political position", which made them "agrarian industrialists". They were also a military caste, and this combination led to a willingness to collaborate with industry in a drive for economic, and national, power. The outcome of the process of accommodation between the aristocracy and bourgeoisie differed in the two countries: liberalism was the victim in Germany, and industrialism in Britain.[9]

One feature which has often been defined as a leading characteristic of the British aristocracy or landed society was its openness, its ability to incorporate new men of wealth.[10] The cultural dominance of the aristocracy would, on this view, be produced by incorporating the newcomers. More recently, the emphasis has shifted to the "astonish-

---

[7] M. J. Wiener, *English Culture and the Decline of the Industrial Spirit, 1850-1980* (Cambridge, 1981), pp. 5, 7, 10, 81, 88, 97, 126, 132.

[8] A. J. Mayer, *The Persistence of the Old Regime: Europe to the Great War* (London, 1981); Anderson, "Figures of Descent", p. 27.

[9] Anderson, "Figures of Descent", pp. 28-30; Wiener, *English Culture*, pp. 8-9.

[10] For example, H. J. Perkin, *The Origins of Modern English Society, 1780-1880* (London, 1969), pp. 61-2.

ing" level of "continuity and closure as a social group". The Stones and Rubinstein contend that new sources of wealth could *not* aspire to enter this landed élite, which should be seen as a closed caste rather than a class which could be entered by anyone with the necessary money. The Stones have claimed that this closure stretched back to the sixteenth century; Rubinstein has concentrated on the nineteenth century, and from an analysis of the estates of millionaires and half-millionaires concludes that only a minority of "new men of wealth" became landholders. The success of the aristocratic capitalists in maintaining cultural and political hegemony therefore rested, at least up to 1880, upon its stability and economic power, rather than its capacity to absorb new wealth.[11] This powerful, wealthy, landed élite faced — so the argument continues — a middle class which was divided between London merchants and bankers on the one hand, and northern industrialists on the other. The fortunes left by the commercial and financial bourgeoisie of the City rivalled those of landowners, and surpassed the fortunes amassed by the industrial bourgeoisie, whose firms remained relatively small scale. The industrialists were accordingly separated from the landowners by the intervening layer of mercantile wealth.[12]

There were, within this general pattern, shifts of emphasis in the 1830s and 1880s. The first was marked by what Rubinstein calls the end of "Old Corruption". As rich financiers rose in importance, so another group of the middle class was falling: those who had made fortunes as clients of the aristocratic state, from sinecures, contracts and government finance. After 1832 this section was displaced and Rubinstein argues that landowners, the commercial middle class and the industrial middle class could go their own separate ways, each largely self-sufficient. The landowners could profit from "high farming", coal royalties and urban ground rents; the commercial middle

---

[11] Anderson, "Figures of Descent", p. 28; L. and J. C. F. Stone, *An Open Elite? England, 1540-1880* (Oxford, 1984); W. D. Rubinstein, "New Men of Wealth and the Purchase of Land in Nineteenth-Century England", *Past and Present*, no. 92 (Aug. 1981), pp. 125-47.

[12] Anderson, "Figures of Descent", pp. 31-5; Wiener, *English Culture*, p. 128. The evidence is provided by Rubinstein from an analysis of probate: see Rubinstein, "New Men of Wealth"; W. D. Rubinstein, *Men of Property: The Very Wealthy in Britain since the Industrial Revolution* (London, 1981); W. D. Rubinstein, "Wealth, Elites, and the Class Structure of Modern Britain", *Past and Present*, no. 76 (Aug. 1977), pp. 99-126; W. D. Rubinstein, "The End of 'Old Corruption' in Britain, 1780-1860", *Past and Present*, no. 101 (Nov. 1983), pp. 55-86. His essays have been republished as *Elites and the Wealthy in Modern British History: Essays in Social and Economic History* (Brighton, 1987).

class turned away from the state and towards financing overseas trade. Perhaps Rubinstein has exaggerated the structural importance of "old corruption", which was already under attack from 1780. By contrast, Anderson emphasizes the *weakness* of the "old corruption" in the absence of a large standing army or absolutist bureaucracy, and argues that this was a factor in explaining the success of the aristocracy in retaining power. Since there was "no huge parasitic outgrowth of office-holding to cut back", it was relatively easy for the landowners *themselves* to effect reforms before the emergence of an industrial bourgeoisie. Accordingly, the Reform Act of 1832 offered only a limited extension of the franchise, and prevented the emergence of "an autonomous bourgeois party". Thus, argues Anderson, the industrialists had not delegated power to the aristocracy: "They remained junior partners in the natural order of things, without compelling economic motives or collective social resources to transform it". Whether the strength of "old corruption" is emphasized or minimized, the general conclusion is the same: in the mid-nineteenth century finance and industry could go their own ways, and there was genuine aristocratic power based on a strong economic position, rather than a delegation of political power to the aristocracy by the bourgeoisie.[13]

The second shift is placed around 1886, when separation came to an end. The commercial and financial bourgeoisie came together with land, while industry remained apart. After 1880 landed incomes started to fall in the face of imports of foreign food, and at this point the prosperity of the City cushioned the aristocracy. Landed magnates and financiers came together in "an increasingly integrated plutocracy" from which industrialists were excluded. "When agrarian property lost its weight", says Anderson, "it was not industry but finance which became the hegemonic form of capital". The aristocracy was no longer so dependent upon the declining rural economy and, unlike Germany or the United States, the fact that the countryside became "empty" made it available as an "integrating cultural symbol" of "a remarkably homogeneous and cohesive elite".[14]

---

[13] Rubinstein, "End of 'Old Corruption'", pp. 55-7; Rubinstein, "Wealth and Land", p. 143; Rubinstein, *Men of Property*, p. 219; Anderson, "Figures of Descent", pp. 25-6, 39-40; J. M. Bourne, *Patronage and Society in Nineteenth-Century England* (London, 1986). G. Ingham, *Capitalism Divided? The City and Industry in British Social Development* (Basingstoke, 1984), p. 9, claims the attack on "old corruption" was led by merchants, not industrialists.

[14] Anderson, "Figures of Descent", pp. 41, 57; Stone, *Open Elite?*, pp. 424-5; Rubinstein, *Men of Property*, p. 220; Rubinstein, "Wealth, Elites and Class Structure",

(cont. on p. 124)

The process of social integration has recently been studied by Lisle-Williams and Cassis, who have both concentrated on the merchant bankers of the City. Both point to the assimilation of bankers to the aristocracy through education, social life and a leisured existence. Their analysis then diverges. Cassis considers the genealogies of a group of banking families, showing the density of networks both within the banking community and with the aristocracy. The result was "the formation of a renewed elite" which added the financial power of the City to the prestige of the old aristocracy, although not on the terms of the aristocracy.[15] Lisle-Williams places less emphasis on intermarriage, which he views as a consequence rather than a cause of cohesion. He starts from the survival of family capitalism among merchant bankers, and the creation of a dynastic structure. The continuity of family possession is explained by the "gentlemanly organization" which led to agreement on "the limits of competition and the desirability of mutual aid as a strategy for collective survival". These merchant bankers, with their dynastic ambition and resistance to loss of control, became firmly entrenched at the Bank of England, which acted to minimize conflict and to preserve a "community-like social system". These merchant-banking dynasties, claims Lisle-Williams, "co-operated with their competitors, who were also their cousins and friends, in a self-perpetuating community of mutual regard". Lisle-Williams's interpretation therefore rests upon a movement away from "competitive openness" in the City during the mid-nineteenth century, which tended to reinforce social distance from the landed aristocracy, and towards an increased concentration within the City, which created the structural conditions to allow the acceptance of aristocratic culture.[16]

(n. 14 cont.)
pp. 112-15; Wiener, *English Culture*, pp. 11-12, 49. Ingham, *Capitalism Divided?*, pp. 2-3, 5-6, 9, accepts the separation of City and industry, but stresses that the City was not simply financial; it was also commercial, involved with mercantile credit, insurance, commodity-broking: "British capitalism has maintained a distinctive dual character — as the first industrial economy and as the world's major commercial entrepot . . . International commercial capitalism has been dominant and has had a determinant impact on its class and institutional structure".

[15] Y. Cassis, *Les banquiers de la City à l'époque Edouardienne, 1890-1914* (Geneva, 1984); Y. Cassis, "Bankers and English Society in the Late Nineteenth Century", *Econ. Hist. Rev.*, 2nd ser., xxxviii (1985), pp. 21-9; Y. Cassis, *La City de Londres, 1870-1914* (Paris, 1987).

[16] M. Lisle-Williams, "Merchant Banking Dynasties in the English Class Structure: Ownership, Solidarity and Kinship in the City of London, 1850-1960", *Brit. Jl. Sociology*, xxxv (1984), pp. 333-62; M. Lisle-Williams, "Beyond the Market: The Survival of Family Capitalism in the English Merchant Banks", *Brit. Jl. Sociology*, xxxv (1984), pp. 241-71. For a different, somewhat curious, view, of this merger of

(cont. on p. 125)

"GENTLEMANLY CAPITALISM" AND BRITISH INDUSTRY 125

A crucial change, it would appear, was the emergence of a "closed caste" of dynastic merchant bankers. There was, according to Wiener, no haemorrhage of ability from such families as the Barings and Rothschilds who could continue from generation to generation, becoming indistinguishable from the old aristocracy, whereas a successful industrial family would experience a loss of ability as a search for social acceptance led to a distancing from industry.[17] Dynastic closure among merchant bankers in the late nineteenth century came at precisely the point at which the aristocracy was, according to the Stones and Rubinstein, becoming more open, and the two social groups came together. The "gentrification" of the middle class in the later nineteenth century, which Wiener treats as an anomalous cultural phenomenon, might in fact be perfectly rational, however inappropriate it might have been for industry. What emerged was a "gentlemanly economy" or "gentlemanly capitalism". Aspirations to gentility did not hamper finance in the same way as industry. Financiers and aristocrats were both wealthy and socially established in the mid-nineteenth century when the cultural counter-revolution to industry was starting. Finance and commerce were removed from production; they involved personal contact with members of one's own class rather than direct control of a large work-force; offered freedom from daily cares; were carried on in fashionable areas rather than in a grimy industrial environment; and were reconcilable with the gentry ideal. The City was distanced from industry, both geographically and socially, and, unlike industry, offered a way of getting rich *and* being a gentleman. "Gentlemanly capitalism", suggest Cain and Hopkins, was a characteristic feature of Britain, alongside industrial capitalism. The aristocracy, they claim, united ideas of authority and status, which had a pre-capitalist basis, with incomes drawn from commercial agriculture. The fusion of traditional authority and the most successful form of capitalism "became the touchstone by which all other economic activities were judged. The more an occupation or a source of income allowed for a life-style which was similar to that of the landed classes, the higher the prestige it carried and the greater the power it conferred". A "gentlemanly capitalist" did not

(n. 16 cont.)

the City and aristocracy, see C. Jones, *International Business in the Nineteenth Century: The Rise and Fall of a Cosmopolitan Bourgeoisie* (Brighton, 1987), pp. 1, 195-6. Jones stresses the demise of a "cosmopolitan bourgeoisie" acting as the agent of a progressive liberal revolution, and the emergence of reactionary nationalism in the later nineteenth century, as merchants sought legitimacy from the aristocracy and power from the state.

[17] Wiener, *English Culture*, p. 145.

despise the market economy, but he did hold production in low regard and avoided full-time work.[18]

The British state, so the argument continues, had become fixed before the onset of industrial capitalism, whereas in other countries the state was remoulded by some crisis which displaced the existing structure of power. "Britain alone", claims Anderson, "was exempt from this process, throughout the whole epoch of industrialization which it pioneered". In consequence, when industry faced competition and decline, the state was "eminently unsuitable as an instrument for redressing the decline of British capitalism". This contention was a theme in a recent collection of essays on the decline of the British economy. An industrial structure dominated by small-scale units could not escape from the production institutions or social relations which were inappropriate to changes in production technology. The financial sector which contributed to the reshaping of industry in Germany and America was not involved with British industry, so that financial leverage was not available. On the contrary, the concentration of financial power in the City, and integration with the élite, produced a more coherent influence over policy than was possible for industrialists divided by sector and region; industrial problems were therefore aggravated by measures designed to benefit the City. "No matter the political colour of the government of the day", Green commented in his analysis of monetary policy in the late nineteenth century, "the British State demonstrated a consistent bias towards City opinion". The general coincidence of interests between City, the Treasury and the Bank of England might, as Ingham has warned, not simply express the City's hegemony, for each had its own interests. There is, however, agreement on the outcome: the interests of industry were neglected.[19]

Such is the orthodoxy of British history — political, social and economic — which has emerged since the mid-1970s. It plays down the impact of the Industrial Revolution in transforming Britain's economy, and suggests a fundamental dualism between industrial

---

[18] Anderson, "Figures of Descent", pp. 41, 57; Wiener, *English Culture*, p. 145; Cain and Hopkins, "Gentlemanly Capitalism, i", pp. 503-10; Ingham, *Capitalism Divided?*, pp. 11-12.

[19] Anderson, "Figures of Descent", pp. 37, 47-8, 57, 75; W. Lazonick and B. Elbaum (eds.), *The Decline of the British Economy* (Oxford, 1986), esp. M. H. Best and J. Humphries, "The City and Industrial Decline", pp. 223-39; E. H. H. Green, "Rentiers versus Producers? The Political Economy of the Bimetallic Controversy", *Eng. Hist. Rev.*, ciii (1988), p. 611; Ingham, *Capitalism Divided?*, pp. 9, 37-8; Wiener, *English Culture*, pp. 128-9.

"GENTLEMANLY CAPITALISM" AND BRITISH INDUSTRY 127

capitalism and commercial capitalism, between the economies of the industrial provinces and the metropolis. There was, it has been suggested, not a single process of growth labelled "the Industrial Revolution", but two fundamentally different patterns. Growth in the industrial areas was based largely on exports, and low wages were needed in order to compete. Consequently, the development of services and domestic industry was frustrated. Growth in the metropolitan economy of the south-east was based on "the twin pillars of accumulated wealth from trade and finance and the land". The wealth and income of the élite and middle class sustained high consumer demand, despite the existence of the casual poor, and required a well-developed service economy. The result was to create self-sustaining growth in the south-east. The metropolitan economy was, claims Lee, not only different in structure but probably bigger.[20] There is nothing very novel about such a view, for it has many similarities with the "new Liberal" critique which developed in Edwardian Britain, and which is associated most obviously with J. A. Hobson. The general elections of 1910 with their themes of the power of the House of Lords and the attack upon land were, he argued, fought between two Englands: the producers' England of the north which was dominated by industry, loyal to free trade and hostile to the Lords and land; and the consumers' England of the south which was dominated by "ostentatious leisure" and "conspicuous waste", supporting tariff reform, the Lords and landowners. "Gentlemanly capitalism" with its dependent service sector was aligned against the industrialists who were "actively engaged" in trades supporting "regular, well-paid intelligent artisans".[21]

This, then, is the case — should it be accepted? Caution might be in order before British history is reinterpreted as a conflict between a dominant "gentlemanly capitalism" and a subordinate industrial capitalism. It is perhaps too readily forgotten who won the general elections of 1910 — not the peers but the people, not the gentlemanly capitalists but their horny-handed opponents. A major theme in Liberal politics was not subordination to a cult of the aristocracy so much as an attack upon the parasitism of landowners on productive capital and labour.[22]

[20] C. H. Lee, *The British Economy since 1700: A Macroeconomic Perspective* (Cambridge, 1986), pp. 131, 136-41.

[21] J. A. Hobson, "The General Election: A Sociological Interpretation", *Sociol. Rev.*, iii (1910), p. 113.

[22] The best account of the "land campaign" is A. Offer, *Property and Politics, 1870-1914: Landownership, Law, Ideology and Urban Development in England* (Cambridge, 1981). He does, however, argue that one motivation was to wrest land from the

(cont. on p. 128)

II

A major prop of the argument for the subordination of the industrial bourgeoisie is Rubinstein's contention that larger fortunes were made in the City. How valid is this? His evidence comes from the probate records which give fortunes at death. One problem is that certain types of property were excluded. Real property was not covered until 1898, and settled personalty (such as marriage settlements which passed to the widow at death) was not included, and these omissions create problems which Rubinstein minimizes.[23] We may, however, impose some check by considering Scottish evidence where the sources are different, and by supplementing the probate records with material from the death duties registers which were not available to Rubinstein. Two Scottish examples might be mentioned. Sir Archibald Orr-Ewing died in 1893, leaving an estate "confirmed" at £1,077,234. But this did not include agricultural land, dye-works, workers' housing, and offices which were, even excluding fixed plant, worth over £300,000. Again, William Pearce left £1,084,000 but this did not include a shipyard worth another £1 million.[24] Much the same pattern is found in England. When Richard Arkwright died in 1843, his will was granted probate at Canterbury at "over £1 million" and at York for "under £20,000". The death duties registers show that his fortune (even excluding real estate which was not covered by the registers until 1853) was in fact £2,278,650.[25] The reliance upon probate could therefore have a major distorting effect, which would appear to be greater for industrialists with large investments in fixed assets, than for merchants and financiers whose concerns were less likely to necessitate investment in fixed plant.

A second problem relates to *inter vivos* gifts. Rubinstein dismisses these as unimportant, for he argues that the motivation was tax avoidance. Since tax levels were low, and all groups of the wealthy had an equal interest in avoiding payment, he claims that his basic conclusion about the level of industrial and commercial estates would not be affected.[26] This is another large assumption. *Inter vivos* gifts

(n. 22 cont.)

landowners so that town-dwellers could enjoy commons, forests and footpaths. The attack upon landowners was therefore justified by the moral benefits of the countryside which Wiener stresses as characteristic of English culture.

[23] Rubinstein, *Men of Property*, pp. 12-15.

[24] N. J. Morgan and M. S. Moss, "Listing the Wealthy in Scotland", *Bull. Inst. Hist. Research*, lix (1986), pp. 190-3.

[25] B. English, "Probate Valuations and the Death Duty Registers", *Bull. Inst. Hist. Research*, lvii (1984), p. 90.

[26] Rubinstein, *Men of Property*, pp. 15-16.

"GENTLEMANLY CAPITALISM" AND BRITISH INDUSTRY 129

were not necessarily designed to avoid tax, and other motivations might indeed affect industrial and commercial estates to varying degrees. One motivation was the smooth transfer of ownership of firms and their direction, which was perhaps of greater relevance in manufacturing partnerships than in banking or finance, where the senior partner often left day-to-day management to junior partners and was content with a supervisory role. A merchant or banker was likely to keep a large part of his wealth in the firm as a loan receiving a fixed interest, which would be caught in the valuation of the estate at death. An industrialist was more likely to hand over the concern during his own life, so that a larger part of his wealth would escape from valuation at death. And estate at death is obviously no indication of total earnings. Peter Denny, the Scottish shipbuilder, withdrew £1,492,527 from his Dumbarton firm between 1845 and 1895, without taking into account his interest in a bank in Liverpool, in marine engineering and in mining. He left only £190,975, and the puzzle is what he did with it. Some could go to the family, some into land, some in philanthropic obligations to the local community dependent on the firm.[27]

Scottish evidence suggests that these distortions affected manufacturing more than finance, although it is too soon to say how much of the discrepancy which is stressed by Rubinstein between industrial and commercial fortunes should be removed. More clear-cut is the rejection of Rubinstein's (and by implication the Stones') view that "new men of wealth" did not invest in land, so that the landed élite up to about 1880 was a closed caste. Rubinstein's case is that "In the world of high politics and government, Britain became more dominated by genuine aristocrats in the half-century after 1832 compared with the half-century before; much of the nexus between the aristocracy and the older business and professional world which marked 'Old Corruption' disappeared in the nineteenth century; the holdings of the largest landowners often became considerably larger in size".[28] Can this rejection of the commonplace view that the British

[27] Morgan and Moss, "Listing the Wealthy", p. 193; see also M. S. Moss, "William Todd Lithgow, Founder of a Fortune", *Scottish Hist. Rev.*, lxii (1983), pp. 47-72. For one example of philanthropy, see J. Reynolds, *The Great Paternalist: Titus Salt and the Growth of Nineteenth-Century Bradford* (London, 1983), pp. 75-6, 278-81. Salt left just under £400,000 on his death in 1876. Charitable gifts during his life included £18,000 for an institute, £7,000 for a Congregational Sunday school, £6,000 to Bradford Grammar School. Salt is a well-known philanthropist, but he was only extending a common practice among industrialists.

[28] Rubinstein, "New Men of Wealth", p. 147; Rubinstein, *Men of Property*, p. 219.

landed élite was much more fluid and open than its counterparts elsewhere be accepted?

Again, it is necessary to adopt caution over Rubinstein's evidence, which is based upon whether the possessors of new fortunes were listed in the survey of landownership compiled by John Bateman. This imposed a high threshold for entry, of 2,000 acres, and Rubinstein concentrates upon the largest of these estates.[29] The term "genuine aristocrats" is significant, for it excludes any movement into the ranks of the gentry and middling landowners. This means that someone like F. G. Dalgety, the wool merchant, who put £313,820 into real estate in England by 1883 simply would not appear.[30] And taking landownership at the date of the death of the person who amassed a fortune is also an unduly rigorous test. How feasible was it both to pursue an active business career *and* to dispose of the fortune within a single life, particularly if education and background had not provided the training for a rural life? It is more realistic to trace the way in which the inheritance was spent in the succeeding generations. F. M. L. Thompson, as a result of a meticulous investigation of the fate of the fortunes left by millionaires, has recently concluded that 90 per cent of millionaires bought land and 80 per cent founded landed families.[31] The notion of a closed caste of landed aristocrats begins to look suspect, and the existence of an "open élite" more plausible.

This conclusion could, of course, be used to support the contention that the bourgeoisie was indeed eager to prostrate itself before feudalism, and might therefore substantiate the belief that a self-conscious bourgeoisie did not emerge. However, this rests upon an overly schematic view of social groupings and a crudely materialistic view of the formation of attitudes, by which ownership of land by definition creates aristocratic values. This is not by any means certain, for there has been a failure to consider *why* land was being purchased. A consideration of one merchant family, that of Gibbs, which left unusually detailed discussions of its investment strategy, suggests that land purchase was designed to prevent overextension of the firm into more risky ventures, and to provide for members of the family

[29] Rubinstein, "New Men of Wealth", pp. 129-34; Rubinstein, *Men of Property*, pp. 214-18.

[30] M. J. Daunton, "Firm and Family in the City of London in the Nineteenth Century: The Case of F. G. Dalgety", *Hist. Research*, forthcoming.

[31] F. M. L. Thompson (paper delivered at Institute of Historical Research, London, 1986).

who were not competent to run the business.[32] The purchase of landed property was part of a strategy to keep the family *in* the City rather than to provide an avenue for escape; it would be wrong to see the Gibbs family as prostrating itself before feudalism. The same point emerges from the investment strategy of the Gregs, the cotton masters. They put money into land, with the aim of offsetting the trade cycle in the cotton industry, providing a safe investment for surplus capital, spreading risk and reducing withdrawals from the capital account in manufacturing. When land was less attractive as an investment, these aims were pursued by putting money in government stocks. The strategy was, therefore, determined by economic considerations rather than a search for social status which served to undermine business success and led to a haemorrhage of talent.[33]

What, after all, was the nature of the aristocracy? It is wrong to see assimilation as a one-way process. Who changed the more, the middle class or the aristocracy? Perhaps the reliability of Rubinstein's figures is not crucial, for "wealth in itself is no simple key to identifying the hegemonic 'fraction' of the ruling class". E. P. Thompson has suggested that the eighteenth-century gentry, as a self-confident capitalist class, united with the industrialists against the parasitism of "old corruption", developing a common ideology of political economy which bridged the interests of land and cotton. Anderson, he claims, neglected the bourgeois culture of political economy and natural science. The bourgeoisie, Thompson believes, enlarged its influence in line with its real socio-economic power. The aristocracy might dominate the army, which was never large, and it kept the church and Oxbridge; but it lost control of local government, the press, and the universities in London and the provinces. The "gentry counter-revolution" of the later nineteenth century was in any case complemented by a movement which Wiener does not mention: the Georgite attack upon land. Landownership was certainly not an "empty" issue, and the apparent rule of the aristocracy had its political uses. What Bagehot called the dignified parts of the constitution might distract attention from the efficient parts and, above all, provide a useful antidote to the possibility of a separate working-class party. The apparent aristocratic hegemony might have a "mystifying role", limiting the development of a working-class critique. The possibility

---

[32] M. J. Daunton, "Inheritance and Succession in the City of London in the Nineteenth Century", *Business Hist.*, xxx (1988).

[33] M. B. Rose, "Diversification of Investment by the Greg Family, 1800-1914", *Business Hist.*, xxi (1979), pp. 79-96.

of attacking aristocratic rule and the share of land in the national income provided a means of uniting tenants in the countryside of the Celtic fringe with the leaseholders of the towns and the miners in the coalfields against the depredations of rent and mineral royalties.[34]

What, if we are to use the term "gentlemanly capitalism", defines a gentleman? Arguably, the criteria changed between the eighteenth and nineteenth centuries in a way which gave primacy to bourgeois rather than aristocratic values. Pocock claims that "civic humanism" was central to the eighteenth century. This stressed the primacy of leisure. Virtue could be developed only through sociability, articulated in the public sphere through the tasks of a citizen. The fear was that opulence and luxury would lead to the onset of corruption caused by devotion to material and private concerns.[35] In the nineteenth century this value-system changed and a Victorian gentleman was judged by different criteria from a Georgian gentleman. The emphasis was on character rather than virtue, and character was tested by striving, self-reliance and the mastering of circumstances. This search for private wealth would contribute to national prosperity and moral worth, whereas civic humanism believed that devotion to private gain meant a loss of leisure and sociability, leading to corruption. Collini has argued that the Reform Act of 1832 was still cast in the language of "virtue", whereas the Second Reform Act of 1867 was cast in the language of "character". The politics of Gladstone may be seen as a rejection of the "ethics of the salon" and eighteenth-century notions of politeness and sociability, with a new emphasis upon the advancement of character by striving and struggle. The value-system was remade between 1832 and 1867, and the outcome was much closer to the views of the business élite than to the traditional standards of the aristocracy.[36]

---

[34] D. Nicholls, "Fractions of Capital: The Aristocracy, the City and Industry in the Development of Modern British Capitalism", *Social Hist.*, xiii (1988), p. 72; E. P. Thompson, "The Peculiarities of the English", in his *The Poverty of Theory and Other Essays* (London, 1978), pp. 245-301; D. A. Reeder, "The Politics of Urban Leaseholds in Late Victorian England", *Internat. Rev. Soc. Hist.*, vi (1961), pp. 413-30.

[35] J. G. A. Pocock, *The Machiavellian Moment* (Princeton, 1975).

[36] S. Collini, "The Idea of 'Character' in Victorian Political Thought", *Trans. Roy. Hist. Soc.*, 5th ser., xxxv (1985), pp. 29-50; P. Smith, "Disraeli's Politics", *Trans. Roy. Hist. Soc.*, 5th ser., xxxvii (1987), p. 72. B. Hilton, *The Age of Atonement: The Influence of Evangelicalism on Social and Economic Thought, 1795-1865* (Oxford, 1988), pp. viii-x, 375-6, accepts that industrial capital was subordinated to "financial and landed-gentry capital of the metropolis", and argues that Evangelicalism was an expression of the former rather than the latter. It was, he claims, not an "enterprise culture", for it argued for free trade as a means of *reducing* the level of economic activity.

There has, indeed, been a lack of subtlety in the interpretation of British culture by those who see it as stultifying the entrepreneurial imperative. Alexander Henderson, who was a newcomer to the City, prospered and purchased an estate of 3,500 acres and a country house at Buscot Park, where he installed Burne-Jones's huge canvases of the medieval legend of *The Briar Wood*. It would be very easy to read into this a rejection of industrial society, a retreat into a chivalric ideal which was aristocratic and backward-looking, an expression of "gentlemanly capitalism" and a surrender to aristocratic values.[37] This is surely a crude interpretation. Burne-Jones was, after all, popular among Birmingham businessmen rather than aristocrats, and Henderson indeed had interests in midland industry as well as in overseas investment. Americans have not been accused of a loss of entrepreneurial dynamism, and were avid profit-maximizers, yet they were not averse to surrounding themselves with the products of medieval and aristocratic societies. J. P. Morgan's library or Vanderbilt's massive château at Biltmore are just as much expressions of admiration for medieval art and aristocratic life as anything in Britain, and it must be wondered whether aesthetic preferences say anything about business dynamism. Certainly, it is a curious view of human nature which so strictly compartmentalizes culture into boxes labelled "aristocratic" or "bourgeois". There seems to be a misplaced determinism implicit in the literature which would suggest that a bourgeoisie is not true to itself unless it adopts some unspecified ideal-type of bourgeois culture. Marxists are often guilty of a crude reductionism which reads culture from the economic base; some recent historians have been equally guilty of a crude reductionism which reads economic success from cultural preferences.

III

A crucial assumption of "gentlemanly capitalism" is the belief that industrialists were distinct from the commercial and financial bourgeoisie, and that "interests" can be neatly separated from one another. This would seem to rest upon two separate propositions. One is that there was only a limited interconnection between industrialists and financial and commercial capital. The other is that the City formed

---

[37] D. Wainwright, *Henderson: A History of the Life of Alexander Henderson, First Lord Faringdon, and of Henderson Administration* (London, 1985); for an account of the ideal of chivalry in the nineteenth century, see M. Girouard, *The Return to Camelot: Chivalry and the English Gentleman* (New Haven and London, 1981).

a coherent group with significant solidarity, so that any internal divisions between different sectors were less important than external divisions between the City and industry. How defensible are these propositions? .

A number of connections may be noted between industrialists on the one hand and the financial and commercial middle class on the other. London banks and financiers, it is often argued, did not provide much fixed capital for domestic industry, and it is usually deduced that the two fractions of capital therefore went their own separate ways.[38] This point may, however, be exaggerated. Banks offered overdrafts to firms, contributing to their short-term credit. The increase in the amount of fixed capital needed by industry made this less significant, yet the needs of industry were not necessarily sacrificed. The joint-stock banks put money at call and short notice on the London discount market and Stock Exchange, so contributing to the ready availability of funds for trade credit, and fuelling the active secondary market in securities which encouraged the purchase of stocks and shares in the knowledge that they could be sold when liquidity was needed.

The benefits of the German banking system in comparison with the British should not be exaggerated. The level of long-term loans was probably lower than critics of British banks have believed, and it should by no means be accepted that decisions were always the most sensible — the allocation of funds might have distorted the German economy. Another factor to consider is the cost of financial instability. "The English banking system", it has been argued in its defence, "may have contributed just as much to economic growth through pursuing a type of banking which did not lead to financial crisis, as the German banks did by facilitating industrial capital formation". Although British banks were not involved in industrial promotions, it should be remembered that the German banks found that risks were high, and their profits were lower. The British banks might therefore have been acting in a way which maximized their profits, maintained financial stability, and contributed to the liquidity of the London money- and capital-markets. The adoption of German

---

[38] The case for the separation, and sacrifice, of industry is presented by W. P. Kennedy, "Foreign Investment, Trade and Growth in the United Kingdom, 1870-1913", *Explorations in Econ. Hist.*, xi (1974), pp. 413-44; W. P. Kennedy, "Institutional Response to Economic Growth: Capital Markets in Britain to 1914", in L. Hannah (ed.), *Management Strategy and Business Development* (London, 1976), pp. 151-83; see the survey of the literature in S. Pollard, "Capital Exports, 1870-1914: Harmful or Beneficial?", *Econ. Hist. Rev.*, 2nd ser., xxxviii (1985), pp. 489-514.

practice might have been inappropriate. German industrial technology was more "lumpy" than in Britain, and the capital-market less well developed. British banks might simply not need to become involved in the long-term capital-market.[39]

The connection between finance and industry might be reversed: profits from industrial enterprise might be channelled into the financial sector. One example is Dundee, whose economy was based upon jute and hemp. The families in these textile trades received fixed interest on the money they left in the partnership, as well as a share of the gross profits. They were inclined to leave profits to accumulate in the firm in order to obtain a steady 5 per cent, so that the problem faced by the firms was not a shortage of funds so much as what to do with their money. It could not all be invested in new plant, and the partnerships might become investment trusts administering a range of investments unconnected with textiles. One such firm — Cox Brothers — started to invest in American railroads in the 1870s, American land in the 1880s, Japanese and Australian government bonds, and various English companies. By 1907 these investments amounted to £147,000. These private, family investment trusts were extended in the 1870s, so that anyone could participate. The most famous example is Robert Fleming's Scottish American Investment Trust of 1873, a business which still exists, relocated from Dundee to the City.[40] It might be suggested that industrial concerns had financial interests which can be understood only in terms of the needs of private partnerships to invest profits outside the firm. Land was one possibility; the strategy of the Coxes was another.

It is often assumed that the City's involvement with overseas investments worked against the needs of domestic industry, which was spurned as funds were diverted into foreign ventures. Most of the overseas investment, it is contended, was portfolio rather than

[39] P. L. Cottrell, *Industrial Finance, 1830-1914: The Finance and Organization of English Manufacturing Industry* (London, 1980), ch. 7; for a critical view of the German banks, see H. M. Neuberger and H. H. Stokes, "German Banks and German Growth, 1883-1913: An Empirical View", *Jl. Econ. Hist.*, xxiv (1974), pp. 710-31; and the response by R. Fremdling and R. Tilly, "German Banks, German Growth and Econometric History", *Jl. Econ. Hist.*, xxxvi (1976), pp. 416-24.

[40] B. Lenman and K. Donaldson, "Partners' Incomes, Investment and Diversification in the Scottish Linen Area, 1850-1921", *Business Hist.*, xiii (1971), pp. 1-18. Scotland was an important source for funds for investment and finance companies: see R. C. Michie, "Crisis and Opportunity: The Formation and Operation of the British Assets Trust, 1897-1914", *Business Hist.*, xxv (1983), pp. 125-47; and J. D. Bailey, "Australian Borrowing in Scotland in the Nineteenth Century", *Econ. Hist. Rev.*, 2nd ser., xii (1959-60), pp. 268-79.

direct: that is to say, it was passive, not securing control over the foreign concerns and not serving British needs beyond the desire of investors to secure a higher return than they could achieve at home, regardless of the social costs.[41] It is, however, possible to put forward an alternative view.

A sizeable part of British overseas investment was not British at all. London's role as a centre for international trade meant that short-term money was held by merchants to cover their commitments, and this money could be placed in long-term securities provided that the Stock Exchange could offer a ready market for their sale when the funds were needed. If this point is accepted, then the Stock Exchange should not be seen as a casino in which speculators sought quick gains at the expense of industry; rather, it provided an active market which allowed the more efficient use of funds, converting short-term money which would otherwise be idle into long-term securities.[42] It might, of course, be that the brokers and the industrialists were *socially* distinct; but this is not the same as saying that they were *functionally* unrelated. There is a tendency in the literature to move from the first to the second.

Neither is it certain that the overseas assets were overwhelmingly composed of portfolio rather than direct investment. Partly this is a matter of definition. Most accounts define direct investment by two criteria: control by the investor in Britain; and investment through subsidiaries and branches rather than the Stock Exchange. But most economists would argue that control *alone* is the criterion, which may be achieved by holding a sizeable block of shares purchased on the Stock Exchange. The present British definition is that an investment counts as direct if the stake is over 20 per cent; the American and Japanese definition is as low as 10 per cent.[43] In any case, many of the shares were in "free-standing companies" which were formed to pursue a particular opportunity abroad, whether a mine or an oil concession. The head office in London usually consisted of a secretary and a board of directors, and services were obtained from a range of specialist accountants, solicitors, mining engineers, trading compan-

[41] See comments by P. Svedberg, "The Portfolio-Direct Composition of Private Investment in 1914 Revisited", *Econ. Jl.*, lxxxviii (1978), p. 763.

[42] R. C. Michie, *The London and New York Stock Exchanges, 1850-1914* (London, 1987), pp. 117-23, 139-40, 156-7; D. C. M. Platt, "British Portfolio Investment Overseas before 1870: Some Doubts", *Econ. Hist. Rev.*, 2nd ser., xxx (1980), pp. 12-14.

[43] Svedberg, "Portfolio-Direct Composition", p. 765; *The Economist*, 20-6 Feb. 1988, p. 73.

ies and merchant banks.[44] The definition of direct investment, and the nature of such companies, suggests that much passive, portfolio investment should be redefined as direct and active. Portfolio investment has often been put at 90 per cent of the total; one recent study of British investment in Latin America would reduce it to 52·2 per cent in 1905.[45]

This figure might still be an underestimate, for while it is easy to measure portfolio investment by aggregating issues on the Stock Exchange, it is not always easy to discover investments made by firms. There was, in fact, a sizeable number of investment groups which are not always readily identified. The parent firm might be a partnership or private company, with overseas activities carried on by junior partners or managers under separate names. An example of this process would be Matheson and Co., which originated in Scotland. By 1914 its head offices were in London: other parts of the group consisted of shipping (the China Coast Steam Navigation and Indo-China Steam Navigation); railway building (the Shanghai-Woosung Railway and the China Railway Co.); financial services (the Canton Insurance Office and the Ewo Bank of Shanghai); mining (Rio Tinto, the Transvaal Exploration Co. and the Caucasus Copper Co.); and, through Jardine, Matheson and Co. in Hong Kong, interests in the China Sugar Co., Hong Kong Land, and the Ewo Spinning Co.[46] The notion of the British overseas investor as a passive "coupon-clipper" has been seriously challenged.

A further functional relationship should be noted, for one of the main roles of the City was to provide raw materials for British industry. There is a danger that the work of Cassis and Lisle-Williams has focused attention upon one part of the City which moved into international banking and overseas loans. There was also a large group of firms involved with handling commodities. A firm such as Frederick Dalgety's, importing wool from Australia, had to be as sensitive to the needs of Bradford as to the state of the clip in New South Wales, and in the 1860s he was to be an opponent of the incursion of finance houses into the business. Dalgety himself had

[44] M. Wilkins, "The Free-Standing Company, 1870-1914: An Important Type of British Foreign Direct Investment", *Econ. Hist. Rev.*, 2nd ser., xli (1988), pp. 259-82.

[45] I. Stone, "British Direct and Portfolio Investment in Latin America before 1914", *Jl. Econ. Hist.*, xxxvii (1977), pp. 690-722; Svedberg, "Portfolio-Direct Composition", pp. 763-77.

[46] S. D. Chapman, "British-Based Investment Groups before 1914", *Econ. Hist. Rev.*, 2nd ser., xxxviii (1985), pp. 230-51.

major investments in Australian and New Zealand land and sheep stations, yet did not see himself as the spokesman of the colonists so much as the defender of the City merchants; the colonists tended to side with the Australasian banks and finance houses which were moving into the City and challenging the dominance of the commission merchants. This provided one significant divide within the City, and Dalgety for all his international links was to be more concerned about the needs of British consumers than of colonial producers. This was even more the case with the larger number of brokers who depended upon the trade. These were divided into two groups, those who acted for the sellers, and those who acted for the buyers in the West Riding. The needs of northern industry were part of the City, and not something alien.[47]

The ties between merchants and industry could be strong: in some cases in the early nineteenth century they were one and the same. William Thompson, alderman of the City and at one time its M.P., the head of Lloyd's, director of the Bank of England, was also the proprietor of one of the largest South Wales ironworks;[48] similarly, the Crawshay family straddled the division between the Cyfarthfa ironworks at Merthyr and the merchant house in the City.[49] The Grenfells, who were to become partners of J. P. Morgan, started as copper-smelters at Swansea;[50] the Barings were initially in the west country cloth industry.[51] Even Nathan Rothschild first came to England to finance the trade in cotton goods in Manchester;[52] and James Morrison made most of his money out of a textile warehouse

---

[47] Daunton, "Firm and Family"; Ingham, *Capitalism Divided?* stresses the commercial as well as financial nature of the City, yet does not develop the connections this involved with industry.

[48] F. Boase, *Modern English Biography*, 6 vols. (Truro, 1892-1921), iii, col. 942; R. S. Ferguson, *Cumberland and Westmorland M.P.s from the Restoration to the Reform Bill of 1867* (London, 1871), p. 443.

[49] J. P. Addis, *The Crawshay Dynasty: A Study in Industrial Organisation and Development, 1765-1867* (Cardiff, 1957), pp. 4-6, ch. 4. The tension between the industrial area and the City took place within the family partnership.

[50] On the development of Pascoe Grenfell's interests in copper and banking, see J. R. Harris, *The Copper King: A Biography of Thomas Williams of Llanidan* (Liverpool, 1974), pp. xvi, 154-7. On the industrial origins of banks, see L. S. Pressnell, *Country Banking in the Industrial Revolution* (London, 1956), pp. 14-36, 322-43.

[51] H. R. Fox Bourne, *English Merchants* (London, 1886), pp. 447-59; R. Hidy, *The House of Baring in American Trade and Finance: English Merchant Bankers at Work, 1761-1861* (Cambridge, Mass., 1949), pp. 4-13.

[52] S. D. Chapman, "The Foundation of the English Rothschilds: N. M. Rothschild as a Textile Merchant, 1799-1811", *Textile Hist.*, viii (1977), pp. 99-115. He left £5 million on his death in 1837, the largest personal estate between 1809 and 1839: Rubinstein, *Men of Property*, p. 44.

"GENTLEMANLY CAPITALISM" AND BRITISH INDUSTRY 139

in the City which marketed goods from the mills of Lancashire.[53] Cotton textiles were crucial to international trade in the early and mid-nineteenth century. The Greek merchant houses, for example, acted as the pivot between a trade in textiles from Lancashire to the Middle East, and in grain from the Black Sea to London. They developed close connections with calico-printers for the first, and with the Baltic Exchange for the second.[54] These patterns of self-contained trading networks disappeared in the later nineteenth century with the emergence of a single multilateral world economy,[55] but this is not to say that merchant banks became separated from the concerns of domestic industry.

The system for marketing British industrial goods which developed after about 1860 was based upon a division between manufacturers, commission agents and financiers. The manufacturers retreated from direct sales, while the larger merchant houses such as Antony Gibbs and Sons or Brown Shipley moved into a financial role as acceptance houses providing trade credit. The actual selling of British goods was in the hands of commission agents who resided in a foreign centre, usually with a partner or agent in Britain. This specialization reduced the need for manufacturers to provide large amounts of trade credit, and encouraged the development of a large army of commission agents spread across the world, to a much greater extent than was the case in Germany and America. The system had advantages of a wide coverage and flexibility, although there were a number of potential drawbacks. The marketing system established barriers between production and selling, between the manufacturer and the consumer. These potential problems emerged less from the fact that the City *ignored* the needs of British industry than from a well-developed *complementarity*.[56]

[53] R. Gatty, *Portrait of a Merchant Prince: James Morrison, 1789-1857* (Northallerton, 1976). James Morrison left £4 million on his death in 1857, the largest personal estate between 1840 and 1879: Rubinstein, *Men of Property*, p. 44.

[54] S. D. Chapman, "The International Houses: The Continental Contribution to British Commerce, 1800-60", *Jl. European Econ. Hist.*, vi (1977), pp. 35-42; S. E. Fairlie, "The Anglo-Russian Grain Trade, 1815-61" (Univ. of London Ph.D. thesis, 1959), pp. 261-91.

[55] S. B. Saul, *Studies in British Overseas Trade, 1870-1914* (Liverpool, 1960), pp. 44-5.

[56] S. D. Chapman, "British Marketing Enterprise: The Changing Role of Merchants, Manufacturers and Financiers, 1700-1860", *Business Hist. Rev.*, liii (1979), pp. 217-31; S. J. Nicholas, "The Overseas Marketing Performance of British Industry, 1870-1914", *Econ. Hist. Rev.*, 2nd ser., xxxvii (1984), pp. 494-5; A. Ellis, *Heir of Adventure: The Story of Brown, Shipley and Co., Merchant Bankers, 1810-1960* (London, 1960); W. Maude, *Antony Gibbs and Sons Limited, Merchants and Bankers, 1808-1958* (London, 1958).

The same point might be made, to a lesser extent, about overseas loans. These might connect with the export of capital goods which formed a major part of British industry in the later nineteenth century. Although the Rothschilds moved into government loan-contracting for foreign states, they could nevertheless remain in touch with British industrial concerns involved with, for example, South African mining.[57] Indeed it is possible to argue that the concerns of finance and industry were in many cases becoming closer in the Edwardian period. A good example of such an interconnection of the City and British industry is Alexander Henderson, first Lord Faringdon, who trained as an accountant in the City before becoming a member of the Stock Exchange. His brother Brodie was apprenticed to James Livesey, the engineer, who was involved in building railways in South America and Africa which were financed by Alexander. It would be wrong to see Alexander Henderson as in any sense opposed to domestic industry, which was benefiting from the activities of Livesey. He was involved with the flotation of the Imperial Tobacco Company; he financed the Manchester Ship Canal; he was concerned with the Great Central Railway; and he was associated with Dudley Docker, the spokesman for British industry, in the formation of the British Trade Corporation; he owned an ironworks in Staffordshire where he stood as a Conservative candidate; he was treasurer of the Tariff Reform League. In some respects, he does look like a "gentlemanly capitalist" for, as noted earlier, he bought a landed estate with an eighteenth-century house; his eldest son became an army officer and married the daughter of an earl; and he was associated with Lord Revelstoke and Sir Ernest Cassel in the formation of the National Bank of Turkey. But this did not mean ignorance of industry: Henderson straddled the lines which have too readily been assumed between land, the City and industry.[58]

In many cases the functional connections between the "gentleman capitalists" and the industrialists were much more obvious and direct. The third marquis of Bute attempted to create a fantasy medieval world and devote himself to Catholicism; but even he could not hide the fact that the ability to indulge his (and William Burges's)

[57] J. Harris and P. Thane, "British and European Bankers, 1880-1914: An 'Aristocratic Bourgeoisie'?", in P. Thane, G. Crossick and R. Floud (eds.), *The Power of the Past: Essays for Eric Hobsbawm* (Cambridge, 1984), pp. 221-2; R. V. Turrell and J. J. Van Helten, "The Rothschilds, the Exploration Company and Mining Finance", *Business Hist.*, xxviii (1986), pp. 181-205.

[58] Wainwright, *Henderson*; R. P. T. Davenport-Hines, *Dudley Docker: The Life and Times of a Trade Warrior* (Cambridge, 1984), pp. 58, 127, 134-5, 137-40, 142-8.

architectural megalomania was based upon the profits from the Bute docks, the ground rents from Cardiff, and the mineral royalties of the South Wales coalfield. He was attacked by South Wales Liberals who followed the Ricardo-George criticism of the share of income taken by rent, which was seen as parasitical upon active enterprise; and one sector of the Welsh industrial middle class did declare independence from the Bute estate by building a separate dock further along the coast. But equally, another part of the Welsh industrial middle class sided with the Bute estate, and was firmly tied to the facilities provided by Bute.[59] The manager of the estate, Sir W. T. Lewis, first Lord Merthyr, was one of the most hard-headed businessmen of the nineteenth century, and straddled the divide between gentlemanly capitalism and industrial capitalism. He served the marquis of Bute as his agent; he ran the Bute docks and railways; he allied with Amon Beasley of the Taff Vale Railway Co. against recognition of trades unions, earning the title of "the best hated man" in Wales for his pains; he was himself a major coal-owner and as chairman of the Monmouthshire and South Wales Coalowners' Association he opposed trades unionism; he was a leading figure, with Beasley, in the Cardiff Ratepayers' Association which opposed the spread of municipal enterprise into public utilities; he was also a medievalist.[60] Bute and Lewis were not alone and were typical of a certain type of enterprise which crossed the landed/industrial divide. Lewis, as a representative of the Bute concerns, was associated with the Liberty and Property Defence League, the brain-child of Lord Elcho (later the earl of Wemyss), which brought together landowners with railway companies, some industries and ratepayers' associations against the Liberal reforms and municipal socialism; its historian has seen in this a proto-Federation of British Industry.[61] The interconnection between land and industry could therefore be active and political, whether or not there was a social fusion.

The existence of a barrier between industrialists and "gentlemanly capitalists" is questionable. The case could be strengthened by a more

[59] M. J. Daunton, *Coal Metropolis: Cardiff, 1870-1914* (Leicester, 1977); J. Davies, *Cardiff and the Marquesses of Bute* (Cardiff, 1981).

[60] Daunton, *Coal Metropolis*; M. J. Daunton, "Inter-Union Relations on the Waterfront: Cardiff, 1888-1914", *Internat. Rev. Social Hist.*, xxii (1977), pp. 350-78; L. J. Williams, "The Monmouthshire and South Wales Coalowners' Association, 1873-1914" (Univ. of Wales M.A. thesis, 1957); D. J. Jeremy (ed.), *Dictionary of Business Biography*, 5 vols. (London, 1984-6), iii, pp. 773-8.

[61] E. Bristow, "The Liberty and Property Defence League and Individualism", *Hist. Jl.*, xviii (1975), pp. 761-2.

detailed consideration of the involvement of aristocratic landowners in port-building, coal-mining, transport undertakings and urban development. However, the literature on this point is extensive. What should be stressed is that the experience of landowners was not constant, and the treatment of aristocracy, City and industry as three coherent interests can be misleading. Landed aristocrats might well be divided. Pastoral areas did better than arable districts in the later nineteenth century, so that they might experience the agricultural depression of the late nineteenth century to a greater or less extent. They might also differ in their ability to benefit from urban and industrial growth.[62] The Liberal attack upon land in the early twentieth century masked these divergences, and helped to create a defensive political solidarity. But what about the City? Was it as internally cohesive as some historians have assumed, and did it adopt a common political stance?

IV

The existence of a merger between City and land might be based upon a biased sample which excludes many sectors of the City. The contention of Chapman is that meritocracy rather than aristocracy was the keynote even of merchant banking and that "the non-aristocratic group were . . . a more significant economic feature. Merchant bankers with aristocratic connections were familiar because the old hereditary leadership were often also prominent in public life, but the vitality and competitiveness of the financial sector was more characteristically drawn from newer arrivals to the City of London". Chapman has compiled a list of merchant banks with a capital exceeding £1 million before 1914. The firms with aristocratic connections — Baring, Rothschild, Grenfell — formed a minority, and even in these cases survival might be due to non-aristocrats. Barings survived largely because of the American partner, Joshua Bates; and Grenfell went into partnership with J. P. Morgan. The bulk of merchant banks did not, according to Chapman, have links with the aristocracy. The Greek house of Ralli Brothers or the Spanish house of Murietta were not obviously integrated into the aristocracy, and Chapman places particular stress upon the larger number of Anglo-German firms who were, he argues, much quicker than the "aristocratic" firms in seizing new opportunities. Members of these families

[62] For a recent synthesis, see J. V. Beckett, *The Aristocracy in England, 1660-1914* (Oxford, 1986).

"GENTLEMANLY CAPITALISM" AND BRITISH INDUSTRY 143

were, claims Chapman, not educated at public school, did not marry English women, had little time for politics or socializing, and had little respect for the Bank. This was not a leisured élite, but was devoted to work, and might consciously repudiate the values of the aristocracy. He cites the German firms, which had a loyalty to the Reich; the Greeks, who had a strong internal cohesion; and the Americans, who were devoted to success. Not everyone in the City, even at the peak of the merchant-banking hierarchy, was a gentleman.[63]

It might be countered that within a generation these "outsiders" would be integrated, but this is to assume that firms and families survived from generation to generation. It must be doubted, however, whether the City could be so dominated by dynastic firms, gentlemanly capitalism and a closed social structure as claimed by Lisle-Williams. Could a dynamic financial and commercial centre, at a time of major changes in the world economy, have long survived the dominance of leisured semi-amateurs? "Statistically speaking", Chapman suggests, "the mortality of family firms, in merchant banking as elsewhere, is more impressive than the continuity".[64] Murietta was bankrupt in 1890, and this firm was not alone. Bankruptcy in the eighteenth century was higher in the City and among commercial concerns than in industry, and it would be surprising if this did not continue to be the case.[65] However, outright failure was less important than a disinclination to continue the firm from one generation to the next. Inheritance and succession in the City were in some ways more difficult than in industrial concerns, and the creation of dynasties was problematical. Family capitalism, contrary to Lisle-Williams, meant a high turnover. Walter Bagehot did not remark upon the presence of dynasties, but rather on the absence of families of merchant princes.[66]

It was only in 1907 that private partnerships could obtain the benefits of limited liability, and for most of the nineteenth century merchants were loath to transform their concerns into companies.[67]

[63] S. D. Chapman, "Aristocracy and Meritocracy in Merchant Banking", *Brit. Jl. Sociology*, xxxvii (1986), pp. 180-93.

[64] *Ibid.*, p. 186.

[65] J. Hoppit, *Risk and Failure in English Business, 1700-1800* (Cambridge, 1987), pp. 68-74.

[66] W. Bagehot, *Lombard Street: A Description of the Money Market*, new edn. (London, 1915), p. 9.

[67] R. R. Formoy, *The Historical Foundation of Modern Company Law* (London, 1923), p. 46.

Unlimited liability and private partnerships were, it was felt by Thomas Baring, the guarantees of "the reputation, honour and credit of the English merchant". Limited liability would, claimed J. G. Hubbard, lead to "reckless and irresponsible speculation", which he was not willing to contemplate: "The honour of a mercantile man was as delicate as that of a woman, and once tarnished could scarcely ever be retrieved".[68] It followed that if family money were left in the firm, it could threaten the entire family with insolvency; yet if the money were taken out of the firm, it could threaten the survival of the business. The succession of the generations therefore required a careful balancing of the interests of family and firm. This task might simply be avoided, and the family could depart from the City and leave very little trace, which makes the task of the historian very difficult.

The process of departure may be illustrated by the example of Philip Flower and Severin Salting, who had formed a partnership in Sydney in 1842. Flower moved to London in 1843 to handle finance and wool sales, and Salting was responsible for the Australian end of the business until he retired to England in 1858. Although the firm was the largest importer of Australian wool in the 1840s, by the 1860s it had slumped to insignificance and the house in the City had only a nominal existence. By then, Flower and Salting had turned to the development of a large housing estate at Battersea. The next generation virtually abandoned the family firm. William Flower led the life of a leisured *rentier*. His brother George, a well-known eccentric who lived in great modesty, spent his days buying works of art which he donated to the Victoria and Albert Museum and the National Gallery; he had also invested shrewdly on the Stock Exchange so that by 1905 he had a portfolio of £1·3 million. Salting had five sons: two devoted themselves to country life and leisure; another caused a scandal by eloping with Viscountess Dupplin; one worked as salaried chairman of a colonial bank; and Cyril married a Rothschild, became Liberal whip, and ultimately Lord Battersea. The Flowers and Saltings had become gentlemen *par excellence*, and in the process the connection between firm and family had, to all intents and purposes, been severed. The families had opted out of the business even before the death of the founders, yet this had been the largest enterprise in the Australian wool trade.[69] Continuity was by no means sought; and even when it was, it was not easily achieved.

[68] *Hansard*, 3rd ser., clxix, cols. 1889-90; clxxii, cols. 830-2.
[69] M. J. Daunton, "Australian Merchants in the City of London, 1840-90", in *The City and Empire*, ii (Institute of Commonwealth Studies, London, Collected Seminar Papers, no. 36, 1987), pp. 136-7.

"GENTLEMANLY CAPITALISM" AND BRITISH INDUSTRY 145

A comparison between two families where dynastic continuity was desired will suggest that success was by no means certain. In the case of the Hubbard family and firm the issues of inheritance and succession from one generation to the next were mishandled. The business comprised two linked partnerships: a Russian branch which controlled cotton-mills and timber estates; and the London house which handled its financial needs. The brothers John and William left contradictory instructions to their sons, who retained the family money in the business without any defined terms for its use. If the money had been paid out of the firm to the beneficiaries, the business could not have survived. As it was, both sons were incompetent businessmen. They were "gentlemen capitalists": Evelyn was a Conservative M.P., a director of the Bank, had married into a landed family, and his father had become a peer and landowner. Although the business was initially rescued, it was not at the behest of a community of interest of the Bank of England, but rather through the intervention of a relative, Stuart Rendel, who was a director of an industrial concern. Rendel complained that Evelyn and Egerton "would have in any case ruined themselves", but they were able to ruin the family as well by the lack of a clear definition of the relationship between firm and family.

The Gibbs family, by comparison, defined the relationship with great care. When William Gibbs decided to retire from active involvement in Antony Gibbs and Sons in 1858, his nephew and partner Henry Hucks Gibbs continued the business. They were both very careful to specify the terms upon which William's capital should remain in the business. The amount should not be too great, for otherwise the firm would be tempted into risky ventures, and William should therefore place some of his money in land. The capital retained in the firm should pay interest at a high enough rate to compensate William for the risk, without absorbing the profits so as to leave little for Henry. And the length of time for the money to remain in the firm had to be clarified. It could not be open-ended, but neither could the period be rigidly fixed in case repayment fell at an inconvenient moment which might lead to insolvency. These were technically difficult decisions, which required a very careful balancing of interests between family and firm, sleeping and active partners. The Gibbs family handled the problems competently and the dynasty survived.[70]

The crucial consideration, it might be suggested, was not the role

---

[70] Daunton, "Inheritance and Succession".

of the Bank so much as the strategy of families in response to the common problems of inheritance and succession. Landed families had a well-formulated strategy based on the strict settlement; merchant families did not. Lisle-Williams's emphasis upon the cohesive, integrated nature of the City would certainly not help explain the contrast between Hubbard and Gibbs families. Henry was, like his close friend J. G. Hubbard, a Conservative M.P., a director of the Bank, a leading Anglican layman, a large landowner — yet the Hubbards fell from the élite of the City while the Gibbs family remained firmly entrenched. Lisle-Williams has placed too much weight upon the Bank of England in maintaining a closed and cohesive social system within the City. Election to the Court of the Bank was usually made when an individual was relatively young, reflecting the mercantile success of the preceding generation rather than the dynamism of the present. In some cases, such as that of Henry Gibbs, the expectation was fulfilled; in others, such as Evelyn Hubbard's, it was not. Membership was not uniformly welcomed. William Gibbs tried to dissuade his nephew from becoming a director, fearing that it would divert his attention from the firm, and Schröder criticized his partner F. C. Tiarks for joining the Court of the Bank. The Bank was not held in high esteem by all members of the merchant-banking community, and was simply not so important in the economic and social functioning of the City as some historians have assumed.[71] It was certainly not crucial in establishing a closed, dynastic structure.

How cohesive, after all, was the City? It has already been noted that merchant bankers were ethnically divided, and had varying degrees of integration with the aristocracy. Even so, this was the sector which was most likely to be marked by continuity, for reputation was crucial. Other sectors were more likely to be shifting and unstable. The important consideration might be the ease or difficulty of access into various City institutions. The London Stock Exchange, for example, was quite unlike its counterpart in New York where there was a limited number of "seats", which were consequently sold at high prices. Since members of the New York Stock Exchange were not forbidden to undertake other functions, the seats tended to fall into the hands of large banks. In London there was no limit to the number of members, but a bar on outside activities. The result was a large number of members with a low capitalization, and a consequently high level of entry and exit. Much the same applied to

[71] *The Economist*, 20 Jan. 1866, pp. 61-2; Chapman, "Aristocracy and Meritocracy", p. 187.

the Baltic Exchange and to Lloyd's. What stands out in London is not the tight, cohesive nature of the society so much as the lack of any rigorous controls and an endemic fluidity.[72]

The structure of the City may be seen as an interplay between two patterns. One was the cycle of inheritance and succession within family firms, which was likely to produce a considerable turnover. The other was the commodity cycle. When a new commodity or area entered world trade, it would usually bring with it a new group of merchants from the periphery of the world economy. In time, a few of these new firms would probably come to dominate the trade as it became more established and demanded larger amounts of capital; and this might also entail a termination of the family cycle if it was associated with the emergence of public companies. The City for most of the nineteenth century operated through private partnerships, and experienced a constantly changing commodity and area composition of trade, quite apart from fluctuations in trade, industry and investment which had a major impact upon firms. In aggregate the picture was one of change and fluidity rather than closure.

The Australian wool trade is a good example of this interplay between the commodity and family cycles. This was a new sector of trade in the 1840s, and a group of merchants arrived in London from Sydney and Melbourne, such as Flower in 1843 and Dalgety in 1854. In the 1850s Flower and his partner Salting faced the problem of succession and, as we have seen, virtually opted out of the wool business; they were succeeded by Dalgety as the dominant firm. In the late 1860s a new style of organization was starting to enter the wool trade: the colonial banks and finance houses which raised funds to provide long-term finance for squatters rather than simply trade credits. These banks and finance houses had larger sums of money at their disposal than independent merchants, for they could utilize deposits or issue debentures. They also acted as spokesmen for the colonies against the City, which was seen as exploiting the growers. Private partnerships such as Dalgety would eventually find it difficult to compete.[73]

---

[72] Michie, *London and New York Stock Exchanges*, pp. 252-3, 256-7; J. A. Findlay, *The Baltic Exchange* (London, 1927), pp. 14, 22, 37; although members were limited to 300 in 1823, this was not adhered to and in 1858 there were 627 and in 1903 1,400 members. For Lloyd's, see F. Martin, *The History of Lloyd's and of Marine Insurance in Great Britain* (London, 1876), pp. 363-5.

[73] A. Barnard, *The Australian Wool Market, 1840-1900* (Melbourne, 1958); R. J. C. Stone, *Makers of Fortune: A Colonial Business Community and its Fall* (Auckland and Oxford, 1973) and H. J. Hanham, "New Zealand Promoters and British Investors,

(cont. on p. 148)

The issue first came to the fore in 1871 when the colonial growers mounted an attack on the London wool merchants. The leading spokesman on the side of the growers was Daniel Cooper, a prosperous Sydney businessman who retired to England in 1861, where he served as director of the Bank of New South Wales. Dalgety, as the leader of the London merchants, was able to frustrate the growers' demand for an enquiry into the functioning of the wool trade, but his success was short-lived. By 1880 the family cycle and the commodity cycle were coming together. Dalgety's partners were retiring or dying, and he wished to take only a supervisory role in the firm; at the same time the needs were mounting for larger amounts of capital to finance squatters buying the freehold of their runs. Dalgety's aim was to continue with family capitalism by recruiting new partners, from the next generation if possible and from outside the firm if necessary. But it soon became clear to E. T. Doxat, a successful wool-broker who was brought into the partnership, that Dalgety's strategy was simply impossible in competition with banks and wool finance houses which had larger, cheaper sources of funds. In 1883 Doxat's ability and dominance within the firm enabled him to force Dalgety to accept the conversion of the business into a company, which could sell debentures in order to compete with the wool finance houses and the banks. Dalgety accepted with great reluctance; and the survival of the firm had been by no means certain. Decline or disappearance had been a very likely outcome, and this was the result in many firms without a figure such as Doxat. Continuity of family firms was highly contingent. Neither was this sector of the City marked by cohesion, for there was a divide between London-based merchants and colonially based banks and finance houses as they competed for the business of the growers. Certainly there was little that was aristocratic or gentlemanly about this sector of the City. The connections were not within British society with landed interests, but with groups in the colonies.[74]

The City was fluid and divided in terms of its economic and social structure, and this point may be continued into the realm of politics. "The City was predominantly Whig-Liberal down to the mid-1860s", remark Harris and Thane, "returned a mixture of Liberal and Con-

(n. 73 cont.)
1860-95", in R. Chapman and K. Sinclair (eds.), *Studies of a Small Democracy: Essays in Honour of Willis Airey* (Auckland, 1963), pp. 56-77, cover one of the most interesting of the colonial ventures; see also J. D. Bailey, *A Hundred Years of Pastoral Banking: A History of the Australian Mercantile Land and Finance Co., 1863-1963* (Oxford, 1966).
    [74] Daunton, "Firm and Family".

"GENTLEMANLY CAPITALISM" AND BRITISH INDUSTRY 149

servative MPs down to the 1880s, and then became continuously Conservative". This puzzles Anderson, for he notes that the City was both committed to free trade and, by the late nineteenth century, Conservative. He attempts to resolve the apparent contradiction between these two attitudes by the City's aversion to popular Liberalism and the belief that "it could neutralize real protectionism" in the event of Chamberlain's gaining office.[75] There is, however, a suspicion that the problem might disappear if the terms are redefined. There has been a confusion between the City *constituency* and the City as a commercial and financial centre. The bulk of the City electorate did not consist of commercial and financial interests, but of small tradesmen and freemen. The constituency represented the world of the corporation and the guild companies, which was concerned to defend privileges which were under attack from Liberal critics.[76] This might give an opportunity to Conservatives among the City merchants, but it did not necessarily entail an overall shift in their allegiance. Although it is true that some bankers did leave the Liberal Party over Ireland in 1886, it is by no means certain that the financial and commercial interests had become predominantly Conservative or Liberal Unionist.[77]

The City as a financial and commercial centre was not united on the issue of free trade versus protection, as was made clear by a memorandum presented to Chamberlain in 1903. This divided the City into four main groupings: dealers in money such as bankers, financiers and stockbrokers; the shipping interests; middlemen and importers; and colonial houses. Within the first group, bankers opposed tariff reform, with some exceptions such as Gibbs and Hambro, while the stockbrokers were "almost to a man in favour". The bankers claimed that free trade was the essential condition for London's dominance of money-markets, and the prominent German houses rejected Chamberlain's contention that protection was the explanation of German progress. German protection was, they claimed, the outcome of political expediency, an attempt by Bismarck to create a strong party by "practically bribing" the landed interest. The shipping interest was more inclined to support tariff reform, on the grounds that an increase in home trade would require more

[75] Harris and Thane, "British and European Bankers", p. 224; Anderson, "Figures of Descent", p. 43.

[76] For example, B. Scott, *The Municipal Government of London* (London, 1884), p. 15.

[77] Harris and Thane, "British and European Bankers", p. 224.

imports of bulky raw materials; others feared that it would reduce the quantity of trade. The middlemen and importers were on the whole opposed to tariff reform. Protection, by fostering the home market, would reduce imports; and higher food prices would tend to increase the cost of exports and so make it difficult to compete in world markets. Although free trade might affect individual industries, it "gave a great elasticity to commerce generally", so that retail business was flourishing. The colonial houses opposed tariff reform so long as it was based on preventing industrial development in the colonies. They also pointed to the problems which would arise in removing colonial tariffs which had been adopted largely to raise revenue; an alternative source of income would have to be found "from more direct and therefore more irksome sources".[78]

These remarks bring out two features. One is that there was no single City view, for even in coming to the same conclusion in opposition to tariffs the argument followed lines which were specific to each sector. The second is that the arguments which were put forward did not refer to the needs of aristocratic landowners for protection. Rather, they were cast in terms of the impact of protection on the demand for various City services as a result of changes in markets for British industry, and readjustments of domestic incomes. This is confirmed by the advice given to Lloyd George by his City advisers when he was chancellor of the exchequer. They argued against the view, held both by Unionists and left-wing Liberals, that overseas investment sacrificed agriculture and industry at home. Instead they argued that overseas investment produced demand for exports in the short term, and promised cheap supplies of raw materials and food in the longer term, which would stimulate the domestic economy. This would generate employment on a basis of free trade and cheap food, instead of Chamberlain's route to employment via protection of home markets.[79]

Tariff reform does suggest that we are not dealing with a simple division between "gentlemanly capitalism" and industry. There were industries which were experiencing foreign competition which might favour protection; the Birmingham metal trades with which Chamberlain was associated were one. There were other trades such

[78] W. Mock, *Imperiale Herrschaft und Nationales Interesse: "Constructive Imperialism" oder Freihandel in Grossbritanien vor dem Ersten Weltkrieg* (Stuttgart, 1982), Appendix IV (memorandum by H. A. Gwynne, Dec. 1903), pp. 393-7.

[79] A. Offer, "Empire and Social Reform: British Overseas Investment and Domestic Politics, 1908-14", *Hist. Jl.*, xxvi (1983), pp. 119-38.

"GENTLEMANLY CAPITALISM" AND BRITISH INDUSTRY 151

as cotton which might be expected to be predominantly free trade. Further, many individuals straddled interests which might *a priori* have been expected to have conflicting views.[80] The idea of a City/ land fusion against industry simply does not help in teasing out the lines of division. The example of Henry Gibbs suggests some of the difficulties. In the 1880s and 1890s he was the leading City proponent of bimetallism. Prices were falling, and he argued that the monetization of silver would reverse this trend. This proposal was welcomed by some agricultural and landed interests as a way of restoring their prosperity, offering a more politically acceptable policy than protection. It might also appeal to the Lancashire cotton industry, whose Indian markets were disrupted by the fall in the value of the silver-based rupee against the gold-based pound. Green has suggested that bimetallism led to a producers' alliance of land and industry against the financial sector of the City, and if he is correct this would obviously contradict the notion of "gentlemanly capitalism". However, Gibbs placed part of the City among the "worker bees" in opposition to the "drones", for he drew a distinction between the money-market, which was not interested in productive industry, and the merchants, who were. "The banks", he remarked, "are but the handmaids of commerce", for they were concerned "with the tools of commerce rather than with commerce itself". Whichever interpretation is adopted, "gentlemanly capitalism" obscures the lines of division in the 1880s and 1890s. Gibbs presented his case for bimetallism in terms of the needs of British industry, and especially Lancashire cotton. Yet he was to become a leading supporter of protection, which divided him from the majority view of the Lancashire cotton industry. City opinion in favour of the gold standard might be seen as hostile to the needs of Lancashire, but the City view in support of free trade was in agreement with Lancashire. The lines of demarcation between City, industry and land were shifting and complex, frustrating any attempt to construct neat formulas.[81]

[80] A. J. Marrison, "Businessmen, Industries and Tariff Reform in Great Britain, 1903-30", *Business Hist.*, xxv (1983), pp. 148-78.

[81] Green, "Rentiers versus Producers?", pp. 588-612; H. H. Gibbs, *A Bimetallic Primer*, 3rd edn. (London, 1896), pp. 179-80; H. H. Gibbs, *A Colloquy on Currency*, 3rd edn. (London, 1894), pp. 179-80, 220. Green, "Rentiers versus Producers?", p. 598 n. 2, uses Gibbs for evidence on bimetallic views, yet denies that the City was fundamentally divided. He cites the list of City supporters of bimetallism in Bodleian Lib., Oxford, MS. Harcourt Dep. 163, fos. 84-8, to support this view. The list may be read as indicating a sizeable City support for bimetallism. Even if they were involved with eastern interests which were particularly affected by the devaluation of silver, this nevertheless suggests that the City did not speak with one voice but had regional concerns.

V

Industrialists, it has been claimed, failed to develop an "autonomous bourgeois party", and were consigned to a "cadet role". Of course, the belief that an "autonomous bourgeois party" failed to emerge begs a major question: it assumes that such a phenomenon *ought* to exist. Leaving aside this basic methodological point, could it be that the existence of a dominant industrial bourgeoisie has been missed for the simple reason that it has been sought in the wrong place? And is it certain that the approach of industrialists to the state was much different from that of financiers and merchants?

The persistent downplaying of the role of the industrial middle class does seem curious, when it is remembered that the large urban, industrial centres of Britain contained the bulk of the work-force and the majority of the population. The nature of the local state has been neglected. It was in Glasgow, Oldham and the other large towns that social structure was remade and the power of the bourgeoisie displayed. Both the Wiener and Anderson interpretations of modern British history are silent on this matter, yet the towns, as Morris has argued, were middle-class creations. They provided the setting where a self-confident middle class built its characteristic institutions and culture.[82] The cotton masters of Lancashire, for example, emerged in the mid-nineteenth century as a hereditary and "cohesive self-sustained elite", with an "overweening confidence" based upon the belief that "the destiny of cotton was to produce the town, and with it the middle class; then would follow a working class made civil by education, a free press, and religious and political toleration".[83] The making of urban society might be achieved by voluntary societies to provide cultural facilities ranging from zoological gardens to libraries; chambers of commerce to establish trade documentation, such as charter parties; the town councils to operate public utilities; or employers' associations to negotiate with trades unions. "The masters' patronage of culture and philanthropy", Howe has suggested, "embodied an ideal of urban and industrial society which supplanted the traditional rural model of the most desirable life. The pursuit of this ideal freed the entrepreneurial middle class from deference to

---

[82] R. J. Morris, "The Middle Class and British Towns and Cities of the Industrial Revolution, 1780-1870", in D. Fraser and A. Sutcliffe (eds.), *The Pursuit of Urban History* (London, 1983), pp. 286-306.

[83] A. Howe, *The Cotton Masters, 1830-1860* (Oxford, 1984), pp. 311, 314; P. Joyce, *Work, Society and Politics: The Culture of the Factory in Later Victorian England* (Brighton, 1980), pp. 146-7.

aristocratic cultural values".[84] Part of the ethic of these industrial cities was the emphasis upon local politics rather than the central government. The central state for most of the nineteenth century accepted the broad parameters of policy which the industrialists desired: free trade; a taxation policy which was equitable between interests; the maintenance of public order and a system of relief based upon a free labour-market. The industrialists preferred to devote their time and efforts to municipal power, which was probably a rational choice in terms of their interests in creating an economically efficient and socially stable urban community. Of course, there were also countervailing forces from the petty bourgeoisie, which might object to an increase in rates, from the central government which might impose public-health measures, from the Trades Council, or from the emerging bureaucracy of local government. The industrial bourgeoisie did not possess unfettered power, yet it should not be viewed as "the poor relation among the British elites, as a subordinate partner in the ruling class".[85]

The argument for the power of the industrial bourgeoisie at the local level could work two ways. On the one hand, the reliance on "private" institutions could be seen as evidence of the alienation of the bourgeoisie from the state. This is the approach taken by Batzel, who argues that trade associations and chambers of commerce established procedures to deal with bankruptcy because they were alienated from the formal rules of law made by parliament and implemented by the courts. "English institutions were not all at one with English industrial society".[86] On the other hand, such behaviour could be interpreted as an indication that industrialists were assertive, self-confident and independent. Perhaps what is at issue is a misspecification of the nature of the state in the nineteenth century which was in some senses "privatized", relying upon semi-autonomous institutions such as trustee savings banks, friendly societies, chartered pro-

[84] R. J. Morris, "Voluntary Societies and British Urban Elites, 1780-1850: An Analysis", *Hist. Jl.*, xxvi (1983), pp. 95-118; Howe, *Cotton Masters*, pp. 313-14; L. Hollen Lees, "The Study of Social Conflict in English Industrial Towns", *Urban Hist. Yearbook, 1980*, pp. 34-43; J. Garrard, *Leadership and Power in Victorian Industrial Towns, 1830-80* (Manchester, 1983); E. P. Hennock, *Fit and Proper Persons: Ideal and Reality in Nineteenth-Century Urban Government* (London, 1973); H. E. Meller, *Leisure and the Changing City, 1870-1914* (London, 1976). But see, for a different view, D. Cannadine, *Lords and Landlords: The Aristocracy and the Towns, 1774-1967* (Leicester, 1980), p. 38.

[85] Howe, *Cotton Masters*, pp. 311-13; Joyce, *Work, Society and Politics*, p. 40.

[86] V. M. Batzel, "Parliament, Businessmen and Bankruptcy, 1825-83: A Study in Middle-Class Alienation", *Canadian Jl. Hist.*, xviii (1983), pp. 171-86.

fessional associations, voluntary hospitals, and so on, to supplement fully public bodies such as the poor law. Voluntarism was a crucial component of the nineteenth-century state, and arguably this reflects bourgeois notions of self-sufficiency and independence. Independence from the state was enjoined upon the working class; should it not also be followed by the middle class? This argument has indeed been extended to the treatment of trades unions which, by the legislation of 1875 and 1906, were given the same sort of legal status as inns of court, universities or clubs.[87] Much the same applies to employers' associations. In Germany agreements by industrialists, for example to determine prices, were legally enforceable contracts; in the United States such agreements were illegal under the Sherman Anti-Trust Act. In Britain it was not illegal to come to some agreement, but neither could it be legally enforced through the courts.[88]

Certainly the industrial bourgeoisie was not alone in placing reliance upon a self-regulatory, privatized state. It was, if anything, even more marked in the City. Factories and mines were at least open to inspection by the state in order to protect the interests of workers; the Stock Exchange and Lloyd's were beyond the purview of the state. The City policed itself, which meant, according to some critics, that it did not police itself at all. This was something which permeated the whole of the City. The corporation and the guild companies had managed to avoid reform, so that they still remained largely beyond government control. The ancient right that the monarch could not enter the City without the permission of the lord mayor survived, and this privilege had, in a sense, been inherited by the commercial and financial institutions of the City. In Paris, for example, the Bourse was closely regulated by the state, whereas in London it was a law unto itself.[89] Similarly, the Bank of England was not a direct arm of the government but a private company which had a large degree of autonomy.

It could nevertheless be argued that the City was able to achieve its ends to a greater extent than industry, on the grounds that it had the benefits of freedom from interference while at the same time

[87] R. McKibbin, "Why Was There No Marxism in Great Britain?", *Eng. Hist. Rev.*, xcix (1984), pp. 297-331.

[88] H. Nussbaum, "Cartels and Syndicates in the Process of Transition from Family to Large-Scale Enterprise", in *From Family Firm to Professional Management: Structure and Performance of Business Enterprise* (Eighth International Economic History Conference, Budapest, 1982, Theme B9), p. 92.

[89] On the Stock Exchange and the Bourse, see *The Economist*, 15 Sept. 1866, pp. 1080-1.

"GENTLEMANLY CAPITALISM" AND BRITISH INDUSTRY   155

national policy was in the interests of the City and land rather than industry. Such an interpretation does not make sense of some of the major issues of political history in the nineteenth and early twentieth centuries, which could be seen as an attempt to secure the support of urban-industrial interests, both laterally by building coalitions between groups of property-owners, and vertically, by tapping working-class electors after 1884. The Liberals might attempt to do this by emphasizing the parasitical nature of land as a drain on productive enterprise. This might therefore unite urban-industrial interests, both of the middle class and working class, against landowners; it also appealed to Nonconformists and supporters of home rule who opposed the power of Anglican landowners. It could unite the particular rural concerns of Welsh farmers and Scottish crofters with the complaints of miners and coal companies against mineral royalties and urban attacks upon ground landlords. This onslaught on the unearned increment as a drain on productive enterprise and labour could form one coalition of lateral and vertical interests. However, there was also a danger that the strategy could be interpreted as a threat to property, which might equally impel some to leave the Liberal camp. The revolt of the Liberal Unionists over Ireland was the occasion, rather than the cause, for such a split. Gladstone's Irish land policy could, in conjunction with Henry George's attack upon the unearned increment, scare property-owners into the Unionist camp. How were the Conservatives to respond? They could not hold power simply by appealing to the landed interests with the support of the City, and their strategy had to be to create a coalition of property-owners by attracting the support of urban and industrial interests. This, Green has argued, explains the emergence of tariff reform in a form designed to appeal equally to agriculture and industry. A policy based upon retaliatory tariffs, such as the "fair trade" movement of the 1880s, might appeal to those industries which faced exclusion from export markets, but was of no value to agriculture which did not export its products. Agriculture wanted protection to exclude imports, which would not appeal to urban-industrial interests which feared the impact of high food prices. The Conservative Party had a difficult, and perhaps impossible, task in attempting to square the circle, but the policy cannot be seen simply as a feudal reaction nor as a device to rescue industry. It was a policy of national economic integration, based upon the interdependence of agriculture and industry in which neither would be favoured. The policy would also offer the prospect of improved employment in a protected home market, so creating, it was hoped, vertical as well as lateral support. The whole point was to devise a tariff programme which would win the adherence of urban-industrial interests without offending land.[90]

Both the Liberal and Conservative Parties had the problem of attracting sufficient support to win elections, and it was obvious to both that reliance upon the landed interest was not enough. A policy designed to appeal to the City would be of little use, for it would win few seats. The solution for both parties was to build a large enough coalition of lateral and vertical support; a policy which was too clearly directed to one group was not likely to succeed. The land question and tariff reform were the two major ways in which this was attempted in the later nineteenth and early twentieth centuries. One was based on an attack upon land within a framework of free trade; the other on a fusion of land and industry within tariff reform. It is difficult to see how, in either case, the intention was to create an alliance of land and the City versus industry. "Gentlemanly capitalism" misunderstands the dilemmas facing politicians as they attempted to secure power.

VI

The aim of this article has been to express scepticism about an interpretation of British history in terms of three cohesive interests — land, City and industry — in which industry remained subordinate. The main focus of the argument has been upon the City, which has been the least considered by social and economic historians, in order to express doubts about whether it was a coherent interest, with a high level of continuity, which fused with landed aristocrats. The secret of its success might, indeed, rest upon the very fact that there was *no* cohesion, and that a high level of turnover created flexibility. The contention that the City could not act as a coherent interest might be extended to the other élite groups of industry and land. Industrialists were divided between export and domestic trades, between capital-intensive and labour-intensive production, between support for tariffs and free trade, between hostility to unions and social reform and their encouragement. Landowners could not necessarily act as one in maintaining closure against outsiders, and might reach a variety of compromises with the forces of economic and social change, involving close political and economic links with industry as

[90] Offer, *Property and Politics*; E. H. H. Green, *The Crisis of Conservatism: The Politics, Economics and Ideology of the Conservative Party, 1880-1914* (forthcoming).

well as the City. The industrial bourgeoisie, even if it did not seek representation in parliament, was actively involved in the difficult task of ensuring political and social stability within the major urban centres; national politicians were concerned with the need to secure support from urban-industrial groups and could not afford to ignore their interests.

Of course, it is easier to be sceptical than to suggest an alternative explanation of British industrial decline. Certainly it is not the intention to exclude social and political considerations, and to return to the narrow, neo-classical economics which have dominated economic history. Much of Wiener's account of British history has been criticized; what may be accepted is his general approach which is based upon the contention that "the question of the causes of British economic decline remains beyond the sole grasp of the economists".[91] The point at issue is not whether social and political factors matter, so much as which are most relevant. If the City-land fusion against industry is displaced from the centre of the explanation, what should be put in its place? Perhaps two points are worth pursuing. One is the nature of the social relations of production within industry, the emergence of a set of institutional practices which increasingly came to frustrate change in technology. These patterns emerged from the slowness of the change to a factory system, and the persistence of older styles of work within the new setting. The contrast which should be developed is between the internal structure of urban-industrial society in, say, Sheffield and Pittsburgh in steel or Oldham and Lowell in cotton.[92] This is not to deny the need to consider the structure of society and politics at the national level, which might well influence the ability of American steel to reshape the social relations of production in the late nineteenth century, whereas the British industrialists could not. The significant factor was not, however, the simple subordination of industrialists. "What was surely different about Britain in the generation before 1914 compared with other societies of the period", Pat Thane has suggested, "was the strength of *all* of the competing economic interests of land, industry, finance and labour; all of them too strong for the state not to take serious account of their interests". Politicians had to keep "a certain critical distance from the interest groups", and the result might well

[91] Wiener, *English Culture*, p. 170.

[92] See, for example, W. Lazonick, "Production Relations, Labor Productivity and Choice of Technique: British and U.S. Cotton Spinning", *Jl. Econ. Hist.*, xli (1981), pp. 491-516, which begins to move in this direction.

be that the state had "a relatively high degree of institutional and ideological flexibility" which, by its response to competing claims, helped to create the stability of British society. The converse might have been that governments "could not consistently promote any set of economic interests, industrial, financial or any other; this may have been to the greater long-run disadvantage of the economy than the assumed hegemony of landed or any other values".[93] The outcome of such an approach to British industrial society and its decline will not have the satisfying neatness of the City-land-industry formula; it will be closer to the reality of British economic, social and political development.[94]

University College, London   *M. J. Daunton*

---

[93] P. Thane, "Financiers and the British State: The Case of Sir Ernest Cassel", *Business Hist.*, xxviii (1986), pp. 94-5.

[94] This will form the subject of a forthcoming book.

[19]

2/ Visible and Invisible Hands in Great Britain

Leslie Hannah

THE DIVORCE of ownership and control in managerial capitalism and the operation of the "visible hand" of the integrated modern corporate enterprise are such ubiquitous phenomena that they seem almost to be part of the natural order of things. Thus, describing their evolution poses a special challenge to historians. Convergence theories, which have held the field in both popular and scholarly analyses until recently, portray the modern corporation as monolithic and universal, without variations among national economies. European economic historians have most often devoted their attention to the similarities between large corporations in Europe and those in the United States; they have failed either to analyze differences or to develop independent theories of historical evolution based on the kind of detailed and broad-gauged national case study Alfred D. Chandler, Jr., has undertaken for the United States.[1] This chapter represents an attempt to sketch the development of managerial capitalism in Great Britain and to test Chandler's theories by an examination of the contrasts between the British and United States economies.

THE ADVENT OF THE MODERN CORPORATION IN BRITAIN

Although the multidivisional organization that characterizes the modern corporation was relatively late in coming to European business, other statistical indicators suggest that many of its characteristics became dominant in British economic life no later than 1930 and continued to expand in importance

41

thereafter.[2] Thus a strong case can be made, I believe, for dating European—or, at least, British—emulation of United States corporate patterns not from the years after World War II, where Chandler has placed it, but from an earlier period. The proportion of manufacturing value added accounted for by the 100 largest firms, which had reached approximately 22 percent in the United States by 1909, attained that level in Britain by the mid-1920s; this index of industrial concentration remained at about the same level in the two countries until about 1955; it rose in the late 1920s, fell discernibly in the 1930s and early 1940s, then rose again in the late 1940s and 1950s. Since that time, the 100 largest firms' proportion of value added has risen much less rapidly in the United States, while industrial concentration in Great Britain has grown to an appreciably higher level; in the early 1970s, the share of the top 100 stood at 43 percent in Britain, surpassing their 33 percent share in the United States.[3] These measures reflect, although only roughly, the combined effect of increases in the vertical integration of operations within individual firms—that is, the integration of production, purchasing, and distribution within a single enterprise—and of the expanded role of the visible hand of management in the horizontal control of markets.

Despite the higher level of concentration in Great Britain, the absolute size of British firms is, of course, generally lower than those in the United States. By international standards, however, Britain had its share of giants. In 1972, each of 30 British manufacturing enterprises employed more than 40,000 people; this is fewer than the United States' 89 but almost as many as all the original six countries of the European Economic Community considered together, though their combined population was more than three times that of Great Britain. Although difficulties arise in measuring industrial concentration in continental Europe—primarily because census definitions and financial structures differ—it is clear that the present level of concentration in Britain is higher than in Germany or the other European countries.[4] The large British corporations have also been active in adopting American management methods. The multidivisional structure and strategies of integration and diversification have been as firmly implanted in the United Kingdom as in Germany and France—even more firmly, in some

VISIBLE AND INVISIBLE HANDS IN GREAT BRITAIN / 43

respects.[5] This was not always the case. Comparable data on concentration for earlier periods are not available for Germany; there is no reason, however, to dispute Jürgen Kocka's view that, at least until the 1920s, the level of concentration and the strategy and structure of large corporations had advanced further on United States lines in Germany than in Britain.[6] At the turn of the century, for example, the largest British manufacturing firm was J. & P. Coats, a sewing-thread manufacturer of Paisley, which employed 5,000 people—only a third or less of the number employed in the largest German corporations at that time.

Merger and acquisition were major sources of growth for large corporations in Britain; certainly after 1950 and probably in the 1920s and 1930s as well, they were more important there than in the United States.[7] This difference was partly a consequence of the United States' discouragement of mergers through antitrust legislation; furthermore, the first wave of mergers in the United States, which began in the 1880s and reached its peak around the turn of the century, had already done much to build up the position of the giants in the United States economy. A movement toward merger took place at the same time in Britain, but both the number of firms involved and their assets were smaller, and it affected fewer and less rapidly growing industries.[8] The real equivalent of the United States merger wave came between 1916 and 1930 in Britain, when major modern corporations such as Imperial Chemical Industries (ICI), Unilever, and English Electric were formed in an unprecedented move toward combination. Compared with the earlier mergers, this second wave involved more "rationalization" of facilities for production and distribution and the creation of more extensive managerial hierarchies to coordinate, monitor, and allocate resources to the component companies or operating units.

Merger is no guarantee of retaining a large share of the market in a competitive economy, however, as the heads of many turn-of-the-century amalgamations in the United States discovered, but the corporations created in the mergers of the 1920s in Britain seem to have been at least as successful as those in the United States in retaining their dominant position in the market. Table 2.1 shows the proportion of the 100 largest British firms that changed or maintained their status between 1919 and 1948; it gives some indication of the chance a large enter-

44 / Leslie Hannah

Table 2.1

Stability and change in the 100 largest manufacturing firms in the United Kingdom, 1919–1969.[a]

	STATUS		
Firms	STILL IN TOP 100	ACQUIRED BY FIRM STILL IN TOP 100	NO LONGER IN TOP 100
Top 100 firms of 1919 in 1930	52	17	31
Top 100 firms of 1930 in 1948	71	5	24
Top 100 firms of 1948 in 1957	71	3	26
Top 100 firms of 1957 in 1969	68	22	10

a. Size of firms determined by market value of securities.

prise had of remaining among the largest over time.[9] As table 2.1 suggests, many of the firms that dropped out of the top 100 during this period did so, not because their size diminished, but because they were acquired by another firm that remained in the top 100; in many cases, they would have remained in the top 100 in their own right if they had continued to be independent. This pattern was particularly prevalent from 1919 to 1930 and from 1957 to 1969. Whether one assumes that all acquired firms would have remained among the largest or that all would have fallen to lower ranks, however, the trend toward greater stability is notable. After 1930, at least two thirds of the largest firms survived undiminished over each period. Greater stability is also evident in the leading ranks of the largest enterprises after 1930; 6 of the "top 10" firms in 1930 were among the 10 largest in 1957 and 1969.[10]

Thus the kind of stability that has been identified among the leading firms in the United States economy beginning in the early 1920s was apparently established in Britain by the early 1930s. The underlying reasons for the increasing corporate stability in the two economies are no doubt similar. Some firms were among the few powerful leaders in an oligopolistic market; their positions were protected by barriers to entry, so that newcomers had great difficulty in dislodging them. On the basis of

VISIBLE AND INVISIBLE HANDS IN GREAT BRITAIN / 45

experience in the first wave of mergers, many large firms abandoned strategies that had earlier proved inimical to growth or even to survival; fewer mergers took place among large numbers of firms, for instance, and vertical integration was attempted less often in industries where it offered no competitive advantage over market coordination. More recently, large corporations in both countries, especially those in stagnant markets, have diversified their output so that they depend less heavily on demand in any single market for continued growth. Diversification has also been accompanied by improved managerial techniques and by the spread of multidivisional organization; thus the large corporations are now managed more effectively than many of their earlier counterparts. By adopting mass production and techniques to coordinate the flow of goods through the enterprise more effectively than was possible for smaller enterprises, the giants have delivered real economic benefits by reducing unit costs and, in the process, have maintained their positions.

THE INDUSTRIAL BREAKDOWN OF THE LARGEST CORPORATIONS

Before examining the response of large British corporations to the problems of managerial capitalism, it is useful to examine their distribution among major industries. Chandler's analysis of the 50 and 200 largest British corporations before 1948, although incomplete, is the fullest analysis available of the broad dimensions of the structure of management in British companies during this period.[11] It covers the 200 largest manufacturing firms, measured by the market value of their capital, in 1919, 1930, and 1948.

Table 2.2 shows the breakdown of the top 200 firms according to the Standard Industrial Classification (S.I.C.) categories of the United States Bureau of the Census.[12] These enterprises vary greatly in size. In 1930, for example, the two largest firms were Unilever and Imperial Tobacco, each with capital valued at more than £130 million, or $650 million; each of the 100 smallest firms valued at less than £3.4 million, or $17 million; with the smallest worth only £1.3 million, or $6.5 million. The 100 largest firms in Britain were comparable in size to the 200 leading United States corporations by the 1930s, but the firms ranking lower than one hundredth in size included many that were significantly smaller than their United States counterparts;

Table 2.2

Industrial breakdown of the 200 largest firms in the United Kingdom, 1919–1948.[a]

Category[b]	Industry	1919		1930		1948	
		Number	% of Top 200	Number	% of Top 200	Number	% of Top 200
19	Ordnance	0	0.0	0	0.0	0	0.0
20	Food and allied products	63	31.5	64	32.0	52	26.0
21	Tobacco products	3	1.5	4	2.0	8	4.0
22	Textile mill products	26	13.0	24	12.0	18	9.0
23	Apparel and allied products	1	0.5	3	1.5	3	1.5
24	Lumber and wood products	0	0.0	0	0.0	0	0.0
25	Furniture and fixtures	0	0.0	0	0.0	0	0.0
26	Paper and allied products	4	2.0	5	2.5	6	3.0
27	Printing and publishing	5	2.5	10	5.0	7	3.5
28	Chemical and allied products	11	5.5	9	4.5	15	7.5
29	Petroleum and energy products	0	0.0	0	0.0	0	0.0

46

30	Rubber and allied products	3	1.5	3	1.5	2	1.0
31	Leather products	0	0.0	0	0.0	0	0.0
32	Stone, clay, and glass products	2	1.0	6	3.0	5	2.5
33	Primary metals	35	17.5	18	9.0	28	14.0
34	Fabricated metal products	2	1.0	7	3.5	8	4.0
35	Nonelectrical machinery	8	4.0	7	3.5	7	3.5
36	Electrical machinery	11	5.5	18	9.0	13	6.5
37	Transportation equipment	20	10.0	14	7.0	22	11.0
38	Instruments and allied products	0	0.0	1	0.5	4	2.0
39	Miscellaneous	3	1.5	4	2.0	3	1.5

a. Size of firms determined by market value of capital.
b. United States Bureau of the Census Standard Industrial Classification category.

this fact is not surprising in view of the relative size of the two economies.[13]

The problems of classifying firms with a wide range of different products by a single industrial category are obvious, but during the period between 1919 and 1930 they were not insuperable. Nonetheless, some lacunae require explanation. British ordnance output was large; much of it came from firms that do not appear under "ordnance" in table 2.2, since all were considered to be engaged primarily in other industries. The absence of certain firms under "petroleum and energy products" is equally misleading. Two of the seven world oil giants, Shell and Anglo-Persian Oil (the corporate predecessor of British Petroleum) were owned, respectively, by Anglo-Dutch and British companies; by the interwar years they held a strong position in British and other world markets for diesel fuel and gasoline. Since significant oil reserves had not yet been discovered in the United Kingdom, these companies were engaged in distribution rather than manufacturing in Great Britain, with their refining and crude-oil production carried on overseas. Thus they do not appear in this list as manufacturing concerns, although they were certainly large British corporations. After 1948, when they built refineries and chemical plants inside Britain, Shell and British Petroleum were among the largest manufacturing corporations in both that country and the world.[14]

Aside from such quirks of classification, the list of the 200 largest British corporations and comparable lists for the United States indicate that the large firms were clustered in much the same types of industry (see chapter 1, "The United States: Seedbed of Managerial Capitalism," for clustering in the United States). In particular, three of the six industrial categories with the largest number of firms were distinctly modern ones: transportation equipment, chemicals and allied products, and electrical machinery. At an early stage, firms in these categories often developed strategies and structures akin to those of their United States counterparts. Within the transportation-equipment group, shipbuilding accounted for more than half the firms in 1919, but automobiles and automobile equipment made up more than half by 1948; aircraft's share also rose. In both 1930 and 1948, the chemicals group was dominated by Imperial Chemical Industries (ICI), formed in 1926 by the merger of the four largest chemical companies in Great Britain. The relatively stable representation of manufacturers of electrical machinery among the top 200 firms conceals a substantial rise in the size of individual firms between 1919 and 1948.

Other industries also show a pattern similar to that in the United States. Some were dominated by giants such as Imperial Tobacco in tobacco products and the Dunlop Rubber Company in rubber and allied products. In such historically small-scale industries as apparel, wood products, furniture, and leather, few of the largest firms in Britain or the United States are represented. The main exceptions by 1948 were the large, vertically integrated mass-tailoring chains such as Montague Burton and Prices, which dominated the cheaper end of the trade in ready-made and custom-made men's suits and which controlled both production and retailing.

Elsewhere, substantial differences appear between the British patterns, indicated in table 2.2, and the industrial breakdown of the largest corporations in the United States. There were far fewer firms manufacturing nonelectrical machinery among the largest enterprises in Great Britain than in the United States, presumably because British factories, offices, and farms depended more heavily on skilled labor and less heavily on capital for their operation—that is, they were less capital-intensive and more skill-intensive; the market for nonelectrical machinery was correspondingly smaller.[15] The few large firms in this category produced textile machinery (a field in which British firms such as Platt Brothers dominated world markets) or imported United States machine technology. (The British United Shoe Machinery Company, for example, was a subsidiary of a United States corporation.) The largest British-owned company distributing or manufacturing nonelectrical machinery in all three years was Babcock & Wilcox, which had begun as a subsidiary of the United States boiler-making firm of the same name but had become financially independent of its parent in 1900. The British offshoot nonetheless depended heavily on the United States company for technical and manufacturing know-how and maintained close links with New York; it exploited the United States company's patents not only in Britain but in the rest of Europe, the British Empire, and other countries outside North America.[16]

Some of the industrial groups with the largest number of

representatives among the top 200 firms also showed significant contrasts to the United States pattern. Food and allied products, for example, accounted for almost a third of the firms in 1919 and 1930 and for more than a quarter in 1948—substantially more than it did in the United States. Over half these firms were manufacturers of alcoholic beverages in each of the three years for which data are given; their predominance is to some extent a statistical illusion resulting from the British approach to licensing public houses. In the late nineteenth century, the temperance forces obtained the enactment of laws that restricted the total number of outlets for alcoholic beverages; during World War I, the times they could remain open were also restricted. In any region, then, the number of pubs was limited, and it was crucial for a brewery to ensure their loyalty. Almost all the breweries met this marketing problem by acquiring pubs; thus, by the interwar period, only a small and decreasing number were owned by independent small businessmen. (The major exception to this strategy was Guinness, which chose advertising and national branding as an alternative.)[17] As a result, the large real-estate holdings of the breweries inflated the market value of their capital. Their dominance in table 2.2 would be significantly reduced if the top 200 were chosen on the basis of value added in manufacturing.

Nevertheless, the remaining firms in the food and allied products industry were also somewhat different from their United States counterparts. More British firms were makers of semiperishable products. Flour, sugar, and chocolate companies had United States counterparts in size and degree of integration. Unlike the United States firms, however, many were processors of imported agricultural products, and many native fresh products were handled by the smaller businesses. Milk combines appeared at an early stage; canners and bakers, later on. By 1928, one of the largest, United Dairies, owned a large number of retail dairy shops in Great Britain, as well as creameries and dairies in that country and in France. In 1919, a large number of fat processors made goods as varied as margarine and soap (they were similar to and competed with Procter & Gamble and American Cotton Oil), but by 1930 almost all had been united by the Unilever merger. The counterparts of firms like Armour and Swift in the United States—such companies as Union Cold

VISIBLE AND INVISIBLE HANDS IN GREAT BRITAIN / 51

Storage, which had extensive meat-producing interests in Argentina and Australia—were mainly distributing firms in Great Britain, where they owned cold-storage plants and chains of retail shops. Because their manufacturing facilities were located in the colonies and in Argentina and North America, they do not appear in table 2.2. Manufacturing meat extract was the major business of Liebig and Bovril, two of the largest firms in 1919; they were still represented in the 200 largest firms at later dates.

Another more striking contrast with the United States appears in the dominance of textile mill products—not surprisingly, in light of Great Britain's share of the world cotton trade. Nor is it surprising that their importance declined as foreign competition grew; they accounted for 13 percent of the 200 largest firms in 1919, 12 percent in 1930, and 9 percent in 1948. Many of the largest textile firms in all three years were horizontal combinations organized as holding companies—that is, federations of small firms legally controlled by a single corporation— operating in one process of production such as bleaching or printing calico, or in special areas like the manufacture of cotton sewing thread. J. & P. Coats, the leading thread manufacturer, was ranked first in 1919 and fifth in 1930 and was still eighth in 1948. The modern textile sector was also represented; Courtaulds, the rayon manufacturer, was already the eighth largest firm in 1919, and British Celanese was in the top 50 throughout the period.

Another industry, primary metals, is also well represented, although no British firm was comparable in stature to Vereinigte Stahlwerke in Germany or to United States Steel.[18] A wide range of medium-sized iron and steel firms served the major industrial districts and maintained strong representation in the top 200 firms; the decrease in their numbers in 1930 resulted largely from the exceptionally adverse movement of stock market prices that reflected the severe depression in the steel industry in that year, compared with the booms of 1919 and 1948. In both 1930 and 1948, the representation of nonferrous metals in this category increase, although the absence of sources of raw materials in Great Britain meant that some of the large British-owned firms in these sectors operated mainly abroad and are not included in table 2.2.

Classifications of this kind make it possible to identify distinct similarities and contrasts between the industrial balance of the British economy and that of others, but they also conceal a great deal. The trend over time, for example, is only imperfectly captured in table 2.2. Although small increases in the proportion of firms in the top 200 in industries like electrical machinery are reflected, these industries' share measured in total output, rather than numbers of firms, increased much more dramatically between 1919 and 1948. Changes that had already taken place among the largest firms by 1930 are also understated in table 2.2. The 50 largest corporations show a clear trend toward the representation of the new growth-oriented industries, including electrical machinery and automobiles, by that date; table 2.2, on the contrary, shows a decline in representation.[19]

The Structure of British Corporations

The data available for determining other characteristics of the British corporate experience—whether or not management was dominated by owners and their families, whether firms served regional, national, or international markets, what internal structures existed for management, or to what extent production was vertically integrated—are less abundant than those on industrial classification. The histories of the majority of firms remain unwritten, and information must be inferred from *Stock Exchange Year Books* and trade journals, a method that leads to significant errors of classification. Before World War I, for example, the names of board members, the addresses of offices, and other information listed for the United Alkali Company imply that the firm was still owned by the family that founded it, was not administered by salaried managers, put out a single product, and was organized as a holding company—a representative of the old style, in other words. More detailed research indicates, however, that the number of professional managers in the higher echelons was increasing and suggests that the company was developing a more diversified range of products, was vertically integrated, was organized according to functional departments, and was centrally administered.[20] Until British business historians have produced a wider range of case studies, then, the generalizations made in this section, based on the imperfect data available, must be considered tentative.

VISIBLE AND INVISIBLE HANDS IN GREAT BRITAIN / 53

Table 2.3 demonstrates the impact of the mergers of the 1920s on the 200 largest manufacturing corporations. In 1919 the single-unit enterprise was the norm; by 1930 the multiunit enterprise, most often organized as a holding company, clearly dominated. Little information is available on the internal management structures within these categories. Some firms identified as holding companies remained extremely loose federations, while others may have created extensive managerial hierarchies that operated through centrally administered, functional departments and in which subsidiary companies were not operating entities but merely legal forms. A few firms, such as ICI, can be identified as distinctly multidivisional by 1930; there were perhaps a dozen by 1948. It is not yet possible to refine the data further. What seems clear, however, is that in 1930 the looser holding company arrangement with only an embryonic managerial hierarchy was still dominant in Great Britain; in the United States during the same period, the centralized, functionally departmentalized structure predominated.[21] In 1948 the federated holding company was still strong in Britain, while the multidivisional organization had made more headway among the leading firms in the United States.

In other respects as well, British industry still conformed to older models. The separation of ownership and control, for instance, had not progressed far enough to displace founding or family directors from company boards; 110 of the 200 largest firms in 1919, or 55 percent, had family board members, as did 140, or 70 percent, in 1930, and 119, or 59.5 percent, in 1948.[22] These statistics do not imply, however, that the families represented on boards owned all, or even most, of the capital; indeed, it was the exception rather than the rule for them to hold the majority of the capital, at least among the larger companies, in the 1930s.[23] Nor does the persistence of family names on the board show that they exercised a dominant role in direction and management. Many were present as important minority shareholders; others, as the price of a merger agreement when their own firms were absorbed. In such cases, family influence was often dwindling in the face of the advance of professional management. In many sectors, however, particularly in brewing, shipbuilding, and food, founding families retained their directorial prerogatives. Many of the multiunit enterprises organized

Table 2.3

Organization of the 200 largest manufacturing firms in the United Kingdom, 1919–1948.[a]

Type	1919		1930		1948	
	Number	% of top 200	Number	% of top 200	Number	% of top 200
Single-unit enterprise	104	52.0	56	28.0	31	15.5
Multiunit enterprise	51	25.5	136	68.0	153	76.5
Unknown or other	45	22.5	8	4.0	16	8.0

a. Size of firms determined by market value of capital.

as holding companies remained federations of family firms. There the founding families still managed "their" subsidiaries, and decisions about production and distribution policies and about allocating resources were usually arrived at by negotiation.

The question of whether continuing family management was a brake on the development of modern management caused much contemporary debate and remains controversial. Where family management proved incapable of generating an adequate cash flow, its strength was, of course, reduced by the need to obtain capital to keep the firm going; the Du Cros family was ousted from control of the Dunlop Rubber Company in the crisis of 1921–22, for instance, and was replaced by professional managers from outside. In other cases family managers were skilled and innovative like the Pilkingtons, who were glassmakers, or like the Kenricks, who were hardware manufacturers, merely skilled at obtaining enough credit to survive even when their firms deserved to go under on general grounds.[24] Perhaps there is as much variation, if not more, within the two groups of firms—those still controlled by family and those run by salaried managers—as there is between them.

The continuing dominance of families in British board rooms is partly a function of the highly developed but diverse capital market. No real equivalent existed in Great Britain, at least before the 1930s, of the investment bankers of the United States or the industrial banks of Germany, which controlled new capital for transportation and industrial enterprises. Even for quite large British corporations, capital came from many sources. Reinvested profit was always a major source of funds, and new capital was raised from stock exchange issues, from private placings with stockbrokers, insurance companies, or merchant banks, and from families and managers themselves. Strong financial interests rarely appeared on the boards. It is, in fact, more difficult in the British context than in any other to distinguish among a founding entrepreneur and his family, the financial interest, and the managerial interest, simply because these roles were not clearly differentiated in Great Britain.[25] Family firms in the shipbuilding industry financed manufacturers of electrical machinery and automobiles and electric utilities. They might appear on their boards as family and might hold a large proportion or even a majority of the shares, but in some cases they were

56 / LESLIE HANNAH

actually members by virtue of their skills in finance or management, rather than as representatives of a family interest. To classify the British entrepreneur who brought together finance, management, and technology as the creator of a family firm may blur the distinction between his services and those of the family directors of a firm inherited from past generations; the latter, of course, is the more traditional version of the family firm as a brake on progress.

In some areas of business, the distinction is clearer. In the electrical-machinery industry, for example, two of the three largest firms had been subsidiaries of General Electric and Westinghouse before World War I; in 1930 they were still controlled by United States capital. The same was true of two of the largest automobile makers, Ford and Vauxhall, the latter a subsidiary of General Motors; their boards, however, had come to be dominated by British managers. Large firms like ICI and Unilever, which still had some members of the original families on their boards in the 1930s, were also dominated essentially by managers and had wide ownership of shares.

In some of the largest firms, however, family management remained a real force; Imperial Tobacco, for instance, was a federation of family firms with little central direction over the two main family branches, the Willses and the Players.[26] Middle-sized enterprises tended to adopt similar federal structures. The history of the Metal Box Company is one of a gradual transition from a federation of family tin-box makers, merged in 1920–1930, to a more centralized structure, necessitated by its decision in 1930 to license can-making technology from the United States firm, Continental Can Company.[27] In the cases of Imperial Tobacco, Metal Box before 1930, and other holding companies that remained federations of family firms, the failure to create a managerial staff meant an inability to take full advantage of administrative coordination and monitoring or of more systematic ways of allocating resources.

Similar loose federations were numerous in the textile industry, where the Calico Printers' Association, Bradford Dyers, and Fine Spinners and Doublers remained horizontal combinations, and in the iron, steel, and metalworking industries, where Guest Keen and Nettlefolds, Stewarts and Lloyds, and Dorman Long remained loose-knit, vertical combinations. Even firms dominated by financiers often preferred to remain loose hold-ing companies that left only residual powers to their main offices. Associated Electrical Industries, formed by merger of four firms under United States ownership in 1926–1928, ran its two larg-est companies—Metropolitan-Vickers and British Thomson-Houston—virtually as independent enterprises, despite the fact that they had similar, and even competing, product lines.

The United States influence on large-scale enterprise in Great Britain was especially noticeable in technology. The adop-tion of modern techniques of mass production and the develop-ment of science-based industries such as steel-rolling mills and the manufacture of automobiles, electrical machinery, and chem-icals have depended largely and increasingly in Britain on links with large United States enterprises, through licensing agreements, consultants, or direct impact on patterns of integra-tion and on management structures. Modern tinplate mills, for example, required larger and more fully integrated manu-facturing processes, and the British firms that took them over usually responded accordingly.[28] The multidivisional manage-ment structure also seems to have evolved in firms that were aware of practices in the United States. Some of these were United States subsidiaries; others, though independent, learned about and emulated organizational innovations in United States corporations like Du Pont and General Motors early in their development. For example, ICI, which had close contacts with Du Pont, had adopted a multidivisional structure by the late 1920s. Others, like Dunlop Rubber, which was managed by Sir Eric Geddes, a former railway executive, apparently developed an advanced, partially functional, partially multidivisional struc-ture largely on their own initiative in the 1920s.

The spread of British business interests abroad can also be seen at an early stage. In 1919, 21 of the 200 largest firms, or 10.5 percent, listed overseas subsidiaries in the *Stock Exchange Year Book* and similar directories. This number had grown to 62, or 31 percent, by 1930, and to 73, or 36.5 percent, by 1948. Since only overseas activities carried on by separately incor-porated businesses, rather than by the companies' branch offices, are listed for many firms, these statistics undoubtedly understate the degree of British involvement overseas. In both absolute and relative terms, Great Britain invested more extensively abroad

in the decades before World War I than the United States. Although much of its outlay was in securities, a substantial proportion was invested directly in operating businesses. Even though
Britain's direct overseas interests exceeded those of the United
States (at least by some definitions), the importance of United
States-owned business abroad was probably somewhat greater
in the manufacturing sector.[29]

Considering the probable omissions (particularly firms not
listed in *Stock Exchange Year Books*) from this data and the
relatively small size of many of the 200 largest British firms, the
nation's degree of international involvement by 1930 is remarkably high. Some of these connections were long established, such
as J. & P. Coats's and English Sewing Cotton's extensive networks of foreign manufacturing subsidiaries or Unilever's subsidiary, Lever Brothers, in the United States. The majority of
listed overseas subsidiaries were new in the 1920s, however, and
many represented an attempt to capitalize on newly acquired
technology and skills by manufacturing outside Great Britain
or by creating sales outlets in international markets. Another
important motive for the expansion of British firms overseas
was the search for raw materials. Vertical integration meant a
move abroad more often for British than for United States firms,
a pattern that obviously reflects the relative wealth of raw materials in the United States and Britain's poverty in this respect.
Thus British steel firms integrated backward to Spanish ore
mine and railways, and Turner & Newall, the dominant asbestos
firm in Great Britain, acquired mines in Quebec, Swaziland, and
Rhodesia.

Within the British economy, the extent to which successive mining and manufacturing processes were integrated and
companies integrated forward by establishing marketing and
sales capabilities is more difficult to assess. In some respects, integration had gone much further by the early 1920s in Great
Britain than in the United States. Shipbuilders commonly owned
steelworks; breweries controlled pubs; margarine manufacturers
operated chains of retail shops (integration with retail chains
was generally more common than in the United States); and
newspaper barons owned newsprint plants. In cases where integration had occurred largely in order to assure outlets or sources
of supply, however, and had produced holding companies that

remained little more than federations of firms, with no central managerial hierarchies, vertical disintegration often came about in the 1930s. Mergers between shipbuilding and steel concerns and newspapers and newsprint manufacturers were dissolved when supplies became more readily available and when outlets proved to be unprofitable. Firms most often turned instead to horizontal combinations in a single industry, such as steel or newsprint, in an attempt to achieve some economies of scale by setting up a central managerial organization and reorganizing plants.

Other kinds of integration common in the United States were absent in Britain. Automobile manufacturers, for example, did not normally own steel-pressing or electrical-components plants; ironmaking was integrated only slowly with steelmaking and finishing; vertical integration between cotton spinning and weaving remained rare. Cases of integration similar to those in the United States do exist, however. Some manufacturers of electrical machinery and cables had substantial interests in the one-third of electric utilities that were not publicly owned. The development of modern road-based distribution, advertising, branding, and sales forces favored the closer interrelationship of manufacturing and distribution and increasingly replaced the earlier reliance on wholesalers and distribution by railway. These trends were clearly strong in the 1920s and 1930s, but the data that are presently available are inadequate as a basis for a statistical summary of their chronological development or for a meaningful comparison with the United States.[30] What is clear is that the choice between integrating vertically related production processes by way of the firm and integrating them by way of the market is revealed to be a complicated one; it depends on many factors, including the degree of monopoly that was achieved, the economies of scale that were possible at various successive stages, and changing technology. It is not surprising, then, that we see much diversity in the experience of different countries at different points in time.

Thus many gaps remain in our knowledge of the structure of the British corporate economy, but the broad picture can be tentatively sketched. In 1919, the characteristics associated with the modern corporate economy were rare in Britain. Large corporations were less common in almost all industries than in the

60 / Leslie Hannah

United States; in some sectors, such as electrical machinery and steel, there were also many fewer than in Germany. Nevertheless, by the early 1930s a substantial merger wave had increased the size of corporations, the number of multiunit enterprises, their degree of overseas involvement, and probably their degree of vertical integration. The degree of functional departmentalization and centralization are uncertain, as is the frequency of multidivisional organization. Both were clearly increasing, but this trend was less evident than in the United States. The loose holding company and the family firm remained much more common structures, despite the development of modern managerial enterprises among some of the largest firms in certain sectors. Corporate development in Great Britain showed distinctive national characteristics, but in the 1950s and 1960s British firms would evolve along a path more clearly similar to that followed in the United States. Substantial reasons remain, nonetheless, for identifying the foundations of the modern corporate economy in the interwar years; postwar evolution built on this already strong base.

The Corporate Economy in Britain and the United States

How well does Chandler's framework of explanation for the contrasting experience of the United States and other countries fit the British case? In Britain there is little evidence of the influence of the central government on the evolution of the modern corporate economy. The local and national telephone services were run as a government department beginning in 1912, and high-ranking civil servants, ministers, and military officers were recruited to senior positions on the boards of large corporations, but state intervention in industrial development was rare before 1945 except in wartime. The major exceptions to this generalization in manufacturing were the activities of the central bank, which was privately owned but anxious to ward off government intervention in its affairs. In the 1930s the Bank of England helped to promote mergers and the creation of larger business enterprises, particularly in the cotton and steel industries. Tariffs, finally imposed in 1932, also contributed to large-scale organization by increasing the monopoly profits that could be gained from domination of the home market. This effect was already evident in Germany and the United States much earlier, however, and it was, in any case, a minor influence.[31]

As Chandler has suggested, the size and the rate of growth of the United States market explain many of the evident contrasts between its pattern of output, and its concomitant corporate structure, and that of Britain.[32] Regional and class tastes generally varied more widely in Great Britain than in the United States, although radio, national advertising, and national brands were already reducing these differences by the 1920s. Significantly, in business sectors in which tastes were probably more standardized and less ethnically differentiated in Britain than in the United States or continental Europe—in the food industry, for example—mass production and mass retailing grew rapidly and probably faster than in the United States.

Moreover, British wages were lower than those in the United States (though higher than in continental Europe); this factor limited the market for automobiles and electrical appliances before World War II. As already noted, low wages and a ready supply of skilled labor in Great Britain had affected the demand for capital goods as well. It was not always economical to substitute electric or mechanical power for manpower; thus the home market for power machinery was restricted, and fewer machinery firms accordingly appeared among the largest corporations. By the 1930s, however, wages and the standard of living had reached relatively high levels. Walt W. Rostow, in his now infamous classification of the stages of economic growth, dated the onset of the "age of high mass consumption" in Great Britain to 1935.[33] It was in the years between the wars that electricity was first installed in most homes and that the middle income groups could realistically aspire to automobile ownership. Appropriately, it was also during this period that the corporate economy emerged in Britain.

Yet the size and growth rate of the British and United States markets can explain the contrasts between the two nations only partially. In some periods the British market was better suited than that in the United States to the development of modern corporations, but they did not evolve. In the 1880s, for example, Britain was more highly urbanized and the nation thus required more street lighting and had a more highly skewed distribution of income (and thus more potential consumers of luxury electric lighting); infant United States electrical-machinery firms under Edison and Westinghouse made more of an arguably less attractive market for early development (though later new mass-market advantages proved greater).[34] No country had as large a market for dyes before 1914 as Great Britain, primarily because of its large, prosperous, and rapidly expanding textile industries, but it was the technically superior German chemical industry that took the opportunity offered by the need for dyes to found modern large-scale firms manufacturing fine chemicals. Historians disagree about the reasons for British entrepreneurs' failure to enter or succeed in these new science-based markets; foreign investment, imperialism, and the social and educational systems have attracted their shares of the blame, while some historians continue to argue that the choices made reflected Great Britain's comparative advantages and thus cannot be construed as mistaken, at least in the short run.[35]

More generally, however, the size or rate of growth of the domestic market is not the best indicator of potential or actual demand. Much more than the United States, Britain considered the world its marketplace, and it exported roughly a third of its output for most of the twentieth century. The major markets of the United States and Germany were in fact closed to it by tariff barriers, and the market made up by its own vast Empire was only partly developed and often not protected by tariffs against competition from third parties. Yet significant market opportunities remained: many United States-made goods, such as electrical machinery, were too expensive to compete in third markets, and chauvinism was often sufficiently strong to exclude German competitors at least from Empire countries. The market faced by British firms, then, was somewhat wider, especially in the white-settler dominions, than its domestic market alone might suggest. (The United States and Germany had also established economic relationships with Canada, Latin America, and central Europe, but these were smaller and less significant.) The rapidly growing British manufacturers of automobiles, chemicals, and electric machinery clearly saw Empire markets as a major field for growth during the interwar years, and the names of such newly formed giants as Imperial Chemical Industries were no accident. International cartel agreements, such as those among Du Pont, I. G. Farben, and ICI, also recognized Britain's claim to large overseas markets even in industries in which its technology was still relatively weak; moreover, attempts by the Soviet and United States governments during World War II to induce Britain to dismantle its Empire were based on the view that it was an economic unit of real significance.[36] In seeing their potential market as a wide one comprising the entire Empire, British businessmen were thus perhaps overly optimistic about the future, but they seemed realistic to their contemporaries.

Other factors made even the British home market larger than a simple comparison with the United States suggests. Especially in the heavier industries, where the cost of transporting goods inhibited competition among regional markets in the United States, the effective domestic markets for a typical British firm—in cement and steel, for example—might be larger than those for comparable United States plants. Market size is thus a complex phenomenon, which can explain only part of the differences between the two economies. The highly compact and urban nature of the British domestic market, however, explains the absence of some types of vertical integration evident in the United States. The economies of speed gained across the Atlantic by the visible hand of the manager were often readily available in Britain through the "invisible hand" of the market. Markets work well where the costs of information and transactions are low, and these are likely to be lowest in the kind of compact, industrialized urban region in which most British industries were located. Sheffield, for example, contained a large proportion of Britain's many ordnance and steel-blade firms, but the area in which they were concentrated was small enough for them to communicate effectively through well-developed, traditional market mechanisms.

Chandler has argued that energy- and capital-intensive industries require hierarchical structures for scheduling in order to ensure a steady flow of work, but similar changes in the nineteenth-century British economy, likewise brought about by the application of coal and steam to industrial processes and by the growth of a railway network, did not lead to an equally noticeable growth of large corporations. This difference resulted at least in part from the highly developed and efficient British

64 / Leslie Hannah

system of markets for commodities, skills, and distributive and financial services, as well as for final products; thus efficient scheduling by market mechanisms was often possible. In Britain, existing institutions were able to obtain the benefits of competition and efficient dissemination of information, making transactions among firms faster and cheaper than before. Thus markets could offer advantages that outweighed the rival benefits of internal organization—primarily economies of scale and efficient scheduling of flows—at least in the short run. When tested by competition in the British context, the invisible hand was often apparently superior to the visible hand of the managerial firm.[37]

A highly developed national and international network of marketing middlemen—including trading companies, commission agents, wholesale and factoring houses, and consultants—was also available to British manufacturing firms. In many cases, they proved more efficient in delivering goods to the point of sale at lower cost than an internal administrative hierarchy.[38] In the absence of import tariffs, which were not imposed generally until 1932, Britain had virtually the status of a free port and was an international center for the exchange of goods and services; strong competitive forces thus created further pressure for efficiency within the market system. Significantly, investigations by the "new" economic historians of production efficiency under these conditions have generally yielded a favorable verdict; in the cotton-textile industry in Lancashire, for example, Lars Sandberg's view is that the market effectively coordinated the competing activities of many small, single-product firms and that the visible hand had a correspondingly small part to play.[39] The picture just sketched of a successful and effective British market system is, of course, complementary to that of Alexander Gerschenkron, developed further by Jürgen Kocka, which argues that continental European economies without similar advantages were obliged to substitute hierarchical coordination by industrial banks, by the state, or by large-scale enterprise in order to economize on scarce coordinating talents.[40]

Nonetheless, market mechanisms were not always superior to managerial hierarchies in Britain, and historians have identified cases of market failure in which hierarchical organization within the firm might have been more efficient. Whether the rate of development of corporate and market institutions in

VISIBLE AND INVISIBLE HANDS IN GREAT BRITAIN / 65

Great Britain resulted from an optimal balance between the two or whether the nation erred on the side of conservatism in its reluctance to adopt the new hierarchical institutions is thus debatable. Modern corporate organization was yielding important gains in efficiency in the economies of countries such as the United States and Germany, although they were quite different. As already noted, Britain may have been mistaken in not developing new technology based on electricity and chemical production, and handling complex technical change is arguably a test that competitive market economies may fail.[41] Later, particularly in the years between the wars, British managers often adopted the view that patterns of organization overseas were more efficient. Indeed, in cases where Britain succeeded in developing new technology it did so through the medium of the integrated corporation; this was the case with British Petroleum and Shell in oil, Turner & Newall in asbestos, Courtaulds in rayon, or Dunlop in rubber. British firms' expenditures for research and development did not begin to rival those of industrial research laboratories in Germany and the United States until after World War I.[42]

Historians have also criticized the performance of the British capital market, especially in allocating resources to new industries. Despite the existence of a securities market in Britain that was more highly developed than similar markets in the United States or Germany, some maintain that market institutions performed their primary functions of bearing risks and encouraging innovation less efficiently than large corporations or industrial banks did elsewhere.[43] The availability of consulting engineers, whose activities may be thought of as a market device for allocating skilled technical and managerial resources among small, unintegrated firms, has also been criticized as leading to the lack of standardization of plant design and equipment and to a failure to take advantage of economies of mass production in some sectors.[44] Whether or not faulty market mechanisms were responsible, even the old industries for which market organization had seemed ideal, such as coal and cotton, were experiencing severe economic difficulties by the interwar period. Competitive market forces might normally have been expected to enforce the required reduction in capacity through bankruptcies, but, in fact, important "barriers to exit" existed; the result was that attempts were made, not always successfully, to substitute the visible hand of administrative coordination by the state or by more concentrated ownership structures for the market processes that were considered to have failed.[45]

The existence of large, urban markets in Britain and the efficient market institutions it inherited not only served as an alternative to multilevel managerial hierarchies but also made it possible for organizations with a less hierarchical structure to coordinate and oversee operations and to allocate resources effectively.[46] The relative costs of market and mangerial coordination depended heavily on the creativity of the entrepreneurs in the economy at any given time and could not readily be predicted. In Britain, however, opportunities for profit through administrative coordination seem to have been more readily seized in distribution than in manufacturing. Retailing, in particular, was strong in the British economy, and Napoleon's gibe that the nation was one of shopkeepers was even more apposite at the end of the nineteenth century than when it was made. Although retailing has been relatively neglected by business historians, the movement to larger-scale operations was at least as vigorous there as in manufacturing.[47] Moreover, although the large retailing groups in the United States—groups such as the Atlantic and Pacific Tea Company and Sears Roebuck—did not generally integrate backward, they were seen in Britain as a natural base from which to build a manufacturing organization or to bolster its position. Thus such firms as Unilever, Union Cold Storage, United Dairies, the brewery combines in the food and drink industry, and Lever Brothers and the major subsidiaries of Imperial Tobacco in soap and tobacco had important distribution and retailing investments that strengthened their market positions.[48] Even in the technically oriented industries, some of the large British corporations developed backward from retailing. For example GEC (the General Electric Company, the major British-owned electrical-equipment manufacturer before World War I) began in the 1880s as a wholesaler and retailer of electric-lighting equipment; Boots, ICI's major rival in the fine-chemical trade, developed its assets, management skills, and cash flow from its chain of retail drugstores in major British towns.[49] In all these enterprises, except possibly the breweries, companies created managerial hierarchies to coordinate high-volume flows and to oversee operating units. Once again, certain industries in which hierarchical organization offered no special benefits in the United States tended to develop large corporations in Britain through the influence of sales; the market power of the British Shoe Corporation and of mass clothing retailers like Burtons depended to a large extent on their chains of High Street shops.

Another difference between Britain and the United States, as Chandler points out, was in their legal situations. Cartels and restrictive practices were legal in Britain, as they were in Germany and France, and effective legislation against them was not enacted until 1956. In important respects—particularly in coordinating sales policies and securing monopolistic control over prices—cartels were an alternative to merger that was open to European entrepreneurs but closed to their counterparts in the United States.[50] Firms that preferred to maintain a single-unit structure in Britain were therefore free to do so while, at the same time, reducing competition by joining a cartel; in the 1930s and during World War II, in fact, these arrangements were actively encouraged by the government. United States industrialists like Gerald Swope, the dynamic president of the American General Electric Company, accustomed to the antitrust tradition, were advised by bankers in Britain that they need not create large, centralized corporations through mergers for their European operations; market competition could be regulated by agreement with other firms, and there was thus no need to acquire them.[51] Such arrangements did not permit careful scheduling of flows among units, but they avoided the creation of large and sometimes overly bureaucratic structures of management; they therefore permitted firms to retain some of the flexibility of medium-sized enterprises.

Tax factors, on the other hand, were probably a more common encouragement to merger in Britain than they were in the United States. Until 1965, Great Britain had no capital gains tax but taxed income heavily; thus independent entrepreneurs or partners had strong incentives to convert the flow of future income from their enterprises into capital gains by allowing their firms to be acquired by corporations. When the former

68 / Leslie Hannah

owner of a firm or his family could continue to operate it as an autonomous subsidiary within a federated holding company, merger became even more attractive.

The factors that encouraged mergers did little, however, to reduce the dominance of family directors on the boards of leading companies. As noted earlier, the pattern of family-dominated enterprise survived longer in Britain than in the United States; even when a family no longer controlled the majority of voting shares, they often retained positions on the board and sometimes took a leading role in management. They continued to be active in part because, as Chandler suggests, many of the enterprises were still small enough to be managed by family shareholder-directors and in part as a result of cultural factors. Still another reason was the relative age of the large British enterprises. In many corporations, such as Unilever, it was only after the death of the founder that professional managers took over leadership. The contrast between Britain and the United States in the 1930s and 1940s arises partly because pioneering entrepreneurs in the United States started their firms earlier and therefore died earlier than men like William Morris of Morris Motors. In some British corporations whose boards were dominated by family members, such as Courtaulds, significant numbers of professional managers already held executive positions by the 1930s; they were not able to consolidate their position, however, until after World War II.

The persistence of family control was not entirely determined by outside factors; it was also a matter of deliberate policy on the part of the controlling families. For example, proposals for a merger between Morris Motors and Austin Motors, the two largest British automobile manufacturers, and for their combined integration backward to steel pressing, were made throughout the 1930s. The pressures to join forces were much the same as those operating in the United States automobile industry. Because of the desire of Morris and Sir Herbert Austin to maintain their independence, however, the merger was not undertaken, and Morris had to abandon his plans for acquiring the Pressed Steel Company. It was not until the 1950s, when Austin and Morris had personally left the scene, that effective integration was accomplished.[52] In the steel industry as a whole, family trusts and family boards still inhibited horizontal and vertical mergers of the kind that were being made increasingly necessary by advances in production technology.[53]

The family firm was not symptomatic of an entirely irrational approach to industrial policy; rather, a case can be made for it on the basis of the alternative resources available for management. Although little is known about changes in the recruitment and training of managers in the twentieth century, the lack of professional development in the field cannot be traced solely to the low demand for managers. Business in Britain was proverbially less prestigious than politics or the professions; although the universities gradually responded to the needs of industry, a substantial gap in the supply of technically trained manpower for management probably remained.[54] Britain's earlier heavy reliance on its market-based industrial organization also led to an underinvestment in managerial talent in the early stages of corporate development. As a result, patronage had to replace professionalism. A young man who wished to learn the business of management could often envisage no better training than in the family firm, where many potential managers both within and outside the family sought it.[55] In some areas, larger, more fully integrated, managerially controlled organizations could probably have developed, but the response was not forthcoming from native British sources. One consequence was an influx of foreign investment, primarily from the United States in the 1920s and 1930s; it continued after World War II. One-sixth of British manufacturing is now foreign-owned and uses imported technology and managerial techniques and, less frequently, non-British managers; this proportion is higher than that in any other European country.[56]

RETROSPECT AND PROSPECT

Theories that the role of the visible hand of management developed in essentially the same way in Western economies, then, are only partially confirmed by an examination of the British case. Perhaps the contrasts between Britain and the United States, or between Britain and other European countries, can best be understood as resulting from a combination of factors that include cultural attitudes, values, ideologies, and social structure as well as the nature of markets and the available technology. Although the British experience broadly confirms Chandler's pro-

70 / Leslie Hannah

posed model of comparative development, some modifications seems necessary if it is to fit the British case. Moreover, considerable further research on individual companies is required before the British corporate experience can be fully compared with that of the United States.

Two more general points are suggested by the data already described. First, a chicken-and-egg problem arises in international comparisons of economies that are continuously in evolution. The fact that the United States market was bigger and was growing more rapidly than European markets may genuinely have resulted from factors exogenous to the strategy and structure of corporations. It market size was, after all, a function of its already high standard of living, and market growth owed much to population increases resulting from immigration and the expansion of the frontier.[57] If, however, the increasing importance of the visible hand is seen as a source of substantial economies of scale, speed, and integration, then the developing corporate economy may be the cause as well as the consequence of rapid economic growth. Between the late 1890s and the 1920s, when Britain experienced the lowest rate of economic growth in its industrial history, the United States and German economies, which were developing large-scale corporations, grew more rapidly. This difference raised the question at the time, as it does now, of whether Great Britain was clinging too long to inherited market structures and failing to develop appropriate integrated and hierarchical coordinating structures in industries where they were being shown to have a comparative advantage in Germany and the United States. Imperfections in the market certainly made such suspicions plausible; and by the 1930s when Great Britain had developed its own large-scale organization, the international rankings in rates of growth were reversed and Britain's relative economic performance improved. The causes of Britain's economic success in that period are themselves to some degree external; the British standard of living, for example, benefited from the fall in world prices for primary products in the early 1930s. Yet it may also be true that the development of the British corporate economy, which allowed new economies of scale, speed, and integration, also contributed to favorable performance.[58]

VISIBLE AND INVISIBLE HANDS IN GREAT BRITAIN / 71

A second point raised by the material reviewed in this chapter—one that conflicts to some extent with the first—is that the consequences of the visible hand of large-scale enterprise were not all benign. Without creating a managerial hierarchy, merger and expansion cannot reduce costs or improve service, a point Chandler has emphasized. Forward integration by breweries to secure pub outlets, motivated by the licensing laws, or merger undertaken for tax reasons may be neutral in their effects on efficiency. Other kinds of considerations, such as horizontal or vertical mergers undertaken to enhance monopoly power, may have negative effects. The arguments on this subject are well known, but economists may have defined them too narrowly. Equally or more important, increases in scale have had social consequences in the form of worker alienation and the loss of freshness and vigor as entrepreneurship has given way to bureaucracy.[59]

Large firms are aware of these problems, and modern multidivisional structures or job-enrichment schemes, for example, may do something to alleviate them, but difficulties clearly persist. On both sides of the Atlantic, there is overwhelming evidence that managers systematically overestimate the gains to be had from contemplated mergers. They undervalue the invisible hand of the market in coordinating activities and overvalue the visible hand with which they plan to replace it in their merged enterprises. Thus a large proportion of mergers are reported to be financial failures.[60] Of course, counterpressures discourage such managerial misconceptions—profit-related executive-compensation packages, stock options, the threat of takeovers or proxy fights for unsuccessful boards—but it is arguable that they work only imperfectly and in the long run.

The two countries with the most concentrated industrial structures and largest corporations since World War II, Britain and the United States, are also those with the least impressive economic performance. The balance between the negative and positive influences of the factors considered here is difficult to assess, and many other factors are involved in determining economic performance. Nonetheless, the questions raised in the 1890s by the early critics of the emerging modern corporations are still properly before us.

72 / LESLIE HANNAH

NOTES

1. See especially Alfred D. Chandler, Jr., *Strategy and Structure* (Cambridge, Mass., 1962); idem, *The Visible Hand* (Cambridge, Mass., 1977); idem, "The United States: Seedbed of Managerial Capitalism," this volume.

2. I have developed this theme at greater length in *The Rise of the Corporate Economy: The British Experience* (Baltimore, 1976).

3. Leslie Hannah and J. A. Kay, *Concentration in Modern Industry* (London, 1977).

4. See S. J. Prais, *The Evolution of Giant Firms in Britain* (London, 1976) pp. 155–162; but see *Economist*, October 8, 1977, p. 97, for data on the absolute size of German corporations, which grew even faster in the 1970s.

5. See Derek F. Channon, *The Strategy and Structure of British Enterprise* (London, 1973); Gareth P. Dyas and Heinz T. Thanheiser, *Emerging European Enterprises: Strategy and Structure of French and German Industry* (London, 1977); Alfred D. Chandler, Jr., and Herman Daems, introduction to *The Rise of Managerial Capitalism,* ed. Herman Daems and Herman Van der Wee (The Hague, 1974).

6. See Jürgen Kocka, "The Rise of the Modern Industrial Enterprise in Germany," this volume; see also Robert A. Brady, *The Rationalization Movement in German Industry* (Berkeley, 1933).

7. Hannah and Kay, *Concentration,* chaps. 5, 6.

8. Leslie Hannah, "Mergers in British Manufacturing Industry 1880–1918," *Oxford Economic Papers* 26 (1974):1–20.

9. For a more complete discussion, see Hannah and Kay, *Concentration,* pp. 103–105.

10. Richard C. Edwards, "Stages in Corporate Stability and the Risks of Corporate Failure," *Journal of Economic History* 35 (1975):428–457; see also Chandler, *Visible Hand,* pp. 371–372.

11. Chandler's preliminary analysis of the data for the 50 largest firms was published as "The Development of Modern Management Structure in the U.S. and U.K.," in *Management Strategy and Business Development,* ed. Leslie Hannah (London, 1976); improved information has led, however, to the reclassification of some of the firms listed there. The extension of Chandler's work is based on estimates of firm size and a list of the 200 largest firms prepared by Margaret Ackrill for the study reported in Hannah and Kay, *Concentration;* the analysis of industrial groups and other characteristics was carried out by Peter Grant.

12. Like the comparable list of United States firms in Chandler's *Visible Hand* but unlike those for Germany prepared by Jürgen Kocka and Hannes Siegrist, that on which table 2.2 is based includes a few subsidiaries of foreign corporations for all three dates. Firms such as Boots Pure Drug Company and Associated Electrical Industries have passed from British to United States ownership and back in the course of the twentieth century. To include only British-registered and British-owned companies would thus have distorted the overall picture and have led to the inclusion of

many companies that operated principally abroad. The criterion for in-clusion—an operational standard, rather than one depending on owner-ship—was that a substantial proportion of a company's assets be in British manufacturing.

13. For a list of the largest United States firms in 1917, see Chandler, *Visible Hand*, appendix A.

14. British Petroleum was still quite small in 1919, however; see Ronald W. Ferrier, "The Early Management Organization of British Petroleum," in *Management Strategy*, ed. Hannah.

15. For a discussion of this industry in the nineteenth and early twentieth centuries, see Samuel B. Saul, ed., *Technological Change* (London, 1970); C. Knick Harley, "Skilled Labour and the Choice of Technique in Edwardian Industry," *Explorations in Economic History* 11 (1974):391–414.

16. Information supplied by Babcock & Wilcox, Ltd.

17. See John Vaizey, "The Brewing Industry," in *The Effects of Mergers*, ed. P. Lesley Cook and Ruth Cohen (London, 1958).

18. See Shin-ichi Yonekawa, "The Strategy and Structure of Cotton and Steel Enterprises in Britain, 1900–1939," in *Strategy and Structure of Big Business*, ed. Keiichiro Nakagawa (Tokyo, 1977).

19. See Hannah, *Rise of the Corporate Economy*, chap. 8; see also Chandler, "Modern Management Structure," pp. 33–35, 41–43. Given the size difference between the two economies, it may be more appropriate to compare the 50 or 100 largest firms in Britain with the 200 largest in the United States.

20. For this example I am grateful to Yuichi Kudo, who has done extensive research in the files of United Alkali.

21. Leslie Hannah, "Strategy and Structure in the Manufacturing Sector," in *Management Strategy*, ed. Hannah; Channon, *Strategy and Structure of British Enterprise*.

22. From data compiled by Peter Grant.

23. Philip S. Florence, *Ownership, Control and Success of Large Companies, 1936–1951* (London, 1961).

24. See, for instance, Theodore C. Barker, *The Glassmakers* (London, 1977); R. A. Church, *Kenricks in Hardware: A Family Business* (Newton Abbot. 1969). See also Kocka, "Modern Industrial Enterprise in Germany," this volume, for a discussion of similar factors in Germany; but compare Channon, *Strategy and Structure of British Enterprise*, p. 248.

25. The interpenetration of finance and manufacturing is a topic worthy of further study. For some illuminating remarks pertinent to the analysis of British business in the twentieth century, see W. D. Rubinstein, "The Victorian Middle Classes: Wealth, Occupation, and Geography," *Economic History Review* 30 (1977):602–623.

26. See B. W. E. Alford, *W. D. & H. O. Wills and the Development of the Tobacco Industry, 1786–1965* (London, 1973).

27. See William J. Reader, *Metal Box: A History* (London, 1976).

28. See Walter E. Minchinton, *The British Tinplate Industry* (London, 1957).

74 / LESLIE HANNAH

29. For comparative data and alternative definitions of direct investment, see, among others, Donald G. Paterson, *British Direct Investment in Canada, 1890–1914* (Toronto, 1976); Irving Stone, "British Direct and Portfolio Investment in Latin America before 1914," *Journal of Economic History* 37 (1977):690–722. Some of the obscurities in the statistics are unraveled in an unpublished paper by Michael Edelstein of the City University of New York.

30. No study has yet been made of changes in the product ranges of large corporations before 1950. For data after 1950, see Channon, *Strategy and Structure in British Enterprise;* for less systematic information on the period before 1950, see Leslie Hannah, "Strategy and Structure in the Manufacturing Sector," in *Management Strategy,* ed. Hannah.

31. See Hannah, *Rise of the Corporate Economy,* pp. 57, 156–157, 169, 188–189.

32. See Chandler, "United States," this volume; see also idem, *Visible Hand,* pp. 498–500; idem, "Modern Management Structure," pp. 47ff.

33. Walt W. Rostow, *The Stages of Economic Growth,* 2nd ed. (Cambridge, 1971), p. xx.

34. See I. C. R. Byatt, *The British Electrical Industry 1875–1914* (Oxford, forthcoming).

35. See, for instance, William P. Kennedy, "Foreign Investment, Trade and Growth in the United Kingdom, 1870–1913," *Explorations in Economic History* 11 (1974):415–444; Donald N. McCloskey and Lars G. Sandberg, "From Damnation to Redemption: Judgments on the Late Victorian Entrepreneur," ibid., 9 (1971):89–108.

36. See J. D. Gribbin, ed., "Board of Trade. Survey of International Cartels, 1944" (London, 1976); William J. Reader, *Imperial Chemical Industries: A History,* 2 vols. (London, 1970–1975).

37. The logic by which the boundaries of market and firm are determined was first clearly enunciated in Ronald H. Coase, "The Nature of the Firm," *Economica,* n.s. 4 (1937):386–405.

38. Many major British firms that bought capital goods—for example, those in the oil and electrical industries—did so through middlemen and other market institutions of this sort rather than directly from the manufacturer. For a less favorable view of the middleman, however, see Peter L. Payne, *British Entrepreneurship in the Nineteenth Century* (London, 1974), pp. 41–45, 53–56.

39. This body of work is summarized in McCloskey and Sandberg, "From Damnation to Redemption."

40. See Alexander Gerschenkron, "Economic Backwardness in Historical Perspective," in *The Progress of Underdeveloped Areas,* ed. Berthold F. Hoselitz (Chicago, 1952); Kocka, "Modern Industrial Enterprise in Germany," this volume.

41. For a general discussion of this issue, see Nathan Rosenberg, ed., *The Economics of Technical Change* (Harmondsworth, 1971); Frederic M. Scherer, *Industrial Market Structure and Economic Performance* (Chicago,

1970), chaps. 15, 16. For an example of contemporary criticism of competition in a technologically developing industry, see British Electrical and Allied Manufacturers' Associations, *Combines and Trusts in the Electrical Industry* (London, 1927).

42. See, for instance, M. Sanderson, "Research and the Firm in British Industry 1919–1939," *Science Studies,* vol. 2 (Harmondsworth, 1972).

43. See especially William P. Kennedy, "Institutional Response to Economic Growth: Capital Markets in Britain to 1914," in *Management Strategy,* ed. Hannah; see also Lance Davis, "The Capital Markets and Industrial Concentration: The US and UK, A Comparative Study," *Economic History Review* 19 (1966):255–272; Chandler, *Visible Hand,* p. 373.

44. See, for instance, I. C. R. Byatt, "Electrical Products," in *The Development of British Industry and Foreign Competition, 1875–1914,* ed. Derek H. Aldcroft (London, 1968), pp. 268–273.

45. See Hannah, *Rise of the Corporate Economy,* pp. 135–137; Neil K. Buxton, "Entrepreneurial Efficiency in the British Coal Industry between the Wars," *Economic History Review* 23 (1970):476–497.

46. See, for instance, Herman Daems, "The Rise of the Modern Industrial Enterprise: A New Perspective," this volume.

47. See Charles Wilson, "Economy and Society in Late Victorian Britain," *Economic History Review* 18 (1965):183–198; Margaret Hall, John Knapp, and Christopher Winsten, *Distribution in Great Britain and North America* (London, 1961); James B. Jefferys, *Retail Trading in Britain 1850–1950* (London, 1954); Derek F. Channon, "Corporate Evolution in the Service Industries," in *Management Strategy,* ed. Hannah.

48. See, for instance, Peter Mathias, *Retailing Revolution* (London, 1967); Patrick Fitzgerald, *Industrial Combination in England* (London, 1927).

49. See Adam G. Whyte, *Forty Years of Electrical Progress* (London, 1930); S. G. Chapman, *Jesse Boot of Boots the Chemists* (London, 1974).

50. In an important sense, however, cartels and mergers also complemented each other. For a fuller consideration of this issue, see Leslie Hannah, "Mergers, Cartels and Concentration: Legal Factors in the US and European Experience, 1880–1914," in *Recht und Entwicklung der Grossunternehmen im 19. und frühen 20. Jahrhundert,* ed. Jürgen Kocha and Norbert Horn, (Göttingen, 1979).

51. See Robert Jones and Oliver Marriott, *Anatomy of a Merger* (London, 1970), p. 124.

52. See Philip Walter Sawford Andrews and Elizabeth Brunner, *Life of Lord Nuffield* (Oxford, 1955); Graham Turner, *The Leyland Papers* (London, 1971); see also R. Church, *Herbert Austin* (London, forthcoming).

53. See, for instance, Peter L. Payne, "Rationality and Personality: A Study of Mergers in the Scottish Iron and Steel Industry, 1916–1936," *Business History* 19 (1977):162–191; idem, *Colvilles and the Scottish Steel Industry* (Oxford, 1979).

54. See Derek H. Aldcroft, "Investment in the Utilisation of Manpower:

76 / Leslie Hannah

Great Britain and Her Rivals," in *Great Britain and Her World,* ed. B. M. Ratcliffe (Manchester, 1975); M. Sanderson, *The Universities and British Industry* (London, 1970).

55. For examples of successful and wide-ranging recruitment of managers by a family, see Barker, *Glassmakers.*

56. See John H. Dunning, *American Investment in British Manufacturing Industry* (London, 1958); idem, *The Role of American Investment in the British Economy* (London, 1969). The high proportion of United States investment resulted in part, of course, from linguistic and cultural affinities, as well as from economic, technical, and managerial factors.

57. Chandler, for instance, makes this argument in *Visible Hand,* pp. 498–499.

58. This is the broader theme of my "Business Development and Economic Structure in Britain since 1880," in *Management Strategy,* ed. Hannah.

59. Hannah and Kay, *Concentration,* chap. 3.

60. For surveys of the literature on Britain, see M. A. Utton, "On Measuring the Effects of Industrial Mergers," *Scottish Journal of Political Economy,* 1974; on the United States, see Thomas F. Hogarty, "Profits from Merger: The Evidence of 50 Years," *St. John's Law Review* (1970). See also Geoffrey Meeks, *Disappointing Marriage: A Study of the Gains from Merger* (Cambridge, 1977).

[20]

BRITISH BUSINESS AND THE TRANSITION TO A CORPORATE ECONOMY: ENTREPRENEURSHIP AND MANAGEMENT STRUCTURES

By T. R. GOURVISH

Business historians, in their work on the single firm – its birth, growth and, where appropriate, decline – have naturally included sections dealing with entrepreneurial response, organisational forms, and, if relevant, the separation of ownership and control and the emergence of managerial hierarchies. That this writing is often, if not invariably, divorced from a more general, theoretical, approach should not surprise us. There is, of course, no obligation on the historian of an individual business to theorise; indeed, many of such studies are commissioned histories, with all the constraints on subject matter which they impose, whether directly or indirectly. Nor is theorising a straightforward matter. For example, conventional neo-classical economics offers little comfort to those who wish to emphasise the role of the entrepreneur and organisational structures in the dynamic process of business develop-ment. Moreover, the situation still persists, notwithstanding the theoretical heritage of Schumpeter and Penrose; the behavioural school of Barnard and Simon; the transaction costs approach pioneered by Commons and Coase; and the imaginative attempts to build constraints into profit-maximising assumptions in micro-economic theory.[1] For many years scholars, whether economists or historians, have often complained that much more empirical work is required before confident generalisations on entrepreneurship and organisational change can be attempted. At the same time, theoreticians remain critical of what they deem the blinkered approach of historians of single business entities.[2]

The behavioural and managerial emphasis of organisation theorists offers some instructive insights into the perceptions of managers, the goals of firms, and the relationship of both to business decision-making. However, where this approach merely replaces the profit-maximisation objective with the maximisation of some other element – whether turnover, capital assets, prestige or whatever – it can be as deterministic and difficult to apply as the conventional neo-classical model. Furthermore, much of this rather eclectic work has the additional weakness of downgrading the consideration of any economic phe-nomena, such as market changes, technological innovation, and protection. For the business historian, the most useful applications of the 'behavioural school' derive from the concept of 'bounded rationality', that is the notion that within organisations intended rational choices or responses are constrained both by uncertainty and by the limited capacity of human beings for computing and processing information. This is important in that it sets defined limits to an efficiency-based model of corporate behaviour, and gives prominence to a study of the activities of individual entrepreneurs and managers, where game theory and conflict models have an obvious relevance.[3]

Penrose has offered business historians numerous insights into the dynamic experiences of the firm, although her discursive treatment certainly does not amount to an integrated theoretical model of either the firm or its growth. On the other hand, she does emphasise the importance of the historical process and the value of using specific case studies, thereby combining the theoretical approach of the economist with the historian's recognition of real situations. Furthermore, her work on diversification strategies and their relevance for an extension of a firm's growth possibilities, and on the managerial costs of and limits to growth, have been major contributions to an understanding of the dynamics of corporate growth. They have been built on and extended by others, notably Marris.[4] Penrose gave considerable attention to the ability of management to cope with the growth process, and this is an area which has been explored in considerable depth by Chandler. His work represents the best example of a quasi-theory attractive both to historians and to other students of corporate development. In *Strategy and Structure* and *The Visible Hand* he focuses upon the emergence of the 'corporate economy' in the USA, characterised by the market dominance of large, multi-divisional companies and their complex managerial hierarchies. The approach is plainly historical, in that detailed case studies are used to demonstrate that entrepreneurial and organisational responses were firmly linked to technological change and market development. The American market expanded in the nineteenth century with the coming of the railroads, which pioneered new organisational structures to cope with the operational complexity arising from size and dispersion and with the separation of ownership and control. They also provided the infrastructure to encourage manufacturing businesses to adopt mass production techniques and vertical integration. The diversification strategies of these growing firms then put pressure on the centralised, departmental or 'unitary' form of organisation, which had been inherited from the early railroads. In the 1920s this produced a structural response in the shape of the multi-divisional or M-form organisation. For Chandler, the organisational structure followed on from the strategy of growth and diversification.[5] An historical approach is also evident in Hannah's *Rise of the Corporate Economy*, which identifies merger activity in manufacturing as the major element in corporate development in the UK.[6]

The 'business history' approach, as Oliver Williamson has dubbed it, has a great deal to offer as a basic framework for the study of particular firms and industries, and has helped to identify specific issues, notably the

20 *Enterprise, Management and Innovation in British Business*

central importance of managerial resources, and the impact of the external economic environment upon those resources. Its relevance is strongest in twentieth-century applications, of course, where with the emergence of large-scale enterprise the 'invisible hand' of the market began to be replaced by the 'visible hand' of management. Whether, as Williamson has asserted, the work of business history can be usefully combined with a transaction costs emphasis is a matter for argument. The assumption that firms will seek to supersede market transactions and the price mechanism until the cost of organising an additional transaction internally equals the cost of transacting in the market is clearly an important one. It has obvious relevance for an understanding of business organisation, particularly when modified by reference to institutions as well as markets. The approach can be employed to analyse decisions to integrate production and selling functions, and it has been used successfully in the study of multinational enterprise, where the highlighting of information costs, uncertainty avoidance, and the relationship between principal and agent is of key importance.[7] At the same time, the information cost emphasis reduces the role of technology in determining the operations of firms inside and outside markets, while the transaction cost model appears to be rather difficult to handle empirically in historical contexts, particularly if quantitative precision is desired.[8] Nevertheless, the work of Chandler, Williamson *et al.* probably offers the best set of ground rules presently available for an analysis of the transition from small family-owned and dominated firms to the giant enterprises and more concentrated industrial structures of 'managerial capitalism', and the increased presence of multinational enterprise.[9]

II

This article draws upon the editors' selection of British company histories in order to explore some of the main themes in corporate development advanced by Penrose, Chandler, Williamson *et al.* These are:

(i) the type of organisational structure employed, the causes of managerial innovation, and the adaptability of management to expansion, technological change and transformed market conditions; and

(ii) entrepreneurial and organisational factors in Britain's apparent 'corporate lag', namely, the delay in emulating, for example, American developments, with particular reference to the persistence of a 'family' presence in management. Equally important, though given less prominence here, are:

(iii) the supply of managerial resources and its implication for the pace of change from entrepreneur-dominated to manager-dominated enterprises; and

(iv) the relationship between organisation and performance, with particular reference to the role of individuals, the relative merits of centralisation and decentralisation strategies in securing control of large businesses, and 'profit' versus 'service' conflicts in public sector enterprise.

The considerable bias in the selection of companies and corporations has been pointed out elsewhere. The 13 businesses to be studied are, with the exception of Archibald Kenrick & Sons of West Bromwich, large concerns. They are still trading, and have an exceptionally long life. Omitting the nationalised enterprises established by legislation in 1946–47, three of the remaining ten companies had roots in the eighteenth century, three were founded before 1837, and three were established in the period 1861–81. All are identifiable today, although Colvilles is now part of the British Steel Corporation, Wills is part of the Imperial Group (itself part of Hanson Trust), and Harland & Wolff has been government-owned since 1975. There is a strong emphasis on manufacturing, where ten of the companies are located. Finally, all have been the subject of a *commissioned* history. Despite the usual protestations of the authors about 'independence', this fact lays them open to some suspicion at least of restraint in the handling of business behaviour and the role of personalities.[10] However, for our immediate purposes the problem should not be exaggerated. While it must of course be conceded that to rely solely on such examples would be to underestimate the importance of failure and of disappearance by merger in business progression, the company attributes of longevity and, ultimately, large size are useful in any examination of the transition from small to large, from entrepreneur-dominated to manager-dominated enterprise. Indeed, it is prominence in the UK economy, coupled with a sense of tradition, that has encouraged these firms to display a statesmanlike attitude to archive-gathering and the commissioning of serious business histories.[11]

III

Our first task is to analyse the evolving organisational structures of the case studies (Table 1 provides an outline analysis). The impression they leave is that before 1914 British firms made very few significant organisational changes to match their growth, technological change, and a competitive world increasingly shaped by the corporativism of the United States and Germany. One searches in vain in our selection of commissioned histories for organisational charts to match those reproduced by Chandler for the USA. 'Organisation' receives compara-tively little attention from our authors; indeed, the word is absent from the index of most of the books dealing with the pre-1945 period.[12] What *is* important, and this emerges clearly, was a general move to limited liability status, a process begun in the 1880s. By 1900 seven of the nine businesses then in existence had registered, three in 1880–85, four in 1891–95; only Bowater and W.H. Smith remained as private partnerships (see Table 1). The new entities were *de facto private* companies, although the legal distinction between 'private' and 'public' was not made until the

TABLE 1

SAMPLE OF BUSINESSES, WITH OUTLINE INFORMATION ON STRUCTURE

Business	Activity	Date of Foundation	Basic Structure	
1. Manufacturing				
Bowater	paper	1881	partnership	
			private limited co.	1910
			public co.	1926
			reconstituted	1932
			holding co.	1947
Colvilles	steel	1861	partnership	
			(private) limited co.	1895
			controlled by	
			Harland & Wolff	1920
			reconstituted	1930
			public holding co.	1936
			nationalised	1951
			privatised	1955
			renationalised	1967
Courtaulds	textiles	1828	partnership	
			(private) limited co.	1891
			public co.	1904
			reconstituted	1913
Harland & Wolff	shipbuilding	1861	partnership	
			(private) limited co.	1885
			public co.	1924
			reconstituted	1937, 1944
			nationalised	1975

Continued overleaf

TABLE 1 (continued)

I.C.I.	1926	chemicals	public limited holding co.
Kenricks	1791	metal goods	partnership (private) limited co. 1883
Pilkingtons	1826	glass	partnership (private) limited co. 1894 / public co. 1970
Wills	1786	tobacco	partnership (private) limited co. 1893 / part of Imperial Tobacco Co. 1901
N.C.B.	1946	coal	public corporation
Electricity*	1947	electricity	public corporation

2. Other (Service, Banking, Distribution)

Railways**	1947	railways	public corporation
Midland Bank	1836	banking	joint stock co. / unlimited co. 1873 / limited co. 1880
W. H. Smith	1792	newspapers etc.	partnership / private limited co. 1929 / public limited holding co. 1949

Key:

*   British Electricity Authority (1948–55), Central Electricity Authority (1955–57), Electricity Council and Central Electricity Generating Board (1958–)

** British Transport Commission (1948–62), British Railways Board (1962–)

Companies Act of 1907. They kept the number of members small, applied restrictions on the transfer of shares, and usually made no appeal to the public for funds. If money *was* required, it was raised by the issue of non-voting loan stock. The controlling ordinary share capital was retained by the participating partners and their families. These moves were part of a general tendency in Britain to adopt the limited liability form. About 132,000 companies were registered in London in the period 1880–1914, and the bulk of them was 'private'. Of the 63,000 on the register in 1914, 48,500 or 77 per cent were of this type.[13]

Why was the decision to register taken? Certainly, by the 1880s the environment was more conducive to incorporation, with the expansion of the financial sector, the adoption of lower share denominations, and the appearance of specialist intermediaries. But a common theme was the concern about future viability after the mid 1870s. Difficulties experienced in the climate of falling prices and squeezed profit margins led firms such as Kenricks (1883), Harland & Wolff (1885), and Courtaulds (1891) to seek the shelter of limited liability. Furthermore, the collapse of the City of Glasgow Bank in 1878 not only encouraged banks to move from *un*limited to limited liability (the Midland, then known as the Birmingham & Midland, did so in 1880), but also persuaded firms in several industries that the advantages of limited liability outweighed the disadvantages.[14] In some cases, growth was the spur. For Wills (1893), Pilkington Brothers (1894), and David Colville & Sons (1895), the context was sustained growth and the need to secure its financing. Limited liability status was a means to increase the number of partners in order to cope with the problems of expansion, an example of response to Penrose's managerial limits to growth. For Wills in particular, the move followed the successful exploitation of new technology – the Bonsack cigarette-making machine.[15] Moreover, the classic case of incorporation to finance growth – brewing – is unrepresented in our case studies. Here, a wave of company registrations in the 1880s and 1890s was both a response and a prelude to growth based on the acquisition of breweries and tied houses.[16] Finally, entrepreneurial or family factors should not be overlooked. The conversion of both Courtaulds and Colvilles to limited liability status owed much to personal circumstances. For Courtaulds it was the death of Harry Taylor in 1890 and the prediliction of George Courtauld III for country life; in Scotland, it was the age of the founder, David Colville, 82 in 1895, and his eldest son's interest in politics.[17]

Limited liability *per se* did little to transform organisational forms and management practices. By the turn of the century, a 'corporate lag' was becoming evident, in the sense of a slowness to adopt large-scale corporate organisations in comparison with the faster rate of change in the United States.[18] But some of the elements which, according to Chandler, stimulated the emergence of 'managerial capitalism' in America, namely the revolution in transport and communications and the creation of urban markets, which unlocked technological opportunities for the integration of mass production and volume distribution, did encourage *tentative* organisational changes in Britain. Thus, both Wills and Courtaulds adopted public company status at the turn of the century, and at Colvilles and Harland & Wolff business pressures were reflected in a degree of managerial adaptation.

In tobacco, the prelude to change was the threat of an 'invasion' of the domestic market by the giant American Tobacco Co. Wills, with a 40 per cent share of that market, led the response of British firms in creating in 1901 the Imperial Tobacco Co. of Great Britain and Ireland, a public concern amalgamating the interests of thirteen leading firms in Bristol, London, Glasgow, Liverpool and Nottingham. Four more manufacturers were added in 1902.[19] The new company, with an issued capital of £17.5 million (in 1905), was the largest in Britain outside the railway industry, and its creation may be seen as an inevitable shift to oligopolistic competition in tobacco. Cigarettes were ideal for low-cost, high-volume production and distribution, and some of Imperial's early moves were entirely consistent with the vertical integration strategy of Chandler's typology, notably the acquisition in 1902 of a key printing/packaging firm, Mardon, Son & Hall, and a large firm of multiple wholesalers and retailers, Salmon & Gluckstein. On the other hand, there were distinct limits to this 'corporate revolution'. In many ways the new giant was a glorified family firm. The Wills family supplied seven of the nineteen Board members and held 70 per cent of the equity capital. Although steps were taken to centralise certain functions, such as tobacco leaf buying and overall financial strategy, action fell far short of the American model, with its central headquarters and complex management hierarchy. Imperial remained essentially a federation of firms, with production and sales policy largely determined by the constituent manufacturers. It was a corporate giant in legal rather than in managerial terms.[20]

The re-registration of Samuel Courtauld & Co. as a public company in 1904 followed a decade of difficulties, including a decline in domestic crape sales and a writing-down of capital. But the change was probably inspired by the decision to move into artificial silk. Viscose patents and licences were acquired in the same year, and a paid-up capital of £600,000 formed the basis for investment in a new factory in Coventry in 1905, and a period of expansion and profitability. Indeed, within ten years profits were high enough to encourage a further reconstruction as Courtaulds Ltd in 1913, with an issued share capital of £2 million. The company also became a multinational enterprise by establishing the American Viscose Corporation in 1910.[21] Nevertheless, as with Wills, Courtaulds still represented a hybrid form of corporate development in comparison with the American model. Although the control of the founding families was diluted considerably, the business was a long way from the complex organisational structures of integrated, functionally departmentalised American companies such as Du Pont and Armour, and of companies moving towards the multidivisional form before the 1920s, such as United States Rubber.[22]

26   *Enterprise, Management and Innovation in British Business*

The modesty of British management changes prior to 1914 can also be seen in the histories of Colvilles and Harland & Wolff. At Colvilles, ownership was widened in 1901–2, but more interesting was the offer of a token shareholding to a number of young managers. The decision gave them a personal stake in the business and was a means to promote the more promising among them to the Board. Indeed, only fourteen years later, in 1916, one of them, John Craig, the son of an iron puddler, emerged as Chairman and Managing Director.[23] In Belfast, Harland & Wolff grew to become the world's leading shipbuilding firm, under the leadership of William (later Viscount) Pirrie, an owner-entrepreneur in the grand manner, who became Chairman in 1895. The firm's rapid growth, together with the industry's complex links with shipping, steel, armaments and marine engineering, encouraged a series of both horizontal and vertical mergers. The need to safeguard supplies of heavy steel forgings and a desire to buy into turbines led to a merger with the Sheffield steel firm of John Brown in 1907. This took the form of an exchange of shares, with 52 per cent of the equity being transferred to the Sheffield concern. The move was one of a series of financial mergers which culminated in Harland & Wolff's conversion to a public company in 1924 and membership of the Royal Mail Shipping Group. However, there is no suggestion that the company's growing complexities produced any significant changes in organisation. Day-to-day management was delegated to a committee of six managing directors, but strategy and financial control remained firmly in the hands of Pirrie.[24]

Thus, corporate change in Britain before 1914 was more legal and financial than managerial, with an emphasis on the retention of control by founding family groups. Business organisation was essentially simple, as far as one can see, based upon a few functionally-structured departments. Policy and planning roles and, in many cases, routine decision-making too, were left to dominant personalities such as Pirrie, and Henry Tetley of Courtaulds, who inspired the move to public company status. Training for management was rare and recruitment could be 'astonishingly casual' in view of the size of the companies concerned.[25] Only in the railway industry is there any indication of 'managerial capitalism' in the sense of dispersed, complex organisations, the separation of ownership and control, hierarchies, and management development by means of training programmes. Even here, the organisational structures themselves remained fashioned upon the departmental model common to both British and American railways in the 1850s and 1860s. In the UK there was little change in response to the move to larger company size and more oligopolistic conditions after 1870, and no fundamental transformation before the government-sponsored mergers of 1921–23.[26]

IV

The inter-war period is generally seen as a fruitful area of study in terms of British corporate development. First, the enthusiasm for 'rationalisation' apparent during the First World War among prominent business leaders was perpetuated in peacetime, although its precise meaning was uncertain. It was used to support strategies ranging from intervention in the organisation of work – the elimination of restrictive practices, for example – to purely defensive reactions to the harsher realities of the post-war economy, from horizontal mergers with minimal change to vertical transformations following the economic hiatus of 1919–21.[27] Second, in manufacturing, a significant merger 'boom' can be detected. As Hannah has shown, the number of firms which disappeared in this way increased significantly in the 1920s, and activity remained at a high level in the following decade.[28] A number of prominent new business entities emerged, not least of which were Imperial Chemical Industries in 1926, Associated Electrical Industries in 1928, and Unilever in 1929. The largest change was outside manufacturing, with the government-sponsored merger of most of the railway industry to form four giant regional enterprises in 1923. This said, how far was the period one of genuine organisational, or managerial innovation? Our case studies point up the steps taken by some of the established or leading firms, but everywhere there is an indication that conservative management practices persisted. The merger wave itself was essentially either (i) defensive, with the aim of stabilising competition and prices, rather than part of a conscious strategy to control the market; or (ii) emulative, inspired by the threat of intervention by leading foreign firms, or encouraged by foreign entrepreneurs active in the British economy. There was real growth, based on new investments such as Ford's at Dagenham in 1932, but more often corporate growth was a matter of 'joining together existing assets'.[29]

The major example of a large-scale merger in manufacturing, fully documented by Reader, is that of ICI. At first sight, there are similarities with the Imperial Tobacco case a quarter of a century earlier. The amalgamation of the four largest chemical firms – Nobel Industries, Brunner, Mond, United Alkali, and British Dyestuffs Corporation – was devised by Sir Harry McGowan (Nobel), in conjunction with Reginald McKenna (Chairman, Midland Bank, 1919–43) and Sir Alfred Mond (Brunner, Mond). While all were rationalisation enthusiasts, the move was prompted by the threat to the British chemical industry presented by the newly-formed German giant, IG Farbenindustrie – and, as in tobacco, was both emulative and pre-emptive in nature. There was no evidence of technological or financial considerations.[30] In a sense there was direct German influence on ICI via the Mond family with its Cassel origins, and German entrepreneurs were also prominent elsewhere, O. Philippi of J. & P. Coats in textiles, Sir Hugo Hirst of GEC in electricity. American influence was also evident in the establishment of AEI in 1928 and in the British motor industry.[31]

But how far did British *management* change in the period? ICI began by moving firmly towards centralised control, led by the two Managing Directors, Mond (Chairman, 1926–30) and McGowan (President,

28   *Enterprise, Management and Innovation in British Business*

1926–30). Using Nobel's holding company model, the first ICI Board presided over an issued capital of £56.8 million with eight executive directors drawn from only two of the constituent companies, Nobel and Brunner, Mond. This was quite different from Imperial Tobacco's 'loose federation' of 1901. Indeed, the evidence suggests that centralisation was taken too far, with the executive directors spending too much time on the routine management of individual constituents, and within four years the company had adopted a more decentralised, multidivisional structure, based on Nobel's Metals Group of 1928, with eight product-based manufacturing groups. It is safe to regard ICI as one of the British pioneers of the Chandlerian modern corporation, and certainly, the organisational steps of 1927–31 ensured that there were no managerial 'limits to growth', in Penrose's formulation. But it is equally clear that these steps, and notably the establishment of a Central Administration Committee and a General Purposes Committee, were designed to strengthen the position of the managing directors, and after Mond (Lord Melchett)'s death in 1930, McGowan dominated the company as Chairman and sole Managing Director until 1937. The bold, energetic Scot, with his high salary (averaging £57,000 p.a., 1931–37), epitomised 'managerial capitalism', but his dictatorial stance, and the continued concentration of authority for finance, marketing and pricing at the centre, ensured that the leaders of the manufacturing groups were merely production directors lacking 'bottom-line' responsibility for commercial performance. ICI, then, fell short of the full multidivisional form. And the early structure of the company was no safeguard against strategic mistakes, as the investment of £20 million in fertiliser plant at Billingham indicates. This was quite simply 'a disaster'.[32]

The ICI example was not taken up enthusiastically in the rest of the UK economy and, in comparison with the USA there were few 'managerial enterprises'. In *Corporate Economy* Hannah refers to three further companies which moved towards a multidivisional form before 1939 by creating regional or product-based divisions – Spillers (milling), Dunlop (rubber) and Turner & Newall (asbestos). Elsewhere he notes that Channon listed only 12 British multidivisional concerns for 1950, eight of which were part of either North American or European multinationals.[33] One of these, Unilever, was the product of a 1920s merger, when the soap and edible fats businesses of Lever Brothers and the Dutch Margarine Unie coalesced in 1929 in 'one of the biggest industrial amalgamations in European history'.[34] The new company, though outside our selection of studies, is a highly instructive example of the transition from owner-dominated to manager-dominated enterprise in a large-scale business. Three necessary ingredients can be found: the determination to maintain family control; the limits to individual control as the firm expanded, contributing to crisis; and the role of crisis in forcing a managerial response.

Lever Brothers Ltd., a public company from 1894, could be regarded in its latter years both as a leading multinational and as a rather ramshackle collection of companies led by an owner-entrepreneur of failing strength. The move after 1912 to an executive board with functional responsibilities and a committee structure did not dent the autocratic rule of William Lever, Lord Leverhulme. His controversial company acquisitions in the early 1920s, not least of which was the Niger Company purchase, at a time of falling prices, produced a crisis; and this was exacerbated by the high gearing of Lever's stock, itself a reflection of the founder's determination to retain control. Liquidity problems forced him to turn to an outsider as manager – Sir Francis D'Arcy Cooper, an accountant from Lever's auditors, Cooper Brothers. It was Cooper, adviser from 1921, Vice-Chairman in 1923, and Leverhulme's successor as Chairman in 1925, who orchestrated the separation of ownership and control and ultimately the Unilever merger.[35]

Thus, crisis produced managerial change, but the process was more complex in that a fundamental shift of company strategy was also involved. Leverhulme's emphasis on internal competition between constituent companies and growth by proliferation was replaced by a policy of retrenchment and a determination to rationalise productive and marketing capacity. In this transformation, organisational adjustment tended to follow, rather than lead, strategy.[36] Nevertheless, changes were made. In Unilever, the challenge posed by *two* large business empires was met by the creation of *two* holding companies, with identical boards (though not identical officeholders), a move based upon the experience of Van den Burghs within the Margarine Unie group. Decision-making at the centre, which focused on finance and marketing, was operated through a small Special Committee, an early 1920s innovation at Lever Brothers (introduced in 1921 to act as a check on Leverhulme). Under Cooper as Chairman (1930–41), Unilever Ltd. and Unilever NV pursued more systematic marketing and production strategies. For example, a rationalisation scheme for the multiplicity of UK soap units, each with its own sales organisation, was introduced under the guidance of Geoffrey Heyworth, another accountant turned successful manager. The firm also encouraged more graduate recruitment to management. There were limitations, of course. The constituent companies, with their world-wide ramifications, took some containing, and the divisional structure was a mixed one, comprising both geographical and product-based units. It took a considerable time before the process of rationalisation was complete. The impression of pre-war Unilever is of a fairly loose federal structure, and as the company's commissioned historian has observed, 'management still had a long way to go before it made radical changes in traditional moulds'.[37] But a measure of what a professional management could achieve in a corporate structure was the bold reorganisation of the company's assets in 1937. In order to adjust for the growing dominance of the UK partner, its non-Empire assets overseas were sold to Unilever NV. The rivalries of the participating families were overcome.[38]

Relatively few firms moved towards a decentralised, divisional form, of course, and by no means all companies responded to the inter-war crisis of recession and over-capacity by adopting manager-dominated organisations. In many cases, family control was maintained, and a crisis did not always provoke managerial change. When organisational adjustments were made, these were often tentative, falling far short of a radical change along Chandlerian lines. Certainly, among our case studies, a number of changes in company form were made. Harland & Wolff (1924), Bowater (1926) and Colvilles (1930) became public companies, and all three experienced managerial or financial crises which necessitated reconstruction – Bowater in 1932, Colvilles in 1930 (after a decade of being controlled by Harland & Wolff), and Harland & Wolff in 1937. The last two were a consequence of the collapse in 1930 of the infamous Royal Mail Shipping Group, a loose conglomerate of financial interests in shipping, shipbuilding and metals built up by Lord Pirrie and maintained, until disaster struck, by Sir Owen Phillips, Lord Kylsant.[39] The period also saw the end of the last partnership in our list, when W.H. Smith & Son became a private limited company in 1929. This might be seen as a belated acceptance of the shortcomings of the partnership form for an expanding national business, but the change was not made for organisational reasons but because there was a need to respond more flexibly to the financial problems left by the death of a principal partner, Freddie Smith. In all four cases, owners continued to participate fully in management, although power was shared with managers. The same is true of Pilkingtons, which survived a management crisis in the early 1930s by restructuring its organisation while retaining strong family control.[40]

The progress, or lack of it, made by our selection of ten companies is set out in Table 2. The assessment must be tentative in view of the reluctance of some authors to conceptualise about organisational form and managerial authority. Nevertheless, the broad picture is fairly clear. Using a crude ranking based on labour force estimates, it can be seen that even the larger companies (those employing 20,000 or more) failed to emulate ICI and Unilever. Harland & Wolff, Imperial Tobacco and Courtaulds all exhibited considerable limitations in organisational capacity and managerial status. Imperial Tobacco and Courtaulds had certainly moved to a larger board of directors, with functionally-structured departments, and some element of managerial hierarchy. But behind these simple delineations, weaknesses were apparent. At Courtaulds, organisational difficulties were fully revealed as the company expanded. The Board retained a complacent, Victorian character in the 1920s and 1930s, increasingly out of step with the company's shift into chemicals and multinational activities. Led by Samuel Courtauld IV, it contained two family members in a group of seven in 1921, and four in an expanded membership of 18 in 1939. Representation was almost exclusively internal, favouring textile production men at the expense of technical experts. The only outside appointment was that of Francis Rodd (Lord Rennell), a banker, in 1935; unsurprisingly, he became one of the sharpest critics of the organisation. Steps *were* taken to improve matters

TABLE 2
COMPANY STRUCTURES, 1939

Company	labour force (approx)	company type	enterprise type[3]	organisational structure	Board composition size	Board composition membership[4]
I.C.I.	57,000(1937)	public holding	managerial	multidivisional	17	mixed
Harland & Wolff	33,000(1939)	public	financial	unitary	6	internal
Imperial Tobacco	30,000(1935)[1]	public holding	family/federative	loose multidivisional	33	internal
Courtaulds	22,000(1938)	public	family	unitary	18	mainly internal
Midland Bank	16,000(1940)	public	managerial	unitary	34	mixed
W.H. Smith	15,000(1939)	private	family	unitary	8	internal
Pilkingtons	13,000(1937)	private	family	unitary	13	internal
Colvilles	7,000(1939)	public holding	family/federative	unitary	9	internal
Bowater	4,000(1936)[2]	public	family	unitary	8	internal
Kenricks	400(1939)	private	personal	unitary	?	internal

Notes

1. Estimate of Christine Shaw/Lewis Johnman: *Business History*, XXVIII, No. 2 (April 1986), p. 239.
2. Bowater and Lloyd.
3. Chandler's typology, namely   Personal: owners dominate
     Based on   Family: owners and managers share power
                        Financial: managers and representatives of investors/banks share power
                        Managerial: managers dominate
4. Typology: Internal: Directors appointed from owners, company managers.
               Mixed: Directors include both internal and external appointments.

32   *Enterprise, Management and Innovation in British Business*

in the late 1930s, with an expanded board membership, the appointment of commercial experts and accountants, the creation of a small advisory group at the centre, and some graduate recruitment. But there was still no clear managerial hierarchy, and, according to Coleman, the company 'was still being run in the manner of an autocratic family business'. A conscious acceptance of the company's shortcomings came with its decision (in 1937) not to take over the rest of the UK rayon industry. This was a clear example of a firm recognising that it was not in an organisational position to reap the benefits of horizontal merger. It took a sharper crisis than the difficult market conditions of the 1930s to provoke further change: this was produced by the enforced sale of Courtaulds's lucrative American subsidiary, AVC, in 1941.[41]

Alford's principal concern is with the operations of the Wills branch inside the Imperial Tobacco group, and he provides comparatively little about the workings of the holding company. However, he indicates that before 1955 very little was done, nor were external market factors pressing enough, to disturb a loose, quasi-divisional structure based on a very large board (33-strong in 1939), recruited, in the main, from the owners of the constituent companies. The Wills family itself gradually surrendered control of Imperial Tobacco as Wills's dominance of the UK tobacco market declined, and the position of John Player & Sons strengthened. There was an organisational response to this change in the balance of power, in the extension of the central advertising function and the creation of a new committee to consider inter-branch matters before they reached the Executive Committee. But the company remained a federation of owner-managers and their firms.[42]

Harland & Wolff is more difficult to categorise. The company's financial weakness in the 1920s, exacerbated by its purchase of Colvilles, was a key factor in the Royal Mail collapse. The crisis was by no means avoidable given the difficult conditions experienced by shipbuilding and steel after the war; but there is little doubt that the scale of the problem was produced by Lord Pirrie's dictatorial pursuit of financial integration, a strategy in marked contrast to the *organisational* integration of best-practice American firms. Pirrie's death in 1924 left Harland & Wolff both financially and managerially insecure. Since 1907 there had been managing directors on the board, working through a committee, but they had little knowledge of the business outside the production process. The initiative passed to Lord Kylsant as Chairman, and the company was forced to go public. Kylsant, assisted by Craig from Colvilles and Sampson from John Brown, concentrated upon finance. Although they exhorted the managing directors to improve tendering and cost control, they had little success. The company was in the worst position of having an overcentralised and compartmentalised control of finance and an inadequate control of production. In 1930, voting trustees were appointed to represent Royal Mail Group creditors, and they installed Frederick Rebbeck as Chairman of Harland & Wolff. An engineer and former works manager, he sought to manage the business as autocratically as his predecessors. The firm cannot be considered a 'managerial enterprise', nor was it an entrepreneurial one. It is best seen as a financial enterprise, in Chandler's typology. The trustees, representing creditors such as the Treasury and the Midland Bank, sought to dictate overall policy and organised the financial reconstruction of 1937. But they failed to control Rebbeck, who exhibited all the defects of the engineer turned manager, in his preference for quality and technical progress over budgetary control.[43]

As for the remaining companies, diversity was the keynote. At one end of the scale there was the Midland Bank which, having expanded in the 1920s by bank affiliations and branch building, developed a more centralised, collectively responsible organisation (from 1929) to control its comparatively large, dispersed labour force. The Board was large, but effective leadership was provided by Reginald McKenna, Chairman, 1919–43, and executive directors such as Frederick Hyde, though there were signs of weakness by 1939. The management style was less assertive than that of Sir Edward Holden, Chairman and Managing Director, 1908–19, but the business was now much larger, the economic environment more treacherous. The Bank appears to have responded to problems of control by improving central accounting, introducing a fully mechanised book-keeping system, and using microfilm in cheque-clearing. The move to a more cautious management was followed by a loss of leadership to Barclays, but it did not mean ossification.[44] At the other end of the spectrum, the owner-dominated Black Country firm, Kenricks, displayed all the classic weaknesses of the personal enterprise: faltering leadership, weak commercial strategies, and the divorce of marketing and production.[45]

Colvilles was different again. The firm became a managerial enterprise from 1916 when led by John Craig. The owners withdrew to become rentiers, and Craig's position, supported by full-time salaried directors, survived the company's purchase by Harland & Wolff in 1920 and subsequent membership of the Royal Mail Group. But reorganisation in 1930, when David Colville & Sons merged with James Dunlop & Co. to form Colvilles Ltd, produced a new board structure which saw a reassertion of owner-participation in the shape of Sir James and Henry Lithgow. The company therefore reverted to a family enterprise, with shared power.[46]

The results in Table 2, drawn from a narrow range admittedly, indicate a continuation of the unitary or departmental form, a preference for internally-recruited directors, and the retention of owners in entrepreneurial positions (the term 'entrepreneurial' is used here to denote strategic decision-making, for example about resource allocation and future growth). Company organisations did develop in the inter-war period, sometimes consciously to improve long-term growth prospects, though more commonly, it seems, as a reaction to crisis. But only two companies in our list had achieved 'managerial status' by 1939, with salaried managers dominating key decision-making at the top, supported

34   *Enterprise, Management and Innovation in British Business*

by a structured hierarchy below. Even large companies, such as Courtaulds and Imperial Tobacco, retained owners in top management roles, and the holding company form was often seen as the remedy for post-merger complexities. Some companies with control problems, such as W.H. Smith, Bowater, and Colvilles, were able to develop managerial hierarchies without deserting the 'family' enterprise.[47] All this suggests that there was a 'corporate lag' in Britain compared with the USA before the 1950s, although its extent should not be exaggerated.[48] Why it occurred is difficult to explain convincingly, and it is impossible to summarise the various arguments in a few lines. A number of macro-economic generalisations, for example about market size and the relative efficiency of communications and capital markets, have their attractions, and not least is Lance Davis's emphasis upon the retarding influence (on concentration) of the ease of obtaining external funds in the UK.[49] It may well be that the external pressures to effect change – and specifically, to adopt the M-form of organisation – were not strong enough before the 1950s; certainly, companies such as Courtaulds appeared reluctant to diversify their production before them. It may be that the immature managerial hierarchies which developed in owner-dominated enterprises were not sophisticated enough or powerful enough to pose the kind of control problems which Williamson identifies as forcing a move to the M-form in order to reassert central control over resource allocation and profitability.[50] But at the root of much of Britain's more cautious response to corporate growth was the persistence of traditional attitudes in top management, whether that management was dominated by owners, or salaried managers, or neither. The 'club' atmosphere of most boardrooms was a key factor influencing attitudes to organisational change. It also provides an explanation for the general diffidence in manufacturing about management training and development in comparison with practice not only in American manufacturing but also in the British railway industry. Some progress can be detected in the inter-war years. ICI established a Central Staff Department in 1927, Pilkingtons introduced a traineeship scheme in 1933, the Midland Bank placed greater emphasis on examinations and entry qualifications in the 1930s. But these rather limited responses were far from typical.[51] Education and training of managers remained separate activities, and even large companies retained a cosy amateurishness. Both must be associated with 'corporate lag' before they were challenged in the post-war years.[52]

V

In post-war Britain the larger enterprises gave much more attention to their organisational structures. There was first of all a move to the holding company type, for example by Bowater in 1947, and by W.H. Smith on taking up public company registration in 1949 (see Table 3). The M-form then gained ground, such that by 1970 four of the nine private sector enterprises in our list had adopted it to some degree (Table 3). Colvilles, which had been nationalised in 1951 and denationalised four years later, also moved to a multidivisional form, in 1963, shortly before it was renationalised in 1967. The task of analysing these developments in detail is hampered by the considerable variation in treatment given to the post-1945 period. There is a whole volume on Courtaulds, covering the quarter-century to 1965, but at the other end of the scale, Reader's history of ICI ends in 1952, and the treatment of post-war Wills (Imperial Tobacco), Pilkingtons and W.H. Smith is far from extensive. What seems to emerge is an acceptance that changed circumstances – the impact of market forces, new technology, etc. – merited a determined organisational response, with new structures, an injection of management theory, and the appointment of 'new blood' managers. Often, these changed circumstances involved policies of acquisition and diversification which placed existing managements under pressure. For Courtaulds, for example, an aggressive merger policy – there were no less than 29 'main acquisitions' in 1957–64, including British Celanese (1957) and Lancashire Cotton Corporation (1964) – was accompanied by the adoption of a hybrid form of holding company, with separate operating units, and product- and process-based divisions. Important changes at Board level followed in the wake of an unsuccessful take-over bid from ICI in 1961. Board committees were streamlined, and two 'Executives', one for Operations, the other for Policy, were established. Both were dominated by Frank Kearton, Chairman from 1964.[53]

Several companies brought in management consultants to advise on necessary changes. The most popular was McKinsey, which invariably recommended a move to a non-executive, planning Board and a multidivisional form. It was on McKinsey's advice that Bowater pursued a diversification strategy in the 1970s; the same company also offered advice to ICI, the Midland Bank and British Rail, though with less success.[54] As organisations changed, there was a significant erosion of the family-dominated enterprise. In Table 2 above, seven firms are listed in the family/personal categories in 1939, but by 1970 it is difficult to use these terms for any but Kenricks. This is not to say that family influences were swept away entirely. Members of the Pilkington and Smith families continued to serve as directors, and to act as chairman. It was not until 1967 that W.H. Smith's chairman, David Smith, renounced his legally established right to nominate a successor.[55]

In many ways the most challenging, and certainly the most publicised, problems of organisation and management in the post-war period concerned the industries taken into public ownership. Not only did nationalisation create sudden and substantial difficulties in controlling such widely dispersed activities as railways and coal-mining, but it also made the debate about the relationship between the type of organisation employed and performance more strident due to the government's close involvement in both. Manpower statistics reveal the scale of these newly-constituted undertakings. In 1948 the British Transport Commission, dominated by the railways, employed 873,000 and the National Coal

TABLE 3

ORGANISATIONAL CHANGES, 1939–70

Company*	Company Type	Organisation Form	Principal Changes
1. Private Sector			
I.C.I.	public	MD/MG	Organisational changes under Sir Paul Chambers 1960-8
Imperial Tobacco	public	MD	MD-form adopted 1964
Midland Bank	public	U	–
Courtaulds	public	HC/MD	Hybrid org. form developed from mid-1950s, streamlined under Kearton in 1960s
Pilkington	public (1970)	MD	MD-form adopted 1969
Bowater	public	HC	Holding co. adopted 1947 Decentralisation after death of Sir Eric Bowater 1962
W. H. Smith	public (1949)	HC	Two-tier Board 1949
Harland & Wolff	public	U	–
Kenricks	private	U	–

Continued overleaf

TABLE 3 (continued)

2. Public Sector

National Coal Board	public corporation	MG	Divisions abandoned 1967
British Electricity Authority/Central Electricity Authority/ Electricity Council, Central Electricity Generating Board	public corporation	MG	Separation of SSEB 1955; Creation of CEGB and EC 1958
British Transport Commission/British Railways Board	public corporation	MD/MG	Attempted decentralisation 1955; Dissolution of BTC 1962; hybrid planning board 1970
Colvilles/British Steel Corporation	private/public corporation	MD	Nationalised, 1951-5, private 1955-67, renationalised 1967 MD-form adopted 1963

Key: U unitary
  HC holding company
  MD Multidivisional on products
  MG Multidivisional on geographical units

Board 776,000. Even the more capital-intensive electricity industry had a workforce of 151,000 (231,000 by 1963), which put it comfortably above that of the manufacturing giant, ICI, with 120,000.[56] From the start, the choice of organisational form was very much a matter for government, and intervention persisted as arguments about the respective merits of centralisation and decentralisation in large enterprises intensified. The problems confronting nationalised transport, coal, electricity, gas and steel were not identical, of course, but certain common features may be identified. First, the legacy of pre-nationalisation structures created enduring headaches for the new corporations; second, the role of individual managers was often decisive in shaping both the organisation and its performance, even in these extremely large enterprises; and third, the government–industry relationship complicates an assessment of management, not only because of state intervention in such areas as pricing and labour relations, but also because governments appointed the senior managers and set (and frequently adjusted) corporate goals.

It is quite clear that the legacy of the past influenced the way in which the organisations of nationalised industries functioned and developed. Coal, in particular, was handicapped by the lack of unity in a large and 'bewilderingly diverse' industry. Although there were large companies in the pre-war period – 14 of them employed about a quarter of the workforce – most colleries were small and independent. The National Coal Board inherited a considerable dispersion, in terms of both ownership and location, with 1,470 colleries and over 800 firms. Unlike the railway and electricity industries, there was no existing administrative structure to work with and, according to Ashworth, little planning for future operation after the war. A dearth of management skills, noted in the inter-war years, was made worse by the unwillingness of many managing directors of private concerns to join the new enterprise. The results were seen in an enduring organisation, a complex and rather remote hierarchy of five/six tiers, which was not substantially modified until 1967; a long span of command; a reluctance to introduce the reform of management techniques; and initial difficulties in controlling the lower tiers (and the Area General Managers in particular) with existing managerial resources, a point noted by the Fleck Committee Report on organisation of 1955.[57] Electricity was initially better placed, in that the industry had moved a long way towards public ownership both in generation, which before nationalisation had been organised by the Grid-owning Central Electricity Board (established in 1927), and in distribution/selling. There was also more support for nationalisation among the senior managers. Nevertheless, there remained the task of taking over nearly 600 concerns, and the experience of the past was reflected in the tension between Area Boards and the British Electricity Authority, since the former's chairmen were recruited primarily from the old public electricity authorities and supply companies and were anxious to retain their autonomy. There was also an appeal to the past by the Conservatives when they encouraged more decentralisation in the 1950s, with the hiving-off of the South of Scotland Electricity Board in 1955 and the separation of generation and distribution elsewhere with the creation of the Central Electricity Generating Board in 1958.[58]

The experience of nationalised transport fell somewhere between coal and electricity. The railways, much the largest element in the British Transport Commission of 1948, had been reorganised into four oligopolistic concerns in 1923. The organisational structures of these companies and in particular the power of the General Manager as chief executive proved difficult to dislodge; and the problems were compounded by the initial organisation of the Commission, a small body which wanted to assume functional responsibilities but which was ill-equipped for more than a planning role.[59]

The post-war experience of these industries, and especially the railways, raises the question as to whether they were too large and too complex to be managed effectively as single enterprises. But they were not beyond the capabilities of the gifted individual to lead and reform. The three commissioned histories identify managers whose role was crucial. In the coal industry, it was Alfred Robens who inspired the reform of the NCB organisation in the 1960s; on the railways, Richard Beeching presided over the break-up of the BTC and the modelling of the new British Railways Board from 1963; in electricity, the centralising tendencies of, first, the BEA, and later, the CEGB were very much identified with the personal initiatives of Lord Citrine and Sir Christopher Hinton. At the same time, some of the organisational weaknesses can be traced to a failure of effective leadership: General Sir Brian Robertson's BTC organisation in the mid-1950s is a case in point. The 'managerial revolution' in the nationalised industries in the 1960s was real enough, and in many ways the public sector out-paced the private in developing investment appraisal techniques and the move to 'corporate planning'. But this 'revolution' was as much about importing single-minded personalities, men such as Beeching who came from the private sector (ICI), as about applying the dictates of business consultants and the management manuals of the business schools. It was also associated with a change in the government's attitude to nationalised industry, in which service goals were subordinated to the need to perform in a 'commercial' manner.[60]

How far, then, had the corporate economy proceeded by *c*.1970? The 1960s saw an intensified merger wave, and a substantial proportion – 72 per cent according to Channon – of the largest companies had adopted the M-form organisation by the end of the decade.[61] The diversification strategies noted by Chandler for an earlier period in the USA had certainly emerged in Britain by this time. The recruitment and training of managers was also given greater attention. In the public sector the complexities of the relationship with government, confusion as to goals, and the legacy of the past should not be allowed to obscure the management gains made in these industries. As stated earlier, it is often difficult to analyse the progress made by the enterprises in our selection

40   *Enterprise, Management and Innovation in British Business*

with any confidence. In general, the literature at our disposal does not place organisation or management at the centre of the analysis. In studies such as those of Harland & Wolff and the Midland Bank, for example, organisational elements emerge at intervals in a rather dense chronological text. Where organisation is given more prominence, for example in the work on Courtaulds and Pilkingtons, there is a reluctance to theorise outside simple Chandlerian formulations of strategy and structure. Elements of an earlier age of British management clearly survived, in the private sector in W.H. Smith and Pilkington, for example, while the traditional approach to railway management proved difficult to reform, as Beeching found in the 1960s, and Peter Parker discovered two decades later. Hybrid forms of the multidivisional approach were adopted in ICI and Courtaulds, and it is clear that in Britain there was a tendency for divisional managers to become involved in strategic decision-making normally reserved for the central headquarters. How far such developments were related to the performance of the enterprise is a vital question, but one which has not been satisfactorily resolved. It is frequently difficult to associate improvements in market performance with organisational type, and evidence for the motor industry suggests that family firms were just as successful as those organised in a more complex fashion. Equally, public bodies such as the British Transport Commission displayed some of the worst traits of the family enterprise.[62] Hypothetical gains from the move to the M-form may be clear enough, but are difficult to prove beyond doubt in an empirical context.[63]

VI

We must guard against the temptation to exaggerate the significance of our findings. It is a common complaint that the case-study approach is limiting. For example, a fair amount of the debate among economists and historians on multinationals centres on the representativeness of case studies drawn from archival material.[64] Here, Penrose's advice remains instructive. While warning that consistent examples were not an automatic proof of a general argument, she suggested that 'the theory of the *process* of growth' (her italics) was 'susceptible to empirical testing against the experience of individual firms'. It is in this spirit, and with a clear understanding of the nature of the material used, that this article has been written.[65] What conclusions should be drawn from the survey? The belated move to complex management hierarchies and, more specifically, the M-form should be given closer attention by business historians. Certainly, the post-war adoption of multidivisional structures appears to have been associated with diversification in many cases, although which came first is more difficult to ascertain, and it may well be that both were a joint response to factors such as market failure and technological change. There are also exceptions to the rule that the move to the M-form was linked to diversification strategies. British Rail, for example, moved towards a product-based or 'business-led' management by 'sectors' after

1982, following the shedding of most of its diversified products, such as hotels, shipping and hovercraft, which were lost in the government's privatisation drive. Another key issue is the nature of an explanation for Britain's 'corporate lag'. This phenomenon may simply be a matter of the comparative number of firms with a diversified product-range and geographically dispersed activities. After all, organisational innovation in the USA was clearly stimulated by the challenge presented by such factors – factors which surfaced on a broader front than in Britain. On the other hand, entrepreneurial explanations focus upon the continuing presence of family members on the boards of many of Britain's major companies. The influence of family participation should not be exaggerated, and it is quite clear that 'family' and 'failure' cannot be closely aligned. But if the term 'family' is broadened to encapsulate the clubby, gentlemanly approach to such elements as management recruitment, staff development, and the application of organisational science to business, then there is much in the thesis that British businessmen displayed a slow corporate response before the 1960s.[66]

University of East Anglia

NOTES

This article is a revised version of a paper given at the Business History Conference held at the University of East Anglia in September 1987. The author would like to thank the participants for their reactions. He is also indebted to Keith Burgess and Stephen Davies for their useful comments.

1. Joseph A. Schumpeter, *The Theory of Economic Development* (Cambridge, MA, 1934), and *Capitalism, Socialism and Democracy* (London, 1943); Edith T. Penrose, *The Theory of The Growth of the Firm* (Oxford, 1959, 2nd. edn., 1980); Chester I. Barnard, *The Functions of the Executive* (Cambridge, MA, 1938); Herbert A. Simon, *Administrative Behavior: A Study of Decision-Making Processes in Administrative Organization* (New York, 2nd edn., 1957); and *Models of Man* (New York, 1957); Ronald H. Coase, 'The Nature of the Firm', *Economica*, new series IV (Nov. 1937), pp. 386–405; Richard M. Cyert and Charles L. Hedrick, 'Theory of the Firm: Past, Present, and Future: An Interpretation', *Journal of Economic Literature*, Vol. X, No. 2 (June 1972), pp. 398–412.
2. It is a common pastime to raise such issues. Cf. Roy A. Church, *Kenricks in Hardware. A Family Business: 1791–1966* (Newton Abbot, 1969), pp. 325–6, citing Ronald S. Edwards and Harry Townsend, *Business Enterprise: Its Growth and Organisation* (London, 1958) and Richard M. Cyert and James G. March, *A Behavioral Theory of the Firm* (Englewood Cliffs, NJ, 1963); Leslie Hannah, *The Rise of the Corporate Economy* (London, 2nd edn., 1983), pp. 4–5 and 'New Issues in British Business History', *Business History Review*, Vol. LVII, No. 2 (Summer 1983), pp. 165–74, and, most recently, Donald C. Coleman, 'The Uses and Abuses of Business History', *Business History*, Vol. XXIX No. 2 (April 1987), pp. 111–56.
3. Simon, *Administrative Behavior*, pp. 79–84; James G. March and Herbert A. Simon, *Organizations* (New York, 1958), pp. 136–42, 203–4; Oliver E. Williamson, 'The Modern Corporation: Origins, Evolution, Attributes', *Journal of Economic Literature*, XIX, No. 4 (December 1981), pp. 1541–2, 1544–6; Cyert and Hedrick, loc. cit., pp. 399–400.
4. Penrose, op. cit. and see in particular the useful preface by Martin Slater, pp. vii–xxx; Robin L. Marris, *The Economic Theory of 'Managerial' Capitalism* (London, 1964);

42 *Enterprise, Management and Innovation in British Business*

Robin Marris and Adrian Wood (eds.), *The Corporate Economy. Growth, Competition, and Innovative Power* (London, 1971). Note also the work of Philip W.S. Andrews, for example, *Manufacturing Business* (London, 1949), and *On Competition in Economic Theory* (London, 1964).

5. Alfred D. Chandler, Jnr., *Strategy and Structure: Chapters in the History of the Industrial Enterprise* (Cambridge, MA, 1962) and *The Visible Hand. The Managerial Revolution in American Business* (Cambridge, MA, 1977).

6. Hannah, op. cit., and note the discussion in Scott Moss, *An Economic Theory of Business Strategy. An Essay in Dynamics Without Equilibrium* (Oxford, 1981), pp. 13, 19–28.

7. Cf. Armen A. Alchian and Harold Demsetz, 'Production, Information Costs and Economic Organization', *American Economic Review*, LXII, No.4 (Dec. 1972), pp. 777–95; Oliver Williamson, loc. cit. and see also his 'What is Transaction Cost Economics?', in *Economic Organization. Firms, Markets and Policy Control* (Brighton, 1986), *Corporate Control and Business Behavior. An Enquiry into the Effects of Organisation Form on Business Behavior* (Englewood Cliffs, NJ, 1970), and *Markets and Hierarchies: Analysis and Antitrust Implications* (New York, 1975). For some applications see Stephen Nicholas, 'Agency Contracts, Institutional Modes, and the Transition to Foreign Direct Investment by British Manufacturing Multinationals Before 1939', *Journal of Economic History*, XLIII, No.3 (September 1983), pp. 675–86, and Peter Hertner and Geoffrey Jones (eds.), *Multinationals: Theory and History* (Aldershot, 1986).

8. Moss, op. cit., pp. 98–103; Mark Casson, 'General Theories of the Multinational Enterprise: Their Relevance to Business History', in Hertner and Jones, op. cit., pp. 49, 59; Peter J. Buckley and Mark Casson, *The Economic Theory of the Multinational Enterprise* (London, 1985). On the need to match the theory employed to the task to be tackled see the seminal article by Fritz Machlup, 'Theories of the Firm: Marginalist, Behavioral, Managerial', *American Economic Review*, Vol. LVII, No.1 (March 1967), pp. 1–33.

9. Note, in particular, Chandler's contributions in: Herman Daems and Herman Van Der Wee (eds.), *The Rise of Managerial Capitalism* (Louvain and the Hague, 1974); Harold F. Williamson (ed.), *Evolution of International Management Structures* (Newark, NJ, 1975); Leslie Hannah (ed.), *Management Strategy and Business Development. An Historical and Comparative Study* (London, 1976); Alfred D. Chandler, Jnr. and Herman Daems (eds.), *Managerial Hierarchies: Comparative Perspectives on the Rise of the Modern Industrial Enterprise* (Cambridge, MA, 1980); Alfred D. Chandler, Jnr. and Richard Tedlow, *The Coming of Managerial Capitalism. A Casebook on the History of American Economic Institutions* (Homewood, IL, 1985); and Kesaji Kobayashi and Hidemasa Morikawa (eds.), *Development of Managerial Enterprise* (Tokyo, 1986). See also his 'The Growth of the Transnational Industrial Firm in the United States and the United Kingdom: A Comparative Analysis', *Economic History Review*, 2nd series, Vol. XXXIII, No.3 (Aug. 1980), pp. 396–410, and 'The Emergence of Managerial Capitalism', *Business History Review*, LVIII, No.4 (Winter 1984), pp. 473–503. All this should not be taken to preclude criticism of the strategy-structure argument. Cf. for example Bernard W.E. Alford, 'The Chandler Thesis – Some General Observations', in Hannah, *Management Strategy*, pp. 52–70.

10. ICI has also been the subject of a non-commissioned history – Andrew M. Pettigrew, *The Awakening Giant. Continuity and Change in Imperial Chemical Industries* (Oxford, 1985) – but its author was very much an insider. Many commissioned works have failed to see the light of day following the withdrawal of company support.

11. Turnover date for 1985–86 reveals that of the 12 companies considered (that is, excluding Midland Bank), seven were in the UK's top 50, each with sales exceeding £1,900 million, and ten were in the top 107 companies. *The Times 1000 1986–1987: The World's Top Companies* (London, 1986). The companies are: ICI, Electricity Council, Imperial Group, British Steel Corporation, British Railways Board, Courtaulds, British Coal (top 50); Bowater, Pilkington, W.H. Smith (top 107).

12. Some writers do refer, however, to 'management structure', 'direction and

management', etc., but the lack of prominence of such entries is still revealing. An obvious exception to the rule is William J. Reader, *Imperial Chemical Industries: A History, Vol. II. The First Quarter-Century 1926–1952* (London, 1975), Figures 3, 5, 6.

13. James B. Jefferys, 'Trends in Business Organisation in Great Britain 1856–1914', London Ph.D. thesis, 1938 (reprinted, New York, 1977), p. 130, and cf. Philip L. Cottrell, *Industrial Finance 1830–1914. The finance and organization of English manufacturing industry* (London, 1980), p. 163 (gives figures for 1915: 73 per cent of cos = private), and Peter L. Payne, 'The Emergence of the Large-scale Company in Great Britain, 1870–1914', *Economic History Review*, 2nd series, Vol. XX, No. 3 (Nov. 1967), p. 520.

14. Anthony R. Holmes and Edwin Green, *Midland: 150 Years of Banking Business* (London, 1986), pp. 60–63; Church, op. cit. p. 71; Donald C. Coleman, *Courtaulds. An Economic and Social History*, I (Oxford, 1969), pp. 150, 274; Michael Moss and John R. Hume, *Shipbuilders to the World. 125 Years of Harland and Wolff, Belfast 1861–1986* (Belfast and Wolfeboro, NH, 1986), pp. 52–3.

15. Bernard W.E. Alford, *W.D. & H.O. Wills and the Development of the U.K. Tobacco Industry 1786–1965* (London, 1973), pp. 183, 466–8; Theodore C. Barker, *The Glassmakers. Pilkington: The Rise of an International Company 1826–1976* (London, 1977), pp. 169, 171; Peter L. Payne, *Colvilles and the Scottish Steel Industry* (Oxford, 1979), pp. 77, 85–6. Cottrell, op. cit. p. 162, suggests that fears of company law reform stimulated company registrations in the 1890s, but this is not mentioned in the case studies.

16. T.R. Gourvish and R.G. Wilson, 'Profitability in the Brewing Industry, 1885–1914', *Business History*, Vol. XXVII, No. 2 (July 1985), pp. 146, 152.

17. Coleman, op. cit. I, pp. 152–3, 175–83; Payne, op. cit., pp. 85–6. In Bristol, too, limited liability status for Wills was seen as a way of strengthening family responsibility in the business: Alford, op. cit., pp. 119, 181–6, 280–82.

18. Payne, loc. cit., pp. 520–24; Chandler, 'Emergence of Managerial Capitalism', loc. cit., pp. 496–7.

19. The four included Ogden's of Liverpool, which had been bought by American Tobacco in September 1901. Its sale to Imperial was part of a deal which involved the transfer of Wills' export business to a new company, British–American Tobacco, dominated initially by the Americans (stakes: ⅔ American Tobacco, ⅓ Imperial). Wills also set up a separate manufacturing enterprise in Australia in 1901, a move consistent with the 'uncertainty avoidance' exhibited by emerging multinationals. Alford, op. cit., pp. 219–20, 250–69, 272.

20. Ibid., pp. 263–4, 272–6, 309–11; Alford, 'Strategy and Structure in the UK Tobacco Industry', in Hannah, *Management Strategy*, pp. 38, 73–4, Payne, loc. cit., pp. 535, 539.

21. Coleman, op. cit., I, pp. 191–3, 220–22; II, pp. 24–32, 37–9, 104–23. In the process the shareholding of the founding families fell to 58 per cent (Courtauld family 32.5 per cent), with 18.5 per cent in the hands of Henry Tetley and Thomas Latham, salaried managing directors who had been brought into the business in 1893. Ibid., II, p. 122, and see Coleman's entries on 'Sir Thomas Paul Latham' and 'Henry Greenwood Tetley' in David J. Jeremy and C. Shaw (eds.), *Dictionary of Business Biography*, III (London, 1985), pp. 662–4; V (London, 1986), pp. 470–72.

22. Chandler, *Visible Hand*, pp. 391–402, 433–41.

23. Payne, op. cit., pp. 87–8, 132–3. Kenricks did much the same thing when Frederick Ryland was given one share in 1883: Church, op. cit., pp. 78–9. However, the firm's capital structure is presented in a very confusing manner, and the precise details of ownership are not clear.

24. Moss and Hume, op. cit., pp. 92, 96–7, 132–3, 135, 173–4.

25. This phrase was used to describe recruitment to the Pilkington board before 1914: Barker, op. cit., p. 241.

26. Terence R. Gourvish, 'The Railways and the Development of Managerial Enterprise in Britain, 1850–1939', in Kobayashi and Morikawa, op. cit., pp. 187–90.

27. See Hannah, *Corporate Economy*, pp. 29–50, and note also John Turner (ed.),

44   *Enterprise, Management and Innovation in British Business*

Businessmen and Politics: Studies of Business Activity in British Politics 1900–1945 (London, 1984).

28. Hannah, *Corporate Economy*, p. 178.
29. Ibid. p. 62.
30. Reader, op. cit., I, pp. 451–66, 476–7; II, pp. 3–21.
31. Hannah, *Corporate Economy*, pp. 37–8.
32. William J. Reader, 'Personality, Strategy and Structure: some Consequences of Strong Minds', in Hannah, *Management Strategy*, p. 122. See also Reader, op. cit., II, pp. 21–30, 133–44; Hannah, *Corporate Economy*, pp. 81–5; R.P.T. Davenport-Hines, 'Harry Duncan McGowan', *Dictionary of Business Biography*, IV (1985), pp. 21–6.
33. Derek F. Channon, *The Strategy and Structure of British Enterprise* (Boston, MA, 1973), pp. 67–9; Hannah, *Corporate Economy*, p. 85, and see also his 'Strategy and Structure in the Manufacturing Sector', in *Management Strategy*, pp. 185–6. The 12 companies were: Vauxhall, Ford, Esso, Mars (US subsidiaries), Massey-Ferguson (Canadian); Nestle, Philips (European subsidiaries), Unilever (European connections); and Smith's Instruments, Spillers, British–American Tobacco, and ICI.
34. *Economist*, 27 Dec. 1930, cited in William J. Reader, *Fifty Years of Unilever 1930–1980* (London, 1980), p. 17.
35. Charles Wilson, *The History of Unilever. A Study in Economic Growth and Social Change* (London, 1954), I, pp. 207–10, 243–312, II, pp. 301–8, and note also his 'Management and Policy in Large Scale Enterprise: Lever Brothers and Unilever, 1918–1938', in Barry Supple (ed.), *Essays in British Business History* (Oxford, 1977), pp. 124–40; David K. Fieldhouse, *Unilever Overseas. The Anatomy of a Multinational 1895–1965* (London, 1978), pp. 24–63; and entries by Reader on 'William Hesketh Lever' and John R. Edwards on 'Sir Francis D'Arcy Cooper' in *Dictionary of Business Biography*, III (1985), pp. 745–52; I, pp. 781–5.
36. This is Wilson's emphasis rather than Fieldhouse's. Cf. Wilson, in Supple, op. cit., p. 124, and Fieldhouse, p. 36.
37. Wilson, in Supple, op. cit., p. 135.
38. Wilson, op. cit., II, pp. 312–15.
39. Edwin Green and Michael Moss, *A Business of National Importance. The Royal Mail Shipping Group 1902–1937* (London, 1982).
40. Charles Wilson, *First With The News. The History of W.H. Smith 1792–1972* (London, 1985), p. 346; Barker, op. cit. pp. 320–45.
41. Coleman, op. cit., II, pp. 222–43. The quotation is from p. 237. Rio Tinto also identified and acted to improve its organisational structure: Charles E. Harvey, *The Rio Tinto Company: An Economic History of a Leading International Mining Concern 1873–1954* (Penzance, 1981), pp. 207–23.
42. Alford, op. cit., pp. 330–34, and Alford, 'Strategy and Structure', loc. cit., pp. 75–7.
43. Moss and Hume, op. cit., pp. 244–50, 270, 278, 282–3, 285–321, and see also entries by Peter N. Davies on 'Owen Cosby Phillips' and Michael Moss on 'Sir Frederick Ernest Rebbeck' in *Dictionary of Business Biography*, IV (1985), pp. 672–4, 853–5.
44. Holmes and Green, op. cit., pp. 122–4, 153–7, 173–4, 190–91, 194–6.
45. Church, op. cit., pp. 144–6, 200–30, and see also 'Family and Failure: Archibald Kendrick and Sons Ltd., 1900–1950', in Supple, op. cit., pp. 103–23.
46. Payne, op. cit., pp. 188–9, 238–49. See also John Scott and Michael Hughes, *The Anatomy of Scottish Capital: Scottish Companies and Scottish Capital, 1900–1979* (London, 1980), p. 85.
47. Wilson, op. cit., pp. 223–6, 280–81, 347–8; Reader, *Bowater*, pp. 90–92, 148–50; Payne, op. cit., pp. 243–9. For the observation that not all firms with managerial hierarchies were manager-dominated, and not all manager-dominated firms possessed hierarchies, see Gourvish, in Kobayashi and Morikawa, op. cit., pp. 282–5.
48. The US lead in diversified firms, M-form companies, and the dominance of managers over owners should not be overplayed. Cf. John Scott, *Corporations, Classes and Capitalism* (London, 1979), pp. 60–65.
49. Lance Davis, 'The Capital Markets and Industrial Concentration: The U.S. and U.K.,

a Comparative Study', *Economic History Review*, 2nd series, XIX, No.2 (Aug. 1966), pp. 255–72.

50. Williamson, *Corporate Control*.
51. Reader, op. cit., II, pp. 74–81, 311; Holmes and Green, op. cit., pp. 133, 193; Barker, op. cit., pp. 323, 330–33.
52. Cf. William Lazonick, 'Strategy, Structure and Management in the United States and Britain', in Kobayashi and Morikawa, op. cit., pp. 101–46.
53. Donald C. Coleman, *Courtaulds. An Economic and Social History. Vol. III. Crisis and Change 1940–1965* (Oxford, 1980), pp. 164, 173, 241–54, 271, 310–11, 321.
54. Reader, *Bowater*, pp. 331–5; Holmes and Green, op. cit., pp. 281–8; Terence R. Gourvish, *British Railways 1948–73. A Business History* (Cambridge, 1986), pp. 368–88.
55. Wilson, op. cit., pp. 391–2.
56. Gourvish, op. cit., pp. 567; Leslie Hannah, *Engineers, Managers and Politicians. The First Fifteen Years of Nationalised Electricity Supply in Britain* (London, 1982), p. 294; *Ministry of Fuel and Power Statistical Digest 1952* (London, 1953), p. 39.
57. William Ashworth, *The History of the British Coal Industry, Volume 5, 1946–82: The Nationalized Industry* (Oxford, 1986), pp. 5–8, 31–3, 138–42, 191–7, 612–29.
58. Hannah, *Engineers, Managers*, pp. 2–4, 7–22, 60–63, 162–3, 183–4.
59. Gourvish, op. cit., pp. 31–60.
60. Ashworth, op. cit., pp. 628–9, 637ff.; Gourvish, op. cit., pp. 144–70, 308–25, 330–43; Hannah, *Engineers, Managers*, pp. 10–11, 42–3, 139–48, 186–90, 264–5.
61. Hannah, *Corporate Economy*, p. 152.
62. Roy Church, 'Family Firms and Managerial Capitalism: The Case of the International Motor Industry', *Business History*, Vol. XXVIII, No.2 (April 1986), pp. 165–80; Gourvish, op. cit., pp. 31–3, 171–2.
63. Cf. Peter Steer and John Lake, 'Internal Organization and Profit: An Empirical Analysis of Large U.K. Companies', *Journal of Industrial Economics*, XXVII, No.1 (Sept. 1978), pp. 13–30.
64. Cf. Hertner and Jones, op. cit., pp. 5–6, 12–13, 60.
65. Penrose, op. cit., p.3, and cf. Hannah, *Corporate Economy*, pp. 4–5, where the warning is put more strongly.
66. These remarks have been influenced by the comments of Donald Coleman and Stephen Davies on an earlier draft.

[21]

British Industrial R&D, 1900-1970

D.E.H. Edgerton
Imperial College, London

Supposed failure in research and development (R&D) has acquired an important place in explanations of the British economic 'decline'. This argument has not, however, been the subject of debate in the same way that the 'entrepreneurial failure' thesis has. This is not surprising since the role of technology in modern societies only rarely causes disagreement. Writing on science and technology, by scientists and non-scientists alike, is dominated by 'technocratic' assumptions. The most important of these is that science and technology have been the major determinants of growth and of differences in performance across nations. 'Technocrats' also tend to believe that the analysis of the historical role of science and technology involves little more than the marshalling of uncontroversial facts. If we were to follow them and bring together all the commentary on research and development and science and technology in twentieth-century Britain we would find, with very few exceptions, a consistent and seemingly convincing story: as a nation Britain has been deficient in its support of research and development and this has been an important cause of 'decline'. Particularly strong is the conviction that British *business* has been bad at supporting R&D. This paper will challenge this interpretation.

The current prevalence of the belief that British industry and the British state have been deficient in technology is closely connected with the influence of the broader 'declinist' literature on Britain. In the 1980s the two most important 'declinists' were Correlli Barnett and Martin Wiener but they were in many cases repeating arguments made in the 1950s by C.P. Snow and others, themselves replays of earlier complaints.[1] These works argue that Britain has been

---

[1] Correlli Barnett, *The Audit of War* (London, 1986); Martin Wiener, *English Culture*

D.E.H. Edgerton

anti-modern in its culture and hence hostile to science and, especially, technology. The 'declinists' have provided us with historical explanations for this anti-modern orientation of British culture, ranging from the character of the public schools (that is, elite private schools) to the nature of British capitalism. But generally they have not provided convincing evidence for the view that British culture, or British industry, or the British state, have indeed been hostile to science and technology.[2] We need to understand what is to be explained before we come up with explanations.

In this paper I will suggest that a careful, critical, reading of the literature shows that the conventional impression about British business is wrong. Indeed, I will show that much of the evidence deployed about R&D is flawed. Typical examples are 1) using arguments about state-funded civil R&D to make points about industrially-funded R&D; 2) using ratio measures of various kinds when absolute measures are needed; 3) taking the nation state as the unit of analysis rather than the region, industry or firm; and 4) making misleading and partial international comparisons. These errors are ones I have commonly come across in academic work, lectures, newspaper articles and so on. To pin them down to their sources is difficult, because there is no clearly defined literature on which people draw and because much of the confusion comes from misreading good sources. To untangle all this is more effort than it is worth. I have therefore avoided, in most cases, attribution. I leave it to readers to confirm (or reject) my view that these errors are common

and the Decline of the Industrial Spirit (Cambridge, 1981); C.P. Snow, *The Two Cultures* (Cambridge, 1959). Other 'declinist' works include D.S.L. Cardwell, *The Organisation of Science in England* (London 1957, 1972) and Hilary Rose and Steven Rose, *Science and Society* (Harmondsworth, 1969).

[2] For critiques see Christopher Harvie, 'Liturgies of National Decadence: Wiener, Dahrendorf and the British Crisis', *Cencrastus* No 21 Summer 1985, pp. 17-23; Bruce Collins and Keith Robbins (eds), *British Culture and Economic Decline* (London, 1990); David Edgerton, *England and the Aeroplane* (London 1991). For critiques of Barnett in particular see David Edgerton 'The Prophet Militant and Industrial: the Peculiarities of Correlli Barnett' *Twentieth Century British History* Vol. 2 (1991), pp. 360 - 79, and José Harris, 'Enterprise and Welfare States: A Comparative Perspective', *Transactions of the Royal Historical Society* 5th series vol. 40 (1990) pp. 175-195.

enough to merit analysis. In the second part of this paper I review the more solidly-grounded literature on industrial R&D, and how it has evolved over time. I have done so in order to guide readers to, and through, material that bears directly on the question of British industry's support of research and development. In the last section of the paper I draw out some 'stylized facts' from this literature.

I

Ignoring Industry

Most of the literature on British R&D in the twentieth century is about a small proportion of the total; it focuses on state-funded civil R&D. It is usually assumed that industrially-funded R&D was deficient and that the state had to finance R&D instead. A very good example is provided by treatments of the interwar years. The usual story goes like this. At the beginning of the first world war Britain found itself short of key products because it had neglected science-based industry. This was recognised and the government acted by establishing the Department of Scientific and Industrial Research which encouraged the formation of, and partly funded, industrial research associations. These spent amounts of money clearly inadequate to deal with the problems in hand. Furthermore, the whole effort was flawed because the cooperative research the research association undertook was biased against innovations which might give individual firms a competitive advantage.

But an examination of the figures shows that in the interwar years the spending of the research associations was trivial by comparison with that of private industry. The research associations were nothing more than a significant detail in the history of interwar research and development. They were established to encourage and establish research in those industries which had no record of substantial industrial R&D, and where the firms were too small to support individual research and development programmes. The research association policy was premised on the fact that some major sectors and major firms supported R&D already — what government had to worry about was the rest of industry. Nevertheless, David Mowery, in an influential article covering industrial R&D as a whole, has suggested that the research association was the typical agent of industrial R&D in interwar Britain, by contrast with the United States where the in-house corporate R&D laboratory dominated.

An undue focus on state-funded civil research and development has also skewed discussion of post-second-world war industrial R&D. Historians and commentators have highlighted the huge state investment in the development of nuclear power stations and civil aerospace, and the fact that these programmes led to huge losses. They also noticed that these programmes consumed a very high proportion of total R&D spending. They then go on to imply that these huge misdirected expenditures led to a 'crowding out' of industrial R&D spending. This argument is often allied to one highlighting the very high levels of government-funded defence R&D. But, as will be discussed further below, until the mid-1960s British industry spent more in absolute and relative terms on industrial R&D than the industry of any capitalist country other than the United States. Indeed, Britain was the strongest European performer of all types of R&D.

A related case of looking at the wrong thing concerns the question of state-funding of R&D. The vast majority of works, when dealing with the period before 1939, focus almost exclusively on civil R&D, in the way discussed above. But the state's funding of R&D was concentrated overwhelmingly in defence — the key government funders of R&D before 1914 were the navy ministry (the Admiralty) and the army ministry (the War Office); in the Great War the Ministry of Munitions funded the bulk of R&D. In the interwar years, the Admiralty, the War Office and a new service ministry, the Air Ministry, responsible for the most technically-oriented of the services, the Royal Air force, spent much more on R&D than civil ministries. The Air Ministry was the largest single spender on R&D in interwar Britain by a very considerable margin. All these ministries, furthermore, spent much of their R&D budgets in industry. One would not know any of this from reading the standard sources on the

52

British state and science; they systematically ignore warlike R&D spending. They also tend to ignore the civil R&D spending by service ministries, for example, the very costly programme to design two airships in the late 1920s, and the finance of aero-engine development through the interwar years.

It is also commonly assumed that the so-called 'Haldane principle' governed the funding of science by the British state. The 'Haldane principle' was that scientists were the best judges of what kind of science should be supported by government and that they should therefore have the most influence in determining spending priorities. But the 'principle' covered only a small fraction of state-funded research, that which was regarded as being of general applicability and which should therefore not be under the control of ordinary ministries. Such research was controlled through the non-departmental 'research councils', which included the DSIR. It emphatically did not cover research funded by mainline government departments like the service ministries, and thus covered only a small proportion of state spending.

The reason for this emphasis on state-funded civil R&D is clear. There was, and is, much more information about it than about business-funded R&D and defence R&D. Indeed, whole books were published on research associations alone. Furthermore, one can easily find historical actors complaining that British business was deficient in supporting R&D. Typically, they were scientists or engineers, organised in pressure groups like the British Science Guild. The emphasis on state support for civil R&D as opposed to defence R&D is also easily explained. In a broadly liberal culture like Britain's it is assumed that science is *essentially* civil, it is a peace-creating progressive force which is the antithesis of military values. Defence R&D is just ignored or regarded as a corruption of science.

A case of misplaced concreteness

By far the most common measure of the R&D expenditure of

D.E.H. Edgerton

a nation, industry or firm is not the absolute amount of R&D done, but rather the ratio of R&D to Gross Domestic Product, the output of an industry, or the sales of a firm. These last two ratios are called the 'research intensity' of an industry or firm. Unfortunately, however, these 'research intensities' are used *as if* they were absolute quantities of R&D. Thus, Chris Freeman has argued that:

> From 1925 to 1933 ..., in absolute terms, ... (IG Farben's) total R&D programme was the biggest in the world. IG Farben's total R&D expenditure averaged just over 7 per cent of turnover from 1925 to 1939. From 1925 to 1931, IG's expenditure was between 7 and 10 per cent, but in the world recession it was cut back fairly drastically to 4.9 per cent in 1933. From 1934 to 1939 it rose again to between 5 and 6 per cent of turnover. [3]

In the first sentence a point is made about IG Farben's R&D in absolute terms. In the second, its R&D expenditure is related to its turnover. But, in the third and fourth sentences 'IG's expenditure' is given in terms of the ratio measure and this is described as if it were the absolute measure. However, because the quotation tells us nothing about changes in turnover we cannot tell how actual R&D expenditure changed, even though we are told it was 'cut back fairly drastically' and then 'rose again'.

Just as common is the use of R&D/GDP ratios to answer the question: how much do countries spend on R&D? Countries with a high ratio are said to spend more on R&D than those with a low ratio. This does not follow. In the 1950s and 1960s the United Kingdom and the US had approximately the same R&D/GDP ratio, but the American R&D effort was in absolute terms many times larger than the British. This was true for the economy as a whole, individual industrial sectors, and individual firms. This is the key fact about any Anglo-American comparison, reflected in the fact that the United States is the most important source of innovations in the twentieth century, especially after the Second World War.

Let me take as an example of another misleading use of ratio

[3] Chris Freeman, *The Economics of Industrial Innovation* 2nd edn. (London 1982), p. 52.

54

measures: David Mowery's comparison of British and American R&D in the 1930s and 1940s. Mowery argues that British industry spent less on R&D than American industry. He justified this by using the ratio of R&D employment to manufacturing employment which yielded the following figures: 1933 - USA 0.18%, UK 0.03%; 1946 - USA 0.39%, UK 0.08%. [4] These figures look quite damning, but most, though not all, of the difference between the British and American figures is probably not due to differences in R&D spending at all. It is probably due to the large gap in labour productivity between British and American industry. If we assume that the productivity of R&D personnel was the same in each country, a reasonable assumption, but remember the productivity of labour was some two to three times larger in America, we can explain away most of the discrepancy. In other words, in terms of R&D expenditure output ratios, the difference is much smaller. But the key point of the Anglo-American comparison remains that American industry, and American firms, spent more than British industry and British firms on R&D. Thus although in the 1930s ICI had a higher research intensity than Du Pont, the latter spent more on R&D than did ICI.

A particularly unfortunate use of a ratio measure in international comparisons is the use of shares of particular kinds of R&D in national totals. It is common to see tables giving shares of national R&D budgets of a given country accounted for by defence and civil R&D, or government-financed and privately-financed R&D. They are useful, but they are often misused. A typical example would be this. In Britain and the USA defence R&D has accounted for around 30% of total R&D since the 1950s, while in Germany and Japan the levels are trivial. Therefore, it is implied, more was spent on civil R&D in Germany and Japan, and this was reflected in higher economic growth in these two countries. This does not follow and, in fact, both Britain and the United States spent more on civil R&D than Germany or Japan into the 1960s, whether in absolute or ratio terms.

[4] David C. Mowery 'Industrial Research, 1900-1950', in B. Elbaum and W. Lazonick (eds) *The Decline of the British Economy* (Oxford, 1986), pp. 191-2.

55

D.E.H. Edgerton

Given these problems with ratio measures, why are they used? The answer is simple: they allow simple international comparisons without the necessity of getting into the complexity of exchange rates. Let me take as an example another ratio measure which is much used: the growth rate of economies. This is the most common comparative measure of economic performance in economic history. It is the increase in output of an economy over a year as a percentage of the output of the previous year. This can be calculated easily for each economy one wants to compare. Confusing these growth rates with actual output, or efficiency, is in fact very common. Thus, because for much of this century British growth rates were behind German it is assumed that Germans were richer or more efficient. Similarly, Japan is often (wrongly) believed to be the richest and most efficient country in the world because its economy has grown fast.

One reason for the misuse of ratio measures is the psychological one. They can be too easily interpreted as measures of commitment, especially in the case of R&D. A high R&D/GDP ratio can appear to represent a nation's great commitment to science, technology and modernity, which is often thought to be a good thing in itself. But, a high R&D/output ratio is not in itself a good thing. It may simply reflect low output. What firms, and nations, presumably want is to invest in R&D which leads to innovations which increase output, thus, at a first approximation, decreasing the R&D/output ratio. In fact, what has tended to happen is that as countries grow richer they tend to invest a higher proportion of output in R&D; that is, their R&D grows faster than their output. But it is not correct to deduce that a high R&D/GDP ratio is essential to rapid growth. One can have too much of a good thing: it is possible to over-invest in R&D, just as it is possible to over-invest in general. Indeed, the former centrally-planned economies provide excellent cases of over-investment, and of high R&D/GDP ratios.

Nations and Nationalism

Although there is an influential rhetoric which claims that

technology is international and internationalising (for example, the standard argument that technical advance creates a 'global village'), most writing on R&D and growth focuses on the nation-state. This is partly explained by the fact that statistics are collected nationally, but it also reveals certain assumptions which are commonly made about the role of nation states. These are often seen as being in competition with each other, with R&D being an important weapon in the economic armoury of a nation. It is also assumed that the interconnections between science, technology, industry and economic growth take place primarily at the level of the nation: one influential formulation highlights the importance of 'national systems of innovation'. Each 'national system' determines the performance of the nation concerned and the world's technological and economic level. Technological breakthroughs are sometimes associated with a particular 'national system': pre-1914 Germany with synthetic organic chemistry, and post-second-world war Japan with consumer electronics.

Such an approach suggests that international comparisons of R&D should be important for analytical and policy purposes, and indeed these have become increasingly common. Nevertheless, systematic international comparisons are rare. Indeed, the most common comparisons made by British analysts appear to be designed to highlight British weakness. A typical comparison made for the period before 1914 is with Germany. In terms of industrial research the Anglo-German contrast relies almost entirely on an analysis of the dyestuffs and fine chemicals industry. The German industry dominated world markets and had very substantial research laboratories, but Britain was by no means unique in not having German chemical industry; neither did the United States or France. For the interwar period, and the immediate postwar period, comparisons are invariably made with the United States. This comparison ignores the sheer wealth and power of the American economy by comparison with all the European economies. More strikingly still analysts ignore the fact that Britain was clearly ahead of Germany, France and Japan into the 1960s: Britain was the R&D

57

D.E.H. Edgerton

powerhouse of Western Europe. And yet studies of changes even of absolute levels of R&D spending between countries from the mid-1960 stress the British relative decline, rather than the very high position from which Britain started.[5] For more recent years the favoured comparison is with Germany and Japan, and not with the USA, or say Italy or Spain.

The choice of comparator has thus varied over time, and for particular time periods particular comparisons are favoured over others. One way of highlighting the arbitrariness of much of what is written is to recall that one country was a specially favoured comparator in two distinct historical periods: in the late 1930s and the late 1950s the USSR was held up as a scientific and technological paragon. Not many would use it today, or use it as a historical comparator. To keep the comparisons in proportion we need to keep in mind that only a few countries were major scientific and technological powers in 1900 and the same ones remain so today with the exception of Japan. In Table I have sketched out some rankings for these major countries excepting Russia/USSR and Austria-Hungary. What the comparison shows, above all, is that the *relative* decline of British R&D is largely a phenomenon postdating the mid-1960s.

However, these international comparisons, even if properly done, may be beside the point. Is the nation-state in fact the proper unit of analysis of R&D and its economic effects? For some substantial amounts of state-funded civil R&D (for example in civil aerospace and nuclear power) that case is a strong one but for industry-funded R&D the case is by no means obvious. Of course, in many cases the R&D programmes of firms will be shaped by the preferences of governments if those governments are prepared to act to create protected markets. A good example is the huge oil-from-coal programmes of the 1930s, which were carried out because many governments wanted to reduce their dependence on imported oil, even when this was cheaper than synthetic oil. But it is remarkable

[5] Keith Pavitt, 'Technology in British Industry: a Suitable Case for Improvement', in Charles Carter (ed.) *Industrial Policy and Innovation* (London, 1981), pp. 88-115.

that even in the interwar period R&D was highly concentrated in large, *multinational* companies. Furthermore the world's major R&D performing corporations had transnational market-sharing and technology-sharing agreements. At least in the interwar years, then, business R&D was not nationally organised. Furthermore, the very high concentration of research in large firms, everywhere in the capitalist world, suggests that the appropriate unit of analysis for industrially-funded R&D is the large firm, not the nation. Two other units of analysis other than the firm suggests themselves. The first is the industrial sector. Thus, it is plausible to suggests that the technical health of, say, the British shipbuilding industry was more dependent on the state of world shipping and the world shipbuilding industry, than conditions characterising the British economy. The second is the industrial district. Thus, is may be more relevant to compare steel-making R&D in Sheffield and the Ruhr, rather than in the United Kingdom and Germany, and so on.

II

In this section of the paper I will review the key literature on British industrial R&D in roughly chronological order. This is not, however, to say that all later work builds on previous work. Indeed it is a feature of our knowledge of industrial R&D that it does not appear to be cumulative. This is ironic since science, technology and R&D are themselves widely believe to grow cumulatively.

J.D. Bernal's *The Social Function of Science* is one of those books more cited than read. [6] It is rightly regarded as a pioneering study of the social and economic relations of science, though it is best known as a manifesto for the planning of science. Bernal was a leading physicist and one of Britain's most important marxist intellectuals of the 1930s. One of the remarkable things about Bernal's book is that it got the broad outlines of the British R&D effort of the 1930s right.

[6] (London, 1939).

D.E.H. Edgerton

More surprising still, given the paucity of contemporary information, it got the scale of industrial R&D approximately right too. Bernal, as a marxist, put great emphasis on the influence of monopoly on industrial R&D, a theme that was picked up again by Lilley in 1948. [7]

It was not until 1943 that reasonable statistics for industrial research in the 1930s were compiled, by the Federation of British Industries. [8] Government surveys started in the mid-1950s and the first academic survey of postwar industrial research was done by Carter and Williams in the mid-1950s; [9] an excellent survey of industrial innovation in the interwar years was published by R.S. Sayers in 1950. [10] The early 1960s saw a very important comparison of British and American industrial R&D in the postwar years by Chris Freeman. [11] The first broader international comparisons were done in the 1960s by the OECD. [12] At the same time the first examinations of the relationship between R&D spending and economic growth across countries were made. They revealed that the links were by no means obvious. [13]

The academic study of the history of British industrial R&D was in abeyance until Michael Sanderson's important paper of 1972. This showed that British industry did much more research before 1914 and 1939 than had by then come to be believed and also made clear that the spending of the research associations was trivial compared with that of firms. The major flaw in the paper was that it did not recognise the concentration of R&D spending in a few large

---

[7] S. Lilley, *Men. Machines and History* (London, 1948).

[8] Federation of British Industries, *Industry and Research* (London 1943); see also *Scientific and Technical Research in British Industry* (London 1947) and *Industrial Research in Manufacturing Industry, 1959-60* (London, 1961).

[9] C.F. Carter and B.R. Williams, *Industry and Technical Progress* (London, 1957).

[10] 'The Springs of Technical Progress in Britain, 1919-1939', *Oxford Economic Papers* Vol. 60 (1950), pp. 275-91.

[11] C. Freeman, 'Research and Development: A Comparison between British and American Industry' *National Institute Economic Review* No. 20 (1962).

[12] OECD, *International Statistical Year for Research and Development: A Study of the Resources Devoted to R&D in OECD Member countries 1963/64* 2 Vols (Paris, 1968).

[13] B.R. Williams, *Technology, Investment and Growth* (London, 1967); D. Landes, *The Unbound Prometheus* (Cambridge, 1969).

firms; it did not mention, for instance, ICI. [14] In 1979 S.B. Saul published a very useful paper of broader scope than Sanderson's which reviewed the case for and against the claim that British industry was poor at innovating. He also debunked the myth that in the postwar years industrial R&D was crowded out by defence and state-civil R&D. [15] The next significant study of industrial R&D in the interwar years was David Mowery's comparative study of British and American industry. [16] This paper, though well received, suffered from a number important weaknesses, some already noted. It assumed that industrial R&D deficiencies were an important cause of the British decline and that American R&D was more efficient than British R&D. Mowery argued that central corporate laboratories attached to modern, large, multi-divisional corporations were the key to successful R&D. David Edgerton, in a paper published in 1987 criticized Mowery, and more generally noted the 'inverted Whiggism' of most writing on science and technology in twentieth-century Britain. He reviewed the coverage of R&D in business histories and found it wanting, but presented new evidence to show the high concentration of R&D in a few firms. [17] Two useful collections of case studies of industrial innovation were also published in the 1980s. [18] More recently Edgerton and Horrocks have provided new data on industrial R&D before 1945, including firm-by-firm figures for expenditure and employment. [19]

[14] Michael Sanderson, 'Research and the Firm in British Industry' *Science Studies* Vol. 2 (1972), pp. 107-51.

[15] S.B. Saul, 'Research and Development in British Industry from the end of the Nineteenth Century to the 1960s' in T.C. Smout (ed.) *The Search for Wealth and Stability* (London, 1979).

[16] David C. Mowery, 'Industrial Research, 1900-1950' in B. Elbaum and W. Lazonick (eds.), *The Decline of the British Economy* (Oxford, 1986).

[17] D.E.H. Edgerton, 'Science and Technology in British Business History', *Business History* Vol. 29 (1987), pp. 84-103.

[18] *Business History* Vol. 26, No. 4 (1984); Jonathan Liebenau (ed.), *The Challenge of New Technology* (Aldershot, 1988).

[19] D.E.H. Edgerton and S. M. Horrocks, 'British Industrial Research and Development before 1945' *Economic History Review* (forthcoming 1994).

D.E.H. Edgerton

III

In this last section of this paper I will pull together this literature to present a brief account of the main features of British industrial R&D. The basic story of British business-funded R&D is that it has grown through the century. The only exceptions were the cutbacks in the early 1930s; the period between 1939 and 1945 when spending was probably static; and after 1967, when there was a fall in spending to 1975. R&D spending grew faster than industrial output, though from the late 1960s growth in R&D was less than in industrial output. In expenditure terms research intensity increased from around 0.4% in 1946 to a peak of 3.27% in 1967. Growth in R&D expenditure was thus extraordinarily fast.

In the years before the Great War it was very difficult to distinguish research from the wider scientific and technological activities of firms. Nevertheless there were a significant number of firms which carried out systematic scientific investigations of their products and processes. Even in the steel industry there were some very significant laboratories. In dyestuffs, British firms' research activities were on a small scale compared to that of German firms, but the Great War saw the creation of two very substantial research organisations in the firms British Dyes and Levinstein. After the war these two merged to form the British Dyestuffs Corporation, and their joint research programme was probably the largest in British industry.

In the 1920s industrial research was a recognised feature of large-scale industry. The great electrical firms, Metropolitan-Vickers, British Thomson-Houston and GEC, all had significant research laboratories. In chemicals Brunner Mond maintained a research laboratory in Cheshire, and the synthetic ammonia programme of its Billingham subsidiary, Synthetic Ammonia & Nitrates had a major research task on its hands. Nobel explosives had an important research facility at Ardeer. These firms, merged together with the United Alkali Company and the British Dyestuffs Corporation, to form Imperial Chemical Industries, from that day to this, Britain's largest private financer of R&D. ICI's most important research programme of the early 1930s was its oil-from-coal programme, but by the late 1930s its largest laboratory was concerned with organic chemistry.

By the mid-1930s *hundreds* of British firms were doing research but business research was, and has remained, heavily concentrated in the electrical and chemical sectors, and in a few large firms. On a crude estimate, in the 1930s four firms accounted for one-third of R&D employment. These were ICI, easily the largest R&D performer, and the large electrical firms mentioned above. After 1939, expansion of research expenditure was largely due to the expansion of existing research facilities rather than to firms starting research from scratch. Many of the largest spenders on R&D in British industry today were in the same position in the 1930s. The pre-eminent example is ICI, but the modern GEC's ancestors, which include the three electrical firms listed above, as well as Unilever, Lucas, BP, Pilkington, and Courtaulds, were among the leaders in the 1930s. The most obvious change between the 1930s and the 1990s is the entry into the very first rank of R&D performers of the pharmaceutical companies, and the relative decline in R&D in the textile and steel industries.

The R&D effort of the major R&D performers of the 1930s cannot be treated as a purely British question. ICI had a close scientific and technical agreement with Du Pont, probably the largest American spender on R&D; Metropolitan-Vickers and British Thomson-Houston were by the 1930s both subsidiaries of General Electric of the United States. and GEC was closely entwined in the world-wide electrical cartels and technology-sharing regimes. If we take the photographic industry we find that by the late 1930s Eastman Kodak was doing more R&D in Britain than the whole of the British-owned photographic industry. The research effort of foreign controlled companies represented a significant proportion of the total. This ceased to be the case after the second world war.

For most of this century, British businesses have been the main source of funds for research and development. To give an indication: in the 1930s ICI's R&D expenditure was about the same as that of the DSIR. The clear exception to this rule is the 1940s and most of the

D.E.H. Edgerton

1950s when state-funded defence R&D was larger. Until the late 1960s state-funded civil R&D was below state-funded defence R&D. Since defence R&D is not directed at economic growth we may state categorically that British businesses have throughout the century paid for the bulk of R&D designed for promoting economic change. A general presumption is made that civil R&D, and within this industrially-funded R&D especially, is an important cause of economic growth. Certainly for American industry economic studies show a positive correlation between R&D and output growth. This is just as we would expect since R&D is an important — though not the only — source of innovation, which itself leads to higher productivity and competitive advantage.

But, it is important to note that this positive relationship between R&D and industrial growth need not hold everywhere. It does not follow that British growth was influenced positively by British R&D, or that, as is often argued, British growth was slow because of inadequate R&D. What became clear to some acute observers in the 1960s was that, across countries, there was no correlation between investment in R&D and economic growth. For example, David Landes noted that in the early 1960s British civil R&D was running at four times the level of French civil R&D, but the French economy had a higher growth rate. [20] An industry-by-industry study of British industrial R&D and industrial performance covering the 1960s found no satisfactory correlation. [21] Indeed in 1968 a British government report argued that Britain and British business was spending *too much* on R&D. [22] Since then it has become clearer that in the 1960s and 1970s Britain was overtaken in absolute economic performance by countries whose firms had spent less on R&D, by any measure, than had British firms.

What needs to be explained by historians is why British businesses invested an increasing proportion of their turnover in

[20] David Landes, *The Unbound Prometheus* (Cambridge, 1969), p. 521.
[21] C.T. Taylor and Z.A. Silberston, *The Economic Impact of the Patent System: A Study of the British Experience* (Cambridge, 1973) chapter 4.
[22] Central Advisory Council for Science and Technoloy, *Technological Innovation in Britain* (July 1968), p. 9.

R&D rather than examine reasons why they supposedly did not do so. Explanations of failure to invest in R&D should focus on the late 1960s and 1970s, not the 1870s. Could it be that one of the reasons was a certain disillusion among British business with R&D?.

IV

To conclude. The story of British industrial R&D is a simple and straightforward one. As the British economy grew and became more efficient, British businesses, especially large firms in chemicals and electrical engineering, increased the proportion of their output going to research and development until 1967. Throughout the century this spending was the main contribution to the total British civil R&D spending. This spending has been either ignored or massively underestimated by commentators on British R&D who have been concerned to argue that deficiencies in British R&D have been an important cause of the British 'decline'. In this, as in many aspects of science, there is a vast gulf between rhetoric and reality. In studying the literature on British R&D we should treat all arguments and evidence with great caution. We should be prepared to believe that the opposite of what is implied could be true. Could it be that in the twentieth century Britain has been the most scientific nation in Europe, and its relative economic 'decline' has been caused by too much R&D?

D.E.H. Edgerton

Further Reading

Peter Alter, *The Reluctant Patron: Science and the State in Britain, 1950 - 1920* (Oxford, 1987).

Correlli Barnett, *The Audit of War: the Illusion and Reality of Britain as a Great Nation* (London, 1986).

J. D. Bernal, *The Social Function of Science* (London, 1939).

Business History Vol. 26, No. 4 (1984).

Bruce Collins and Keith Robbins (eds), *British Culture and Economic Decline* (London, 1990).

Charles Carter (ed.) *Industrial Policy and Innovation* (London, 1981).

C.F. Carter and B.R. Williams, *Industry and Technical Progress* (London, 1957).

Central Advisory Council for Science and Technology, *Technological Innovation in Britain* (HMSO, July 1968).

D.E.H. Edgerton, "Science and Technology in British Business History", *Business History* Vol. 29 (1987), pp. 84-33.

David Edgerton "The Prophet Militant and Industrial: the Peculiarities of Correlli Barnett" *Twentieth Century British History* Vol. 2 (1991), pp. 360-79.

David Edgerton and Kirsty Hughes, "The Poverty of Science" *Public Administration* Vol. 67 (1989), pp. 419-33.

D.E.H. Edgerton and S.M. Horrocks, "British Industrial Research and Development before 1945", *Economic History Review* (forthcoming 1994).

David Edgerton, "Liberal Militarism and the British State", *New Left Review* No. 185 Jan-Feb 1991, pp. 138-169.

David Edgerton, *England and the Aeroplane: An Essay on a Militant and Technological Nation* (London, 1991).

Christopher Freeman, "Research and Development: A Comparison between British and American Industry" *National Institute Economic Review* No. 20 May 1962.

Christopher Freeman, *The Economics of Industrial Innovation* 2nd edn. (London, 1982).

Christopher Harvie, "Liturgies of National Decadence: Wiener, Dahrendorf and the British Crisis", *Cencrastus* No. 21 Summer 1985, pp. 17-23.

P.D. Henderson, "Comment", in Charles Carter (ed.) *Industrial Policy and Innovation* (London, 1981).

P.D. Henderson, *Innocence and Design* (London 1986).

David Landes, *The Unbound Prometheus* (Cambridge, 1969).

Jonathan Liebenau (ed.), *The Challenge of New Technology* (Aldershot, 1988).

S. Lilley, *Men, Machines and History* (London, 1948).

David C. Mowery "Industrial Research, 1900-1950", in B. Elbaum and W. Lazonick (eds) *The Decline of the British Economy* (Oxford, 1986), pp. 191-2.

Donald McCloskey, *Econometric History* (London, 1987).

Manchester Joint Research Council, *Industry and Science: A Study of their Relationship* (Manchester, 1954).

R.C.O. Matthews, "The Contribution of Science and Technology to Economic Development" in B.R. Williams (ed.) *Science and Technology in Economic Growth* (London, 1973).

OECD, *International Statistical Year for Research and Development: A Study of the Resources Devoted to R&D in OECD Member countries 1963/64* 2 Vols (Paris, 1968).

K. Pavitt (ed.) *Technical Innovation and British Economic Performance* (London, 1980).

K. Pavitt, "The Size and Structure of British Technology Activities: what we do and do not know" *Scientometrics* vol. 13 (1988), pp. 329-46.

Hilary Rose and Steven Rose, *Science and Society* (Harmondsworth, 1969).

Michael Sanderson, "Research and the Firm in British Industry" *Science Studies* Vol. 2 (1972), pp. 107-51.

S.B. Saul, "Research and Development in British Industry from the end of the Nineteenth Century to the 1960s" in T.C. Smout (ed.), *The Search for Wealth and Stability* (London, 1979).

C.T. Taylor and Z.A. Silberston, *The Economic Impact of the Patent System: A Study of the British Experience* (Cambridge, 1973), chapter 4.

B.R. Williams, *Technology. Investment and Growth* (London, 1967).

Martin Wiener, *English Culture and the Decline of the Industrial Spirit* (Cambridge, 1981).

Table 1

RANKINGS OF ABSOLUTE R&D BY COUNTRY

(EXCLUDING RUSSIA AND USSR)

1900-1914	1918-1935	1935-1945	1945-1965	1965-1980
Gross expenditure				
Germany	USA	USA	USA*	USA*
UK	UK	Germany	UK*	Japan*
				Germany*
				UK/France*
Defence				
UK	UK	USA*	USA*	USA*
Germany	USA/France	Germany	UK*	UK*
		UK*	France	France*
				Germany*
Industry-Funded				
Germany	USA*	USA*	USA*	USA*
USA	UK*	Germany	UK*	Japan*
UK	Germany	UK*	Germany*	Germany*
	France			UK/France*

Figures before 1960 are largely guesses. Certain comparisons are marked*

Name Index